Hasidism on the Margin

MODERN JEWISH PHILOSOPHY AND RELIGION

Translations and Critical Studies

Barbara E. Galli and Elliot R. Wolfson, series editors

Hasidism on the Margin

Reconciliation, Antinomianism, and Messianism in Izbica/Radzin Hasidism

Shaul Magid

THE UNIVERSITY OF WISCONSIN PRESS

The University of Wisconsin Press
1930 Monroe Street
Madison, Wisconsin 53711

www.wisc.edu/wisconsinpress/
3 Henrietta Street
London WC2E 8LU, England

5 4 3 2 1

Printed in the United States of America

Library of Congress Cataloging-in-Publication Data
Magid, Shaul, 1958–
Hasidism on the margin : reconciliation, antinomianism, and messianism in Izbica and
Radzin hasidism / Shaul Magid.
p. cm.—(Modern Jewish philosophy and religion. Translations and critical studies)
Includes bibliographical references and index.
ISBN 0-299-19270-9
1. Hasidism. 2. Hasidism—Poland—Izbica. 3. Hasidism—Poland—Radzyń Podlaski.
4. Judaism and philosophy. 5. Antinomianism. 6. Reconciliation. 7. Messianism.
I. Title. II. Series.
BM198.M24 2003
296.8′332—dc21 2003007232

For Nancy

Property and wealth are bequeathed to the fathers, but an "enlightened partner who enlightens" comes from God.

Proverbs 19:14

בית והון נחלת אבות ומיי אשה משכלת

משלי יט:יד

לפי סוד ישרים על התורה דף מד

It is the will of God that a man's helpmate should come from that which challenges him most.

אעשה לו עזר כנגדו—כי כן הוא רצון הבורא ית״ שיצמח לאדם עזר וסיעתא מדבר שהוא כנגדו—

מי השילוח א דף ד

Table of Contents

Acknowledgments

Although I began my academic work on the Izbica/ Radzin Hasidic tradition as a doctoral dissertation at Brandeis University in the early 1990s, I was exposed to Polish Hasidism and Kabbala more generally during the late 1970s and 1980s while studying in Jerusalem and Brooklyn, New York. I would like to thank the many friends and teachers who brought me into the world of Hasidism and Kabbala, both as a textual tradition and a source of religious devotion.

My choice to leave the haredi (ultra-Orthodox) world and enter the academy was quite tumultuous. While I feel my place is in the academy, I still hold dear the experiences and memories of the communities and friends I chose to abandon. The love, passion, and intensity of that world is rare, and it remains a constant source of inspiration for me as I continue to study and examine the texts that serve as the foundation of their religious lives and mine. Of special note is Dovid Din z'l, without whom I would not and could not be where I am or who I am. He was a true teacher in heart and mind and I remain forever grateful.

I cannot begin to offer thanks to those who have supported me in this project without first mentioning Rabbi Shlomo Carlebach z'l, who almost single-handedly brought Izbica Hasidism into the modern world. His ability to render these texts relevant to the contemporary context is unparalleled, and his inspirational readings are a mainstay for anyone who takes these texts seriously. He never saw this work, and it is likely he would have disagreed with some of my readings. However, in his ever-gracious manner, I am sure he would have appreciated a close reading of this material.

I have been blessed with many friends who have read and commented on this work and some who have simply been supportive of my work more generally. They include: Professor Aryeh Cohen, Rabbi Shai Held, Professor Talya Fishman, Professor Marvin Fox z'l (who advised on my dissertation "Hasidism in Transition"), Gloria Greenfield, Rabbi Jacob Lainer (who readily shared with me his intimate knowledge of his family history),

Rabbi Moshe Mykoff, Dr. Ely Stillman, Professor Peter Ochs, Professor Neil Gillman, Chancellor Ismar Schorsch, Professor Barbara Galli, Professor Elliot Wolfson, my students and colleagues at Rice University and the Jewish Theological Seminary, and the members of the Fire Island Synagogue in Seaview, New York. I want to especially thank Professors Rob Eisen, Pinhas Giller, and Hava Tirosh-Samuelson for their close readings of this manuscript and their invaluable comments. I also want to thank Jane Rosen and Hila Ratzabi for their skilled editorial work and Hila for the index, and the staff at the University of Wisconsin Press for their help, guidance, and support.

My father did not live to see this work to completion but his encouragement will be remembered always. To my mother, for her undying support and love. To my children, Yehuda, Chisda, and Miriam, for bringing their own unique light to the world. To Kinneret, for her laughter and the joy she brings us. Finally, to Nancy, this is my gift to you. May you find something in it of value. Your light has brought forth a New Morning, may it shine on and on.

General Introduction

I

The scholarly study of Hasidism is almost as old as Hasidism itself. Already in the mid-nineteenth century, when Hasidism was still quite young, western-trained scholars began to examine this new movement of Jewish pietism that had emerged in the traditional communities in Eastern Europe. Many of these initial studies were critical of Hasidic innovations and spirituality, some even claiming Hasidism to be an extension of the subterranean Sabbatean movement that was still in existence in many parts of Eastern Europe. Other studies were quite positive, even apologetic, viewing Hasidism as a fresh new approach to Jewish religiosity and life, correcting the infatuation with rabbinic legalism that had permeated Eastern European Jewish traditionalism. Most of these early studies, both critical and apologetic, focused on the early period of the movement and its charismatic founder, Rabbi Israel ben Eliezer, known as the Baal Shem Tov (or "Besht").

The early period of Hasidism was most intriguing for scholars because they believed it exhibited Hasidism's most radical doctrines, perhaps influenced by, or even emerging out of, Sabbateanism and challenging many of the conventions of classical Judaism and the rabbinic elitism that had become dominant in many areas of Eastern Europe. Committed to the historicism that was popular in the study of religion at that time, many of these scholars focused their attention on the origins of the movement, primarily on the predynastic masters of the Besht and his disciples.

Simon Dubnow, an early-twentieth-century historian of Hasidism, illustrated this predilection for the early period when he proclaimed that the fertile period of Hasidic creativity ended in 1815 (beginning in earnest in the 1750s), after which Hasidism lost its critical edge and largely became reabsorbed into traditional Jewish society. While twentieth-century scholars of Hasidism produced important studies on Hasidism after 1815, even into the twentieth century, Dubnow's proclamation still looms large in the field of Hasidic research.

This study intends to contribute to the end of Dubnow's hegemony on what is and is not creative and even radical (for most scholars the two categories are identical) in Hasidic literature. I will argue that, at least in some cases, Hasidism's social and even intellectual reabsorption into traditional Jewish society did not result in a loss of creativity. To the contrary, the most radical Hasidic doctrines may have emerged precisely in the relative calm of the mid- to late nineteenth century, in a Hasidic community no longer plagued by the Mithnagdic and Maskilic critiques of previous decades.

This study presents an analysis of one Hasidic dynasty known as Izbica/Radzin (the names of two small hamlets), which flourished in Congress Poland from the mid-nineteenth century until that century's end. Inaugurated by Rabbi Mordecai Joseph Lainer of Izbica in his posthumous teachings *Mei Ha-Shiloah,* first published in 1860, this dynasty produced numerous Hasidic works that exhibited a doctrine of determinism and antinomianism unparalleled even in the early, more footloose Hasidic schools. Scholars such as Joseph Weiss, Rivka Shatz-Uffenheimer, and Morris Faierstein have written about this "radical" Hasidic tradition, attempting to unpack its rather opaque comments on the questions of free will and antinomianism (i.e., overcoming the need for mitzvot). While building on these informative studies, I will begin with different assumptions and take this literary tradition in a very different direction.

First, I argue that the real ideological architect behind the Izbica/Radzin dynasty is Rabbi Gershon Henokh Lainer of Radzin, grandson of R. Mordecai Joseph. This is not simply because R. Gershon Henokh collected, redacted, published, and perhaps even wrote some of his grandfather's teachings. He also published his own voluminous commentaries on the Torah, the Zohar, and reflections on the Jewish calendar. More importantly, he wrote *Ha-Hakdama ve Ha-Petikha* (Introduction and Preface), a long, systematic introduction to the entire Izbica/Radzin tradition that has been ignored by scholars in the field. I argue that this Introduction and Preface is the programmatic foundation of the entire Izbica/Radzin system, without which the radical doctrines of determinism and antinomianism cannot be understood. Moreover, it is one of the first systematic attempts, internal to Hasidism, that seeks to place Hasidism in the trajectory of metahalakhic Jewish literature, incorporating both medieval Jewish philosophy and Kabbala. Therefore, the first three chapters of this study analyze and interpret this monograph as a prelude to the more well known exegetical writings of both grandfather and grandson. The advantage of studying the

Izbica/Radzin tradition, compared to other Hasidic dynasties in this period, is that we have such a programmatic work written by the author himself, systematically mapping the foundations of what he understands to be the Hasidic contribution to Jewish life and literature.

Second, I argue that the opaque and sketchy comments in R. Mordecai Joseph's *Mei Ha-Shiloah* are not conducive to careful scholarly analysis without reference to R. Gershon Henokh's more voluminous writings on the Torah and the Zohar. This is not to say that R. Gershon Henokh merely reiterated his grandfather's ideas. On the contrary, I show many instances where he departs from his grandfather's approach and moves out on his own. R. Gershon Henokh often reformulates older ideas into a new approach, which, because of his prolific pen, better lends itself to scholarly inquiry.

Chapters 4, 5, and 6 are devoted to close textual analysis of both masters' exegetical writings, paying close attention to the hermeneutical techniques employed to read both religious determinism and antinomianism into the biblical narrative. Or, perhaps, to read the Bible in such a way that determinism and antinomianism organically grow out of its narrative structure.

The final chapter is devoted solely to the question of antinomianism. While scholars of Judaism who work on Sabbateanism and other Jewish heresies have addressed antinomianism, it has not been explored in Jewish movements that remained true to Judaism. I view antinomianism in this study through two distinct lenses. First, I view it through the comparative lens of Christian antinomianism and Christianity's struggle over the relationship between faith *(sola fide)* and the efficacy of works as prerequisites for salvation. Second, I look at Izbica/Radzin antinomianism through the lens of a recent reading of Maimonides, arguing that Maimonides' "reasons for the commandments" *(ta'amei ha-mitzvot)* were largely Maimonides' response to the danger of philosophical antinomianism, a danger that, from a very different perspective, our Hasidic author shared. This is not to say that Maimonides and R. Gershon Henokh were unequivocal defenders of nomos (halakha) against antinomian doctrine. In fact, this study argues that they were not. Rather, it is to say that the philosopher (for Maimonides) and the Hasidic pietist (for R. Gershon Henokh) both lived in the shadow of antinomianism and, as such, had a different relationship to mitzvot than their nonphilosophical and nonpietistic brethren. Antinomianism *in* Judaism, I will argue, is not merely expressed by the overt abrogation of the commandments for the sake of redemption (which would take it *out* of Judaism), but it can also be a belief that one's devotional life no longer needs the commandments, even though one may choose to continue to live by them.

Finally, I show that while this Hasidic tradition does not exhibit any overt messianism—that is, it does not calculate the end or make any proclamations as to the messianic vocation of its leaders—it is messianic to the core. Its entire exegetical project is devoted to constructing the messianic personality out of the biblical narrative of Genesis, a person who must live in the protomessianic world having already overcome it. This is an extension of, but not identical to, what Rivka Shatz-Uffenheimer called "self-redemption" in Hasidism. The difference here is that the messianic person in Izbica/Radzin Hasidism is tied to a particular spiritual lineage, building on the Lurianic idea of soul inheritance *(gilgul).* The exegetical texts of this tradition trace the spiritual lineage of the messianic soul as it travels from Abraham to Jacob and then becomes fragmented in Jacob's sons, reappearing in the biblical Judah. While surely an *apologia* for Hasidic pietism and the ways Hasidism sometimes plays on the margins of the law, I argue it is more than that. It also seeks to make the anxiety of living with the law not only a result of human desire that must be confined, as is the case in much of classical pietism, but makes that desire, under certain circumstances, a sign of the immanent redemption. That is, to enact or at the very least to affirm the desire that takes one temporarily outside the law may be acting in light of redemption. In this sense, this study contributes to the ongoing discussion about the messianic nature of Hasidism, arguing (contra Buber and Scholem) that the messianic in Hasidism in general, and in Izbica/Radzin in particular, is an integral part of the Hasidic project.

II

A brief note on method. Most studies of Hasidic literature are interested either in: (1) exploring the historical context of Hasidic literature; (2) presenting the contribution of Hasidic ideas in relation to the larger Jewish discourse of pietism, mysticism, and devotional literature; or (3) presenting Hasidism as a living tradition, responding to intellectual, social, and cultural trends of its time. While I traffic in, and benefit from, all these types of analysis, I will focus on three other components of Hasidic spirituality that have not gotten as much attention.

The first is Hasidism's understanding of secrecy and epistemology as philosophical categories that underlie its claim of being the final unfolding of Jewish esotericism and thus the prelude to redemption. This includes understanding what is at stake epistemologically when Hasidism speaks of "faith" and devekut (communion with God). In chapters 1 and 2, I explore R. Gershon Henokh's understanding of faith and knowledge and investigate his claim that only Hasidism fully discloses the esotericism that underlies all of Jewish literature. His notion of Hasidic faith as a primordial and experiential faith that is only achieved through devotional praxis contributes to the larger epistemological question of knowledge addressed in classical Jewish texts such as Maimonides' *Guide of the Perplexed* and the Zohar. While the *Guide* and the Zohar serve as the basis of this Hasidic analysis, R. Gershon Henokh argues that the Besht discloses those heretofore concealed elements in the Zohar that enable an overcoming of conventional faith by a more primordial faith, resulting in an experience that reconciles the human soul with its divine source, a reconciliation necessary for redemption. This is not simply the reiteration of the Hasidic doctrine of devekut, because it is founded on an intellectual foundation lived in a devotional (i.e., praxis-oriented) context. Reason is only overcome through reason—it can never be circumvented.

The second component explores the ways that the Izbica/Radzin tradition utilizes, re-reads, and adapts the medieval philosophical tradition, particularly Maimonides, into its Hasidic program. Maimonides loomed large for R. Gershon Henokh, not only as a canonical Jewish thinker but also as a recipient of a partial esoteric tradition that was intentionally concealed in the garments of philosophical discourse. The Hasidic master (here a reference to himself) who holds the potential for redemption is obliged to reveal Maimonides' esoteric source in order to erase the bifurcation of classical nonlegal Jewish discourse (i.e., the philosophical and the Kabbalistic). While many Hasidic masters cite Maimonides in their writings, even his *Guide of the Perplexed,* none closely examine the *Guide* as a systematic esoteric text. At most, Hasidic authors use the *Guide* (or other medieval philosophical texts) when it serves them either as a lemma for particular issues they wish to discuss or as a proof-text of a particular point in their lesson. R. Gershon Henokh's introduction is one of the only systematic studies of the medieval rationalist tradition in the history of Hasidic literature. While its clearly apologetic and sometimes simplistic reading of the *Guide* will not satisfy serious scholars of Maimonides, when seen in the context of his larger redemptive program, R. Gershon Henokh's analysis of Maimonides is intriguing and worth scholarly investigation.

Finally, and most importantly, this study seeks to develop the almost nonexistent field of Hasidic hermeneutics. That is, in many of my readings I am less interested in what the Hasidic text actually says than how it says it as an outgrowth of its reading of the Bible and the Zohar. I have found that many if not most studies of Hasidism, while impressive and complex in their analysis of Hasidic ideas and texts, do not pay enough attention to the hermeneutic practices inherent in Hasidic reading. Therefore, rather than merely citing texts and getting to the ideas expressed therein, I concentrate on how these ideas are constructed from the Hasidic reading of Scripture or the Zohar, or how these texts use ideas in Lurianic Kabbala as tools to interpret biblical episodes. While many studies focusing on these hermeneutic questions exist in Talmud and midrash, medieval Jewish philosophy, and Kabbala, almost none exist in Hasidism, even as this may be its most creative and constructive dimension. Therefore, while I do frame the relevant issues in the language of contemporary scholarship on religion, I concentrate more intensely on the hermeneutical questions as they arise, reading texts closely to illustrate the intricacies of Hasidic reading. Getting inside the text's own world, as it were, will yield a more nuanced and sophisticated understanding of Hasidism as both a literary and revolutionary movement in the history of Judaism.

Biographical Introduction

I

This study focuses on one Hasidic dynasty in Congress Poland that flourished from the first third until the end of the nineteenth century. As is common in Hasidism in general, this dynasty is primarily known by the name of the town where it emerged, in this case, the town of Izbica, a relatively small hamlet located in the Radom province of Poland, southeast of the city of Lublin. In fact, the dynasty is known by the names of two towns in that province, Izbica and Radzin. Both were centers for the Lainer family; the first was the home of Rabbi Mordecai Joseph Lainer (1800–1854), author of *Mei Ha-Shiloah,* and the second was the home of his grandson Rabbi Gershon Henokh Lainer (1839–1891), author of many works, most notably the multivolume *Sod Yesharim, 'Ayin Tekhelet, 'Orhot Hayyim, Sidrei Taharot,* and *Ha-Hakdama ve Ha-Petikha.*[1]

The Izbica /Radzin Hasidic dynasty flourished in the Congress during a particularly tumultuous period in modern Polish history.[2] The Polish rebellion against Russian domination in 1830 ushered in a new era of qualified Polish tolerance toward Jews.[3] This was followed by Pope Pius IX's ascendancy to the Vatican in 1846 and the coronation of Alexander II as Czar of Russia in 1855, both of which contributed to a rapid period of modernization in the entire area that had a profound effect on the Jews, both secular and traditional. In some sense, this culminated in the partial emancipation of both Polish peasant farmers and Jews in the aftermath of the 1863 Polish rebellion (in which Jews participated), resulting in an era of tolerance that the Jews in Poland rarely, if ever, knew before.[4]

The overt impact of this progressive period on Hasidic communities in the Congress is hard to determine. Hasidic Jews did not generally participate in Polish culture and politics, nor were they very optimistic about the more open access to Enlightenment thinking that was filtering into Poland from German-speaking Europe in the aftermath of Poland's modernization and emancipation.[5] This included, parenthetically, required military service that Hasidic masters fought hard to prevent. Hasidim, however, both intellectuals and laymen, readily took advantage of the technological advances, opportunities for travel, and increased availability of books and manuscripts that came with these progressive changes.[6]

More significant, the impending threat of the Jewish Enlightenment became a significant part of their intellectual lives. One cannot fully understand the development of mid- to late-nineteenth-century Polish Hasidism without understanding the power and force of all aspects of the Jewish Enlightenment in the lives of Hasidic communities in the Congress.[7] I argue in this study that the influence of modernity, albeit covert, was particularly important for R. Gershon Henokh of Radzin. Living in a transformed Poland at the end of the nineteenth century, R. Gershon Henokh took on the Jewish Enlightenment by reconstructing the medieval philosophical hero Moses Maimonides as a thinker supporting and not contradicting the pietism of the Zohar (the classical thirteenth-century Jewish mystical text). He also located a renewal of Judaism in the Baal Shem Tov, the founder of Hasidism.

Whereas early Hasidism fought against both the Mithnagdic critique and the Enlightenment, the Enlightenment was, for the most part, not in their backyards. By the latter third of the nineteenth century, particularly in Congress Poland, modernity was literally knocking at the door of every Hasidic home, offering all the advantages that come with being a member of a revitalized and advancing society, including the beginnings of Jewish nationalism in the nascent Zionist movement. As a result, Hasidism had to reconstruct itself as a pietism that could stem the tide of modernity, a pietism refracted through a wider lens that included all the great Jewish philosophers and mystics of the classical period. This reframing was a fundamental part of R. Gershon Henokh's project and serves as an underlying principle of this study.

II

The Izbica/Radzin dynasty grew out of what was known as the Pryzsucha School of Hasidism, founded by Rabbi Simha Bunim of Pryzsucha (a small town near Warsaw) in the early nineteenth century.[8] R. Simha Bunim, a disciple of R. Isaac Jacob Horowitz (the Seer of Lublin), was R. Mordecai Joseph's teacher and a leading Hasidic figure in that period. Izbica Hasidism began after R. Simha Bunim's death, with a rift between R. Mordecai Joseph and his close friend and mentor, R. Menahem Mendel Morgenstern, known as the Kotzker Rebbe, on the festival of Simhat Torah in 1839 (the Jewish year 5600). Both R. Menahem Mendel and R. Mordecai Joseph were disciples of R. Simha Bunim, R. Menahem Mendel inheriting R. Simha Bunim's Hasidic court after his untimely death in 1827.[9]

It was rare that one individual would inherit an entire dynasty in this period of Hasidism. Usually, a son inherited part of the court, and one or two of the more prominent disciples inherited the remainder.[10] When the founder of the Pryzsucha dynasty R. Jacob Isaac ben Asher Rabinowitz (known as the Yehudi Ha-Kadosh or Holy Jew) died, a small circle of disciples remained with his son Yerahmiel while most went with R. Simha Bunim. R. Mordecai Joseph joined R. Simha Bunim's circle at that time.[11] After R. Simha's death, smaller offshoots of this dynasty emerged in Alexander, Warka, and Sokhachov, although Kotzk became the center of Hasidic activity emerging from this tradition. The Izbica dynasty can thus be seen as an offshoot of the Pryzsucha School, filtered through the dynasty of Kotzk.

The contentious split between R. Menahem Mendel and R. Mordecai Joseph in 1839–1840 had strong messianic undertones. It happened in a year fraught with both personal and communal turmoil. Polish Hasidim in particular and Hasidic Judaism in general greeted the Jewish year 5600 with great expectations. Messianic fervor swept through Eastern Europe, as many mystically oriented Jews awaited the fulfillment of the promise stated in the Zohar 1.116b–117a and 119a, "the wellsprings of wisdom will be opened in the year 5600 [1840]."[12]

In 1840 (actually the final months of 1839, which was the beginning of the Jewish year 5600), R. Menahem Mendel began his thirteenth year as Rebbe of Kotzk.[13] Some time after the festival of Simhat Torah (autumn 1839) and before January 1840, R. Menahem Mendel went into complete seclusion, where he remained for the final twenty years of his life. While R. Menahem Mendel left no writings or account of the reasons for his self-imposed exile, it seems that R. Mordecai Joseph's sudden departure from Kotzk that autumn had a profound effect on him.

R. Mordecai Joseph's disciples saw his thirteen years in Kotzk as having great mystical and messianic significance.[14] According to rabbinic legend, Rabbi Shimon bar Yohai spent thirteen years in a cave during the Hadrianic persecutions in the first century C.E., hiding from the Romans and disclosing the teachings of the Zohar. The Hasidim thus viewed the number thirteen as the necessary period of concealed preparation before revealing oneself as the redeemer. Izbica tradition has it that the thirteen-year period meant that, for R. Mordecai Joseph, "the time had not yet come for him to teach Torah publicly," and his sudden departure from Kotzk signified the beginning of his final concealment before emerging as a redeemer.[15]

Accounts disagree over what caused the breach between R. Mordecai Joseph and R. Menahem Mendel.[16] A later Izbica tradition interprets the split to be the moment of R. Mordecai Joseph's revelation as a messianic figure. R. Hayyim Simcha Lainer writes in his *Dor Yesharim,* "[R. Mordecai Joseph] began to awaken and illuminate a new and pure light, revealing the secrets of the Torah that had been hidden until then."[17] This is an allusion to the Zohar passage above regarding the messianic import of the year 5600 coupled with a common Kabbalistic theme in the anonymous *Sefer Temunah* (early fourteenth century), expressed somewhat differently in the Zohar and subsequent Kabbalistic literature, that the messianic era will bring forth "new" Torah not previously revealed.[18]

After leaving Kotzk, R. Mordecai Joseph returned to Tomaszow (his hometown) for a short time, after which he settled in Izbica, a small hamlet near Kotzk in the province of Radom.[19] His young married son Jacob, together with his wife and infant son, Gershon Henokh, soon moved to a house close to the Study House *(Beit Midrash)* in Izbica.[20] R. Jacob remained there until R. Mordecai Joseph's death on the Seventh of Tevet, 1854. It was there that the young Gershon Henokh studied with R. Mordecai Joseph and obtained his fundamental education.

After R. Mordecai Joseph's death, his circle of close disciples scattered. Many of the more established ones moved to Lublin, a prominent Hasidic center at that time known as "the Jerusalem of Poland," anointing R. Leibele Eiger (the grandson of the illustrious Talmudist R. Akiva Eiger) as their new master. R. Jacob Lainer and the still-young Gershon Henokh remained in Izbica, maintaining R. Mordecai Joseph's small community there.[21]

R. Jacob Lainer led the community in Izbica for the next twenty-four years, during which time he moved to Radzin, a small city almost due north of Kotzk and Lublin in the northern corner of the province. This brought him closer to the growing Izbica community already established in Lublin. R. Jacob Lainer remained in Radzin until his passing in the summer of 1878. Although his younger brother, R. Schmuel Dov Asher of Biskovitz (author of *Neot Deshe*), was well known for his piety and scholarship, it was R. Jacob Lainer's eldest son Gershon Henokh, then thirty-nine years old, who was chosen to continue the dynasty.

III

R. Gershon Henokh's literary career focused on four main projects. The first was a collection of all the material on the laws of ritual purity in rabbinic literature, resulting in the creation of a pseudo-Talmudic tractate on subject matter for which there is no extant Talmudic collection. This resulted in his *Sidrei Taharot,* first published in Petrikow in 1902.[22] The second project was the alleged discovery and documentation of the *tekhelet,* the dye used to make the blue thread of the fringed garment *(zizit)* traditionally worn by Jewish males (Numbers 15:37–41). The snail (called *hilazon* in rabbinic literature)[23] from which this dye is extracted was said to have been lost some time in the Gaonic period (eighth to tenth centuries).[24] R. Gershon Henokh claimed to have discovered the snail in an aquarium in Naples and was able to extract the dye necessary for the production of *tekhelet.*[25] He subsequently oversaw the production and dissemination of this blue dye and wrote extensively on his discovery; he also analyzed the relevant literature on this matter, including extensive responses to all his contemporaries who doubted the veracity of his claim. This project resulted in three books: *Shipunei Temunei Hol* (1952), *Ma'amer Petil Tekhelet* (1952), and *'Ayin Tekhelet* (1954), all devoted to the renewal of *tekhelet.* (For all publishing data, see bibliography.)[26]

His third project was to show that many esoteric and mystical traditions that comprise classical Kabbala are buried in the halakhic and midrashic discourses of rabbinic literature. In *Sod Yesharim, Sod Yesharim Tinyana,* and *Tiferet Ha-Hanokhi,* his collected commentaries on the Pentateuch, the Jewish festivals, and the Zohar, he consistently works to show the ways in which the Zohar and subsequent Kabbala illumine classical midrashic literature. In these sometimes labyrinthine Hasidic commentaries, the Zohar serves as the foundation of all biblical exegesis, without which the biblical narrative is closed. These volumes also serve to expand and elaborate on the collected teachings on the *Mei Ha-Shiloah,* a text he redacted and published in 1860.

His fourth project, completed at the end of his life, was an attempt to synthesize the philosophical and Kabbalistic traditions of late antiquity and the Middle Ages, claiming that Hasidism served as the final frontier of Jewish esotericism. In his *Ha-Hakdama ve Ha-Petikha,* written as an introduction and preface to his father's commentary on Genesis, *Beit Ya'akov 'al Sefer Bereshit,* R. Gershon Henokh presents a new analysis of the relationship between faith and knowledge, based on the teachings of the Baal Shem Tov, and attempts to prove that Maimonides' philosophy is consistent with the Zohar. While his synthesis of medieval mysticism and rationalism never explicitly addresses the contemporary spiritual crisis of Hasidism living in the shadow of the Jewish Enlightenment, these contemporary events underlie this exercise. Responding to the ways that the Jewish Enlightenment thinkers used Maimonides, R. Gershon Henokh attempts to counter the claims of Haskalah rationalism with a more philosophically engaged Hasidic mysticism, one that does not ignore the rational tradition of the Middle Ages. He was surely not the first Hasidic master to reclaim Maimonides for Hasidism, but he is the only Hasidic thinker to systematically read the *Guide of the Perplexed* through the lens of the Zohar and subsequently through Hasidic thought.[27]

The Maskilim, or Enlightenment Jews of Germany, Poland, Hungary, and Galicia, viewed themselves as the rightful inheritors of the Maimonidean tradition. They found support from historians in the *wissenschaft des Judentums* school like Henrich Graetz, who placed Maimonides' "rational" philosophy against the mystical trend in Judaism which they argued was largely the result of "external" influences not compatible with "normative" Judaism.[28] Contemporary scholarship has both refuted the accuracy of this claim as well as uncovered its ideological bias.[29] Nevertheless, the Enlightenment often used Maimonides as a foundation for liberal, rational Judaism in the eighteenth and nineteenth centuries. R. Gershon Henokh was well aware of this literature, as the Jewish Enlightenment had already permeated Congress Poland by the final third of the nineteenth century.

Throughout his analysis of Maimonides in *Ha-Hakdama,* R. Gershon Henokh believes he has transformed Maimonides from a philosopher to a mystic along the lines of the Zohar. The implications of such a position are significant in a world where the Jewish Enlightenment posed a serious challenge to Hasidic continuity, especially when it claimed to be rooted in a rational Maimonidean "method."[30] R. Gershon Henokh challenges the Enlightenment thinkers' use of philosophy as well as their claim to root their ideology in Maimonidean thought. To accomplish this he had to disengage Maimonides from the Enlightenment notion of philosophy. By making Maimonides a mystic, R. Gershon Henokh distanced him from the philosophical agenda of the Maskilim, who saw no place for mysticism in the authentic history of Jewish thought.

After his discovery of *tekhelet* in 1888, R. Gershon Henokh continued to teach and lead the Hasidic community of Radzin until his death in the winter of 1891. After a short tenure as the Rabbi of Ostrow, he returned to Radzin, where he responded to the many letters he received on *tekhelet* and oversaw the completion of his other scholarly work.[31]

The dynasty of Izbica/Radzin attracted the attention of scholars of Hasidism because of its radical doctrine of determinism, its brush with antinomianism, and its audacious readings of biblical episodes and characters. None of these scholars paid close attention to an overarching system or ideology that may underlie this tradition as it emerged in the writings of R. Gershon Henokh. In particular, no one has yet attempted to view this radical tradition within the larger fields of heresiology, esotericism, phenomenology of religion, and, especially, Hasidic hermeneutics. On these issues, Izbica/Radzin is not merely one tradition among many in the history of nineteenth-century Polish Hasidism, but serves as its radical apex—one important instance where Hasidism is presented as a systematic response to the challenges of modernity, a Hasidic ideology that carves out the margins of Judaism.

A Note on Translation

Many scholars who have written on Kabbala or Hasidism in the English language (or have translated Hebrew works into English) have confronted the difficult challenge of rendering the opaque and symbolic language of the Jewish mystical tradition into a language that does not share its tradition or context. English is a far richer language than Hebrew, while Hebrew is a much more pregnant language than English. Words in Hebrew can mean many different things depending on context and situation. This is particularly true of the premodern Hebrew of Kabbala and Hasidism, a sometimes-awkward language that has a fairly limited vocabulary. The English language has a far deeper vocabulary, enabling one to express nuanced distinctions through a simple choice of words. I have thus found it constraining to be absolutely consistent in rendering important Hebrew terms into English equivalents. In this work I have taken the liberty of using various English words to express a singular Hebrew term. Here are a few examples: The term *yerah* in Hebrew literally means fear, as in *"yerat Ha-Shem"* (fear of God). Yet it also means reverence or awe, which, while similar to fear, are not identical to it. The Hebrew term *tikun,* used so often in Kabbala and Hasidism, can mean many things, including fixing, rectification, reconciliation, and completion. Another example particularly relevant to this study is the term *berur,* which can mean clarification, cleansing, separation (e.g., evil from good), or purification. Given the complex and multivalent ways these terms are used in these texts, I found it impossible to maintain a one-to-one correspondence in my translation and analysis of many passages. Therefore, taking into consideration the specific context and hinted allusions of the term as employed in specific passages, I chose the English equivalent I felt best represented the intent of the author. To avoid confusion I often include the transliteration of the Hebrew term alongside the English to enable the reader to evaluate my choice of translation.

A Note on the Absence of Gender-Inclusive Language

In the past two decades it has become commonplace, and appropriate, for scholars to present their research and analysis in gender-inclusive language, working under the assumption that engendered language, even if unintentional, contributes to an imbalance in societal systems and norms. Having that in mind, I intentionally chose to keep the language in this book gender *exclusive* because I believe that the writers and thinkers I treat in this study, and the mystical and legal systems that underlie their worldview, are primarily, if not exclusively, intended for a male audience. These texts are written exclusively by men and primarily for men. Their world is a male-centered and hierarchical world, built on an essentialist ideology of gender distinction drawn from the metaphysics of Kabbala. I feel it would be disingenuous to the texts and a misrepresentation of their worldview to make their comments and analysis equally inclusive to both men and women. In maintaining gender exclusivity, I also hope to challenge this mystical worldview's appropriation of gender and invite scholars to confront the engendered nature of Hasidic discourse as a topic for future scholarly analysis.

Part I

The Piety of Secrecy

Esotericism, Faith, and the Hasidic Construction of Origins

As a religious ideology steeped in the mystical tradition of the Kabbala, Hasidism is an esoteric discipline. By that I mean its understanding of human nature and the trajectory of its textual tradition (both of which are, for R. Gershon Henokh, along the same continuum) are born out of a belief in the secrecy of truth. This means that the core experience of divine truth and the origin of all literature that points to that truth are concealed and thus outside the parameters of conventional human experience. Accessing this concealed truth, or revealing the secret, requires a combination of factors. First is the ability, through devotional living and practice, to transcend the confines of the empirical world, a world that includes what we conventionally call faith, and access a dimension of God that is the origin of all existence yet cannot be experienced through existence. Second is the ability to read Jewish texts, in particular classical Jewish philosophy and Kabbala, through the lens of a third hidden source, partially available as a consequence of devotion, which is the origin of all metahalakhic (supralegal) discourse.

The substance of this secretive third source is never fully disclosed but, according to R. Gershon Henokh, it is partially revealed through the juxtaposition of the two apparently disparate disciplines of philosophy and Kabbala. This way of reading for, and toward, the secret is a way of reconstructing that original source, the result of which will yield the redemption of the world. Yet this disclosure is itself a kind of concealment, as the secret only remains an incommunicable remnant within the consciousness of the devotee and never filters into the understanding of one who has not already experienced it outside the text. Reconstructing this secret, or "Sod," requires both extratextual and textual dimensions.

This part contains three chapters, each dealing with a different dimension of secrecy and its momentary disclosure. Chapter 1 deals generally with the question of the origins of Kabbala and its relationship to a primordial, and secret, Abrahamic Torah, which is called "Sod" (secret). The argument is that Kabbala as a written textual tradition only partially reflects an unwritten and originary Abrahamic Torah that precedes Sinai and thus exists before the emergence of commandment (mitzvah, halakha). Kabbala is an attempt to filter this Abrahamic Torah into the Sinaitic world of commandment and also provide a first step toward the reconstruction of Sod, thus overcoming the Torah of Sinai. Chapter 2 serves as a test case for this theory of redemptive reading by interpreting Maimonides' *Guide of the Perplexed* through the lens of the Zohar, thereby revealing hidden fragments of this primordial Torah buried, one might say exiled, in the language and argumentation of philosophy. Chapter 3 is an extension of chapter 1 in that it also deals with the question of origins. Chapter 3 focuses on the origin of Hasidic devotion as an overcoming of faith, devotion as the embodiment of secrecy that discloses the secret of origins to the devotee outside the text. One who has this secret knowledge (Sod) can then apply it to his reading of classical Jewish literature, reconstructing the lost Abrahamic core that lies at the source of Jewish theological reflection.

1 Retrieving the Origins of Kabbala

Gershon Henokh of Radzin's "Primordial Torah of Abraham" and Its Dialectical Disclosure

Revelation and (to a lesser extent) prophecy are the revolutionary challenges to an order founded on revelation

Robert Cover

In 1890, R. Gershon Henokh of Radzin published an introduction to his father's Hasidic work, *Beit Ya'akov 'al Sefer Bereshit.*[1] This introduction, entitled *Ha-Hakdama ve Ha-Petikha* (Introduction and Preface), is a lengthy monograph divided into three major sections.

Part 1 presents an argument for the origins and authenticity of Kabbala, integrating medieval attitudes but seen through the prism of the author's Hasidic perspective. Part 2 is a technical and careful attempt to outline the affinities between the Zohar and Moses Maimonides' *Guide of the Perplexed* by arguing that both classical texts draw from an unknown third source, a concealed esoteric tradition originating with the biblical patriarch Abraham. This concealed source served as the foundation for R. Gershon Henokh's Hasidic theory of esotericism, which held that the Jewish philosophical and mystical traditions in the Middle Ages are attempts to reconstruct this lost pre-Sinai esoteric tradition, only fragments of which survived.

The goal of this exercise—which R. Gershon Henokh believed was an extension of the Baal Shem Tov's program of showing the unity, or at least mutuality, between God and the world—was to overcome the oppositional nature of classical Jewish literature by understanding the relationship between philosophy and Kabbala dialectically rather than dualistically.

Part 3 takes the dialectical approach as a way of understanding canonical postrabbinic Jewish literature and extends it into the realm of human devotion. It does this by constructing a devotional framework of faith, awe, and miracle as the basis for one who seeks an experience of mystical communion (devekut) through mitzvot *and* through the world. R. Gershon Henokh's understanding of this experience of enlightenment departed radically from the Neoplatonic medieval notions of *unio mystica* (Kabbala) or conjunction with the Active Intellect (philosophy), both of which necessitated a detachment of the body from the soul in order to enable the soul to act independently of physical appetites. The Neoplatonic model produced a mystical and philosophical asceticism that underlies both Kabbalistic and medieval philosophical models of human perfection. The Baal Shem Tov's anti-ascetic pietism informs R. Gershon Henokh's attempt to construct a theory of piety based on engagement with, and not separation from, the world.[2]

In this chapter I will explore the reasons underlying R. Gershon Henokh's renewed interest in searching for the origins of Kabbala, a medieval activity that had largely become obsolete by the eighteenth century, and his belief that the discovery of an Abrahamic "Sod" (secret) tradition could rectify the oppositional attitude of Kabbala and philosophy among Jewish mystics. This all contributed to his construction of Hasidism as the final completion of the project of Kabbala.

I will begin by briefly surveying the trajectory of this Hasidic rendition, starting with the myth of origins in medieval Kabbala, then moving to the stark dualism of postexpulsion Kabbala, and finally to the "myth of confluence" adopted by many Renaissance mystics. All of these phases contributed to R. Gershon Henokh's myth of "esoteric reconstruction."

The medieval model of asceticism is built on the principle that the domination of the spirit and dissolution of materiality is an act of emulating the incorporeality of God.[3] R. Gershon Henokh suggested that devekut is not achieved via separation of the body and soul, but by each perceiving the sameness in the other, or by understanding one extreme as the condition for its opposite. That is, devekut is achieved dialectically and not dualistically. The unity of opposites in human devotion, which R. Gershon Henokh understood was the Baal Shem Tov's fundamental contribution to Jewish spirituality, became the foundation for what our author called his "Introduction to Izbica/Radzin Hasidism," which *de facto* was a new introduction to Hasidism in general.

The dialectical reading of the classical Jewish canon, which R. Gershon Henokh believed was the necessary outcome of reading Kabbala through the prism of Hasidism, served as a prelude to his discussion of Hasidic devotion. He begins this exploration by revisiting the quest for the origins of Kabbala as a way of unifying its traditions with those of philosophy. The goal was to diffuse the mutual exclusivity of both traditions that resulted from the detachment of philosophy from Kabbala in the Zohar and later in fifteenth-century Kabbalists such as R. Meir ibn Gabbai. This became more pronounced in light of R. Isaac Luria's more emphatic disdain of philosophy, coupled with the demonization of philosophy by ultratraditional societies in the wake of the Jewish Enlightenment in the nineteenth century.

Throughout the Middle Ages and Modern periods, Jewish mystics have engaged in searching for the origins of their mystical tradition. This search for origins is not unique but finds expression in almost every society and religious tradition, especially by those that traffic in esotericism.[4] In the Jewish mystical tradition, this search is accompanied by the claim that the manifold forms of extant mystical literature constitute levels of an ancient esoteric (oral) tradition, reaching back to the distant, even mythic, past. In the Middle Ages, when Kabbala was vying for authority in a world dominated by philosophy and/or rabbinism, this search also had a polemical agenda: to root Kabbala in the very belly of Judaism, either as transmitted at Sinai or, more audaciously, as the product of the biblical patriarchs, specifically Abraham.

The religious investment in origins is often tied to a quest for authenticity that could convince skeptics or counter accusations of deviance wielded by conservative voices in the tradition. The search for origins among mystics is complicated by the fact that the object of the search can never be known. The mystical search thus perpetuates the mystery even as it tries to reveal its source.[5] As Antoine Faivre suggests, "[e]soterics *knowingly* [my emphasis] cultivate mystery."[6] That is, the search for the unknown never concludes with its "discovery," but only connects that which is known (i.e., a body of literature) to the mystery of the unknown (Revelation) and the unknowable (God). In biblical religions, the quest to connect the known with the unknown is often based on a genealogy of apostolic transmission, utilizing mythic personalities from the body of authoritative literature (Bible or Sages) as the sources of the secret the esotericists are trying to reveal. Such is the case with the genealogy of rabbinic authority (Mishna Avot 1:1), as well as the transmission of Kabbala. In both cases, the known (Mishna/Kabbalistic literature) is connected to the unknown (Sinai) through a belief in the claim of the purity and accuracy of transmission. The unknown is the root of the authoritative tradition, and the one who makes the claim of access to that tradition, through the purity of transmission, makes claim to that (divine) authority.

In the case of Kabbala, as opposed to rabbinic authority, transmission is often accompanied by inspiration and not linked historically through generations. That is, lost transmission can be recovered by supernatural means, inspiration serving as a corrective *(tikun)* for corrupted transmission, restoring the tradition to its original state. This is the case both in the circle of the Zohar and later in the Lurianic fraternity in sixteenth-century Safed. In the Zohar, after several of R. Shimon's disciples expound on the beauty of the *sephirotic* world, their master responds, "I now know for certain that the Holy Spirit vibrates within you. . . . Torah has been restored to her original state!"[7] The case of Luria is more explicit. While maintaining that an ancient esoteric tradition did exist, Luria's disciples claimed that it had been corrupted and subsequently retrieved by Luria, via illumination, through *gilluy Eliyahu* (a direct communication with Elijah the Prophet).[8]

In the introduction to his recension of the Lurianic corpus, Luria's disciple and scribe R. Hayyim Vital made the audacious claim that the tradition of Kabbala from Moses Nahmanides (thirteenth century) until Luria (sixteenth century) should be disregarded because it contained only fragmented dimensions of a full tradition *(kabbala shelamah),* a tradition restored by Luria through Elijaic revelation.[9] Luria's system, achieved through divine inspiration, was not viewed merely as an explanation or elaboration of an ancient tradition received through transmission, but rather it was seen as a revelation that recaptured and restored the spirit of a lost tradition no longer recoverable solely through conventional means of transmission. The authority of Lurianic Kabbala among post–Lurianic Kabbalists was based on the belief in this claim.

While this did not result in erasing Kabbalistic literature from the thirteenth through sixteenth centuries, it instituted a shift in the post–Lurianic mystic's orientation to the large body of medieval Kabbalistic texts, represented most prominently by Luria's teacher R. Moses Cordovero, whose Kabbalistic system was largely an elaborate organization and systemization of earlier Kabbalistic material. By the eighteenth century, the reading of medieval Kabbalistic literature, specifically the Zohar, was largely viewed through the lens of Lurianic nomenclature and interpretation coupled with Cordovero's broad-based system adopted from earlier material.[10] The unspoken assumption of most post–Lurianic Kabbalists was that the fragments of truth in the corrupted tradition could be corrected through Luria's inspired reading. Scholem's observation that Luria's major contribution may have been his charismatic personality is significant here.[11] Luria's authority as the recipient of an illumination of the prophet Elijah served as the foundation of his rereading of the entire history of Kabbalistic literature and profoundly affected the extension of that tradition into Hasidism.

In one sense, Luria's claim of authentic illumination (the truth of which is not at issue here), and the subsequent dissemination of Kabbala from the sixteenth through the eighteenth centuries founded on that authoritative claim, stifled the search for the origins of Kabbala among many Hasidic thinkers. The authority of Kabbalistic interpretation now rested squarely on the shoulders of Luria's interpretation of the Zohar (the *textus classicus* of Kabbala, believed to be the product of second-century Palestinian sage R. Shimon bar Yohai). R. Gershon Henokh underscores the necessary correlation between R. Shimon and Luria. "[Luria] illumined and explained the words of R. Shimon bar Yohai, as it is written in *Shivhei Ha-Ari:* Everything he achieved he acquired from the Zohar. God granted him the gift of language to communicate the word of God."[12] The search for origins further lost its momentum when Kabbala became the dominant metahalakhic foundation of Judaism. By the time Hasidism emerged in the late eighteenth century, the mystical search for origins in Judaism had ceased being a major concern for Jewish mystics, if for no other reason than that the authority of Kabbala was now uncontested. Kabbala was at the center of metahalakhic Jewish discourse in traditional Jewish circles of Eastern Europe; indeed, it was the *de facto* "philosophy of Judaism."[13]

Even given Luria's dominance, Hasidism leaned on the entire Kabbalistic tradition as the source of its inspiration. As Moshe Idel has recently argued, apart from the theosophical tradition extending from Gerona through the Zohar and Lurianic Kabbala, Hasidism drew from the ecstatic school of Abraham Abulafia and Joseph ibn Gikatillia filtered through the work of Moses Cordovero, Elijah da Vidas, and others.[14]

I would argue, however, that the Lurianic corpus, especially after much of it had been printed in Karetz in the mid–eighteenth century, still remained the dominant grid through which Hasidic ideology drew its inspiration.[15] Luria's inspirational reading of the Zohar was accepted uncritically by most Hasidic masters as the Kabbalistic foundation of Hasidic ideology.[16] The dominance of Luria's corpus also played a mythic role in the very genesis of Hasidism. According to one legend, Dov Baer, the Maggid of Mezeritch (who generated the spread of Hasidism as a movement), became a disciple of the Baal Shem Tov after hearing the latter interpret a passage from Luria's *Etz Hayyim.*[17] Although the truth of such a claim is highly unlikely and the book studied is different in other versions of the story, this legend speaks to the weight of Lurianic Kabbala, not only as the substantive foundation of Hasidism but also as its original spark.[18]

The Baal Shem Tov's contemplative *kavvanot* for immersion in the *mikve* (ritual bath), and his famous commentary on Psalm 107, both of which drew heavily on Lurianic symbols and substance, became signposts to Hasidism's dependence on the theosophical tradition.[19]

The relationship between Hasidism and medieval Jewish philosophy is more subtle and, surprisingly, has largely been ignored by scholars. Portrayed as a "user-friendly" interpretation of Kabbala or, as Scholem preferred, a "mystical psychology," Hasidism drew from the variegated traditions of medieval Kabbala and utilized earlier attempts to integrate the medieval Jewish philosophical tradition into its mystical-pietistic program. Yet Hasidism also emerged in a world where Kabbalistic-philosophical polemics were a relic of the past. Most canonized medieval "rationalists" were securely integrated into the pious program of Eastern European traditional Jewry. In the tradition of the Zohar and Lurianic Kabbala, both of which had little use for philosophy and did not engage in polemics against it, Hasidism in the eighteenth and early nineteenth centuries had no use for philosophy or the medieval debates on the relationship (or lack thereof) between philosophy and Kabbala.

The uncritical symbiosis between Kabbala and medieval heroes like Maimonides, so common in Hasidic writing, came to a screeching halt in the middle decades of the nineteenth century, when the Jewish Enlightenment began making deep inroads into Eastern Europe using medieval rationalism as a basis for their religious reforms.[20] Medieval attempts to "Kabbalize" Maimonides, uncritically adopted by many early Hasidic thinkers, were challenged by historical scholarship. A new response to the relationship between Kabbala and medieval Jewish philosophy was needed in light of this Enlightenment critique.[21]

In this context, the question of origins once again emerged. Could a new theory of the origins of Kabbala embrace philosophy while defending the Hasidic way of life? Could a different approach to the origins of Kabbala break new ground in defending these medieval heroes through widening the vision of the Baal Shem Tov's redemptive program, which highlighted dialectical rather than dualistic readings of medieval Kabbala? Could a new attempt to theorize the origins of Kabbala also preserve (or even sanctify) the medieval philosophical tradition by deconstructing the oppositional presentation of philosophy and Kabbala that many traditionalists had adopted?

This is the context of *Ha-Hakdama ve Ha-Petikha,* R. Gershon Henokh's new "introduction to Hasidism." In it, he attempts to extend the Baal Shem Tov's program of unifying God and world and also his grandfather R. Mordecai Joseph Lainer's attempt to see the dialectical relationship between the premessianic and messianic personalities in *Mei Ha-Shiloah.* R. Gershon Henokh unifies the disparities between philosophy and Kabbala, seeing them both as drawing from a third esoteric source.[22] The rationalist program of Maimonides is defended against the reformers by seeing it as a reasoned attempt to reconstruct a fragmented ancient tradition. The Zohar, understood as containing the fullest (but still incomplete) explication of this esoteric tradition, becomes the lens through which medieval Jewish philosophical texts are reread and thus rescued from the hands of the Maskilim.

While R. Gershon Henokh's quest for the origins of Kabbala has precedent in the Middle Ages, his goal is quite different, perhaps even antithetical, to his medieval predecessors. For many Kabbalists, especially in light of the Jewish expulsion from Spain, the medieval quest for the origins of Kabbala sought to separate Kabbala from philosophy, seeing the former as a product of pure revelation and the latter as a product of human reason.[23] This is surely true among postexpulsion, antiphilosophical polemicists such as R. Meir ibn Gabbai, but also true (to a lesser extent) of earlier mystics such as Abraham Isaac ibn Latif and Abraham Abulafia, both of whom valued philosophy as a tool or stage in the mystical quest.[24]

Uncharacteristic of most Hasidic masters, R. Gershon Henokh viewed the literary tradition of Kabbala, specifically the Zohar, as only a partial expression of an unknown (and perhaps unrecoverable) esoteric doctrine. He viewed philosophy, specifically but not exclusively the work of Maimonides, as a rational attempt to reconstruct this lost tradition, fragments of which survived and served as a foundation for Jewish philosophical reflection.[25] Medieval Kabbalists, influenced by a dualistic Neoplatonic spirit and a belief in the viability of pure transmission, often sought to justify Kabbala by seeing its origins as absolutely distinct from philosophy.

R. Gershon Henokh, infused with the quasi-dialectical spirit of Hasidism, applied this principle to show that "authentic" philosophy, that is, the work of Maimonides and others like him, contained seeds of that lost tradition rationally reconstructed without the aid of divine illumination or pure transmission. By illuminating the lost fragments in Maimonides' philosophical discourse, R. Gershon Henokh believed he was redeeming philosophy by exposing its roots in revelation, thereby preparing for this lost tradition's full disclosure in the imminent messianic era.[26]

By the middle decades of the nineteenth century, two important changes took place in Hasidism that served as the foundation for revisiting the question of the origins of Kabbala. First, Hasidic communities had attracted young students from non-Hasidic Lithuanian backgrounds for whom Torah study was central. This was coupled with the educational reforms of more modern traditional communities, including medieval poetry and philosophy, not normally part of the traditional Jewish curriculum.[27] The result was a widening of the Jewish canon among more traditional thinkers, not only for the elite (where it was always wider than in popular circles), but also for the larger educated community. This new canon was not limited to the study of Talmud and legal codes but also included a wide array of metahalakhic Jewish literature, including medieval pietistic texts, Kabbala, modern *Mussar* literature, and Jewish philosophy.[28] As the canon of Talmud Torah widened beyond the limited scope of rabbinic literature, the apparent differences and even contradictions between these metahalakhic materials, and the myths that argued for their unanimity, had to be justified.

Second, the Enlightenment had already made deep inroads into the minds of many intellectually curious Jews who were finding new spiritual life in the communities of Hasidism. To simply ignore the reformers' claims of innovation would not suffice since, for some, these very reforms arose out of their readings of medieval philosophical classics such as Maimonides' *Guide of the Perplexed.* A Hasidic response to the above questions would have to emerge as a response to these two substantive challenges.[29]

R. Gershon Henokh's choice to define his monograph as an "introduction" is curious. Why did we need a new introduction to Hasidism? What end does an introduction serve? By the mid-nineteenth century, R. Gershon Henokh believed Hasidism had moved into a new phase, what he determined was its final phase—expanding the Hasidic message of dialectical unity into the construction of a unified tradition of "canonical" Jewish literature. Underlying this theory was a belief that Kabbala, specifically the Zohar, served as the most authentic, albeit deficient, expression of religious truth.

Extending R. Hayyim Vital's observation about the corrupt transmission of Kabbalistic tradition in the Middle Ages, R. Gershon Henokh argued that even the Zohar (as it has been transmitted to us) is not the fully embodied "Sod" tradition of the ancients, even as it may be its most authentic representation. Therefore, Kabbala did not have exclusive rights to this Sod tradition. Authentic metahalakhic Jewish reflection, which included canonized medieval Jewish philosophy, drew from the esoteric tradition that had survived in a fragmented form through the ages. By reading the *Guide through* the Zohar, as opposed to reading it *in contradiction* to it, he believed he could show how the former was drawing from fragments of this lost tradition and reconstructing it through reasoned analysis.

Underlying this exercise was a belief that the Besht's dialectical approach to God and world must be applied to the Jewish literary tradition. The mutuality rather than opposition of philosophy to Kabbala (even as Kabbala remained superior) would accomplish two goals.[30] First, it would undermine the reformers' attempt to co-opt Maimonides for their heretical ends. This is because the reformers were very invested in the distinction between philosophy and Kabbala, believing the latter to be an inauthentic myth that did not reflect rabbinic Judaism.[31] Second, it would extend the Baal Shem Tov's messianic project of dialectical unity to the Jewish literary canon, completing yet another part of the redemptive drama.[32] The challenge of the Jewish Enlightenment in general, coupled with the increased intellectual nature of Hasidic communities indicative of mid-nineteenth-century Polish Hasidism, created the conditions that made R. Gershon Henokh's new "introduction to Hasidism" a desideratum.

The body of this chapter will be an analysis of R. Gershon Henokh's theory of retrieving the origins of Kabbala as a primordial esoteric doctrine called "Sod" (secret), originating with the patriarch Abraham, dialectically disclosed and concealed (only fully disclosed through orality, then concealed through writing) throughout Jewish history.[33] This "Sod" tradition is the silent third source that will be viewed as the bridge between Kabbala and philosophy and the foundation of all authentic metahalakhic speculation. The full disclosure of this tradition which, according to R. Gershon Henokh, can be accomplished through the innovation of the Hasidic interpretation of Kabbala, will overcome the dualistic presentation of Kabbala and philosophy as incompatible, resulting in the full disclosure of their concealed esoteric sources. This will be the final prelude to the messianic Torah.

The Authenticity of Kabbala in Izbica/Radzin Hasidism

One may justifiably ask why a Hasidic thinker like R. Gershon Henokh Lainer would deem it necessary to argue that Kabbala is an authentic part of Judaism. Someone raised and educated in the Hasidic communities of mid-nineteenth-century Poland should have taken this for granted. However, there are at least three historical factors, particularly regarding Congress Poland in the middle decades of the nineteenth century, which may shed some light on his motivation. First is the fact that Lithuanian Orthodoxy by the latter decades of the nineteenth century, whose polemic against Hasidism had subsided by this time, had largely ignored Kabbala as the foundation of its religious worldview.[34] The centrality of Kabbalism in Lithuanian Judaism in the previous decades—in the writings of R. Elijah ben Solomon Zalman (the GRA),[35] R. Hayyim of Volozhin, and the GRA's students in Sklov and Palestine—had been supplanted by a Lithuanian tradition that was deeply rooted in the psychological approach of the growing *Mussar* movement and less based on the metaphysics of Zoharic and Lurianic Kabbala.[36] While Hasidism continued to use Kabbala as its metaphysical foundation, by the latter decades of the nineteenth century, it too had lost some ground to alternative models of Hasidic piety, such as the Pryzsucha/Kotzk schools and later the Ger dynasty, which were less inclined toward pure Kabbalism.[37] Political reforms in Poland and Russia in the middle decades of that century resulted in more fraternal interaction between Polish and Lithuanian Jews. Actually, the permeability of the borders between Hasidic and Lithuanian communities had occurred decades earlier, bearing fruit in the Hasidic court in Lublin, led by R. Jacob Isaac Horowitz (the Seer of Lublin), where many Lithuanian Jews found a home in search of Hasidic piety.

Second, by the latter decades of the nineteenth century, the Jewish Enlightenment (with little tolerance for any mystical interpretation of Judaism) became a driving force in the Congress. Kabbala was accused of being a foreign myth based on primitive superstition, the cause of everything wrong with traditional Judaism in Eastern Europe. Third, R. Simha Bunim of Pryzsucha, mentor of R. Mordecai Joseph of Izbica and a whole generation of Polish Hasidic masters, was reticent about Kabbala in general and Lurianic Kabbala in particular.[38] He believed that Kabbala was often misused and frequently served to distract its adherents from the Hasidic piety espoused by the Baal Shem Tov.[39] This attitude was supported, and even expanded, by R. Simha Bunim's disciples, R. Menahem Mendel Morgenstern of (Tomaszow) Kotzk and R. Isaac Meir Alter of (Warsaw) Ger. While R. Gershon Henokh's grandfather, R. Mordecai Joseph Lainer of Izbica, who initially was a friend and later a disciple of R. Menahem Mendel, was more interested in Kabbala than his teachers, it was not until R. Gershon Henokh (and his contemporary R. Zaddok Ha-Kohen of Lublin) that Kabbala once again became the dominant foundation of Congress-Poland Hasidism in this period.[40]

R. Gershon Henokh's reintegration of Kabbala into the psychological Hasidism of the Pryzsucha tradition is crucial to understanding the motivation underlying his *Ha-Hakdama ve Ha-Petikha.* This introduction to Hasidism is an attempt to present classical Kabbala in a post–Beshtian age, an age that had orchestrated a marked psychological shift in both Hasidism (Pryzsucha) and Mithnagdism (*Mussar* and Talmudism). This included a defense of the traditional foundations of medieval Jewish philosophy in response to the religious reforms of the Jewish Enlightenment, many of which were based on philosophical principles.[41] In R. Gershon Henokh's exegetical writings, his reading of Scripture is almost exclusively enacted through the lens of the Zohar. Almost every section in his commentary to the Torah in *Sod Yesharim* begins with a quote from the Zohar, utilizing the Zoharic passage to offer his Hasidic rendition of a scriptural verse or midrashic observation.

A companion volume to *Sod Yesharim,* entitled *Tiferet Ha-Hanokhi,* is a running commentary to the Zohar containing both original material and more developed versions of interpretations of the Zohar found in his earlier work. The function of the Zohar and Lurianic Kabbala in R. Gershon Henokh's writings is a complex matter that will be taken up in more detail in later chapters. Here I simply want to suggest that R. Gershon Henokh is attempting to achieve the most complete disclosure of Scripture as possible by rereading and reconstructing it through the prism of the Zohar, which he believed was the most complete extant version of the ancient esoteric tradition of Abraham.

Adopting the Zohar's own claim to be the "soul of the Torah," R. Gershon Henokh believed that by reading Scripture through the Zohar, he could strip away the outer layers of the text to reveal its hidden meaning. In essence, this is what the Zohar is claiming to do in its own teachings. What this means for one who uses the Zohar as a tool of mystical disclosure is that the Zohar is not merely an inspired interpretation of Scripture but the interpretive blueprint to deconstruct, and thereby reveal, what Scripture is trying to hide. R. Gershon Henokh uses the Zohar to read Scripture the way some Renaissance Kabbalists used philosophy to understand Kabbala. In both cases the interpretive scheme, in the form of a body of texts (philosophy, Zohar), is used as a grid to unlock the secrets of the text being read (Kabbala, Scripture).

Regarding R. Gershon Henokh's theory of the Zohar as an incomplete but authentic remnant of this Abrahamic tradition, this interpretive grid is neither humanly determined nor simply divinely given concomitant with the text. Rather, it is a fragmented version of another text, given earlier and now unknown, which expresses a more pristine and direct message of divine will than the text it is reading. In this instance, the Torah as we know it is really a substitution or garment of pre-Sinaitic Torah, remnants of which appear in the Zohar. This should not be surprising, as the Zohar makes a similar claim about itself.[42] However, R. Gershon Henokh is suggesting something quite different. While the Zohar claims that the entire Torah, both esoteric and exoteric, is concealed in the written law (and merely needs to be exposed by revealing the secrets), R. Gershon Henokh suggests that, while that may once have been true, exile has made access to that truth impossible. That which needs to be retrieved is fragmented and appears in various forms of Torah, Kabbala and philosophy being the most dominant. Only by seeing how each reflects fragments of that Sod tradition can it be reconstructed and subsequently revealed. Therefore, the question of the authority and origin of the Kabbala, ignored by the Mithnagdim, challenged by the Maskilim, and marginalized by R. Gershon Henokh's Polish Hasidic predecessors, becomes his central concern. To discover the origins of Kabbala (the ancient Sod tradition) is to discover the origins of Torah itself! In fact, the entire discourse of metahalakhic Jewish thinking rests on the origin of this esoteric tradition.

According to R. Gershon Henokh, without the Zohar (representing Kabbala in general), including a full understanding of its nature and origin, the Baal Shem Tov's project to unify God and the world in the experience of the Hasid could never be accomplished. The Zohar serves as the archetypal bridge: between the Torah and Israel's Abrahamic past (the primordial Sod tradition), between Israel and the Torah (disclosing the Torah's hidden meaning), and between Jewish philosophy and other modes of thinking that are seen as "outside" the authentic canon. The mutuality of both traditions is accomplished by viewing philosophy and the Zohar as rooted in one source, a source still unknown but partially disclosed, a source that holds the true secret of redemption.

Implicit in R. Gershon Henokh's exegetical writing is an entire historiography of Jewish redemptive reading. The history of the scriptural exegesis of the rabbis (Talmud/midrash) is viewed as part of a dialectical process whereby the Torah is revealed and subsequently concealed through its very disclosure. What is revealed are garments that contain fragments of the inner message, yet the garments prevent the message from being disclosed. This trajectory culminates in the Zohar, not because the Zohar is the product of the most brilliant and inspirational rabbinic mind, but (1) because it is the most complete composite of an esoteric tradition that reaches back to Abraham, and (2) because it reverses the rabbinic program by revealing the secrets and then concealing them. From this perspective, one could argue that the Zohar's depiction of R. Shimon's anguish and suffering about "revealing secrets" was precisely because he knew that he was transgressing the entire rabbinic program, but he also knew that he had to do it ("Woe if I reveal them. . . . Woe if I do not reveal them").

However, the concealed nature of the Zohar's composition also prevented the full disclosure of what it contained. The act of R. Shimon bar Yohai's disciples writing down the lessons of their master distorted the purity of R. Shimon's inspirational teaching. What remained were fragments of truth, disorganized and unexplained, containing only veiled hints of what R. Shimon intended. According to R. Gershon Henokh's historiography of Kabbala, the history of the interpretation of the Zohar takes a paradigmatic turn with R. Isaac Luria.[43] R. Gershon Henokh and many of his Hasidic contemporaries viewed Lurianic Kabbala as a reconstruction of the true nature of the Zohar, putting together disparate pieces and adding missing sections. In this schema, the innovations of the Lurianic system are seen as interpretive tools to reconstruct the Zohar's original message. However, Luria's project does not complete the process, as his highly mythic and symbolic language conceals the very secrets it reveals.

> The language of the Ari was only understood by his disciple [Vital] because he taught in a very abbreviated fashion and only spent a very short time with him. In this short time, however, he transmitted all the secrets. . . . In later generations his [Luria's] teachings were made more accessible and all who wanted could engage with them and understand them. However, everyone who wholeheartedly strove to understand his teaching [comprehensively] and construct a worldview on its foundations found it very difficult. There are numerous attributes given to one thing and several things labeled with many attributes, until one who reads them without a deep understanding [of the entire system] will find many contradictions. This is especially true if one wants to build on these principles [*hadesh b'da'to*]. . . . His teachings began spreading to many countries, each country copied and understood them in their own way.[44]

The nature and method of Lurianic transmission concealed the very things it was trying to reveal. Vital's expansive and detailed presentation did not resolve this dilemma; it may have even made it worse. To fully understand any part of the system one had to know the entire system. Yet, the full system was never explained in any systematic way; it could only be learned from the texts themselves. This "catch 22" resulted in a variety of different schools, each emerging from the one closed (but also open) system of

Vital's and Luria's disciples. Luria thus accomplished what R. Shimon had done in the Zohar—his secrets were transmitted but not revealed.

The penultimate phase of this reconstruction is inaugurated with the Baal Shem Tov. "The gates of wisdom, understanding, and knowledge, were opened for him. Using them, he began to explicate the 'unblemished esoteric Torah' [*Torat Ha-Shem Temimah*] compelling himself to explain the concealed wisdom in them, reaching to the outer limits of one's ability to understand in those days."[45] The Besht's contribution to the process of redemptive reading was his ability to explain the inner meaning of the Kabbala without the use of its intricate metaphysical terminology. The mythic and symbolic language of the Kabbala was viewed as a garment used by mystics to protect its sacred message.[46] This idea reflects earlier Kabbalistic theories of language, most notably that of Abraham Abulafia, for whom language was an important distinction between philosophy and Kabbala.[47] The Besht, having plumbed the depths of this esoteric tradition, was able to transmit its message without its protective garb. In R. Gershon Henokh's mind, R. Mordecai Joseph of Izbica is the Hasidic master who most fully discloses the Besht's true intention, thus completing his program. R. Gershon Henokh appears at the end of this process, playing the role of the interpreter of this intellectual and spiritual trajectory and bringing it to its final conclusion by completing the last leg of this marathon of exile—synthesizing the Zohar and the *Guide,* thus unifying the mystical and rational sources of Judaism. His *Ha-Hakdama ve Ha-Petikha* is the introduction to this final stage and thus the final introduction to Hasidism.

Before undertaking a careful synthesis of the Zohar and the *Guide* in order to show their common roots (which will be discussed in chapter 2), R. Gershon Henokh establishes the authenticity of the Zohar as an example of this incomplete primordial text.[48] His history of redemptive reading begins with a claim about the origins of the Zohar. This part of his introduction constitutes a classic illustration of religious esotericism. His overarching thesis—that a buried Sod tradition underlies the entire corpus of metahalakhic Jewish literature, appearing most prominently in the Zohar—illustrates what the English esotericists called *perennialism,* that is, that a "primordial tradition" exists, overarching (and impacting) all other forms of religious literature.[49] The vocation of the esotericist is to uncover or reveal this primordial tradition within the various permutations of canonical texts. Locating this tradition requires one to go beyond the "exoteric foundations that are the religions" and search for their common root.[50] In the history of western esotericism, this is often a call for the transcendental unity of global spirituality.[51]

Unlike many of his predecessors in the Renaissance, R. Gershon Henokh had little interest in the universalistic project of breaking down barriers between Jew and Gentile or Judaism and Gentile religions. His unification project was wholly internal to Judaism. For this reason, he had no use for the oft-cited myth of confluence between Plato and the prophet Jeremiah. As far as I know, this medieval myth, which seems to have been known (and rejected) by Maimonides, plays little or no role in Hasidic reflections on origins of the Kabbala or mystical genealogies of transmission. As an inheritor of the early Hasidic notion of the unity of God and world, R. Gershon Henokh argued that mystical and philosophical traditions in the "Jewish" Middle Ages were all drawing from an unknown esoteric source, rooted in a pre-Sinai tradition. With this, the early Hasidic notion of unity now extended to the corpus of Jewish canonical literature.

The messianic implications of this theory lie close to the surface. Exile was understood by early Hasidism (drawing from its Kabbalistic roots) as the illusion of fragmentation, what the Zohar calls "*'alma d'peruda*" (the world of disparity). Psychologizing the cosmological notions of *zimzum* (divine rupture) and *shevirat ha-kelim* (breaking of the vessels),[52] the two central components of Luria's creation myth, the Hasidic tradition viewed this fragmentation, and thus exile itself, primarily from a psychological rather than an ontological perspective, meaning that the exilic personality (or community) creates and/or perpetuates its own exile by viewing the world in a fragmentary manner.

This internalization of historical exile was emblematic of Hasidic spirituality in its early years and was absorbed by Polish Hasidism in the nineteenth century.[53] R. Gershon Henokh's attempt to unify the apparently disparate Jewish canon extends the classical dualistic categories of body/soul, God/world, holy/profane, and good/evil to include different modes of spiritual and rational cognition, that is, between mysticism and philosophy. Just as the fragments of the world are rooted in the transcendent One, the divergent literary traditions of Jewish philosophy and Kabbala are rooted in "one" primordial tradition. R. Gershon Henokh refers to this tradition simply as "Sod" (secret).[54]

In early Hasidic thinking, where monism is introduced into the dualistic framework of Lurianic Kabbala, the bifurcation of good and evil is viewed as the exilic and deficient perception of reality. Whereas most medieval Neoplatonic/Gnostic (i.e., classical Kabbalistic) notions of returning to the One required an annihilation of the "many" by subverting the demonic for the sake of the Good, the Baal Shem Tov (at least as he is constructed in the Hasidic imagination) instituted a notion of integrating rather than subverting evil that subsequently draws out the good contained therein. While this idea is clearly an interpretation of the Lurianic notion of "elevating the sparks," in Hasidism such an elevation is not limited to sparks of holiness in evil but evil itself.[55] Thus, the redemptive act of unification of God and world which stands at the center of early Hasidic thinking speaks about redemption via the sanctification of the mundane, a sanctification that retains evil (the extraneous husks of Lurianic Kabbala) even as it transforms it.

While many medieval Kabbalists accepted philosophy as partially legitimate, to my knowledge few viewed the symbiosis of philosophy and Kabbala in such a redemptive light.[56] In the Renaissance, the interdependence of these two disciplines did have a universalist and therefore redemptive agenda, but the redemptive quality of this universalism was more a product of humanism than an exclusively Jewish notion of the messianic. Reflecting Hasidic sentiment at every instant, R. Gershon Henokh's project is clearly geared toward a messianic end, conceived solely through classical rabbinic and Kabbalistic literature, exhibiting no humanistic sentiment.

Underlying his synthetic thesis of redemption is the fundamental belief in the early Hasidic idea of sanctification, whereby the fragmented world will return to its pristine state of oneness by seeing the mutuality of incompatible opposites, resulting in reconciliation. This idea is the basis of his grandfather's *Mei Ha-Shiloah* (which R. Gershon Henokh collected and edited), and his own *Sod Yesharim on the Torah and Festivals,* illustrated by interpreting the preredemptive characters in the Bible in opposition to their messianic counterparts.[57] Transferring this to the Jewish literature in *Ha-Hakdama,* R. Gershon Henokh juxtaposes the premessianic literature of philosophy to the messianic teachings of pre-Sinaitic esotericism, embodied in the Kabbala (especially in the Zohar and Luria). The messianic nature of the Zohar is that it contains the secrets necessary to unify the Jewish canon by revealing the esoteric teachings of the Sod tradition reaching back to Abraham. This task can only be fulfilled, however, when the premessianic literature is understood as compatible with and not in opposition to its messianic counterpart.

Before speaking about Kabbala as a literary tradition, R. Gershon Henokh presents what he understands to be the theoretical foundation of Kabbalistic esotericism. He suggests that the theoretical goal of Kabbala is to reveal that which is hidden. He finds this idea rooted in the biblical tradition of Abraham, beginning with Melchizedek, Abraham's teacher in the Genesis narrative.[58] Melchizedek, the King who is called the "Priest of the Highest God" (Genesis 14:18), is depicted by R. Gershon Henokh as the first real monotheist. By this he means that he is the first biblical character who identifies the monotheistic underpinnings of the world in which he lives. Given that the Bible tells us almost nothing about Melchizedek, R. Gershon Henokh's observation is necessarily gleaned from the midrashic tradition and, more specifically, from the Zohar.

Seeing Melchizedek as the prelude to Abraham, who we normally understand as the "first monotheist," R. Gershon Henokh simultaneously elevates and equivocates Melchizedek's stature. As his name indicates, Melchizedek relates to God as "the Highest God" or, in R. Gershon Henokh's reading, the "God who is only transcendent." Abraham, however, extends Melchizedek's monotheistic "discovery" and develops what may be called a useable or "covenantal monotheism."

> Abraham, our father began to reveal to the world that God is to be found in this world as well [as in the heavens]. Melchizedek, from the genealogy of Noah [*Ben Noah*] served God as transcendent, as it says [Genesis 14:18] *He was the priest of the God, Most High. And he blessed him* [*Abraham*] *and he said, "Blessed be Abraham of the God Most High, maker of Heaven and Earth, be blessed from the God Most High, who delivered your foes into your hand."* The term Most High [*elyon*] refers to the dimension of God which is beyond the limits of human knowledge. Therefore, the study of Torah and worship before Sinai [*Matan Torah*] required a great deal of self-denial, pushing one's own limitations [*nisyonot*] and great patience. By means of these traits one can comprehend the existence of God whose actions are rooted in this higher source [*b'midat elyon*].[59]

Anyone familiar with the polemical way Hasidism uses exegesis can immediately see how Abraham is constructed here "in the image" of the Baal Shem Tov, at least in the way he is conventionally presented in Hasidic thought. More pointedly, Abraham's interpretation of Melchizedek's monotheism squares with how R. Gershon Henokh understands the Besht's innovative reading of Kabbala. Abraham's discovery of God in the world is presented here as a prelude to the movement from dualistic to dialectical thinking common in Hasidic interpretations of Kabbala. Abraham could not accept Melchizedek's monotheism because it did not contain the covenantal reciprocity that requires permeability between the apparently incompatible categories of God and world.

The distinction between Melchizedek and Abraham can be framed as a distinction between rational and miraculous monotheism. Reason can posit, at least according to our author, that a Creator exists who is infinite and therefore transcendent of existence. This is the underlying principle of monotheism in Maimonides' writings. While accepting its basic premise,

R. Gershon Henokh's Abraham challenges this model. He concludes that only miraculous monotheism, that is, monotheism whereby the infinite is also accessible to the finite, is true monotheism; for monotheism to be covenantal, it must bridge the sharp distinction between two realms of existence which are, on the surface, incompatible.

Although Maimonides also makes this claim both in his *Guide of the Perplexed* and *Mishneh Torah,* he never claims that God "fills the world" and can be found in it.[60] For Maimonides, what is found in the world is the consequence of God's action or divine attributes. R. Gershon Henokh's depiction of Melchizedek and Abraham is a depiction of the philosopher (Melchizedek) and the mystic (Abraham)—the exilic Jew, who is correct but incomplete, and the redemptive Jew. In our passage, Abraham's monotheism demands the overcoming of a certain kind of logic, one that posits God's existence and providence but does not allow His presence in the world.

The depiction of Abraham's Hasidic monotheism as an extension of Melchizedek's rationalism is more refined than the conventional notion of Abraham as the one who discovers or rediscovers the monotheistic tradition of Adam and the first generations of humankind.[61] In our Hasidic rendition, Abraham is not a revolutionary figure who breaks with the past but an interpreter of the past who initiates an evolution in human understanding of both God and world. Abraham's interpretive turn in this text is developed in the second part of this treatise, which is devoted to divine worship. It is also bolstered in other parts of R. Gershon Henokh's corpus that discuss the different forms of heresy among other nations as representing the arrested development of pre-Abrahamic theological discourse. For example:

> Each nation is like an outer garment from the source of holiness . . . each nation is recognized from its form of faith that serves to embody the holy. There are so many mistaken beliefs among them. There is one nation who denies the existence of God completely. Others acknowledge the existence of a Creator but deny Providence, i.e., they believe that the world has no Ruler and is subject only to natural law. Others argue the exact opposite—that God directs everything and all is in the hands of heaven, even the actions of individuals and his desires. This is the belief of the ancient peoples [*anshe bnei kedem*]. . . .You will not find one theological position that leaves room for the necessity of divine worship.[62]

Abraham becomes God's chosen representative on earth and the father of Israel by taking the lessons of his teacher and expanding them into a monotheism that is relational. The notion of the immanent God, which

Abraham introduced, was inscribed in the act of circumcision.[63] The entire Izbica/Radzin Hasidic tradition adopts and develops the Zohar's reading that the theoretical nature of the act of *brit milah* (circumcision) is that it reveals the concealed phallus, inscribing the covenant on the male Jewish body.[64] In our texts, this inscription is the physical manifestation (and result) of Abraham's discovery that God is not only transcendent but also immanent. It also serves as the model of Hasidic esotericism, disclosing the concealed presence of God in the world and the concealed Sod tradition enveloped in the garments of the textual tradition.[65]

> Moreover, Abraham our father recognized that God "fills all the worlds" and removed the sheath [*'orlah*], which concealed the light of God from the minds [*hasagot*] of men.[66]

> Until Abraham was circumcised he only achieved a certain level [of clarity] [Zohar 1.98a]. This means that he only saw from the concealed realm [*ha-hester*], which is *Malkhut*. What he did not see [and what he subsequently saw after circumcision] was that from this cloudy realm [*Malkhut*], [God's] light can also be found.[67]

The result of Abraham's circumcision in the Zohar citation (which is the base text of our second text above) is that Abraham, through circumcision, became connected to the *sephirah yesod* (the phallus) and through it the entire upper realm of the cosmos.[68] This enabled him to see that light also was present in the darkness of *Malkhut,* which has no light of its own. R. Gershon Henokh uses the Zohar's approach to Abraham's circumcision, coupled with his own construction of his relationship to Melchizedek, to present a new way of envisioning the world that paved the way for the covenant at Sinai. Sinai was, for the collective, what Abraham had recognized as an individual.[69] The result of this experience was the exoteric Torah, that is, the Pentateuch. The correlation between circumcision and Torah (Sinai) is implied in midrashic literature and becomes prominent later in the Zohar:

> Come and see: It is not said of Abraham before he was circumcised that he observed the Torah. But once he was circumcised it is written, *Because Abraham listened to My voice, and kept my charge, My commandments, My statutes, and My Laws* [Genesis 26:5]. And because he was circumcised and the holy mark was on him, and he maintained it in the proper manner [the Torah] regards him as if he kept the entire Torah.[70]

The Zohar's discussion of circumcision and Torah in this context is largely concerned with equating proper sexual behavior *(shemirat ha-brit)* with the entire body of mitzvot. In other places, however, the Zohar sees circumcision as an inscription of God's name on Abraham's body resulting in a new level of apprehension.[71] R. Gershon Henokh uses this perspective but suggests that what resulted was not only a new vision but an entire esoteric tradition built on that new understanding, a tradition that survived and contributed to all realms of classical Jewish metahalakhic thinking.

The literary tradition of Kabbala is understood by R. Gershon Henokh as a fragmentary remnant of this Abrahamic tradition that was overshadowed by the dominance of the exoteric Torah at Sinai. Although it continued to function as an interpretative grid of the exoteric Torah, Sod became maculate in the rabbinic period when the rabbis intentionally tried to conceal it in order to protect its purity. While the Torah of Sinai (both written and oral) had the same goal as this esoteric tradition, revealing the immanent nature of God in the world, it was enveloped in protective layers of narrative and mitzvot.

For R. Gershon Henokh, even the esoteric tradition of Kabbala developed protective layers, consisting of mythic and symbolic language. On this reading the Baal Shem Tov was the new Abraham of this "Sod" tradition, one who was capable of transmitting the inner meaning of the Kabbala without its external garments. The classical Kabbala, with its focus on cosmogony and cosmology, thus represented a post-Sinaitic Melchizedekism, authentic and holy, but still deficient. The Baal Shem Tov, depicted mythically here as the new Abraham, inaugurated a new era no less significant than that of the biblical Abraham by disclosing the Kabbalistic worldview, stripped of its concealing garments, in order to bring this ancient tradition full circle.[72]

R. Gershon Henokh's rendering of the act of circumcision (cutting the foreskin—*'orlah*) as "revealing the light" *('ohr)* concealed from the "minds of men" is significant. The intention, I believe, is to connect the act of circumcision to the act of cognition, specifically referring to the cognition of Torah. As a close reader of the Zohar, R. Gershon Henokh utilized the Zoharic etymology of the word "Torah" (TRH) as "light" (OHR-*ohr*) rather than the Talmudic understanding of Torah as "teaching" (HRA—*hora'ah*).[73] The light of Torah—or Torah as light (TRH—OHR), understood by R. Gershon Henokh as the immanence of God in the world—was, until Abraham and Sinai, concealed. The purpose of Torah as the product of Sinai *(brit)* was to accomplish what Abraham began by means of circumcision *(brit),* that is, to reveal and uncover the presence of God in the world, which was "hidden from the minds of men."[74]

In this context Kabbala, often referred to as the hidden secrets of Torah *(Sitre Torah),* is really Torah itself.[75] Torah as Kabbala is viewed as that which can reveal the immanent nature of God in the world by revealing the hidden meaning of the Torah. The mystic removes the foreskin of Torah (i.e., its protective shield), as he reads Scripture through the lens of Kabbala. The mystic, like Abraham, is the one who fulfills the commandment of intellectual circumcision. The next step for R. Gershon Henokh is to more precisely explain the difference between the exoteric or legal tradition of Torah and its esoteric counterpart. He does this by using the rabbinic categories of written and oral law.

He begins to develop his position on Kabbala using the two conventional rabbinic categories of the written law and the oral law, redefining each category to serve his particular needs.[76] The oral law in the following text is not rabbinic law (Mishna and Talmud) but the "law of the Prophets," that is, the explication of the written law according to its oral (secret) meaning.[77] In R. Gershon Henokh's view, from the moment of Sinai onward, Judaism was in a dialectical state of trying to reveal or unravel the written law (the Pentateuch) while ensuring that certain dimensions of the law remained concealed. The oral law was just as much about concealing the written law as revealing it.

Prophetic tradition is the first stage in this dialectical process. Prophecy was an attempt to uncover the true meaning of Sinai through prophetic experience and teaching, subsequently taking on a literary form in the Prophets.[78] In order to fully disclose the tradition of Sinai, the Prophets had to revert back to remnants of an earlier primordial tradition of Abraham that preceded Sinai. Sinai itself was not the full disclosure of the pre-Sinai, esoteric Torah but was a frame through which one could recover that ancient teaching. To fully disclose Sinai required reviving its pre-Sinai, esoteric roots.

The transition between the first and second commonwealth (the first with prophecy, the second without) was viewed as a transition from one form of oral law (the Prophets) to another, more concealed form of oral law (the rabbis).

> In the days of Ahashveros, the time between the First Temple and the Second Temple, the Jews needed to acquire a new possession, i.e., oral law. During [the time] of the First Temple [the era of the Prophets] the light [of this law] was completely revealed. The revealed state of light is called written law in that the hand of God wrote everything. When the light was concealed it is called oral law. That means that the written law was concealed

> and enveloped in the oral law. . . . After the destruction of the First Temple the revealed nature of the written law was hidden in the oral law, which is the Second Temple.[79]

This perennial esoteric Sod tradition, described here simply as the written law, or "when the light was completely revealed," is concealed after prophecy (the first oral law) ceased, requiring a new oral law for the Second Temple at the beginning of the rabbinic period.[80] This Sod tradition served as a bridge between the prophetic message and the written law—that is, it was used by the prophets to disclose the written law. Having nothing more to work with than scattered references in the Zohar, R. Gershon Henokh constructs a hypothesis of concealment and disclosure that is aligned with the existence and absence of prophecy, which he then uses to build the framework for his reading of the development of the more formal category of what he calls "Kabbala" in the rabbinic period.[81] What is implied, however, is that methodologically the more formal Kabbala is the continuation of a process that served as the foundation of ancient Israelite religion from its inception. It is an attempt to retrieve and reconstruct the prophetic teaching from its concealed state in rabbinic Judaism.

When R. Gershon Henokh begins to describe the rabbinic period, he introduces a new phenomenon. Whereas in the prophetic period, the prophets were openly utilizing this Sod tradition in order to reveal the hidden message of Scripture, the agenda of rabbinic Judaism is understood as a deliberate attempt by both doctrine and method to conceal this Sod in Jewish literature.[82] An antecedent to this stance already appears in R. Hayyim Vital's introduction to *Sha'ar Hakdamot,* when he states:

> Their words [the sages in the Talmud] are like a dream with no interpretation. The secrets and hidden traditions [i.e., Kabbala] are called the "soul of the Torah." These are the interpretations of the dream . . . this is the Babylonian Talmud which is not enlightened [understood] without the Zohar. These are the secrets of the Torah upon which the verse says, *the Light of Torah.*[83]

A significant difference between R. Hayyim Vital's polemical statement above and R. Gershon Henokh's dialectical principle developed in *Ha-Hakdama* is that Vital's claim about the deficiency of Kabbalistic transmission is not the result of any intention to conceal but a general statement about the nature of esoteric transmission. That is, the deficiency of rabbinic literature, at least on the question of the transmission of esotericism, is not calculated. "The wisdom of the Zohar illuminates them [the words of the Talmud] and explains the words that are stated in the Talmud which are enveloped [*m'lubashim*] as if they deal with physical things, upon which it is said, *the Torah of light*."[84]

For R. Gershon Henokh, this apparent absence is calculated as a necessary part of the dialectical redemptive process. This is suggested by juxtaposing a passage from the Zohar with a Talmudic passage from the Tractate Sanhedrin:

> Rabbi Shimon said, "When I am with the community of scholars from Babylonia, they come to me and I teach them things in a revealed manner. Then they take the teachings and place them in a sealed chest with hard iron shackles, closed from all sides" [Zohar 1.224b]. This is the nature of the Babylonian Talmud, as it states, *"He has made me dwell in darkness, like those long dead"* [Lamentations 3:6]. R. Jeremiah said, "This is the Babylonian Talmud" [Tractate Sanhedrin 24a]. [In Babylonia] they conceal their Torah in garments of *peshat* [plain-sense meaning], in order to conceal the Torah in matters of this world. These secrets are passed on to the initiated.[85]

He argues that the rabbis were successful in concealing the prophetic Sod tradition within halakha, integrating it into a system of praxis and law. However, the price of concealing this tradition solely in a body of praxis was that it made the experiential bridge back to Sinai inoperable. What was offered in place of direct experience of God's will was halakha, a religious system that protected the tradition of Sinai precisely when access to the Sod tradition could not be disclosed. This suggests the notion that halakha is the only legitimate path to God in a world of *deus absconditus (hester panim)* and human alienation, that is, exile. However, this state of alienation and absence is temporary and, in the Kabbalistic imagination, overcome suddenly at the moment of, or perhaps even moments before, redemption.

The dialectical process, which lies at the core of this theory of Jewish literature, suggests that the light of Sod must be revealed progressively, becoming more and more a dominant part of Judaism until it is finally overcome completely in the messianic era.[86] Hasidism uses the Zohar's idea of "opening the gates of [esoteric] wisdom" as a signpost for its popularization of Kabbala. In the following interpretation of Tikkunei Zohar (*tikun* 28), R. Gershon Henokh alludes to this point: "Before the [divine] light was received, it [Torah] was only enveloped [in a concealed state]; this is halakha. Halakha is the garment [*levushim*] of the words of Torah. When the light was received and the inner meaning [of Torah was understood] this is Kabbala."[87] Essentially he argues here that although the rabbis may have successfully concealed the Sod tradition, here called the oral law (I have called it the second oral law, the first oral law being the prophetic law), its disclosure began again from within its own discourse, in the teachings of the rabbinic sage R. Shimon bar Yohai, later taking the form of the Zohar.[88] The Zohar was intended to reveal that which is concealed in rabbinic literature. It took the oral law, or the concealed Torah, to renew that tradition, which lay at the very core of the essential message of Torah, back to its original, esoteric form.

> R. Shimon bar Yohai was unique in having knowledge of all the secrets of the Torah, which he received from Elijah the Prophet in the cave. He had reached the stature of Moses, our teacher, upon whom it is said "mouth to mouth I will speak to him, and show him wonders." All who achieve an understanding of divine secrets can only do so through R. Shimon bar Yohai, who received these secrets, as the Zohar states [3.61b]: "R. Shimon bar Yohai's wisdom had dominion over the entire world. All who aspire to his level, only do so to complete that which he began." . . . The Torah revealed to R. Shimon is the revelation of the written law. There is nothing in the world outside Torah, everything comes from Torah, as is made explicit in the Zohar [3.287b].[89]

The text of the Zohar served as the bridge to accomplish the disclosure of the original (written) tradition, a tradition that was closed after the culmination of prophecy and further concealed in rabbinic literature. The act of disclosing secrets and retrieving origins is understood ritualistically through the act of circumcision and the motif of the shofar at Sinai, both serving as metaphors for disclosure.[90]

As a rabbinic text, the Zohar is thus unique in that it reverses the trajectory of rabbinic discourse that, according to R. Gershon Henokh, sought to conceal rather than to reveal. The relationship between the Zohar and other rabbinic literature is thus problematical. The Zohar is envisioned as engaged in a somewhat contentious relationship with the larger rabbinic narrative, of which it is mythically a part, in its attempt to reverse, and thus complete, the entire rabbinic project.

The dialect that unfolds carries redemptive implications and sets the stage for R. Gershon Henokh's view of the development of Jewish literature in the Middle Ages and the apparent bifurcation of philosophy and Kabbala. The Zohar represents the prophetic tradition after prophecy (i.e., as a corrective to the rabbis), while philosophy represents the rabbinic tradition. R. Gershon Henokh presents the Zohar as an attempt to undo the rabbinic literary project of concealing and thus protecting the esoteric tradition of Moses from the larger Jewish community. The consequence of this rabbinic enterprise was that it concealed the very secret it wanted to reveal.

On this reading, the esoteric message embedded in rabbinic Judaism is obscured in a complex web of legal discourse. The Zohar discloses the secret in rabbinic literature, hidden in the garments of law, by creating its own garments, that is, Kabbalistic language. Subsequent generations of philosophers and mystics, both of whom inherit parts of this unrabbinic product of the rabbis (i.e., the Zohar), attempt to unravel the esoteric discourse transmitted in the Zohar and thus complete the process of simultaneously completing and undoing the rabbinic project of concealing the secret.[91] The dialectical process of concealing and revealing lies at the core of Judaism itself and becomes, for R. Gershon Henokh, the fulcrum of Jewish intellectual activity.

There is, I believe, a more radical claim being made here that becomes apparent in the exegetical writings of R. Gershon Henokh and his grandfather R. Mordecai Joseph. It appears from this interpretation that rabbinic Judaism not only concealed that which brings one back to Sinai; its very program is in tension with the telos of Judaism, that is, revealing the Sod tradition of Abraham. Whereas Judaism should reveal the nature of God as *memalei kol 'olmin* (one who fills all worlds), rabbinic Judaism, by embedding esoteric tradition in the body of halakha, concealed the tradition of Abraham, thus limiting the dominion of God to the "four cubits of halakha."

In his typology of Jewish intellectual history, Scholem suggested that rabbinic Judaism emerged at least partially as a result of a deep sense of alienation in the postprophetic world of divine silence. Halakha served as a model of covenant no longer tied to prophetic or mystical experience.[92] R. Gershon Henokh's history of Jewish esotericism at least partially affirms this observation. According to his model, however, rabbinic Judaism should not be viewed negatively. It necessarily concealed the Sod tradition to enable it to be transmitted orally and reemerge at a later time. The exile of the Sod tradition was a direct outgrowth of historical exile. To conceal this tradition became the condition for its disclosure.

Acutely aware of the radical implications of such an argument, R. Gershon Henokh recoils from the consequences implied in his theoretical presentation and offers a more temperate, but not less provocative, reading. He argues that rabbinic Judaism did not attempt to destroy the path back to Sinai, but rather embodied the Sod tradition in rabbinic legalism in order to protect it, so that it could be disclosed in the future. He is not willing to entertain the possibility that the rabbis were unaware of this essential component of divine revelation, nor of the part they played in concealing it. Yet he is also not taking the more conventional stance that the descendants of the rabbis (in the Middle Ages, for example) were continuously aware of what they were doing.

I would argue that he would have considered it plausible that the rabbinic enterprise, at some later point in time, lost track of the larger picture in its ongoing (and noble) effort to conceal the Sod tradition from the larger community. In short, rabbinic Jews in the centuries after the rabbinic period lost the dialectical principle that underlies the rabbinic project. The extension of this resulted in empty rabbinic legalism, the root of the early Hasidic critique of Lithuanian Jewry. By re-presenting the history of Sod as rooted in the rabbinic period, R. Gershon Henokh is essentially presenting Hasidism as a natural corrective for the distortion of rabbinic Judaism promulgated by these latter-day Talmudists and sages.

It seems that R. Gershon Henokh believed that the rabbinic enterprise of concealment and disclosure, had it retained its dialectical posture, could have constructed a path back to Sinai and subsequently to Abraham, obviating the need for the contribution of Kabbala.[93] In some sense, Kabbala also reflects the rabbinic program in that it represents the important move that reveals the Sod tradition within the body of a legalistic tradition *(ta'amei ha-mitzvot),* making the inner meaning accessible to a larger constituency.

The proximity of the Kabbalists to the rabbis, at least in method, reiterates that the calculated concealment of the rabbis was not viewed pejoratively. Reflecting the general sentiment of Hasidic polemics, negativity about the rabbinic project only emerges when it sees itself as self-sufficient and self-contained. R. Gershon Henokh understood the need for concealment in order to protect the sacred Sod tradition from distortion and abuse. However, redemption necessitated that it turn outward, whereby the tradition would be revealed and facilitate the final purification of the exilic psyche of the Jewish people. The failure of rabbinic Judaism to turn against itself in order to complete its own project gave birth to the esotericism of the Zohar. The act of concealment resulted in the emergence of an esoteric tradition, that is, the Zohar (or perhaps transformed a previously exoteric tradition into an esoteric one [Zohar]) setting the stage for the emergence of what is formally known as Kabbala and its completion in Hasidism. As noted above, this reading of rabbinic Judaism as the calculated concealment of this Sod tradition also carries strong messianic implications. Jewish esotericism, and consequently the messianic process that Torah is supposed to fulfill, begins in the very moment of rabbinic restraint.

Restraint as a necessary part of the redemptive process is not a new observation. In his seminal essay on Maimonidean messianism, Amos Funkenstein argues that Maimonidean messianism is based on Maimonides' message to the Jews of Yemen to constrain and limit messianic anticipation and speculation. According to Funkenstein, cautious restraint was a necessary component in the messianic process.[94] Underlying Funkenstein's theory of Maimonidean messianism and R. Gershon Henokh's theory of rabbinic Judaism is a firm commitment to the dialectical process as a condition for the eschatological climax of redemption—that is, that redemption occurs through rupture and the very reversal of the project that created the conditions for its possibility. Whereas Funkenstein's dialectical stance is drawn largely from Hegel, R. Gershon Henokh's dialectical view of perfecting the world is rooted in his dialectical reading of the Lurianic theory of *shevirah* and *tikun* (rupture and repair).

According to Luria, *tikun* is a slow process of emanation and retraction of light, each emanation and subsequent retraction strengthening the vessel until it is able to be a permanent receptacle for divine emanation.[95] R. Gershon Henokh adopts this cosmological theory as the basis of his concept of the trajectory of the Sod tradition as it travels through Jewish history. Rabbinic legalism and later medieval Jewish philosophy were two stages in the concealment of this tradition. Whereas the rabbis may have been at least partially conscious of their actions, the medieval philosophers were not.[96]

Rabbinic caution and restraint, which became manifest in the calculated concealment of the Sod tradition in the body of law, prevented the problematic messianic tragedy of "forcing the end."[97] In R. Gershon Henokh's panoramic view, the dialectical process that served as the core of Jewish intellectual activity in the Middle Ages also allowed Torah as light—that is, revealing the concealed—to remain present yet not fully disclosed.

The first step beyond the legalistic activity of the rabbis, which constituted concealment, appears in the work of the second-century rabbinic figure, Rabbi Shimon bar Yohai, who, in the mind of R. Gershon Henokh, is the author of the Zohar. The figure of R. Shimon in the Zohar initiated a process of revealing the mystical doctrine cloaked in rabbinic legalism.[98] The essential task of R. Shimon bar Yohai is likened to that of the patriarch Abraham. Just as Abraham had to expand the boundaries of Melchizedek's transcendent God to include an immanent God, R. Shimon had to expand the rabbinic notion of God as limited to the "four ells of halakha" (rabbinic legalism) to include divine presence in the mundane.[99]

Sensitive to the radical nature of such a claim, R. Gershon Henokh suggests that R. Shimon was only revealing that which already existed in a concealed state in the rabbinic tradition.[100] Esoteric innovation is thus always about breaking boundaries for the sake of extending a true doctrine beyond its own limits, while also seeing the extension as already implied in the system being interpreted. Innovation in this light is envisioned as renewal, embodied in the ancient liturgical dictum *hadesh yamenu k'kedem* (renewing our days like those of old), reaching all the way back to Abraham.[101] The subtle retrieval of this Abrahamic tradition lies at the root of R. Gershon Henokh's dialectical/mystical enterprise.

An important distinction emerges from this reading of the development of the Jewish intellectual tradition. Referring to the oft-quoted Talmudic dictum that "the first 2,000 years of Torah begin with Abraham," R. Gershon Henokh suggests that the Torah of Abraham is the Torah of pure spirit or the Sod tradition, which is reflected in the teachings of the Zohar and not in the rabbinic teachings of halakha.[102] Halakha becomes a post-Sinaitic phenomenon while Kabbala, taking a literary form in the Zohar, is viewed as having its roots in the pre-Sinaitic teaching of Abraham.[103]

Not unlike other architects of sweeping religious ideologies, R. Gershon Henokh often rearranges categories to fit into his new historiosophy. Earlier we pointed to how he drew a distinction between the Torah of Abraham and the Torah of the rabbis, suggesting that the former is reflected in the teachings of the Zohar, which is a combination of the pre-Sinaitic Abrahamic tradition and the revelation of Elijah the Prophet to R. Shimon bar Yohai.[104] Next, he draws a distinction between the mystical tradition in pre-Zoharic Judaism and the mystical tradition of the Zohar itself.

Although he argues that the text of the Zohar is a renewal of the pre-Sinaitic tradition of Abraham filtered through the revealed mystical tradition of the prophets that was concealed by the rabbis, he does not champion a position of pure restoration. Each new stage of this esoteric tradition offers a revision of the old system. Hence the Zohar, in the act of revealing the concealed nature of God as immanent through rabbinic legalism, interprets the pre-Sinaitic tradition in a new way.

Before the Zohar, R. Gershon Henokh argues, Jewish tradition was developing along two separate paths—halakha (legalism) and Kabbala (mysticism). Implied in this bifurcation of mysticism and legalism is the fact that pre-Zohar Kabbala (i.e., Hekhalot literature, *Sefer Yezerah, Sefer Bahir*) does not generally integrate the legal tradition or engage in *ta'amei ha-mitzvot* like the Zohar. R. Gershon Henokh, of course, held all these texts to be of ancient origin. Nonetheless, he appears to have taken note of the Zohar's unique interest in halakha and mitzvot and integrated it into his history of the Sod tradition. While R. Gershon Henokh views all these texts as "rabbinic," he appears to view the Zohar as a text that moves away from the (rabbinic) bifurcation of legalism and mysticism.

According to this theory, halakha before the Zohar was the exoteric tradition while the Kabbala was its esoteric counterpart,[105] even as Kabbala was concealed within the halakhic tradition.[106] This all changed as a result of R. Shimon's decision to unveil the mystical tradition embedded in the legalism of the rabbis. In the imagination of R. Gershon Henokh, R. Shimon set the agenda for all subsequent mystics. He understands that this shift, divinely directed, ushers in a new stage in the unfolding of the Sod tradition that climaxes in the Besht's interpretation of Luria.

Once Kabbala is revealed as part of the rabbinic tradition, the Kabbalist must always seek to uncover the mystical nature of the exoteric rabbinic text.[107] In the theosophical tradition of which the Zohar is a central part, *ta'amei ha-mitzvot* became a focus of mystical reflection. The dialectic of concealing and subsequently revealing this mystical tradition concealed in the legal discourse of halakha (*ta'amei ha-mitzvot,* according to its Kabbalistic construction) continued throughout Jewish history, reaching new heights in the teachings of R. Isaac Luria.

Just as R. Shimon revealed the subliminal mystical meaning of rabbinic Judaism, the contemporary mystic must reveal the esoteric tradition from within its newly concealed state, that is, from the Zohar and medieval Jewish philosophy. This is the underlying impetus behind R. Gershon Henokh's treatment of the medieval rationalist tradition, particularly Maimonides' *Guide of the Perplexed.* R. Gershon Henokh understands that *ta'amei ha-mitzvot,* which became a dominant theme in medieval philosophical literature and in Maimonides in particular, originated in the late antique esotericism of the Zohar. The exercise of inquiring into the meaning of the mitzvot *(ta'amei ha-mitzvot),* even in its rational form, emerges from the mystical program of reconstructing the Sod tradition of Abraham out of the exoteric Torah of the rabbis.[108] Rationalism serves as the medieval correlate of rabbinic halakha, enveloping the esoteric tradition in order to make it accessible to the widest possible audience. By revealing the esoteric underpinning of the *Guide,* R. Gershon Henokh claims to be doing to the *Guide* what R. Shimon did to rabbinic literature.

Before moving on to the Middle Ages, I would like to set the stage for this next phase of R. Gershon Henokh's dialectical hypothesis. I suggested earlier that he held that the Zohar accomplished two things. First, it revealed the mystical tradition hidden in rabbinic Judaism. This, in essence, unified two traditions that shared the same source yet had been developing separately, a common theme in the general history of esotericism. The separate and alienated state of these two traditions before the Zohar symbolized historical and psychic exile. Historical exile was founded on the alienation of the mystical and legalistic traditions in Judaism. The unity of these traditions in the Zohar, accomplished by revealing how each contains its opposite, created the possibility for redemption. Thus, in the Idrot sections of the Zohar, R. Shimon is viewed as a messianic figure.[109] Second, since it drew from oral traditions that preceded Scripture, the Zohar integrated all the pre-Sinaitic teachings that had no scriptural base into a Judaism based on Scripture. In short, it created a synthesis between the revealed and the concealed and between Sinai and what preceded it.

Accordingly, one could argue that all human knowledge contained in the Torah of Sinai exists in the Zohar in a more complete and pristine way. This is because the Zohar reveals the hidden meaning in the exoteric tradition (i.e., rabbinic law) and integrates that which preceded Sinai into Scripture. This point will become clear when we analyze R. Gershon Henokh's synthesis of rationalist medieval philosophy with the Zohar in the next chapter.

Underlying his entire Hasidic presentation of Judaism is the notion that the substance of Jewish philosophy, even as it uses the language of Greek philosophy, is rooted in the Sod tradition of Torah that preceded Sinai. Moreover, although he never states so explicitly, he would appear to accept the position held by other mystics that the knowledge of the Greeks could be found in the Torah, in that the Torah includes all that could be rationally known, albeit through the superrational experience of revelation. This stance is highly uncommon among Hasidic thinkers, who generally did not include secular wisdom in their dialectical understanding of the relationship between God and the world. On the question of secular knowledge and Torah, most Hasidic masters adopted the position of the incompatibility of Torah and secular wisdom championed by R. Meir ibn Gabbai and the other postexpulsion Kabbalists.[110] In this sense, R. Gershon Henokh is uncharacteristic and may represent an important example of a Hasidic nexus with modernity, albeit quite attenuated.

R. Gershon Henokh makes an important distinction in *Ha-Hakdama* between the original orality of the Zohar and the construction of the Zohar as a written text.[111] When we refer to the Zohar we usually mean the written text we call *Sefer Ha-Zohar,* which, according to R. Gershon Henokh, is an accurate albeit limited transcription of R. Shimon's teachings.

The full disclosure of the Sod tradition accomplished by R. Shimon bar Yohai in the Zohar lasted only as long as R. Shimon was alive.[112] Throughout the Zohar we read that R. Shimon's death destroyed the pristine quality of his teachings: "When R. Shimon departed [died] the fountains of wisdom were closed" (Zohar 2.149). Using this and other examples, R. Gershon Henokh suggests that the loss of orality with the death of the master once again concealed an important element of his teaching. Therefore, the bridge from the oral law back to the written law and finally back to the Sod tradition can never be maintained textually. The full disclosure of Sod must include an oral component in the figure of an inspired master.[113] The inspired interpreter (R. Shimon/Luria/the Baal Shem Tov) is able to transmit knowledge that could not be retained or maintained through mere study and repetition (that is, through the text of the Zohar).[114] Hence, the students of R. Shimon, in their interpretations of their master, conceal (albeit unconsciously) the revelatory nature of those very teachings as those teachings move from oral transmission (orality) to text (literacy).[115] The deficiency resulting from R. Shimon's death replays a similar theme in rabbinic literature, the loss of memory after Moses' death.[116] For R. Gershon Henokh, who sees the Zohar as the best textual representation of the Sod tradition of Abraham, R. Shimon's departure resulted in the deficiency of all subsequent Kabbalistic doctrine, initiating another level of concealment of this tradition in the literary form of the tradition of its disclosure. This renewed state of concealment is rectified only through the oral teachings of the Baal Shem Tov.

> We also find this with the commentaries to *Sefer Yezerah* . . . and afterward with other Kabbalistic works that speak in a concealed language, such as *Sefer Ha-Kaneh* and Rabad's commentary to *Sefer Yezerah.* In subsequent generations Kabbalistic works were written that contained reliable traditions [*kabbala shelamah*] which were concealed in philosophical language [*lashon ha-mehkar*]. In places where they had a reliable tradition they alluded to it in their writings. In places where they did not have a reliable tradition, they wrote in a confusing manner [*gimgamu b'lshonam*].[117]

Although this point is never developed systematically in *Ha-Hakdama,* it appears that the experiential dimension of transmission plays a critical role in the method of uncovering the concealed secret. With Abraham and at Sinai, direct intervention by God served as the experiential component that transformed the concealed into the revealed. In the case of R. Shimon and perhaps other mystics after him (Luria, for certain), Elijah the Prophet intercedes and points toward the proper way of reading an exoteric text in order to reveal its esoteric meaning.[118] R. Shimon's death, as described in detail in the Idra Raba and Idra Zuta, is an essential part of this dialectical process and therefore receives a great deal of attention in the Zohar. His death resulted in the retraction of the experiential component of the transmission of esoteric doctrine, yielding a new era of concealment represented in the literary textual formulation of *Sefer Ha-Zohar*. In this rendering, the Zohar embodies a new form of esotericism—a text which hints at a message that consistently eludes its readers, because its message can only be fully disclosed by the inclusion of an experiential transmission via the master. The Zohar is the most complete exemplar of this Sod tradition, but, as text, cannot reflect its entire content. Textuality results in a new form of exile, but one that serves as a vehicle for the final disclosure of esoteric wisdom. The textuality of Sod becomes a new veil hiding the secret it contains. The construction of a text, especially in esoteric traditions, is often accompanied by lamenting the loss of a cherished leader. The tendency toward insularity is common among many mystical schools when its charismatic leader dies. The text, which is the sole vehicle of transmission, is also the veil of secrecy.[119]

While textuality by itself is viewed here an act of concealment, R. Gershon Henokh also suggests that the death of R. Shimon resulted in a conscious move by his disciples to conceal the oral traditions of their teacher (even those that were not lost as a result of his departure). The text of the Zohar, as opposed to the original oral teachings upon which it is based, subsequently houses the hidden message of Sod, not unlike that of rabbinic literature. This phenomenon also creates symmetry between the Zohar as text and medieval Jewish philosophy (the *Guide of the Perplexed* being its best exemplar), even as the form of the Zohar contains a more complete rendition of the tradition that both conceal. On this reading, the *Guide* and the Zohar as texts are different only in degree and not in kind. Both contain fragments of the esoteric Sod tradition that the Hasidic reader is required to reveal.

The Zohar is more complete than the *Guide of the Perplexed* in that it has already been partly revealed through Lurianic Kabbala; it also uses language that more accurately transmits its hidden message.[120] For this reason R. Gershon Henokh leans heavily on the Lurianic reading of the Zohar in order to disclose the secrets of the *Guide,* an idea I will develop more fully in the next chapter. He believed that the Jewish philosophical tradition was yet another part of the concealment of the esoteric tradition. Jewish philosophy contains only a portion *(kabbala helkit)* of that full doctrine *(kabbala shelamah),* since it is not founded on divine oral transmission but is solely the product of the human intellect coupled with fragments of incomplete received traditions.[121] R. Gershon Henokh's overarching project in *Ha-Hakdama*—to reveal the places in Maimonides' *Guide of the Perplexed* that he believed were derived from the Sod tradition embedded in the Zohar—is devoted to exhibiting the symmetry and mutuality of both texts, resulting in the full disclosure and liberation of the Sod tradition that underlies both.

Philosophy is understood by R. Gershon Henokh as an attempt, by way of reason alone, to reveal the esoteric nature of the written law. Philosophy is necessarily flawed in that it carries no full tradition *(kabbala shelamah)* via oral transmission or divine inspiration. Its attempt at disclosure (i.e., to attain clarity about the truth of revelation), while it may contain constructive elements, more often than not results in a new level of concealment.

> Philosophical inquiry [*hakirah 'iyunit*] contains a great deal that is extraneous. Philosophy is built upon empirical proofs and theories [that which is known from the senses] to understand that which exists above nature. As such, that which is not known to the senses cannot be understood. However, that which is not empirical also cannot be understood. Yet, it seeks to arrive at knowledge by going from the effect to the cause [*Ha-Alul el Ha-Ilah*]. Therefore, in most cases it [philosophical discourse] is mistaken.[122]

For R. Gershon Henokh the deficiency of philosophy is not only the fact that it is solely the product of the intellect. Philosophical language inherently limits one's understanding of the presence of God in the world because it uses limited language to describe the empirical or logical realms, neither of which contain direct access to divine presence.[123]

In short, R. Gershon Henokh argues that philosophical language in general is not inspired. However, even as he limits philosophical discourse and method (in line with earlier medieval Kabbalists), he legitimizes the agenda of philosophy as part of the dialectical process of revealing and concealing the authentic Sod tradition. This is all predicated on his belief that an esoteric pre-Sinai tradition was in the hands of an elite group of Jewish philosophers in the Middle Ages.[124] Without offering any significant explanation or providing any textual examples, R. Gershon Henokh suggests that the symbolic language of the Zohar and Lurianic Kabbala is preferred to the philosophical language of philosophy:

> Even if a "complete and reliable Kabbalistic tradition" [*kabbala shelamah*] would be written in the language of philosophy, the language would not

> be sufficient to explain [the issue]. In most cases, it would miss the proper intention. . . . For example, a number of chapters in *The Guide of the Perplexed* deal with the denial that God has any corporeal properties and with the problem of homonyms. The Zohar, in its language, can explain in one or two words all that we learn in these chapters [in the *Guide*].[125]

This text raises numerous issues that require careful attention. First, it acknowledges that philosophy and Kabbala have, in many cases, a similar agenda—the agenda of revealing the divine in the world. Second, it implies that both philosophy and Kabbala attempt to complete their respective tasks through language. The essential difference between them is the linguistic form each chooses to transmit this tradition.

The deficiency of philosophy (here represented by the *Guide*) is, first, that it does not possess a complete and reliable transmission of this esoteric doctrine *(kabbala shelamah),* because philosophers were not recipients of any revelation, prophecy, or illumination but instead used reason as a method of reconstructing fragments of the tradition they received.[126] Second, the linguistic tools that Jewish philosophers borrowed from the Greeks are not as succinct or as pregnant as the symbolic language of the Zohar.[127] In discussing the presence of God in the world, a presence that is not given to empirical evidence, philosophical language fails to adequately convey the human experience of the divine realm. The language of myth and symbol—mystical or poetic language—more accurately depicts the nature of the divine realm.[128] What is interesting here is that R. Gershon Henokh, in opposition to many pre-expulsion Kabbalists, does not claim that the difference between Kabbala and philosophy is that the former represents a complete and reliable transmission of the concealed Sod tradition. Both Jewish philosophy and Kabbala are reconstructive projects born from the necessary failure of any written transmission to fully embody its oral beginnings following the rabbinic project of concealment. While the revelatory inspiration of Kabbalists (Luria, for example) can aid in this reconstructive endeavor, it cannot complete the tradition that has already been lost.

The theoretical first part of R. Gershon Henokh's treatise is an attempt to trace the history of Jewish esotericism from its origins in the pre-Sinai tradition of Abraham to its bifurcated state in the Middle Ages in the realm of philosophy and Kabbala.[129] Throughout this historiography, however, we are never given any insight into the substantive content of this Sod tradition. We are told that methodologically Sod is focused on revealing the aspect of God as *memalei kol 'olmin* (He who fills all worlds), reflected in the act of the circumcision of Abraham and the voice of the shofar at Sinai.

It seems obvious that R. Gershon Henokh is not concerned with the substance of this tradition. Sod merely serves as a mythic foundation that creates the condition for his projected synthesis of philosophy and Kabbala. Moreover, it creates the foundation for Hasidism in general as the final frontier of the Jewish mystical tradition that completes the Zoharic project by fully disclosing the esoteric roots of Sod that underlie both Kabbala and Jewish philosophy. For this reason, the treatise in question is presented as a preface to his father's Hasidic work *Beit Ya'akov,* and is presented an "introduction to Izbica/Radzin Hasidism," implicitly intended to be a new and final introduction to Hasidism in general. As we will see in the following chapters, the dialectical theory of transmission (disclosure and concealment) is also intended to serve as the vindication of his grandfather's denial of free will in *Mei Ha-Shiloah.* The polemic against *Mei Ha-Shiloah,* which was already in full force before this treatise was written, hovers over R. Gershon Henokh's entire literary corpus.

For R. Gershon Henokh, classical Kabbala did not emerge until the Sod tradition of Abraham and Sinai was intentionally concealed in the rabbinic legalism of halakha. In fact, rabbinic legalism creates the conditions for Kabbala, whose main purpose is revealing the secrets embedded in rabbinic literature.[130] Halakha is not understood here as merely containing this Sod tradition of Abraham. It is a body of literature that intentionally conceals it, yet does so in a way that enables future generations to reconstruct it.

The reversal of rabbinic concealment occurs in the belly of the rabbinic fraternity in the person of R. Shimon bar Yohai, who, threatened by the possibility of annihilation at the hands of the Romans, discloses the secrets to his hidden fraternity. For the generation after Noah, Abraham, and later the generation of Sinai, what needed to be revealed was the presence of God in nature, perhaps explaining the correlation between the covenantal promise to Noah in the rainbow, the covenantal promise to Abraham in the ritual of circumcision, and the covenantal experience of Sinai in *seeing the sounds . . . of the Shofar* (Exodus 20:15). After the development of halakha (i.e., through Rabbinic Judaism), itself a product of exile and divine concealment resulting from the culmination of prophecy, it is the halakha that hides the presence of God.

The job of the Jewish mystic is then to reveal the Sod tradition embedded in halakhic discourse. This is, for R. Gershon Henokh, the agenda and program of R. Shimon bar Yohai in the Zohar and subsequently the Kabbala. The act of disclosing God's will in the halakha is completed by reconnecting the pre-Sinai tradition of revealing God in nature (Noah and

Abraham) as an outgrowth of Kabbalistic literature. In a sense, the completion of this program is the overcoming, but not the erasure, of halakha. This project is championed by the Baal Shem Tov who serves as the last hero before the advent of the messianic era.

In exile, the two poles of the dialectical process of revelation and concealment become embedded in the Jewish literary tradition in rabbinic Judaism (halakha) and in the Zohar (Kabbala). R. Shimon began to deconstruct the rabbinic concealment of the Sod tradition by revealing the secrets therein. R. Shimon's death and the culmination of any direct revelation of Elijah the Prophet set the stage for the philosophical centuries of the Middle Ages.[131]

The most telling consequence of R. Shimon's death, and the concealment of his disclosure of Sod in the body of the Zohar as a text, is that subsequent Kabbala must reconstruct the Sod in the Zohar without the aid of divine revelation. The program of post-Zohar Kabbala (at least until Luria) and medieval Jewish philosophy is the attempt to recover this Sod tradition buried in the metahalakhic Jewish literary corpus without the aid of divine intervention or a fully extant tradition. This was an important phase in the redemptive process, in that this metahalakhic enterprise of reconstruction is an inversion of the rabbinic program of concealment. Kabbala and medieval Jewish philosophy, as recipients of fragments of this ancient tradition, provided the context enabling these hidden fragments to rise to the surface and be reconstructed as a post-Sinai Abrahamic religion, completing the history of Jewish esotericism.[132]

Accepting R. Hayyim Vital's statement that the transmission of Kabbala was corrupted after Nahmanides (in the late thirteenth century) and was renewed with R. Isaac Luria in sixteenth-century Safed, R. Gershon Henokh adds that this revelation extended to the Baal Shem Tov as well. Luria succeeded in reconstructing the fragmented tradition embedded in the Zohar, and the Baal Shem Tov illuminated that tradition by stripping it of its symbolic language and re-dressing it in what R. Gershon Henokh determined was a more Abrahamic style.[133] These two developments set the stage for the final exoneration of the last vestige of God's concealment—medieval Jewish philosophy. R. Gershon Henokh's synthesis of the partial tradition embedded in medieval Jewish philosophy with the Zohar was understood by him as the final phase of reversing (and thus completing) the rabbinic project which was, in at least a historical sense, the construction of exilic Judaism. The illumination of the Sod tradition of Abraham intended to bring out the primordial Jewish relationship to God; natural, fluid, and liberated. This idea is subsequently the foundation of the protomessianic and messianic personalities of biblical figures, as depicted in his grandfather's *Mei Ha-Shiloah* and his *Sod Yesharim*.

In sum, R. Gershon Henokh's theory of esotericism, the disclosure of the Sod tradition of Abraham, requires: (1) the admission that no extant literary tradition, even Kabbala, contains a verifiable and complete transmission of Sod; (2) that a reconstruction of such a tradition is only plausible by reading the best forms of Jewish metahalakhic literature (the Zohar and the *Guide*) side by side; (3) that Luria, by reconstructing the fragments embedded in the Zohar, and the Baal Shem Tov, by stripping Kabbala of its garments that conceal its essence, set the stage for this last synthetic phase; (4) that the synthesis of the *Guide* and the Zohar would complete the dialectic of concealment and disclosure initiated by the rabbinic sages, resulting in the overcoming of the intellectual dualism of post-rabbinic Judaism and the redemption of Jewish consciousness; and, finally (5) that this synthesis would filter down into Jewish devotion, enabling Jews to reconstruct the categories of human will, worship, and commandment and retrieve a more pristine form of Abrahamic religion, lived through, but not limited by, halakha. This last point, that is, the translation of intellectual synthesis to pietistic praxis, is envisioned as the goal of Hasidism after the Baal Shem Tov, the telos of R. Gershon Henokh's "Introduction to Hasidism."

2 Recircumcising the Torah

The Synthesis of the Zohar and the *Guide of the Perplexed* and the Hasidic Reconstruction of Esotericism

In viewing Hasidism as a "new approach to Torah," one could posit that it sets out to rectify an overemphasis on study and the all-encompassing nature of the law as the sum total of living within the covenant (a somewhat exaggerated characterization of eighteenth- and nineteenth-century Lithuanian Jewry).[1] Living in the shadow of the Sabbatean heresy of the seventeenth century and thus acutely aware of the antinomian implications inherent in such a critique, Hasidism also stresses a strong commitment to the codified law *(Shulkhan Arukh)* and consistently affirms that mitzvot are the exclusive, legitimate framework of Judaism.

What resulted from this dual allegiance (i.e., to a critique of the law and allegiance to the law) was an internal critique of halakha, based on the assumption (drawn from classical prophets) that the commandments (temple ritual/halakha) create the possibility of religious behaviorism, whereby individuals could outwardly observe the law yet inwardly desecrate it.[2] This internal critique of the law, which arguably becomes the emblem of Hasidic spirituality, focuses on the deficiency of the law when observed without any experiential component (devekut). The Hasidic alternative is structured as an extension of the prophetic critique of ancient Israel. The prophetic chastisement of ritual practices void of internal devotion and moral living was translated to Hasidism as a critique of halakhic observance void of devekut.

As close readers of Scripture, Hasidic masters used biblical characters, creating them in their own image, to root their critique in the most sacred text of the tradition. In particular, the pre-Sinai characters of Genesis, most notably the patriarch Abraham, were especially compelling to Hasidic thinkers. Abraham is often presented in Hasidic literature as the inverse of the religious personality Hasidism criticized in that he is a figure who was able to fulfill God's will independent of any external framework of law or commandment. Abraham becomes the Hasidic hero and a central model of Hasidic spirituality. His intuitive skill, born from his unwavering faith and his commitment to spread his own awakening in an intimate and accessible manner, serves as the template of Hasidic Judaism's reconfiguration of authentic Jewish religiosity.[3]

Another important facet of Abraham as the hero for mystical Judaism in general, and Hasidim in particular, is his identification with the act of circumcision, the first "covenantal commandment," often viewed as the archetypal mitzvah. The physical act of circumcision, removing the foreskin to reveal the hidden crown of the penis, is used as a trope for esotericism in medieval Kabbala, particularly the Zohar, surfacing again in Lurianic Kabbala and later in Hasidism. The Zohar places great emphasis on the cutting of the foreskin and the disclosure of the penis as emblematic of its own hermeneutic of disclosure, the redemptive act of revealing the secrets hidden in the biblical narrative.[4]

In the Kabbalistic imagination, the act of circumcision is a physical manifestation of the purpose of Torah study in general, revealing the secrets of God's existence by peeling away the external layers hiding the "true" meaning of the text. Redemptive Torah study or, according to Luria's disciple R. Hayyim Vital, true *"torah lishma"* (Torah study for its own sake) can only be achieved through the study of Kabbala, the literature that reveals the hidden message of Scripture.[5] Kabbala, along with its medieval counterpart, philosophy, developed an esoteric hermeneutic that seeks to unveil the scriptural text and thus enable Israel to understand God's full intention.

In Hasidism, however, circumcision is only one part of the Abraham leitmotif. Also included is Abraham's intimacy with God, his unwavering faith (exhibited most prominently in the binding of Isaac),[6] and the ancient tradition that he composed a secret teaching that survived as esoteric lore, albeit transmitted in a maculate form, throughout Jewish history.

R. Gershon Henokh's Hasidic esotericism is based on the assumption that all legitimate metahalakhic Jewish literature is an attempt to reconstruct that ancient Sod tradition. Jewish exile is the result of this unfinished task. The history of esoteric literature can thus be viewed as the continual circumcision and recircumcision of this ancient tradition, whereby this tradition is revealed and subsequently concealed (for numerous reasons), each new phase posing fresh challenges and possibilities for redemption. In

R. Gershon Henokh's thinking, the Baal Shem Tov and subsequently his own grandfather, R. Mordecai Joseph of Izbica, are the latest arbiters of this circumcision process. His vocation was to take their own synthetic work into another arena—the realm of medieval Jewish philosophy and Kabbala.

In an attempt to diffuse the dualism between Jewish philosophy and Kabbala constructed by many postexpulsion Kabbalists, the Hasidic esotericist must carefully peel away the "foreskins" that cover all the permutations of the ancient Abrahamic tradition underlying both literary traditions (i.e., philosophy and Kabbala), revealing their common source. The result will be a full reconstruction of this Abrahamic tradition, yielding the culmination of Sinai and thus the end of Jewish exile. In this chapter I will analyze both the theory and substance of this synthetic exercise, arguing that it is the foundation of the entire Izbica/Radzin project of Hasidic renewal, and maintaining that the anti-intellectualism that may have existed in Hasidism's early phase is no longer prominent in Hasidism's more mature mid-nineteenth-century period.

Redemption through Cutting/Uncovering

The second section of part I of *Ha-Hakdama ve Ha-Petikha* is the textual application of R. Gershon Henokh's theory of esotericism (discussed in the first section of part I). Here, R. Gershon Henokh attempts to illustrate the similarities between medieval Jewish philosophy and Kabbala in order to prove that they share a common tradition and a similar agenda. The purpose of this synthetic enterprise contains two complimentary components. First, it is to show the affinity between philosophy and Kabbala as two forms of Jewish esotericism that dialectically disclose and conceal the secrets of an ancient Abrahamic tradition. Second, the synthesis of philosophy and Kabbala (or, more accurately, subsuming philosophy into a monistic Kabbalistic project) seeks to complete an essential component of the Baal Shem Tov's tacit deconstruction of the Platonic dualism of medieval Kabbala. Until these apparently incompatible traditions (philosophy and Kabbala) are seen in light of one another, and even as dependent upon one another, the complete unfolding of the Abrahamic Sod tradition via the Baal Shem Tov cannot be achieved. That is, until the Beshtean process of sanctifying the profane is extended to include the disclosure of the primordial antecedents that lie beneath the surface of Jewish rational and mystical discourse, the redemptive process will remain incomplete.

In the previous chapter I argued that R. Gershon Henokh held that the medieval Jewish philosophical tradition, like its Kabbalistic counterpart, attempted to explain the fragments of the Sod tradition it had inherited. However, since it did so via philosophical discourse, which is not able to adequately express these secrets, the result is that the secrets become even more concealed in their attempted philosophical disclosure. This point remains opaque in *Ha-Hakdama* because R. Gershon Henokh never illustrates his theory with any concrete evidence. Rather, he adopts earlier Geronese (Nahmanides), ecstatic (Abulafia), and postexpulsion (Ibn Gabbai) Kabbalistic models that claim that the failure of philosophy is at least partially due to the fact that rational (i.e., philosophical) discourse is unable to transmit the secrets of the esoteric tradition.[7]

R. Gershon Henokh's utilization of these antiphilosophical models is not merely a repetition of these older positions because it is couched in an esoteric theory that views the *Guide* as an authentic embodiment of the Mosaic and even Abrahamic traditions, not purely the result of rational interpretation and reasoned opinions. In opposition to these earlier models, many of which present a highly dualistic portrait of philosophy and Kabbala, R. Gershon Henokh advocates serious engagement with the *Guide,* not to illustrate its shortcomings or exhibit its limited success in achieving correct interpretation through rational inquiry, but to disclose the ancient Sod tradition that underlies its failed delivery and to offer a more dialectical interpretation of the complex relationship between these two metahalakhic traditions.

While R. Gershon Henokh's critique of philosophical language reflects earlier Kabbalistic critiques of Maimonides, it is founded on a different premise. Moshe Idel recently argued that the Kabbalistic critique of philosophical language is the foundation for much of the antagonism against Maimonides by medieval Kabbalists.[8] This critique, I would add, is couched in the firm belief that the *Guide* was an authentic, albeit deficient, text. This is especially true among pre-Zohar Kabbalists, whose worldview was more compatible with the basic philosophical premises of the *Guide,* especially as interpreted through the lens of Neoplatonism.[9]

The authenticity of the *Guide* for many of the medieval Kabbalists resulted from their belief that reason, when properly used, played an important role in the acquisition of, or preparation for, mystical knowledge. This is especially true for Kabbalists such as R. Abraham Isaac ibn Latif, Abraham Abulafia, and Joseph ibn Gikatillia, but also true for Nahmanides and even Yehuda Ha-Levi who, while not a Kabbalist, exhibits a predilection for mystical reflection.[10]

In Hasidism, due in part to its historical proximity to the Jewish Enlightenment, reason as a vehicle for mystical knowledge does not have the same stature as it did for medieval Jews. Strongly influenced by the Zohar and the post-Zoharic imagination, the notion of authenticity in Hasidic literature is largely limited either to bona fide transmission or divine inspiration. R. Gershon Henokh never claims that Maimonides is the recipient of divine inspiration like R. Shimon bar Yohai in the Zohar or R. Isaac Luria.[11]

Therefore, the truth of the *Guide* for R. Gershon Henokh lies in Maimonides' access and use of an esoteric tradition, even as that tradition may only be accessible in fragments (*kabbala helkit*). Therefore, R. Gershon Henokh never states that medieval Kabbalists opposed Maimonides because they felt he was philosophizing and thus defiling an ancient esoteric tradition.

This rejectionist theory, as Idel argues, appears late in medieval Kabbala, perhaps due to the influence of the Zohar. R. Gershon Henokh maintains that the *Guide*'s philosophical apparatus is merely a veil to conceal the esoteric tradition that flows underneath the entire treatise. Curiously, *Ha-Hakdama* appears more aligned with the pre-Zohar Kabbalists on this matter, albeit with a different agenda. The *Guide* is legitimate for R. Gershon Henokh because it represents a concealed text, one that can be opened by reading it through the lens of a more revealed (yet not fully revealed) text, the Zohar. What results is a Hasidic position on the legitimacy of the *Guide* that reflects pre-Zohar Kabbalistic sentiments toward Maimonides utilizing the textual structure and stature of the Zohar and its Lurianic interpretation, both of which have little use for philosophy in general and Maimonides in particular.

In his attempt to mark new boundaries in order to construct a compatibility or mutuality between the Zohar and the *Guide,* R. Gershon Henokh reconstructs a pre-Zohar debate on the viability of the *Guide* in a world dominated by the canonization of the Zohar. He argues that Maimonides had at least fragments of some ancient tradition which informed the basis of his philosophical discussions.[12] Rational discourse (i.e., philosophical language) is viewed as a garment concealing, sometimes unwittingly, the true Sod foundations of any position in the *Guide,* and not as an independent mode of reasoning toward truth void of any esoteric foundation. Although precedent for this position appears in Kabbalists such as Ibn Latif, Moshe Botreil, and Abraham Abulafia, it was overshadowed by the dominance and popularity of thinkers like Ha-Levi and Nahmanides, the Zohar, and finally the antiphilosophical Kabbalism that emerged in the wake of the expulsion from Spain at the end of the fifteenth century. Moreover, the medieval Kabbalistic positions do not generally maintain that Maimonides was the recipient of any esoteric tradition.[13] At best, they viewed the *Guide* and philosophy as a stage toward the acquisition of mystical knowledge—a stage eventually to be overcome by the study and practice of Kabbala.[14]

By the middle of the nineteenth century, Hasidic Kabbalism begins to cohere as an alternative Kabbalistic ideology among the other mystical schools in Eastern Europe. In general, the Kabbala is viewed as the authentic transmission of an ancient tradition conceived orally and later canonized in Kabbalistic literature. In Hasidism, the Jewish philosophical canon in general and the *Guide* in particular are sometimes interpreted to express basic Kabbalistic ideas; or, more frequently, they are ignored or cited only sporadically as proof-texts for some unrelated point. In Hasidism, medieval Jewish philosophy is severed from its metaphysical foundations and intellectual context, and it is used canonically only as it supports a body of texts built on very different foundations.[15]

In the case of Radzin Hasidism, the literary tradition called Kabbala is conceived largely as an authentic version of a Sod tradition not yet fully revealed. The deficiency of the Zohar as a text is due to its written form and also to the long exile which made its proper interpretation impossible. Luria's teaching, via inspiration, while clarifying some obscure elements in the Zohar, also conceals some of those ideas in opaque mythic language. The Baal Shem Tov begins to disrobe Kabbala of its concealing and obfuscating language, inaugurating the final era of esoteric restoration. R. Gershon Henokh situates himself along that continuum, both historically and ideologically.

R. Gershon Henokh's reading of the philosophical and Kabbalistic traditions is informed by the common Hasidic claim that the Baal Shem Tov sought to complete Luria's program by revealing that the vessels not only contain divine light but are themselves composed of divine light. The redemptive act is then not confined to separating or liberating the sparks from the vessels (a foundation of Lurianism, which is also the case in Hasidism) but also to transforming the vessels themselves into light by revealing that, in essence, they are light.[16] The claim that the Besht was able to reveal the divine nature of the veils *(masakhim)* that covered the light is extended to his reading of the Kabbala. That is, the Besht is able to translate the secrets in Luria's teaching in a this-worldly manner, making the secrets accessible to the uninitiated and more readily translatable into a language of devotion and faith.

> Even in our lowly generation God revealed to him [the Besht] a language that could communicate the secrets of Torah in a complete manner. God opened the inner gates that were closed until that time. He subsequently transmitted them [i.e., the secrets] to all Israel. . . . He opened the gate of the supernal Zohar [*Zohar Ha-Rakiya*], which is the [the text of the] Holy Zohar [*Sefer Ha-Zohar*], and the writings of the Ari [R. Isaac Luria] in order to teach them in a direct and accessible manner.[17]

Opening the secrets of the Kabbala is also intended to expand the canon of Torah. "There is nothing in the entire Torah that is not relevant to every Jew and not worth striving to understand."[18] Following this dictum, R. Gershon Henokh introduces the entire Jewish medieval philosophical tradition into Hasidic discourse, a tradition that had largely been excluded from systematic analysis in Hasidic literature. Integrating philosophical literature into the mystical tradition of Hasidism is now possible because the secrets of the Kabbala, revealed through the Besht, made Kabbala and philosophy more compatible. Underlying this claim is the curious notion that the incompatibility of Kabbala and philosophy, which partially causes the disappearance of philosophy from the purview of Jewish schools founded on the tradition of the Zohar, is the result of the concealed nature of both traditions. Ironically, the Lurianic tradition, perhaps the most nonphilosophical of all Kabbalistic schools, enables the Besht to unveil the esoteric sources of the Zohar, setting the stage for R. Gershon Henokh's unveiling of the shared esoteric sources of the Zohar and Maimonides' *Guide of the Perplexed*.[19]

In my view, the subtext of this whole enterprise is a reconstruction of traditional defenses of the *Guide* builton new foundations. Many defenders of the *Guide* in the Middle Ages and early modern period justify Maimonides' use of philosophical language and ideas as a tool to reach those alienated from the truth (and language) of tradition. The "secret" of the *Guide,* according to these defenders, is the body of tradition conceived by the rabbis, nothing more.[20] Alternatively, many antiphilosophical Kabbalists (including Hasidic masters) who denigrated the *Guide* did so because they misunderstood Maimonides' use of philosophical language and ideas, fooled by Maimonides' own esoteric game.

> I have spoken at length about Maimonides to protect his honor. He is no closer to me than his interpreters, all of whom were holy. Even if I have to suffer from the baseless hatred of those that seek to blot him out—they will also have to come after me. It is not because of this that I value him even more than his interpreters, but because in truth his critics have not understood him. I come only to justify the righteous [*l'hazdik 'et ha-zadik*]

> and shut the mouths of those who speak about the righteous one [Maimonides] in a debasing and false manner. Even now there are groups who have such a tradition and feel commanded to ridicule him. . . . This is all because of their faulty understanding.[21]

These critics of Maimonides view his philosophical project as corrupt because it does not contain either a transmission of truth through tradition (i.e., *kabbala shelamah*) or the acquisition of truth through revelatory inspiration *(gilluy Eliyahu).*

R. Gershon Henokh offers another perspective founded on three principles: first, that Maimonides is the recipient of at least a partial transmission of true doctrine *(kabbala helkit);* second, that the completion of the esoteric project cannot be accomplished solely through transmission but also requires inspirational reading (*gilluy Eliyahu,* lit., the revelation of Elijah the Prophet); and third, that human reason (philosophy) can be a legitimate substitute, albeit one that is inferior, in the absence of *gilluy Eliyahu.* That is, while the lack of *gilluy Eliyahu* is a deficiency that often results in mistaken understanding, reason is not, in and of itself, corrupt.

Reason is only corrupt when it is not founded on any transmission whatsoever. "He who thinks he can innovate and add words to the Torah [*l'hadesh u l'hosif divrei Torah*], independent of what he received is like one who comically ridicules Torah [*mitlozez 'al divrei Torah*]. For this person, the Torah is not a serious matter."[22] Philosophy fails when it is not founded on or has no access to some element of transmission *(kabbala).* This is not the case with the *Guide.* R. Gershon Henokh claims that Maimonides' philosophical discourse, and that of others like him, is a tool to explain or reveal, in a concealed and incomplete manner, fragments of this Sod tradition to those educated in the philosophy of the Greeks. According this line of reasoning, the tradition Maimonides is revealing, albeit covertly, is not the tradition of the rabbis (halakha) but the very tradition the rabbis intentionally conceal (Abrahamic Sod).

The irony here is that on this reading, while Maimonides seems to support the halakhic system in the *Guide,* he is not, in fact, supporting it but is in some way subverting it by revealing esoteric elements that the rabbis concealed in the halakha. In this sense, Maimonides has more in common with the Zohar, although the Zohar is superior in at least three ways: the Zohar is more linguistically competent; the Zohar is more committed to disclosing its secrets; and the Zohar is far more informed in the Sod tradition than is Maimonides.

According to this, both the rabbinic anti-Maimonideans and the anti-Maimonidean Kabbalists misunderstand Maimonides because each are wedded to their ideological positions, neither of which properly construe the fundamentals of esotericism as a lost tradition transmitted in fragments via exoteric rational means. The rabbinic anti-Maimonideans misread Maimonides because they have no concept of esotericism. The anti-philosophical Kabbalists misread him because they wrongly understand esotericism as purely the result of direct transmission. R. Gershon Henokh argues that Maimonides' philosophical program, which contains an esotericism aligned with the Kabbala,[23] continues with R. Isaac Arama (ca. 1420–1494) and R. Isaac Abrabanel (1437–1508), two Spanish Jews who are openly critical of philosophy, even as they venerate Maimonides.[24]

Like other close readers of Maimonides throughout the centuries, R. Gershon Henokh is acutely aware of the esoteric nature of the text, as explained by Maimonides himself in his introduction. Like other readers of the *Guide,* he seeks a method to unravel the contradictions and find the true intention of its author. His approach differs from his predecessors in conflating Kabbalistic and Maimonidean esotericism, viewing the Zohar as the key to unlocking Maimonides' secrets. As opposed to other mystical and nonmystical readers of the *Guide,* R. Gershon Henokh frames his reading on the internally unsubstantiated but nonetheless intriguing assumption, reflected in his version of *philosophia perennis,* that Maimonides' *Guide* and the Zohar shared a common esoteric (Sod) tradition which underlies both texts, and that the redemption of both texts can be achieved by reading them through one another.[25]

This method is not solely about understanding Maimonides (or the Zohar), but has a much larger goal. It is about completing the process of unification initiated by the Baal Shem Tov. It is the job of the Hasidic reader, R. Gershon Henokh believes, to uncover the fragments of this subterranean esoteric tradition in order to unify the disparate traditions of philosophy and Kabbala, redeeming the postrabbinic literary tradition and subsequently redeeming the world.

R. Gershon Henokh begins by collecting all the contradictory statements made by Maimonides on any given issue. He then finds a passage in the Zohar that deals with the same issue. Looking back into the *Guide,* he finds the Maimonidean position that most closely resembles the position of the Zohar and concludes that this must be Maimonides' true opinion because it was the one he inherited.

From a critical perspective, this method admittedly seems banal, especially if we are interested in learning Maimonides' true opinion on any particular matter. However, this is not R. Gershon Henokh's primary interest. His interest is the discovery of textual compatibility that supports his unwavering belief in the principle of esoteric transmission. Beginning with the *prima facia* "belief" that Maimonides and the Zohar share a common tradition, even as the Zohar's was purer, R. Gershon Henokh sought to rend the veil of Maimonides' esoteric project, revealing its compatibility with the Zohar, thereby liberating Maimonides both from his mystical critics and rational defenders. According to R. Gershon Henokh, it was only when Maimonides had no tradition that he resorted to human reason which, while valid, often does not reach the correct conclusion. In those cases, R. Gershon Henokh tries to locate a fragment from the Zohar that may serve as a corrective to Maimonides' deficient opinion and reveal the holes in the fragmented tradition Maimonides may have inherited.

In many cases in classical Jewish literature, contradictions are resolved through a method of casuistry, resolving a disagreement of two sources by reframing one position in the argument or by invoking a third source to dispel one side of the argument. In *Ha-Hakdama,* R. Gershon Henokh's method is less casuistic and more a reflection of the esoteric perennialist's attempt to discover and subsequently reconstruct the hidden source embedded in the exoteric texts they read.

Talmudic casuistry does not work here because the third source that could resolve the disagreement is concealed and thus inaccessible, only reconstructed through a reading of the two sources together. Therefore, the third source cannot be invoked to resolve a contradiction but arises out of the juxtaposition of two opposing sources.

The third source or resolution to the disparity can only become evident through the disparity itself, read with the underlying belief that an analysis of the common thread of the two contradictory sources can reveal the third concealed source. The opposing spiritual visions embodied in contradictory worldviews (Maimonides and the Zohar) are understood as a consequence of exile that must be reconciled before the advent of the messianic era. Therefore, the synthetic method of resolving metahalakhic contradictions through rabbinic casuistry is insufficient for this Hasidic master, because such resolutions come either through revision or through the erasure of incorrect opinions, even as those rejected opinions may still remain part of the discourse (as is the case with the structure of talmudic literature). R. Gershon Henokh was only interested in the erasure of mistaken opinions reached solely through reason. All other "opinions" received through tradition or inspiration would be absorbed into a larger mystical worldview whose roots lie in a pre-Sinaitic Sod tradition.

His redemptive agenda is focused on revealing that the illusory nature of the contradiction is the result of the concealed nature of the Sod tradition.

It is, therefore, not sufficient to suggest a resolution of two apparently inconsistent texts. Rather, the redemptive reader—the one who makes the esoteric, exoteric—must show how both approaches are deficient manifestations of the Sod tradition embedded in the narrative. If the concealed source embodies the full disclosure of truth, then all legitimate extant texts are both right and wrong. They contain fragments of that concealed truth but are deficient in the part of that truth that remains concealed. To uncover this tradition is to redeem the Torah and subsequently to redeem the world.

As previously mentioned, redemptive reading is an act of cognitive circumcision, whereby removing the sheath (philosophical or symbolic language) reveals the secret of the text. The knife that circumcises is the text that stands in opposition to the text being read. Juxtapositional or intertextual reading (i.e., reading one text in light of another) is enacting circumcision on the Torah itself. The Zohar is the knife for the *Guide,* and the *Guide,* albeit to a lesser extent, is the knife for the Zohar.

The Mirror That Reveals: The *Guide* Read through the Zohar

Let us now turn to some examples of how this method functions in an attempt to evaluate its efficacy. In *Guide* 1:73 (sixth premise), Maimonides makes his case for free will against the position of the Ash'ariyya, a position he later deems as "mockery." He sums up their position as follows:

> Accordingly, God creates at every one of the instants—I mean the separate units of time—an accident in every individual among the beings, whether that individual be an angel, a heavenly sphere, or something else. This He does constantly at every moment of time. They maintain that this is the true faith in God's activity; and in their opinion, he who does not believe that God acts in this way denies the fact that God acts. With regard to beliefs of this kind, it has been said in my opinion and in that of everybody endowed with an intellect: "Or as one mocks a man, do you so mock him"—this being in truth the very essence of mockery.[26]

The rejection of the position of determinism in the Ash'ariyya is strengthened in *Guide* 3:17 (469), where Maimonides states:

> It is a fundamental principle of the Law of Moses our Master, peace be on him, and all those who follow it that man has an absolute ability to act: I mean to say that in virtue of his nature, his choice and his will, he may do everything that is within the capacity of man to do, and this without there

> being created for his benefit in any way any newly produced thing. . . . This is a fundamental principle about which—praise be to God!—no disagreement has ever been heard within our religious community.

This unequivocal affirmation of free will in the *Guide* has no direct parallel in the Zohar, whose position on free will is much more ambiguous. Aware that these sources seriously challenge the Zohar's equivocation of free will and the more blatant determinism of his grandfather R. Mordecai Joseph of Izbica, R. Gershon Henokh begins his analysis of the *Guide* by drawing our attention to *Guide* 3:51 (625), where Maimonides speaks of the overarching reach of divine providence. Providence is intended here to complicate Maimonides' position on free will:

> We have already explained in the chapters concerning providence that providence watches over everyone endowed with intellect proportionately to the measure of his intellect. Thus providence always watches over an individual endowed with perfect apprehension, whose intellect never ceases from being occupied with God. On the other hand, an individual endowed with perfect apprehension, whose thought sometimes for a certain time is emptied of God, is watched over by providence only during the time when he thinks of God; providence withdraws from him during the time when he is occupied with something else.

This notion of providence, while surely not contradicting Maimonides' position on free will, lends itself to interpretation through the lens of the Zohar. Or, at the very least, it can be compared to the Zohar's position on the same issue. On this passage, R. Gershon Henokh finds a parallel in the Zohar 1.103a/b:

> The creatures of the earth think of Him as being on High, declaring, *His glory is above the heavens* [Psalms 113:4], while the heavenly beings think of Him as being below, declaring, *His glory is over all the earth* [Psalms 57:12], until they both, in heaven and on earth, concur in declaring *Blessed be the Glory of the Lord from His place* because He is unknowable and no one can truly understand Him. This being so, how can you say *Her husband is known in the gates* [Proverbs 31:23]? But in truth, the Holy One makes Himself known to everyone according to the measure of his understanding and his capacity to attach himself to the spirit of Divine wisdom; and thus her husband is known not *in the gates* [*shearim*] but, as we may translate, "by measure" [*shiurim*] though a full knowledge is beyond the reach of any being.[27]

The Zohar's notion of God revealing Himself to an individual "according to his measure" *(shiurim)* is understood in this context to be aligned with

Maimonides' idea in *Guide* 3:51 that providence is linked to one's apprehension of the divine ("the measure of his intellect"). R. Gershon Henokh reads the passage as follows:

> Later on [in a Zohar passage cited later] it will be explained that from the perspective of a believer and a servant of God, everything is subject to providence, even a leaf falling from a tree. . . . In truth, from the perspective of God everything exists with particular providence to meet His purpose. It is only from the perspective of the creation that providence is received according to its capacity. However, from God's perspective, there is no distinction.[28]

Distinguishing between the divine perspective and the human perspective in treating the paradox of God as both transcendent and immanent,[29] as well as the problem of free will and determinism, have been the subjects of Kabbalists and philosophers for centuries.[30] R. Gershon Henokh uses the perspectivity argument, at least as it is implied in the Zohar, as an exegetical tool, a way to read *Guide* 3:51 on providence that would not contradict the unequivocal affirmation of free will in *Guide* 3:17 (and the explicit rejection of the determinist view in *Guide* 1:73). The Zohar suggests that being "attached to God" or, in Maimonides' terminology, being "occupied with God," is the vehicle for "knowing God." The knowledge of God to which the Zohar refers is not knowledge in the discursive sense of acquiring and analyzing information about an object but the experiential unity with the object being observed.[31]

The more one "knows" in this nondiscursive sense,[32] the more one sees the unity of Creator and creation and thus recognizes the overarching nature of providence.[33] This perspective on providence subsequently nuances any free will position, because providence, at least for R. Gershon Henokh, suggests divine intervention at every instance in one's life. On this reading, Hasidic devekut becomes a mode of "knowing" an object that cannot be known in a purely cognitive way. Or, in the case of free will, of knowing that the truth (i.e., "all is determined") is the opposite of what it appears to be.[34]

For R. Gershon Henokh, devekut is seeing things from God's perspective—that is, seeing that free will is nonexistent. He uses the concept of devekut as interpreted by early Hasidism to unpack the esotericism that underlies Maimonides' affirmation of free will and the Zohar's notion of mystical knowledge. According to him, it is not that devekut *enables* one to "know God"; devekut *is* the knowledge of God, in that devekut is being able to see the world through God's eyes. Maimonides' statement on free will in *Guide* 3:17 is now contextualized in a pre-devekut perspective, while

Guide 3:51 (on providence) is Maimonides' tacit (and esoteric) acknowledgment that another perspective is possible.

R. Gershon Henokh surmises from his reading of *Guide* 3:51 that Maimonides must have been aware of a tradition that one's knowledge of God and one's recognition of the limitlessness of providence were related. When Maimonides states, "Thus providence always watches over an individual endowed with perfect apprehension" (*Guide* 3:51, 624), R. Gershon Henokh understands him to mean that the individual is not only protected via conjunction with the Active Intellect but is also acutely aware of that which protects him. That is, he is conscious of providence as it happens. This is the nature of devekut. However, if R. Gershon Henokh's reading of Maimonides is accurate, how could Maimonides have been so critical of the Ash'ariyya in *Guide* 1:73, who claim that everything was under the constant influence of divine providence, thus denying the capacity for free will?

On this point R. Gershon Henokh is far less explicit. It would appear, however, that he would hold that Maimonides' rejection of the Ash'ariyya position is directed to those who are not "occupied with God" (that is, those not in a state of devekut) and thus do not have the apprehension of the all-pervasive nature of providence. As one becomes more aware of God (i.e., God as present in the world, or providence as outgrowth of devekut), the more free will disappears, for such an individual is in a constant state of "perfect apprehension," encompassing all of human experience and will.[35]

At that moment, free will ceases to exist, as its "existence" is the result of one's inadequate knowledge due to the absence of devekut. Yet to make such a claim, as the Ash'ariyya do—without it being the result of an experience of divine omniscience (devekut)—is, in Maimonides' words, "mockery." The mockery lies not in the substance of the claim but in the way it is determined. From a purely discursive, empirical point of view, the Ash'ariyya's conclusion that free will is nonexistent is absurd, since the imperfect soul who has not gone through the process of purification (*berur,* in Izbica/Radzin Hasidism) will always understand himself to have free will. For R. Gershon Henokh, the logical and rational conclusion of the existence of free will can only be overcome when the individual's authentic experience takes him beyond the limits of rationality as implied in the Zohar passage cited above. This Hasidic rendition of the Zohar is grafted onto the discussion in the *Guide*. Moreover, the law is founded and resides in a world of imperfection, a world where the nondiscursive knowledge implied in the Zohar and read into the *Guide* is not commonplace and cannot serve as a foundation for Torah. Therefore, the servant of God who realizes this must be silent and not allow his experience to change the nature of the law.[36]

Let us examine another similar case. In this instance, R. Gershon Henokh chooses to utilize a Lurianic reading of the Zohar rather than a passage from the Zohar itself.[37] As mentioned earlier, this is quite common, as most Hasidic masters generally accepted Luria's reading of the Zohar as canonical. Maimonides speaks about the chariot *(merkavah)* in the introduction to part 3 of the *Guide* (416):

> On the other hand, as has been stated before, an explicit exposition of this knowledge [of the chariot] is denied by a legal prohibition, in addition to that which is imposed by judgment. In addition to this there is the fact that in that which has occurred to me with regard to these matters, I followed conjecture and supposition; no divine revelation has come to me to teach me that the intention in the matter in question was such and such, nor did I receive what I believe in these matters from a teacher. But the texts of the prophetic books and the dicta of the Sages, together with the speculative premises that I possess, showed me that things are indubitably so and so. Yet it is possible that they are different and that something else is intended.

Maimonides then proceeds to interpret the prophetic vision of the chariot of Ezekiel as representing metaphysics, reading the imagery and symbolism of Scripture into the philosophical framework of Aristotle.[38] The whole tone of Maimonides' introduction and the philosophical interpretation that follows raises a number of issues that R. Gershon Henokh was likely exposed to through the standard medieval commentaries to the *Guide*.

R. Gershon Henokh asks, if we take Maimonides at face value—that the chariot in Scripture (Ezekiel's vision) is a description of metaphysics and can be understood through the interpretation of Scripture—then why is there a strong prohibition against such speculation? R. Isaac Abrabanel first raised this question in his commentary to the *Guide*.[39] R. Gershon Henokh suggests that reading the chariot as metaphysics, and thus within the realm of human reason, is not only plausible but can be supported by Kabbalistic interpretations of the chariot. In Luria's corpus, the chariot of Ezekiel is depicted as a stage in the downward emanation from *eyn sof* and represents a relatively low rung on the ladder of this supernal process. Given the chariot's low status in the supernal realm, R. Gershon Henokh argues that the Maimonidean depiction of the chariot as philosophical metaphysics is not as problematic as critics of Maimonides claim.[40] Below is a summary of the Lurianic position cited by R. Gershon Henokh, followed by a description of the method used to read it back into Maimonides' introduction to part 3 of the *Guide*.

Lurianic theosophy is a system largely built on the Zohar's metaphysics of emanation. This is founded on the notion that the Infinite God *(eyn sof),* who is undifferentiated, constructs finitude by emanating light from His infinite being into a world not yet created. Creation is the result of the distancing of divine light from its source, resulting in the formation of the cosmos and finally the material world. In the Zohar, the light extends from God but is never severed from its divine source. In Luria, due to his theory of rupture and divine fragmentation *(shevirat ha-kelim),* the extended light's relation to its divine source is more complex. This latter development adds a Gnostic component to the Lurianic system. In both instances, however, Neoplatonism serves as the dominant ideational foundation of such a system, while the Jewish tradition, from the Bible through the rabbis, serves as its substantive core.

For our limited purposes, Luria's innovation and contribution to Zoharic metaphysics is at least fourfold. First, he makes the concept of *zimzum* (the self-contraction of God as the initial move toward creation) the centerpiece of his theosophy.[41] Second, he introduces rupture, that is, "the shattering of the vessels" *(shevirat ha-kelim),* as a preamble to existence thus making *tikun* the overarching trope of the human endeavor. Third, he moves away from the largely *sephirotic* grid of the Zohar in favor of *parzufim* (lit., faces), which are clusters of *sephirot* that each have a unique character and purpose. And fourth, he focuses on the intricate details of the inner workings of the cosmic world instead of a more general scheme of the Zohar.

In *Etz Hayyim,* R. Hayyim Vital delineates the basic premise of the Lurianic notion of revelation *qua* emanation as a relative and progressive unfolding of the metasupernal world *(eyn sof)* into the supernal world below it *('olam ha-sephirot).*[42] In the Lurianic scheme (largely drawn from different parts of the Zohar),[43] there are four main worlds, each containing two elements which are broken down into five subelements. The four worlds are *azilut* (emanation), *beriah* (creation), *yezerah* (formation), and *asiah* (action), drawing from three dominant verbs used in the Bible to denote the creative act (excluding *azilut*). The two basic elements are direct light *('or yashar)* and surrounding light *('or makif).*[44] These dimensions of light either emanate into, or hover above, the vessels that constitute existence. The five subelements—also presented as the architecture of the soul—are *nefesh, ruah, neshama, haya,* and *yehida,* five components that constitute the sum total of spiritual (i.e., nonmaterial) existence. Relativism and relationality are the overarching tropes of Lurianic hermeneutics, particularly in its Vitalian recension.[45] This means that these elements and light are dynamic and not static. They are labels that denote relation rather than identity. For example, a thing can be called *nefesh* in relation to one object and *ruah* in relation to another.

What is outer light in one world becomes inner light in the world below it. What is hidden in one world or in one dimension of one world becomes revealed as it descends to the spiritual dimension below it. This relationality creates a fluidity that makes any definitive statement about any particular manifestation of these elements difficult if not impossible. In the Lurianic system, definitions of spiritual elements are inextricably tied to the geographic space they occupy (their cosmic world or vertical position in a particular world) and the nature of their relational components (within one world—their horizontal interactions).

Vital records that Luria told him that the interface, permutation, and transformations of these categories are constantly changing depending on at least two factors, time and the performance of mitzvot. No unification *(yihud)* can ever be replicated, from the moment of creation until the end of time. Every unification is progressive. Repetition has no place in the Lurianic system.

This theory of emanation is founded on the principle that all permutations of cosmic reality are ultimately connected to the Infinite God *(eyn sof),* who exists beyond the boundaries of this supernal system. As the process of emanation is ongoing, it is never disconnected from its source (although not identified with it); each moment in time discloses a new dimension of *eyn sof* not previously revealed. In *Etz Hayyim,* Vital explains that Ezekiel's vision of the chariot is a vision of the third world from the top, the world of Formation *('olam yezerah),* which is the realm immediately above the lowest (fourth) world, the world of action *('olam asiah).*[46] This prophetic vision was a vision of a realm below the second angelic world, the world of creation *('olam ha-beriah).* Vital summarizes as follows:

> All the higher worlds [referring to *azilut* and above] are one holiness [*kedusha ahat*] and one divinity [*elohut ehat*]. There is no distinction in them, God forbid. However, in the three lower worlds [*beriah, yezerah,* and *asiah*] the soul [*neshama*] [or third level of the soul] is divine [*elohut*] but, while from the spirit of that soul [*ruah*] downwards all are still divine, they are called *Serafim, Hayot, Ofanim,* and the Seat of Glory, whether in the world of creation, formation, or action—understand this well.[47]

Vital's delineation of these realms is important for our discussion. The highest world *(azilut)* is beyond the realm of human experience because in it there is no distinction or fragmentation of the Godhead. While the three lower worlds are still divine, divinity is fragmented into distinguishable parts. As the emanation moves downward, even within one world, this distinction becomes more pronounced and therefore becomes more accessible to human experience. While the three upper levels (from the top down, *yehida, haya, neshama*) of the lower three worlds *(beriah, yezerah, asiah)* still lie beyond the realm of human experience, from the fourth level *(ruah)* in the three lower worlds, the distinction between divine realms is clear enough as to become accessible to human experience.

R. Gershon Henokh suggests that the telos of Ezekiel's vision was to reveal the place where divine concealment *(koah ha-hester)* begins to reveal itself, resulting in the realization that divine absence is itself divine.

> At that time it was God's will to show Ezekiel how God fills the entire creation. Therefore, he showed Ezekiel the first [highest] place where He could be apprehended until the place that was necessary, i.e., the place of His concealment. That is, until the world of formation [*'olam ha-yezerah*]. As it is explained . . . in the world of emanation, holiness and goodness are dominant. This is also true in the world of creation. In the world of formation, however, good and evil are balanced. Therefore, it is only in the world of formation that the power of divine concealment begins. God wanted to show Ezekiel that the power of concealment is itself from God.[48]

R. Gershon Henokh utilizes the Lurianic notion that the chariot is housed in the world of formation *(yezerah)*—the first world where good and evil appear as distinct—as a support for the Maimonidean claim that the chariot represents metaphysics.[49] That is, metaphysics is the highest realm of speculation of the divine because it is the first place where God is hidden. Divine absence becomes the first stage of our apprehension of God. The first human apprehension of God is His absence. For R. Gershon Henokh, the purpose of the vision is for Ezekiel to see and communicate that God's absence (evil) is the result of divine will.[50]

The Lurianic interpretation of the chariot of Ezekiel lowers the status of the prophetic vision to a place that is accessible to the human intellect and experience, that is, the angelic world where good and evil are already distinct. Here, this Lurianic text is used to defend Maimonides' explanation of the vision of the chariot as metaphysics against those who argue that such an interpretation profanes the supernal nature of the prophetic vision.[51] Introducing his interpretation, Maimonides, perhaps in an attempt to preempt opposition, states that "I followed conjecture and supposition; no divine revelation has come to me . . . nor did I receive what I believe in these matters from a teacher" (*Guide,* 416). Using Luria's delineation of the cosmos and ignoring Maimonides' own disclaimer, R. Gershon Henokh suggests that the philosophical interpretation of Ezekiel's vision given by Maimonides is actually rooted in an ancient tradition he refuses to openly disclose. Perhaps this can shed some light on Maimonides' curious acknowledgment in the same introduction that, while he is fully cognizant of the rabbinic prohibition to engage in speculation of the chariot, he will proceed to explain it so that "nothing in it will remain hidden from him" (*Guide,* 416).

Implied in R. Gershon Henokh's reading is the question: How can Maimonides so blatantly transgress a rabbinic decree?[52] Some interpreters of the *Guide* surmise that the prohibition only applies when one is revealing the meaning of a received tradition.[53] Or, as Maimonides says, it is only prohibited when what is offered is an "explicit explanation." However, Maimonides continues, he is saying nothing "over and above what is indicated by the text" devoid of any tradition or revelation.

Hence, philosophical speculation, even on prohibited matters, does not fall under the rubric of the rabbinic prohibition as long as it remains conjectural—that is, as long as it is speculative and does not disclose any received esoteric doctrine. From R. Gershon Henokh's point of view, one could argue that the rabbinic prohibition against revealing the true nature of this vision (*sitrei torah*—secrets) was a prohibition against disclosing a Sod tradition that was concealed in the body of rabbinic discourse. By juxtaposing Maimonides' rendering with the Lurianic system, he implies that Maimonides is not merely translating the verses from one language to another (Maimonides' claim in the introduction) but revealing, in a concealed fashion, the underlying tradition.

If this is so, how is Maimonides not transgressing the rabbinic prohibition? To R. Gershon Henokh's way of thinking, while Maimonides generally supports the rabbinic project of concealment, he also subverts it by dialectically disclosing things in a manner that simultaneously reveals and conceals them. R. Gershon Henokh's suggestion that Maimonides uses philosophical language to conceal the tradition of the meaning of the chariot from full disclosure may justify how the *Guide* is aligned both with the rabbis (and not in blatant violation of the prohibition) and with the Zohar (which may indeed transgress the rabbinic interdiction). In this way, Maimonides may be transgressing the formal rabbinic warning, strictly defined, without transgressing its spirit.[54] Philosophical language both conceals and reveals. It is the garment of concealed disclosure that enables Maimonides to explain the vision of the chariot, revealing its secrets, but he does so in a way that does not transgress the rabbinic decree.[55]

As to whether Maimonides was aware of the tradition that underlies his discussion, and is therefore misleading (if not lying) about having received no tradition on these matters, R. Gershon Henokh is silent. But this, of course, is beside the point. What matters to our Hasidic writer is that the veil concealing the esoteric source of Maimonides' discussion is lifted when juxtaposed to the Lurianic teachings on the chariot, revealing the underlying source of Maimonides' philosophical speculation.

In another case dealing with the vision of the chariot, R. Gershon Henokh defends Maimonides against Abrabanel's critique by using Lurianic Kabbala as a way of illustrating Abrabanel's misunderstanding of the *Guide's* intention. In *Guide* 3:1 Maimonides states:

> It is known that there are men the form of whose faces resemble that of one of the other animals, so that one may see an individual whose face resembles that of a lion and another individual whose face resembles an ox and so forth. It is according to the shapes that tend to have a likeness to those of animals that people are nicknamed. Thus his saying: "the face of an ox and the face of a lion and the face of an eagle . . ." [Ezekiel 1:10] all of them merely indicate the face of a man that tends to have a likeness to forms belonging to these species [417].

The problematic nature of this metaphorical interpretation is obvious. Maimonides strips Ezekiel's vision of its plain-sense meaning by interpreting the animal faces as different perceptions of the human being. Abrabanel's problem is more textual than exegetical. Addressing the fact that Scripture explicitly states that each face has four faces, how can Maimonides ignore an explicit scriptural reference, even to offer the more reasoned interpretation that each human face resembles one of the animals—that the animal faces are (merely) metaphors for the human face? He raises the problem in his fourth argument in his commentary to *Guide* 3:1.[56]

> How could the Rav [Maimonides] have explained that some of the animals had the face of man, some the face of a lion, some the face of an ox and some the face of an eagle? It is explained in Scripture that each one of the forms had all of the faces, the face of a man, a lion, an ox, and an eagle. Therefore, if it is that all of them were the face of men [as Maimonides claimed] they would also all have to be the face of an ox and the other forms. The scriptural verse is explicit, "and the face of the lion was to the right of the four and the face of the ox to the left of the four. . . ."

> Therefore, they were all the face of man and the face of an ox, a lion, and an eagle.

Although Abrabanel understands the logical problem of one face simultaneously being four, he wonders how Maimonides can ignore the plain-sense meaning of the verse in order to enable the vision to align itself with rational thinking. That is, that the four faces were all faces of men, the animal faces only a metaphorical likeness or expression of the human face.

R. Gershon Henokh responds to Abrabanel's question by invoking the well-known Zoharic idea (whose roots lie in earlier Kabbala) that the four worlds mentioned above are each subdivided into ten *sephirot*. He suggests that Maimonides was aware of this distinction, although he veiled it in philosophical language, citing the *Guide* 2:10 (271), "The spheres are four; the elements moved by the spheres are four; and the forces preceding from the spheres into that which exists in general are four, as we have made clear."

The notion of four spheres in the *Guide* is understood by R. Gershon Henokh as a philosophical correlation to the four worlds of the Zohar.[57] Making this correlation, which is admittedly quite spurious unless you have already accepted his basic premise of an underlying third source, he uses the entire Kabbalistic grid of the four worlds to liberate Maimonides' ambiguous statement about the prophetic vision from its philosophical language.

The fact that each world contains the ten *sephirot* is taken here to mean that each world is a reflection of the world below and above it, as each set of ten *sephirot* correspond to or are a reflection of the ten *sephirot* above and below them. Therefore, the four faces of the chariot are, like the four supernal worlds, reflections of each other, each one reflecting all the others. And, each one *(sephirah)* embodies the characteristics of Adam Kadmon (Primordial or Cosmic Man, the most lofty manifestation of God in the cosmos), in Maimonides' depiction, the face of a man. The different forms on the chariot (i.e., the face of an ox, eagle, etc.) are merely the different stages of emanation they occupy.[58] Thus the forms of the faces of the chariot do not fully reflect their essence (which may very well all be man, who is the image of God) but merely the particular stage of emanation. Yet each is, as Maimonides claims, ultimately the face of man (Adam Kadmon).

R. Gershon Henokh argues that Maimonides' statement on the chariot is a reflection of the Kabbalistic interpretation of the verse in Genesis, *Let us make man in our image and form* (Genesis 1:26), to mean that the creation is a microcosm of the human form in general and of the human face in particular.[59] Hence, the vision of the chariot, which is only a glimpse into the complex fabric of divine emanation, must take on the "face of a man." Abrabanel's mistake, according to R. Gershon Henokh, was that he was not aware that Maimonides' comment must be seen within the Kabbalistic notion of the entire creation, and not just the human being, as "the form of man." While every manifestation of divine emanation carries a particular valence (the face of an animal), it is always a depiction of its source (the face of a man). While it may be true that each valence contains all the others, its dominant trait becomes its label. According to R. Gershon Henokh's reading of Maimonides, each face of the chariot is the face of man, which also carried the face of all the animals, and therefore is called lion, ox, et cetera because of its particular place in the emanation process.

Let us take another example where R. Gershon Henokh attempts to unravel the esoteric nature of the *Guide* by what he deemed were direct parallels in the Zohar. What distinguishes this case from those already discussed is that Maimonides' positions here are (1) not necessarily problematic for the Kabbalist and (2) seemingly have no source in rabbinic literature. This gives R. Gershon Henokh license to locate the source of Maimonides' position in the purer and more complete tradition *(kabbala shelamah)* of Sod embedded cryptically in the Zohar and absent in the rabbis.

In his discussion of the various levels of prophecy in *Guide* 2:45 (402), Maimonides claims that the prophecy of Abraham at "the time of the binding [of Isaac] (Genesis 22) is the highest form of prophecy known to man excluding the prophecy of Moses."[60] Although Maimonides begins his sentence with the words "[I]n my opinion," R. Gershon Henokh attempts to show that the stature of Abraham's prophecy in the *Guide* is, in fact, rooted in the Zohar (Idra Rabba, Zohar 3:130 a/b):

> We learned that the name of *atika* [the ancient one—the concealed realm of the divine] is closed to all and not explained [revealed] in the Torah except in one place where *zeir anpin* swore [*d'umei zeir anpin*] to Abraham.[61]
>
> The name of *atika* is the most concealed name of all. It is only revealed in the Torah once, when *zeir anpin* swore to Abraham, as it is written *By Myself, I swear, God declares* [Genesis 22:16]. The declaration is the declaration of *zeir anpin*. . . .[62] At the moment the angel uttered, *do not raise your hand against the boy* [Genesis 22:12] this supernal light [*atika*], which is beyond all boundaries, was revealed to him. This light remained intact in Isaac and his seed.[63]

The superiority of the prophecy of Moses is stated in Scripture, affirmed in rabbinic literature, and finally codified in Maimonides' *Mishneh Torah*.[64] However, the notion that the prophecy during the Akedah is second to

Moses' prophecy or, as in our second text, is the prototype for all subsequent illumination, *even* the prophecy of Moses, is not explicit in Scripture, rabbinic literature, or classical medieval exegesis. R. Gershon Henokh argues that Maimonides did not reach his conclusion from his own "opinion," as he wants us to believe. Rather, he was aware of the tradition expressed in the Zohar (Idra Rabba, Zohar 3:129a, 3:130a) and masked this tradition in the form of an "opinion."[65] By veiling his position as "opinion," Maimonides is able to transmit this esoteric tradition without revealing its source. Accordingly, his use of philosophical inquiry is a veil the way halakha was a veil for the rabbis. Halakha, like philosophy, conceals the very roots that serve as its foundation. Just as R. Shimon in the Zohar unveils the embedded Sod in rabbinic literature, R. Gershon Henokh unveils the Sod in Maimonides' philosophical discourse.

Ta'amei Ha-Mitzvot: Turning Philosophical Rationalism into Mystical Knowledge

Another important category treated in R. Gershon Henokh's synthesis of the *Guide* and the Zohar concerns the notion of *ta'amei ha-mitzvot* (reasons for the commandments). While both Maimonides and the Kabbalists, unlike the rabbis, engaged in detailed explorations of *ta'amei ha-mitzvot,* Maimonides is strongly criticized by Kabbalists for his "rational" *ta'amei ha-mitzvot* in the *Guide.*[66] It is not the practice itself that is considered spurious but the method of his analysis. In fact, the whole enterprise of attempting to give reasons for the commandments (metahalakha) is a common concern for both Jewish philosophers and mystics in the Middle Ages.[67] *Ta'amei ha-mitzvot* is arguably one of the fundamental areas of medieval Jewish reflection on Judaism.

The act of giving reasons for the commandments is often viewed as an attempt to rationalize mitzvot and thus is mistakenly considered largely the product of philosophical interpretation. In fact, Lurianic Kabbala and Hasidism (in the tradition of medieval Kabbala in general) are deeply invested in *ta'amei ha-mitzvot* from a different perspective and see this enterprise as a centerpiece of their presentation of Judaism.[68]

Lurianic Kabbalists are particularly, and uniquely, committed to *ta'amei ha-mitzvot* as the backbone of their cosmology. Whereas *ta'amei ha-mitzvot* among medieval philosophers and pre-sixteenth-century Kabbalists can generally be categorized as philosophical and/or mystical teleology, Luria integrated the theoretical enterprise of *ta'amei ha-mitzvot* into the practical realm of performing mitzvot, including the concretization of specific guidelines for established mitzvot and the innovation of many new rituals.[69] That is, in the Lurianic corpus the entire complex web of *kavvanot,* or the contemplative mapping of the descent and ascent of divine effluence as a consequence of performing a mitzvah, work within the general framework of *ta'amei ha-mitzvot.*[70] In this way, Luria offers a practical alternative of *ta'amei ha-mitzvot* distinct from the more rational form offered by Maimonides or the more purely theosophical form of the Zohar. For Luria, *ta'amei ha-mitzvot* became the foundation for contemplative practices *(kavvanot)* that accompanied the performance of mitzvot. They became inextricably tied to devotional practices and serve as a principle foundation of Hasidism even though many Hasidic masters abandoned the detailed application of Lurianic contemplative practices.[71]

The problematic nature of philosophical or teleological "reasons" for the commandments is that such an approach can result in subordinating the commandment to its reason, yielding a relativistic orientation toward commandments.[72] Maimonides, both in his *Mishneh Torah* and *Guide of the Perplexed,* consistently tries to avert such relativism that by itself may indicate his own recognition of the vulnerability of his enterprise.[73]

In Lurianic *ta'amei ha-mitzvot,* the structure is not social and/or psychological but cosmological/relational. The "reason" or telos *(ta'am)* for any commandment is the way the performance of a particular mitzvah at a particular time aids in repairing the cosmic world that is fragmented as a result of the sin of Adam and Eve.[74] The mitzvot serve as the relational matrix between Jews and the cosmos. In Lurianic Kabbala, the Hebrew term *ta'am* in the expression *ta'amei ha-mitzvot* is best translated as efficacy rather than reason, referring specifically to the cosmic effects of the performance of mitzvot.

Because the functions of mitzvot are cosmological and not this-worldly (even as this world is affected by those cosmic changes), Luria's "reasons for the mitzvot" are unchanging in that the supernal worlds are unaffected by natural law or the trajectory of human history. That is, Kabbalistic "reasons for the mitzvot" are largely independent of any historical or cultural context. Therefore, the danger of relativism or equivocating any particular mitzvah due to changing historical or cultural circumstances—the critique waged against philosophical *ta'amei ha-mitzvot*—was rarely a challenge to the Kabbalistic program of *ta'amei ha-mitzvot.*

According to Luria, each mitzvah functions to repair a different aspect of the supernal world, which subsequently affects the world below. Lurianic Kabbala focuses on designated "functions" for each mitzvah in the cosmic order (or disorder), reflected in the different meditations that apply to any particular mitzvah. By understanding the cosmic function of a particular mitzvah (requiring an intimate knowledge of Kabbala), one can understand the purpose and thus meaning of the mitzvah. Whereas medieval philosophers attempted to rationalize the meaning of unexplained mitzvot through philosophical interpretation, the Lurianic Kabbalists attempted to uncover the mystical nature of mitzvot by discovering the particular function they play in the cosmic process of *tikun*. Whereas Maimonidean *ta'amei ha-mitzvot* serve under the rubric of the midrashic dictum that the function of the mitzvot are to purify humanity *(l'zaref 'et ha-bri'ot),* for the Kabbalists the mitzvot serve to unify the cosmos *(l'taken 'et ha' olamot).* As a result the distinction between ethical and ritual mitzvot does not play a significant role in Zoharic and Lurianic *ta'amei ha-mitzvot*.[75]

Adopting the cosmic framework for understanding the nature and "reasons" for mitzvot in Lurianic Kabbala, which becomes dominant by the eighteenth century, most Hasidic authors have little interest in and use for the philosophical rationalization of the mitzvot.[76] Although they respect these medieval philosophers and accept them as halakhic authorities, where applicable, they were unwilling to take their philosophical views seriously, at least at face value.[77] Even among the many Hasidic writers who mention Maimonides' *Guide* and use Maimonidean positions to support theories of their own, we rarely find a systematic attempt to justify the philosophical activity of the medieval Jewish philosophers in Hasidic literature.[78] This may be because Hasidic spirituality had so deeply absorbed the Zoharic/Lurianic understanding of metahalakha (or *ta'amei ha-mitzvot*) as delineating the cosmic function, rather than the rationalization of mitzvot. This is coupled with the disdain they had for the Enlightenment, which used "reason" as its fundamental principle of interpretation. The absorption of the Lurianic worldview served to eclipse the more intellectualist model, even as espoused by authoritative Kabbalists such as R. Moshe Cordovero. This is not only true in Hasidism but in Lithuanian non-Hasidic Kabbala as well, particularly in the Kabbala of the Vilna Gaon and his student R. Menahem Mendel of Sklov. The ideational structure of the Zohar and its Lurianic interpretation so permeates post-sixteenth-century traditional Jewry engaged in mysticism at any level that the pre-sixteenth-century notion of *ta'amei ha-mitzvot,* whether philosophical or mystical, is no longer a significant part of the conversation.

In this schema, R. Gershon Henokh is both unique and conventional. His uniqueness is that he addresses the problems of Maimonides' philosophical views in their specifics. He is conventional in that he is not willing to read them independent of any connection to authentic (i.e., mystical) tradition. His esotericism is his way of acknowledging the philosophical (and problematic) nature of Maimonides' corpus while maintaining Maimonides' stature as the medieval Jewish hero. R. Gershon Henokh's use of *ta'amei ha-mitzvot,* one of the more problematic dimensions of the *Guide,* is an attempt to confront Maimonides head-on by attempting to show: first, that the philosophical reasons given by Maimonides are not in conflict with the Kabbalistic reasons presented in the Zohar and Lurianic Kabbala; and second, that Maimonides' reasons are mostly not his "opinions" (even when Maimonides says they are) or rational positions—as is conventionally thought—but part of a pre-Sinaitic Sod tradition to which Maimonides had at least limited access. In short, R. Gershon Henokh is attempting to synthesize the philosophical agenda of "rationalization" of the mitzvot with the functionalist program of *ta'amei ha-mitzvot* of the Kabbala. Philosophical teleology is viewed as the veil used by Maimonides both to reveal and conceal his sources.[79]

The Unwritten in the Written: Unlocking Secrets through Inspired Reading

In numerous places throughout his lengthy monograph, R. Gershon Henokh reminds his reader of the introduction to the *Guide,* where Maimonides enumerates the types of contradictions the reader can expect to encounter when reading the *Guide.* Maimonides warns his readers not to reveal the secrets discovered by resolving these contradictions, particularly in cases that seem to contradict the "famous sages of our law."[80] What remains unclear, of course, is exactly what Maimonides is trying to hide. More radical philosophical readers argue that Maimonides' personal inclination is philosophical (even when in contradiction to the law). On this reading Maimonides is not an unequivocal defender of the tradition but is, in fact, a sharp critic of tradition. He uses the method of contradiction to hide his true opinion from his traditionalist readers.[81] Traditionalist readers argue that Maimonides' true opinion was also that of "the sages of the law." What is innovative in his project is that he reconstructs the rabbis under the guise of philosophy in order to make the tradition palatable to those already alienated from it.[82]

R. Gershon Henokh would have held that both radical and traditionalist readers were mistaken, each misunderstanding both Maimonides and the rabbis. He believes that Maimonides' true opinions derived from a received Sod tradition that is intentionally concealed in rabbinic discourse and revealed in a concealed (limited) manner in Maimonides' philosophical treatise. As I argued earlier, the act of disclosure is also an act of concealment, in that philosophical language can convey the esoteric message while not revealing it as a source of transmission. By explaining/revealing/concealing this esoteric tradition philosophically, Maimonides hopes to convey it in a way that could easily be understood by his contemporaries, both philosophical and nonphilosophical.

The disclosure of the concealment of Maimonides, which R. Gershon Henokh attempts to reveal in *Ha-Hakdama,* is accomplished through the Zohar, whose secrets are also concealed; but they are more accessible than Maimonides because of the Zohar's linguistic schema coupled with Luria's inspired interpretation. In opposition to many other interpreters of the *Guide,* R. Gershon Henokh is not interested in explaining Maimonides as much as using him to illustrate his own esoteric theory—to take the theory of mutuality of God and world which lies at the root of the Hasidic tradition and apply it to the history of Jewish literature. This attempt to diffuse the opaque borders between philosophy and Kabbala, largely constructed after the Spanish exile at the end of the fifteenth century, reopens the canon of Jewish literature that he believed would enable the Sod tradition to rise to the surface of Jewish literature.

One cannot overestimate the messianic implications of this enterprise. The exile of the Jewish people and the exile of the Torah are viewed as mutually dependent phenomena. Redemption for both occurs when the Sod tradition, concealed and perhaps even forgotten as a result of exile, emerges, via reconstruction, to overcome the illusory fragmentation of Jewish literature. R. Gershon Henokh's synthetic method is directed toward this very end—the redemption of Torah via the uncovering of the Sod tradition, inaugurating the redemption of Israel.[83]

According to R. Gershon Henokh, all authentic Jewish carriers of this Sod tradition fall into one of three categories. The first is the one who possesses a full Kabbalistic tradition *(kabbala shelamah)* as the direct product of divine illumination. Examples are R. Shimon bar Yohai (as depicted in the Zohar) and R. Isaac Luria. The second is an attenuated *kabbala shelamah,* which is the transmission of this full tradition without an inspired reader. An example would be the Zohar as text. The third is a partial Kabbalistic tradition *(kabbala helkit)* received through oral transmission that diminished over time. This partial tradition is explicated or interpreted through the medium of human reason and philosophical language. Examples include Maimonides and most other medieval Jewish philosophers.

The distinction between the latter two categories—*kabbala shelamah*'s uninspired transmission and *kabbala helkit* explained via human reason—is the way the uninspired reader transmits the secrets.

For example, in the case of the text of the Zohar, which is the second category above (*kabbala shelamah* without an inspired reader), the text accurately retains the esoteric message because it is transmitted without the intervention of reason. As such, R. Gershon Henokh considered it more accurate and more valuable than philosophy as it provided a more unadulterated reproduction of the concealed secrets. Its disadvantage is that it cannot be fully understood without an inspired reader serving as its interpreter. In the third category *(kabbala helkit),* the partial tradition is explained and presented through human reason. Its advantage is that while the secrets remain concealed, the reader has easier access to a partial understanding of them by studying the text, which is more accessible because it is rational. The disadvantage is that human reason and philosophical language often distort the "tradition" embedded therein, making it seem like something other than it really is. That is, what is understood is not the secret, or even a portion of it, but a mistaken idea born out of a true esoteric teaching.

The philosophical enterprise can never contain a full tradition, precisely because it is interpreted through the human intellect and is not the result of an inspired reading of a received tradition. R. Gershon Henokh values philosophical language as a valiant, albeit failed attempt to rend the veil of the secret tradition that, in spite of itself, manages to transmit some elements of that tradition. Although he acknowledges that the pure tradition is not fully revealed, even in Kabbalistic texts, he would surely reject the more radical position of R. Moses Isserles (1530–1572), in his *Torat Ha-Olah,* that contemporary Kabbala is merely the product of human reason *(s'vara)* and not the remnant of any ancient tradition.[84] The ancient Sod tradition, initiated by Abraham and transmitted orally, is the product of a direct communication between God and the individual. Although this tradition requires an inspired reader to reveal its secrets, its authenticity as a product of inspiration remains intact even without an inspired reader. An individual who is the recipient of such an inspiration and uses it to interpret the esoteric text (i.e., Luria's interpretation of the Zohar) has the potential to reconstruct the complete tradition *(kabbala shelamah)* and to elevate the second category to the first. One who receives this Kabbala through transmission, however corrupt and incomplete, but has no inspiration himself (i.e., Maimonides), may use philosophy as a tool to both disseminate and conceal what he received, without acknowledging it as received. The work of such an individual, even as it may succeed in revealing certain elements of the concealed esoteric tradition, is inferior to Kabbala in two ways: first, it is founded on a partial tradition; and second, it is devoid of any inspired interpretation and must depend solely on reason, which is inherently flawed, in order to unlock the secrets of the tradition.

It is imperative that the Zohar, which is the most authentic reproduction of the Sod tradition (even as it is still closed as a text), be accompanied by an inspired interpreter. Therefore, R. Gershon Henokh's entire project of reading Maimonides through the Zohar rests on his belief in Luria's inspired reading of the Zohar. That is, the Zohar is a closed text (i.e., its secrets remain concealed) until Luria, who, via inspiration *(gilluy Eliyahu),* is able to unveil its true meaning. This creates the condition for using the Zohar as a tool to reveal the esoteric components of the *Guide*. It is only through Luria that the secrets of the Zohar can be understood. Luria thus brings the text of the Zohar from category two to category one, enabling the Zohar to become the lens through which the secrets embedded in the *Guide* can be disclosed.

Moreover, as stated earlier, it is the Besht's reading of Luria that finally opens the concealed nature of Luria's own reading of the Zohar. Therefore, the Besht makes Kabbala (Zohar, Luria) an accessible *kabbala shelamah* and thus a tool to reveal the Sod that underlies the medieval philosophical tradition. In *Ha-Hakdama,* R. Gershon Henokh believes he is merely utilizing the possibilities already extant through the Besht's opening of Luria's interpretation of the Zohar in order to complete the Hasidic project of unveiling the secret of the tradition, returning Judaism to a full-bodied Abrahamic religion.[85]

The innovation of Luria's inspired reading as revealing the underpinnings of the Zohar, creating the conditions for redemption, is a cornerstone of R. Gershon Henokh's entire oeuvre and, arguably, the centerpiece of his Hasidic ideology. To illustrate the restorative nature of Lurianic discourse as the final period of esoteric disclosure, R. Gershon Henokh juxtaposes him to Nahmanides, who is viewed by R. Hayyim Vital as the last inheritor of a full tradition *(kabbala shelamah).*

> Many of the *Ba'ale Ha-Tosafot,* as can be seen from their language, concealed many things, likened to the concealing of *Atik Yomin*. They hinted at these things with their words. Nahmanides emerged after the *Ba'ale Ha-Tosafot* and began to [explicitly] hint at these lofty things [by using the phrase] "by way of truth" [*'al derekh ha-emet*]. He hinted at things that can clearly be seen to contain deep and holy secrets, as he indicated in his introduction to his commentary to Genesis. The Ari [R. Isaac Luria] attested

> to the fact that Nahmanides indeed received as full tradition [*kabbala shelamah*] yet greatly concealed his words. Nahmanides raised many disciples, many of whom received this full tradition from him. However, according to the Ari, all Kabbalistic works written after Nahmanides do not contain this full tradition, even as the authors were giants in Torah and piety. Luria even cites their works. However, he [i.e., R. Hayyim Vital] wrote that one should not study their works. This is not because they contain any deviant opinions, God forbid, but because all of their words are included in the teachings of the Ari who ordered them and added to them elements that were revealed in his day. Therefore, it is worth [only] studying that which contains everything. . . . He [Ari] was the chosen of God. The hidden light was in him, reaching from one end of this world to the next. He was able to illumine and explain the words of R. Shimon bar Yohai [the Zohar]. As it is written in *Shivhei Ha-Ari,* everything the Ari achieved came from the Zohar.[86]

It is well known that Nahmanides' use of Kabbala is very opaque.[87] Nahmanides often hints at Kabbalistic interpretations but rarely expounds on the substance of those readings. Building on the idiosyncratic tenor of Nahmanides' Kabbalistic method, Moshe Idel suggests that Nahmanides offers a Kabbalistic interpretation only when he receives such an interpretation from tradition and, in at least some cases, may have not even known its meaning.[88] On R. Gershon Henokh's reading, Idel's thesis would align Nahmanides with Maimonides. However, R. Gershon Henokh draws an important distinction between his reading of Maimonides and Nahmanides by adopting the Lurianic opinion, as stated by R. Hayyim Vital, that Nahmanides was the last medieval Jewish thinker in possession of a full Kabbalistic tradition *(kabbala shelamah),* as opposed to Maimonides, who only possessed a partial tradition *(kabbala helkit).*

According to our author, neither Nahmanides nor Maimonides were inspired readers like Luria. Both concealed their works, albeit in different ways. Nahmanides was more reliable because he largely transmitted what he received (at least according to Idel), but what he received was often not understood because he lacked the requisite inspiration needed to bring the secrets to life. Maimonides was less reliable because of what he received (i.e., only a *kabbala helkit*), but he explained what he received in a manner more accessible to his reader. Nahmanides' method of concealment requires the inspired reading of someone like Luria to open and reveal his hints.[89] This may be why Vital, in his introduction to *Sha'ar Ha-Hakdamot* (printed as the introduction to *'Etz Hayyim*), situates Luria as the next inheritor of the Nahmanidean tradition. It may also shed light on

Luria's marked lack of interest in philosophy in general and Maimonides in particular. Luria was only interested in Kabbalists who received a full tradition *(kabbala shelamah)* that needed further disclosure through his inspired reading. Therefore, for Luria the *Guide* is a useless text or at best an uninteresting one. Alternatively, R. Gershon Henokh had no interest in Nahmanides because Luria had already succeeded in revealing his secrets. However, he does have an interest in Maimonides precisely to exhibit the partial tradition he possesses in order to include him in the circle of authentic Jewish carriers of the ancient Sod tradition. On this reading, Luria's disinterest in Maimonides set the stage for Hasidism's reengagement with Maimonides' philosophical corpus.

It would appear, then, that the final stage of illumination has occurred in Luria's disclosure of the secrets of the Zohar. However, for R. Gershon Henokh the dialectic continued, in that R. Isaac Luria's illumination of the full tradition is expressed in highly symbolic and mythic language that equivocated its full disclosure. Hence, the study of Lurianic Kabbala is fraught with apparent contradictions and intricate symbolic categories that, as the Kabbalistic dictum goes, "reveals a handbreadth and conceals two."[90]

There are many reasons given to explain why Luria's discourse is as opaque and as jargoned as it is. First, the fact that Luria spent less than eighteen months with his students before his early death from an epidemic of the plague (on 15 July [5 Av] 1572) appears to have left his disciples to resolve discrepancies in his lectures without him. Second, following the tradition of the Zohar, especially the Idrot that were foundational texts for Luria, he intended his teachings to remain within a closed circle, accessible only to those who had the tools to truly understand them. This second reason may also reflect Luria's messianism (also an extension of the Idrot) and his desire to resist full disclosure of the messianic Torah until the coming of the messianic age and not a moment before. In fact, drawing from the Zohar's interpretation of Adam's untimely copulation with Eve in the Garden of Eden, premature disclosure could yield further destruction if the world is not yet adequately purified *(m'vurar)* in order to absorb the sanctity of the secret.[91]

For R. Gershon Henokh, the concealed nature of Lurianic Kabbala sets the stage for what he believed was the final unveiling of this ancient esoteric tradition and thus the final phase of Jewish exile ushered in by the appearance of the Baal Shem Tov. R. Gershon Henokh viewed the Besht's contribution to this disclosure as the final stage in the age-old dialectic of Jewish esotericism. It is with the Besht that the Sod tradition of Abraham, having taken on a highly intricate and complex form in the history of Kabbala, is translated back into the language of faith and awe to be shared and experienced by all of Israel. In the final stage of exile, the synthesis and integration of the *Guide* and the Zohar, representing the redemption of the Sod tradition from its bifurcated exilic state, is finally overcome. In this final stage, faith and awe, the pillars of the devotional life of Jews throughout history, become the carriers of this Sod tradition through the teachings of the Baal Shem Tov. Hasidism is viewed as the culmination, completion, and "overcoming" of Kabbala as a literary tradition, resulting in the flowering of the messianic personality cultivated by devotional practice rather than mystical speculation.

3 What Is Hasidism?

A Hasidic Search for Origins

. . . halakha is an exoteric discipline.
Isadore Twersky, *Rabad of Posquiéres: A Twelfth-Century Talmudist*

The Erasure of Knowledge and the Hasidic Construction of Piety

This chapter will examine the centrality of worship in the Hasidic imagination and its place in R. Gershon Henokh's theory of esotericism. The second part of R. Gershon Henokh's *Ha-Hakdama ve Ha-Petikha* describes how the Baal Shem Tov completes the circle of Jewish esotericism, preparing the world for the final redemption. The Hasidic contribution to Jewish esotericism described in this treatise, a tradition whose trajectory extends from rabbinic Judaism's concealment of Sod in the law through R. Isaac Luria's initial disclosure of the secrets of the Zohar, is meant to show that the final full disclosure of this esoteric tradition can only be accomplished through piety (devotional praxis) and not solely through study (Talmud Torah), cognition (philosophy), or mystical contemplation (classical Kabbala).

This piety is not distinct from philosophy or Kabbala but is the full integration of those ideas into behavioral practices—acts that hold the potential to elevate the worshipper above the limits of human intellectual activity. On this reading, the uniqueness of Hasidism is not in its ideas per se but in its orientation and prioritization of what it means to live Jewishly, that is, the translation of thought into practice. I call this Hasidic contribution to Jewish esotericism the "piety of secrecy" because it claims to complete the intellectual and contemplative trajectory of Sod by bringing esoteric knowledge, through praxis, back to its origins in the religion of Abraham.

The flow of this discussion will revolve around the question, "what is Hasidism?" This question is only asked by later masters who inherited the

Beshtean tradition and the first few generations of disciples. My contention is that Izbica/Radzin Hasidism in general, and *Ha-Hakdama ve Ha-Petikha* in particular, constitute the first systematic attempts to address the question of "what is Hasidism?" from inside Hasidic Judaism. It is a product of late-nineteenth-century Polish Hasidism that had already survived the Mithnagdic polemics of the early part of that century and had grown to become a dominant force in Eastern European Jewry.

The question "what is Hasidism?" considers the larger issues surrounding the Hasidic contribution to Jewish life and letters that were not the focus of Hasidism's formative period. Other questions—such as "what are the larger literary, philosophical, and theological issues at stake in Hasidism?" or "what is Hasidism trying to accomplish as an inheritor of the Jewish mystical and pietistic tradition?"—became relevant only for later masters who lived in the safe haven of Hasidism's communal and intellectual success throughout Eastern Europe. In a sense, Hasidism inadvertently began writing its own intellectual history as a way of drawing boundaries between its innovative spirit and the surrounding non-Hasidic world.[1]

Without making explicit reference to innovation, R. Gershon Henokh utilizes Hasidic doctrine and teaching to reexamine the mystical and philosophical literature of the Middle Ages in his quest to demonstrate the integration of the metaphysical claims of philosophy and Kabbala into the practice of Hasidic piety.

The first part of this treatise is devoted to a theory of Hasidic esotericism, presenting the argument that an unknown (or, at best, partially known) esoteric tradition informs the philosophical and Kabbalistic literature of late antiquity and the Middle Ages. Maimonides' *Guide of the Perplexed,* the Zohar, and Lurianic Kabbala are chosen as the three best exemplars of how esotericism survives as a subterranean tradition influencing metahalakhic literature. This first part of *Ha-Hakdama,* examined in previous chapters, consists of a detailed comparative analysis of the *Guide* and the Zohar in an attempt to expose their similar positions and shared influences. At the end of this first part, Hasidism is presented as closing the circle of Jewish esotericism by returning the Sod tradition to its Abrahamic origins via the Besht's ability to translate and thereby disclose this Sod tradition by severing it from the linguistic and ideational garments constructed to conceal its message.

The second part of this treatise constructs an edifice of Hasidic piety on the foundations of the philosophical and mystical ideas examined in part 1. This second part exhibits what I argue is an attempt to shift the trajectory and orientation of medieval philosophy and Kabbala, including *ta'amei ha-mitzvot,* to include Hasidism's praxis-oriented approach to esotericism. The implicit assumption in this second part is that medieval philosophical and Kabbalistic texts explicate their respective systems, both rational and cosmological, in order to justify, explain, or accompany the practice of mitzvot. As exemplars of *ta'amei ha-mitzvot,* these systems create an ideational context for the commandments, even to the point of mapping their cosmic efficacy (as in theosophical Kabbala). However, both philosophy and Kabbala maintain a distance from the act itself, even as they support its performance. They serve to foster knowledge of the inner meaning of mitzvot, intentionality *(kavvanah),* or contemplative states *(yihudim)* that accompany the performance of mitzvot.[2]

While it is true that Zoharic cosmology includes the practical component of the performance of mitzvot, Lurianic cosmology more fully integrates the performance of mitzvot and ritual than its medieval theosophical predecessors. Even though these contemplative states stand at the center of the Lurianic system, I would argue that in Luria's translation of cosmology to mystical psychology (i.e., *kavvanot* and *yihudim*), such states still only function to make the worshipper conscious of the cosmic shift that occurs as a result of the performance of a particular religious act.[3] That is, the cosmos, in one form or another, is still the focus of the worshipper's intention. In Hasidism, at least the way it is presented by R. Gershon Henokh, the cosmology of the Kabbala is even further detached from its theosophical and theurgic moorings. Cosmology is translated into a human orientation toward God and becomes a grid for a behavioral response to that orientation, embodied in the form of faith and reverence for/to God.[4] The Hasid worships from the existential place between the poles of faith and reverence and pays less attention to the cosmic realm. The Hasidic focus as presented here is more psychological than cosmological or theurgic.[5] Faith and reverence are not validations or explanations of the mitzvot, nor are they merely principles that are affirmed; they are the building blocks of human volition, the very vehicles that propel the worshipper to act. The devotional act is a response to, and an outgrowth of, the experiential consequences of faith and reverence, born out of the existential posture procured by constructing an aesthetic of worship from the metahalakhic ideas in Jewish philosophy and Kabbala. The cosmos becomes a grid upon which one understands the human condition of faith.

The basic difference between Kabbala and Hasidism, according to R. Gershon Henokh, is the claim that cognition (philosophy) and mystical knowledge (Kabbala) cannot yield the full disclosure of the Sod tradition and therefore cannot facilitate redemption. In fact, one may go as far as to say that the philosophical worldview is not messianic at all! Even as it strives for an ideal that is messianic, the fact that it uses reason as its primary vehicle of transmission actually prevents the achievement of the ideal it seeks to disclose. Full disclosure can only be accomplished through devotion *(avodah),* the translation of ideas into behavioral norms that, when performed in the correct "state of mind," can elevate the worshipper beyond the limits of the human intellectual endeavor and expose him to a vision of redemption.[6]

The assumption here is that exposure to the ideal, albeit in a momentary and veiled form, is a requirement for the ideal to remain the object of human desire. One must "know" what one is striving for or the striving is futile. This "knowing," according to our Hasidic critic, is only achieved via devotion since the object of knowledge (God as Infinite) cannot be known any other way.

The result of devotion enacted through this mystical state of mind is called by our author perfect faith (*emunah shelamah,* the fleeting glimpse of the perfect above-ordered existence that informs one's entire religious life). This glimpse remains as a trace *(reshimu)* as the worshipper reenters the world of limits. The faith experience fosters the messianic personality, one who still lives in the world of doubt *('olam ha-safek)* but has experienced a glimpse of the ideal that lies beyond it.[7] According to this Hasidic view, redemption can only be desired if it has already been achieved.

While mitzvot may remain obligatory for the enlightened, they become less and less a central part of his/her religious life. The religious models of Moses and Rabbi Akiba are slowly transfigured via a retrieval of Sod into the religion of Abraham. Abraham was able to serve God fully without the need for the formality of obligatory acts. This transfiguration cannot take place via cognition, as human knowledge, being created, is too limited to reach beyond itself. This, R. Gershon Henokh argues, is the mistake of the philosophers and, to some extent, the classical Kabbalists. The Besht understood this, he says, and reoriented Judaism toward the fully integrated act by presenting the act itself as having the potential to transcend the limits of human cognition and offer a glimpse of the idealized divine world.

In many ways, this Hasidic critique deconstructs the Neoplatonic revision of Plato that served as the backdrop of the medieval Jewish philosophical tradition.[8] In a recent study of the Jewish philosophical tradition, Kenneth Seeskin makes the following claim that is relevant to our discussion:

> The transcendence of the Rational, which might also be called "anti-anti-incarnationalism," asserts that it is impossible for the ideal to be realized in a sensuous medium. This principle is the philosophic equivalent of the basic Jewish conviction that God is separate from the world and cannot be depicted with images of things found in the world. According to Deuteronomy 5:8, *You shall not make for yourself a sculpted image, any likeness of what is in the heavens above, or on the earth below, or in the waters below the earth.* In this respect, the second thesis is similar to the first: God is never *in* heavenly bodies or earthly phenomena but is a moral will who stands *above* them. In philosophic terms, this means that everything in the world is fallible and subject to critique. The most that can be claimed on behalf of anything in the world is that it strives for the ideal; but to strive for something is to admit that one does not have it. In this way, Jewish thought is appropriately described as messianic. Instead of defending the world as it is at present, it puts forward a standard which has not been achieved and may never be achieved until the end of time.[9]

The subject of Seeskin's observation is the classical Jewish philosophical tradition and does not include its Kabbalistic counterpart. The limits he draws for philosophy ("that everything in the world is fallible and subject to critique") is aligned with R. Gershon Henokh's critique of philosophy. However, unlike the philosophers, R. Gershon Henokh would include human reason in the category of "everything in the world."

Inheriting the implicit Jewish Neoplatonic critique of the philosophical tradition in the Zohar, R. Gershon Henokh argues that these very limitations make the philosophical pursuit unmessianic for the exact same reasons that Seeskin sees them as messianic. Messianism for R. Gershon Henokh only begins with the overlap of the real and the ideal—when the latter begins to infiltrate the purview of the former. In this Hasidic rendition, messianism is a critique of the real, albeit a "real" that has already reached beyond itself. In Judaism the realm of the "real" is comprised of the mitzvot that direct Israel toward the ideal (redemption). Maimonides and the Jewish philosophical tradition add reason to this mix as a way to understand the commandments and thereby understand divine will.

Our Hasidic author agrees that the mitzvot are the path to the ideal, but he suggests that mitzvot alone can never ultimately get us there. "Getting there" is only achieved by fully actualizing human potential through devotion and faith, resulting in a vision of unity between the human and divine will. This potential begins to be actualized in Abraham's vision at the Akedah (Binding of Isaac) (as understood according to the Zohar), the vision being the reward for his piety (i.e., his willingness to sacrifice Isaac).

This vision, dormant in the souls of Israel, is the only path that reaches beyond the human and thus the only path that yields the fully human. Based on various passages from the Zohar, R. Gershon Henokh claims that the end is only realized when devotion overcomes cognition, reenacting the piety of the Akedah, and resulting in a vision of the Infinite that is then absorbed back into the unredeemed world. Piety, and not reason or even contemplation, is the only vehicle to overcome exile.

Faith before Faith: Striving to Overcome Cognition

R. Gershon Henokh holds that the dialectical nature of the Sod tradition (represented in fragmented form in both philosophy and Kabbala) is the consequence of a premessianic world where God is eclipsed by creation and thus inaccessible without the intervention of prophecy or divine illumination. It is for this reason that a "full tradition" is always only the property of the mystical elite who insures that it remains concealed. Thus, R. Shimon bar Yohai's statement (and the ensuing discussion) in b.T. Shabbat 138b, 139a, that "Torah will not be forgotten in Israel," is taken to mean that Torah will not be utterly forgotten but will be concealed until the world is ready for its complete disclosure. For the mystics, the "Torah" referred to in the talmudic passage is the concealed tradition of Sod. As a support for esotericism, the talmudic statement is read to say, "Torah will not be forgotten in *all of* Israel, but will be forgotten (or concealed) in most of Israel."[10]

According to R. Gershon Henokh, many Jewish thinkers, including many medieval Jewish philosophers, inherit only fragments of this tradition *(kabbala helkit),* enveloping these fragments in philosophical language and categories in order to insure their protection. Both of these traditions (philosophy/Kabbala) are kept away from the uneducated masses for fear that they would distort the message therein and defile the sanctity of the secret. In concert with the populist nature of Hasidism, R. Gershon Henokh's entire project is built on the assumption that redemption can occur only by disclosing this secret to the entire nation.[11] This invention of the Besht, at least the way Hasidism understood it, was the foundation of R. Gershon Henokh's "Introduction to Hasidism."

The vocation of the latter-day Kabbalist is to reveal the true Sod tradition and use it to facilitate the mystical experience. The Kabbalist traditionally attempts to unveil the Sod tradition embedded in either the body of sacred literature, that is, Scripture or rabbinic literature; the philosophical language of the medieval Jewish philosophical tradition; or the symbolic language of classical Kabbala. All three alternatives require considerable familiarity and training in the classical texts of Judaism coupled with a commitment to pietism, often constructed as a type of mystical asceticism.[12]

For R. Gershon Henokh, the Besht introduced another avenue whereby the aspiring devotee could reach beyond the limits of the intellect to achieve an experiential unity of creation and Creator. This new "method" was called devekut.[13] While Hasidic devekut shares a great deal with pre-Hasidic models, the centrality and focus in early Hasidic literature led many scholars to surmise that it was the most innovative element in Hasidism. Devekut is achieved in Hasidism through the devotional life, lived with the intention and belief that devotion, specifically but not exclusively prayer, could foster an experience of communion with God that could not be achieved by any other means.

The notion of devotion as a catalyst for devekut serves as the foundation for the second half of R. Gershon Henokh's introductory treatise.[14] His unique approach to the efficacy of devotion and its relation to the intellectual trends in classical Kabbala and medieval Jewish philosophy complete what he deemed was the final phase of the history of Jewish esotericism, the ultimate transfiguration of the cognitive to the experiential.

This second part of *Ha-Hakdama* serves as a radical departure from the intellectual world of the Middle Ages, including both the rationalism of Maimonides and the theosophy of the Zohar. However, as we will presently see, the intellectual synthesis of part 1 serves as the foundation of part 2's focus on devotion and praxis as the overcoming of both faith and reason.[15]

R. Gershon Henokh begins his discussion of Hasidic faith with the oft-cited verse from Psalms 111:10: "The beginning of wisdom [*hokhma*] is the fear [*yeriah*] of God." While accepting fear of God *(yeriah)* as the prerequisite for knowledge of Him *(hokhma),* he suggests that fear cannot be the origin of all human apprehension. "Faith [*emunah*] is the root of fear and fear is the vessel that contains faith. The root of fear [in Psalms 111:10] comes from faith."[16] The insertion of faith before fear subverts the psalmist's literal message as well as the Zohar's reading of this verse. However, the faith mentioned here is not a conventional notion of faith as believing "in" something but one that has a unique pietistic/Hasidic valence. In order to carve out this niche, R. Gershon Henokh must interpret the various passages in the Zohar that highlight Psalms 111:10, extending its meaning as a foundation for the body of mitzvot. The Zohar (1.11b; 2.68b–69a; 2.51b) claims that fear of God is the foundation of the human relationship to God and thus the groundwork of the covenant (mitzvot). The notion of fear in Psalms 111:10 is described in the Zohar as the first mitzvah and the basis of creation *ex nihilo.*

> *In the beginning God created. . . .* This is the first mitzvah. This mitzvah is called fear of God [*yeriat Ha-Shem*]. It is the first point upon which the psalmist states, *The beginning of wisdom is the fear of God. . . .* Upon this mitzvah the entire world stands. This fear has three dimensions, two of which do not have a sufficient foundation and one that has such a foundation. There is a person who fears God in order that his children live and not die. Or, he fears physical or financial retribution. He is one in a constant state of fear. This fear of God, however, never reaches its root. Another may fear God from punishment in this world or the next. These two types of fear are not fundamental. The type of fear that is fundamental is the fear that stems from God as the foundation and arbiter of all the worlds, and that all those worlds are nothing compared to Him, as it is written, *all earth dwellers are naught compared to Him* [Daniel 4:32]. One should place his desire and will in that place—which is called fear [*yeriah*].[17]

This extended interpretation of Psalms 111:10 is the foundation for R. Gershon Henokh's reading, but ultimately it does not satisfy his search for a Hasidic foundation for piety no longer tied to the theosophical language of the Zohar. The problem is simply that fear requires an object that is, in some sense, known. The Zohar is not blind to this difficulty, addressing this problem in another context: "If a person does not know Torah, the reward of its mitzvot and punishments of its transgressions, and does not know who created Torah and gave it to Israel, how can he fear it and protect its statutes. Therefore, David said to his son Solomon, *Know the God your father, and serve Him* [Chronicles 1:28:9]."[18]

R. Gershon Henokh's unwillingness to accept the *prima facia* meaning of the Zohar—on fear of God as the origin of mitzvot—is now understood as a problem internal to the Zohar itself. His turning away from the Zohar's interpretation of Psalms 111:10 should not be viewed as contesting the Zohar's reading of the passage in Psalms; rather, he is importing into this case what the Zohar says in another place (regarding mitzvot in general). The Hasidic proposition of faith that precedes fear is constructed as a disclosure of the Zohar's intent, perhaps even an element of a lost fragment of its Sod foundation, and not simply the invention of one Hasidic reader of the Zohar. If the first mitzvah is the fear of God as absolute creator (i.e., *ex nihilo*), something must enable the individual to experience a glimpse of that creative power beyond the created world. In fact, this reading suggests that such an experience is the necessary prerequisite for fear and thus for mitzvot in general. Therefore fear, while "a" beginning, cannot be "the" beginning. "The foundation of this fully rooted fear [*yeriah ha-ikarit*] is faith, whereby one can come to understand, believe, and know, the greatness of God, after which he can fear Him. Only then will fear be complete."[19] The type of faith presented here as a prerequisite for fear of God is not a "belief in" or a "belief that."[20] It is, rather, an existential posture that grows out of the illumination of a perfected world, enabling one to fear the God who is experienced in that illumination even as that God does not remain present. R. Gershon Henokh calls this "perfect faith" *(emunah shelamah).* "The faith that is the root of fear of God, is the perfect faith [*emunah shelamah*] that God brings forth all of creation *ex-nihilo* . . . he also establishes, apportions, and measures human knowledge and intellection, with the limits he distributes to the rest of creation."[21]

The use of faith language as a supplement to and precursor of fear, which the Zohar argues is the first mitzvah, is R. Gershon Henokh's attempt to integrate Maimonidean language into his construction of Hasidic piety. Moreover, using Maimonidean language to supplement the Zohar's rendering of faith addresses one of the more curious things about the Maimonidean discussion of both faith and knowledge: the conspicuous absence of creation *ex nihilo* in the *Mishneh Torah* and *Sefer Ha-Mitzvot.*

Although Maimonides does seem to come out on the side of creation *ex nihilo* in *Guide* 2:25 and 2:26, he excludes any mention of creation, including any description of God as Creator, in the beginning of *Sefer Ha-Mitzvot* and the *Mishneh Torah* passages above.[22] Fear of God is listed as the fourth positive commandment in *Sefer Ha-Mitzvot,* referring primarily to fear of retribution and providence, interestingly the two categories of deficient fear mentioned in the Zohar. For Maimonides, then, the first mitzvah is the belief that the God whose existence can be "known" via philosophy is the same God who reveals Himself at Sinai. For the Zohar, the first mitzvah is the fear of God who is creator *ex nihilo*. From the Zohar passages we have seen, no previous knowledge of Him is assumed.

Circling back to R. Gershon Henokh's discussion, we can begin to unravel the oblique notion he calls "perfect faith." In the passage cited above, the Maimonidean language of faith, which applies to God as a source of revelation, is assigned to the Zohar's notion of creation *ex nihilo.*[23] This faith is not merely doctrinal but can (or will) result in the "understanding, belief, and knowledge of the greatness of God." This faith seeks to answer the question regarding how one can fear what one does not know. If, as both Maimonides and the Zohar assume, the Creator God cannot be known in any conventional sense, superrational experience of this God (from the perspective of the Zohar) must precede fear of Him.[24] The perfect faith presented here is a faith that is a vehicle for overcoming cognition, creating a foundation for the Zoharic fear of God as Creator. This perfect faith is a faith before faith—that is, a belief about the nature of the individual that precedes a "belief in" or a "belief that," both of which are about believing in an object or an idea outside the believer. Experiencing this faith before faith is understood as the momentary actualization of full human potential which culminates in the direct, albeit fleeting, experience of God.

> One must believe with perfect faith and establish that faith permanently in one's heart and soul that all human knowledge is created—that one's intellect is a product of creation and that all apprehension is created. [One must believe] that God directs the world at every moment, is providential at every instant, and renews all worlds, powers, emanations, creations, formations, and actions. God also gives life and renews our knowledge and ability to apprehend. Through this knowledge we will be able to serve him with free will, because [that knowledge] necessitates free will. . . . Understanding this insight [*hasaga ha-zot v'sekhel ha-zeh*] results in free will. This is the will of God—that we serve him with free will.[25]

Perfect faith is two-tiered. First, it is the recognition that human knowledge itself is created, thus limited. Therefore the intellect, only able to function within its own created limits, can never apprehend the roots of creation, that is, God as Creator. Second, faith is a belief that our empirical and logical understanding of the world as regulated and ordered *('olam k'minhago noheg)* is incorrect yet the inevitable product of our own created minds.[26] This limitation exists, according to R. Gershon Henokh, in order for us to serve God willingly (free will), or at least with the illusion that we serve Him freely. So far this is all quite conventional. However, the extension of this claim yields some new results.

> Also, one must believe with perfect faith that God can change one's apprehension so that he understands things different than before—whether this is a sweeping change that alters one's understanding of the order of all activity which would nullify free will—or whether it only affects one's apprehension while retaining free will. [One must believe that] God can give an individual a different perspective [*sekhel 'aher,* lit., another intellect] enabling him to see things differently [*hasaga 'aheret*] so that he will understand everything the opposite of how he understands it now. . . .that is, one should believe with perfect faith that nothing is impossible for the Creator. Even the human intellect is always in the hands of God.[27]

R. Gershon Henokh wants to draw from the observation of the perennial instability of human knowledge that all knowledge is "in the hands of God." Therefore, he surmises, it must be possible that an individual can also become privy to that which lies beyond the limits of the human intellect. While this supernatural apprehension is clearly the result of divine will (as is all human apprehension), it is fostered by the perfect faith that is the root of the Zohar's fear of God's greatness *(yeriah shelamah).*

> One must see the supernal power over all of creation. When it is seen that what one understands is the opposite of his neighbor, he will understand that even that which is agreed upon by all is still [only] created [and thus fallible]. At that moment he will understand creation itself exists only from the perspective of the created. From God's perspective, there is no nature, it is only creation that is veiled in the concealment [of natural law]. God can [also] change what is felt and established [in human experience] until someone can understand the opposite of what he thought was true. This will result in "strong fear" [*yeriah 'azuma*]. . . . [Moreover] one is obligated to ask *who created all this?* [Isaiah 40: 26]. This is the entire purpose of human existence—to come to understand this concealed power and that there is an essential existence to everything. This can become known by seeing [and understanding] how everything [in existence] can change.[28]

Fear of God in the Zohar is understood by R. Gershon Henokh not merely as an ontological proposition but as the experience resulting from the successful human inquiry into that which lies beyond empirical and cognitive reason. Instead of the natural world being the object of human contemplation of God, as was common in the Middle Ages,[29] R. Gershon Henokh uses the instability of nature as a correlate to the deficiencies of human understanding, both of which inspire one to seek God's perfection and submit to the human dependence on that perfection. However, that dependence does not yield a religious posture reminiscent of the romanticism of the nineteenth-century Protestant theologian Friedrich Schleiermacher. Rather, the submission of createdness and thus the fallibility of human understanding is the first step toward elevating oneself above those very limits. "Seeing how things change, from one extreme to the other, is the source of human devotion and the root of the fundamental question *who created all this*?"[30] This observation is based on Zohar 2.231b, where the Isaiah verse is read within the context of medieval metaphysics, as understood by the theosophical tradition, that symmetry exists between the supernal and material realms.

> If one raises his eyes and gazes above he can know and absorb [*l'minda u l'istakla*] that which he was not able to know and envision. It is written *lift up your eyes to the heights* [*and see who created all this*] [Isaiah 40:26]. He that desires to gaze and know the works of God should turn his eyes upward and see the myriad of angels and supernal beings who serve God one to the other in their entire multitude. Only then will he see and rightly question and know who created these.[31]

R. Gershon Henokh uses the Zohar's interpretation of Isaiah 40:26, but he significantly changes its direction.[32] The vision one achieves is not a vision of the supernal realm of nonmaterial matter (the angelic world) but what lies above even that—a glimpse of the God who is Creator. This vision is achieved through faith in the limitations of human knowledge and the ability to rise above those limits. This faith will enable one to have a super-rational experience on which to base his or her fear of God as Creator (*rav v'shalit,* in the Zohar). This observation is used to explain the nature of miracle in the Bible. Referring to the Exodus narrative and the experience of the miracle of redemption from Egypt, R. Gershon Henokh writes: "Israel's fundamental connection to God is through faith. Faith can bring one above the limits of what the human being can know. Faith is pure interiority [*penimiut*] that is not enveloped in any garment. Therefore, Israel can be redeemed purely on the merit of faith, even if it is not accompanied by explicit acts of goodness."[33] The relevance of miracle and redemption and its relationship to Israel's understanding of historical events will be analyzed later on. What is important here is that the layers *(levushim)* in this passage can be understood as different facets of human reason.[34] This faith before faith does not merely acknowledge the limits of human reason but facilitates an experience beyond those limits. This experience, whether it is of the Creator God, the limits of natural law, or the deterministic nature of the universe, momentarily lifts the worshipper out of the darkness of doubt that serves as the general forum for human devotion.

The darkness of exile in the Exodus narrative, which is the context of the above-cited passage, is identical to the darkness of creation and the darkness of human doubt, understood by many Kabbalists and Hasidic masters as the natural exilic human condition. This darkness is the veil that separates the perfect God from His creation, which is temporarily rent by means of perfect faith. The Zohar states: "There is no possibility of serving God except through darkness—there is no good without the existence of evil."[35] While the human being is a product of that darkness and must serve God from that place of doubt *('olam ha-safek),* R. Gershon Henokh argues that one can momentarily overcome doubt through perfect faith *(emunah shelamah)* and integrate that experience back into the darkened world. The initial experience of this darkness is fear. Overcoming cognition through perfect faith is the accomplishment of Abraham and the foundation of the messianic personality that the Izbica/Radzin tradition seeks to nurture.[36]

Living the Life of Sod: Devotion as the Vessel for Faith in a World of Darkness

Throughout his treatise, R. Gershon Henokh stresses that perfect faith must become permanently embedded in the heart of the devotee, becoming the very source of his devotional life. This idea has both a historical and an experiential component. Historically, this act of integration is viewed as the accomplishment of Abraham, the result of which was his acquisition of a Sod tradition. The experiential component is that all Israelites, as descendants of Abraham, have the potential, and should strive to actualize, Abraham's faith experience and accomplishments. However, actualizing this potential cannot be attained solely via cognitive or contemplative means.

Since Abraham achieved this faith through the act of the Akedah, it can only be achieved through the devotional life centered on devotional praxis.[37] The biblical depiction of Abraham as a man of piety and faith and not necessarily a man of knowledge and wisdom is the foundation of this model of Hasidic devotion.[38] While it remains true that postrabbinic Jewish piety is predominantly based on halakhic practice, that is, the laws of Moses, simple adherence to the life of halakha will not suffice for R. Gershon Henokh. Halakha must be directed toward an end whereby the fulfillment of the law can be accomplished without the formal practice of the law, even as the practice of the law remains intact. This protomessianic vision, while admittedly not in concert with rabbinic models of piety, is not absent in ancient and medieval Judaisms.[39] In R. Gershon Henokh's Hasidic thinking, for example, halakha must be directed toward the Abrahamic end of fully integrating one's experience of the perfect God, achieved by actualizing Abraham's religiosity. This produces a Judaism where the external halakha, while still obligatory, is no longer the sole (or even primary) vehicle for human perfection.

The completion of Abraham's piety of integration and the full-bodied acquisition of perfect faith is exhibited in the Zohar's rendering of God's response to the Akedah (Genesis 22). The Zohar suggests that Abraham's willingness to sacrifice his son resulted in a revelation of divine presence that was only revealed at one moment in history.

> We learn that the name of God called *atik* is absolutely concealed. *Atik* is only revealed in the Torah in one place: when God grants [lit., swears] *zeir anpin* to Abraham, as it says, *By Myself, I swear, God declares* [*because you have done this and not withheld your son, your favored one*]. *I will bestow my blessings on you and make your descendants as numerous as the stars of heaven and the sands on the seashore . . .* [Genesis 22:16, 17]. *I Myself,* this is *zeir anpin*.[40]

R. Gershon Henokh reads this passage to suggest that the divine disclosure of *atik* after the Akedah becomes a part of Abraham and his seed forever, serving as the basis for the possibility of perfect faith.

> From the moment it was said, *Do not raise your hand against the boy, or do anything to him* [Genesis 22:12], Abraham received this supernal light [*atika*] that was above all manner of limitation. This light became established in Isaac and his seed. In truth, Isaac was a perfect sacrifice [*'olah temima*] after he, in concert with Abraham, agreed to be sacrificed. His entire life [after the Akedah] was lived from the verse, *Do not raise your hand against the boy*. From this verse his seed would always hold the potential to receive this light [*atika*] whenever needed, as we have explained at great length in our comments on the Akedah. All of this is possible by means of the full integration of faith in the heart of man. This faith binds one to God in a place that is beyond all manner of comprehension. Therefore the power of prayer can activate even that which nature prevents and can arouse God's will, the effects of which can be seen with the naked eye and be experienced within the limits of human knowledge.[41]

The use of Genesis 22:16 to depict God's revelation of *atik* stems from a linguistic problem in the verse, at least from perceptive of the Zohar's symbolic reading. In most cases, the highest dimension of the Godhead that addresses Israel is *zeir anpin* (YHVH in Scripture). In our verse, God is swearing on Himself, "Himself" understood by the Zohar as *zeir anpin*. Therefore, some other dimension of God (the "I" in the verse) must be doing the swearing if *zeir anpin* ("Myself") is sworn upon. The Zohar concludes that the "I" in the verse must be *atik* (a more lofty dimension of God's essence than *zeir anpin*), making this the only instance in (mythic) history where this essence is revealed to humankind.

R. Gershon Henokh claims that the moment of disclosure of *atik* is not actually Genesis 22:16, as the Zohar suggests, but is embodied in the earlier verse, *Do not raise your hand against the boy* (Genesis 22:12), after which Abraham and Isaac integrate this experience of divine perfection and subsequently transmit it to their descendants. Genesis 22:16 is merely the result of this disclosure, enabling God (as *atik*) to use *zeir anpin* as a vehicle for His oath. The more interesting Hasidic turn in this interpretation is how the dimension of God called *zeir anpin* in the Zohar is understood to represent human devotion *(avodat Ha-Shem),* which now becomes the vehicle for actualizing the revelation of *atik* in the soul of Abraham's descendants. R. Jacob Lainer, R. Gershon Henokh's father, develops this notion.

> Therefore [God's blessing] was aroused from *atika kadisha* and God swore from the place that is severed from any connection to the creation. *Atika kadisha* is above the influence of human devotion, which is called *zeir anpin.* [*Atika*] is above the influence of worship [*zeir anpin*] because its existence precedes worship. . . . This is the place that God shone on Abraham according to his measure [*mida b'mida*] because his own act of worship [i.e., the Akedah] was also above [against?] human nature.[42]

What is significant here is a transformation of the term *zeir anpin* from its cosmic referent in the Zohar to Abraham's devotional act (the Akedah), resulting in the disclosure of a previously unknown dimension of God *(atika kadisha).* Moreover, *zeir anpin,* the collateral of God's oath in the Zohar's reading of Genesis, is also the vehicle for actualizing the dimension of *atik* (the highest level of the divine anthropos) in every Jew. Abraham's willingness to sacrifice his son, and Isaac's willingness to be the sacrifice, resulted in God's granting Abraham and his descendants the ability to use devotion *(avodah, zeir anpin)* as a vehicle to know God beyond the conventional limits of human understanding.

Whereas the verse in Genesis states that the blessing God bestows on Abraham is the birth of a nation from his seed, in the Zohar and in R. Gershon Henokh's interpretation of the biblical blessing, it is the revelation and integration of *atik* (the concealed aspect of God) and the ability to access that dimension of God through worship. The covenant is an outgrowth of that apprehension. God's saving Isaac from the knife of sacrifice was precisely because, having willingly succumbed to God's will, Isaac also embodied the potential to use devotion *(avodah, zeir anpin)* to achieve enlightenment. This orientation toward devotion, that is, actualizing the experience of *atika kadisha,* serves as the foundation of the messianic personality developed in the exegetical writings of this Hasidic dynasty *(Mei Ha-Shiloah, Beit Ya'akov,* and *Sod Yesharim)* which I will explore later.

In *Ha-Hakdama,* R. Gershon Henokh argues that the Besht initiates this new praxis-oriented approach to Jewish esotericism. The Besht's integration of Kabbala (the most complete embodiment of the Sod tradition), with the devotional life enacted in the space between faith and fear, brings Judaism back to its Abrahamic origins, closing the circle of Judaism's spiritual history. Philosophy and Kabbala were two later manifestations of this Sod tradition. Hasidism, as argued here, overcomes these later manifestations by using them to develop an edifice of piety that returns to the tradition's original message.

This interpretation deliberately turns away from medieval models of knowledge and faith and the Lithuanian notion of study as the predominant vehicles for human perfection. The acquisition of philosophical truth (Maimonides), mystical knowledge (Zohar), or the act of *Talmud Torah* (Lithuanian Mithnagdism) are all part but not the apex of a Judaism that seeks to return to its Abrahamic (and secret) roots. R. Gershon Henokh, by systematically using the writings of Maimonides and the Zohar, presents a Hasidic model built on, but significantly departing from, those earlier traditions.

The question "what is Hasidism?" is now understood as pointing to a new Judaism bridging the gap between metaphysics and piety. The medieval models are deficient either because they limit human perfection to the intellect (philosophy) or argue that human perfection can only be achieved by an elite few who are initiated into an closed esoteric fraternity (Kabbala). The Hasidic claim is that devotion, which is accessible to all, holds the potential to overcome these earlier systems, enabling all to achieve a glimpse of the perfect God *(atik)* and to fully actualize their latent Abrahamic potential.

> The order of creation enables one to comprehend beyond that which is revealed in this world. This can only be achieved through worship and faith. [Through worship and faith] one can elevate oneself above the realm of ordered existence and absorb this [supernal] light that [later] descends into the limits of human comprehension. Therefore, everything is dependent upon one's faith and worship. When one is diligent in faith and worship, the supernal light is revealed [to the worshipper] and becomes established in ordered existence.[43]

Although the specific context of this text is about miracles and the supremacy of Abraham's prophecy, it depicts the general tenor of R. Gershon Henokh's turn away from cognition and contemplation as vehicles for acquiring divine knowledge. Reflecting on one of the perennial problems in Jewish philosophy and theology—the existence and explanation of miracles—R. Gershon Henokh argues that a miracle is a divine gift that enables the witness to perceive a glimpse of the redeemed world without requisite preparation. Devotion enacted from "perfect faith" enables the individual to see the miraculous in the mundane and to independently apprehend that which was only apprehended through a collective miracle.

Faith functions here on multiple levels. As mentioned earlier, the first dimension of faith (faith before faith) is a prelude to worship and is aligned with the Zohar's notion of fear *(yeriah)* as the first mitzvah (Zohar 1.111b cited earlier). To briefly reiterate, devotion first demands the individual's acknowledgment of his own limitations. One must first acknowledge the existence of and dependence on that which is beyond human comprehension. This is both the context of human devotion *(avodah)* and what separates the mere fulfillment of mitzvot (halakha) from piety. Mitzvah as halakha may be fulfilled simply as a response to divine command. Piety *(avodah)* assumes that the act is efficacious in the cosmos and creates the possibility for transcending the limits of human knowledge. That is, piety is the religious act performed as a vehicle to apprehend its divine source. Religious acts become devotional only when they are believed to be efficacious, both cosmically and existentially. Yet R. Gershon Henokh acknowledges that the efficacy of a religious act can never be fully traced at the outset. Therefore, Hasidic devotion begins in a shroud of darkness and doubt, drawn from the Zohar's depiction of Abraham's choice to sacrifice Isaac. This notion is developed in R. Mordecai Joseph's *Mei Ha-Shiloah:*

> The essential dimension of this test [the Akedah] was that the transgression of murder [*lo tirzakh*] was clear to Abraham. [Even so] if it would have been clear to Abraham that God wanted him to slaughter his son, it would have been easy for Abraham to do so with all his soul. However, as the Zohar states, [Zohar 1.130b] the commandment to slaughter Isaac came from a speculum that does not shine [*aspaklaria d'lo nahara*]. That is, God did not command him in a clear fashion. Abraham was confused and could have resolved the doubt by choosing any number of options.[44]

The second dimension of faith, that is, the faith the results from action, only emerges from the devotional act. This faith that is realized through devotion serves as a bridge between first faith, that is, "faith before faith" that precedes devotion, and perfect faith, the synthesis of the two. This second dimension of faith is the beginning of the acquisition of perfect faith, the actualization of how the Zohar reads Genesis 16:17. This first faith results in *da'at,* or consciousness, the experience of the greatness of God *(romemut)* or, in the Zohar's rendition, the revelation of *atika.* This first stage precedes what we conventionally call "the fear of God." The human response to this realization is fear (or awe) of that experience, which is the motivation for an integrated ritual life of piety. The relationship between consciousness *(da'at)* and fear *(yeriah)* is alluded to in Genesis 22:12 in the conclusion of the verse. R. Gershon Henokh argues here, against the Zohar, that "fear as consciousness" is the real moment of illumination. This fear is not like the fear of God in the Zohar. This fear as consciousness in Abraham is an act of *imitatio dei:* "*For now I* know [*y'dati*] *that you are one who* fears *God* [*yerei elohim*]" (Genesis 22:12). God becomes conscious *(y'dati)* that Abraham served Him from a place of fear *(yerei elohim),* thereby fully actualizing his potential.

Devotion is the vehicle for and consequence of the actualization of Abrahamic religion. The initial act of devotion is an emulation of the Akedah. Subsequent acts of devotion serve to integrate the illumination of *atika,* resulting from the first act of piety, enabling the devotee to continually access that moment of clarity in the natural world of doubt. Although it is never made explicit, I assume that this process is dynamic and ongoing—there is no single moment of illumination out of which everything else flows. As is the case with Kabbalistic and Maimonidean notions of illumination, these moments are always fleeting. In this Hasidic case, illumination can be reproduced through devotional activity.

Earlier I mentioned what I took to be the subliminal presence of Maimonides in R. Gershon Henokh's analysis of the Zohar. That assumption is important here in order to exhibit how R. Gershon Henokh's critique of Maimonides and philosophy in general, accompanied by his use of philosophical language, constructs the notion of Hasidic piety. In *Sefer Ha-Mitzvot,* Maimonides speaks of the commandment to believe in God. According to R. Gershon Henokh's synthetic approach, Maimonides is alluding to the concept that appears in the Zohar (Introduction to Genesis 1.11b), which says that faith is the commandment that establishes and maintains the world.[45]

At the beginning of the *Mishneh Torah,* Maimonides states that the foundation of all true wisdom *(hokhmot)* is knowledge of the supernatural First Existent that unifies all creation. The problem with R. Gershon Henokh's attempt to read this into the Zohar is that Maimonides never states that the essence of the First Existent can ever be known. Maimonides only says that human beings, via reason, can determine its existence. God is known, according to Maimonides, through His works *(peulot Elohim).*[46]

Only the existence of His essence can be philosophically determined. Moreover, whereas the Zohar asserts that the God who is feared *(atika)* is the God who creates, Maimonides refrains from all manner of describing the knowledge of God as the God of creation (at least *ex nihilo*) when discussing what one must know about God.

Interestingly, R. Gershon Henokh still prefers Maimonides' faith language to the Zohar's language of fear. He is also cognizant that the Zohar refers to faith as the "foundation of the world" and also to fear as the "first mitzvah." He reads Maimonides in *Sefer Ha-Mitzvot* as parallel to Zohar 1.11b by dividing faith into at least two categories: faith as a context for mitzvot (first faith) and faith as the outgrowth of mitzvot (second faith). The first faith is the germ of perfect faith that is only achieved through second faith, a faith that results from action. R. Gershon Henokh regards Maimonides' faith, the first mitzvah, as the recognition of one's human limitations. This faith is the identification of the First Existent (whose existence can be "known") and the unknowable providential God of revelation, who said *I am the Lord your God* (Exodus 20:2). For this to hold, one would have to claim that the God of creation in Zohar 1.11b is identical to the God of revelation in *Sefer Ha-Mitzvot*'s positive commandment 1. However, the Zohar and Maimonides part ways when the Zohar argues that this first mitzvah yields a revelation of God beyond creation (i.e., divine essence). No real parallel exists in the Maimonidean corpus to match that assertion. In the mind of R. Gershon Henokh, this is precisely the failure of philosophy as a vehicle for esotericism.[47]

> This is precisely where the philosophers fail. Even though they believe and acknowledge that everything comes from God and that nothing is deficient in Him, this does not lead to an acknowledgment and belief that their own knowledge is also always in God's hands. Therefore, they think their knowledge and thought are in unison with God's knowledge. Therefore, all this is difficult for them to comprehend. One who believes and knows that all powers are the product of creation, including the human intellect and everything that it produces, will not be disturbed by the notion that something can come from nothing.[48]

R. Gershon Henokh wants to construct his Hasidic piety as an antidote to the failure of philosophy as he understands it. However, his position is not antiphilosophical in the classical sense. Philosophy and philosophical language are needed as a supplement to the Zohar in order to understand the relationship between faith and knowledge. Faith is not in opposition to knowledge but is the vehicle for a knowledge that reaches beyond the cognitive realm. The language and substance of philosophical knowledge is required as a prelude to that faith-moment. Note that R. Gershon Henokh does not merely use the word "believe" when speaking about the nature of God above creation but also includes the word "knowing." This, I would argue, is intentional, as he understands this "belief" (first faith) to lead to apprehension of the perfect God via the illumination of *atik.* Human perfection, or the integration of Abrahamic religion, comes about when the recognition of human deficiency (this first faith) results in the recognition of divine perfection via a revelation of *atika,* enabling the individual to internalize the mitzvot and achieve the religion of Abraham. The recognition of this deficiency is made possible by the study of the world and human knowledge (i.e., philosophy).

> Apprehending the purpose of praising God only comes about via [the verse] *From my flesh I will see God* [Job 19:26]. *From my flesh* teaches the deficiency of humanity. It is [only] from the recognition of human imperfection that the existence of the One who contains all manner of perfection arises. It is this Perfect One who has the power to complete the imperfection of humanity. This is the root of divine praise and prayer which is directed toward completing the deficiency in the one who prays. As to the essence of divine perfection—we have no knowledge of this at all. This is because all types of divine perfection that are present in this world exist only in order to enable the individual to complete his deficiencies.[49]

For R. Gershon Henokh, the final stage of divine disclosure only comes about when the perfection of God *(atika)* is experienced through the recognition of human imperfection (first faith), serving as the motivation for human action in the devotional life of the Hasid.[50] Seeing devotion as a vehicle for divine disclosure becomes the foundation and motivation for continued worship as a means toward integrating the mitzvot and retrieving the religion of Abraham. This is all built on but also subverts the entire medieval intellectual tradition of Jewish philosophy and Kabbala, much of which viewed devotion as either: (1) the realization and expression of philosophical truth (philosophy); (2) the act that initiates cosmic shifting (Zohar); or (3) the forum for contemplative practices, witnessing the cosmic effects of one's action (Lurianic *kavvanot*).[51]

As is the case for many religious traditions, early Protestantism for example, Hasidism's religious critique claims to retrieve the lost spirit of the tradition's spiritual origins. In this case, the retrieval is accompanied by an esotericism positing that the secret spirit of the tradition has always been concealed under layers of philosophical and Kabbalistic literature, each of which contains fragments of these secrets. The intellectual exercise of uncovering these sources, either in philosophy or Kabbala, cannot complete the disclosure of God. That must finally come from devotion and faith that makes God's perfection above creation *(atik)* accessible, finally returning the worshipper to the secret origins of Abrahamic religion. This is the crux of R. Gershon Henokh's answer to the question, "what is Hasidism?" What follows is an analysis of how the experiential dimensions of faith and fear are rooted in the biblical notion of human sin (Adam and Eve) and collective miracle (the Exodus narrative).

Individual Perfection, Collective Transformation, and the History of Israel

According to the Izbica/Radzin tradition, a person of Hasidic faith sees reality as bifurcated between the world that is known and the divine realm, which is unknowable yet constantly directs, and even controls, human existence. While the category of the known or knowable includes empirical and logical knowledge, it also includes metaphysical knowledge (in Kabbala, *'olam ha-sephirot*).[52] Even though the *sephirot* constitute the intermediary realm between the Eternal God *(eyn sof)* and creation, as created, the *sephirot* are within the realm of human experience.[53] According to the theosophical Kabbala, adopted by many Hasidic masters, since these *sephirot* are the most divine form of creation, they are the true catalysts for the knowledge of God.[54] Studying Kabbala is thus imperative for this idea of Hasidic faith. But, unlike many classical Kabbalists, for Hasidic masters Kabbala is not sufficient because, as created, it too is still too limited to complete the final *tikun*.[55] The final *tikun* will only take place when the worshipper is elevated above the limits of human apprehension, accessible through the wisdom of the Kabbala.[56]

Hasidism begins with the underlying principle that the human being functions, and thus serves God, in the world of doubt *('olam ha-safek)* or divine concealment.[57] While this state was not the initial condition of humanity, it became so as a result of the sin of Adam and Eve. The biblical narrative describes Adam hiding from God after the sin (Genesis 3:8). According to certain Kabbalistic interpretations of midrashic traditions about God's concealment *(hester panim),* it was not Adam but God who hid his face as a consequence of Adam and Eve's deviant behavior. The human condition outside the garden is thus founded on divine absence. However, the innate human desire for divine presence, a product of the human essence as *zelem elohim,* remained a fundamental part of humanity's condition. This desire is expressed in divine worship *(avodat Ha-Shem)* as retrieving the lost state of the garden while living in exile.[58] Through devotion, human beings may retrieve the lost essence of *zelem elohim* that survives in the state of divine concealment *(hester panim).* This is accomplished by the latent potential of devotion's ability to offer worshippers a glimpse of the divine essence that they can retain as they return to the world of divine absence. This divine essence is not something outside them but a realization of the identities of the divine will and human will that inspires them to continue in their devotional lives. The messianic era is depicted in these texts as a time when the sin of Adam will no longer veil the presence of God, making human devotion, at least as we now know it, obsolete.[59] Devotion will be extended to all human action as all human action will be a reflection of divine will.

Even as the biblical narrative, especially in Genesis, presents us with informal and even congenial interactions between God and human beings, this all takes place in the realm of *hester panim.* As the biblical narrative widens its lens and focuses on the collective (the People of Israel) in the Book of Exodus and beyond, this absence becomes more pronounced, resulting in the increased formality of the divine-human relationship, finally limited strictly to prophecy.

As the informal relationship to God in Genesis gives way to the collective relationship to God in Exodus, miracle as a collective moment of illumination emerges as a relational tool, momentarily bracketing the condition of divine concealment. These moments, most typically represented in the events associated with the Exodus from Egypt and the theophany at Sinai, are, in the rabbinic imagination, redemptive moments in the context of exile and serve as hints of the future redemption. In the Bible, miracles serve as the vehicles for a collective moment of clarity, understood by midrash and Kabbala as a prelude to a future where the miraculous moment will be the norm rather than the exception.

Miracles are exceptional moments in time because they occur in a world otherwise absent of God. Once they become the norm and lose their exceptional status they are no longer "miraculous." Throughout history, individuals have claimed to witness miraculous moments or events where the natural order appears to be suspended. These events are all exceptional precisely because the witness experiences them from the vantage point of the natural order. In his model of Hasidic faith and piety, R. Gershon Henokh argues that one who serves God with perfect faith has the potential to see and live in a world beyond miracles. That is, one may attain a temporary awareness of the future state where miracle is the norm resulting in a transformation of his orientation toward the present norm. While this awareness is only momentary, it becomes an integral part of one's devotional life, slowly diffusing the world of doubt and uncertainty. The mentality where one's perception and experience of the world stand in stark opposition to the world as we know it is the foundation of the messianic personality in the Izbica/Radzin tradition.

The two foundational biblical events, sin (the Garden of Eden) and miracle (Exodus and Sinai), are the two poles of R. Gershon Henokh's Hasidic piety. Beginning with the sin, we will examine how these biblical events are understood as the foundation for human devotion and its eventual obsolescence. In the Kabbalistic tradition, Adam's sin is viewed as an act of premature abrogation of devotion. Put another way, Adam's sin is a correct understanding of his own essence *(zelem elohim)* and an incorrect understanding of his condition living on the penultimate day before creation's conclusion. The sin is living and acting "as if" the world was redeemed when, in fact, it is only on the cusp of redemption (the sixth day of creation). Adam's sin was thus the prototype of a kind of heresy founded on human miscalculation. Thinking he had risen above the need for human devotion, his sin becomes the very source of the need for obligatory acts (mitzvot). However, the consequence of Adam's sin, that is, mitzvot, can repair the sin only if the worshipper sees that mitzvot too are temporal. Only by seeing that devotion arises in, and is dependent on, the world of doubt, can one see beyond it and therefore understand its telos.

> This is the essence of the sin of Adam according to the writings of Ha-Ari z'l in *Etz Hayyim* and *Likkutei Torah*.[60] The sin of Adam was the desire to expand the realm of *keter* of *zeir anpin* before the proper time and not [first] fill it with light. Therefore, the sin was in the feminine dimension [*b'nukva*], which turned the masculine into the feminine. . . . It states in the Zohar, "what is essential is the four letters and the ten letters that are in *malkhut,* which includes all ten *sephirot.* In her [*malkhut*] all ten *sephirot* must be included. One who takes *malkhut* without the other nine is a heretic [*kozez b'nitiot,* lit., cutter of the shoots]. Anyone who takes the ten *sephirot* without *malkhut* is a non-believer [*kofer b'ikar*]."[61]

R. Gershon Henokh understands the Zohar's comment about "taking the ten *sephirot* without *malkhut*" to mean the mistaken assumption that one can fulfill God's will, and thus repair the cosmos, without devotion *(avodah).* This is the mistaken belief that the human being, who lives in the world of doubt while his essence *(zelem elohim)* is beyond it, can facilitate cosmic repair solely from that essence.

> Adam, in his sin, did not embrace the worldly service of God [*malkhut shamayim*] as an act of devotion to God. One must act as a divine servant, even in the outermost realm [*levush aharon*]. However, after Adam surmised that he was the most cherished [of God's creatures] he believed that all human desire must also be from God. The notion of *malkhut* [in the Tikkunei Zohar] is bringing God into the world through free-will [i.e., *avodah*]. That is, one should restrict oneself for God's sake and purify oneself in the realm of free will.[62]

In the Izbica/Radzin, tradition, free will and the world of doubt *('alma d'sefaka)* are interchangeable. Free will exists as the condition for human action but is not part of human essence *(zelem elohim).* The sin of Adam is his attempt to live outside his condition. The result is that his condition (i.e., doubt/free will) becomes the norm of his existence.

> Since God created him [Adam], he believed he could [automatically] beautify his Creator in the lower parts of creation. Therefore, he thought that he was a necessary [and not contingent] part of creation [*m'huyav b'meziut*] and did not need devotion. Since all the attributes of God were included in him, any action he performed would result in the beautification of God [*kavod shamayim*]. This is an abbreviated presentation of the words of the Ari z'l.[63]

The sin is founded on Adam's assumption, using the language of the Zohar and Luria, that while the world may still be incomplete on the sixth day of creation, Adam, as God's precious creation, is already complete (i.e., he embodied the fully matured *malkhut,* including all the other nine *sephirot*). Referring back to Luria's description, Adam tried to emulate the fully enlightened cosmic man *(zeir anpin)* before he was prepared to receive its highest light *(keter of zeir anpin).* This light, depicted as the expansion of *keter* of *zeir anpin,* can only be absorbed through devotion. As we will presently see, this miscalculation is the root of a particular kind of heretical behavior.

> This was the mistake of Ben Zoma, who thought his devotion had reached the level of *bina* of *hokhma*.[64] He felt that since he apprehended the roots of all the divine attributes [*sephirot*] in *bina,* he could enlighten all the attributes in their particulars, thinking that *bina* was the place where all the attributes were bound together. [His mistake was] that while the realm of *bina* is the place where the attributes are indeed bound together, [in *bina*] they are still in the realm of attributes—it is only that they are no longer in opposition to one another. This is all explained in *Etz Hayyim*. In truth, to complete this process one must use devotion in order to reach the roots of

> these attributes in *hokhma,* where they are pure *hesed.* . . . In that place they are no longer called attributes. They are only called attributes when they descend to levels below *hokhma.*[65]

This text offers a reading of the famous talmudic discussion in b.T. Hagigah 14b/15a about the four sages who entered Paradise *(Pardes).* Only Rabbi Akiba "entered in peace and left in peace" (or "whole"). One died, one became a heretic, and Ben Zoma went insane.[66] In this Kabbalistic rendition, Ben Zoma's mistake, which led to his insanity, is twofold. First, he believed he had completed the cosmic repair by simply envisioning the unification of the *sephirot* in their source in *bina* (the primordial feminine—understanding). This supposedly gave him license to act as he wished, thinking his will was completely aligned with divine will. Second, even when he acknowledged the incomplete nature of his apprehension of the divine attributes in *bina,*[67] he believed he had reached the apex of human experience, coming as far as he could in rectifying the cosmos. "When Ben Zoma apprehended the distance between the attributes [in *bina*] and their roots in *hokhma,* he imagined that it was impossible for anyone to unify them through devotion to the point of complete unification [*yihud gamur*]."[68]

While R. Gershon Henokh does not explicitly state that Ben Zoma's failure is his attachment to human cognition and his inability to see how devotion transcends human knowledge, this is, in my view, implied. Immediately following this passage he discusses at great length the failure of philosophers to acknowledge the ability to know beyond knowledge. This is significant because this Talmudic legend, read through the lens of Adam's sin, distinguishes between heresy proper, which we will see below, and human miscalculation which, while not heresy, is depicted as the foundation of Adam's sin. This miscalculation of Adam is now likened to the mistake of the philosophers. In these selections, the sin of Adam and its repetition in Ben Zoma is the inability to see how human knowledge, as created, can never fully achieve human perfection—or, that it can achieve perfection of the human condition but not the perfection of the human essence. The latter requires perfect faith—the acknowledgment of the deficiency of the human condition and the belief in one's ability to be elevated above it through devotion.

> In truth one must know and understand that from God's perspective, everything is one. Concealment and distinction only exist from the

> human perspective. And [one must know and understand] that God gave the human being the power to worship Him freely, which can result in the full unification of all divine attributes in their root [in *hokhma*] until they can no longer even be called attributes. This is why the Talmud in Hagigah states that "Ben Zoma is still outside. . . ."[69] However, [we know either from Mar Zutra or R. Assa that the separation of the upper and lower waters in heaven is like] "two cloaks spread over the other . . . or two cups tilted over one another."[70] That is, there really is no separation [between the higher and lower waters] at all! However, it is only through human devotion that the [perception of] separation disappears.[71]

It is significant that Ben Zoma, who here represents Adam, is not the heretic in this rabbinic story. Rather, he is the one who goes insane. According to R. Gershon Henokh's reading, his insanity is expressed as disbelief *(kofer b'ikar)* as opposed to heresy (*kozez b'nitiot,* lit., "cutting the shoots"). This disbelief has two parts: one, an inability to see that truth can undermine human understanding and lie beyond the realm of human cognition; and two, an inability to accept that human devotion can result in an apprehension that lies beyond the limits of human cognition. In short, one who lacks perfect faith is in danger of insanity when inquiring into matters of divine wisdom. Ben Zoma is an example of one who embodies the consequences of Adam's sin.

The implied distinction between heresy, depicted in the Talmudic story in the sage Elisha ben Abuya, and disbelief *(k'firah)* in R. Gershon Henokh's description of Ben Zoma's mistake, is quite telling. Formal heresy is not a mistake or miscalculation—it is a calculated choice to defy the clear message of divine will. The Genesis exemplar of the heretic is the serpent or, in some traditions, Esau.[72] The biblical description of the serpent as "shrewd" (Genesis 3:1) and the rabbinic depiction of Esau as deceitful illustrates this view. Disbelief, however, is the inability to live fully in one's condition (the world of doubt) while believing that one is not totally limited by it. Human beings, like Adam, and Israel as a nation, are perennially vulnerable to this miscalculation.

The interpretation of Adam's sin sets the stage for the interpretation of miracle. Miracle offers a momentary glimpse into a world void of the condition of sin, a world where God is not concealed. Sin places both the human being and God in the world of doubt. Sin-consciousness limits the human intellect and subverts Adam and Eve's being created in "God's image." This occurs because sin results in divine concealment. The divine image, now void of substance, can be falsely interpreted to imply a premature identity between human and divine will, thus obviating the need for devotion as an act of free will. In exile, that is, in sin, the full embodiment of this image, being aligned with divine will, only exists *in potentia* (at least in the descendants of Abraham) and can only be actualized by (temporarily) overcoming this condition of limits via devotion, that is, by the transcendence of the intellect. The desire to do so, which is part of the human being's "divine image," is always challenged by one's inability to grapple with the instability and fallibility of human knowledge. This can lead to two conclusions: hopelessness in the human capacity for perception, or disbelief in the efficacy of devotion. Alternatively, it can result in a belief in premature perfection erasing the need for devotion, the very thing that can achieve the desired goal. Acting "as if" one's condition is one's essence—that one has completed the repair within the limits of one's intellect—gives rise to Adam's sin of miscalculation. This only deepens uncertainty and makes the human being more dependent on devotion as commandment. Only perfect faith, R. Gershon Henokh contends, can overcome this condition. This perfect faith, embodied in devotion, is both conditioned on and functions within the imperfect condition of human sin. In the history of Israel, miracle is the temporary transcendence of the condition that fuels the essential desire for divine presence.

Miracle functions in this system as a communal moment where the human condition of sin (doubt) is bracketed in order to offer a glimpse of the telos of devotion, that is, its transcendence. It is significant that the two archetypal miracles, the Exodus and Sinai, are preludes to the giving of the law (i.e., devotion) as the vehicle for redemption. The law functions best as a vehicle for redemption only when it is understood at the outset that its purpose is temporal. That is, the law is given to Israel precisely because they are imperfect yet contain the seeds, via Abraham, for their own perfection. This temporality is conveyed in the collective experience of miracle that precedes the law. Biblical miracles are understood in this Hasidic system as recognition of Israel's premature state and need for divine guidance in order to apprehend and absorb the requisite perfect faith needed for proper adherence to devotion. R. Gershon Henokh intentionally frames his discussion of the Exodus on the "hasty" and premature departure of Israel from Egypt (Exodus 12:11; Deuteronomy 16:3). He utilizes the Zohar's rendering of the Hebrew *b'hipazon* (hastily), describing the Exodus, as *kodem zim'na* (before the appropriate time), in order to connect the Exodus, and subsequent miracles, with Adam's sin, which was an act performed "before the appropriate time." Miracle is a lesson both in the future of the world and in the essence of humankind.

> What comes out of all of this is that the essence [and purpose] of miracle is only to reveal in this world the divine action that is above time and beyond human comprehension. At that moment, it will be seen clearly that opposites do not exist. [It will be understood that] even that which appears oppositional in nature exists as such only according to a lower order. When this supernal activity is revealed, all who witness the miracle [will know] that there is no change in divine will.[73]

Miracle is not presented here simply as an objective event. Rather, it is a perceptual moment, an interpretation from the vantage point of the witness.

> In truth, even natural law [*hanhagat ha-teva*] is miraculous in that it is always the result of providence. However, God conceals this, resulting in the appearance of natural law. One who believes with excessive faith [*emunah yetera*] that God acts on all things will believe that everything is miraculous, even those concealed miracles. For the believer, nature is as miraculous as revealed miracles.[74]

Excessive faith *(emunah yetera)* is, as far as I know, another expression of perfect faith *(emunah shelamah).* I take it to be excessive in the sense that it demands an eclipse of reason before one has experientially overcome reason. The revelation of *atika* to Abraham (the consequence of the Akedah) resulted in planting a seed of faith in the hearts of Israel that enables them, through devotion, to actualize this redemptive state of mind even as they continue to live in the exilic world of doubt.

> God established a point [in the hearts] of Israel [that contained] this type of sustained faith [*emunat kevuim*] by which they can bind themselves to the realm of the divine above nature. . . . With this faith in their hearts they can reach above the limits of human comprehension and arouse God to open the highest light [*'or elyon*] which is above time and all worldly boundaries.[75]

This potential apparently exists in Adam but is misused in the sin and becomes concealed in Adam and Eve's exile from the garden. It reemerges in Abraham's actions at the Akedah. Adam's misuse of faith was his attempt to hastily draw down the light of *atika* before the proper time. This seed of faith, only actualized in Abraham and potentially in his descendants, elevates the witness above human limits, allowing one to see the miraculous in all things. Since miracle is "above time," its collective occurrence happens "hastily," or "out of time." Thus Israel was redeemed from Egypt *b'hipazon* (hastily), which the Zohar reads as "before the appropriate time."

> With this faith [planted] in the heart one is able to reach beyond the limits of cognition and arouse God's will to open the supernal light that is above time and above all natural limitations, as we see in the redemption from Egypt. [The Exodus] was before the appropriate time [*kodem z'-manah*], as it says, "skipping on the mountains and jumping on the hills." In the Zohar its says, "The Exodus from Egypt was without time [*b'lo z'-manah*]" [Zohar 1.61b.]. . . . We also see that the Exodus was actualized through the screaming of the heart, as the Zohar says "Screaming is always from the heart. [lit., "screaming is the heart"] and *Their heart screamed out to God* [Lamentations 2:18]. Screaming and crying is the same thing and are more precious to God than prayer. Through this "faith in the heart" one is able to reach this scream that is inside the heart, even though one cannot express [that] in prayer. This is the lesson of the scream; it is something that cannot be enveloped in the reason of the heart [*higayon ha-lev*] or the letters or words of prayer . . . the arousal of this supernal will can only come from this faith embedded deep in the heart. . . . The essence of miracle is the strong expression of faith, which results in a vision above nature. . . . The ability for devotion to be efficacious is in accordance with the actualization of this faith in the heart because the power and actuality of miracle [*kol koah ha-peulat ha-nisim*] is through the strength of this devotion in the depths of the heart.[76]

The wordless expression of anxiety and frustration that exemplifies the depth of the Israelite experience in Egypt and the beginning of liberation serves here as a leitmotif for the actualization of the perfect faith in Israel's hearts, originating in Abraham's heart at the Akedah.[77] The scream that could not be enveloped in words or even controlled [*higayon ha-lev*][78] illustrates an elevation above the natural order, likening the order of time to the natural linguistic state of human expression. By lifting these biblical expressions out of their narrative context and juxtaposing them to passages in the midrash and Zohar that connect the Exodus to an abrogation or erasure of time, R. Gershon Henokh presents the miracle of the Exodus as one of perception rather than historical occurrence. It was not, as the Bible clearly states (Exodus 3:8–9), that God heard the cries of Israel and decided to redeem them before the appropriate time, but that redemption as miracle was the very expression of the cry, the actualization of the perfect faith of Abraham whereby Israel actualized the human potential to rise above the human condition. Juxtaposing two Zoharic statements, "the Exodus was without time," and "the scream *is* the heart," R. Gershon Henokh constructs miracle as a moment above time that is initiated by the human actualization of perfect faith. Israel, like Dorothy in the *Wizard of Oz,* redeemed itself, always having had the potential to simply "go home."

The discussion about sin and miracle, focusing on the biblical narrative, is never severed from the larger issue of esotericism. The model of miracle in the Bible, including its telos of collective *tikun,* is brought back to R. Shimon bar Yohai's revealing the secrets in the Idrot.[79]

The event of the Zohar as esoteric transmission is understood as a miraculous event, viewed by R. Gershon Henokh as a progressive moment in the perfection of the individual through the disclosure of secrets to the collective.[80] In the following text, R. Gershon Henokh juxtaposes other cases of divine illumination with the illumination of R. Shimon bar Yohai during the transmission of the teachings that comprise the Idra Rabba, considered the Zohar's most enlightened (and concealed) discourse. The text suggests that fear, the first mitzvah in the Zohar and the foundation of devotional life, is overcome by divine love *(hesed)* through the disclosure of divine secrets, all resulting from an illumination of the highest order *('or elyon).*

> Rabbi Shimon said, *God, I have heard of your renown, I am awed by your deeds* [Habakkuk 3:1]. According to this verse, it is proper to have fear. For us, however, all is dependent on God's love [*b'havivutah talya milta*], as it says, *Love the Lord your God* [Deuteronomy 6:5], *And God loves you* and *I* [*God*] *love you* [Malachi 1:2] [Zohar 3.138a, Idra Rabba]. In order to understand this we must invoke [another Zohar passage], "Where you find perfection, there you will find fear" [Zohar 2.79a]. There was no greater state of perfection [in the world] than that which was attained by R. Shimon bar Yohai and his circle at the time of the holy Idra Rabba.[81] At that time the phrase *All is dependent on God's love* was applicable. At the outset [before the Idra], fear was the only means by which perfection could be attained. After an individual achieved this state of perfection by means of divine worship [*avodah*] fear continued to be necessary in order to maintain the level [of sanctity] achieved [through devotion]. This is what is meant by "where you find perfection, there you will find fear." However, there is a level of perfection [i.e., that which was attained by R. Shimon and his circle] which is embodied in *all is dependent on God's love* [*for us*]. At the time of the Idra, God imparted to R. Shimon and his circle all kinds of perfections, all of which were permanently [embedded in their consciousness] and would not be diminished even as many levels of concealment followed them. When God imparts precious light to an individual that cannot be maintained, that individual must increase his fear [of God], which will strengthen his ability to receive and maintain that light. The ability of an individual to receive and maintain [divine] light is dependent upon fear as it says *Fear of God* [*yerat Ha-Shem*]*—that was his treasure* [Isaiah 33:6].[82] If a person receives this precious light without the proper

> readiness, i.e., without the necessary level of fear, this is likened to the first world that was destroyed because the light was too strong for the vessels.[83]

Fear, which in R. Gershon Henokh's thinking is both the basis and consequence of faith, provides the deficient individual with the necessary tools to construct their own vessel in order to receive and maintain divine illumination (the "precious light" [*'or yakar*] described above). In the deficient state of the premessianic world, fear continues to function even after the illumination in order to secure the unstable and frail state of that illumination in a yet unredeemed world. What is striking in this passage is the unique quality of R. Shimon and his circle, all of whom were privy to a different kind of perfection, one that was permanently integrated and absorbed into their consciousness. What is implied here is that this unique state of perfection, that is, messianic perfection in the premessianic world, no longer requires the otherwise necessary faith/fear dichotomy precisely because it has overcome it through the illumination. The consciousness of God's love for Israel replaced the fear and awe of His absence.

Yehuda Liebes argues that the Idra Rabba is an event held on the festival of *Shavuot,* reenacting the theophany at Sinai.[84] This claim departs from Luria's earlier claim that the Idra Rabba was held on *Lag B'Omer.*[85] Liebes shows that the *Shavuot* scenario, while not in concert with Luria and his disciples, is widely accepted by later Kabbalists and becomes a central part of the *Tikun Leyl Shavuot* liturgy, recited throughout the night on the eve of *Shavuot.* This is significant because it may shed important light on why the Idra passage was used as an example of miracle in R. Gershon Henokh's sermon, delivered on the eve of the seventh day of Passover, commemorating the miracle of the parting of the Red Sea, the apex of the Exodus narrative.

In the midrashic imagination, the miracle of the sea revealed a dimension of God "not even seen by [the prophet] Ezekiel son of Buzi," although the substance and stature of this revelation is never fully explained. The Idra is a text focused on the *tikun* of *atika kadisha,* the very same realm said to have been revealed only once to Abraham at the Akedah.[86]

What may be at play here is R. Gershon Henokh's weaving together three (historical) moments: the Red Sea, Sinai, and the Idra, three moments where miracle transcends the very bounds of human understanding and is subsequently integrated back into the devotional life of the witnesses. The Idra also becomes the vehicle for this full integration of the Abrahamic Sod tradition, as its focus, the *tikun* of *atika,* is precisely that which originated with Abraham at the Akedah. The limitations of Adam's sin are overcome in the visual moment of the parting of the sea, the audiovisual moment of God's voice at Sinai, finally filtering down into the intellectual apprehension of R. Shimon's teaching of the Idra interpreted as devotional praxis by the Hasidic tradition. The devotion that follows from the Idra is not identical to halakha because, unlike halakha it is not based on obligation. That is, it does not dwell in the tension between the will and the "ought." The basis of the obligatory character of mitzvot is that the limits of human understanding can never fully grasp how the mitzvot function. The "ought" is always commanding the will to act, even or precisely against its natural inclinations. Thus fear is the necessary starting point of a life of mitzvot, as will alone could never overcome its desire to act independently of commandment. In the Idra, however, R. Shimon acknowledges that the event itself changes the orientation of the witnesses by having them momentarily witness the end, which is God's love for Israel as the foundation of devotion. R. Shimon and his disciples have overcome the need for fear, a sign that they have overcome any distinction between human will and "ought." This experience becomes the basis of their devotional lives.

R. Shimon's personal transmission of his esoteric doctrine in the Idra Rabba represents the fullest disclosure of the Sod tradition along the trajectory of the Red Sea and Sinai, the likes of which have never again occurred in Jewish history. This phenomena in the history of Judaism, where the pillars of Jewish worship (faith and fear) are overcome, became the fulcrum of R. Gershon Henokh's belief in the culmination of this esoteric tradition in the Besht and his disciples. The Besht reinstitutes the centrality of devotion over cognition and contemplation, which had been eclipsed in the medieval traditions of philosophy and Kabbala. The Besht serves, according to this Hasidic analysis, as the culmination of R. Shimon at the Idra, claiming that his illumination of *atika* can be reenacted through Hasidic devotion.

Sin, Desire, and God's Command: The Dialectics of Free Will

Sin and miracle as framing the human condition and its transcendence circles back to the main issue confronting the Izbica/Radzin tradition: the existence or illusion of free will. The details of how this question is addressed in Hasidic exegesis and the antinomian implications therein are the subject of the following chapters. In *Ha-Hakdama* free will is only addressed parenthetically. However, considering that this "Introduction to Hasidism" was written after the publication of *Mei Ha-Shiloah,* and therefore in the wake of the controversy on free will that ensued, the brief comments on free will presented here are surely an initial rejoinder to the critical responses to *Mei Ha-Shiloah.*

Throughout *Ha-Hakdama,* free will is invoked as the foundation upon which human devotion is built. It is the human response to the ontological reality of divine absence and the centerpiece of the human condition. Adopting a quasi-Maimonidean stance, R. Gershon Henokh argues that belief in free will is a prerequisite for the possibility of mitzvah.[87] Yet, departing from Maimonides and others on the nature of the redemptive era, he posits that while free will is a foundation of Judaism in exile, it is not a permanent nor an essential part of human existence. Moreover, while the full disclosure of redemption may be a future event in history, the actualization of the redemptive personality, which already exists *in potentia* in the hearts of Abraham's descendants, emerges gradually through perfect faith, devotion, and miracle. The more humanity realizes its potential, the more free will disappears.

Yet, this notion is fraught with dangers for a community committed to the life of mitzvot. According to this model, drawn from the sin of Adam as acting prematurely on a correct principle, timing is everything. Premature absolution of free will results in antinomianism. A belief in the permanence of free will, and thus the perpetuity of the nomian tradition, is also a mistake in that it prevents the actualization of the telos of devotion, that is, the dissolution of the law in the messianic era. In this treatise, and throughout the exegetical writings of this tradition, free will is dialectically constructed as a prerequisite for, yet potentially an impediment to, Hasidic piety. Free will is only true when it is temporal, that is, when it is based on the possibility of its disappearance at the appropriate instant. If it is prematurely denied, the possibility of its denial is thwarted. If its affirmation is overextended (i.e., if it is viewed as a permanent element of the human essence), the efficacy of devotion is impossible. Below are two brief examples of how this is presented.

> God can change our minds and give our hearts a better understanding to see that even the past can change. God gave all this as a part of free-will. If one chooses the good, he will see, as a result, that that was God's intention at the outset, i.e., to bestow upon him goodness. So too, with the opposite.

> The ability to see the will of God [lit., *divrei Ha-Shem,* the words of God] is determined by human action. If one's actions bring forth good results, it

> will be understood that the act was a correct response to God's words, as the Zohar states, "All of your words are conditional."[88] One cannot apply the language of change to the root of divine will. All human free will [where change is applicable] is only according to the limited perspective of the individual. All human acquisition of perfection, goodness, and happiness is the result of that free will. An individual can only acquire for himself within the orbit of his limitations. God's will acts [upon him] even if he transgresses God's will. Therefore, even if one transgresses divine will according to his understanding, God directs his life above the limits of his own knowledge.[89]

The assumption is that free will is a function of human limitations arising, as discussed earlier, from Adam's sin, resulting in divine concealment. Free will, like mitzvot, is thus predicated on the human inability to determine divine will. God's will can only be understood, if understood at all, in retrospect—that is, according to the providential stance that all consequences are divinely determined.

As presented earlier, perfect faith, or the full actualization of human essence, elevates one above the very limits that require free will. Miracle is the momentary collective state of an identical illumination. However, as they are fleeting, both perfect faith and miracle cannot serve as the foundation of human experience in an unredeemed world. The individual or collective (via illumination or witnessing a miracle) necessarily descends back into the human condition of the premessianic world. However, a trace of that transcendent moment remains a central part of their devotional life. Therefore, the illumined individual or group behaves within the devotional system while internally living beyond it.

What happens, however, if that momentary elevation out of the human condition also induces a directive for action that counters the devotional system? Can one enact that antinomian behavior while still living in accordance with divine will dictated by halakha? This question will be addressed in the final chapter of this study. As a conclusion to the present discussion, this next text sets up the problem that arises from a belief in the temporality of free will.

> This is likened to what we read in Hosea, *Go marry a whore and children of a whore,*[90] *because the land will stray from following God. So he went and married Gomer, daughter of Dibliam* [Hosea 1:2, 1:3]. God further said to Hosea, *Go love a woman who, while loved by her husband, is the lover of another. . . .* [Hosea 3:1],[91] and fulfill the commandment of God outside the orbit of permissible behavior [*derekh heter*]. Hosea surely did not desire this, that is, he did not act (sin) from desire nor seek to gain pleasure

> outside the framework of mitzvah. Therefore, when God made known his will, the action was a clear result of God's words [and thus permissible]. This is also the case with thievery. What happens, for example, when it is decreed that the victim of theft was destined to lose property via this particular thief, at this very moment in time? If the thief did not desire to steal because he did not want to transgress, he would have to be explicitly commanded by God to do so. Or, he would have to construct a reason why this act of theft is not forbidden. From the perspective of the victim, the loss is something that was decreed from heaven. From the perspective of the thief, however, it would be the result of his evil intention [to steal], and he would be appropriately punished. Therefore, the power of free will only exits in the orbit of one's limited understanding, which would enable one to choose the good or not.[92]

What emerges from this text is that an act performed outside the orbit of halakha is only a transgression when it is done for one's own benefit or pleasure. If it is done for the sake of heaven, it is not a sin. This is because an act performed without any desire for benefit is not solely an expression of human will, assuming that we choose what we desire when given the freedom to do so. This is not unprecedented but has roots in the medieval pietistic tradition and even rabbinic literature. However, in this strain of Hasidism it plays a more prominent role than in these earlier and more nomian traditions.

In the case of the prophet Hosea, God's command to marry a forbidden woman is a divine decree and thus an expression of divine will. The permissibility of that act, according to our author, is only in the fact that the transgressive union is not desirable to Hosea. If it had been desirable for him, such an act, even though commanded by God, would have been a sin. Since this divine decree is against the law, it also must be against Hosea's own will. For such an act to be permissible, perhaps even obligatory, depends solely on Hosea's own antipathy for the act.

The case of thievery raises a slightly different point. Barring an explicit decree by God (or, I suppose, a rabbinic injunction), one must refrain from stealing, even if the victim determines (however that may be) that it is God's will that he be the victim of this particular individual at this particular time. That is, one individual cannot be the vehicle of another person's experience of divine will. One is held responsible even as he transgresses in order to fulfill the divine will of another. This last case is actually closest to our situation—where the illumined individual knows that all actions are really the result of God's will and that it is God's will that this person be a victim. In such a case he should still refrain from acting outside the devotional framework of halakha because he knows that the world is still unredeemed and that, while living in such a world, he cannot be completely liberated from the human condition of doubt. In this case, illumination does not hold the authority of prophecy that allows for the temporary abrogation of the law.[93] However, as we will see, in certain cases, and for certain ends, it does create the possibility for extrahalakhic behavior, especially when no one else is affected negatively. I will argue in the following chapters that there are cases where R. Mordecai Joseph in particular uses this model to advocate for such extrahalakhic behavior. This is the cornerstone of the "deterministic (anti)nomianism" of the religion advocated by the Izbica/Radzin tradition.

Conclusion

This chapter analyzes the status of the devotional life as a vehicle for the transcendence of human cognition and apprehension that lies at the root of the philosophical and theosophical Kabbalistic traditions. My claim is that the underlying question "what is Hasidism?" served as the basis for R. Gershon Henokh's construction of Hasidic piety as the final phase in the retrieval of the esoteric Abrahamic tradition. Hasidism is viewed here as the final chapter in the history of Jewish esotericism because it completes the circle of Abraham's devotional beginnings at the Akedah. The Akedah, and the subsequent revelation of *atika kadisha,* results in the formation of an esoteric tradition that filters through the prophets and was intentionally concealed in the rabbis, resulting in halakha. The consequence of this rabbinic concealment, coupled with the failure of R. Shimon bar Yohai's disciples to accurately record his full oral transmission of that esoteric tradition, resulted in the fragmentation of Sod and the beginning of Jewish esotericism.

Fragments of this tradition remain as subterranean strands in metahalakhic literature, reemerging in the concealed disclosure of Jewish philosophy and particularly Kabbala, illustrated in the *Guide,* the Zohar, and the teachings of R. Isaac Luria. The Besht both inherits and overcomes this tradition by translating Jewish esoterica into the existential categories of faith and fear, returning the Sod tradition to its original devotional roots in Abraham, making way for its full disclosure.

According to this theory, the inability of this final phase of history to be achieved prior to the Besht is the fact that both philosophy and (theosophical) Kabbala function within the constraints of the capacity of the human intellect. As created, human knowledge could never fully actualize the revelation of *atika kadisha,* that is, God as infinite being. Accepting the epistemological constraints of his mystical predecessors vis-à-vis human knowledge, the Besht maintains (according to R. Gershon Henokh's reading) that devotional acts, born out of a particular kind of faith in and fear of God, prepare the individual for the revelation of *atika kadisha* which would enable them to see the telos of devotion. This would in turn erase the obligatory nature of halakha, bringing us back to the internal piety of Abraham. The Besht (and subsequently Hasidism in general) is presented here as the return of Abraham (pure faith) into the world of Moses (law), preparing the world for its final redemption by cultivating messianic personalities through the teachings of Hasidism.

R. Gershon Henokh presents this idea by drawing a sharp distinction between the human condition, resulting from the sin of the Garden of Eden, and human essence, the divine nature of humankind that sees that all is divine will (the full actualization of *zelem elohim*). The protomessianic process matures as these two psychological states, the exilic and the redemptive, begin to overlap. Miracle is the momentary rupture of this progressive model, replayed to a lesser extent in the enlightenment of smaller collectives (i.e., the circle of the Idra) and the personal illumination resulting from devotion enacted from perfect faith (Hasidic piety). It is Abraham, according to the midrashic and Kabbalistic imagination, who begins the *tikun* of Adam's sin in earnest. To return to Eden, we must first return to Abraham. This requires full disclosure of his Sod tradition actualized through the devotional life of Hasidic piety. The way Hasidic piety and the cultivation of the messianic personality unfold in the exegetical writings of the Izbica/Radzin tradition and its antinomian implications are the focal points of the remaining chapters of this study.

Part 2

Hasidism and the Hermeneutical Turn

Reading Scripture against Itself

Hasidic masters think with and from Scripture. The scriptural narrative and its Kabbalistic interpretation, the latter of which serves as the lens of Hasidic reflection, is also the foundation of the Hasidic imagination. All philosophical and theological ideas are articulated through the lens of the Kabbala, read into and onto the episodes and personalities of the Hebrew Bible. While the use of Scripture as a foundation for theological reflection is at least as old as midrash, and likely older (e.g., Philo of Alexandria, first century B.C.E.), the Hasidic use of Scripture has a few unique characteristics. First is the simple fact that Hasidic printers choose the weekly Torah portion as the context of Hasidic publishing. In my view, this is significant. The choice to produce books of "Jewish thought" framed as homilies on the Torah has had a profound and lasting affect on modern Judaism's relationship to the Pentateuch. In some sense, Hasidism marks an important return to the Bible in the modern period. This return, however, is not a return to the genre of scriptural exegesis that marks much of medieval Jewish literature, nor is it a reflection of the genre of Hebrew homiletics in the medieval and early modern period. It is also not a return to late antique midrash, which offers its readers short creative readings of biblical passages or more formalistic renderings of Torah passages in proemic form. Hasidism is a meditation on and of Scripture generally, and on biblical personalities in particular (not on verses or biblical episodes). Biblical figures come to life in this literature, created in the image of the devotional personality Hasidism wants to foster.

This return to Scripture is also more than merely a reification of Hasidic aspirations. It is also the theater of serious reflection on perennial philosophical and theological issues, topics that captured the attention of Jews throughout postrabbinic Jewish history. Someone like Moses Maimonides confronts these dilemmas directly through philosophical argumentation, employing biblical verses to bolster his position for Jewish readers. By contrast, Hasidic masters use the biblical narrative as a forum for grappling with philosophical and theological issues. The construction of a biblical personality, the underlying intention of his or her actions, and the complex relationships between biblical persons all contribute to the Hasidic construction of what it is to be a Jew. In Hasidism, exegesis is not a tool to understand Scripture. Rather, the object of Hasidic exegesis is the aspiration of the Jewish pietist, the devotional reader who constructs his devotional life, both externally and internally, based upon these biblical archetypes. While this process is aided by the Zohar's reification of the Torah into a cosmological map, Hasidism, while adopting many of the Zohar's constructs, focuses more intensely on the biblical personality as personage, as a mirror of the human condition and model for human devotion. Since this devotional life is founded on the mitzvot and the heteronymous covenantal relationship forged at Sinai, Hasidic readings often address the tension between the human aspiration of devekut (communion with God) and the obligatory system of law known as halakha.

In these next three chapters I explore the exegetical development of various biblical and rabbinic figures as they are used to construct a deterministic religion whereby free will dissolves as the messianic personality emerges in the protomessianic world. The theater of this perennial question is an extended meditation on the trajectory of the Zaddik (righteous man), beginning with Abraham (perhaps even Melchizedek of Salem) and culminating with Jacob. Jacob's sons, instead of taking the biblical story to its redemptive conclusion, represent the refragmentation of the fully integrated personality of Jacob and, as a result, form the core of Jewish exile, both spiritual (existential) and physical (historical). The notion of sin has been eradicated by Jacob's spiritual achievement (i.e., his self-consciousness that unifies human and divine will), and the overcoming of sin has been inherited by his progeny. Sin is now the exclusive property of the non-Israelite. This has an interesting resonance with Christianity, which I explore in part 3.

Chapter 4 deals with the Hasidic relationship to Scripture and explores the question of free will as it emerges in the stories of the Garden of Eden and Noah. To bridge part 1 and part 2, I also discuss the relationship between faith, fear of God, and determinism in setting up the dissolution of free will in the messianic personality (not necessarily the messianic person). Chapter 5 begins with the pre-Abrahamic origins of the devotional life (Noah and Melchizedek), illuminating the spiritual deficiencies of Abraham's predecessors that are rectified by Abraham. Much of this chapter deals with two major themes: Abraham's circumcision as the biblical metaphor of having attained divine consciousness, and the perfection of Jacob as one who acquires self-consciousness, the final step in the pursuit of unity between human and divine will. Chapter 6 looks at the fragmented trajectory of Jacob's perfection as depicted in the dysfunctionality of his sons and various other figures (biblical and postbiblical) that embody the post-Jacobean world of Jewish exile. The chapter concludes with a long analysis of the Pinhas-Zimri story in Numbers—surely the most provocative and arguably the most misunderstood episode in Izbica/ Radzin exegesis. I argue that this reading is not an aberration but actually the very core and culmination of the entire project, an episode that is typologically foretold in numerous Genesis narratives, shaping the larger vision of this messianic and quasi-antinomian Hasidic school, embedding it in the foundational narrative texts of the Torah.

4 The Redemptive Foundation of Sin

A First Step in Recovering Determinism

One must also learn to read books against their declared intentions.

Gershom Scholem

The Bible is not a history of the Jewish people, but the story of God's quest of the righteous man.

Abraham Joshua Heschel

The Hasidic Return to Scripture

One of the positive consequences of the popularity and proliferation of Hasidism is that it has brought Jews, especially those interested in Jewish mysticism, back to Scripture. While classical medieval philosophical and Kabbalistic literature are surely rooted in Scripture and engaged in intricate methods of scriptural exegesis, their focus is arguably more focused on systematic thinking. Even the Zohar, whose main body is a running commentary on Scripture, teaches us less about the biblical narrative than about its own cosmology.[1] Coupling this cosmology with the midrashic imagination, Hasidic writers turn their attention back to Scripture, using it as a template for constructing their pietistic and devotional program. Cosmology gives way to anthropology, and biblical characters move from cosmic topoi to human models for religious behavior.[2] Hasidism succeeds in merging Kabbalistic and even philosophical Judaism with the passion and personal drama of the biblical narrative.

The fact that Hasidic texts are primarily redacted and printed as commentaries to the weekly Torah portion was no accident.[3] This publishing decision was a calculated attempt by Hasidic masters and their printers to bring Scripture back into the center of Judaism, not as a source of law or history, but as a source for constructing the Hasidic personality. This Hasidic return to Scripture, however, does not circumvent the Kabbalistic and philosophical traditions and simply return to the midrashic program of the ancient rabbis. Rather, it incorporates these non-Scripturally based Judaisms into its Scripture-centered approach. Therefore, all the philosophical problems raised and addressed by medieval philosophers and Kabbalists—problems such as providence, revelation, prophecy, reward and punishment, and free will—were on the minds of Hasidic exegetes. What Hasidism offers, then, is a postphilosophical, pietistic, midrashic Judaism, working out some of the perennial problems of the classical period through a mystically informed midrashic reading of the biblical drama, focused largely on biblical personalities and their spiritual development.[4]

The overarching issue looming over the exegetical works of Izbica/Radzin Hasidism is the question of free will; its existence, its limits, and its transcendence. In light of the claim that the Bible serves as the template for Hasidic thinking, this chapter and those that follow are devoted to tracing the way the Izbica/Radzin tradition utilizes the Bible as the backdrop for its discussion of the dissolution of free will as a prelude to the messianic era. The unfolding of the prehistory of Israel, from the sin of Adam and Eve until the final reconciliation of Jacob and Joseph at the end of Genesis, exhibits what the Izbica/Radzin tradition implicitly argues is the recovery of determinism—the true stance of piety that was lost as a result of the sin in the Garden of Eden.[5]

These next three chapters will examine R. Mordecai Joseph's and R. Gershon Henokh's readings of sin as the origin of human freedom and how the book of Genesis exhibits the initial stages in the recovery of determinism as a way of hastening redemption. I will emphasize that, while Hasidic exegesis integrates the full spectrum of Jewish approaches to Scripture, including midrash, medieval Jewish philosophy, classical pietism, and Kabbala, it is unique in its use of biblical narrative and characters as exhibiting stages in the progressive development of one personality type—the messianic man (not necessarily the Messiah)—who, by fully actualizing his potential, rectifies the sin of Adam even before redemption. This results in the illumined individual living simultaneously inside and outside exile. Torn between his inner perfection and the exilic environment, he embodies the archetype of the biblical Judah. In the Hasidic imagination, this messianic figure is represented in the figure of the Baal Shem Tov (the Besht), who, as the messianic figure before the Messiah, serves as the bridge between halakha and its final overcoming.

Before turning to our Hasidic texts, I will briefly outline the ways in which the Bible and the rabbis of the Talmud and midrash simultaneously address and ignore the question of free will and then show how their tepid recognition of this underlying issue, coupled with medieval Jewish philosophy and Kabbala, serves as the foundation for our Hasidic reading.

Free Will in the Bible: The Rabbinic Ambivalence of an Implied Dilemma

As I argued in previous chapters, the Izbica/Radzin tradition is engaged in an intricate construction of Hasidic piety that assumes the dissolution of free will as a prerequisite for "redemptive devotion." More generally, I argue that Hasidic exegesis is not merely an example of a free-wheeling postrabbinic midrash but is built on a very particular worldview expressed through the prism of the biblical drama. Therefore, in order to understand the subtext of the exegetical writings of R. Mordecai Joseph and R. Gershon Henokh on the question of free will, one must consider three things: first, what role does free will play in the biblical narrative; second, how does free will (i.e., human freedom) square with divine omniscience; and third, how does rabbinic and medieval Judaism understand the problem of free will in Scripture. Addressing these three questions will better equip us to see the creative and provocative contribution of Hasidic exegesis in general and of Izbica/Radzin Hasidism in particular.

Free will as a philosophical problem has a long history in Jewish literature, reaching back to the Hebrew Bible. However, the Bible, while it surely grapples with philosophical issues in general and free will in particular, rarely if ever confronts these issues outside its limited narrative scope.[6] The reader of the biblical text is invited, perhaps even expected, to explore these issues in a more theoretical manner as they emerge from the biblical story. For example, free will underlies the story of Adam and Eve in the Garden of Eden and the Joseph stories (Genesis 37–50), as well as the hardening of Pharaoh's heart and the heart of the Amorite King Sihon (Exodus 9:12, 10:20, 11:10, 14:4, 14:8, 14:17; Deuteronomy 2:30).

Yet, the theoretical problem of free will in a world that apparently affirms divine omniscience (even as the term may be a bit anachronistic here) is never explicitly addressed in any of these episodes. More fundamentally, while the biblical depiction of the covenant clearly assumes and requires human autonomy, the difficulties inherent in that autonomy juxtaposed to the divine heteronomy introduced at Sinai are never explored. It would seem that the Bible's lack of consistency on this and many similar issues leaves a philosophical reader wanting. Yet the subterranean philosophical issues that lie beneath the surface of the biblical narrative are the foundation of the medieval Jewish philosophical project.[7]

This is not the case with the rabbinic sages. While the rabbis are more reflective about the underlying philosophical elements of the biblical narrative than the Bible itself, they too are generally unwilling to address those philosophical questions independent of Scripture's narrative context. Frequently, particularly in midrash, the rabbis expand on a philosophical problem in Scripture by recreating the Bible's narrative in the form of parable or *mashal.*[8] The advantage of midrash over the Bible in this regard is that the *mashal* often includes a *nimshal,* or lesson to be drawn from the parable.[9] This *nimshal* is sometimes the place where the underlying (philosophical) problem of the *mashal* is addressed. This parabolic method, even as it gives us more than the Bible, still falls short of what could be called philosophical discourse.[10]

The reasons that rabbinic literature largely refuses to engage in philosophical reflection about issues it seems acutely aware of is not relevant to this analysis.[11] What is of importance here is the rabbis' understanding that, in order to interpret and comprehend the Bible's message, which is arguably their main concern, certain philosophical issues, free will among them, must be brought to the surface, even if left unresolved.

One illustration of this is the rabbinic depiction of the covenant at Sinai. The rabbis assume that the covenant forged at Sinai (Exodus 19–21) is founded on human freedom—the notion that Israel must choose to obey God's command in order for that obedience to be considered covenantal. While this claim is never stated outright, it emerges out of a striking depiction of the Sinai event as deficient precisely in that regard. In Babylonian Talmud Shabbat 88a, the rabbis (re)construct the theophany at Sinai as an act of divine coercion.

> *And they stood under the mount* [Exodus 19:17]. R. Abdimi ben Hama ben Hasa said: This teaches that the Holy One, Blessed be He, overturned the mountain upon them like an inverted barrel, and said to them, "If you accept the Torah, it will be well with you, if not, this place shall be your burial." R. Aha ben Jacob noted: "This furnishes a strong protest against the Torah."[12]

According to this statement, the result of the Sinai event is that the covenant is not sufficient because it is not predicated on human freedom, that is, Israel's choice. The Talmud, in the name of R. Aha ben Jacob, acknowledges this fact. "The protest against the Torah" is that coercion is a just excuse for nonobservance. Since Israel's acceptance of the Torah was not an act of free will, Sinai is an unfinished bond requiring a future corrective. The corrective suggested in this Talmudic story is the episode of Purim, reinvented in the midrashic imagination as an event where Israel freely chooses the covenant, thereby erasing the rabbinic coercion narrative read into Sinai. The Talmud continues, "Yet, even so, they re-accepted it [the Torah] in the days of Ahashveros, for it is written [*the Jews*] *confirmed and took upon them* (Esther 9:27). That is, they confirmed [willingly] what they had accepted long before" (b.T. Shabbat 88a).

The motive behind these rabbinic inventions and the hermeneutical intricacies underlying how these juxtaposed events (Sinai, Purim) reflect one another are not at issue. What is at stake, in my view, is the unspoken rabbinic recognition that free will is a necessary component in the covenant and that, for whatever reason, the Sinai narrative did not achieve that standard.[13] In order to communicate this, the rabbis corrupt the event of Sinai by making it coercive and then save the covenant instituted there by imagining Purim as correcting Sinai. It is also significant that the Purim story is the preamble to Israel's return to Eretz Israel and the Second Commonwealth, reviving the redemptive possibility that Sinai offered, at least in the minds of the rabbis.

What is achieved here is twofold. First, free will is the foundation of the covenant. Second (and more curious), the ultimate moment of divine revelation and prophecy occurs at the expense of free will. While free will is necessary for the purposes of obligation, which is why Purim is so important to the rabbis, it remains, in the minds of some, precisely that which needs to be effaced in order to achieve human perfection (redemption, the return of prophecy). This suggests, perhaps, a tripartite covenant. Sinai is the result of coercion, the lack of freedom. Purim is the result of human freedom resulting in Israel's choosing God. The future redemption will be the realization of the illusion of that freedom and the unity of the human will with the divine. That is, it will be a freedom not conditioned on any distinction between the human being and God. While this may sound far-fetched (and is surely beyond the purview of the sages), many Jewish mystics and pietists in the Middle Ages, and some Hasidic masters in the modern period, pick up on this thread as they construct their ideas about mystical experience, be it devekut or *unio mystica,* as the prelude to redemption.

Philosophical (i.e., rationalist) interpretations of Judaism (e.g., Sa'adia Gaon, Maimonides, Gersonides, and Joseph Albo), almost all argue in favor of free will in their defenses of Judaism. However, most recognize that human freedom and divine omniscience are not easily reconciled. Perhaps the best illustration of this tendency is found in Maimonides' affirmation of free will in his *Mishneh Torah.*

> Perhaps you will say, "Doesn't God know everything that will happen before it happens? Does He or doesn't He know whether one will be righteous or wicked? If He knows that one will be righteous how can those people be anything but righteous?" If you say, "He knows that one will be righteous but he could also be wicked, then that would be saying that He doesn't know the thing in its root." Know that the answer to this question is as long as the earth and as wide as the sea. [You do not know] how many foundational principles [*'ikarim gedolim*] and lofty mountains depend on this. But, you must know and understand this thing the way I have explained it.[14]

Maimonides offers an answer to this theoretical query by making an absolute distinction between God's knowledge and human cognition, using semantics as an attempt to diffuse his own rhetorical question.[15] He concludes by saying, "Just as we cannot apprehend the true [essence] of God, we cannot apprehend the nature of divine knowledge. . . . Therefore, we can never know how God knows everything about all His creatures and their actions [and still maintain the truth of free will, my addition]."[16]

Perhaps it is precisely because medieval Jewish philosophers understand the extent to which the doctrine of free will is vulnerable to critique that divine omniscience becomes such an important issue to defend. The defense, in most cases, was that the existence of free will *and* divine omniscience, without distinguishing between divine and human knowledge, is rationally indefensible but a true principle nonetheless. On this point, Gersonides is the exception that proves the rule.[17] He is the lone medieval Jewish philosopher who limits divine foreknowledge in order to protect against the collapse of free will. In this sense, Gersonides is often considered the most "rational" (and in some circles the most problematic) of medieval Jewish philosophers because his uncompromising commitment to rationalism and dissatisfaction with Maimonides' semantic distinction forced him to sacrifice divine foreknowledge for the sake of human freedom.

What is interesting for our concerns is the trajectory of the discourse on this and other philosophical questions in the history of classical Judaism, literature that our Hasidic authors are surely aware of. The Bible conceals its philosophical questions in historical narrative. The rabbis cautiously bring some of these issues to the surface but rarely engage in philosophical reflection. The medieval Jewish philosophers, pietists, and mystics confront these issues more directly, each examining them according to their particular agendas.

Emerging in the eighteenth century from the belly of traditional Judaism in Eastern Europe, Hasidism carries this whole literary history on its back, philosophical, Kabbalistic, and pietistic. It inherits the canonized philosophical texts of Sa'adia Gaon, Maimonides, and Judah Ha-Levi, and was influenced by the pietistic treatise *Duties of the Heart* by Bahya ibn Pakuda, as well as the entire history of Kabbala constructed through the lens of the Zohar and its Cordoverean and Lurianic interpretations. To my mind it is far too simplistic to posit that Hasidism ignored, or even rejected, its philosophical predecessors, and instead adopted the worldview of the Kabbala at the expense of all other Jewish metahalakhic systems. While the Kabbala is surely the dominant framework of Hasidic discourse, the Hasidic masters, as close readers of the Bible and its interpreters, also grapple with the philosophical ideas inherent in the Bible and subsequent interpretations.

As stated above, Hasidism engages with the Bible in a way that recaptures the midrashic imagination while incorporating medieval philosophical and theological concerns. Unlike rabbinic literature in general (e.g., midrash and Mishna), Hasidism does more than merely acknowledge these philosophical issues. However, like midrash, it rarely treats them as distinct from the Bible. Unlike medieval Jewish philosophy (and Kabbala), Hasidism does not generally engage in systematic thinking. Whereas medieval Jewish philosophers and mystics often viewed the Bible as the occasion for more theoretical and systematic analysis, Hasidic masters see the Bible as the occasion for developing their particular notion of piety and devotion, which sometimes requires taking positions on various philosophical issues. Finally, in line with midrash but with significantly more exegetical license, Hasidism refracts biblical episodes through its own particular lens, focusing more on personalities than events, developing its stance on perennial philosophical issues as they emerge in biblical personality archetypes.

Fear, Faith, and the End of Free Will

It would be audacious and even heretical for any Jewish thinker working inside the complex web of canonical Jewish texts to openly and unequivocally deny the existence of free will. Such a denial would take us back to R. Aha ben Jacob's response to the Talmud's coercive reading of Sinai: "This furnishes a strong protest against the [viability of the] Torah." Without free will, the covenant simply could not be sustained. However, the rabbinic suggestion that Israel's accepting the Torah at Sinai was in fact coercive, and thus not volitional, could lead one to question whether free will is a part of human perfection or merely a consequence of human limitation. The upshot of the distinction is whether free will can survive redemption. Therefore, even as the more determinist-minded thinkers in Judaism support a doctrine of free will in some form, we must consider how much this support belies an esotericism that, in fact, holds the opposite.[18] In our examination of Izbica/Radzin Hasidism, which comes as close to an explicit denial of free will as we have in Judaism (even as it argues for the temporal need to retain it), we must maintain a healthy skepticism about the positive affirmations of free will in these texts and see how these affirmations may veil an esoteric determinist position.[19]

In *Mei Ha-Shiloah* and more poignantly in *Sod Yesharim,* the biblical characters in Genesis embody various stages in the progression of a redeemed personality, one who has overcome the illusion of free will and understands that unity with the divine is precisely to comprehend that everything is determined. This progression reaches its climax in the patriarch Jacob. However, the rectification of Adam's sin in Jacob is only temporary. His sons, all of whom inherit only fragments of his personality, cannot maintain their father's perfection. As a result, their contentious actions, specifically their sibling rivalry and jealousy, reflect another stage of exile, one that now contains a redemptive remnant fully realized in Jacob, but unrealizable without him. The final perfection and redemption of Israel now requires a historical event in the lives of Jacob's descendants (i.e., the descent into Egypt and the Exodus) to finally realize what Jacob had attained internally. These twelve sons, who constitute the collective body of the Israelite nation, are presented in this Hasidic discourse as representing two distinct and incompatible personality archetypes, the messianic archetype of Judah and the protomessianic archetype of Joseph. The final reconciliation of these personality types is Joseph's understanding of how Judah's relationship to God cannot be expressed solely within the confines of the halakhic life. The inability of the Judah archetype to live solely within the halakha results from his inner drive to act outside it and his understanding that that drive (i.e., his will) is identical to God's will.

As a final preamble to my analysis of the Garden of Eden narrative in the Izbica/Radzin tradition, I want to briefly return to R. Gershon

Henokh's discussion of faith in *Ha-Hakdama,* since his exegetical writings develop how faith is the tool with which to overcome free will.[20] In *Ha-Hakdama,* faith is presented as the vehicle that enables the individual to have access to an experience of divine unity in the world. In the exegetical texts *Mei Ha-Shiloah* and *Sod Yesharim,* this same faith also serves as the agent that dissolves free will, given that free will is seen as a consequence of sin, which occurs because of a lack of perfect faith *(emunah shelamah).*[21]

In this sense, faith is not about submission to doctrine but is the means toward enlightenment. On this reading, enlightenment also has a devotional component; it requires a completion of the requisite refinements *(berurim)* that are only achieved through discipline and devotion. Sin, both in the garden and beyond, is the product of a lack of faith *in* and fear *of* God. Fear and faith are often conflated. R. Gershon Henokh views them as two distinct stages of enlightenment. He divides faith into two preliminary categories, culminating in a third synthesis: first faith, the primordial faith of illumination; second faith, the faith that comes as a result of fear; and perfect faith, *emunah shelamah,* the synthesis of these two categories, the redemptive faith that dissolves free will and creates the opportunity for a full expression of the human will as divine.[22] That is why he puts so much emphasis on Abraham's tests as the prelude to his illumination at the Akedah, and why God's response to Abraham (via the angel) at the Akedah is that he is one who "fears the Lord" (Genesis 22:12). Abraham's faith enables him to ascend Mount Moriah in order to sacrifice Isaac. God's response to this act of faith is to call him "one who fears God." Through faith, Abraham achieved a revelation of *atika,* the highest dimension of God. As a result of that illumination, Abraham achieves fear. This fear is then the foundation of wisdom and results in what we conventionally call faith.

In much of postbiblical Judaism, faith and fear are actualized and filtered through the performance of mitzvot. In our Hasidic texts, mitzvot serve to retrieve Abrahamic enlightenment by purifying the soul of its deficiencies, reflecting the midrashic description of mitzvot as "perfecting (or purifying) God's creatures [*l'zaref 'et ha-beriot*]." However, these mitzvot are not the goal of devotion; they are only the means. The goal of human devotion is devekut, and while it is achieved through mitzvot it is not solely achieved through them. Since Abraham achieved the goal without them, the mitzvot may nullify themselves when they complete their task. They may become obsolete once the enlightened person successfully integrates the mystical experience in a manner that enables him to sustain the experience of a unity of wills (divine and human)—that is, when he fully recovers Abrahamic religion. In classical Jewish mysticism, this "enlightenment" is often relegated only to the messianic era. What is peculiar in Izbica/Radzin Hasidism is that this messianic personality already exists in exile, emerging slowly, living in tension with normative Judaism in the proto-messianic world.[23]

Surprisingly, Abraham is not the prototype of this messianic personality, although he achieves its highest goal. Rather, he is the first stage in retrieving the lost status of humanity embodied in Adam before the sin. The fact that the initial disclosure of this messianic personality (i.e., through the revelation of *atik* at the Akedah) is not achieved through mitzvot is significant in the eyes of our Hasidic thinkers. While halakha is envisioned as the vehicle to retrieve that moment of revelation, allowing it to filter into and finally saturate the normative tradition, halakha is not the origin of that illumined state and, as such, may not survive its full recovery.

This idea is so fundamental to the entire Izbica/Radzin project that it serves as the subtext of many of its commentaries to Scripture, and it is the leitmotif of its interpretation of Hasidism in general. One explicit example of this proclivity can be found in R. Mordecai Joseph's distinction between fear of Elohim *(yirat Elohim)* and fear of God *(yirat Ha-Shem)* in *Mei Ha-Shiloah*.

> *Now I know that you are one who fears God* [*Elohim*] (Genesis 22:12). The difference between fear of YHVH [the Lord] and fear of *Elohim* [God] [is as follows]: Fear of *Elohim* is embodied in one who refrains from acts like eating because he has not yet reached the appropriate state of perfection. He therefore limits himself according to his own self-understanding. This is called fear of *Elohim*. Fear of YHVH is as follows: Even though a person understands that it is permissible for him to do such and such a thing since his soul has been purified from the deficiency that would prevent him from doing so, [he refrains from such an act] because God has forbidden it. God commands just commandments [*pekudim yesharim*] for all men [*l'kol nefesh*] precisely because there are individuals who have not yet reached this state of purity. Hence God does not permit such acts [for the perfected individual] because He is not equal for all.[24] Such an individual is obligated to suffer [*l'sbol*] limitations [*issur*] for the sake of his friend. This is called fear of God.[25]

Characteristic of Hasidic exegesis, this comment reaches far beyond the context of the biblical narrative it interprets. What is particularly interesting in R. Gershon Henokh's expansion of his grandfather's cryptic observation above is R. Gershon Henokh's saying that fear of *Elohim* and fear of YHVH are not mutually exclusive categories. Rather, the former yields the latter. Only by fearing *Elohim* and acting for the sake of human perfection can one fear God and live inside halakha solely for the sake of one's neighbor. The distinction between these two orientations toward mitzvot yields an ongoing tension between the one who needs the mitzvot and one who "suffers the limitation [of mitzvot] for the sake of his [not-yet-perfected] friend." It is precisely the proliferation of the spiritual orientation of the one who fears God and not *Elohim* that is a sign of the impending era of redemption.

Following this line of reasoning, R. Gershon Henokh hints that when mitzvot function properly, they nullify themselves. This is also true of faith. Faith, which serves as the foundation and motivation for the performance of mitzvot, is a temporal, albeit necessary matrix of religious worship. Both mitzvot and faith serve to complete a process of reconciliation between human and divine will which yields a redemptive illumination. Properly integrated, this leads to the obsolescence of both. "God gave man the ability [*koah,* lit., strength] to serve Him by way of his free choice in order that he unify all of the traits [*middot*] to their [appropriate] place only to see that they are not to be described as traits at all."[26] Adopting the Zohar's position that mitzvot are divine directives [*'ittin d'oraita*],[27] R. Gershon Henokh suggests that mitzvot generally serve a purpose *only* in the unredeemed world of doubt.[28] Whereas many other Jewish thinkers make a similar claim,[29] R. Gershon Henokh goes further to state that, in opposition to an external rupture (i.e., the advent of the messianic era), the mitzvot, when properly observed, nullify themselves even in the not-yet-redeemed world.

Many Jewish mystics, drawing from selected sources from the rabbinic corpus,[30] suggest that while mitzvot remain the necessary framework for Jewish worship in the imperfect world of exile *(galut),* they will be nullified, in part or in total, at some future time *(geulah).* Antinomianism emerges when this "future time" is seen as attainable in the present or, as in the case of Saint Paul and Sabbateanism, when the future breaks through into the present.[31] Both R. Mordecai Joseph and R. Gershon Henokh attempt to find a middle ground between the permanence and obsolescence of mitzvot in this world by distinguishing between human perfection and historical redemption. In their view, human perfection, understood as the full actualization of the messianic archetype, precedes the advent of the messianic era or the arrival of the Messiah. Therefore, certain individuals must live in the historical time of exile while having integrated a unity of human and divine will that render mitzvot obsolete. The future nullification of mitzvot in the messianic era, which is a more popular trend in Jewish mysticism and far less problematic because it always pushes off the dissolution of mitzvot to an undetermined (and perhaps unrealizable) future,[32] is supplanted here by the experience of unity in the yet unredeemed world. In this case, human perfection is not totally dependent on historical time. Redemption and exile are dialectical rather than historical categories.

The relationship between faith and mitzvot, so central in R. Gershon Henokh's *Ha-Hakdama,* is that the latter secures a permanent status for the former in the hearts of Israel.[33] This is not to say that the recipient of this illumination is no longer bound by the mitzvot. Rather, he is no longer *personally* bound, even as he still remains bound as a member of an unredeemed people. The human trajectory of redemption can thus overcome the historical and collective trajectory of redemption. Ironically, his living according to the mitzvot in an attempt to remain in the collective results in a state of double alienation: he feels as if he is living outside himself, and he is marginalized by his community, which senses his ambivalent relationship to the mitzvot. This is the dimension of "suffering" alluded to in the *Mei Ha-Shiloah* passage cited above. The anguish of the messianic person is that he must live in a world (and thus by its rules—i.e., halakha) that lags behind his own spiritual achievement.

Creation and Sin: Cosmic Fragmentation and Human Alienation

Hasidism's fundamental understanding of cosmology and cosmogony is derived primarily, albeit not exclusively, from the Zohar, R. Moshe Cordovero, and Lurianic Kabbala. In many cases, the cosmological teachings of Luria and his disciples are used as a template for Hasidic observations about human nature and devotion. Luria's rendering of creation and the sin in the Garden of Eden narrative is a central part of his cosmology and looms large in postmedieval Jewish literature.[34] The Lurianic construct of rupture *(zimzum)* and fragmentation *(shevirat ha-kelim)* results in the subsequent exile of God *(eyn sof)* from Himself *(sephirot),* creating disharmony, cacophony, and finitude.[35] This is viewed as the fabric of exilic reality that is repaired through the performance of mitzvot accompanied by contemplative practices *(kavvanot* and *yihudim).* The relationship between *zimzum* (creation) and human sin in Genesis, viewed as two separate but correlative stages in the development of material existence, is a fundamental principle in Lurianic Kabbala but not really a central issue for most Hasidic interpreters.[36] Hasidism is generally more interested in human life than the life of God. These two stages (the first cosmological, the second psychological) are interpreted by Hasidic masters in creative ways. R. Gershon Henokh, for example, understands creation and sin as representing two distinct phases of human history exemplified by the dominance of the preredemptive and redemptive personality archetypes.

The first phase of this divine process is manifest as the fabric of creation after the sin of Adam and Eve, that is, the unredeemed world (the world of the Tree of Knowledge, *'ilana d'sfaka*) or the world of doubt *('olam ha-safek)*.[37] The second phase is the reintegration or reconciliation of the human soul, with God represented as the Tree of Life or the world of certainty.[38] The history of redemption is the first phase of repair *(tikun)*—beginning with the life of Abraham. Noah represents the prehistory of redemption; until Noah, human civilization lived in the shadow of Adam's sin, but Noah turned the trajectory toward redemption through his faithful act of building the ark. Noah's act of righteousness is rewarded with a covenant, a sign of a new direction (Genesis 9:8–17). However, Noah's covenant is limited, reflecting his own limitations. He cannot transmit his faith into the lives of his offspring. His initial act of faith thus meets a tragic end (Genesis 9:20–27). Abraham's covenant with God (the Akedah), resulting in a blessing to Isaac, extends Noah's covenant by transmitting it to future generations.

Lurianic language and nomenclature permeate this Hasidic reading, even as the cosmological symbols are transformed into stages of human development. For example, R. Gershon Henokh distinguishes among four related but distinct dimensions of light in the Lurianic myth of creation as a way of exhibiting the development of the human personality from alienation to reconciliation. He uses the more common Lurianic terms of "surrounding light" *('or igullim)* and "direct light" *('or yashar),* coupled with "external or hovering light" *('or makif)* and "inner light" *('or penimi)*.[39] The distinction in Luria's teaching between these two sets of divine emanations is that the first set generally relates to emanation from God to the world, while the second set relates to the status of divine light (and its vessels) inside creation.[40] R. Gershon Henokh rephrases the Lurianic idea that creation *(zimzum* and then *shevirat ha-kelim)* is really about the emergence of evil. Wanting to frame evil solely within human experience he calls it alienation, both from God and from the divine element (i.e., the essence) of the self.[41]

The dialectical relationship between the external light and the inner light in the Lurianic story of creation is taken to mean that there is a dimension of divinity that is not integrated into the world and, more importantly, not experienced by humanity. The Lurianic construct of the "hovering light" *('or makif)* is transformed into an alienating light, a light that remains outside human experience, alienating the individual from God. In Lurianic terms, this is the result of the breaking of the vessels *(shevirat ha-kelim),* yielding a vessel too weak to contain the fullness of that which fills it.

R. Gershon Henokh reads the shattering of the vessels back into the biblical narrative. *Shevirat Ha-Kelim* is depicted by R. Gershon Henokh as the most alienated and alienating character in the Bible, the serpent in the garden narrative, a character who is described in the Bible as *'arum* (Genesis 3:1). *'Arum* (ARM) is conventionally translated as "shrewd" but more literally means "naked."[42] Therefore, divine rupture is embodied in a character who, as alienated from God (naked), seeks to reconcile his alienation with the image of Adam and Eve, the image of the divine in the garden.

Characteristic of the hyperliteralism of Jewish mysticism, the Kabbalists and their Hasidic interpreters maintain the more literal rendering of *'arum* as "naked," avoiding the more idiomatic translation of "shrewd" when referring to the serpent. Viewing the serpent as naked implies that it was not enveloped in creation—it was not clothed in divine garments *(levushim).* The serpent thus personifies the shattering of the vessels and the hovering light that ensues. Victimized by divine alienation, the serpent seeks reconciliation with God through Adam and Eve. His desire, and Adam and Eve's identification with that desire, is the origin of human sin. Adam and Eve's identification with the homelessness of the serpent, hovering outside creation but still being a part of it, results in the homelessness or uncanniness *(unheimlichkeit)* of humanity, forced to live outside the garden by defying God's command in an attempt to emulate Him (Genesis 3:4–5).

There are two things in the garden narrative that threaten the unity of the human being and God. The first is the biblical serpent, who is defined as the "hovering light." The serpent is viewed in this Hasidic perspective as the creature who is alienated—hovering, in search of a vessel to contain or envelop him and integrate him into the rest of creation. R. Gershon Henokh translates Luria's understanding of the serpent as the human condition of alienation, perhaps also a Hasidic play on the Zohar's translation of the serpent as darkness.[43] The human being (Adam), having ingested the serpent through the sin, incorporates the serpent's alienated status as part of his own condition.

The second object in the garden narrative that threatens the reconciliation between the human and the divine is the Tree of Knowledge that the Izbica/Radzin tradition, utilizing the Zohar, calls the "Tree of Doubt" *('ilana d'sfeka)* or the "realm of doubt" *('olam ha-safek).* "This tree and the realm of existence [lit., *'olam*] that is represented by this tree is the place of doubt."[44]

The danger of the incomplete creation of the first six days lies in the human submission to the alienating power of the serpent by ingesting the fruit of the Tree of Knowledge, thereby seeing the world solely through the prism of knowledge *(ratio),* that is, distinct (naked/alienated) from God. The consequence of heeding the call of the serpent (alienation) is the permanent alienation of the human soul from its source in God, yielding a world of doubt where God's will is veiled and hidden.[45] The result of this concealment is human freedom.

The rub of the Garden of Eden narrative is that, after consuming the fruit of the tree, Adam and Eve in essence *become* the serpent (in opposition to the serpent's promise that they would become divine!).[46] Ingesting the fruit is read symbolically—they ingest the serpent (through sexual union) and thus become alienated from God.[47] For R. Gershon Henokh, the act of ingesting the fruit of the Tree of Knowledge transforms Adam and Eve into the serpent. This is the beginning of evil,[48] precisely because the serpent is now empowered by interacting with and sustaining itself on the holiness of the human soul.[49] By entering into the divine image in the garden, the serpent becomes less alienated from God at the expense of alienating Adam and Eve. The sin, although destructive, was not irredeemable. In fact, it may even have been necessary in order for the good to engage with evil and subsequently redeem it. The human being is viewed here as the nexus between the alienated serpent and God. The center of this nexus is the place of "human desire," simultaneously the root of human sin and the very potency necessary for the entire creation (including the serpent) to be redeemed.

> *When the woman saw that the tree was good for eating and a delight to the eyes, and that the tree was desirable as a source of wisdom, she took of its fruit and ate. She also gave some to her husband and he ate* [Genesis 3:6]. This is the first action that is mentioned in the Torah that comes about by means of desire. This was the birth of desire. [Desire] is the intermingling of good and evil. It is impossible for man to receive goodness unless it is enveloped in the garment of this world. Therefore, goodness is also found in evil in that goodness fell into evil as a result of this action.[50]

For R. Gershon Henokh, the sin of Adam and Eve represents a necessary part of the redemptive process in that the alienated light (*'or makif,* the serpent) needed to be integrated into the inner light (*'or penimi,* humanity) in order to return to its source and thus bring the world to its final state of resolution.[51] The alienated light cannot undergo the process of transformation until it intermingles with the integrated light of divinity inside the human being. Apparently, this would have happened naturally, as the six days of creation culminated in the Sabbath. Adam, however, seeks to quicken this natural occurrence. Consequently, he alienates his divine nature from its source in God and initiates exile. Evil, or the human alienation from divine will, is thus the result of a premature push for redemption *(dekhiat ha-ketz).*[52] Humanity is always the catalyst for creation's reconciliation with God. Before the sin, humanity facilitates *tikun* through restraint (i.e., not engaging with the serpent and the Tree of Knowledge). After the sin, human beings must *transform* the evil within their own souls, returning it to its source in God. The sin gives birth to human suffering, that is, humanity's suffering is the consequence of living in doubt, alienated from the divine will. This is the context of *tikun*.[53]

On this reading, the relationship between the serpent and Adam (via Eve) is a confrontation between two elements of divine light—one that has successfully integrated into the vessels of corporeality (the human soul, *'or penimi*), the other which remains outside the vessel of creation (the alienated serpent, *'or makif*). If this process had not been interrupted by Adam and Eve's ingesting or coupling with the serpent, the vessels of materiality would have become strong enough to house the serpent, making the serpent's longing for an encounter with humanity obsolete. The serpent (hovering light) would be absorbed into humanity (integrated light) and subsequently redeemed. The serpent's desire for Adam and Eve would have thus been erased by human restraint. This would have subsequently resulted in the return of the divine light of creation back to its source in *eyn sof.*

According to the Zohar and Luria, this is also Adam and Eve's intention in the sin. That is, Adam wanted to accomplish what would have naturally unfolded in time. The Zohar states that Adam "took *malkhut* without the other nine *sephirot.*" Luria reads this as trying to "grow *Keter* of *Zeir Anpin* before the appropriate time." R. Gershon Henokh uses these Kabbalistic models as the basis of his reading of the sin.[54]

> Luria states that Adam wanted to expand *keter* of *zeir anpin* before the appropriate time. He [Adam] thought that he would be able to draw down Wisdom to all his appendages in order that they all [naturally] act in accordance with divine will [at all times]. [Therefore], he took *malkhut* [alone]. *Malkhut* is the power of nature without the higher nine [*sephirot*].[55] If Adam would have taken it [*malkhut*] through the other nine [*derekh ha-tesha sephirin*] he would have successfully constructed the kingdom of heaven [*malkhut shamayim*] including *keter* of *zeir anpin*. As a result, fear of God would have been permanently established in human nature and in all of creation. This would have also included *keter* of *zeir anpin*.

> All human action would thus have risen from a perfected consciousness [*da'at shelamah*], which would have discerned what humans are forbidden to do in order to rectify things in their root without fear of God, and, what humans would be permitted to take [in order to facilitate *tikun*] as we explained. However, because Adam took [*keter*] before the appropriate time, he entered [the demonic realm—i.e., he interacted with the serpent] prematurely, wanting to elevate the material world before it was ready. As a result, he and the world fell into a darkened state of consciousness [*hester da'at*], forgetting, and other dimensions of materiality [*gashmiut ha-olam*]. This is [what the Tikkunei Zohar calls] "taking *malkhut* without the other nine *sephirot*."[56]

Here the failure of Adam and Eve is not an act of defiance against God per se but a miscalculation of the strength of their own ability to withstand the alienated light of the serpent. The sin is viewed here as a premature effort to unify the world. The result is the prolonged state of alienation, not only of the serpent, but also of humanity (Genesis 3:14–19). Historical redemption can now only grow out of human perfection, realized through piety. Piety actualizes human potential, thereby nullifying the demonic power of the serpent within the human being and resulting in the realization of the innate identity of human and divine will, that is, Adam before the sin.

The final question R. Gershon Henokh addresses on the narrative of the sin is to explain why the transformation did not take place immediately—why couldn't Adam, having ingested the alienated divine light of the serpent, elevate the admixture of integration and alienation to its source in God and prevent permanent damage to the creation and humankind.[57] His answer is based on the common Lurianic interpretation of primordial sin, combined with the correlation of cosmic rupture with human error. According to Luria's interpretation of the Zohar (based on various midrashic sources), Adam was forbidden to have sexual intercourse with Eve until the Sabbath. Luria's reason for this prohibition is that the "shattering of the vessels," which produces the fabric and texture of creation, also makes the union of the two opposite poles represented in man and woman dangerous until the world itself has undergone reconciliation with God through the completion of creation on the Sabbath.[58]

> Eve was forbidden to Adam until the Sabbath. However, he came upon her before the Sabbath.[59] From there rose his sin in that he [Adam] had not yet reached the appropriate state of perfection. On this it is stated that the serpent was naked ['*arum*].[60] Therefore there is a tradition [b.T. Berakhot 61a] "that the evil inclination is likened to a fly that resides between

> the two entrances of the heart." [This means that the fly] is not in the heart for if it were, man would be able to overpower it.[61] Rather, it sits between the two openings of the heart where there is an element of choice. Wisdom [*hokhma*] is in the mind and understanding, [*binah*] is in the heart. From their union emerges consciousness [*da'at*]. Consciousness [*da'at*] is the power of choice. And this is the meaning of, *the serpent was 'arum* (Genesis 3:2).[62]

This reading of the garden narrative is an attempt to give meaning to the biblical phrase *and the serpent was 'arum* (Genesis 3:2), focusing on the similarity between the serpent, Adam, and Eve, all three being described as *'arumim* (naked) (Genesis 3:1).[63] R. Gershon Henokh frames this narrative through the Talmudic statement that the evil inclination resides not in the heart of man but just outside its grasp, hovering, as it were, like the serpent in the garden. In our terminology, the consumption of the alienated light (the interaction with the serpent) does not result in the temporary absorption of the serpent into Adam, immediately followed by a return to its proper place in God. Rather, the serpent remains alienated *inside* Adam and alienates Adam as well.

This, however, is the necessary first step toward resolution, in that the alienated light now directly encounters the integrated light. In short, for R. Gershon Henokh, unless Adam and Eve commit the sin, the possibility for redemption would never exist. Sin and exile give birth to redemption. Of course, as has been argued throughout Jewish literature, if they had refrained from sexual relations until the Sabbath, redemption would never have been needed. However, various Lurianic texts go further to suggest that, had Adam and Eve not sinned, the creation would have been incomplete and God's will unfulfilled. This is because the sin gives humankind (as opposed to nature) the opportunity to elevate the fallen sparks.[64] Therefore, the premature sexual act, resulting in the birth of evil,[65] is simultaneously the beginning of exile and the beginning of the redemptive process.

As mentioned, the term *'arum* in R. Gershon Henokh's reading of Genesis 3:2 is best translated in its most literal sense as "naked" or "exposed" in that the serpent is not enveloped or clothed in the light of God. Alternatively, *'arum* can represent a dimension of divine light not contained in a vessel, a form of hovering. Nakedness takes on the meaning of alienation, understood psychologically as a false sense of independence.[66] Hence, when God discovers Adam hiding in the garden, Adam says, *I heard the sound of You in the garden and I was afraid because I was naked* [*'arum*](Genesis 3:10). Adam, after having ingested the serpent through his sexual encounter with Eve, now defines himself *as* the serpent (i.e., naked [*'arum*]).[67] Our Hasidic reading collapses the contextual distinction between the word *'arum* in Genesis 3:1 (referring to the serpent) and Genesis 3:10 (referring to Adam). Refraining from an encounter with the serpent (and subsequently with Eve) would have resulted in the natural diffusion of the danger of evil by never allowing it to transcend the initial stage of potential *(koah).* Committing the sin empowered evil and expanded its influence by engaging with holiness.

R. Gershon Henokh further identifies the alienated light of the serpent with reason, adopting Onkelos's translation of *'arum* as *hak'im* (wise) in Genesis 3:1. Knowledge, perhaps more accurately in this context rationality, is the result of the consumption of the alienated light without elevating it to its source in God. Knowledge is thus viewed as a barrier separating the integrated light (the will of man) and the transcendent light (the will of God).[68] Freedom, as a product of the fragmentation of the integrated light from the transcendent light, becomes the matrix of man's and woman's relationship to the world as a result of this action.[69] In short, free will, here manifest as choice, is the offspring and product of sin.[70]

We may sum up this first stage of creation as follows: The world before the sin is incomplete and unredeemable because the alienated light (*'or makif,* the serpent) has no relation to the integrated light (*'or penimi,* Adam and Eve). If Adam and Eve had refrained from their ill-timed action,[71] the Sabbath would have been enough to facilitate the integration of the alienated light into the appropriate vessels, uniting it with the integrated light, and culminating in the completion of creation. Instead, God chooses to facilitate this resolution through humanity. Therefore, it is decreed that Adam and Eve ingest the alienated light (the fruit of the Tree of Knowledge by means of the advice of the serpent), thus cutting off the already integrated light (the human soul before the sin) from its source above (God).[72] This results in humanity's own alienation from God and from the divine self, manifest in doubt, choice, and rationality. Hiding from God in the Garden of Eden becomes indicative of humanity's alienation from God outside the garden (i.e., in exile). For Adam and his progeny, God becomes a stranger once the world becomes real.[73] The reality of the world (which requires the effacement of God) is the world outside the garden. This period of history (depicted in b.T. Sanhedrin as the 2,000 years of confusion [*tohu*]) culminates with the reinstitution of God's relationship with humanity in the incomplete covenant with Noah and finally in the integrated covenant with Abraham. It is to these two covenants we must now turn.

The Covenant with Noah and the Prehistory of the Retrieval of Determinism

For R. Gershon Henokh, the alienation of man (Adam) from God becomes manifest in the illusion that he is independent of God, meaning that he can come to know truth via reason and that he has free will.

> The one who is close to the source of God [*ha-makor*], which includes even the realm of God that is hidden, will see from this perspective that nothing is outside the encompassing light of God. Even that which appears to be the result of his own intentions [i.e., free will], one who cleaves to God will understand that God directs even that. However [God's] actions are beyond the intellect of man.[74]

This alienation that is manifest as the illusion of independence comes to a climax in the generation of the Flood.

> And so it was in the days of the Flood that the divine influence had become so materialized by those who received it that the light of God was not seen at all. This climaxed in the appearance that there was no Ruler. The covenant that God made [with Noah] was [intended] to create a connection between the lower world and the upper world.[75]

The first covenant God makes with Noah is understood by R. Gershon Henokh as the result of the inability of humankind to initiate a covenantal relationship by seeing the divine source of creation.[76]

> And God further said, "this is a sign that I set for the covenant between Me and you, and every living creature with you, for all ages to come. I have set My bow in the clouds, and it shall serve as a sign of the covenant between Me and the earth. When I bring clouds over the earth, and the bow appears in the clouds, I will remember My covenant between Me and you and every living creature among all flesh, so that the waters shall never again become a flood to destroy all flesh" [Genesis 9:12–16].

R. Gershon Henokh understands this covenant as illustrating two essential points. The first is the rainbow, which, as opposed to the circumcision of Abraham, is an object that "hovers" outside the individual and is only a half-circle in need of completion.[77] The second, which is not included in the biblical verses, is Noah's sin after the covenant (Genesis 9:20–24).

> The consequence of the sin of Noah [Genesis 9:21] reached Ham so that God's light would be hidden in a manner that would appear to limit His

> ability to sustain the entire world. That is, when God would sustain one [realm], another [realm] would be diminished. When God is viewed as contingent [and not necessary] His ability is limited. This is represented in the sin of Ham, who castrates his father so that he would not bear any more children [Genesis 9:22–23].[78] Therefore his punishment was that he [Ham] should be in a perpetual state of servitude. That is, he would receive divine effluence only through an intermediary and not directly [*b'ha'arat panim*].[79]

Noah's sin points out the limited efficacy of his covenant. His son's actions exemplify an attitude that cannot overcome the alienated nature of the fragmented human soul. Both of these elements in the narrative (the rainbow and the sin of Ham) lead R. Gershon Henokh to suggest that even though the very notion of covenant *(brit)* is a step toward the reconciliation of humanity with God, the covenant with Noah (as depicted in the rainbow) does not represent its full actualization.

Although recognizing the presence of God in the world, the consequence of the externalization of Noah's covenant in nature (the rainbow) is that he still views himself as independent of the divine scheme and thus lacks the will to take an active role in the world's salvation.

> *Listen to me, you stubborn of heart, who are far from victory* [Isaiah 36:12].[80] *Stubborn of heart,* those are the ones who depend upon their own nature [*yesodom*] without any action. They say that since God created the world and desires that creation, if He chooses to remain veiled and His will hidden, it should remain so. [They ask,] "If He wanted to be revealed, why did He create the veils which hide Him?"[81]
>
> In truth both [the positions of Rav and Shmuel] are correct.[82] One who acts in an arbitrary manner is called "stubborn hearted," because he says that since God created the world as it is, He must have wanted it to be this way. If He wanted it to be different, He wouldn't have created a world where He would be hidden. We find that [such a person] is *far from righteousness*[83] as it states in the Zohar 1.76b, ". . . and they do not want to come close to God, therefore they are *far from righteousness.*" Moreover, they are far from the Torah . . . and since they are far from righteousness, they have no peace.[84]

Although the covenant with Noah introduces God back into creation via nature, human civilization is still unable to permanently integrate that recognition and use it to retrieve a pre-Adamic status. In other words, the rainbow (being an external sign) cannot produce perfect faith *(emunah shelamah).* As a sign, the rainbow is both fleeting and unpredictable. While it serves as a spontaneous sign of divinity for human civilization that otherwise feels alienated from God's presence, its ethereal nature makes it unable to efface the impact of Adam's sin.

This last point is the focus of R. Jacob Lainer's reading of the rainbow narrative.

> *When I bring clouds over the earth, and the rainbow [keshet] appears in the clouds* [Genesis 9:14]. *The clouds over the earth:* This is a time of great concealment, when darkness will cover the earth. At that time, the rainbow will appear in the clouds [from within the darkness] and reveal the great light [of God] which was hidden. . . . So too, with man. If he falls away from knowledge and, as the result of great fear, asks himself, "Maybe God doesn't want my actions? Who am I in comparison to God?" At that moment, God will enlighten his mind with great power and trust. Therefore, [a tradition relates that] a rainbow never appeared in the generation of Hezekiah and the generation of Rabbi Shimon bar Yohai, as it is written, "Because they were on the level of [the Hebrew letter] *vav,* the letter which connects [two opposites]."[85] Their [righteousness] illuminated the world so that a great darkness [the likes of which existed after the Flood] never appeared in their time. Therefore, they never needed the rainbow because the essential message of the rainbow was that light exists in the darkness. Their generations were never void of light.[86]

Here the rainbow is seen in a far more positive light than in R. Gershon Henokh's rendition. However, the implications are similar. On R. Jacob Lainer's reading the rainbow serves as an external sign of divine presence for a generation that had not yet integrated the hovering light of alienation. In both R. Gershon Henokh and R. Jacob Lainer, this only begins with circumcision and the covenant with Abraham.

Finally, the limitation of Noah's covenant is substantiated in his actions following the Flood (Genesis 9:20–25). Noah's behavior as well as those of his children proves, for R. Gershon Henokh, that Noah's covenant cannot sustain itself.[87] The initial recognition of God's presence in the world could not be maintained solely through a sign of God in nature. Although this may be the first step in the renewed relationship between the human will and the divine will which was severed after the sin in the garden, for the covenant to become permanent and thus facilitate reconciliation, the promise has to become a part of man himself and not merely of man's perception. This first takes place in the biblical character of Abraham via circumcision.

R. Gershon Henokh's view of Noah as initiating the beginning of the integration of God into creation after the sin of Adam and Eve departs from the teaching of his grandfather, R. Mordecai Joseph Lainer of Izbica.

In *Mei Ha-Shiloah,* R. Mordecai Joseph states explicitly that Noah achieves perfection during his time in the ark. Therefore, his unconventional behavior after the Flood (Genesis 9:18–28) must be evaluated in a new way.

> This is the meaning of the verse, . . . *put the entrance to the ark on its side; make it with bottom, second, and third decks* [Genesis 6:16]. This means that God commanded Noah regarding the proper way to behave with his three sons [i.e., bottom, second, and third,] each one according to his level [of development]. With Ham, who was "bottom," to speak only in a restricted superficial manner [*l'panim*]. Yafet was second and Shem was third. This means that Noah should speak to Shem with depth and should reveal to him all his secrets. This advice was given to Noah before he reached perfection. That is, God commanded him in the appropriate way to conceal Himself. Immediately after he exited the ark and achieved perfection, he was able to do exactly the opposite from what God commanded him, as it says, *He drank of the wine and became drunk, and he uncovered himself within his tent* (Genesis 9:21) . . . *When he woke up from his wine and learned what his youngest son (Ham) had done to him, he said, "Cursed be Canaan; the lowest of slaves, shall he be to his brothers."* Noah became angry with Ham but did not transgress His directives (lit., the attributes of God). The reason is that when a person has achieved perfection he is permitted to move beyond the boundaries of permissible behavior [*l'hitpashet,* lit., to be expansive] because at that juncture everything [the person does] is the will of God.[88]

The difference between R. Gershon Henokh and his grandfather in their respective interpretations of this biblical episode is significant. R. Gershon Henokh has a more systematic approach to his reading of Scripture (particularly Genesis) and attempts to show the progressive development of the messianic personality from Adam through Joseph. He uses the deterministic model of his grandfather but is selective in its application. Therefore, the positive appreciation of Noah in the classical tradition and in Hasidic discourse is limited in *Sod Yesharim* to indicate only the beginning of a process toward reconciliation. R. Mordecai Joseph does not share his grandson's progressive approach and utilizes the determinist model more freely or at least more unsystematically. In this selection from *Mei Ha-Shiloah,* Noah's achievement does not differ in any substantive way from the achievements of Abraham or Jacob.

In sum, in this Hasidic tradition, among many others, the biblical narrative is the template for the reconciliation of God with humankind. In Izbica/Radzin Hasidism, this reconciliation initiates and fulfills the covenant. This includes two basic components: first, the recognition of the unity between the human will and the divine will that results in a determinist religion; and second, a belief in the possibility of achieving that state before historical redemption, thus making possible the obsolescence of mitzvot as the exclusive frame of human devotion. Before moving on to Abraham who, with Jacob and Judah, is a pivotal character in R. Gershon Henokh's ideology of determinism, I want to suggest an important distinction regarding determinism in the texts we have read thus far.

The recipients of the covenant of Noah all share a similar characteristic. They recognize God, yet see themselves as independent of Him and also unable to reveal His presence in the world. In the Noahide world, God's presence in the world is only the extent to which He chooses to reveal Himself. Regarding Noah's feeling of impotence, I would suggest that the Noahides (a term that refers in R. Gershon Henokh's work to all non-Israelite characters in the Bible until Esau) are essentially theological fatalists.[89] This theological fatalism, which is not viewed in a totally negative light (Noah is still a covenantal partner with God), is the first stage in the reconciliation between the human being and God in that it recognizes both God and providence. However, it is incompatible with the Torah of Abraham and later the Torah of Sinai because it accepts the empirical concealed state of God as a permanent part of creation. Abraham challenges the theological fatalism of Noah by concluding that the concealment of God must indeed only be a temporary state that can (and must) be reversed by human devotion *(avodat ha-shem).* For R. Gershon Henokh, it is only with Abraham that the Zohar's reading of Torah as "uncovering what is hidden" truly begins.[90]

Abraham's challenge to the theological fatalism of his forbearers results in the realization of one's ability to reveal God in the world (i.e., Torah). Living in this new covenant subsequently results in a realization that the will of the carrier of Torah, one who lives inside the covenant of Abraham, is one with God. Here we find the foundation of a determinist position that eventually dissolves free will even as it applies to the performance of mitzvot.[91] Just as the theological fatalism of the Noahides was a stage in the human-divine reconciliation, so Torah, as a catalyst for illumination, is an extension of that process. When God is revealed through illumination, Torah, as we know it, will have served its purpose and will become obsolete.

The notion of the Torah being supplanted by the revelation of divine will and the removal of the barrier that distances us from God is also a central idea in the Zohar and other Kabbalistic literature. The question of antinomianism arises when this experiential state is seen as attainable in the unredeemed world and subsequently becomes the framework out of which the individual serves God. The question that remains unresolved is whether the affirmation of such an experience is itself the nullification of the mitzvot; or is it that the experience of unity, which indeed nullifies the mitzvot in principle, is only accessible through the practice of the mitzvot, that is, remaining rooted in the fragmented world of doubt and thus preserving the need for the mitzvot. This question and others relating to the antinomian tendencies in Izbica/Radzin Hasidism will be discussed in the final chapter of this study.

5 Human Perfection and the Fulfillment of Abrahamic Religion

From Circumcision to Abraham's Death

It is the glory of God to conceal a matter—And the glory of a king to reveal it.

Proverbs 25:2

When God reveals something to an individual, that individual must conceal it.

R. Moses Maimonides, Introduction, *Commentary on the Mishna*

It is time to reveal everything . . .

R. Shimon bar Yohai, Idra Zuta, Zohar 2.290a

The Covenant with Abraham and the Beginning of Reconciliation

The image of Abraham looms large in Hasidic exegesis.[1] Abraham is envisioned by Hasidic masters as the quintessential "man of faith" whose relationship with God is personal, informal, and intimate. In some cases, he counters the legalistic and more structured leadership of Moses. While Moses is surely valorized in Hasidism as the lawgiver and leader of Israel, he does not fully capture the texture of Hasidic religiosity the way Abraham does. In *Ha-Hakdama ve Ha-Petikha,* R. Gershon Henokh uses Abraham, and particularly the Zohar's rendition of the Akedah, as a leitmotif for his Hasidic position on faith in, and fear of, God. Abraham is the hero of faith whose intimacy with God serves as the foundation both for the collective covenant at Sinai and for the goal of Hasidic spirituality. Therefore, to retrieve Abraham's religiosity, which does not include formalized commandments, is to achieve the telos of mitzvot, understood here as divine directives *('ittin d'oraita)* that are given precisely because humankind has lost the sense of God in the world that Abraham "lived" so fully.

In the midrashic and Kabbalistic imaginations, the heroic characters in the Bible (especially in Genesis) are often understood as reflecting different stages of human perfection. Each character comprises a distinct personality type (especially in Kabbala, where these types are reified as part of the Godhead), which reflects a particular dimension of the fully enlightened human being. In the exegetical writings of the Izbica/Radzin tradition, specifically in *Sod Yesharim* and *Tiferet Ha-Hanokhi,* the conventional Kabbalistic model is somewhat altered.

In R. Gershon Henokh's writings the biblical characters are not viewed as distinct personalities or cosmic potencies but as one developing personality, culminating in Jacob, who achieves the final state of self-consciousness representing the messianic person. According to this trajectory, Abraham represents the initial stage of that perfection, exhibiting the first stage in retrieving the lost personality of Adam before the sin. Because Abraham is the beginning of a process that only culminates with Jacob, his life as a servant of God is by definition flawed or at least incomplete. In *Sod Yesharim* and *Tiferet Ha-Hanokhi,* these flaws are an important part of understanding the biblical Abraham. In these Hasidic texts, even though Abraham is still the hero of pre-mitzvah Jewish spirituality, his own flaws are readily apparent, serving as the foundation for the next stage of development in Isaac and finally in Jacob. Whereas the episode of the deluge and the personality of Noah illustrate the prehistory of human reconciliation with God, the history of that process begins in earnest with the emergence of Abraham and God's charge to him to temporarily leave humanity behind and begin the process of becoming a new man (Genesis 12:1, 18:1).

R. Gershon Henokh sees Abraham as making significant progress toward the rectification of the Adamic sin, that is, the reconciliation of the alienated light of the serpent *('or makif)* with the integrated light of God in the human soul *('or penimi).* The result of Adam and Eve's sin in the garden, understood as ingesting the serpent through the serpent's insemination of Eve and then Eve's subsequent copulation with Adam, results in the conflict of these two lights inside the human being.

In *Ha-Hakdama,* R. Gershon Henokh illustrates the uniqueness of Abraham in his encounter with the biblical king Melchizedek of Salem (Genesis 15:18), presenting Abraham as the one who develops an inherited tradition that becomes the foundation of covenantal monotheism.[2] In *Sod Yesharim,* Abraham is largely viewed in comparison to Noah. Whereas Noah recognizes the presence of God in nature, he views himself as both independent of God and unable to facilitate change in God's world. He never internalizes or embodies the divine like Abraham. Abraham, through circumcision as the embodiment of the divine on human flesh, realizes that nothing human, not even freedom, is independent of God (extending Noah's perception of divine presence in nature by collapsing the distinction between God and world), and that the human being has the capacity both to unify the apparent fragments of creation and subsequently to experience that unity. Abraham challenges Noah's position that human freedom is synonymous with separation from God (or the inability to approach Him) and proposes a notion of freedom founded on the principle of human power. The human being, free yet bound to God (through covenant via circumcision), has the obligation to reveal God in the world and thus make the world less and not more separate from its source.

For Noah, both God and world exist as separate and distinct entities, albeit relationally tied to one another. God could (and does) intervene in nature but the individual has no power to influence God. Humanity is a part of nature and can never reach beyond it. Abraham simultaneously expands the presence of God in the world, collapsing any distinction between them, thus challenging Noah's idea of human freedom as separation from God. He then envisions humanity as having the power (and obligation) to influence the divine via pious living. This realization is the origin of a covenant of reciprocity that begins with circumcision and is concretized at Sinai.[3]

For R. Gershon Henokh, then, Abraham's contribution is essentially twofold. First, he posits that God and the world are essentially unified although not identical. This includes even those aspects of the world that seem to be void of God (i.e., evil). Second, he empowers the individual to become the catalyst to make the presence of God known through human devotion *(avodat ha-shem)* in order to bring about salvation through redemption. "From man's perspective, one must remove the garments and reveal the light of God even in the dark. . . . When that happens it will be revealed that everything is from God."[4] The phrase, "one must remove the garments and reveal the light of God" is the central message in this statement. It is clarified in the following text:

> A comprehensive covenant was not attained with the children of Noah as it was with Abraham. With Abraham, the covenant was with *words of Torah* out of which God began to reveal the light of Torah. With Noah, the covenant was only with *derekh eretz* [ways of the world/nature]. Therefore, it was only possible to gaze at the light of God through [the covenant with] Abraham.[5]

R. Gershon Henokh, unlike many Hasidic commentators on Scripture (including his father, R. Jacob Lainer), does not utilize the Noahide covenant of the rainbow as a trope for Jews. The rainbow, as an external sign, is contained solely in the prehistory of integration, a preliminary stage in the reconciliation between the hovering light of the serpent in the Garden and the inner light in the consciousness of humanity. Therefore, the rainbow is only the covenantal trope for the Gentile world, which is still bound by pre-Abrahamic civilization's limited capacity to redeem the world.[6] As I discussed in the previous chapter, the three limitations of the rainbow as a covenantal sign are: one, it is only a half-circle, revealing God in part but not all of the world; two, it is in nature and not an integral part of the human experience; and three, it is ethereal and unpredictable, still "hovering" over the world and not a permanent part of it.

On this reading, Abraham's breakthrough is that he comes to realize that the concealment of God in the world is not an end in itself but a framework out of which one can reveal the presence of God, removing the veil behind which He was concealed. This realization is what R. Gershon Henokh calls the covenant of Torah, described as "words of Torah" above. The term "Torah" in the above citation is juxtaposed to the term "*derekh eretz*" (lit., the way of the world), invoking a correlation between Torah study and "living in the world" *(derekh eretz)* initially made in Mishna Avot 2:2. In our text, *derekh eretz* refers to the covenant with Noah that was made in nature (i.e., through the rainbow, Genesis 9:8–11). Implicit in this formulation is that Noah, as the carrier of this covenant of nature, could only view the covenant through nature. Abraham, however, internalizes the covenant by inscribing God on his body (circumcision). As a result, he is no longer dependent on nature for an affirmation of his covenant with God; God becomes an internalized presence on the central part of the male human anatomy.

The term "Torah" in the text above does not refer to any body of law or obligatory behavior. Rather, Abrahamic Torah is a state of mind, a belief in the ability to uncover what is hidden. The Torah of Abraham is a spiritualized Torah that only later becomes manifest in a Torah of law (Moses). As we will see, this point is pivotal in understanding how the determinism of

Izbica/Radzin Hasidism challenges the authority of the halakhic system.[7] Commenting on the midrash's (Leviticus Rabba 13) reading of Isaiah's statement, "The [new] Torah, when will it emerge?" (Isaiah 51:4),[8] R. Gershon Henokh writes:

> Even though the Torah is eternal, that which is in this world as commandment will be in the future established permanently.[9] In this world the Torah is in the state of *zimzum* and divine service [*avodah*] is in the realm of the negative commandments. In the future the Torah will be revealed in the hearts of Israel who, in the depths of their hearts, house no anger or desire. Therefore, that which is in this world *faith in the heart* will be, in the future, explicitly revealed to man [italics mine].[10]

For R. Gershon Henokh, this "new Torah" of Isaiah is, in a sense, a retrieval of the spiritual Torah of Abraham.[11] Abraham, by means of internalizing the covenant, comes to realize the omnipresence of God, even in that which appears as its opposite. "Abraham strove in his worship in the trait of *hesed* [kindness] to reach its utmost depth until he realized that the trait of *gevurah* [judgment], the opposite of *hesed* is also included in *hesed.* With that [realization] Isaac [who represents *gevurah*] was born, resulting from the all the trials and tribulations [of Abraham's worship]."[12] Faith, like mitzvot, is the catalyst for the divine illumination of unity. The fragmented nature of our material existence is to be superseded by the experience of unity, both of the world and God, and, more importantly, between human will and divine will.

Before moving on to discuss the larger implications of this reading, it is important to note that while R. Gershon Henokh draws much of his thinking from the Zohar and Luria, a significant difference in orientation emerges between his work and those earlier texts in the case of circumcision and the covenant with Abraham. The Zohar, largely following various elements in the midrashic tradition, suggests that circumcision initiates (or perhaps symbolizes) Abraham's vision of "seeing God" (Genesis 18:1).[13] Genesis Rabba attempts to correlate Abraham's vision of God in Genesis 18:1 to the very act of circumcision. This trope is repeated and expanded in the Zohar.[14] Although R. Gershon Henokh is well aware of this Zoharic tradition that focuses on the correlation between mystical vision and circumcision, he intentionally moves in a different direction in his understanding of that phenomenon. His interest is not one of mystical vision or illumination but rather of a refined consciousness of the divine will and the presence of God in natural phenomenon.

In Hasidism more generally, Kabbalistic theosophy is translated into what Gershom Scholem called "mystical psychology." Consciousness of God is not the result of a mystical vision of the cosmos or soul elevation into the supernal realms as much as a new sense of the world as an outgrowth of understanding the presence of God through human experience *in* and not *beyond* the world. Kabbalistic motifs become psychic and psychological tropes out of which a new sense of the self is constructed.

While Hasidic literature is replete with soul elevations and reports of mystical experiences by Zaddikim, I would argue that the mystical notion of "seeing God" so prevalent in medieval Kabbalistic literature is not dominant in Hasidic literature, especially from the mid–nineteenth century onward.[15] R. Gershon Henokh attempts to exegetically map the transformation of the sign of the covenant from nature (rainbow) to flesh (phallus) in order to illuminate the internalization of an element of divine light, which, up to this point in human history (i.e., Abraham), was not integrated into the consciousness of man.[16] The implications of circumcision are far wider than merely a sign of the covenant between God and Israel. Circumcision is a signpost for a new stage in the history of human civilization. The one who is circumcised inherits and internalizes a higher level of consciousness, a development that brings him closer to the purpose of creation and the age of redemption.

The distinction between the acosmism so common in early Hasidism (implied in the unity of God and world) and the determinism implied in the unity of the human will with divine will deserves closer scrutiny.[17] Although the portrait of Abraham as one who recognizes the omnipresence of God implies the recognition of the unity of God and world, it also (and more importantly) points to the beginning of the reconciliation between the human will and the divine will, separated as a result of Adam and Eve consuming the "hovering light" of the serpent in the garden. The internalization of the covenant, represented in the bodily sign of God on the phallus, transforms man from one who is passive *(m'kabel),* as exhibited in Noah, to one who is active *(mashbiah),* exhibited in Abraham.[18]

For R. Gershon Henokh, the source of this activity is the activation of the human will after being reacquainted with divine will. Abraham's *hidush* (innovation) is the dissolution of Noahide passivity. The procreative phallus is now empowered with a divine sign. Human creativity is now about revealing God through human action.[19] As long as human will is independent (i.e., alienated) from divine will, it has no motivation to act. Hence Noah is described as passive. In the previous chapter I interpret this passivity as fatalistic. In a sense, Noah begins to deconstruct the alienation he inherits from Adam by recognizing God in nature; but, not having internalized the covenant, he cannot see himself as an active part of the process.[20] He remains an observer of God through the lens of nature and thus cannot see himself as an active participant in God's relationship with the world. He still envisions his will and divine will as distinct. Therefore, whereas before Noah, at least from the generation of Enosh, humanity is in such a deep state of alienation that it cannot even recognize the unity of nature in a single divine power, Noah introduces a monotheistic notion of God but could not extend that monotheistic idea to the unity between his will and the divine will. On this reading, Noah's essential problem is that he did not see himself as distinct from any other part of the natural world. Like nature, humanity had to simply accept its destiny. Noah's worldview is depicted in the midrashic construction of Melchizedek, King of Salem. Abraham receives Noah's theological worldview through Melchizedek and expands to it achieve covenantal monotheism by separating humanity from nature and aligning it with God.

Dark Unity and Human Desire: The Limited Perfection of Abraham

The immediate consequence of Abraham's innovation is not the full integration of the divine will with the human will. Rather, his contribution is the initial illumination of their unity and, more importantly, the emergence of human desire for full reconciliation.[21] Even after the Akedah and his vision of God, Abraham still lives in a "world of doubt" dominated by the consequence of the primordial (original) sin of Adam. The emergence of the human desire for reconciliation with the divine still requires a medium whereby one can facilitate this reunion. This medium or vehicle is Torah, defined now not only as spirit but also as mitzvot. Through the mitzvot, the seed of Abraham exhibit their innate desire to reunite with divine will by seeking out God in His most material and mundane manifestation.

Rather than overcome doubt, Abraham represents the important place of doubt in the developmental process toward self-consciousness. The insecurity of Abraham's personality enables him to overcome the false security of reason that seduces Eve to eat from the Tree of Knowledge and blinds the generation of the Flood from heeding Noah's message of impending doom.

> *Happy is the one whose transgression is forgiven; whose sin is covered over* [Psalms 32:1]. This verse speaks about the precious soul who serves as a chariot for the divine presence [*Shekhina*]. It has no will other than fulfilling the will of God that descends upon it. This is the meaning of the verse *He made darkness His screen: dark thunderheads, dense clouds of the sky* [Psalms 18:12]. As we explained earlier,[22] doubting something [lit., darkness] evokes the desire to apprehend that which is concealed. [As a response] God reveals and enlightens one's eyes to the world. This is like Abraham our father . . . who asked "who created all this?"[23] God answers, "I am the Master," as we explained in the first volume.[24] God further said, "You will see for yourself that your question is not like the questions of the philosophers who also ask and inquire [about these things]. Why is this so? Because you raised your voice about this [question] more than anyone else in the world. This [pure desire] enabled you to know that [the world] is from the [same] God who dwells in your heart. This aroused [the desire] in your heart to lift your voice and cry "*Who created all this*?" [Isaiah 40:26]. This is the meaning of *He made darkness His screen* in which He revealed to him [His] concealed [Nature]. *Dense clouds of the sky* . . . [this means] God reveals [Himself] to those souls who have no other desire [other than God]. To those souls [alone] God reveals that which surrounds them.[25]

The centrality of doubt implicit in the above citation is made even more explicit in the following text:

> This is the meaning of *If you follow My Laws and faithfully observe My commandments* [Leviticus 26:1]. *If*, is understood to imply the language of doubt. Even when a person follows the ways of Torah, he must maintain an element of doubt, saying, "Perhaps I am not fulfilling God's will completely? For the ways of God are very deep." *He made the darkness His screen* [Psalms 18:12]. The doubt and darkness one maintains by saying "perhaps I did not fulfill His will completely"—by means of this [posture] the concealed nature of Torah will be revealed to Him.[26]

The realization of doubt as the first step toward the reconciliation of the human will with the divine will is a central motif in the entire Izbica/Radzin tradition. The messianic personality, who is fully embodied in the patriarch Jacob and then later in the biblical Judah, having overcome the doubt exhibited by Abraham, never falls prey to the false certainty of "knowing" God's will, the germ of the sin of Adam and Eve. In fact, the potential (and also desire) to act outside the "four ells of halakha," which is the significant characteristic of the messianic personality in Izbica/Radzin Hasidism, is based on the unwillingness to accept a stagnant depiction of

God's will. What the messianic personality does intuit is that his will and God's are identical. For R. Mordecai Joseph, Abraham sets the stage for this process in the test of the Akedah.

> *And God tried Abraham* [Genesis 22:1]. The trial of the *Akedah* has to do with the greatness of Abraham's faith in God. Even though God told him [that his seed would be great] and that the covenant would be established through Isaac, and now he is told to offer him up as a sacrifice, nonetheless, he believed in the first process as before, and did not lose faith in them. And this faith is beyond the intellect. For in truth, Abraham did not receive a clear command from God to slaughter his son. Therefore, the Torah does not say that "YHVH" [the Lord] tested Abraham, but that "Elohim" [God] tested him, meaning that the word came to him through a dim glass.[27] Therefore, it says "Elohim" referring to *tekufot*.[28] That is why the trial is also a trial for Isaac. Isaac believed Abraham when he said that YHVH had given the command. Hence, for Isaac it wasn't a test. But for Abraham it was a trial, for he did not receive an explicit command. Now, had he had any emotive interest, of a father to a son, he would have had mercy on him [on Isaac, and could not have agreed to sacrifice him]. In truth God did not intend Abraham to sacrifice Isaac. The test was only to "enlighten the eyes of Abraham."[29]

According to R. Mordecai Joseph, the pivotal message of the trial is not that Abraham was challenged to hold two contradictory truths simultaneously, nor is it a command to act one way while believing that the opposite result would ensue.[30] Rather, the test is whether Abraham would be able and willing to act with certainty within the realm of doubt. If he had been certain of what God wanted from him, the episode would not have been a test.[31] Hence the term "trial (NSH)" is not used regarding Isaac, who believed that Abraham had achieved clear prophecy, commanded by YHVH instead of Elohim. If Abraham had been overcome by doubt he would not have agreed to sacrifice his son. This is what is meant by R. Mordecai Joseph's observation that "had he had any emotive interest, of a father to a son, he would have had mercy on him [on Isaac, and could not have agreed to sacrifice him]." Had Abraham not acted "as if" he was certain of God's intent, that is, had he become absorbed in doubt, his love for Isaac would have prevented him from fulfilling God's command.[32] Alternatively, if he had been sure of God's voice, it would not have been a trial.

On this reading, Abraham's greatness is his ability to recognize the unalterable state of uncertainty and still act with conviction. This is precisely why R. Mordecai Joseph adopts the Zohar's rendition of Abraham's prophecy in Genesis 22 as experienced through a "dim glass," while rejecting the Zohar's embedding this image in the verse *He saw the place from afar* (Genesis 22:4). The trial here is not about "seeing God" or having a vision of His presence. Rather, R. Mordecai Joseph stresses the use of the term "Elohim" and calls it *tekufot,* a central term in Izbica/Radzin Hasidism that implies ever-expanding boundaries of divine will. The notion of *tekufot* as it is used here creates the possibility of fulfilling divine will outside the law, because it suggests that all boundaries (even those sanctioned by God) are ever-expanding and expandable. What Abraham envisions and understands in this episode is the extent to which God's paradoxical request (and Abraham's inability to comprehend it) lies at the core of what it means to be in a covenant with Him. To be God's covenantal partner, one must always be uncertain of what He requires, since all boundaries are temporary and subject to change. As the midrash relates, the entire trial is to "enlighten the eyes of Abraham"—not, as the Zohar suggests, to offer Abraham a vision of God, but rather to show Abraham that the covenant must be lived with conviction without the vision of certainty.

What, then, does Abraham understand from the Akedah according to this approach? It is not that Abraham clearly understands that God did not want him to sacrifice his son, nor is it that he believes that God did want him to sacrifice his son. Rather, Abraham understands that doubt and uncertainty lie at the core of the covenant, and that living in the covenant is about acting with certainty in the realm of doubt, not denying doubt and deluding oneself into a false certainty, nor becoming paralyzed in the uncertainty endemic to the human condition. However, as we will see, acting with certainty in a world of doubt is only one stage in the progression of the enlightened personality. Abraham's doubt is not a permanent part of Israel's experience of the covenant. Jacob, who embodies the final, albeit temporary, state of human perfection, overcomes this doubt and achieves the fully realized self-consciousness of the messianic person where the self (human will) and the Other (divine will) are reconciled. However, the failure of Jacob's sons to actualize Jacob's accomplishment sets the stage for the final phase of exile, where redemption latently exists in the messianic souls of the biblical lineage of Judah.

Doubt in the Izbica/Radzin tradition is thus a stage in the progression of consciousness. When one achieves full integration of the hovering light of the serpent and the inner light of the human soul, doubt dissolves and results in a level of confidence that enables one to act in any manner one wishes, for "God is [surely] with him." The patriarch Jacob is the first to achieve this stage of full integration. This is later revisited in Judah and then Moses and subsequently serves as a subterranean and subversive strain in individual personalities until the onslaught of the messianic era.

> *You will go in my statutes* [Leviticus 26:3]. As long as the holiness of God is not engraved in his heart he is called "standing" [*'omed*]. One must focus [*l'zamzem 'et 'azmo*] on all his actions as to not to [prematurely] expand his will, for "sitting and not doing" [*shev v'lo ta'ase*] [i.e., passivity] is better [than premature action]. When one integrates the Torah to the point where it is engraved and permanently [embedded] in the heart, then one can be expansive and go in any way that one wishes, for God is [surely] with him, as it states in the midrash.[33]

Both R. Mordecai Joseph and R. Gershon Henokh are quick to note that will and consciousness are not identical.[34] In fact, nonintegrated will, which is the central characteristic of Abraham, results in intuitive rather than reasoned action. Even though, in retrospect, this act of pure will may be aligned with the will of God, the uninitiated (in this case, the uncircumcised, represented by Melchizedek) cannot understand such activity, even intuitively. Abraham attains this intuitive sense from the Akedah, but he lacks the self-consciousness of knowing his desire to fulfill God's will *is* God's will. The covenant (more specifically, the Akedah) empowers Abraham with the desire and will to reveal God in the world. This is based on the realization that God's relationship to the world is reciprocal, and that human action has the power to facilitate change. However, even in this empowered state Abraham is never fully aware, or sure, of what he is doing. Although this phenomenon repeats itself in other messianic personalities in the Bible, it is particularly true of Abraham, for whom the only expression of divine will is the urge (what Joseph Weiss calls "the unusurpable urge") inside him. Abrahamic desire begins a process toward self-consciousness, a process that Abraham initiates but cannot complete. The Talmudic dictum that states that the 2,000 years of Torah begins with Abraham is understood by R. Gershon Henokh as the beginning of human history initiated by Abraham's desire for God.[35] It is fulfilled in Jacob, and it becomes concretized collectively at Sinai.[36]

The Torah of Spirit (based on intuition) is thus the Torah of Abraham. It is enveloped in the Torah of Action (mitzvot) born at Sinai.[37] This Torah of Action provides a context for the reconciliation of the divine will with the human will. However, the development of biblical religion in R. Gershon Henokh is focused on the development of human consciousness as it moves to reunite with the divine will, making commanded action (mitzvot) obsolete. This final stage of integration takes place in the biblical figure of Jacob.

"Jacob the Perfect" *('Eish Tam)*: The Perfection of Jacob and the Consciousness of the Human Will as Divine: The Beginning of a Determinist Religion

The notion that Jacob is the balance and synthesis of Abraham and Isaac has its origins in rabbinic literature and becomes foundational in the Zohar and subsequent medieval and postmedieval Kabbala.[38] In the *sephirotic* scheme of classical Kabbala, especially in the Tikkunei Zohar and Idrot, Jacob represents *tiferet,* the third *sephirah* of the *parzuf* of *zeir anpin.* Jacob is also used as a generic term for the entire *parzuf* of *zeir anpin,* representing the (male) body of the divine anthropos.[39] As a *sephirah, tiferet* is the balance and synthesis of *hesed* (Abraham) and *gevurah* (Isaac) as well as being aligned with the higher *sephirah* of *da'at* (Moses) and *yesod* (Joseph).[40] In the Zohar, *zeir anpin* is also the model of masculinity and the foundation of the phallus that unites with the feminine *malkhut (Shekhina)* to initiate divine everflow *(shefa)* to the world below. Luria, basing himself on the *parzufim* first presented in the Idra Rabba and Idra Zuta, develops the figure of Jacob in his own system of *parzufim.*[41] Jacob represents the *parzuf* of *zeir anpin* (the small faces),[42] which combines the six lower *sephirot* from *hesed* to *yesod.* The *parzufim* above Jacob *(abba, imma, arikh anpin,* and *atik yomin)* are more pristine and not vulnerable to demonic forces. The *tikun* or rectification of cosmic dysfunctionality results from the constant infiltration of these higher forces into the cosmic body of Jacob, who then emanates these higher forces downward through *yihudim* (cosmic coupling) with the two female *parzufim* Rachel and Leah. For Luria, closely following the Zohar, Jacob is the nexus of God's encounter with His creation.[43] The *parzufim* above Jacob are stages in the process of emanation from the *eyn sof,* which only take concrete form in the *parzuf* of Jacob.[44]

This very brief outline of the biblical figure of Jacob in the symbolic system of Lurianic Kabbala is merely intended to contextualize R. Gershon Henokh's depiction of Jacob as the culmination of cosmic as well as human alienation from God. In Lurianic Kabbala, the stress on theosophy often results in the formulation of biblical personalities as mythic figures rather than personality types.[45] Hasidism in general, and mid- to late-nineteenth-century Polish Hasidism in particular, is not focused on the theosophical framework of the Kabbala as much as on using Kabbalistic literature and nomenclature to further its own program, which is more psychological and anthropological in nature. The reason for this change in orientation by Hasidic masters has been a constant source of scholarly debate.[46] I only want to raise it here to highlight how our Hasidic masters utilize the Kabbalistic cosmology for their own exegetical and pietistic ends.

The final maturation of the messianic archetype arises in the patriarch Jacob, who is the symbol of cosmic Israel in the Kabbala. In one of his two articles on R. Mordecai Joseph, Joseph Weiss notes almost in passing that R. Mordecai Joseph considered Jacob the perfected patriarch:

> R. Mordecai Joseph once said that of the three patriarchs only Jacob, not Isaac and Abraham, attained the level of complete enlightenment. Abraham and Isaac had to rationalize and elaborate the enlightenment bestowed upon them. . . . This was not so with Jacob, who was subject to continuous and ever-renewed guidance.[47]

Although I agree with the general thrust of Weiss's claim, I would argue that R. Gershon Henokh developed this distinction in a different and more nuanced way. This more textured view, the origins of which I believe can be found in a subtle reading of R. Mordecai Joseph's *Mei Ha-Shiloah,* will constitute the remainder of this chapter. To begin, Weiss's claim about Jacob must be augmented by the fact that the state of continuous illumination in Jacob is not permanent but immediately becomes fragmented in his sons. The constancy of Jacob's illumination is thus concealed in the hearts of Israel, only to be fully disclosed in the messianic era.[48]

I say "fully disclosed" because both authors maintain that certain pious individuals can actualize this potential even before the messianic era, resulting in the inner-Israelite controversy between the actualized messianic souls and those souls whose actualization depends on the historical unfolding of redemption. Even as Jacob's sons could not maintain the perfect consciousness of their father, there is a substantive difference between the fragmented and dysfunctional nature of human civilization before Jacob and the refragmentation of Jacob's perfected consciousness in his sons.

The refragmentation of Jacob's sons and the world they create and inhabit after the perfection of Jacob is different than the world before Jacob attained the full reconciliation between the human and the divine. After Jacob, exile already contains a latent redemptive strain that Jacob achieved and, in broken fragments, bequeathed to all his sons. Moreover, Jacob's enlightenment and his son's refracting parts of that enlightenment create an insurmountable difference between the descendants of Jacob (the Jews) and everyone else (the Gentile world). The possibility of Torah (Sinai) is only possible as a vehicle for *tikun* after Jacob completes the reconciliation and reconstructs the Adamic soul before the sin. What Torah can accomplish is the reconstruction of Jacob by gathering all of his parts from the disparate souls of his progeny. As we will see, the vocation of Israel as a nation is to engage in the internal struggle to reveal the concealed dimension of Jacob that holds the secret of the message, "all is in the hands of Heaven—even the fear of Heaven."

In Abraham we find the origin of the "urge" or redemptive desire for reconciliation with God, the intuitive expression of human will to reveal the divine in everything. It is only in Jacob, however, where this will becomes integrated and produces self-consciousness.[49] As suggested earlier, Abraham looked beyond the world in order to draw God into it, because, for him, the world was transparent. Yet this transparency was something he never really grasped; that is, he never fully integrated what he accomplished into his consciousness. Abraham still utilizes the transcendent notion of God, an idea he inherits from Noah and Melchizedek, as the matrix for his new notion of divine immanence. For Abraham, the world is always pointing beyond itself, but that very notion seems beyond Abraham's grasp. Alternatively, Jacob, while accepting Abraham's basic monotheistic approach, understands the world in a way that Abraham does not.

The essential difference between Abraham as the initial stage of the reconciliation between the human and divine will and Jacob as its culmination is illustrated in the following text:

> It is cited in Bereshit Rabba 60:12 [T. Albeck, ed., 639], *Who among you reveres the Lord and heeds the voice of His servant? Though he walk in darkness and have no light, let him trust in the name of the Lord* [Isaiah 50:10]. Who is it that fears the Lord? This is Abraham. *Who hears the voice of His servant?* This is God, who heard the voice of His servant [Abraham] who was walking in the dark. Abraham went from place to place and did not know where he was going, like a man immersed in darkness. Who was it that showed him the light? It was God, who showed him the light in every place that he went. In that way, He began to draw out the uniqueness of Israel from the darkness that was covering them from the nations. This began in earnest with the birth of Jacob, who was pure of any extraneous forces [*pesolet*]. . . . The vocation of Abraham was to develop the knowledge of the kindness [grace] of God in the world. However, the establishment of this grace of God was in the birth of Jacob, whose characteristic of "truth" gave the covenant permanence.[50]

R. Gershon Henokh uses Isaiah 50:10 in order to draw a distinction between Abraham who "walked in darkness" and Jacob who gives the covenant "permanence." This notion of Jacob as the beginning of perfection is found in the Zohar without any reference to Abraham.[51] Jacob's comparison to Abraham in this context is an important Hasidic addition to the Zohar, as it illustrates the Hasidic tendency to exhibit how each patriarch overcomes the deficiency in the other. Moreover, the midrashic portrait of Abraham "walking in darkness," only to receive divine light moment to moment, plays quite well into R. Gershon Henokh's whole scheme of integration and his belief that the biblical characters all depict the emergence of the archetype of the messianic person.[52] The covenant is internalized by Abraham (through circumcision) but lacks the continuity and consciousness of Jacob. This distinction is made from another vantage point in the following passage.

> *God parted* [*vayeal*] *from him at the spot where He had spoken to* [*i'to*] *him* . . . [Genesis 35:13]. [The phrase] *God parted from him* also appears regarding Abraham, *God was gone from Abraham* [Genesis 17:22]. This means that [Abraham] was likened to a chariot that God sat [dwelled] upon.[53] Notice, however, that [this verse] does not say, *from the place that he spoke to him.* In parting, even from a place upon which God dwelled there always remains a trace [*reshimu*] that is beyond human comprehension [consciousness]. Therefore, the phrase *from the place where he spoke to Him,* only appears with Jacob. Speech is the most comprehensive stage of human understanding. [Regarding Jacob] it is from this place [of understanding] where God parted. It is well known that when the holiness departs from any holy place, a trace [of that holiness] remains below. In this manner, the divine will in its complete state remained in the consciousness [of Jacob].[54]

The midrashic image of Abraham as "walking in darkness" until he receives the light from God is intensified in R. Gershon Henokh's reading that Abraham's consciousness of God ("darkness") is dependent on God speaking "with him." For Jacob, however, the experience of the conversation "with" God is maintained even after God departs. This ability to maintain the vision of God's presence even after it departs is what we have termed "consciousness," which R. Gershon Henokh, following the Zohar, calls "perfection" *(shelemut)* and which may be translated in our Hasidic rendition as "integration."

This notion of Jacob as the synthesis of Abraham and Isaac, as well as the collective body of Israel (in *zeir anpin*), is common in Kabbalistic literature after the Zohar. The creative contribution of Hasidism in general and Izbica/Radzin Hasidism in particular is the way this Kabbalistic model is used to suggest a new approach to religious life and a new attitude regarding the perfection of the religious personality.[55]

Jacob's personality is complex for various reasons. Unlike Abraham and Isaac, the Torah develops its portrait of Jacob against many other biblical personalities, such as Esau, his wives Rachel and Leah, his father-in-law Laban, and his sons and daughters. Linguistically, Jacob's uniqueness in the Pentateuch is that he is the only character who retains his original name after it is changed to Israel by divine decree. For our Hasidic authors, the ability to simultaneously maintain two names (Jacob/Israel) points to a unique integrative and synthetic personality.

In the theosophical structure of the Zohar and Lurianic Kabbala,[56] Jacob's two names (Jacob and Israel) represent two very different symbolic clusters, both contained within the larger *parzuf* of *zeir anpin*. R. Gershon Henokh's portrayal of Jacob as the biblical archetype of his determinist religion is built on the division of *zeir anpin* into two distinct but related parts (Jacob and Israel), coupled with midrashic readings that result in three basic principles. First is his relationship to his twin brother Esau. Second is his dual nature, as implied in his two names. Third is the final overcoming of rationality in his struggle with the angel in Genesis 32:23–33. R. Gershon Henokh's notion in his reading of the Eden narrative—that intuition overcomes rationality, resulting in a new mode of understanding after the final integration of the alienated light with its source in God—is most fully viewed as embodied in the biblical personality of Jacob. Jacob represents a stage in human development embodied in the fully formed *sephirah tiferet,* integrating the *sephirah da'at* (consciousness), resulting in the synthesis of *hokhma* (wisdom) and *binah* (understanding). After surviving three transformative events (his encounters with Laban, Esau, and the angel), Jacob achieves the full actualization of *zeir anpin,* thus creating the human foundation for redemption.

As already stated, the process of reconciliation that becomes necessary as a consequence of Adam and Eve's sin does not culminate in Jacob because of his failure to pass on his perfection to his sons. Jacob's sons simply cannot see how each of them reflects the perfection of their father. In short, they cannot maintain Jacob's state of self-consciousness. Two distinct personality archetypes emerge from this familial flaw. The first is one whose consciousness of divine will can only be maintained within the framework of halakha (Joseph). The other is one whose consciousness of divine will is maintained even outside the framework of the law, even as it may contradict halakha (Judah). The bifurcated consciousness of the perfect Jacob in these two personality types embodies the new state of exile, an exilic category that already contains its own redemption. This new exilic state is protoredemptive, since it no longer represents the alienation of the "hovering light" from the "inner light" of God in the human soul (as is the case in pre-Abrahamic and Abrahamic religion). Rather, it manifests itself in the inability of these two religious archetypes (Joseph and Judah) to recognize the truth in each other's religious personalities. The vertical nature of pre-Jacobian religion (man's alienation from God) now manifests as a horizontal alienation between Jacob's sons, who comprise the distinct personalities of the nation of Israel. Jacob's perfection, even in its deficient transmission, significantly changes the entire nature of human devotion by making sin (understood as acting against divine will) obsolete. After his initial reconciliation, which overcomes the alienation of divine will from the human will, sin is no longer possible for his descendants. All Israel's actions, however problematic, are aligned with God's will:[57] "all of the sinners [of the Gentile nations] are drawn from a source which appears to be separated and has an independent source of will. . . . Israel has no sin in its source. Therefore [what appears as sin] is only like a peel that surrounds the fruit."[58] Jacob annihilates sin by achieving total integration of the human and divine will.[59] After Jacob, only those who do not inherit the innovations of both Abraham and Jacob (i.e., the Gentile nations)[60] are bound to the unredeemable theological framework of Esau, Noah, and Melchizedek. "In truth, the heart of the Jew is purified from any blemish [*sig*] or extraneous intention [*pesolet*] and is not [naturally] drawn to err in the will of God. Those instances where Israel acts against the will of God do not come from them but rather from the influence upon them from the nations."[61]

The sharp distinction between Israel and the nations, a division that permeates almost every realm of Jewish mystical thinking, is understood here as the result of Jacob's repairing Adam's sin. The descendants of Jacob, that is, the nation of Israel, become the embodiment of human/divine reconciliation as opposed to the sons of Noah and Esau, who remain in a fragmented state unable to absorb the "hovering" divine light and thus unable to achieve redemption.[62] What stands in the way of the culmination of redemption is not sin but Israel's inner battle between law (Joseph) and spirit (Judah).

Returning to our analysis of Jacob, one of the more striking comments in both *Mei Ha-Shiloah* and *Sod Yesharim* is the claim that initially Jacob and Esau were identical.

> *Isaac favored Jacob because he had a taste for game* [Genesis 25:28]. It is explained, "He would trap his father [by asking him], 'How does one tithe

salt and straw?'" [Bereshit Rabba 63:10, 693].[63] One should not understand this passage simply. It is certain that Isaac did not err if he [Esau] was blatantly a liar. Rather, in the beginning, both [Jacob and Esau] were equally great men. However, Esau chose to make himself beautiful in his father's eyes in order that Isaac should pray for him to be blessed with *wisdom in his heart.* Jacob, in his simple way, said, "Why should I do this, if I am fit in the eyes of God, He will move in my father Isaac's heart to pray for me." Esau's way was not proper in the eyes of Jacob, for [to attempt what Esau did] requires clarification [*berur*]. How is one to know whether his intentions are pure or an attempt at trickery? Jacob, removing himself from all doubt [*safek*], relied only on God.[64]

In this rendition of the story of Jacob and Esau, Esau's selfishness makes him unable to move toward human perfection and is therefore unfit for Isaac's blessing. Fully cognizant of the importance of Isaac's blessing, for both physical and spiritual reasons, Esau attempts to coerce Isaac to pray on his behalf. Jacob's refusal to replicate Esau's desperate attempt to receive his father's blessing illustrates the fundamental difference between them. Jacob's greatness is exhibited here in his unequivocal refusal to try to convince God (or his father) that he is worthy of the blessing. On the surface, it would seem that Jacob's bizarre passivity would result in his exclusion from the covenant. Is Jacob acting here as a fatalist, more a reflection of Noah than Abraham? To surmise that Jacob's choice to "rely solely on God" is fatalistic (a trait more reminiscent of Isaac) is, in my view, imprecise. In this text, Jacob's reliance on God is a focused kind of passivity. He only relies on God in the context of attempting to fulfill His will—that is, in giving him the strength and direction to accomplish what God desires. Jacob knows that ultimately, regardless of human volition and action, God determines who is worthy of the blessing. This deterministic truth seems to have eluded Esau, effaced by his burning desire to be his father's chosen son. Jacob's response to this dilemma was twofold: first, to trust himself (something Isaac could not do); and second, to recognize that his understanding is limited (which he learned from Abraham). Within that delicate matrix of self-reliance and an understanding of his own limitations, Jacob served God in order to reveal His presence in the world. If that devotion is worthy of God's blessing, surmises Jacob, so be it.

A similar idea is developed in R. Gershon Henokh's *Sod Yesharim.* In *Ha-Hakdama,* he interprets faith as the recognition of the limitation of the human intellect as the catalyst for divine illumination. More than the other patriarchs, Jacob is the individual who most fully absorbs this faith and is able to integrate it into his *ratio,* resulting in self-consciousness.

Abraham has the desire to reveal God in the world but, following his blind intuition, often "walked in darkness," unaware of the purpose of his actions and the source of his own desire.[65] Abraham is one who walks *in* faith, albeit a dark faith of uncertainty. Isaac recognizes his imperfection (a central criterion for faith) but lacks the volitional drive necessary for divine illumination. According to R. Gershon Henokh, Isaac's problem is that he is not able to sufficiently recognize and affirm the tension between God and the world so as to achieve reconciliation between them.[66] He cannot recognize divine absence enough to be motivated to reveal more of God than already exists, and he cannot understand the nature of his own potential. This is captured in R. Gershon Henokh's provocative quip, "Isaac our father did not believe in himself at all."[67] Hence, Isaac is not willing to enter into the world of doubt, a realm necessary for revealing God. Jacob is the figure who combines the activist desire of Abraham with the passive God-consciousness of Isaac. He moves beyond Abrahamic faith by integrating the God-consciousness of his father into the tension between God and world. This is something Isaac simply could not achieve due to his passiveness toward the world.

R. Gershon Henokh develops the full implications of Jacob's personality in contrast to the personality of Esau. As expressed in the text cited above, he suggests that the failure of Esau is rooted in his theological conclusions rather than in his essential nature. This is expressed most poignantly in Esau's intention in selling his birthright to Jacob.

> The midrash states [Bereshit Rabba 69:29, 694] *And Jacob made a porridge.* Esau asked, "What is the purpose of this porridge?" Jacob responded, "The elder [Abraham] has died." Esau said, "The elder has become subject to judgment!?" Jacob answered, "Yes." Esau then said, "If this is so, there is no reward and there is no resurrection." This means that, after Abraham's failure [to attain immortality in this world], Esau could no longer justify Abraham's great pious achievements and all the tests for which he was subject, and all the miracles which he experienced, with the fact that he was unable to repair the root of the sin of Adam and reach the clear light which would no longer have been concealed. Even Abraham's body should not have been able to conceal it [that is, he should have overcome death]. When Esau saw that Abraham had died he lamented, "There is no judge and there is no judgment." This means that Esau concluded that the concealed state of God in the world must be permanent and there is no way to reveal Him. Even if He would be revealed in the [redemptive] future, it would not be through human action. [Esau concluded:] Human action can have no part in redemption at all.[68]

The midrashic reading that serves as the lemma of this Hasidic reflection ascribes two critical flaws to Esau. The first is his inability to acknowledge that Abraham's death might very well be part of the divine plan. I will call this Esau's "rationalist flaw." Second is his conclusion that, since Abraham's perfection did not result in redemption, God's concealment must be His will and human beings cannot and should not seek to alter it in any way. This is his "fatalist flaw."

This is quite a different Esau than the one portrayed above by R. Mordecai Joseph, who attempts to coerce Isaac to pray on his behalf. Here, Esau's response to Abraham's death is fatalistic in that it severed him from both the motivation and the desire so central to Abraham's personality (which apparently was part of Esau as well).

Combining these two texts, the reader will note a marked change in the depiction of Esau before the incident of Abraham's death (exhibited in his active attempt to coerce Isaac to pray on his behalf) and the fatalistic stance Esau takes as a result of Abraham's death. In R. Gershon Henokh's portrayal Esau, confronted with Abraham's death, responds like Isaac without the dimension of Abraham! Isaac believes in God but has no faith in humanity. Having lost faith in humanity, specifically in humanity's ability to transform the world, Esau subsequently loses faith in God (the very dimension he inherits from his father). Esau's loss of faith in humanity leads him to fatalism. In a sense it leads him back to Noah, who is now refracted through the Abrahamic line. Isaac also has no faith in himself or humanity, but he holds fast to a belief in God that he inherits from Abraham. Isaac appears to have the Abrahamic drive to reveal God in the world, but he is unsure how to utilize that desire. On this reading, Isaac is a spiritually deep, even profound, figure whose very depth paralyzes him. As a result of this dormant Abrahamic desire, Isaac remains within the Abrahamic fold in spite of his passivity. However, he is ultimately unable to take Abrahamic religion to the next level. Isaac may have a dimension of the "fatalist flaw" exhibited fully in Esau, but he did not have Esau's "rationalist flaw," that is, he never abandons the notion that humanity can transform the world, even though he never understands how.[69]

Both R. Mordecai Joseph and R. Gershon Henokh stress the essential contribution that each biblical character plays in the collective process of human reconciliation with the divine. This is largely modeled after the Kabbalistic portrayal of these figures as facilitating cosmic unity. However, in this Hasidic rendition, these cosmic symbols become archetypes of human personalities struggling to understand the nature of human devotion. Isaac without Abraham yields Esau. Jacob inherits the blessing, but not because, as is conventionally argued, he is the true biological firstborn.[70] On this reading, both sons are born with equal potential to earn the blessing. Jacob only merits the blessing after he reaches spiritual maturity and integrates the necessary characteristics of both his father and grandfather.

Although the problematic issue of the explicit statement in Scripture (Genesis 25:28) that places Isaac's favor with Esau over Jacob is never directly addressed, an interpretation may be drawn from our reading of this episode. Isaac loves Esau because Esau is an unadulterated representation of himself. That is, Esau inherits Isaac's skepticism about humanity. In terms of Esau's lacking the intuitive faith of Abraham, this is the "blind spot" Isaac cannot overcome. In short, Esau shares Isaac's weaknesses but not his strengths. Isaac has sympathy for his son because he identifies, perhaps overly so, with Esau's ultimate limitations. Alternatively, the self-consciousness that Jacob attains—by integrating the characteristics of Abraham and Isaac—is alien to his ailing father. The irony in this episode, as it emerges from this Hasidic reading, is that the very element in Jacob that makes him fit for the blessing, that is, his unique contribution to this process of reconciliation, is the very trait that Isaac cannot understand.

In one sense, Esau and Isaac are quite similar. In another sense they are very different. After Abraham's death, which Esau could not accept, he concludes that the world, as he knows it, is all there is. Although this is the opposite of what Isaac concludes from his experience at the Akedah, the outcome is similar. For Isaac (the human sacrifice who survived), the world does not really exist, there is only God. In both cases (Isaac's experience of the Akedah and Esau's experience of Abraham's death), the correlation between God and the world is severed and human beings are disempowered. Both Isaac and Esau exhibit an absolutist mentality that limits their ability to integrate opposites, a fundamental principle of self-consciousness.

In R. Gershon Henokh's portrayal, Abraham's "walking in darkness" is accompanied by a beacon of divine light shone as a result of his blind intuition to reveal God in the world. Thus, "walking in darkness" may have been Abraham's fate but not his desire. Though limited, he strove to overcome his limitations. This spiritual activism is Abraham's greatness. It is precisely this desire that gives birth to Jacob and finally the covenant. Esau, in responding to Abraham's death, submits to this Abrahamic "walking in darkness" as an ultimate and unalterable reality. He cannot accept the fact that his grandfather did not achieve the final reconciliation of the human and the divine that would have made him the messianic figure. As a result, he loses (or relinquishes, as the Bible relates) the desire he inherits from Abraham after concluding that Abraham's death cannot be squared with his own fatalistic vision of the world. This decision culminates in the sale of his birthright which, according to his new worldview, loses all meaning.[71]

Jacob's reaction to Abraham's death, depicted in his cooking of the lentil soup in his tent (Genesis 25:30–33), is very different. Returning to the Lurianic distinction between "direct light" *('or yashar)* and "surrounding light" *('or makif)* discussed in the story of the Garden of Eden, R. Gershon Henokh suggests that Jacob's choice of the round-shaped bean (lentil) was an expression of his recognition of the reconciliation of the unintelligible "surrounding (circular) light" and the intelligible "direct light" of reason and knowledge. In short, Jacob takes the unintelligibility of Abraham's death and views it as a part of and not in opposition to the "direct light" of knowledge. It is this decision, represented in the circular shape of the lentil, that completes the process of reconciliation initiated with the half-circle of the covenant with Noah (the rainbow) and the integration of the alienated light in the circumcision of Abraham. On the roundness of the lentil, R. Gershon Henokh writes:

> This is another reason why the lentil was round. God created two kinds of lights; surrounding light and direct light. The surrounding light symbolizes that which man cannot understand since it is hovering above the creation without internal differentiation. Direct light descends in lines like the form of man, the head [the top] controlling the rest of the body. The direct light is the root of all human activity by which a man draws to himself [divine light] as a consequence of those actions. [The surrounding light] (that which is beyond human comprehension), represents [God ruling] in the realm of circles [*'iggulim*]. God also creates this realm. However, there emerges through faith a direct line [*kav*], which enables the surrounding light to become integrated into the direct light and thus insert the "inner light" into man.[72]

This text is pivotal in understanding R. Gershon Henokh's reading of the biblical Jacob (i.e., the community of Israel) as completing the process of reconciliation necessary as a result of the sin of Adam and Eve.[73] More importantly, however, this text is a window into R. Gershon Henokh's idea of faith as the catalyst for divine illumination. On this reading, if Abraham can rightly be called "the man of faith," Jacob could be called "the man of consciousness." Jacob's intuition is no longer the unrefined blind urge of Abraham but an enlightened consciousness that, through faith, draws the "surrounding light" into itself, yielding self-consciousness and reconciliation. In Jacob, faith and reason merge, yielding the recognition of the divine nature of the human will. In R. Gershon Henokh's words, Jacob embodies knowledge "beyond human comprehension."

Because this new awareness cannot rightly be called knowledge in any rational sense, I will refer to it simply as intuitive consciousness. Whereas Abraham's life was centered on his unyielding faith in the omnipresence of God, Jacob's life is devoted to making the unity of God and world consciously known. According to R. Gershon Henokh, Abraham spreads faith while Jacob spreads self-consciousness. As we will see, the tragic culmination of Jacob's life is the stark confrontation of Jacob's sons Judah and Joseph. Each character represents one dimension of Jacob's personality, one hidden (Jacob, the lower portion of *zeir anpin*), the other revealed (Israel, the upper portion of *zeir anpin*). As the revealed dimension of Jacob, Joseph cannot understand the concealed dimension of Jacob (and thus the concealed dimension of himself), Judah. Joseph inherits Isaac's "blind spot" that first emerges as a flaw in Isaac's inability to distinguish between Jacob and Esau. This blind spot now becomes an integral part of collective Israel, constituting the internal nature of Jewish exile.

R. Mordecai Joseph notes that the world, even in its imperfect state, is truly real for Jacob because he sees and comprehends the divinity of the world. More importantly, only Jacob understands the human being as both free and yet bound to the will of God. Jacob's freedom (or perhaps liberation) is precisely that he can only act according to divine will. Therefore, the world poses no threat to him, exhibited in the ease with which he approaches his work with his father-in-law Laban (Genesis 29:15–30).[74]

Jacob's consciousness of reconciliation between the human and divine will should not be taken to mean that he believes human actions are irrelevant. For Jacob, the more the human being acts, the more God's presence is felt in the world. All human action, whether mitzvah or sin, is part of the process of *tikun*. The ability to perceive divine will in any particular act is dependent on one of two factors, both of which arise from Luria's focus on the transmigration of the soul [*gilgul*]: first, the root of the individual soul; and second, the level of that soul in the developmental process.[75]

In order to reconcile both God and world and the human will with the divine will, Jacob must remain deeply embedded in the world, even though he understands that it will be transformed in the future. Jacob, unlike Isaac, never views the world as something to be transcended but only something to be disclosed. This points to the Hasidic depiction of the Baal Shem Tov's attempt to "sanctify the mundane," a Hasidic rendition of the Kabbalistic notion of "raising the lost sparks of exile."[76]

The continuous affirmation of the divinity of the world by means of unveiling its hidden dimension is central for R. Gershon Henokh. As stated earlier, the reconciliation in question is not between nature and God but between the human will and divine will. Only by affirming and subsequently overcoming the apparent paradox of the fragmentation of the human soul can unity be fully achieved and maintained. Because Jacob is conscious of the unity between his will and God's, he is not puzzled by the apparent incongruity between what God desires and what he understands to be true. Whereas before Abraham's death, the young Jacob refused to enter into doubt and chose faith in God instead of trying to argue for his blessing,[77] the mature Jacob is willing to act because he has overcome doubt by constantly being conscious of it.[78] That is, he knows that all his actions are "in the hands of Heaven," even as they may seem otherwise. By overcoming doubt, Jacob transcends free will and thus is truly free. That is, his freedom is fully absorbed in divine will. Therefore, according to R. Gershon Henokh, Jacob lives in the shade of the Tree of Life (redemption/reconciliation) and not the Tree of Knowledge (exile/separation). He carries the consciousness of redemption even as he walks in a world unredeemed. Even (or precisely) in Egypt, Jacob is already redeemed.

The unique ability of Jacob to walk in the world as he experiences divine illumination is exhibited by R. Gershon Henokh in the Talmudic reading of the biblical passage that recounts Jacob being left alone after crossing the river Jabbok (Genesis 32:24):[79]

> Even though he [Jacob] drew down to the world the light of God, it is impossible, while still in the physical body, that this can be accomplished without forgetting [human imperfection].[80] *After he crossed the river Jabbok;* this means that after he had reached the level of drawing the divine light even into the forces of nature, Jacob needed to complete this action [to return for these small vessels] so that he wouldn't think that God is constantly drawn down by him [alone]. Therefore, he returned to complete this action called the small vessels in order that he would be aware that this power [to reveal God] and its vessel [i.e., Jacob himself] are [still quite] small.[81] He also needed to understand that the light [he draws down] is not constant and without interruption.[82]

This text accomplishes two things. First, it illustrates the inherent danger of losing one's perspective when experiencing a divine illumination. The "small vessels," as well as Jacob forgetting them, points to the need to remain aware of one's limitations even during the mystical experience so as not to become severed from the world. Second, we find a hint here that returning to the world in order to integrate one's illumination is an essential part of Jacob's character and thus an essential part of the redemptive character of Israel.[83] Remaining in touch with the world during such a conscious state of illumination is not intended merely to guard one against the danger of radical transcendence. Rather, the purpose of the experience (here, crossing the river) is to return for the forgotten vessels. It is as a result of that action that the wrestling with the angel occurs and the new Jacob (i.e., Israel) is born.

According to R. Gershon Henokh's Hasidic/Kabbalistic interpretation, the aforementioned passage suggests that the word "Jabbok" (*ya'abok*—YBK) refers to Jacob successfully breaking through the veiled emanation of God in nature and experiencing a vision of God from a source above nature and thus (until now) inaccessible to human beings: "If a man purifies himself to the best of his ability, God will reveal to him that which is beyond what can normally be understood. This is the realm of Jacob our father that is also *yesod d'abba*. He may reveal even more until [he realizes that] there is no place void of His light."[84]

In the biblical narrative, after crossing the river Jacob goes back to gather his possessions on the other side. It is this very act (i.e., returning to illuminate the world) that is the unique quality of Jacob and the final integration of the alienated light (over the river) with its source in God.[85]

The final dimension of R. Gershon Henokh's exegetical formulation of his determinist religion, using Jacob as the pivotal character, is the dual nature of Jacob as a biblical patriarch and as a Kabbalistic symbol. As mentioned earlier, Jacob is a unique biblical character in that, unlike Abraham and Sarah, who also received new names in the Bible, Jacob retains his old name even after receiving his new one. This is fundamental in the Zohar's and Luria's formulation of the *parzuf* of *zeir anpin* (Jacob/Israel) as the cosmic body of the nation of Israel. Jacob as an individual and as a symbol *(zeir anpin)* contains both a hidden and a revealed dimension.[86] This is built into the Lurianic framework that distinguishes between the upper half of *parzuf* of *zeir anpin*, from the *sephirah* of *hod* above, and the lower half of *zeir anpin*, the *sephirah yesod* (and, to a lesser extent, *malkhut*).[87] In the Izbica/Radzin tradition this dual nature of Israel (one revealed and one concealed) is the foundation of the split between the premessianic personality of Joseph (the revealed) and the messianic personality of Judah (the concealed). The alienation between God and the individual that began with the sin has now entered a new phase as a result of Jacob's perfection: the alienation between one camp in Israel (the Joseph Jews) and the other (the Judah Jews).

R. Gershon Henokh uses the dual nature of Jacob/Israel, an idea mythologized in Luria's reading of the Zohar, to suggest a new stage in the process toward the final reconciliation between the human will and the divine will. The consciousness of Jacob remains hidden in the lower half (actually lower two-thirds)[88] of *zeir anpin* (called Jacob) and revealed in the upper half (called Israel).[89] The concealment of the divine will is understood to mean that *parzuf abba* (taken to be a purer form of divine essence than *imma,* his female counterpart) remains concealed in *parzuf imma,* after her descent into *zeir anpin,* until the *sephirah hod* in the *parzuf* of *zeir anpin.* The lower half of *zeir anpin* (i.e., *hod, yesod, malkhut*) is the first place in the divine emanation where the light of *parzuf abba* is disclosed from within the garments of *imma.*[90] That is, it is unveiled from its feminine closure in *imma* and can impact *zeir anpin* directly. However, this is also the place where *zeir anpin* is severed from *imma* (her descent ends at *hod* of *zeir anpin*), resulting in the loss of maternal consciousness in the bottom half of *zeir anpin.*

The mythic language of the Lurianic tradition is interpreted in our Hasidic texts as indicating the dual nature of Jacob. Jacob is able to achieve his developed state of consciousness in his upper half (i.e., concealed in the maternal consciousness of *imma*), but cannot completely integrate it into the whole of creation, as indicated in the fractured state of his children. The reconciliation of the divine and the human exists in both parts of Jacob but is only revealed in one. In Izbica/Radzin Hasidism, this is taken to mean that the Judah Jews, those who see all Israelite action as aligned with divine will, represent the upper concealed part of *parzuf* Jacob (which contains both maternal and paternal influences); while the Joseph Jews, who cannot comprehend God's will outside halakha, embody the lower revealed part of *parzuf* Jacob, which represents the paternal influence severed from its maternal covering. There is an inherent imbalance in the bottom part of *parzuf* Jacob, an imbalance that is the root of Joseph's limitations in viewing divine will as inextricably tied to halakha. Exile results from the fact that Joseph Jews cannot understand the source of their brother's religiosity, which also points to the fact that they cannot understand the concealed part of themselves. Put another way, Joseph Jews cannot comprehend the full integration of *abba* and *imma* and are thus dominated by a masculinity that views the world solely through the lens of the law.

It is significant to note here how the hidden (upper) part of Jacob is different from the unconscious "walking in the dark" of Abraham. Since consciousness of the unity between human will and the divine will has already been achieved in Jacob, the hidden aspect of his nature is the last stage in the messianic process toward redemption. Whereas Abraham, who is living before the reconciliation, is trying to reach beyond the world to seek its unity, the children of Jacob, living after reconciliation, seek to reach within themselves to uncover the unity that already exists.

R. Gershon Henokh develops this last point in a long discourse on the meaning of *tefillin* (phylacteries). *Tefillin* share two traits with the symbolic portrait of Jacob. First, they are objects that bind divine will (represented by the biblical verses contained in the *tefillin*) with the human will (represented by the injunction to wear them opposite the heart, the place of human will). Second, the contents of the *tefillin* are covered, corresponding to the concealed nature of the upper half of the *parzuf* of Jacob.[91] R. Mordecai Joseph interprets this dimension of concealment as the human need for *zimzum* or introspection in order to detect the will of God in the human heart.

R. Gershon Henokh extends his grandfather's insight to distinguish two dimensions of this *zimzum*.[92] The first is an emotional-cognitive *zimzum* (i.e., meditative introspection). The second is behavioral (i.e., piety, mitzvot). Whereas Abraham practices the first, it is only Jacob who introduces the second. This is because the cosmic *parzuf* of Jacob contains all the limbs of the human body. Thus, the embodiment of God consciousness (i.e., piety) only begins with Jacob, for whom the cognitive quest for God is integrated into the human action of mitzvot. For both R. Mordecai Joseph and R. Gershon Henokh, the redemptive Jew begins with the assumption that his will and God's are identical (the product of cognitive *zimzum*). The life of mitzvot (behavioral *zimzum,* here represented by one particular mitzvah, *tefillin*) enables the individual to embody a form of meditation or introspection (noted here as an act of *zimzum*) in practice in order to become conscious of the unity between his will and the divine. This can only take place in a world where God is still hidden. However, whereas before Jacob, divine concealment results in the apparent distinction between God and the world, after Jacob, the concealment of God is contained solely within the individual. The integration of the alienated light of the serpent *('or makif)* and the inner light of the human soul *('or penimi)* is finally complete in Jacob.

The piety of individual devotion facilitates but does not cause God's ushering in the final reconciliation between the human and God by revealing the divine nature of His will.[93] Devotion as facilitating this last movement is represented by the years Jacob worked for his father-in-law Laban. Although Scripture explicitly states that Jacob worked for Laban for twenty years (Genesis 31:38), R. Gershon Henokh adds to this calculation the years following Jacob's departure from home before his employment with Laban to arrive at the significant number 33. According to the *sephirotic* calendar of the counting of the *'omer* (constituting the forty-nine days between Passover and Shavuot, Leviticus 23:15–16),[94] the thirty-third day represents the *sephirotic* calculation of *hod sh'b'hod (hod* of *hod),* the final place where the forces of *abba* are enveloped within *imma.* According to rabbinic lore, this day marks the anniversary of R. Shimon bar Yohai's death, ending the deaths of the disciples of R. Akiba during a tragic plague in the first century. For post-Zohar Kabbalists, R. Shimon is the mystical hero who dies as a result of revealing the secrets of the Torah. The anniversary of his mystical death marks a shift in the process of revealing divine secrets, holding the potential for even further divine disclosure.[95]

> When Jacob completed his refinements [*berurim*] with Laban he also completed his own *berurim.* This was the 33rd year from the beginning of his journey, which is *hod sh'b'hod.* On this it is said that the refinements of man which he can complete can only reach until [the *sephirah* of] *hod,* as it says, *and the words I placed in your mouth, shall not be absent from your mouth, nor from the mouths of your children, nor from the mouths of your children's children* [Isaiah 59:21]. . . . From this trait until its innermost manifestation, which is *hod sh'b'hod,* there are no clear *berurim,* only the screaming of the heart to God to be saved and to complete the process for the good. From that point onward [i.e., from *hod sh'b'hod,* or the thirty-third year of Jacob's departure] even the heartfelt scream is not within the power of the individual but only of God.[96]

At this stage, which is the culmination of the human capacity to act on one's own behalf, the will of God is no longer concealed either in the texture of the world or the deep recesses of the human heart. Only when the will of God is liberated from the garments that conceal it can the individual experience unity and the final stage of reconciliation. This moment also holds the potential to be the final moment of human action after which, "from that moment on, God guides him forever."

One could ask, according to R. Gershon Henokh's depiction of the alienation of the sin and the reintegration of the alienated light in Jacob, what remains left to accomplish before redemption? He seems acutely aware of this question. In the next chapter I argue that his reading of the remainder of Genesis and beyond, focusing on the complex relationships between the sons of Jacob, their descendants, and the sons of Esau, all address this question.

The descendants of Esau (generally referred to as the Gentile nations) continue to play a major role in the Torah, suggesting that the alienated light of the serpent had not completely become integrated and reunited with its source in God. A few brief words of summary are in order before discussing how these two sets of relationships (the sons of Jacob and Israel and the nations) are interpreted by R. Mordecai Joseph and R. Gershon Henokh as the final stage of exile.

I began my examination of R. Gershon Henokh's reading of Scripture with what he suggests is the alienation of the "hovering light" of the serpent in the Garden of Eden from the "inner light" of the human soul, as a result of the process of *zimzum* and the "breaking of the vessels." By reading Lurianic cosmogony into the biblical narrative and its characters, R. Gershon Henokh remains true to the classic Hasidic tendency, influenced by the Zohar in this regard, to build its ideology out of Scripture, rather than the Lurianic tendency to formulate a cosmology and then read it onto Scripture.[97] As a result, the symbolic categories such as "hovering light," "surrounding light," and "inner light" become alive in the biblical characters of the serpent, Noah, Abraham, Esau, and others. Moreover, Adam before the sin (the archetype of the future Israel) is portrayed as that creature who houses the integrated divine light which can only be reunited with the alienated light through his actions (mitzvot).[98]

The drama becomes more complex as Abraham's intuition (the initial stage of the integration) yields a state of consciousness that is close to the God-consciousness of Jacob, except that it remains in a prerational intuitive stage and never becomes fully integrated into Abraham's person. The descendants of Noah develop to their full capacity within the limited confines of their covenant, a covenant that recognizes God in nature but cannot recognize the part that humans must play in the covenant in bringing creation to its conclusion.

Esau represents a new part of this dichotomy (between the descendants of Abraham and the nations), in that he is a descendant of Abraham who relinquishes his right to Abraham's covenant. Esau errs as a result of his inability to view the death of Abraham as part of the divine plan. What is interesting about Esau in R. Gershon Henokh's reading is that his rationalism and fatalism, and the conclusions he draws concerning the impotence of humanity to facilitate change, point the reader back to the descendants of Noah who lived in a pre-Abrahamic covenant.[99] Esau's post-Abrahamic reversal back to a pre-Abrahamic covenant suggests that Abraham's intuition was not enough to finalize the change it began. Ironically, Esau's reversal results from his inability to make sense of Abraham's death. Thus Abraham indirectly plays a role in Esau's failure.

Esau's tragic flaw suggests that as long as the intuition remains unconscious and not completely absorbed into the fabric of the religious personality, it can always be denied or, alternatively, become the source for deviance. Such denial becomes fatalistic in Esau, shared to a lesser extent by Melchizedek and Noah. Reconciliation is only accomplished by Jacob, illustrated in his response to Abraham's death (the cooking of the lentil soup) and his crossing back over the Jabbok ford to gather the "small vessels" left on the other side (resulting in the confrontation with the angel and his new name, Israel, representing the revealed consciousness of God). Only Jacob's accomplishments solidify and make permanent the covenant made initially with Abraham.

However, this does not result in Jacob's emergence as the Messiah. One could argue that Jacob's life achieves enough to enable his descendants (Israel) to complete the task. As I will argue in the next chapter, the consciousness Jacob achieves in his tumultuous and tragic life is not fully understood by his progeny and is therefore eclipsed, as exhibited by his sons' failures. Esau's choice to relinquish his covenantal ties, however, is no longer possible for the sons of Jacob, who are products of either the hidden or the revealed dimensions of their father as *zeir anpin*. The inability of Jacob's sons to understand each other now serves as the context for the final phase of exile and, more importantly, as the basis for some of the most heretical statements in Izbica/Radzin Hasidism on the questions of religious determinism and antinomianism. The integration of the divine will with the human will, accomplished in the personality of Jacob, creates a firm foundation for a determinist religion. Among other things, such a foundation fractures, or at least threatens, the correlation between divine will and the four ells of halakha. Thus, for R. Mordecai Joseph and R. Gershon Henokh, the realization that "every [Israelite] act is the will of God" simultaneously points to the messianic era and the culmination of Torah as we know it.

6 Reconciliation and Fragmentation

The Second Rupture and the Final Stage of Exile

. . . that which redeems us is also that which ought not to have taken place.

Georges Bataille

But what is duty? Duty is simply the expression for God's will.

Soren Kierkegaard

As inheritors of the patriarch Jacob, the nation of Israel is depicted in the Izbica/Radzin tradition as an imperfect body (i.e., Jacob's fractured progeny) that contains perfection (Jacob). As illustrated in the last chapter, Jacob achieves the complete reconciliation of the human and the divine will that begins with Abraham's transformation of Noahide monotheism (expressed in the *brit* of nature) through Melchizedek's recognition of divine transcendence (*Blessed be Abram of God Most High, Creator of Heaven and Earth. And blessed be God Most High, who has delivered your foes into your hand* [Genesis 14:18–20]). The result of Jacob's achievement is an understanding that human will, when acting inside Abraham's covenantal monotheism, is perfectly aligned with divine will, even if one's actions appear to be in conflict with established law (halakha). What this does is eradicate any conventional notion of sin (sin understood as acting against God), making all deviant behavior an expression of concealed divine will. Sin in the conventional sense is only relevant to those who do not inherit Jacob's perfection (i.e., the Gentile nations).

Jacob's perfection, however, is not transmitted in its fullness to any of his sons. Each son inherits a portion of Jacob's perfected state. The fragmentation of Jacob in his sons yields two personality archetypes, one embodied in

Joseph, the other in his half-brother, Judah. Joseph lives according to the letter of the law, following his father's understanding of devotion as the fulfillment of divine will in halakha. Judah also lives by the law but is unwilling to accept it as the exclusive vehicle for human devotion. He constantly tries to renew the law. This emphasis on human subjectivity sometimes brings Judah to the conclusion that he must live outside the law in order to fulfill God's will, which he understands, via Jacob, as a concealed expressed of His will. According to this, one can say that the Joseph archetype is an extension of Jacob through Isaac, and the Judah archetype is an extension of Jacob through Abraham.

The Israelite exile in Egypt is depicted as the internal struggle between these two factions of Jacob's progeny for the mantle of his spiritual inheritance. There is a momentary reprieve when Jacob descends into Egypt, once again bringing his sons together. Once Jacob dies, however, the division continues, and with this division the exile intensifies until the appearance of Moses. In this Hasidic rendition, the notion of the imperfect in the perfect, the twelve sons as inheritors of Jacob, is the unique character of the Jewish people.

The Sons of Jacob: Refragmentation and the Final Stage of Exile

Izbica/Radzin exegesis is a reading of the Bible from the vantage point of Judah. Until Joseph, Jews understand the Jacobean source of Judah Jews and comprehend that, until they understand how halakha is a necessary but insufficient condition for the covenant, they will never understand the Judean roots in their own personalities. As the revealed dimension of Jacob, Judah holds the key to Joseph's redemption and subsequently the historical redemption of Israel. Judah Jews do not need redemption because, as we will see, they are already redeemed. What Judah Jews need is to be liberated from the confines of their brother's limited vision. As part of Israel, they cannot sever ties with their exilic brother but also cannot succumb to his boundaries.

The internal struggle of Israel as a nation consists of a deep misunderstanding between these two personality archetypes. In a sense, fragmentation constitutes an essential part of the Jewish psyche and is the root of Jewish exile. This is partly exhibited in Jacob's painful life, most tragically depicted in his son's inability to see the unifying nature of their diverse personalities.

> It is taught in the midrash [*Shir Ha-Shirim Rabba* 1:1.9], "Just as wisdom makes a crown for the head, humility [the trait of Jacob] makes a sandal for the heel." The trait of humility is very precious. Therefore Jacob was satisfied when he achieved humility in that he knew his character was complete. However, God then showed him, [*T*]*hese are the generations of Jacob . . . Joseph.* This implies that here starts a new generation [*holadah hadasha*] and a new vocation [*'asek hadash*].[1]

R. Gershon Henokh suggests that the essential difference between the pre-Jacobean traits of Abraham and Isaac *(hesed* and *gevurah,* the upper half of *zeir anpin)* and post-Jacobean Israel, represented in the *sephirotic* realm as *netzah, hod,* and *yesod* (the bottom half of *zeir anpin*), is that the latter all contain complete parts of each other. Jacob's sons' inability to understand one another, and subsequently themselves, is the very root of Israelite exile. Such exile is the result of one trait in each personality (the dominant *sephirah*) dominating and effacing all the other traits. Thus, each brother sees the other, and subsequently himself, in a distorted way. This illustrates a lack of self-consciousness, the very foundation of Jacob's perfection.

> In Israel, every soul includes all of the character traits [*middot*] [of all the other souls]. [The difference lies] in one trait being more pronounced [in a particular individual.] . . . Judah is the strongest of his brothers. However, [being a son of Jacob] Judah also shares the trait of Joseph. After the clarification [apparently after Joseph disappeared] it appeared to Judah that Joseph [the trait of Joseph in all the brothers] was lost. Consequently, there was a deficiency in the connection of all the brothers to God until it was ascertained that Joseph was still alive. It then became apparent that the covenant that God made with the patriarchs would shine forever and its light would never be extinguished.[2]

Using the Talmudic legal principle that teaches when one can and cannot learn a general rule from specific cases *(klal u perat),* R. Gershon Henokh suggests here that the result of Jacob's integrated life was that all his sons shared part of each other's characteristics. Their differences only lie in the degree to which one trait is dominant over another.[3] This notion of integration is bolstered by the fact that in classical Kabbala, the *sephirah tiferet,* representing Jacob, is also used as a generic term for the entire body of *zeir anpin,* which includes all the other traits (the bottom six *sephirot*). All the traits embodied in Jacob need to function in harmony for at least two reasons: first, to complete the messianic personality by nationalizing the individual person of Jacob; and second, to retain the preredemptive nature of the covenant (law) *and* its messianic counterpart (spirit). In short, the brothers need each other because they are all part of each other. However, as the biblical narrative unfolds we see that they are unable to see themselves in the other. That is, they cannot accept each other as equal and legitimate inheritors of their father's perfection. Our text suggests that Judah is the first to recognize this defect after the disappearance of Joseph (Genesis 37:26–28).

This background serves as the groundwork for both R. Mordecai Joseph and R. Gershon Henokh's determinist religious ideology. The idea of human will as independent of its divine source is the consequence of the lack of self-consciousness exemplified in the sons of Jacob and exhibited in their continuous feud. The conflict of the sons of Jacob in the biblical narrative is viewed in the Hasidic imagination as the inability of each to see how the other is also acting according to divine will. Judah realizes this when he feels a deficiency in himself after Joseph disappears. However, our text goes further. It is not only that Judah realizes that Joseph, as different as he may be, is acting in accordance with God's will; Judah also realizes that his ability to act, that is, his devotional life, is in need of Joseph, his typological antagonist.

Before examining how these personality types are constructed from biblical, rabbinic, and Kabbalistic literature, it is important to emphasize that the inability of these two archetypes to understand and accept each other is the foundation of R. Gershon Henokh's reading of the spiritual and historical exile of the Jewish people. Both R. Mordecai Joseph and R. Gershon Henokh identify with the character of Judah who, constructed in the image of the Baal Shem Tov, is viewed as the forerunner of the Davidic kingdom and the messianic era.[4] The polemical undertone throughout is that historical exile is a consequence of the spiritual descendants of Joseph and Ephraim (the Mithnagdim?) and their inability to accept the validity and viability of the descendants of Judah and David (the Hasidim?).[5]

Sibling Rivalry and the Internal History of Israel: Judah and Joseph

The most fundamental division in the fragmentation of the sons of Jacob is between Judah and Joseph. This is not new in Izbica/Radzin Hasidism but appears throughout rabbinic, midrashic, and Kabbalistic literature. These two individuals and their respective tribes represent the two messianic figures in ancient Israelite history, the Messiah of Joseph (or Ephraim), ushering in the final redemption, and the Messiah of David (from the family of Judah).[6] Judah and Joseph represent the two archetypes of all of Israel, each the product of a particular spiritual inheritance of Jacob. There is a latent deterministic twist to the Izbica/Radzin construction of this motif. Any individual, as inheritor of either the spiritual nature of Judah or the spiritual nature of Joseph, can only perfect themselves within the predetermined confines of that spiritual inheritance. The juxtaposition of Judah and Joseph is the most explicit presentation of spiritual predisposition found in the Izbica/Radzin school and serves as the underlying theme of both R. Mordecai Joseph's and R. Gershon Henokh's stances on the alienated nature of Israel in the protomessianic world.

This following passage is perhaps the most explicit of this juxtaposition:

> This is what is meant by [the verse] *Ephraim shall not envy Judah, And Judah shall not harass Ephraim* [Isaiah 11:13]. In truth these two tribes are always in opposition to one another. The nature [*hayyim*] God gave to the tribe of Ephraim is to seek out everything according to the law [*ma'aseh 'al ha-din*] and halakha without deviating from it. Therefore, when it is written that the purpose of the Torah is not to sin it states, *Else He will rush fire upon you, the House of Joseph* [Amos 5:6]. This means that you [Israel] should make sure [your actions] are not opposed to the actions [of the House of Joseph]. The root of the life of Judah is always to search after God in every action regardless of what the law requires. [Judah] always looks to God in order that He will reveal to him the depth of the truth [*'omek ha-emet*] in any particular situation. It could be that even though the decree [*din*] may be true according to the arguments of the litigants, it may not ultimately be true in that their testimony may be based on false assumptions, as we see in *kinyan d'Rabba* [b.T. Nedarim 25b]. This can be true in all such matters. This is the root of the life of Judah, i.e., to seek out God in everything and not to act according to the dictum, *a commandment of men—learned by rote* [Isaiah 29:13].[7] Even though he performed a certain act in one way yesterday, today he will not depend on himself but only seek out God to reveal His will anew. This [mode of behavior] sometimes requires acting in opposition to the halakha [*neged ha-halakha*] for [it is written] *It is the time to act for God for they have abandoned Your Torah* [Psalms 119:126]. This is the reason these two tribes oppose one another. However, in the future it is stated, *Ephraim will not envy Judah and Judah shall not harass Ephraim* [Isaiah 11:13]. This means that Ephraim will not oppose [the actions] of Judah when he

> acts outside the realm of halakha. He will not harass him because God will show Ephraim that Judah's intentions were for the sake of heaven and not for his own benefit. As a result there will peace between them.[8]

As suggested earlier, both R. Mordecai Joseph and R. Gershon Henokh identify with the character of Judah. In his lengthy essay on R. Mordecai Joseph, Joseph Weiss notes that while R. Mordecai Joseph never explicitly associates himself with the archetype of Judah, such an association underlies the scope and trajectory of *Mei Ha-Shiloah*.[9] Morris Faierstein argues that it is quite clear from a number of biographical sources that R. Mordecai Joseph saw himself, and was viewed by his disciples, in the messianic/Judah model.[10] I would suggest that even without the lineage of the Lainer dynasty that allegedly points to the Judah-David family, we could see the author's identification with Judah in the above-cited passage.

The verse in Isaiah (11:13) is constructed as reciprocal in nature. It implies an inherent antagonism between the two tribes. R. Mordecai Joseph uses this verse as the basis of his interpretation. The verse states that in the redemptive future, *Ephraim shall not envy Judah and Judah shall not harass Ephraim*. This means that presently both tribes are acting wrongly toward one another, the consequence of Ephraim's envy and Judah's harassment. This verse is cleverly read in *Mei Ha-Shiloah* to yield a different result. If we look closely at the conclusion of R. Mordecai Joseph's statement, we will see that the term "harass," which, in the verse, applies to Judah's attitude toward Ephraim, appears to be reversed. He (Ephraim) will not harass him (Judah) when he sees him acting outside the halakha.

According to R. Mordecai Joseph, Ephraim will not harass Judah because he will see that Judah's actions are for the sake of heaven. On this reading, the reciprocal nature of the verse disappears. Judah appears innocent and the victim of Ephraim's shortsightedness (both his envy and harassment). In R. Mordecai Joseph's reading of the Isaiah verse, the exile of Israel rests solely on the shoulders of Ephraim, Judah having already integrated the reconciliation of his father. Judah's failure is his inability to see how his brother lags behind. At worst, he is guilty of impatience.

The depiction of Judah as the messianic figure who inherits the messianic personality of his father and overcomes free will is illustrated in the various juxtapositions of Judah to his brothers in the Izbica/Radzin exegetical tradition. The following text is taken from R. Mordecai Joseph's comment on Moses' blessings to the twelve tribes of Israel, offering the reader a national rendition of the familial blessings Jacob gave his sons in Genesis

49 and Genesis 50. Here the juxtaposition is no longer only between Judah and Joseph but between Judah and his other brothers, each of whom suffers from a unique spiritual deficiency.

> *And this is to Judah. And he said, "God heard the voice of Judah. . . ."* [Deuteronomy 33:7]. This verse hints at the blessing given to Simeon. The twelve tribes are the limbs of the Shekhina, as it says in the Zohar [1. 241b]. Reuven is the eyes of the Shekhina as he has a clear vision of God. Simeon is the ears of the Shekhina and Judah is the heart, for he has a pure and refined heart [*m'burar*]. This is the meaning of the verse, *God heard the voice of Judah.* It is a directive that Simeon should hear the voice of Judah as Simeon always needs clarification [*berurim*][11] as we explained in the verse, *And Isaac loved Esau* [Genesis 25:28].[12]

This text cannot be understood without revisiting R. Mordecai Joseph's comment on Jacob's blessings to Simeon in Genesis 49. Before turning to that text, however, what is set up here is that Judah, being the heart and emotional center of the *Shekhina* (whose limbs are the twelve tribes), serves to direct his brothers (i.e., the nation of Israel) away from exile and toward redemption; or, he directs them from the deficient protomessianic personality to the perfected messianic personality whose life is driven by the identification of the human heart and divine will. As previously mentioned, this is the technical nature of the term *berurim* (clarification) in the Izbica/Radzin corpus.[13]

> It is also the case in Israel that there are Jewish souls for whom it is more permissible to enter into tenuous situations [*s'fakot*] than other souls, even though both are from the seed of Jacob.[14] Such is the case with Simeon and Dina. Levi did not want to redeem her [and destroy Schem (Genesis 34:25–31)] for he feared that his intentions might not have been pure [lit., for the sake of heaven] as the tribe of Levi embodies the attribute of fear. Entering into a tenuous situation for the tribe of Levi is likened to the verse in Malachi 2:5, *I had with him a covenant of life and well-being, which I gave to him, and of reverence, which he showed Me. For he stood in awe of My name.* As a result, the tribe of Levi became priests who entered into the Holy of Holies. . . . But Simeon entered into this tenuous situation and said [to himself], "God forbid that I should be associated with sexual impropriety." He redeemed Dina and subsequently entered into a situation that required clarification [*berur*]. He claimed that he trusted God unequivocally and that his actions [i.e., slaughtering Schem] were purely for the sake of heaven in order to rescue Dina from Schem. However, the tribe of Simeon required further clarification in these areas, like Zimri, who also claimed his intentions were noble. When Simeon's nature is purified in the future, his status will rise above Levi's.[15]

Not only does this passage clarify the ambiguous statement regarding Simeon in the text cited above, it further develops the hierarchy of the messianic personality in Simeon and Levi the way R. Mordecai Joseph does with Judah and Joseph. This text is built on inferences about Jacob's blessing to his sons before his death, juxtaposed to Moses' blessings to the twelve tribes before his death at the end of Deuteronomy. In Genesis 49:5–7, Simeon and Levi are the dual recipients of one blessing that mentions, with indignation, the incident with Dina. There is no apparent distinction between Simeon and Levi in Jacob's blessing (Genesis 49:5).[16] In Deuteronomy 33:4–10, Moses overlooks Simeon completely yet blesses Levi with the priesthood. On R. Mordecai Joseph's reading, this occurs because the tribe of Levi has succeeded in rectifying the deficiency of their namesake in order to merit the priesthood. R. Mordecai Joseph draws our attention to the absence of Simeon in Moses' blessing, suggesting that the dichotomy between Simeon and Levi reflects the larger dichotomy between Judah and Joseph. The difference is that in the Judah and Joseph case, the messianic personality of Jacob who is fully actualized in Judah is at odds with the protomessianic archetype of Joseph. Unlike Jacob, Judah is not pure enough to make his own spiritual inheritance understandable to his brother. In Genesis 49, both Simeon and Levi are unprepared for the unity of the human and divine will. However, in his passion, Simeon contains the potential for full clarification by hastening to Judah's voice (Deuteronomy 33: 7). Levi, in his caution, merits the priesthood but is eventually usurped by his comparatively unrefined yet ultimately superior brother Simeon.[17] As we will see in our discussion of Moses, who is from the tribe of Levi, he is the character who fully integrates the passion of Simeon, the vision of Judah, and Levi's cautious demeanor. In this sense, he shares the messianic vocation of Judah even though he is not from the messianic tribe.

The fact that R. Mordecai Joseph uses this episode in Genesis to draw our attention to his most radical comments in the Pinhas-Zimri narrative in Numbers (25:1–10) is not coincidental. As I will argue later in this chapter, the Pinhas-Zimri narrative is the epicenter of the Izbica/Radzin worldview and not merely a curious aberration. The comments on that biblical event should not be seen as independent of the entire Izbica/Radzin project. In fact, I will argue that the development of the messianic personality in Genesis, creatively yet largely conventionally argued, is the groundwork for R. Mordecai Joseph's daring comments about Pinhas and Zimri in Numbers. The classic definition of the Messiah as unappreciated and misunderstood (and even rejected) is the backdrop for the sibling rivalries of Jacob's sons, centering on Judah and Joseph. This comes to a radical head in the vindication of Zimri and the merit, yet shortsightedness, of the heroic figure of Pinhas.

R. Gershon Henokh takes his grandfather's distinction between Judah and Joseph and develops it in at least two distinct ways. First, he suggests that Joseph represents the synthesis of Jacob as it is presented to the Gentile world. This is obviously drawn from Joseph's life in Egypt and his close relationship to Pharaoh and the Egyptian aristocracy. In Genesis, Joseph is far more appreciated by Egyptian society than his own family. The reconciliation between Judah and Joseph (Genesis 44:18–24), which results in Jacob's reunion with his sons in Egypt, is short-lived. Soon after Jacob's death, the brothers once again feel estranged from their "Egyptian brother" (Genesis 50:15–21). Second, R. Gershon Henokh suggests that Joseph embodies the service of God from the standpoint of reason, while Judah represents the service of God from a stance of intuition.

Both of these devotional models are explicated in R. Gershon Henokh's interpretation of his grandfather's reading of b.T. Sotah 21a, which distinguishes between the candle of mitzvah as temporal and the light of Torah (the study of Torah) as eternal. In its presentation of the superior nature of Torah study, the distinction the Talmudic discussion suggests is that the eternal light of Torah protects an individual even when studying, while the light of mitzvah is only protective when one is involved in the act of mitzvah.[18] R. Gershon Henokh uses this passage and transforms the categories of "Torah as study and mitzvah as action" in the Talmud, to "Torah as divine consciousness" and "mitzvah as rationality and halakha." Reading this back into his biblical anthropology, Torah becomes Judah and mitzvah becomes Joseph.

> The character of mitzvah is that a person is able to fulfill a mitzvah with only a garment [i.e., externally] yet it is still seen as if he fulfilled a mitzvah. This is because even one who fulfills the mitzvah with all of the appropriate intentions [*kavvanot*] still does not reach the essence of the *kavvanah*. God intended that the mitzvot require a physical act embedded in the lowest realm of human existence. The foundation of [the concept of] mitzvah is Joseph Ha-Zaddik (Joseph the Righteous One), who sustained and served as a filter for the entire world."[19]

As described here, mitzvah is not the most pristine form of worship because it is intrinsically bound to a physical object or to a specific time or place. The transference of mitzvah to the biblical Joseph is strengthened by the Zohar's assertion that *yesod* (Joseph) is "orphaned."[20] In the Bible, Joseph's status as orphan is the result of his being severed from all family ties during his stay in Egypt. The orphan is viewed here as an individual having limited perspective—one whose internal sense of self can never be fully supported by one's external environment. Even while in Egypt Joseph knows that he is a son of Jacob, but being severed from his familial roots, he is limited in his ability to understand his familial status and his place in the world. R. Gershon Henokh uses the image of orphan to assert that while both Joseph and Judah perform the mitzvot, only Judah can see beyond them. Joseph cannot fully wed his internal life (his passion for God) with his external life (mitzvot).[21] The "orphaned" nature of Joseph, biblically depicted as abandoned by his family and Kabbalistically rendered as empty of the influx of feminine consciousness from *parzuf imma,*[22] is reread by R. Gershon Henokh to imply that, through his separation and exile, Joseph lost the intuitive vision of his father Jacob. That is, he lost the messianic consciousness that would have enabled him to see the temporality of mitzvot.

> At the time when the light is not clear it is necessary to be adamant concerning the performance of mitzvot. Through the mitzvot one will be able to draw down the light of "Torah" to the mitzvot. . . . [However] when the light is clear and God openly [makes accessible] this clarity, the individual can receive the "general light" [Torah] and from this light come to know the particulars [mitzvot] in one glance. Hence, when the light is not clear one must arouse its clarity through divine worship and the performance of mitzvot and, through them, come to understand the particular. . . . However, this is very difficult and requires great effort. This is the character of Joseph and his exile.[23]

This passage suggests that in a world where God is hidden, the way to understand and experience His omnipresence (the light of Torah) is only through the particular (mitzvot). Joseph's life in exile is viewed as the biblical model of Israel in exile. Joseph not only lives most of his life in exile but also is unaware of the condition of his brothers and his father (i.e., he is, in a sense, unaware of his own exile).[24] This is the essential part of his being orphaned. Therefore, Joseph's understanding of God can only come through the mitzvot (i.e., the law), having been "orphaned" from the general Torah of Spirit. In Izbica/Radzin Hasidism, this limited personality represents the person who is in constant conflict with the spiritualistic type of Judah, the one who never severs his ties with his father and thus fully inherits the messianic consciousness of his father. As a biblical personality and a cosmic trope, Joseph is depicted as the one who remained devoted to the mitzvot in order to survive the darkness of exile, resulting from the absence of divine presence and connection to his family. The disciples of

R. Gershon Henokh develop this point further in their reading of the miracle of Hanukkah.

> Israel is only [redeemed] with a strong arm [*zeroah*] when they are fulfilling the mitzvot [midrash Tanhuma, *parshat ki tavo,* 1]. Therefore, any person who is far from knowledge [of God] should hold tightly to the simple mitzvot as it says, *And Moshe took the bones of Joseph with him* [Exodus 13:19]. Joseph represents the clarity of light that illuminates how one is connected to God in a revealed way. Therefore, when the lights are concealed, that is, when the realm of Joseph is absent, he [Moshe] took his bones. Joseph's bones represent the simple mitzvot.[25]

Joseph embodies the miracle of Hanukkah. R. Gershon Henokh is cited as saying, "The miracle of Hanukkah and the loss of Joseph are the same thing. What was temporarily lost [in both instances] was the revealed nature of connection between Israel and God. It is only via divine service [the simple performance of mitzvot] that the hidden light will once again become revealed."[26] The strict legalism of Joseph is always that which precedes the illumination embodied in the messianic figure of Judah.

The moment of confrontation between Judah and Joseph (Genesis 44:18–24) is the pivotal moment of redemption in general, and redemption from Egypt in particular, as well as the paradigmatic shift required to usher in the final historical redemption of Israel. According to rabbinic tradition, the Jews in Egypt occupied "the forty-ninth level of defilement." For our Hasidic masters the inability to comprehend the depth of exile is depicted in the archetype of Joseph, the Kabbalistic concept of *zimzum,* and the boundaries of halakha and the Tree of Knowledge of Good and Evil *('Etz Ha-Da'at Tov ve Ra).* Judah, with his visionary nature and self-consciousness inherited from Abraham through Jacob, is the messianic character, the power to overcome *zimzum* and to bring Israel back to the Tree of Life.[27] Although Judah needs to remain rooted in the world, his task in the confrontation with Joseph in Genesis 44:18–24 was to finally break the Israelite people out of the mode of Joseph (the hidden dimension of Jacob) and turn them toward the mode of Moses (the revealed dimension of Israel).[28] The stark and tense confrontation between Judah and Joseph in Genesis forces Joseph (representing the concealed state of God) into a negation of concealment, forcing him to reveal his true identity as the son of Jacob. This revelation/disclosure is the "redemption" of Joseph (and his spiritual inheritors) and prepares Israel for the emergence of Moses (the true inheritor of Jacob via Judah) and subsequently the redemption from Egypt.[29] In short, R. Gershon Henokh reads the confrontation of

Judah with Joseph, and the ultimate victory of Judah, as the moment that enabled Israel to experience the Exodus from Egypt and subsequently receive the Torah at Sinai. Here the Messiah does not come at the end of exile but at the very beginning.

The implications of this reading are far-reaching, and the polemical tone is more apparent here than in other parts of his commentary. As stated earlier, the radical notion present here is not in suggesting that, at some future messianic time, the strictures of halakha will be altered or even become obsolete. The obsolescence of mitzvot in the future appears both in Talmudic and midrashic literature and is expanded in the Kabbalistic imagination in texts such as *Sefer Temunah* and, of course, in Sabbateanism. It is greatly equivocated in other medieval texts, such as Maimonides' "Laws of Kings" in his *Mishneh Torah*, and in R. Isaac Abrabanel's *Yeshu'at Meshikho*.[30]

The Izbica/Radzin Hasidic reading offers another alternative that stands between Maimonidean conservatism and Sabbatean heresy. The character of Judah, who acts out of his desire for God even if such desire takes him beyond the boundaries of halakha, is not a consequence *of* redemption but a prerequisite *for* redemption.[31] Again, messianism (and not Messiah) comes at the beginning. It is the effacing of halakha *in potentia* that inaugurates the beginning of the redemptive process. The consequence of redemption is Joseph's realization that Judah's transgressive behavior is aligned with the will of God and that Judah is the true inheritor of Jacob's perfected personality. The stage for this confrontation and subsequent realization of Judah as the true messianic archetype does not occur in the messianic age but in the very depth of exile (i.e., in Egypt). These passages suggest that Judah and his spiritual descendants take this postredemptive attitude in the protoredemptive world and, in doing so, destabilize the entire halakhic system.[32]

Using this framework, R. Gershon Henokh explains the problematic behavior of every biblical character, from Er and Onan (the sons of Judah who die as the result of illicit sexual behavior in Genesis), to Aaron's sons Nadav and Avihu, and finally to Pinhas and Zimri. As mentioned earlier, for R. Mordecai Joseph and R. Gershon Henokh, the whole concept of sin as transgression is impossible for Israel in the post-Jacobean world. Jacob reconciled the alienated light (embodied in the serpent of the creation story) with the integrated light of the divine (human) soul, and thereby made sin, understood as acting against divine will, impossible for his descendants. Therefore, the apparent sins of biblical characters, as inheritors of Jacob, serve as the essential challenge for the exegete who believes that sin is no longer possible. I will show that even the illusion of sin only exists for those with the soul of Joseph, that is, those who are living in the preredemptive world. For those with the soul of Judah (and later Moses and David), sin is only a historical remnant of the concealed state of creation (via *zimzum*) that must be overcome. As I stated at the outset, Izbica/Radzin Hasidism is, to a large degree, a reading of the Bible from the vantage point of Judah. This Judean framework, which is messianic before the Messiah, serves as the basis for R. Gershon Henokh's entire exegetical enterprise, culminating with the most oft-cited interpretation in Izbica/Radzin Hasidism, the story of Pinhas and Zimri.

Sexual Deviance and the Final Purging of Judah: Er and Onan

The story of Judah and Tamar (Genesis 38:12–30) is one of the more intriguing episodes in the latter half of Genesis, posing a serious challenge to any biblical exegete devoted to defending the righteousness of all the biblical characters. I will focus on the sins of Er and Onan (Genesis 38:6–9), in what appears to be a straightforward prelude to the narrative, in order to show how Izbica/Radzin Hasidism vindicates both sons of Judah and subsequently Judah himself. I mentioned above that the Izbica/Radzin tradition reads the Bible from the vantage point of Judah. Thus, as sons of Judah, Er and Onan could never be guilty of the actions of which they are accused, regardless of the explicit accusation found in the biblical text. Any conclusions resting on Er's and Onan's guilt must therefore be a misunderstanding of the Bible based on a reading from the Joseph (i.e., exilic) perspective. Esotericism has become the Torah according to Judah!

The Talmudic tradition understands Er's and Onan's sins to be sexual in nature. In one sense, as we will presently see, Er's and Onan's sins are the inverse of Adam's sin in the Garden. Adam comes upon Eve too soon and is punished for following his desire. While Er dies for reasons that are unknown (Genesis 38:7, *But Er, Judah's firstborn, was displeasing to the Lord, and the Lord took his life*), Onan subsequently refuses to engage in sexual relations with Tamar as an act of levirate marriage, and is killed by God. From Scripture itself, we only know one thing about Onan: he refuses to fulfill the apparent obligation of levirate marriage. The "thing" that *displeased God* about Er is never made explicit. The Talmud (Yebamot 34b) makes this "displeasing act" (committed both by Er and Onan) sexual:

both Er and Onan spill their seed rather than copulate with Tamar.[33] Without much textual evidence to the contrary, this position quickly becomes the standard reading of these verses.

Zohar 1.186b attempts to bring support to the Talmudic reading, drawing a parallel between the words describing Er's action, *ra b'eynei Ha-Shem* (evil in the eyes of God) (Genesis 38:7), and the same word *(ra)* in Genesis 8:21 referring to the inappropriate sexual behavior of the generation of the Flood *(the devisings of man's mind are evil* [ra] *from his youth)*. Rashi, citing b.T. Yebamot 34b, suggests that Er did not want to impregnate Tamar for fear that her pregnancy would destroy her beauty. This last comment, couched in the Zohar's linguistic reading, becomes the basis of R. Mordecai Joseph's vindication of Er and Onan.

R. Mordecai Joseph interprets Genesis 38:7, which is explicit in its vilification of both Er and Onan, in such a way as to suggest that Er and Onan were acting out of pious restraint, a trait they inherited from Jacob. That is, they did not want to come upon Tamar until they felt sure their intentions were pure. This act of pious restraint only becomes a sin when taken to an extreme. Referring to the Talmudic explanation of Er's and Onan's intentions cited by Rashi, R. Mordecai Joseph vindicates them by replacing Tamar in the story with the *Shekhina*. Er and Onan's intentions are thereby spiritualized and reinterpreted as devekut with the *Shekhina*. The phrase cited by Rashi, that Er and Onan refused Tamar "so as to not damage her beauty," is reread here to refer to the beauty of the human ability to achieve devekut. Tamar's beauty now refers to the beauty of the experience of unity with God. The adjective "beauty" which, in the rabbinic reading, refers to Tamar, is transformed into an adverb describing the experience of devekut. The transference of adjectives to adverbs is a fairly conventional midrashic move, especially popular in Kabbala and Hasidism. The un-midrashic result here is that this midrashic/Hasidic twist results in a complete reformulation of the whole incident, transforming biblical villains into pietistic heroes.

What is intriguing here and highlights a characteristic of Hasidic (as well as other postrabbinic) hermeneutics, which differs from classical midrash, is that the status of Rashi's comment on the verse, essentially an adaptation of a Talmudic text, is elevated from an interpretation of the text to the text itself. According to R. Mordecai Joseph, there is no longer any distinction between the verse—which mentions nothing of Tamar's beauty as a motivating factor for Er and Onan's actions—and Rashi's interpretation of that verse. What our Hasidic text does is to allow Rashi's interpretation of the verse to become the exclusive lens through which the verse is read and then turns Rashi against himself via Kabbalistic nomenclature (i.e., reading Tamar as the *Shekhina*), in order to construct a radical rereading of the entire episode. What results is the vindication of Er and Onan, a reading Rashi would surely have rejected. Once the adjective "beauty" describing Tamar becomes an adverb, describing one's experiential closeness to God, the entire motivation of Er and Onan moves from the inappropriate and base infatuation with her physical beauty to the protection of the pietistic value of devotion.[34]

Perhaps aware of the tenuous nature of such a reading, R. Mordecai Joseph roots his position in the Mishna (Mishna Avot 2:1), which states that proper action is the combination of that which is done for one's own benefit and to benefit others. R. Mordecai Joseph suggests that "to benefit others" in the Mishna means to give credence to the true nature of the human being and the telos of human behavior, communion with God (devekut). R. Mordecai Joseph continues:

> The life force [lit., "drop of life"—the origin of semen] descending from the mind cannot result in birth until it has become physical in the semen of man.[35] At that moment there is a break [and thus a forgetting] in [the] human consciousness [of God]. If one constantly has his mind on the Creator, he cannot bring himself to engage in this concealment and forgetting of God which is necessary for pro-creation. Therefore Er was focused on "benefiting the form of man." This means that he had a clear mind that was always involved in communion with God and thus did not want to destroy that experience. This is the meaning [in Rashi] of not wanting to destroy her beauty, i.e., the beauty of Israel [in their ability to commune with God].[36]

The apparent sin of both Er and Onan is no longer a sin of selfishness or inappropriate sexual behavior (as the Bible intimates and the rabbis affirm) but an extreme example of the character of Jacob, who asks God for a tranquil life void of doubt and decisions.[37] This resembles the classic Hasidic depiction of Nadav and Avihu, the sons of Aaron, who, as pietistic heroes, are killed as a result of bringing "strange fire" before God (Leviticus 10:1; Numbers 3:4, 26:61).[38] For R. Mordecai Joseph, the episode of Er and Onan is surely a tragedy of acting against divine will, but one that has pure pietistic intentions. It is born out of an unwillingness to temper the yearning for devekut with a commitment to the world, an overextension of Jacob that results in the imperfect temperament of Isaac without the compassion of Abraham. Er and Onan become overly spiritualized descendants of Judah, exhibiting a critical flaw in the messianic personality that is not yet fully and permanently actualized.

Judah steps in to redeem his son's mistakes by having intercourse with Tamar, who subsequently gives birth to Perez and Zerah and initiates the messianic lineage (Genesis 38:27–30). Judah's decision to copulate with Tamar (which is formally forbidden according to the biblical laws of incest) is the result of his ability to maintain a state of devekut even during the very moment (i.e., sexual intercourse) that yields forgetfulness. The unique ability to simultaneously be in the world and beyond it is the trait of the fully actualized human being and is the personality of the Messiah. Judah's quasi-transgressive liaison with his daughter-in-law (Tamar) is the full actualization of Jacob. Judah is able to understand that this behavior, which is outside the halakha, was needed to fulfill God's will. What results is nothing less than the beginning of the Davidic line. Parenthetically, it is not insignificant that this trait of being able to maintain a state of devekut during moments of distraction is also reflected in Maimonides' depiction of the unique prophetic quality of Moses, who also has a messianic vocation.[39]

R. Mordecai Joseph's correlation between Moses and Jacob, implying Judah as well, may very well have been influenced by Maimonides' position on Moses, although no explicit reference is made to Maimonides in these texts. It is more likely that he is commenting on the Zohar's correlation of Moses and Jacob that is developed in Lurianic Kabbala, adding to this mix the messianic figure of Judah.[40]

As interesting an interpretation of Er and Onan as this may be, our Hasidic masters cannot simply ignore God's explicit dissatisfaction in the narrative. Basing his reading on a Zoharic and Lurianic interpretation of similar texts, R. Mordecai Joseph concludes that Er and Onan are redeemed in their death because Perez and Zerah, the sons of Tamar and the beginning of the messianic Davidic lineage, inherited their souls through reincarnation *(sod ha-yebum).*[41] Perhaps the most telling comment in this reading of the story is the following passage:

> On those two [Perez and Zerah] God said, *She* [*Tamar*] *is more right* [*zidka*], *than I* [*mimeni,* lit., from me] [Genesis 38:26]. . . . A voice [*bat kol*] went forth [regarding] these secret matters [*devarim kevushim*].[42] This means that even though Er and Onan were not fit in His eyes, those two [i.e., their souls] were fit. Even though it appeared that Perez acted against the halakha as we find in the Kingdom of David, God testified that their actions were justified, according to the verse, *It is the time to act for God, for they have forsaken my Torah.*[43] Even though it appeared that the sin of Er was greater than that of Onan, nevertheless, the soul of Er was greater than that of Onan since from his soul was born the soul of the Kingdom of David.[44]

What is suggested here is that Er's behavior was an extreme example of the "urge" of Abraham not properly filtered through the integrated personality of Jacob. Er's sin was his unwillingness to sacrifice a moment of devekut in order to fulfill the mitzvah of levirate marriage and procreation through the act of sexual intercourse, even as that act of procreation would result in the birth of the messianic lineage. From this Hasidic perspective, Er's action is both transgressive and heroic simultaneously!

This reformulation of a problematic personality in the Bible is not new in the Izbica/Radzin tradition. For example, in both Hasidic and Kabbalistic exegesis, there is a whole tradition that attempts to argue for the viability of Korah's position in his confrontation with Moses for the right of being High Priest (Numbers 16:1–35). However, even as rabbinic tradition vilifies Korah beyond the biblical narrative, his rebellion has some legitimacy. In the case of Er, however, nothing redeemable is readily apparent, either in the Bible or in the Talmud or midrashim. Although the Bible never tells us why Er was killed, perhaps *precisely* because the Bible never tells us why he was killed, the rabbinic and Zoharic readings are taken by later readers as the simple meaning of the text.[45] For example, this gives license to the Zohar to draw a correlation between Er and Onan and the generation of the flood, linking pre-Abrahamic and post-Jacobean civilization. R. Mordecai Joseph, unlike the Zohar, refrains from drawing any correlation between Er and the generation of the flood. For our Hasidic writers, who view post-Jacobean Israel as purified of sin, Er's and Onan's behavior, while transgressive, must be rooted in a deeper sense of mistaken piety. This behavior, while punishable in this world, will be rewarded in the next. In a sense, not unlike Judah, Korah, and Zimri, Er is the victim of overextending his redemptive personality in a world yet unredeemed.

The Messianic Hero Reconstructed: Moses and Rabbi Akiba

The next manifestation of the determinist religion in Izbica/Radzin can be seen through a radical rereading of the midrash which speaks of the relationship between Moses and Rabbi Akiba.[46] The correlation between Moses and Rabbi Akiba is quite common in classical rabbinic literature. Moses is the giver of the law and Rabbi Akiba is its master interpreter.

> Rabbi Yehuda said in the name of Rav: When Moses ascended on high he found the Holy One, blessed be He, engaged in affixing crowns to the letters. Moses said, "Lord of the Universe, who stays Your hand?" God answered, "There will rise a man at the end of many generations, Akiba son of Joseph will be his name, who will expound upon each title, and draw out heaps of laws." "Lord of the Universe," said Moses, "permit me to see him." God replied, "Turn around." Moses went and sat down in the eighth row [and listened to the words of Akiba]. Not being able to follow his argument he became discomforted, but when they came to a certain subject, and the disciples said to their teacher, "From where do we know this?" the latter replied, "It is a law given to Moshe at Sinai!" Moses was then comforted. He turned to God and said, "Lord of the Universe. You have such a man and yet You give the Torah to me?" God replied, "Be silent, for such is My decree!" [47]

This mythic meeting of the two great figures in the Jewish imagination plays an important role in Lurianic Kabbala.[48] In some early mystical texts, Rabbi Akiba's and Moses' names are even interchanged. The substance of the aforementioned Talmudic midrash in b.T. Menahot 29b sets Rabbi Akiba against Moses, praising Rabbi Akiba's talent in exegesis yet warning the reader that his creative method of "innovative exegesis drawn from the crowns of the letters" does not supersede the authority of Moses' prophecy *(halakha l'moshe m'Sinai).* However, Moses appears to remain somewhat unnerved even after Rabbi Akiba submits to his authority. It is, perhaps, not only Moses' inability to understand the exegetical technique of Rabbi Akiba but the strangeness of the whole rabbinic enterprise.[49] Viewing Moses in the spiritual lineage of Judah and Rabbi Akiba in the lineage of Joseph, R. Mordecai Joseph and R. Gershon Henokh transform this midrashic reading from a praise of Rabbi Akiba (and thus a praise of rabbinic legalism and exegesis) to a praise of Moses as one who gives the law through revelation yet cannot fully understand the purpose of the law outside of revelation.

The portrayal of Moses in *Mei Ha-Shiloah* begins with a comparison of Moses and Isaac. As mentioned earlier, Isaac is viewed as the archetype who could not see beyond the letter of the law, illustrated by his failed attempt to bless Esau simply because he is his biological firstborn. Isaac is a kind of pre-Jacobean prelude to the character of Joseph. This observation of Isaac is used to justify his sincere attempt to give Esau the blessing, as conventional tradition dictates that the firstborn indeed inherit the father's primary blessing:[50] "*When Isaac was old and his eyes were too dim to see* [Genesis 27:1]. The idea [character] of Isaac is the opposite of Moses. Isaac was not permitted to leave the Land of Israel, but the power of sight was taken from him. Moses was not permitted to enter Israel, but it is said of him, *and see with your eyes* [Deuteronomy 3:27]."[51] This text must be compared with two others where R. Mordecai Joseph implies that Moses might have attained a purer state of prophecy even than Jacob in that, for him, the distinction between intellect and intuition had entirely disappeared.[52] Jacob is able to fully integrate his intellect with his intuitive faculty and thus able to apprehend the presence of God in the world. He is also able to see the need for devotion outside of his own illumination. That is, although he has intellectually achieved full reconciliation, recognizing the illusory nature of the fragmented world, for him, the distinction between divine and human will still remain intact, even as he sees them as aligned. That is why he is able to tolerate those not yet refined. Moses, described as the mouth of God,[53] like Judah, cannot maintain this compromising position. He finds it difficult to comprehend any sense of disunity between the human and the divine and consequently is in constant conflict with his constituency, all of whom live within the very disunified consciousness he finds intolerable.

This reading of Moses is perhaps best expressed in R. Mordecai Joseph's comparison of the wisdom of Moses to the wisdom of Solomon. Solomon's wisdom represents a wisdom that is available to the whole world. However, Solomon feels that when he communicates his wisdom, he does not fully comprehend it. This emerges as a play on the verse in Ecclesiastes 7: 23, *All this is tested with wisdom, I thought I could fathom it, but it eludes me.* Moses, however, has fully integrated his own wisdom and understands it perfectly but cannot communicate it to others (*But Moses said to God, "Please, O God, I have never been a man of words"* [Exodus 4:10]). As we saw earlier with Jacob, the perfected personality, or the personality of redemption, is by definition deficient in the preredemptive world. Without some deficiency, he would have surely brought about redemption. In R. Mordecai Joseph's understanding of the responsibility of the messianic personality, the goal is to move Israel from the wisdom of Solomon to the wisdom of Moses. At such time, the proper communicator will emerge.[54]

While it appears that R. Mordecai Joseph maintains that Moses is even more spiritually refined than Jacob, R. Gershon Henokh, using the identical model, suggests that Moses' constant state of illumination was actually a deficiency:

> *Moses is from the inside and Jacob is from the outside* [Tikkunei Zohar, *tikun* 13, 29b]. This means that for Moses there was no difference between the garment and what it enveloped. For Jacob, even though internally he

> possessed the same light as Moses, the light was distinguishable from what enveloped it. Therefore, he wanted to bring the "*small vessels*" from over the Jabbok ford, the letters in the word Jabbok [YBK] symbolizing all the permutations of God's Name. . . . He wanted to shine the light even to the farthest corners so that he would be able to possess them and thus bring out the light [of God which was in them].[55]

The deficiency in Moses is his inability to communicate his realization of unity or tolerate those who have not achieved that unity. Having unified his imaginative and rational faculties (this is Maimonides' definition of the uniqueness of Moses' prophecy in *Mishneh Torah*), Moses loses the ability to tolerate those who do not share his experience. The depth of Moses' inability to understand his constituency and be understood *by* them is illustrated in the mythic narrative between Moses and his older brother Aaron.

> It can thus be explained. Moses our teacher recognized that God first chooses an individual only after he attains the power of choice [*koah habehira*] in his worship [*b'avodato*]. Hence [he realizes] that *everything* is from God. This is what is meant in the midrash Tanhuma [parshat] Zav: 8, "*baharu ve lo kirvu*" [he is chosen yet is not drawn near].[56] Rather, he draws himself near. Aaron the Priest recognized that God's choosing an individual is the consequence of the individual's worship and passion to draw himself near to God. This is called "*kirvu ve lo baharu*" [he is drawn near and not chosen].[57] In truth, even if at first blush these models appear in opposition, in truth they come from the same source.[58]

In this text, Moses' experience of revelation and the unity of his will with the divine diminishes his ability to understand human worship as the foundation of and condition for devekut. According to Moses, the passion and focus of human devotion is the externalization of already being chosen and not a condition for being chosen. That is, devotion should be an expression of and not a preparation for devekut. The human struggle for perfection and the battle between human desire and divine will is foreign to Moses. In a sense, Moses' achievement results in his transcending his humanness and, as a result, he cannot fully understand the challenge of human imperfection, the very foundation and condition for mitzvot.

This Mosaic trait is then used to explain the numerous instances in the Torah where he appears to be unable to fully comprehend the people's failure to absorb the Sinaitic revelation. R. Mordecai Joseph illustrates this feature in the need for the second commandment of the Decalogue. The opaque typology of Judah and Joseph now becomes fully transparent in the mythic encounter between Moses and Rabbi Akiba. Commenting on the statement in b.T. Menahot 29b discussed earlier, he states:

> [Moses was troubled because] he saw how Rabbi Akiba developed the word [commandment], *There shall be no other gods before Me* to include so many "fences." It is known that the root of everything is *I am the Lord Your God* and *There shall be no other gods* only exists to protect one from becoming distant from God.[59] Moses was troubled until he [Rabbi Akiba] reached one halakha whereby Moses saw why all of these "fences" were necessary. [Rabbi Akiba] said "this is a law from Moses at Sinai." This reinforces that *I am the Lord your God* is the foundation of the Torah as it is written, *Hear O Israel*. . . is the foundation of the Torah. *There shall be no other gods* . . . is only to protect Israel from drifting away from *I am the Lord your God.* At that moment, Moses was appeased [*nitka'ara da'ato*] for he realized that he [Moses] had been given the fundamental principle [*ha-ikkar*].[60]

The last statement displays Moses' coming to understand the need for what we have come to know as halakha. His initial reaction to halakha ("fences") is one of bewilderment. For one who has fully integrated the commandment of *I am the Lord your God,* the second commandment and thus the fences derived from the exegetical practice of Rabbi Akiba seem superfluous. The resolution of the law comes about only when Moses realizes that the "fences" (halakha) are necessary for those who have not fully integrated the revelation. It is only then that Moses recognizes that the Jewish people as a whole still live in a fragmented world.

The above-cited texts, both by R. Mordecai Joseph and R. Gershon Henokh, portray Moses as the true inheritor of Judah. Rabbi Akiba, the rabbinic hero and perhaps the archetype of the Lithuanian Mithnagdim, reflects the outlook of Isaac, Joseph, and Ephraim. Ephraim's inability to understand Judah is reflected in Moses' inability to understand the vocation of Rabbi Akiba. In short, the integrative personality, whose search for God cannot be limited by the confines of halakha, can only accept the need for halakha when he understands that most others do not share his vision of God. This is what finally appeases Moses in the midrash. Alternatively, the ability of the halakhic personality to accept the viability of the integrated messianic personality can only truly come about when he too shares the illumination of unity.

Arguably this reading turns the Talmudic midrash on its head. The Talmudic sages, as inheritors of Rabbi Akiba, create this myth in order to validate and even celebrate the rabbinic enterprise. Moses' eventual acquiescence to Rabbi Akiba, after realizing that he (Moses) is still the foundation of the Talmudic dialectics he does not understand, is meant, in one reading, to connect rabbinic Judaism to Sinai. In a sense, R. Mordecai Joseph offers an antirabbinic reading of the story. Moses, as the Judah archetype, only accepts Rabbi Akiba (who is, after all, "ben Joseph") after realizing that Rabbi Akiba and his spiritual inheritors simply cannot understand the first commandment (the reconciliation of the human and the divine) without the aid of the second commandment ("fences," or halakha). R. Mordecai Joseph's reading appears to be based on a Lurianic rendition of this midrash taught by R. Hayyim Vital, which attempts to maintain Moses' superiority in light of his inability to understand Rabbi Akiba.

> It is written in Bamidbar Rabba 19:6, "That which was revealed to R. Akiba was not revealed to Moses." But the rabbis said, "even that which a faithful student will ask his teacher in the future was revealed to Moses."[61] This raises a [significant] discrepancy. It can be explained thus: Moses was aware of everything that would be revealed in the future—he knew the entire Torah. However, all that he knew he knew [solely] "by way of the mouth" [directly via revelation]. He did not know how to draw out this knowledge via *drush* or hints from verses in Scripture, each one in its proper place. This began with the sages. Each sage was able to draw out the appropriate *drush*. So it was with R. Akiba. He knew all of those crowns of the letters, implying *halakhot*. The substance of each one was revealed to Moses. What wasn't revealed to him was what each crown hinted to in Scripture. R. Akiba came and drew them out from the points [of the crowns] of the letters by saying "this point hints to this *drush*—and this to this. . . ."[62]

Vital reads the midrash in Bamidbar Rabba (and by implication b.T. Menahot 29b) in opposition to the midrash about Moses' overarching knowledge of Torah, even the Torah that will emerge in the future. In a general sense, what is implied here is a dichotomy between the prophet and the sage, a conventional trope played out throughout rabbinic exegesis.[63] Here Moses' knowledge was solely the result of revelation, and thus he is puzzled by Rabbi Akiba's rabbinic enterprise of interpretation. Whereas Rabbi Akiba is the one who acquires knowledge of God's will via Torah (he is the prototypic Torah sage), Moses has little need for Torah in the conventional sense. Torah for him is the externalization of the revelatory experience, but it is not a tool to explicate the substance of that experience.

This reading by Vital may also be an attempt to transform the prophet/sage dichotomy in rabbinic literature into the inspired mystic/rabbinic model in sixteenth-century Kabbala. In numerous places Vital argues that the authority of Luria's teaching is rooted in *gilluy Eliyahu* (revelation of the prophet Elijah). Gershom Scholem sets this claim within the context of trans-scriptural authority:

> And yet, for all their glaring novelty [i.e., the creative innovations of Luria] they were not regarded as a break with traditional authority. This was possible because the authority of the Prophet Elijah was claimed for them—a claim that was widely recognized thanks to Luria's impressive personality and piety. Thus Luria's source of inspiration became a new authority in its own right. . . . The mystical experience that was his source is still as authentic as any, and as high in rank as any earlier phenomenon in the world of Rabbinic Judaism.[64]

Thus Luria's Kabbalistic discourse is not, and need not be, exegetical in nature as his authority is rooted in mystical inspiration unmediated by Scripture. Moses is depicted here as a similar type of inspired individual who is not as disturbed by Rabbi Akiba's conclusions (trans-scriptural) as much as the method he utilizes to draw out those conclusions and the general need for them. Thus, when Rabbi Akiba invokes the rabbinic dictum, "This is a law from Moses at Sinai [*halakha l'Moshe m'Sinai*]," Moses is appeased precisely because this is the way Moses received the entire body of divine teaching. That is, *halakha l'Moshe m'Sinai* is a basis for law purely via revelation without any source in Scripture.[65]

In the Izbica/Radzin tradition, drawing from implications embedded in Lurianic Kabbala, the depiction of Moses as the inspired prophet who cannot fathom the need for either Scripture or halakha is indicative of the messianic personality in general, for which Moses is the archetype. Torah and its explication are essential for one who has not attained (or cannot maintain) the intimate unity with divine will. For such an individual, God's will is always mediated through Scripture and its authoritative interpretation. The integrated personality—Judah/Messiah—has transcended the need for Torah even as he continues to live in a world where Torah is necessary. Therefore, as cited above, "he [the messianic person who has achieved complete clarification] can be expansive in his actions, for surely God is with him." We can see how Vital's text, which has its own polemical agenda, serves the Izbica/Radzin tradition as an authentic voice in understanding the inner-Israelite tension in the protomessianic world.[66]

Pinhas and Zimri: The Naive Hero and the Messianic Underside of the Villain

The exegetical trajectory introduced in this chapter can now help us understand the problematic interpretation of R. Mordecai Joseph's reading of the incident with Pinhas and Zimri in Numbers 25:6–9, an interpretation that has caused so much controversy in the study of this Hasidic literature.[67] I am less interested in the bold and provocative vindication of Zimri's action in *Mei Ha-Shiloah* and *Sod Yesharim,* as such vindication is not unprecedented in rabbinic, medieval, and early modern Jewish literature. What is indeed striking and, in my mind, a clear example of how Izbica/Radzin determinism is implemented in its exegesis, is the mythic dialogue between Moses and Pinhas immediately preceding Pinhas' zealous murder of Zimri, a dialogue that is born in the rabbinic imagination and subsequently finds its way into Rashi's commentary to the Pentateuch.

The biblical narrative is quite short and unfolds as follows: While encamped in Shittim, immediately following the episode with Balak and Balaam, the Israelites came under the influence of the Moabite tribes and began partaking of their idolatrous practices, including ritual prostitution. God was incensed and ordered Moses to "impale" the deviants guilty of this abomination. Moses immediately orders his tribal leaders to slay those in his tribe who were guilty. At this time an anonymous Israelite ("one of the Israelites") approached the tent of meeting with a Midianite woman. What he did with her is not made explicit. However, given that Midianite women were forbidden to Israel, the implication was that he engaged in a public display of sexuality as an act of unabashed rebellion against Moses. Pinhas, who was a grandson of Aaron the Priest, followed the two "into the chamber" and stabbed both of them to death. As a result of this act of violence, the plague, which God brought on the Israelites, subsided. Pinhas' apparent heroism resulted in God granting him a special pact of the priesthood, both for him and his generations. Only after the description of Pinhas' reward are the identities of the two transgressors made known. The man was Zimri, son of Salu, the chieftain of the tribe of Shimon. The woman was Kozbi, daughter of Zur, the head of the Midianite tribe.

The rabbinic tradition takes advantage of the thinness of the biblical narrative by creating a mythic encounter between Moses and Pinhas that serves as the foundation of almost all postrabbinic readings of this episode. According to b.T. Sanhedrin 82a, when Pinhas witnesses Zimri and Kozbi engaging in an illicit sexual encounter in front of the entire assembly (Numbers 25:6–8), he approaches Moses and demands immediate action. The Talmud presents the following narrative:

> He [Pinhas] saw the action and was reminded of the halakha. He approached Moses and said, "We have received from you [the halakha] that one who has sex with an Amorite woman, should be attacked by the

zealous." Moses replied, "You have learned the law [lit., you have read the document] so you must act upon it."[68]

The central question here is why Moses refuses to fulfill the halakha himself. That is, why does Moses not, both as leader of the nation and recipient of God's command, stop this egregious behavior and enact judgment against Zimri and Kozbi? The rabbinic introduction of the Zimri episode creates the question that marks the beginning, and stands at the center, of our Hasidic reading. The following is how R. Mordecai Joseph understands this question.

> *It shall be for him* [*Pinhas*] *and his descendants after him a pact of priesthood for all time, because he took impassioned action for his God, thus making expiation for the Israelites. The name of the Israelite who was killed, the one who was killed with the Midianite woman, was Zimri son of Salu. . . .* (Numbers 25:12–14) . . . This means that after the act, God revealed to Pinhas with whom he was doing battle so that he should not think that he [Zimri] was a complete adulterer [*no'ef*], God forbid. Pinhas, because he was from the seed of Joseph who is perfected through trials and tests and through these very acts [of illicit behavior] viewed this act of Zimri as evil.[69] On this it is said, *I fell in love with Israel, When he was still a child* [Hosea 11:1]. This refers to Pinhas who judged Zimri as merely guilty of inappropriate sexual behavior. Therefore, he judged him according to the principle, "the zealous should attack him." However, the depth of this whole incident was hidden from him [Pinhas] for she [Kozbi] was his [Zimri's] soulmate from the sixth day of creation, as it is written in *Kitve Ari z'l.*[70] Therefore, Moses did not explicitly dictate that he should be killed.[71] In this action, Pinhas was like a naive one [lit., child, *na'ar*].[72] He did not know the depths of this incident and only judged Zimri according to his rational faculties. Nevertheless God loved him, and agreed with him, in that he acted according to his reason and risked his life.[73]

As mentioned above, most of the earlier sources vindicating Zimri, including the Lurianic passage referred to in our text, offer a retrospective reading of the episode suggesting that, whatever Zimri's intentions may have been, his copulation with Kozbi was destined to have taken place. I will briefly summarize three earlier vindications of Zimri to show that, while certainly provocative, they fall short of the radical interpretation of R. Mordecai Joseph.

In his *Tiferet Yonatan,* the eighteenth-century halakhist and Kabbalist R. Yonatan Eyebshutz goes further than most to claim that Zimri's intentions are indeed *correct* in principle, even as he was *mistaken* in taking the divine decree of such a union as applicable to him (i.e., to Zimri) at that particular time. The provocative nature of this reading is that the transgressive nature of the act (as a Midianite, Kozbi was forbidden to an Israelite) is maintained. Eyebshutz's attempt to justify the act, in principle but not in practice, is founded on the rabbinic reading of Moses' ambiguity. That is, Moses refuses to hold Zimri accountable and to enact justice himself, but permits, or even advises, Pinhas to do as he wishes. Eyebshutz surmises from this ambiguity that while Zimri was wrong to perform the act, the act itself, in another time and place, may be appropriate. Knowing this, Moses does not want his actions to be interpreted as a general proscription of such a union.

In the Lurianic rendition, and in its adaptation in Eyebshutz, Zimri's act is viewed as an unintentional act of transgression *(shegagah)* but not a sin. That is, Zimri's intentions and intuitions were correct that he and Kozbi were destined to be together, even though the act may have been "mistaken." This again appears to be the result of Moses' inaction and unwillingness to do what God told him to do (*Take all the ringleaders and have them publicly impaled before the LORD, so that the LORD's wrath may turn away from Israel.* [Numbers 25:4]). By employing the transmigration of souls *(torat ha gilgul)* as a hermeneutical trope, Luria views Zimri and Kozbi as soulmates. However, he too cannot let go of the mistaken nature of the act, applying the law of "unintentional sin," thereby liberating both Zimri and Kozbi from the death penalty. Thus, Moses refuses to act.

R. Zaddok Ha-Kohen of Lublin, a disciple of R. Mordecai Joseph and contemporary of R. Gershon Henokh, reads this incident in a similar way, citing *Tiferet Yonatan* rather than *Mei Ha-Shiloah* as his source. R. Zaddok apparently feels more comfortable seeing the act as a mistake, as opposed to R. Mordecai Joseph who views it as necessary and even praiseworthy. A close reading of R. Zaddok will show that by importing Eyebshutz into *Mei Ha-Shiloah*'s more radical reading, he is attempting to soften his master's startling rendition of the story.

R. Mordecai Joseph suggests that Moses' refusal to personally punish Zimri is due to his knowledge that Zimri's behavior is essentially correct, both in principle and in actuality. Only R. Mordecai Joseph dares to suggest Moses' full acknowledgment of the correctness of Zimri's action. Pinhas, embodying the Joseph lineage in Numbers 25, is unable to understand the correctness of Zimri's action, thereby justifying the implementation of the halakhic principle, "the zealots will render justice [lit., they will/should attack and destroy the sinner]." What *Mei Ha-Shiloah* does not provide is an original justification of Zimri's behavior. R. Mordecai Joseph simply refers in passing to a comment in Lurianic Kabbala (without any reference) linking Zimri and Kozbi as fated soulmates.

The missing link in the Izbica/Radzin reading of this episode is the fully disclosed reference to the lineage of Zimri expressed in a Lurianic text. We find a subtle reference to that text earlier in *Mei Ha-Shiloah,* 1:13:

> *Jacob arrived safely in the city of Shechem . . . and he encamped before the city* [Genesis 33:18]. *Before the city* refers to the honorable among its residents. Who were they? They were Shechem and Hamor. The language *encamped* [*ve'yihen*] can be read to mean that they found favor [*hen*] in his [Jacob's] eyes. It is said in the writings of the Ari [R. Isaac Luria] that Shechem was reincarnated in Zimri son of Salu son of Dina.[74] Therefore, he [Shechem] desired her [Dina] even now. However, it says, *My son Shechem longs for your daughter* [Genesis 34:8]. This means that he didn't want to marry the daughters of his land but only Dina. This also explains why Jacob was fond of him, for he had some connection to Jacob.[75]

R. Mordecai Joseph's mention of Zimri's lineage in his commentary to Genesis as well as the connection between Zimri (through Shechem) to Jacob is significant for an understanding of our passage in Numbers. This is especially true in light of Moses being a fully actualized dimension of Jacob in the Moses/Rabbi Akiba midrash discussed above. The Jacob/Moses connection places Moses and Zimri on the same continuum. This also explains why Judah, who, according to the Kabbalists, is the spiritual ancestor of Moses, refuses to be involved in saving Dina and destroying Shechem (Genesis 34:25–31). The story of Dina and Shechem is an important intertext to the Pinhas episode, at least as read by R. Mordecai Joseph, in that the latter seems to replay the drama of the former.

The subtle allusion to the Lurianic reference in the Pinhas narrative is integrated into the wider interpretive scheme here. Luria states that Zimri is the son of Dina and Shimon and the spiritual inheritor of Shechem ben Hamor, transmitted through his insemination of her before her marriage to Shimon.[76] We can now read the episode of the rape of Dina and subsequent marriage to Shimon against the Pinhas narrative and its rabbinic reading. Moses, viewed as the recipient of Jacob's integrated personality in both *Mei Ha-Shiloah* and *Sod Yesharim,* refrains from punishing Zimri, whose connection to Dina and Shechem has been established. Instead he allows and even encourages Pinhas (i.e., the Joseph personality) to act instead. What Luria has accomplished through *gilgul* is the creation of a direct line from Moses to Zimri through Shechem, Dina, and Jacob.

Stepping back for a moment from Moses in Numbers to Jacob in Genesis, Shimon and Levi, both of whom are viewed by R. Mordecai Joseph in a pre-Jacobean mode (Shimon as Abraham and Levi as Isaac),[77] carry out the punishment on Shechem, while Jacob is openly angry at both of them for their violent behavior. Like Moses, Jacob seems unable, or at least unwilling, to enact justice on Shechem for his desire for Dina. In short, R. Mordecai Joseph views the Pinhas/Zimri episode in Numbers as a replay of the Dina/Shechem incident in Genesis. Jacob and Moses are aligned as the integrated messianic personalities, both of whom refrain from punishing what each views as a necessary, albeit problematic, encounter (Jacob with Shechem, Moses with Zimri). Judah's part in this story is less clear. He is aligned with Jacob in Genesis in that he refrains from aiding his brothers in the rescue of Dina and the slaughtering of Shechem. Judah's passivity in light of Shimon's and Levi's revenge of Shechem is likened to Jacob's unwillingness to punish Shechem for taking Dina as a wife. Jacob's silence in the Dina episode, Judah's passivity in the revenge of Shechem, and Moses' unwillingness to kill Zimri are all viewed as actions of the messianic person who sees that God's will is sometimes manifest outside the normative framework of what we can anachronistically call "halakha."

Shechem and Zimri are aligned Kabbalistically as having blood ties through Dina that translate in our Hasidic narrative as having noble, albeit overly ambitious, intentions. One significant difference between the messianic personality as exemplified in Jacob and that of Moses in our two stories is that Jacob is openly angry with Shimon (and Levi) for avenging Dina's fate, while Moses is at best ambivalent about Zimri and Kozbi and shows no emotion when Pinhas finally kills them. However, R. Mordecai Joseph nuances the oddity of Moses' detachment by noting that Jacob denies Shimon (and Levi) a blessing in Genesis 49:5–7.[78] Moses, in his blessings to the Israelite tribes in Deuteronomy 33, extends the wrath of Jacob by denying the tribe of Shimon a blessing, rebuking them for not modeling themselves after the tribe of Judah.

> *Hear, God, the voice of Judah and restore him to his people* [Deuteronomy 33:7]. Here we have a hint to the blessing to Shimon. The 12 tribes constitute the appendages of the *Shekhina,* as was taught in the holy Zohar.[79] Reuben is the eyes of the *Shekhina* as he has clear vision of God. Shimon is the ears of the *Shekhina* and Judah is the heart of the *Shekhina,* for his heart is pure and has undergone the necessary refinements [*berurim*].[80] This is the meaning of the verse *Hear, God, the voice of Judah*—the tribe of Shimon should heed the voice of Judah, for Shimon is in constant need of refinement [*berurim*] as was explained regarding the verse *And Isaac loved Esau* [Genesis 25:28].[81]

The comment at the end of Genesis 25:28 is an important part of the larger exegetical scheme of R. Mordecai Joseph's reading of the Pinhas/Zimri narrative. The issue being discussed there is the danger of entering into a precarious situation (doubt) as opposed to remaining safely within the realm of certainty (the four ells of halakha). I will pick up in the middle of this long text, where the dichotomy between Jacob and Esau is reflected in the incident with Dina in Genesis 33.

> [The difficulty Isaac had with Jacob was that Jacob] avoided entering into the realm of doubt, relying solely upon God. Every time one enters into the realm of doubt in his worship of God or things that require clarification [*berur*], if proper refinement was achieved he becomes greater than one who never entered into doubt at all. This is only the case for the seed of Jacob [i.e., excluding Esau who sold his birthright to be an inheriting seed of Jacob]. For the seed of Jacob has a strong trust in God that everything is for the good.[82] This allows them to enter into the realm of doubt. One who does not have this trust cannot enter into doubt. . . . One who is not from the seed of Jacob, it is better to confine himself with all manners of limitations [*zimzumim*] as it is said that converts should not enter into the realm of doubt.[83]. . . The nation of Israel also has souls who can enter into areas of doubt more than others even though both are from the seed of Jacob. An example would be the incident with Shimon and Dina. Levi did not really want to rescue her for he feared that perhaps his intentions were not for the sake of heaven. The tribe of Levi embodies the attribute of reverence [*yerah*] and the avoidance of doubtful situations as it is written about them *Know, then, that I have sent this charge to you that My covenant with Levi may endure—said the Lord of Hosts. I had with him a covenant of life and well-being, which I gave to him, and of reverence* [*yerah*], *which he showed me*. (Malachi 2:4,5). Therefore the priestly class emerged from Levi who could enter the Holy of Holies. . . . Shimon, however, entered into the realm of doubt and said to himself, "I am not doing this for selfish reasons, God forbid!" He then married Dina and entered into a relationship that required further refinement [*berurim*]. Since he [wrongfully] thought that his intentions in rescuing Dina from Shechem were noble and pure, his descendants [the tribe of Shimon], had to undergo a continuous process of clarification. This emerges again in Zimri [Shimon's descendant] who also thought his intentions were noble as I explained in its place. However, when Shimon undergoes this process of refinement, their place will be higher than that of Levi.[84]

This text both deepens and expands our understanding of the Pinhas/Zimri episode in the Izbica/Radzin tradition. Guilty of hubris, Shimon is juxtaposed to Zimri not only genealogically (via Luria's reading), but ideologically as well. Even more strongly, Zimri's action and his subsequent murder at the hands of Pinhas are now viewed as a necessary step in repairing Shimon's avenging Dina by killing Shechem and the inhabitants of his city. Shimon and Zimri's mistake was not their action (as Shimon was also destined to marry Dina and needed to get her away from Shechem to do so) but entering into a dubious situation *(safek)* without adequate self-scrutiny *(berurim).*

These two episodes include three passive characters, all of whom represent the messianic personage: Jacob, Judah, and Moses, all of whom understand the wrongful nature of the act in question but also see the necessity of the respective episodes having taken place. Pinhas plays a critical role here. According to our Hasidic reading, he is the spiritual inheritor of Joseph, the *na'ar,* or innocent one whose intentions are noble but who does not see the divine hand at work.[85] Pinhas' violence toward Zimri is reminiscent of Shimon and Levi's murderous act of Shechem (as depicted by Jacob in Genesis 49:6) yet exhibits a significantly more refined dimension. Before acting rashly, Pinhas approaches Moses (the Jacobean/Judean character in Numbers) and asks him what to do about what is unfolding before his eyes. It is only after Moses' tepid approval that Pinhas acts.[86] Shimon and Levi never take council with Jacob before murdering the people of Shechem, whereas Moses permits, and even witnesses, Pinhas' act of retribution. However, the Izbica/Radzin tradition is unwilling to go as far as to acknowledge that Moses agrees with Pinhas' action. Rather, both R. Mordecai Joseph and R. Gershon Henokh view Pinhas in the model of the Joseph archetype, the premessianic personality who simply cannot see beyond the confines of conventional legalistic (halakhic) norms. It is not inconsequential for R. Mordecai Joseph that the issue of Zimri's action is formulated in the mouth of Pinhas as "halakha" in the Sanhedrin passage cited by Rashi on the verse. The conflation of halakha and Pinhas' desire to kill Zimri (fulfilling the letter of the law) is precisely the point!

Moses' call to the tribe of Shimon to heed the voice of Judah at the end of Deuteronomy is read by R. Mordecai Joseph and R. Gershon Henokh as an implicit reaction to the Zimri episode in light of the Dina narrative. In *Tiferet Ha-Hanokhi,* R. Gershon Henokh's commentary to the Zohar, this is made explicit: "The tribe of Shimon was in constant need of refinement [*berurim*] because Shimon entered into the dubious marriage with Dina. So too with the incident with Zimri, as the Ari z'l explains in *Ma'amar Pesiuto el Avraham* printed at the end of [R. Abraham Azulai's] *Hesed l'Avraham.*"[87] The entire Torah is read through the prism of the messianic person who lives in a protomessianic world. Jacob's evolution, resulting in the important distinction between the Israelite (Jacob) and the Gentile (Esau), sets the stage for a refragmentation of the Jacobean (i.e., Israelite) personality into Judah and Joseph and subsequently the Israelite nation. Jacob, having achieved human perfection, erases the possibility of sin, making all deviant behavior in his progeny at most a "mistake" *(shegagah).* The source of such error is the individual's inability to see how extrahalakhic behavior is also fulfilling the will of God.

In sum, I would argue that what appears to be a problematic and idiosyncratic interpretation of the Pinhas/Zimri episode in Numbers is, in fact, directly in line with the larger archetypal framework of the Izbica/Radzin reading of Scripture as a whole. Moreover, it is a fine example of a determinist stance that views messianism as a living mode of consciousness in the protomessianic world. In line with the rabbinic statement that the potential for the Messiah lives in every generation, both R. Mordecai Joseph and R. Gershon Henokh might say that the consciousness of the integrated messianic world lives on in the inheritors of Jacob, Judah, and Moses in every generation. However, whereas in the messianic world the revealed portion of Jacob will be recognized, in the protomessianic world the hidden dimension of Jacob is, at best, vague and the revealed dimension of Jacob remains hidden.

Conclusion to Part 2

The purpose of the last three chapters has been to exhibit how Izbica/Radzin Hasidism weaves its ideological stance of determinism into the biblical narrative. As stated at the outset, my contention is that this determinist ideology unfolds by first positing the rational and nonrational dimensions of human experience in R. Gershon Henokh's *Ha-Hakdama ve Ha-Petikha*. It is then applied to illustrate the integration of the nonrational (in this case messianic) dimension as the central element of religious life and the achievement of Jacob and his progeny.

Hermeneutically, this emerges in R. Gershon Henokh's and R. Mordecai Joseph's portrayal of the non-Jacobean biblical characters (the descendants of Noah and then Esau) and the lineage of Joseph. In all three of these personality archetypes we see variant permutations of a religious perspective rooted in empiricism and reason. Noah recognizes a divine presence but cannot understand (according to his rational faculties) how the human being could relate to this God and how he could change divine will. In some sense, Noah's position resembles a quasi-Aristotelian view of the divine, existent but impersonal. Esau, unable to overcome Abraham's death, becomes lost in a fatalism that results in his willful relinquishing of his covenantal inheritance because he believes it is no longer viable.

The lineage of Joseph (the halakhists) are firmly planted in the covenant but do not have the capacity to see that God's will is the fabric of all of creation and thus transcend the four ells of halakha, and that human will and divine will are joined after Jacob's reconciliation, meaning that divine will can sometimes be fulfilled outside the realm of halakha.

In short, the halakhist's position is an exilic one that may be necessary until the messianic era, when the Joseph Jews will recognize their myopic perspective. The halakhists, however, unlike the Noahides or the descendants of Esau, embody the potential to understand the determinist position of the lineage of Judah because they are descendants of Jacob. As Jacob's sons they already contain his perfection, dormant and enveloped in their limited perspective. Their inability to be conscious of this latent determinism in their own personalities is the result of the unfinished state of creation. As inheritors of the concealed portion of Jacob's personality (as represented in the lower half of the Lurianic *parzuf* of Jacob/*zeir anpin*), the halakhists must wait for the final redemption in order to fully comprehend the limitlessness of divine will, its unity with human will, and the internal nature of their (seemingly transgressive yet truly messianic) brethren, the inheritors of the revealed state of Jacob.

What emerges from this reading is a quasi-nomian determinist religion whose boundaries are permeable, unstable, and always on the verge of collapsing. In light of this, various issues remain unresolved. First, how does being theoretically freed from the constraints of halakha square with the clearly halakhic life of the Izbica/Radzin community? We have no indication that the antinomianism inherent in this teaching ever had any behavioral manifestation as it did, for example, in the Sabbatean heresy of the seventeenth century. Yet, in my view this is not enough to justify the apologetic view taken by Shlomo Zalman Shragai in his *Be-Netive Hasidut Izbica/Radzin,* which attempts to soften the determinist position by finding precedent for it in rabbinic and medieval Jewish traditions. Nor is it legitimate to take Joseph Weiss's view that this represents an example of traditionalist "religious anarchy." The Izbica/Radzin position is quite subtle and slippery and can only be understood by exploring its hermeneutic, that is, by closely examining how its positions arise from its readings of classical Jewish literature. Taken outside of its exegetical context, Izbica/Radzin Hasidism loses the very edge that makes it so interesting. One could extend this to include Hasidism more generally.

In one sense, this Hasidic reading moves beyond the provocative tenor of later Kabbalists. Even the cosmological map of Luria and his disciples, filled with slippery reincarnations of biblical figures, falls short of the radical move made in the Izbica/Radzin reading of the Pinhas/Zimri episode. In *Mei Ha-Shiloah* and *Sod Yesharim,* the Lurianic material merely lends credence to a much larger exegetical and ideological program. In our Hasidic texts, and many others like it, the developmental nature of the discourse, that is, the interface between the biblical persons and events and their Hasidic reformulation, necessitates a more programmatic and comprehensive analysis that would span the entire width and breadth of the biblical narrative. To see one frame of this narrative (i.e., Pinhas/Zimri) as an isolated instance in the hermeneutic scheme is to miss, in my view, the innovative contribution of Hasidic hermeneutics. The Pinhas/Zimri narrative is not an aberration in Izbica/Radzin—it is either everywhere or nowhere. To see more precisely if and where antinomianism fits in here and if it coincides with the other religious antinomianisms, we must first examine antinomianism as a religious phenomenon and, through close readings, formulate Izbica/Radzin's relationship to that doctrine. This will be the focus of the final chapter of this study.

Part 3

The Law and Its Discontents

As a revivalist movement, Hasidism set out, at least in part, to critique the rabbinic culture of eighteenth- and nineteenth-century Eastern Europe, which was founded on Talmudism and the exclusivity of the law (halakha) as the sole arbiter of covenantal living. In doing so, Hasidism had to carefully negotiate its relationship to halakha as the telos of all Jewish worship. As a pietistic movement built on the foundations of the Jewish mystical tradition, Hasidism's critique had to grow out of, and not in opposition to, Kabbala's commitment to the law (in conjunction with Torah more generally) as the vehicle that brought cosmic effluence to the physical world. Moreover, its birth and growth took place in close proximity, both historically and geographically, to the Sabbatean heresy in the seventeenth century and the radicalization of Sabbateanism in eighteenth-century Eastern Europe.

While rarely mentioning the Sabbatean movement specifically, Hasidic writers were acutely aware of the fate of this heretical movement and cognizant of the ways in which its own critique contained certain parallels with Sabbateanism. When Sabbateanism (more specifically Sabbatai Sevi is mentioned in Hasidic literature it is often to draw sharp distinctions between itself and its heretical predecessor. By itself this is a sign of Hasidism's awareness of its own marginality. Sabbateanism was also founded on the Kabbala, and its heresy was at least in part the result of an amalgam of Kabbala and acute messianism. Early Hasidism succeeded in circumventing the accusation of Sabbateanism by personalizing and thus dehistoricizing messianism, using Kabbala as a metaphysical grid through which one could understand the complex nature of the human condition and not as a historiographic sign of the impending redemption of the world. While these sweeping observations are still the source of scholarly debate, there is consensus that these three issues—Kabbala, halakha, and messianism—loom large in the Hasidic depiction of Judaism.

Revivalist movements, especially those built on mystical foundations (e.g., radical Protestantism and Sufism) have often been accused of antinomianism, loosely defined as a religious position that protests against the law as the sole mediation between the individual and God. Protestant antinomians such as Anne Hutchinson in the seventeenth century argued that works, while important, are not salvific. Salvation comes solely through faith (Luther's *sola fida*). This is often accompanied by the claim of unmediated religious experience, inspiration, or revelation, whereby the antinomian is able to realize divine will directly, that is, outside any accepted nomos.

There are not many Jewish studies on antinomianism. Besides Gershom Scholem's magisterial *Sabbatai Sevi: The Mystical Messiah,* few works have appeared that treat the subject as it relates to the Jewish literary tradition (e.g., recent studies by Elliot Wolfson, Yehuda Liebes, and Moshe Idel). Some claim that Paul, and by extension Christianity, is an example, perhaps the first, of Jewish antinomianism. While the truth or falseness of that claim is beyond this work, I use Paul as an example of one whose interpretation of Judaism is antinomian to the extent that he erases the law as the vehicle of covenantal worship. The Sabbatean case is the most obvious, because it arose from deep within postrabbinic Judaism and, in its Kabbalistic interpretation, eventually moved outside it (either to Islam with Sabbatai Sevi or Christianity with Jacob Frank). What I do here is claim that antinomianism, at least in Judaism, requires a more subtle definition. That is, the narrow rendering of antinomianism as requiring an overt and systematic rejection of the law may not fully capture the history of antinomianism in the Jewish pietistic tradition.

I argue that Izbica/Radzin Hasidism, and to a lesser extent Hasidism in general, is a kind of soft antinomianism, whereby the law is undermined yet protected. The law is supplanted yet not erased, resulting in twin mediations, halakha for the unenlightened and devekut for the enlightened. It is precisely the erasure of the law by the enlightened, even though they by and large keep the law, that prepares the world for the final fulfillment of the law as an overcoming of the law (this is the Hasidic innovation, part of which it shares with Sabbateanism). Curiously, this position in part finds precedent in medieval philosophical antinomianism, especially that which arose from Averroism and Averroist interpretations of Judaism. Hence, Maimonides' comments on *ta'amei ha-mitzvot* (reasons for the commandments) are an example where antinomianism is rejected but also subtly accepted, at least in principle. I argue that R. Gershon Henokh's interpretation of his grandfather's work reflects the Maimonidean model as interpreted in a recent study on Maimonides by Joseph Stern. In short, any study of Hasidic spirituality and textuality, especially in this tradition, must seriously consider the question of antinomianism, redefined, as a central part of the Hasidic project. The fact that Hasidism remains inside traditional Judaism does not determine its rejection of an antinomian doctrine. In fact, as I argue in the conclusion, Hasidism presents a religious critique, founded on piety, that sets the stage, at least ideationally, for future religious reform.

7 In and Around the Law

Antinomianism and Mitzvot in Izbica/Radzin Hasidism

To live outside the law you must be honest.
Bob Dylan, "Absolutely Sweet Marie"

What is radicalism? The attempt to draw boundaries.
Gershom Scholem, Letter to Erich Brauer, 17 July 1916

In the previous three chapters I examined how R. Mordecai Joseph and R. Gershon Henokh develop a determinist ideology out of their reading of Scripture. Their understanding of the biblical characters in Genesis constitute the basis of two distinct religious personality archetypes, the exilic (Joseph) and the messianic (Judah). Both R. Mordecai Joseph and R. Gershon Henokh use this dichotomy to understand the disharmony between the individual who lives solely within the framework of halakha and the messianic person (not necessarily the Messiah) who comprehends the divine will and acts on it even as it may take him outside the boundaries of halakha. The future messianic era is constructed as the final reconciliation between these two persons, unifying the fragments of the Israelite nation.[1]

Human and divine will are unified within this messianic perspective, resulting in the dissolution of free will. However, Izbica/Radzin Hasidism does much more than reiterate the more common position that free will is a premessianic phenomenon that will be nullified in the future. For both R. Mordecai Joseph and R. Gershon Henokh, the messianic personality already lives in the protomessianic (contemporary) world. Combining spiritual inheritance and pious devotion, facilitated by spiritual refinements *(berurim),* these persons have already achieved redemptive consciousness while trapped in a world not-yet-redeemed. These illumined individuals have broken the barriers of the fragmentary and exilic nature of creation and have experienced the unity of human and divine will.[2] Their behavior, as long as it is for the sake of heaven, is aligned with the will of God even as it may contradict normative halakhic practice. These messianic persons embody the personality archetype of the biblical Judah and must live in constant tension with the still-binding halakhic system. Living in the protomessianic world, they are bound by the confines of halakha while having overcome the need for any external system of law.

The legitimacy of extrahalakhic behavior in Izbica/Radzin is not simply to "permit the forbidden" *(matir 'issurim),* a concept popularized by the Sabbateans in the seventeenth century, as much as it is to legitimate and even sanctify the tension of living simultaneously inside and outside the law.[3] This tension, however, is not purely theoretical, even though the literature never provides any concrete examples of sanctified transgression in their contemporary world. My claim is also that the Judah/Joseph paradigm is not purely a hermeneutical tool to decipher the tensions underlying the biblical narrative. Like other forms of classical Judaism, Hasidism often constructs its world through the lenses of the classical texts it interprets. However, the Hasidic masters do not live in a social and cultural vacuum. The social and political agenda of Hasidism lurks behind much of its seemingly apolitical homiletics.[4] Early accusations by some of Hasidism's detractors that Hasidism loosens the law in order to cultivate individual pietism still resonate in the mid- to late-nineteenth-century Hasidic tradition. What is significant here is that even as the tension between conforming to both a normative system and pious desire may sometimes mandate acting outside the system, it never normalizes extrahalakhic behavior. Acutely aware of the Sabbatean heresy and perhaps also aware of Hasidism's close ideational proximity to the Sabbatean critique of the conflation of legalism and piety, our Hasidic authors are careful in the ways they formulate their doctrine.[5] The reader is invited to enter a world where holy transgression is ever-present but never explicitly manifest.[6] In short, this Hasidic dynasty re-presents halakha as a system with permeable boundaries, enabling certain individuals to traverse between normative religious behavior (halakha) and sanctified transgression.

This notion of sacred transgression raises various issues that this chapter will address. First, if halakha no longer functions as the sole arbiter for acceptable Jewish behavior or as the sole vehicle for divine will, how can Izbica/Radzin Hasidism still claim to carry the mantle of ultratraditional Judaism? Second, free will in Judaism is based on the assumption that the human being has the ability and capacity to act against divine will, that is, to sin. The entire covenantal framework of Judaism and Christianity is built on this foundation. If I am correct in my reading of *Mei Ha-Shiloah* and *Sod Yesharim* in previous chapters—that "overcoming" of free will is a spiritual goal that is attainable *before* the end and is not merely a result *of* the end—then how can that be squared with the biblical model of reward and punishment and the rabbinic application of that model as existing exclusively in allegiance to the halakhic system? Third, how radical is this assertion? Is the ability of the pious to transcend or perhaps circumvent the law in order to fulfill the will of God really such an aberration from classical Jewish sources? Or is there a latent antinomianism that underlies much of Jewish mystical literature, even in its most normative incarnations? This final chapter will examine these issues and others in an attempt to understand the implications of Izbica/Radzin spirituality and to determine whether the initial protests against the appearance of *Mei Ha-Shiloah* in 1860, as well as during the entire career of R. Gershon Henokh, were justified.

Pious Transgression as a Spiritual Critique of Religion: Antinomianism, Neonomianism, and Libertinism

The history of antinomianism is at least as old as the appearance of Hellenistic thinking in Palestine. In his treatise on Abraham, Philo of Alexandria, living in Egypt in the first century B.C.E., was already aware of the danger that spiritualistic (mystical?) interpretations of Judaism posed to the authority of Jewish law.[7] Cognizant of this danger, Philo tried to navigate around the ever-present antinomian threat in his presentation of (pre-Talmudic) Jewish law and its roots in the biblical and prophetic tradition.[8] Although many references in noncanonical biblical literature point to the possibility of a messianic antinomianism in classical and late antiquity, it was Paul, in his scathing critique of Pharisaic Judaism, who first popularized Jewish antinomianism as a critique of normative (Pharisaic?) Judaism as it was taking shape in the early stages of rabbinic Judaism.[9] Although the first concretization of Jewish antinomianism may appear parenthetically in the various works of Paul, it is in Paul's sustained critique of the law in his *Epistle to the Romans* that antinomianism enters center stage.[10] Paul's formulation of the religion of law (Pharisaism) versus the religion of spirit (Christianity), a formulation arguably built on a Jewish notion of antinomianism, became a signpost for the development of Christian doctrine, particularly after the Reformation.[11]

It does not serve our purpose to trace the history of antinomianism as a critique of rabbinic Judaism in Christianity, as Hasidic antinomianism is clearly not an outgrowth of, or response to, the early Christian critique of the law. However, since antinomianism plays such an integral role of the development of Christian faith and doctrine from its inception through the Reformation and beyond, Christians, unlike Jews, are far more sophisticated in their evaluation of the nature and boundaries of antinomianism. A careful analysis of Jewish attitudes toward antinomianism has much to gain from Christianity's understanding of this phenomenon.

In Christianity, antinomianism has been defined as ". . . the denial of the relevance of the moral law to the Christians because of the ability claimed for the Holy Spirit to separate persons directly and radically from the obligations of ordinary worldly existence."[12] In much of Protestant thinking, the moral law functions either as the way toward salvation or, for Calvinists, the physical expression of faith. The antinomian Christian believes that one can achieve salvation without adhering to or practicing the moral law but merely by being "one with God" through faith. This doctrine becomes antinomian and heretical when adherence to the law or nomos is seen as preventing the fulfillment of divine will.[13] John von Rohr makes this point quite clear when he states regarding the Antinomians, "Salvation is entirely by God's act, and thus there is no place for human effort, or even for human participation. The law and its demands have no proper part in all of this, either before or after the coming of God's captivating Spirit; even faith itself is solely a divine creation."[14] This definition suggests two possibilities: either as a result of experiencing their "effectual calling," these individuals are incapable of sinning, and are thereby released from the constraints of the moral law;[15] or these individuals may indeed "sin," but having been chosen by God, they are no longer held accountable for their transgressions.[16]

Christian doctrine and debate on the necessity and efficacy of works is largely based on Paul's critique of the law and his claim that grace alone is the vehicle for salvation.[17] Antinomianism is thus a belief in the ability to be released from the constraints of the moral law while still being assured of salvation. The Christian notion of "assurance," a complex theological term that serves as a foundation for some Protestant theories of antinomianism, is often employed to define this occurrence. Since Jewish antinomianism does not focus on the assurance of salvation in the Christian sense but on the viability of defining and fulfilling God's will outside the law, the Christian idea of assurance as a justification for antinomian behavior does not speak directly to our Jewish sources. However, for both Jews and

Christians, the individual who claims to be the recipient of this "effectual calling" or "illumination" must justify himself or herself to those who still feel bound by the moral law.[18] As much as assurance remains a central motif justifying antinomian Christians, no objective criteria is ever established to certify the purely subjective experience of sanctification that lies at the root of antinomian behavior. In any case, the antinomian lives within the framework of his own experience and the community of those who determine that such an experience is authoritative. The community's acceptance of these marginal individuals rests on the willingness of the unsanctified to accept the validity of their sanctification. This description resonates to some degree in *Mei Ha-Shiloah*'s depiction of the Judah archetype in his struggle to attain legitimacy with his nonmessianic brethren.

In opposition to the Christian justification of "effectual calling," our Hasidic texts justify antinomian behavior through religious determinism. By positing that "all is in the hands of heaven—even the fear of heaven," illumined individuals may permit themselves to act outside (or even against) halakha, believing that such action has divine sanction. My assumption is that there is a tight correlation between determinism and antinomianism, similar to the relationship between atheism (as the negation of the biblical God who acts in history) and nihilism. The atheist and the determinist represent two opposite poles of the same doctrine. Any theological justification for living in accordance with the divine law dissolves for the atheist who denies God's existence (or at least divine providence).[19] For the theological determinist who negates free will, every action has the potential to be an expression of divine will (if done for the right reasons); thus all action, regardless of its conformity to ethical or legal standards, can be seen as divinely sanctioned. Just as the atheist can (but does not necessarily) justify immoral behavior by denying any divine retribution (i.e., Fyodor Dostoevsky's quip, "if there is no God then all is permitted"), so too the determinist can justify unconventional, even immoral behavior, by denying any limitation of divine influence. Whereas the atheist may be accused of believing too little, the determinist may be accused of believing too much. Both positions threaten divinely decreed systems of law by justifying actions outside any theological system, either because all systems are humanly contrived or because no system can fully contain divine will.

As an "overbeliever," the determinist may challenge religious norms as having exclusive rights to divine will. This may manifest itself in at least two distinct ways: antinomianism, or living outside the boundaries of conventional religion by abrogating the law; or hypernomianism, redefining the norms of religious behavior in a supererogatory manner.[20] Medieval

Jewish pietists such as Bahya ibn Pakuda and Abraham Maimonides rub against the margins of conventional Jewish notions of free will, often coming close to a determinist position, yet remain steadfast in their pietistic behavior. This type of Jewish pietism is often founded on a hypernomian ideology, which arises from a quasi-determinist position coupled with a mystical orientation of asceticism as a way of purifying the soul and the will. Although we normally do not link pietism with antinomianism, these two critiques of religious culture often share common ground in that both often have determinist underpinnings. As we will see in the Izbica/Radzin tradition, pietism as asceticism *(berurim),* built on determinist foundations, is a prerequisite for acting outside the confines of halakha. In this schema, the ascetic vocation, expressed by refusing to partake in permitted pleasures and benefits, frees the pietist from the confines of the law.

The sixteenth-century Christian theologian John Calvin constructed a determinist ideology that challenges conventional Christian ideas of free will but does not yield to the lure of antinomianism. Our interest in the determinist doctrine of Calvin is that it stresses the importance of affirming undeserving grace but holds onto the importance of adhering to the moral law. Battling against the Armenians, who held that salvation is determined by works alone, Calvin argued that works, although necessary, can never assure salvation.[21] Salvation is the product of God's grace alone, independent of the individual's actions. What then is the importance of righteousness (i.e., works) for Calvin? Calvin argues that righteousness (works) does not *bring about* salvation but is its *justification*. When one is justified through Christ, one is sanctified and thus acts righteously.[22] The attainment of righteousness, produced by faith, is exhibited through works. Therefore works (moral behavior) are signs that one has been sanctified through grace, but they are not a prerequisite for salvation. Conversely, immorality is an indication of a lack of sanctification.

According to Calvin, we can begin to evaluate the spiritual status of an individual by witnessing their actions. Calvin's theory of works suggests that the sanctified individual (who achieves sanctification through faith and grace) will only act according to the moral law because his/her soul will naturally be attracted to moral acts.[23] Calvin's reading is important for us in that it views "works" (the Christian correlation to halakha) as necessary for salvation even though they does not produce it. Moreover, the fact that Calvin holds that the sanctified soul is inherently moral, and therefore acts morally, speaks to our texts, which struggle with the external system of halakha and the will to act outside it. Izbica/Radzin Hasidism moves in a more antinomian direction than Calvin, in that it justifies extrahalakhic behavior as a viable expression of the illumined (or sanctified) soul. Calvin's theory that the sanctified soul will naturally act morally may shed light on the ambiguous idea in the Izbica/Radzin tradition that the "works" of the purified soul are, by definition, aligned with divine will. In a sense, for our Hasidic thinkers, divine will is not only expressed *through* law but can also be determined by the actions of these illumined individuals, whose very actions *create* law.

The category of neonomianism is another alternative in the Christian interpretation of the Pauline critique of the law that may help us understand the strange case of Izbica/Radzin Hasidism. Neonomianism, as opposed to antinomianism, does not focus on breaking the strictures of the normative system. Rather, it claims that a new nomos emerges to replace an old one, changing the precepts decreed by God.[24] This position supposes a paradigm shift, whereby a new era or set of historical circumstances demands a radical shift in the ways a religion is practiced. For the neonomian, to live in accordance with the old law is, in essence, to live against it.

In most Jewish cases, messianism is the paradigm shift that lies at the root of radical shifts in halakhic behavior. This is the case with Paul in the first century and the Sabbateans in the sixteenth and seventeenth centuries, some of whom argued that the onslaught of the messianic age in the figure of Sabbatai Sevi demanded a change in religious behavior, such that (at times) a sin is a mitzvah and vice versa. One can view the Sabbatean heresy from a neonomian rather than from a purely antinomian perspective. According to some Sabbateans, the law is not abolished but transformed, requiring behavior that previously had been forbidden.[25] Thus, some Sabbateans argue, they are the true nomians, and the traditional communities are antinomian as they are acting "against" the nomos of the messianic era![26] To some extent, this idea reflects Paul's response to the Pharisees concerning the status and relevance of the law. According to this neonomian reading of the Sabbatean movement, to live *by* the law (in its premessianic form) after Sabbatai Sevi is an antinomian act, in that it denies the transformative nature of the law in response to changing historical circumstances (i.e., the messianic era), an idea which has at least theoretical precedent in rabbinic literature.[27]

When speaking of antinomian trends in Judaism, especially in traditional societies, we must consider the extent to which these movements are also neonomian and whether moving outside or even against the law is really replacing one law with another. Conrad Cherry's definition of neonomianism may be helpful here: "[Neonomianism is conceiving] faith as a new kind of obedience and the gospel as a new kind of law. The grace sufficient for salvation is viewed as conditional on the human performance of faith."[28]

The substitution of one human act for another as a way of understanding the need for the abrogation of the law may be useful in our attempt to define the complex nature of R. Mordecai Joseph's and R. Gershon Henokh's relationships to halakha. Temporarily acting outside the law may be an attempt to extend the elasticity of the law, preparing the community for the transition to a new redemptive era. The importance of the messianic personality in the Izbica/Radzin tradition, especially as it rises to the surface immediately preceding the messianic era, may be to introduce such a new kind of obedience, or at least a new relationship to obedience. So as not to overstate the present claim, I will argue later in this chapter that Izbica/Radzin Hasidism does not adopt an orthodox neonomian position, in that a new law is never presented as a replacement for the old. Rather, the sanctified person begins to stretch the boundaries of the old law, challenging the claim that the existing law is the exclusive carrier of divine will. Before looking more closely at how this claim emerges, however, I want to briefly discuss libertinism (the polar opposite of pietism), which often accompanies antinomian ideologies.

Libertinism is the performance of licentious or immoral acts, often but not always buttressed by antinomian or fatalistic ideologies.[29] Christians who polemicize against alleged antinomianism often conflate libertine behavior with antinomian doctrine.[30] The simple reason for this assumption is that the liberation from the confines of moral or behavioral strictures, which may define antinomianism in its most simplistic formulation, potentially justifies the expression of the uninhibited fulfillment of inner desires (Nietzsche's "Dionysian spirit"), which may constitute immoral behavior. Antinomian trends, especially in the ancient world, often lead to such libertine behavior. According to Hans Jonas, "[u]nlike the ordinary purely 'psychic' individual, the pneumatic [Gnostic] is a free man, free from the demands of the Law . . . and, inasmuch as it applies a positive realization of this freedom, his uninhibited behavior is far from being a purely negative reaction."[31] Yet it is also the case that the intent of many antinomians is to answer to a higher moral and spiritual calling, a calling that cannot be fulfilled by normative works or law. In many cases of postmedieval Jewish "antinomianism," including early Sabbateanism, piety (hypernomianism) and not libertinism is the standard behavioral model. The freedom from external constraints of normative behavior makes antinomians vulnerable to the libertine critique, but their higher calling often had the reverse consequence. As W. B. Stover notes in his study of the antinomian controversy in the Massachusetts Bay Colony in the seventeenth century, "It was possible, however, to hold antinomian doctrines without in practice committing or condoning moral excess, and not everyone who might technically be labeled 'antinomian' ended in libertinism."[32] Robert Cover makes a similar argument. "[T]he rejection of the 'covenant of law' for that of grace does not imply an absence of laws from the internal functionings of earthly communities. Indeed, the coherent and normative force of Amish doctrine is argued forcefully in the Amish brief in *Yoder.*" [33]

In Judaism most instances of antinomianism are accompanied by a severely ascetic pietism that results in supererogatory rather than libertine behavior.[34] The fact that antinomians challenge the authority of normative religion is often overlooked, intentionally or not, in that many who advocate antinomian doctrines hold themselves to a higher standard of religious and social behavior.[35] This notion is exemplified by the following text.

> Then Judah [said to his brothers], *"What do we gain by killing our brother [Joseph] and covering up his blood"* [Genesis 37:26]. The Talmud states [b.T. Sanhedrin 6b], "all those that bless Judah are called beneficiaries [*boze'ah*]." We learn in the Talmud [b.T. Nedarim 32b] "when the evil inclination has dominion the good inclination is not recognized." That means, when God wants to test an individual He causes that individual to forget the nature of the transgression that is the subject of that trial. This was also true of Jacob's brothers [*ha-shevatim*]. When they wanted to kill Joseph they forgot the fact that such an act was forbidden.[36] The only thing [that saved them was a moral code] that was external to Torah.[37] This is because Judah was wise in the ways of the world. Therefore, he rose up and said, *What do we gain. . . .* This means, [he realized that] even though it may have appeared to him that this act was permissible from the perspective of pure halakha [*m'zad ha-din*], as it was explained, he still inquired as to the benefit that would result [from such an act]. [Thus Judah said] will our father love us more [for killing Joseph]? Immediately after the brothers decided not to kill Joseph, the gravity of the sin they were about to commit became apparent to them. This teaches a lesson that it is only permissible to depend on worldly wisdom [*hokhmot akum,* Gentile wisdom] at the time of a trial, that is, when one has no other alternative. However, when one knows something is forbidden, one should separate themselves from that act because it is commanded by God and not because of some external wisdom. . . .[38]

Here Judah is viewed as the model of the perfected personality because he is able to ascertain divine will by extrahalakhic means (the substance of which is never discussed) in a case where divine will was concealed. Judah is beloved by his father, because Jacob recognizes his own completion in him more than in any of his other sons. The brothers' recognition of Judah's prowess only becomes apparent to them after the fact, hinting at the messianic era, when the evil inclination will be effaced and the trial of Israel will become clear. The irony in this reading is that the messianic archetype of Judah, who saves Israel from further suffering by making decisions outside the normative system, is the one who enables the community to remain in the system, until which time it reaches its completion. Judah's search for God's will outside, and even in opposition to, halakha enables the brothers to make the correct choice, which is to not kill Joseph, even though they believed (correctly) that it was permissible to do so. In our text, Judah's actions outside the system are supererogatory in that it *appears* to Judah and his brothers that killing Joseph is halakhically permissible. Only by utilizing a pious sensibility external to the halakhic system does Judah enable his brothers to understand the true nature and requirements of the system itself. This is one example of how antinomian actions (here acting against that which *appears* to be nomian) are supererogatory and not libertine. On this reading, the controversy over antinomianism in both Christianity and Judaism is perhaps less about the fear of libertine behavior than about challenging theological and legal doctrine, thereby weakening the binding force of law as the sole expression of divine will. In Judaism—a religion without the Messiah—this often results in touching the emotional nerve of messianism, which carries the potential for a paradigm shift in religious behavior.[39]

For the defenders of tradition, the popular conflation of antinomianism and libertinism is often used as a polemical tool. Although the antinomian doctrines of Sabbatai Sevi, especially as they are interpreted by Jacob Frank and other so called "radical" Sabbateans, do indeed lead to licentious behavior,[40] the normative Jewish mystical tradition (including early Sabbateanism) largely averts the libertine consequences of antinomianism while affirming legitimate spiritual life outside the confines of rabbinic legalism. As Elliot Wolfson has recently argued, in this sense excessive pietism or hypernomianism is also a form of antinomianism. Potentially antinomian statements of this nature exist in early anonymous Kabbalistic texts (thirteenth and fourteenth centuries) such as *Sefer Ha-Kaneh, Sefer Peliah,* and *Sefer Ha-Temunah.* These texts illustrate the underlying tension that exists between law and mysticism. Another example is *Ray'ah Mehemna,* one of the later strata of the Zohar, which develops the notion of a "Torah of emanation" *(torat azilut),* in opposition to the legalistic "Torah of creation" *(torat ha-beriah).* In early Hasidism, Arthur Green has noted that the tension between "mystical religion" and "mediation" is perhaps the central concern of Hasidic masters.[41] Although the tension between experience and mediation may indeed be generic to Jewish mysticism as a whole, Green points out that Kabbalists have almost always found ways to protect the sanctity of halakha while espousing doctrines that threaten it. As implicitly radical as these doctrines may seem, they rarely if ever lead to the public abrogation of halakha or the justification of sustained abrogation of the halakhic system.

This curious phenomenon must be considered as we attempt to unravel the antinomian tendencies in Izbica/Radzin Hasidism. Soft antinomianism (a category I will employ to define antinomian strains in highly nomian systems) does not necessitate any substantive rupture in the halakhic system, even as it justifies interim abrogation of halakha.[42] Its purpose is twofold: First, soft antinomianism is an attempt to experientially bridge the gap between the fragmented past and the unified future, between life in exile and the experience of redemption. This goal is aligned with most antinomian doctrines in Judaism, which are almost always couched in messianic language and doctrine.[43] Second, in opposition to the rare cases of hard antinomianism in Judaism that validate or even obligate deviant behavior (Frankism, for example), Izbica/Radzin Hasidism is primarily interested in highlighting the tension between the spiritual personality (whose sole focus is divine worship) and the halakhic system.[44] This Hasidic ideology in general problematizes the conventional rabbinic notion (present in medieval pietism and *Mussar* anthropology, contemporaneous with mid-nineteenth-century Hasidism) that the human desire to act outside the halakhic system is, by definition, the byproduct of the "evil inclination" *(yezer ha-ra)* and should be controlled or nullified. In Izbica/Radzin Hasidism, such desire, coming from an individual who inherits the soul of the biblical Judah and has undergone a strenuous process of spiritual purification *(berur),* may indeed be the will of God. Finally, the tension and anxiety that accompanies living the halakhic life points to the more evolved nature of the individual's soul.

In sum, I have presented two basic types of antinomianisms in Judaism. The first, which I call "hard antinomianism," is advocated by those who indeed want to usurp the authority of the legal and/or moral code that limits their activities. Practical messianism, combined with dormant antinomian doctrines embedded in their respective traditions, enables these parties to justify unconventional and even immoral behavior as a part of the unfolding eschaton. The goal of these communities is to forge a severe and permanent rupture in the system in which they exist. The rupture itself is the redemptive act. Alternatively, there are antinomian ideologies that are not intended to "liberate" their adherents from any mode of obligatory behavior; they are directed at introducing a subjective, experiential source of authority that may temporarily be in conflict with an external body of law or norms but does not comprehensively supplant it. This I call "soft antinomianism," a religious ideology that lies at the root of some of the mystical and revivalist religious movements in Judaism. It is the phenomenon that I believe is most common in Jewish mysticism, perhaps including early Sabbateanism (which eventually overcomes its "softness"), and that best represents the antinomianism of Izbica/Radzin Hasidism.[45] If the experience of divine unity (in Izbica/Radzin Hasidism, the illumination) is to be taken seriously, it cannot be subjected to the authority of any external system, even if such a system is itself the product of divine revelation.

The elevated stature of the human will and its unwillingness to be confined by halakha in Izbica/Radzin Hasidism is not a double-truth theory or sign of an irreparable conflict between two sources of truth (external/halakha and internal/human will). Rather, the claim is that the halakhic system, even for these individuals, is divine; but the human will, which may compel the individual against the halakha, is also divine. Thus the halakha can be temporarily bracketed if it conflicts with an inner drive that cannot be silenced. This position does not dissolve the halakha nor deny its divine nature. Rather, it argues that God's omnipotence, which by definition transcends the boundaries of halakha, can be intuitively felt by certain individuals and can, in certain circumstances, serve as an alternative source of divine authority and human action. The consequence is that these individuals, who have internally overcome the *need* for halakha, yet remain externally *bound* by its directives, live in a perpetual state of anxiety. As messianic personalities, they are strangers in our premessianic world, a world driven by the doctrine that halakha is the sole arbiter of divine will.

The Elasticity of the Law: The "Soft" Antinomianism in Izbica/Radzin Hasidism

Following this brief clarification of some medieval and early modern antecedents of antinomianism as they relate to Izbica/Radzin Hasidism, I now turn to some of the more provocative texts by R. Mordecai Joseph and R. Gershon Henokh in an attempt to see how their presentation of the tension between illumined experience and the authority of halakha constitutes an example of soft antinomianism. Before doing so, however, I want to offer a general rubric of soft antinomianism articulated by the legal theorist Robert Cover. Cover states:

> If a law reflects a tension between what is and what might be, law can be maintained only as long as the two are close enough to reveal a line of human endeavor that brings them into temporary or partial reconciliation. All utopian and eschatological movements that do not withdraw to insularity risk the failure of the conversion of vision into reality and, thus, the breaking of the tension. At that point, they may be movements, but they are no longer movements of the law.[46]

In my view, Cover captures what our Hasidic authors feel but do not have the tools or language to articulate. The tension of the law (what is) and the vision (what might be) is precisely what the Izbica/Radzin tradition wants to highlight. It wants to be a "movement of the law," but a movement that always pushes the law beyond itself; from the real to vision, from what is to what is waiting to be. They implicitly argue, always through the opacity and protective veil of biblical exegesis, that the development of halakhic societies (perhaps the Mithnagdic communities are a case in point) often fall prey to subsuming all religious life to a life of the study and practice of the law. In doing so, the law becomes tighter (resulting in halakhic stringencies for their own sake), and piety is determined by external practices alone. Soft antinomianism is an attempt to reverse this process by redefining piety as acting in accordance with divine will, which can extend beyond the law. To have holy transgression as a perennial possibility enables the law to function as a rope between the present and the future—as a temporary means toward but never the permanent end of human perfection.

Most scholarship on R. Mordecai Joseph argues that his son, R. Jacob Lainer, and his grandson, R. Gershon Henokh, considerably softened R. Mordecai Joseph's radical stance on the question of antinomianism and religious anarchy. By "softened" I simply mean that the cryptic and often sharp references to acting outside the halakha in *Mei Ha-Shiloah* are interpreted as squaring with conventional notions of the binding nature of halakha in nineteenth-century Hasidism. While this may indeed be the case for R. Jacob Lainer, I will argue that R. Gershon Henokh's position is not an apologetic revision of his grandfather.

It is true that on the issue of divinely sanctioned behavior outside or even against halakha, the most provocative idea in *Mei Ha-Shiloah,* R. Gershon Henokh presents this antinomian perspective within the framework of a highly nomian system. In line with the earlier chapters of this study that highlight the strong influence of Maimonides on R. Gershon Henokh's thinking, I will argue here that R. Gershon Henokh's interpretation of the antinomianism in *Mei Ha-Shiloah* is a unique combination of mystical messianism and Maimonidean rationalism that acknowledges one's ability to overcome the need for the law while maintaining that the binding nature of the law plays an essential role in such an enlightened state.

One of the ways this is done is to read *Mei Ha-Shiloah* as presenting a protomessianic world where the exilic and redemptive eras clash. In its opposition to medieval messianic antecedents, *Mei Ha-Shiloah* is not interested in interpreting historical events as an illustration of the transition from exile to redemption. Its author lives in the "self-redemptive" world of classical Hasidism, focusing on the individual as the lens through which redemption unfolds.[47] The question of whether human will, purified from the *kelippot* through hyperpietistic behavior *(berurim),* can directly perceive divine will, even outside the confines of halakha, is the place where this clash becomes most pronounced. As is the case with Sabbateanism, the antinomianism of *Mei Ha-Shiloah* is couched in a neonomian context. As the messianic era approaches, these messianic archetypes, representing a new nomos of the covenant, begin to challenge the exclusivity of the halakha. Commenting on the highly personalistic nature of *Mei Ha-Shiloah*'s messianism, Morris Faierstein draws a distinction between the "personal messianism" in *Mei Ha-Shiloah,* largely influenced by his teacher R. Simha Bunim of Pryzsucha, and the collective messianism of R. Gershon Henokh, which returns to a more medieval model of universal redemption.[48] Although Faierstein may be slightly overstating the case when he says, "[m]essianism, in the conventional sense, plays no role in the *Mei Ha-Shiloah,*" his observation that R. Gershon Henokh interprets his grandfather in a more conventional messianic manner is essentially correct. I will show that he turns to Maimonides, rather than classical Kabbalistic approaches, in order to root his position in such a normative framework. In fact, it is precisely this leap backward to Maimonides that enables the radicalism of *Mei Ha-Shiloah,* otherwise enveloped in its own ambiguity, to be absorbed in the Hasidic community in Poland.

In his two influential studies on the Izbica tradition, Joseph Weiss argues that R. Mordecai Joseph introduces a theory of personal illumination that may necessitate or even obligate the individual to move outside the framework of halakha in order to fulfill the will of God.[49] Weiss's thesis has three main components, ideological, spiritual. and historical. Weiss argues that R. Mordecai Joseph's thinking emerges out of a combination of religious determinism (ideology), a Hasidic version of messianism that focuses on the personal redemption of the individual (spirituality), and the sincere belief in the advent of the messianic age (history).[50]

Morris Faierstein contributes to Weiss's third component by showing the ways in which historical messianism is more the product of R. Gershon Henokh than of his grandfather. However, I believe Weiss also errs in his assertion that R. Mordecai Joseph proposes a religious anarchy that pits the authority of religious illumination *against* the authority of halakha and thus constitutes a case of what we may call "hard" antinomianism.[51] My contention is that R. Mordecai Joseph is not an antinomian in the strict sense of the word, as he does not fit comfortably into any of the categories discussed at the beginning of this chapter. However, he is clearly a religious determinist who feels that, as a chosen individual inheriting the spiritual legacy of Judah, he can intuitively perceive the omnipotent will of God outside the limits of rationality and religious norms. More strongly, he believes that individuals with such a calling *must* seek to fulfill that divine will, even as it may force them to temporarily transgress halakha.[52] He is not an antinomian in the classical sense, because he believes in the continued binding nature of halakha, even as he makes the boundaries of the halakhic system permeable (sometimes even transparent), especially for the illumined messianic personality. He understands halakha to be in a state of transition, moving from its strict, coercive, premessianic construction to a messianic fluidity that allows God's will to be determined *through* and not solely *by* the law.

The initial prototype for this messianic personality is the patriarch Abraham, who R. Mordecai Joseph portrays as an individual driven more by his intuition than by reason.[53] In *Sod Yesharim,* R. Gershon Henokh reads this to mean that Abraham's impulse is correct, but that he lacks the self-consciousness to understand the nature of his own actions. R. Mordecai Joseph is well aware of the dangers inherent in the assertion that one may have to transgress in order to fulfill God's will. In order to avert any legitimization of libertine behavior, he stresses the ascetic quality of Abraham's personality, whereby Abraham, unsure of the divine sanction for his actions, refrains from gaining any benefit or pleasure from such unconventional behavior. In explaining Abraham's negotiation with the king of Sodom, R. Gershon Henokh discusses the requirement of asceticism as the necessary condition for extrahalakhic behavior.

> This is the meaning [of the Talmudic statement, "The inheritance of a woman is her husband's" [b.T. Ketubot 65b/66a]. A wife represents a help to her husband ['*ezer k'negdo*]. When he is required to listen to her advice he is fulfilling [the verse] *Now is the time to act for God* [Psalms 119:126].[54] This is explained in the story of Adam and Eve. Eve was given to Adam as a helpmate in order that he listen to her words. In that case [in the eating of the fruit] he did not sin [by benefiting from her advice] in that the desire [i.e., the intention to sin] was not from her but from the serpent. This is what [the Mishna] means when it says, "The inheritance of the woman is her husband's." When a person acts [intentionally] against the law, following the dictum, *Now is the time to act for God* . . . it is forbidden for him to gain any pleasure [from such action]. Rabbi Akiba states that [her actions and advice] are hers [and not his], therefore a man can indeed gain pleasure from them. However, since Abraham, at the time of the action, did not know the full intention [of his act to save Sodom], he did not want to gain any pleasure from the act.[55]

This text raises numerous issues relevant to our topic. First, it acknowledges that one must sometimes act outside of the framework of the law (defined here as *mishpat*). However, in order to avert the unjustified abrogation of the law for pleasure and/or benefit (i.e., to avoid libertinism), R. Mordecai Joseph stresses that an action outside the law must be done without any intent to benefit from its consequences. Abraham represents an individual who was driven by his intuition to act outside the law and who lived by a higher standard than the law required in order to secure that such actions were within the context of fulfilling the divine will.[56] This does not necessarily mean he always refrained from transgressive acts, only that his supererogatory behavior served as a filter to assure that his intentions (and desire) were pure.

As is common in other soft antinomian (and hypernomian) positions in Judaism and Christianity, the mystical fraternity who elevate their own subjective sense of divine will as authoritative, even as it transgresses halakha, must answer to a higher spiritual and behavioral standard than those who live solely within the framework of halakha. Asceticism is thus a necessary criterion for any Jewish antinomianism that seeks to remain within the confines of normative Judaism. In order to be an antinomian inside Judaism, one must be a pietist. To live outside the law one also has to live beyond the letter of the law. In Bob Dylan's words, "To live outside the law you must be honest."

Asceticism counters the danger of libertinism, always a potential outcome of being freed from the confines of the law. This text and others like it attest to the acute awareness of the marginality of the position presented. Given that our texts never make any overt claims as to the advent of the messianic era, which would give rabbinic sanction to transgress halakhic norms or even usurp the halakhic system, their orientation is constantly scrutinized within the system, even or precisely as it diminishes the system's absolute authority.

This first type of soft antinomian tendency in *Mei Ha-Shiloah,* embodied in the patriarch Abraham, I will call nonintegrated antinomianism. Abraham is never quite sure whether his actions are the result of his own desire or divine will.[57] By refraining from gaining any benefit from his actions, he insures the pure intentions of his abnormal behavior. The second stage of this antinomian personality, more refined because it is more self-conscious, I call integrated antinomianism. This type is represented by the religious personality of the biblical Jacob and more prominently by his son Judah.[58] Inheriting the messianic lineage, the Judah archetype who acts outside the law is no longer concerned with the need to set artificially higher standards for himself, because he understands that his extrahalakhic behavior is aligned with divine will. Whereas Abraham (and even Jacob) needed to set ascetic standards in order to assure their behavior was aligned with divine will, Judah, as the true messianic personality, need not take such precautions. Below are two examples of this type of activity from *Mei Ha-Shiloah:*

> It states in Psalms [105:3], . . . *let all who seek the Lord rejoice.* A rejoicing heart [*yismakh lev*] is one heart [singular]. *All who seek the Lord* is two [plural]. . . . Abraham rejoiced when he saw that the spirit of prophecy was present even in his servants. It was then that he understood that God dwells in all of his actions, even all of his supralegal actions [*hitpashtutav*][59] and possessions. This is exhibited also in Rabban Gamliel's response as to why he washed on the first night after the death of his wife [b.T. Berakhot 16b].[60] [When questioned] he responds, "I am an *'istanit* [one who is sensitive]," even though the law states that an *'istanit* is permitted [to wash during the mourning period] such a law had not yet been issued. Rabban Gamliel was so refined [*m'burar*] that God dwelled in all of his actions. On this account, the law was established that a sensitive person [*'istanit*] can wash [during mourning]. Similarly, slaves and maidservants were never referred to as father of "x" or mother of "x" except the servants of Rabban Gamliel. The light of God was so integrated into his being that all permutations of his actions and possessions [i.e., even his slaves] were filled with holiness.[61]

Abraham, who in our first text appears to be driven by an unconscious impulse rather than a clear understanding of God's presence in all of his actions, now claims to apprehend the divine nature of the world through the presence of the prophecy of Sarah's servants. More important, however, is the case of Rabban Gamliel, who is able to decide legal matters (i.e., institute halakhic practice) by reflecting on his actions rather than first turning to the halakhic tradition to determine if such actions are warranted. This is a reflection of the integrated personality of Jacob and finally of Judah described in the previous chapter. In this example, Rabban Gamliel's will is so aligned with God's that he is readily able to establish legal standards (the expression of divine will) without deferring to the formal legal process. R. Mordecai Joseph suggests that his very actions determine halakha, as his will is synonymous with the expression of the divine will. The following text makes this point even clearer:

> This is the root of the life of Judah, i.e., to seek out God in everything and not to act according to the dictum *A commandment of men, learned by rote* [Isaiah 29:13]. Even though he performed a certain act in one way yesterday, today he will not depend on himself but only seek out God to show him his will anew. This [mode of behavior] requires sometimes doing things *against the halakha* [emphasis mine], for [it is written], *It is the time to act for God for they have abandoned your Torah* [Psalms 119:126].[62]

This text supports Weiss's contention that R. Mordecai Joseph's major contribution is his belief in what Weiss calls the "unusurpable desire" that forces one to act outside the halakhic system but not outside the framework of divine will.[63] *Mei Ha-Shiloah* consistently attempts to avert the danger of religious behaviorism by stressing the importance of being prepared for enlightenment at any moment.[64] The polemical strains against rabbinic culture so common in early Hasidism still resonate in this mid-nineteenth-century dynasty. Perhaps more than others, the Izbica/Radzin tradition is willing to entertain the underlying possibility that such critique may indeed shatter the system it wishes to uphold. Yet we must ask ourselves, does this constitute a true antinomianism? Played out in the complex world of biblical exegesis, the ideological tension between spontaneity of worship and the obligatory nature of halakha is often loosened just when it reaches its breaking point. Taking cover in rabbinic notions of the future, R. Mordecai Joseph often softens his radical doctrine with a more conventional understanding of the nature of Torah as halakha, where the abrogation of the halakhic system is pushed off to some future (messianic) era.

> *Take for yourselves a red heifer without blemish* [*t'mimah*], *in which there is no defect and on which no yoke* [*'ol*] *has been laid* [Numbers 19:2]. In the future

> God will reveal His glory to Israel without any garment [*levush*]. This sustaining life force [*hayyim*] is also now found in the depths of Israel but it is only revealed via garments. The garments are Torah and mitzvot. One is not able to come to recognize the depths of God's will without Torah and mitzvot. . . . This is all referring to the present when [the divine will] is enveloped in Torah and mitzvot. However, in the future God will show Himself without garments as it states in b.T. Niddah 61b, "mitzvot will be nullified in the future" [*mitzvot betalot l'atid l'vo*]. God will reveal to Israel that they do not have any yoke as it will become clear that God is directing them. [In our present state] He is concealed. This is the meaning of the phrase [referring to the red heifer] *It never had a yoke* [my emphasis].[65]

In a subtle fashion, R. Mordecai Joseph suggests that Israel is likened to the red heifer in that: (1) they are (as sons of Jacob) perfect; (2) they are unblemished by sin; and (3) they have never (really) had a yoke, meaning that the construct of mitzvot as a yoke (the burden of Torah and mitzvot or the yoke of heaven) is illusory. The phrase "God is directing them" implies that their fate is not solely the result of their adherence to the mitzvot, that is, the consequence of free will. It is significant that R. Mordecai Joseph likens Israel to the red heifer whose meaning, according to rabbinic tradition, will remain concealed until the messianic era.[66] The red heifer, which purifies Israel from the defilement of death, allowing them to render service in the Temple, is an analogue to the eternal pure state of Israel in the cosmos *(Knesset Israel)* that is concealed in the defiled body of exilic Israel.

Despite the intriguing correlation between the red heifer and Israel, and the notion that Torah and mitzvot are a temporary model of Jewish devotion to be supplanted in the future by the unity of the divine and human will, this text still lies within the acceptable boundaries of classical Judaism supporting the possibility of nullification of mitzvot in the messianic era (b.T. Nidda 61b). However, I would suggest that R. Mordecai Joseph moves beyond the secure boundaries of rabbinic discourse on this matter in his justification of the temporary yet intentional act of transgression. His justification goes beyond the conventional rabbinic model of transgression for the sake of continuity or even transgression for the sake of heaven.[67] He constructs an inner tension between the knowledge of the transgressive nature of the act and the "unusurpable urge" to perform that act. The following text reflects such a precarious move:

> *The Israelites marched on and camped at 'Obot* [Numbers 21:10]. '*Obot* represents the general principles of Torah and mitzvot from the language *Av l'Hokhma* [lit., the father of wisdom]. It states in the Talmud [b.T. Berakhot 54b] *Now is the time to act for God, they are desecrating Your Torah*

> [Psalms 119:126]. Rabbi Nathan says, "They are desecrating your Torah in order to 'act for the sake of God.'" This is what it means. The words of our Holy Torah [suggest that] there are times when it is clear [*m'vurar*] to an individual to "act for the sake of God," like Elijah on Mount Carmel.[68] At such a time one must nullify the general principles of Torah and behave only in accordance with God's explicit demands. R. Nathan states that when this understanding is not clear in the mind of an individual he is obligated to act according to the general principles of Torah and mitzvot without deviating from the boundaries of halakha. R. Nathan speaks of a case of one who is drawn after the will of God after all manner of obstacles are removed [from his path]. God presents him with the opportunity to act in a manner that appears to him to be outside the confines of halakha, God forbid. On this R. Nathan states that since his heart is drawn to fulfill the will of God and all obstacles are removed, it is surely the case that the act is not a sin at all, God forbid. At that moment he knows with clarity that it is a *time to act for God* [emphasis added].[69]

The individual can justify the viability of a marginal and even a transgressive act in two distinct ways: either by the inner drive to perform the act, or by the opportunity to perform the act. This opportunity is interpreted as divine sanction for acting counter to the halakhic norm. This highly unusual and provocative reading of this Talmudic passage, which is conventionally rendered as the rabbinic recognition of the fact that the end does not always justify the means, takes R. Mordecai Joseph to the boundary of normative Judaism. Yet I would still maintain that antinomianism does not apply here, as the mitzvot are never supplanted in any permanent way nor viewed as a barrier standing between the individual and God. The mitzvot are not abolished (as they are, for example, in Paul's critique of the law) but only viewed, under certain circumstances, as having limited authority over devotional behavior. Moreover, the legitimacy and even obligatory nature of the transgressive act is still a temporary lapse and not a permanent uprooting of the system. What does occur here, however, is another attempt to blur the boundaries between the messianic era and the messianic person. Uncertainty *(safek)* and the continued need for spiritual refinement *(berurim),* both exhibited in the traits of humility and piety, are necessary conditions for the messianic archetype to act outside the confines of halakha in a premessianic world.

My contention is that as much as we see R. Mordecai Joseph's tendency to challenge the authority of the halakhic tradition as the sole arbiter of divine will, we do *not* see an antagonistic attitude toward the halakhic system as a whole. From the brief overview of antinomian trends discussed earlier, antinomian doctrines almost always claim that the individual desire, illumination, or experience, coupled with changing historical circumstances (the advent of the messianic era or the second coming, for example), challenge the body of law as a whole. This is why scholars have labeled Paul the first real "Jewish antinomian." This also lies at the root of the later Sabbatean notion of "redemption through sin."[70] Both movements are antinomian and heretical because their messianism is interpreted as a substitution for the law as a whole.[71] Jewish antinomians (including Paul) generally argue that the law (or at least part of the law) has been overcome and is obsolete, no longer functioning as a medium of divine worship, and that it has been supplanted by a "new" law for a new era *(Torah Hadasah, Brit Hadasah).*

The legitimacy of the antinomian claim is often dependent on the diminution or erasure of the binding system that it challenges.[72] This is clearly not the case in Izbica/Radzin Hasidism, which entertains the permanent nullification of the law only in the messianic era, an idea whose roots lie in the Talmudic tradition. Distinct from the rabbinic tradition and subsequent normative Judaism, however, it does claim that extrahalakhic behavior for the sake of heaven (sanctified transgression) may point to the immanent arrival of that era, an idea whose roots lie in earlier Kabbalistic literature.[73] However, it does not claim this era has arrived and therefore does not condone any *permanent* abrogation of halakhic practice. The provocative and marginal twist in both *Mei Ha-Shiloah* and *Sod Yesharim* is that the messianic archetype lives in the protomessianic era and, as such, is tortured by an inner drive that may sometimes result in extrahalakhic behavior while still living within the confines of halakha. That is not transgression *of* the law but sanctified transgression *in* the law.

Hasidic Modernism: The Individual as Authority

Another antinomian streak in Izbica/Radzin Hasidism is its theory of radical individualism, whereby the experience of one individual holds the potential to supplant the communal experience at Sinai. R. Mordecai Joseph's thinking suggests that the revelation at Sinai can be broken down into diverse elements, each individual receiving a different portion according to the nature of his/her soul.[74] Although this is not a new idea in Judaism, the Izbica/Radzin adaptation of this doctrine as a justification for the authenticity of the individual's experience as his/her own personal Sinai is quite innovative.[75] Joseph Weiss views this as the portico to the Izbica/Radzin tradition's religious anarchism:

> According to Mordecai Joseph's conception, each individual is summoned to his directing illumination from above; he alone is its sole recipient and no one can transfer to someone else the illumination allocated to him. This, of course, implies the total liquidation of the system of commands and prohibitions; the doors to religious anarchy stand wide open.[76]

Weiss's startling assessment requires closer examination. First, it is not at all clear why individual illumination necessarily liquidates the halakhic system. I have not seen any source where R. Mordecai Joseph places halakha as a system in strict opposition to illumination. Rather, he suggests that if we assume first that God's will transcends the fragmentary world in which halakha resides, and second, that certain individuals, via spiritual inheritance and ascetic piety *(berurim),* have access to that unified dimension of divine will via mystical illumination, extrahalakhic behavior for those individuals is justified. However, for those less fortunate individuals who cannot reach this mystical height, and for those who may have fleeting moments of that experience but cannot sustain it, the halakhic life remains the exclusive avenue for accessing divine will and is unequivocally binding. Furthermore, the sacredness of the halakhic system remains intact even for "illumined" individuals, although their perception of divine will may not be subsumed solely within the confines of that system. Weiss is correct that R. Mordecai Joseph amplifies the tension between halakha as one mode of spiritual behavior and illumination as another (even higher) mode of the religious life. However, such a view is not new in the Izbica/Radzin tradition in particular or Hasidism in general.[77] Gershom Scholem argues in numerous studies that this tension is a generic part of the Jewish mystical tradition.[78] To conclude from this that such a tension (essentially the fabric of the exilic life which will be rectified in the future) constitutes a new "religious anarchy" is, in my view, unwarranted. In fact, I would argue that in most cases R. Mordecai Joseph would agree that divine illumination and halakha dictate parallel modes of behavior. That is, even one whose spiritual existence is dictated by his personal illumination can live comfortably inside the halakhic system. The potential for "holy sin" outside the halakha may be the necessary consequence of almost any mystical interpretation of a legalistic religion. The Izbica/Radzin tradition may be unique in explicitly stating what remained unsaid in many other mystical Judaisms, enabling its readers to more courageously explore the dimensions of such an assertion. Such provocation, however marginal, does not constitute "religious anarchy."

I would suggest that Izbica/Radzin Hasidism represents a marginal Judaism that challenges the conflation of divine will and halakha and strives to extend the elasticity of the halakhic system by elevating the stature of individual experience. This Hasidic school presents a religious ideology built on the antinomian impulses of R. Mordecai Joseph, tempered by R. Gershon Henokh's attempt to contain those impulses in light of the binding halakhic tradition. From *Mei Ha-Shiloah,* R. Gershon Henokh attempts to re-present halakha as a mode of worship which by and large embodies divine will even though, under certain circumstances and with certain individuals, it comes into conflict with it. In my view, this is not an apologia intended to protect *Mei Ha-Shiloah* from a damning critique of the religious establishment, but an attempt to flesh out what is left unsaid in *Mei Ha-Shiloah*'s terse style, illuminating its provocative claims and setting them in a context of the devotional life of a traditional Jew. In fact, as Morris Faierstein correctly notes in his study of R. Mordecai Joseph, R. Gershon Henokh is a far more avid messianist than his grandfather, which radicalizes rather than diminishes the antinomianism in *Mei Ha-Shiloah*.[79]

Curiously, it is precisely this messianic impulse that leads R. Gershon Henokh to view extrahalakhic behavior as a *companion to* and not an *opponent of* the halakhic system. The one who, following the prescribed ascetic preparations *(berurim),* temporarily acts outside the halakhic system, does not act against halakha but alongside it. The underlying assumption here is that the protomessianic world is the nexus of two conflicting nomoi (halakha and the will of the messianic archetype). The challenge of the protomessianic generation is to allow these conflicting forces to coexist in dialectical tension.[80]

Thus far I have outlined a different reading of the antinomianism of Izbica/Radzin Hasidism from the one suggested by Joseph Weiss in his claim of "religious anarchism." I have argued that R. Mordecai Joseph's ideology, expanded and deepened by his grandson, is an example of a soft antinomianism capable of living with halakha while challenging its basic tenet—that is, its exclusive right to divine will. This attenuated status of halakha is a sign of the evolving state of redemption. The spiritual challenge to the halakhic system, embodied in the rise of Hasidism in the late eighteenth century and its widespread influence in mid-nineteenth-century Poland, is viewed by our Hasidic thinkers as the final shift in the ideological paradigm preceding the advent of the Messiah. I argue that such an assertion, while provocative, is hardly unprecedented or heretical in a society that had absorbed such diverse mystical movements, each containing underlying tensions between the mystical experience and the normative tradition.[81]

What stands out in R. Mordecai Joseph's ideology is that personal illumination appears to be independent of the normative mode of devotion, that is, the performance of mitzvot. Most mystical interpretations that exhibit antinomian tendencies not dissimilar from those of R. Mordecai Joseph attempt to integrate the mystical experience back into the framework of mitzvot.[82] Joseph Weiss and others claim that illumination in R. Mordecai Joseph is not only independent of the halakhic system but sometimes works in opposition to it. I argue that R. Gershon Henokh's position is that the halakhic system is integral to maintaining the illumination of his grandfather, thus enabling the antinomian undercurrent of *Mei Ha-Shiloah* to remain intact while inhabiting the normative, albeit destabilized, world of protomessianic Judaism.

R. Gershon Henokh's understanding of his grandfather's discourse reflects, I believe, Maimonides' elaboration of *ta'amei ha-mitzvot* as a preventative against the dangers of the philosophical antinomianism of his day. Maimonides is acutely aware of the dangers inherent in presenting the philosopher as one who can ascertain truth without the law, and he responds to this peril in his elaboration of *ta'amei ha-mitzvot* in his *Guide of the Perplexed.* R. Gershon Henokh understands the marginality of his grandfather's radical doctrine (and is in agreement with it!), yet maintains that halakha can survive even in a Jewish ideology where it is no longer absolute.

Two basic problems emerge from the theory of personal illumination and the antinomian tendencies championed in *Mei Ha-Shiloah.* First, what part does the halakhic system play in the attainment of personal illumination that enables its recipients to reach beyond halakha? Second, what is the purpose of continuing to fulfill mitzvot for one who has inherited the spiritual legacy of the biblical Judah and has attained a personal illumination aligning his will with that of the divine? These questions can be framed in another way. First, what do the mitzvot mean for the illumined individual, and how do the mitzvot benefit the enlightened worshipper? Second, what would motivate such an individual to practice halakha if he has already achieved its purpose, knowing and performing God's will? This can be compared to the two-tiered basis for *ta'amei ha-mitzvot* developed in the Middle Ages. Joseph Stern formulates it in this way: "These reasons [for the commandments] could be of two kinds: either those of the legislator (or Legislator), explanations why the commandments were legislated, or those of the performer, reasons that would justify or move an agent to perform the commandments."[83]

While medieval philosophers engage in the rationalization of mitzvot in order to answer both of these questions, our Hasidic thinkers only address the second, and do so exegetically rather than philosophically. The reason that the first question is largely ignored by Hasidism is due to the influence of the Kabbalistic tradition it inherited from the Zohar and also from Cordovero and Luria, which presents a complex cosmology built on the foundations of *ta'amei ha-mitzvot.*[84] For our thinkers, the first question of *ta'amei ha-mitzvot* (why these mitzvot were legislated) is answered by medieval Kabbalistic theosophy, which constructs its cosmology around the mitzvot, understanding them as the vehicles for human theurgy and divine effluence.[85] Moreover, unlike their Kabbalistic predecessors, Hasidic writers are less interested in God's intentions and more focused on human behavior and devotional precepts embodied in the second dimension of *ta'amei ha-mitzvot* mentioned above. In a recent study on *ta'amei ha-mitzvot* in Maimonides and Nahmanides, Joseph Stern argues that Maimonides' discussion of *ta'amei ha-mitzvot* in the *Guide* 3:26–49 (or, in Stern's reading, *Guide* 3:26–53) is intended to combat the potential antinomianism that existed either without *ta'amei ha-mitvzot* (Kalam) or with too much *ta'amei ha-mitzvot* (Averroism).[86] Stern's innovative reading of Maimonides is based on the inclusion of *Guide* 3:50–53 as a part of Maimonides' *ta'amei ha-mitzvot,* albeit speaking to a philosophical as opposed to a general audience.

Before turning to R. Gershon Henokh's revision of his grandfather's provocative comments on antinomianism, I will briefly digress to outline Stern's claim vis-à-vis Maimonides in order to view R. Gershon Henokh's revision in a philosophical frame. My claim is that the fear of antinomianism underlying both Maimonides in the *Guide* and R. Gershon Henokh's interpretation of *Mei Ha-Shiloah* is an answer to the second question of *ta'amei ha-mitzvot,*—that is, why should the philosopher or the recipient of illumination be motivated to abide by halakha? Maimonides' answer lies in *Guide* 3:51–52, which is understood by Stern as *ta'amei ha-mitzvot* for the philosopher for whom certain mitzvot are irrelevant. R. Gershon Henokh's answer lies in his *Sod Yesharim* and *Tiferet Ha-Hanokhi,* showing why halakha applies even to one who has overcome it.

Disclosure as Overcoming: *Ta'amei Ha-Mitzvot* and Antinomianism

Throughout this study I argued that Maimonides plays an important role in R. Gershon Henokh's construction of Hasidic piety. Here I argue that R. Gershon Henokh's interpretation of his grandfather's work reflects Maimonides' understanding that *ta'amei ha-mitzvot* serves to prevent what Maimonides believed was a latent, two-dimensional antinomian threat. The first threat is from the open philosophical examinations of the commandments that lead to the contextualization and, in some circles, relativization of certain mitzvot. The second is from the Kalamist claim that mitzvot (as God's will) have no "reason," which leads to the diminished motivation for practicing the mitzvot.[87] While an ardent defender of the *ta'amei ha-mitzvot* project, Maimonides understands that engaging in such philosophical interpretation and speculation is precarious and that using philosophy as a microscope to examine mitzvot threatens the foundation of mitzvot as the exclusive context for Jewish devotion.

In his *Introduction to the Code of Maimonides,* Isadore Twersky, reviewing Maimonides' *Hilkhot Me'eila* 8:8, sets up two distinct kinds of antinomian threats that arise from the study of *ta'amei ha-mitzvot* and also provides three solutions to these threats. The first threat is philosophical; finding the reason for a commandment and understanding that what it seeks to achieve may obviate the need to perform that commandment. This is the classic antiphilosophical attack against *ta'amei ha-mitzvot* waged against Maimonides, to which he partially responds in the *Guide.* The second threat Twersky calls "agnostic antinomianism," defined as "[a] rejection of religious law because it has become trivial in man's eyes after he was unable to motivate or spiritualize it."[88] This results either from the failure to find a compelling reason for the mitzvah or from finding a reason, usually historical, that deems the mitzvah irrelevant. The underlying principle for both of these reasons is that *ta'amei ha-mitzvot* invariably destabilizes the halakhic system, because the viability of the mitzvot too easily becomes dependent upon their underlying reason.[89] If the reason is convincing, the mitzvah may become obsolete because the philosopher may argue that he no longer needs the action to accomplish its purpose. If the reason is too weak, that is, if it is unconvincing, the mitzvah may become meaningless and thus lose its authority and divine status in the community.[90]

Although outside the formal parameters of our discussion, it is worth noting that Maimonides chooses to engage in *ta'amei ha-mitzvot* because he believes that the alternative of not seeking reasons for the commandments was either philosophically wrong,[91] an affront to the divine nature of the mitzvot,[92] or far more dangerous for the continuity of halakhic practice.[93] Maimonides believes that the intellectual exercise of *ta'amei ha-mitzvot* is a fundamental component of the law that, if ignored, threatens the very roots of the law as a framework for the religious life. However, he never lets his readers forget the dangers of *ta'amei ha-mitzvot,* constantly reiterating these dangers throughout his analysis.[94]

Isadore Twersky argues that Maimonides cautions his searching interpreter who fails to find good reasons for a commandment in three ways: first, he warns him not to ignore the law because he fails to find a reason for it; second, he advises him to be scrupulous in his search, not settling for inferior or indiscriminate explanations; and third, he urges him not to treat his subject as he would treat mundane matters. Thus, he emphasizes that one's observance of a commandment should never be allowed to depend upon its reason. One must continue to observe the mitzvah even if one thinks "that the commandments are worthless."[95] Twersky argues that these three admonitions point to Maimonides' requirement that the seeker who has failed at the task of *ta'amei ha-mitzvot* should yield to tradition, which he defines as "the purposiveness of the law," even though its justification may escape human inquiry. Twersky assumes that Maimonides' program of *ta'amei ha-mitzvot* is largely directed at the first reason given, the intention of the Legislator (i.e., God).[96] As for the motivation for performing these mitzvot, Twersky would likely have argued that Maimonides' position is clear; the motivation for performing the commandments is the "perfection of the body and soul" (*Guide* 3:27) and that even the philosopher is in need of acquiring such perfection.[97] When the utility of a commandment to achieve this purpose is threatened due to the failure to find a reason for it, tradition becomes the default position in that it is founded on the assumption that all commandments serve some purpose, always relevant, regardless of our ability to understand what that purpose is.

Joseph Stern presents a broader understanding of Maimonides' project of *ta'amei ha-mitzvot*. Like Twersky, he believes that Maimonides is talking to two different audiences, the masses and the elite. Unlike Twersky, he does not believe tradition serves as the answer for the elite on the question of motivation for performing mitzvot (the second reason cited above). One underlying difference between Stern and Twersky is that Stern maintains that, for Maimonides, the fear of antinomianism goes far deeper for the philosopher than Twersky would like to admit. For the philosopher who has achieved "correct opinions," parts of the halakhic system (the *hukim*) largely become obsolete.[98] Therefore, even as the call to tradition may have considerable weight, it cannot ultimately compel the philosopher to stay inside the system of mitzvot if remaining inside means performing acts that are either philosophically nonsensical or historically irrelevant.[99] In other words, according to Stern, some mitzvot lose their religious meaning when they are "understood" by the philosopher. For the philosopher to continue to perform these acts as religious acts would require the philosopher to live a lie. Another reason besides the default position of tradition must be found for antinomianism to be averted. Stern argues that Maimonides' response to his first audience and to the first reason for *ta'amei ha-mitzvot* can be found in *Guide* 3:26–49. He responds to the elite, who are interested in the question of motivation and not the intention of the Legislator, in *Guide* 3:50–53.

According to Stern, Maimonides' fear of antinomianism resulting from misinterpretation, lack of respect, or philosophical hubris, all discussed by Twersky above, does not apply for the truly enlightened ones (the philosophers). In fact, the entire first reason for *ta'amei ha-mitzvot* does not apply. Rather, "Maimonides [in *Guide* 3:50–53] directly responds to the more specific question [the second question asked above]: Why should and must the philosopher at the highest stage of worship continue to observe all, or certain commandments, one, when he can worship God through the higher form; and two, when he knows that certain commandments are even opposed to the requirements of that higher form of worship?"[100]

Stern argues that Maimonides' answer to the philosopher can be found in its most concise form in *Guide* 3:51 and 3:52. In order to avoid antinomianism, the philosopher must find another motivation to continue to perform commandments that he knows to be no longer relevant (i.e., the *hukim*). According to Stern, Maimonides does not adopt the fairly narrow definition of the *hukim* offered by the rabbis. Rather, the *hukim* comprise any mitzvah whose reason is not evident, is not rational (like prayer, for example), or whose reason no longer applies (like sacrifices).[101] Stern argues that Maimonides' answer to the philosophical danger of antinomianism can be found in *Guide* 3:50–54. In these final chapters of the *Guide,* Maimonides states that the purpose of the mitzvot is "to occupy yourself with these commandments . . . rather than with matters pertaining to this world. You should act as if you were occupied with Him . . . and not with that which is other than He (*Guide* 3:51)."[102] Or, "He . . . has explained that the end of the actions prescribed by the whole Law is to bring about the passion which is correct that it be brought about, as we have demonstrated in this chapter *for the benefit of those who know the true realities* [my italics] (*Guide* 3:52)." Stern argues that these last chapters are responding to the one for whom some of the commandments (usually the *hukim*) no longer apply, either because they know the true reasons (which are now irrelevant), or because the perfection the commandments sought to achieve has already been achieved. Therefore, they are no longer directed toward "perfection of the body" or "perfection of the soul." Regarding this, Stern states, ". . . precisely because these practices do him 'no good' in his circumstances 'in his existence'—and because he knows this—they are ideally suited for him to use instead as means to train himself to occupy himself with God's commandments as opposed to 'matters pertaining to the world.'"[103]

The distinction between "mitzvot" and "piety" underlying Stern's thesis is suggestive. The philosopher is one who knows too much and thus cannot subjugate himself to commandments that are irrelevant and no longer part of his own spiritual perfection. In *Guide* 3:51–52, Maimonides attempts to prevent the philosopher's abnegation of these commandments (to avert antinomianism) by suggesting that these commandments (*hukim* in the larger sense) serve as the foundation for piety precisely because they are irrelevant; that is, they are meaningless as tools for perfection. These mitzvot enable the philosopher to train himself to concentrate only on spiritual matters, permanently separating him from the mundane. While the masses still think these *hukim* are part of the larger framework of what we may call halakha, the philosopher sees them as supererogatory precepts that are directives solely for one who has already been spiritually refined via philosophical speculation. Piety is the submission to the overarching principle of mitzvot—to occupy oneself with God, even as the specific mitzvah may no longer serve any constructive function.

While our Hasidic texts live in a very different ideational universe and have a different notion of spiritual enlightenment, they share two important components with this presentation of Maimonides. First, they contain the belief that an individual can, in the course of his life, become so attuned to divine will as to transcend the need for the entirety of the halakhic system, even as he continues to live inside it. Second, these Hasidic texts (particularly the writings of R. Gershon Henokh) promote the belief in the binding nature of the law and construct a defense of it that includes transparency but not obsolescence. The reconstruction I present in this discussion of R. Gershon Henokh is not apologetic in the defensive sense, in that it takes R. Mordecai Joseph's deconstruction of the absolute nature of halakha as a fact.[104] It is, rather, a clarification of an antinomianism *in* halakha and not *outside* halakha. Just as Stern maintains that traditionalist critics of Maimonides are essentially correct in their appraisal of the status of the philosopher in the *Guide* but misunderstood the intention of *Guide* 3:50–54,[105] I am suggesting that R. Gershon Henokh would have been sympathetic to Joseph Weiss's appraisal of R. Mordecai Joseph as a religious anarchist but that he would also claim that Weiss misunderstands the purpose of mitzvot within that antinomian system.

As mystical exegetes and not philosophers, both R. Mordecai Joseph and R. Gershon Henokh construct their worldviews via biblical exegesis and not logical argumentation. These exegetes view the Jewish people through biblical archetypes, constructing personality paradigms that serve as the foundation for their understanding of both human nature and history. There is little doubt that they see themselves as embodying the integrated messianic personality of the biblical Judah, interpreted in *Mei Ha-Shiloah* as one who cannot be bound by the external norms of halakha. The depiction of Abraham and Isaac as the first stage of messianic integration is a model that is overcome by the sons of Jacob, each of whom complete another facet of their ancestor's personality, culminating in Judah's relationship to Tamar (Genesis 38:6–26) and his confrontation with Joseph in Egypt (Genesis 44:18).

The unconscious intuitiveness of Abraham and Isaac becomes self-consciousness in Jacob, only to be carried to its messianic (and antinomian) conclusion in Judah. The radical theology of Izbica/Radzin Hasidism is not merely a justification of *unconscious* and therefore inadvertent transgression (Abraham, Isaac), but the justification of *conscious* actions outside the halakhic framework as fulfilling the will of God (Jacob through Judah). As opposed to Abraham and Isaac, Jacob and later Judah consciously act against conventional norms, knowing full well the implications of their behavior. It is this integrated state of "a time to act for God" which represents the most provocative dimension of the Izbica/Radzin tradition.

R. Gershon Henokh is acutely aware of the dangers of his grandfather's opaque comments in *Mei Ha-Shiloah* on this matter and attempts to preempt some of the criticism that he is certain will follow. Yet he does so without softening the sharpness of R. Mordecai Joseph's claims. A central theme in *Sod Yesharim* is to penetrate and even deepen the latent antinomianism in *Mei Ha-Shiloah* precisely by placing it on the margins of legitimate Judaism, that is, halakha. In concert with Hasidic homiletics in general, R. Gershon Henokh never confronts this explicitly but leads us through an intricate exegetical web of observations on the Bible born out of the midrashic and Kabbalistic traditions. The permanent status of mitzvot plays an important role in the soft antinomianism that deconstructs the exclusivity of the system they represent. One of the more explicit assertions by R. Gershon Henokh in this regard is as follows:

> The will of God envelops his precious Torah in garments and gradations such as "two that make a claim on a prayer shawl" [b.T. Metzia 1:1].[106] These garments are called "Truth" [*torat emet*] and "Eternity" [*hayye 'olam*] to hint that these garments [halakha] will never become obsolete, even after the "precious depths" [God's will] will be revealed from within these garments making them unnecessary. In the future, there will be no need

> for these physical garments [of God's will]. Nevertheless, these garments of Torah. . . like "two who make a claim on a prayer shawl" will never be nullified.[107]

Prima facie this statement is quite normative, even conservative, in its appraisal of the divine will enveloped in the mitzvot and the mitzvot as the outer garment for that will. It appears to support the rabbinic notion that divine will lives solely within the "four ells of halakha," and also Maimonides' claim in his Thirteen Principles of Faith that the law will never be nullified, even in the messianic era.[108] Such a remark can also be located in any number of sources that are founded on the Kabbalistic notion of the mitzvot as the garments of Torah.[109] However, coming from R. Gershon Henokh, who is reared in the Izbica tradition that counters this conservative claim, the above statement must be seen in light of, and not in contradiction to, the antinomian spirit of R. Mordecai Joseph.

The first way R. Gershon Henokh justifies the continued relevance of halakha for one who has attained personal illumination is by making it clear that the illumination itself is temporary and cannot be sustained while living in the imperfect premessianic world.[110] To illustrate this, he invokes the Lurianic notion that the cosmic world contains two types of sexual unions. The first is the higher union between the *parzufim* (*sephirotic* clusters) of *abba* and *imma* (cosmic Father and Mother), a union that is constant *(yihud temidi)* and is not affected by human action. The second is the lower union of the *parzufim* of *zeir anpin* (Jacob) and *nukva* (Rachel), a union that is temporal and dependent upon the performance of the mitzvot.[111]

Generally, in theosophical Kabbala from the Zohar through Luria, the temporal union between *zeir anpin* and *nukva,* and not the perpetual union of *abba* and *imma,* facilitates the mystical experience (the latter is beyond the realm of human influence). As I argued earlier, the complexity of these theosophical ideas does not concern our Hasidic masters. However, these principles become the conventional nomenclature out of which Hasidic ideology takes form.[112] For example, regarding the temporal nature of the lower union that is open to human experience, R. Gershon Henokh states:

> This illumination is only in parts, whether it be in space [*'olam*], time [*shana*], or spirit [*nefesh*].[113] As long as an individual lives in his body, it is impossible to sustain a clear vision of God as eternally present. Such [a vision] would nullify one's ability to serve God. Therefore, he would have no place in the world.[114]

Although R. Gershon Henokh stresses that the illumination is always experienced through the prism of the temporal lower union of *zeir anpin* and *nukva,* enabling one to survive without a permanent loss of self, he also notes that the true illumination is like a flash rather than a sustained light.[115] He extrapolates on this notion of the temporal state of illumination from a halakhic disagreement about Shabbat Hanukkah. R. Gershon Henokh comments on a Talmudic passage (b.T. Shabbat 23b), where Rava asks whether, on Shabbat Hanukkah, one should light the Sabbath candles on Friday evening before the Hanukkah candles (because the Sabbath candles are more common [*tadir*]) or vice versa (because the Hanukkah candles publicize the miracle of Hanukkah). He states:

> The Hanukkah candles shine light into the darkness, therefore they are not permanent [lit., *tadir*] but only temporal, the result of the performance of a mitzvah that raises the consciousness of the individual. Hence, it states in b.T. Sota [21b], "*The candle is mitzvah, the Torah is light* [Proverbs 6:13] because the candle only [shines] temporarily." However, *Kiddush Ha-Yom* [Shabbat candles] symbolize the continuous actions done for God's Glory. All that one accomplishes in fulfilling the precepts of Shabbat is fixed and established. Anything added to that [established] holiness will increase the [already] established sanctity in one's soul resulting in an elevation to a higher place. This is what is called permanence [*tadir*]. The [Talmud] decided that the Hanukkah lights should be lit first because they publicize the miracle. Publicizing the miracle is exposing the power of God, which is hidden in every person. . . .Therefore, in human beings, sometimes the light [of God] will be aroused from the darkness. They [the rabbis] decided that the Hanukkah lights should be lit first because of publicizing the miracle. Even though this [arousal] is not fixed and established, nevertheless that which was aroused at that moment, i.e., the light [of God] from within the darkness, will remain as a sign and a remnant. This is very precious even if the light itself does not remain clear. . . .[116]

R. Gershon Henokh uses this atypical halakhic case, where the rabbis decide that an uncommon mitzvah (Hanukkah lights) takes precedence over a more established one (Sabbath candles), to make a point about the permeable boundaries of halakha. He suggests that the symbolic nature of the Hanukkah lights, as the momentary illumination of God in the dark recesses of creation, is important enough to override the normative halakhic principle regarding the order of mitzvot. This interpretation is a play on the nature of the Hanukkah lights as embodying the personal illumination of God's will. The illumination is such that it cannot be sustained in its fullness (i.e., it can never become normative). Nonetheless, its remnant *(reshimu)* remains in the consciousness of the one who receives it. The permanent result of the reception of this remnant of illumination is the psychic "overcoming" of the mitzvot, understood here as overcoming the normative halakhic principle of "*tadir ve 'eyno tadir, tadir kodem.*"[117]

Whether this new orientation is ever externalized by advocating a temporary abrogation of halakhic norms is not at issue here and is never made explicit either by R. Mordecai Joseph or R. Gershon Henokh. Moreover, R. Gershon Henokh does not draw the antinomian conclusion that the "illumined" experience of the unity of God in the fragmented creation (i.e., the exposure of divine light represented in his interpretation of publicizing the miracle of Hanukkah) would override the need to light the Sabbath candles (i.e., continue to live in the established framework of halakha). Both are necessary—halakha and its dissolution. However, this remnant does change the nature of the community's enactment of the mitzvot and the individual's relationship to halakha in that an experience of God that is not facilitated through halakha (Hanukkah candles as publicizing the miracle) now becomes part of one's devotional life. Even as R. Gershon Henokh advises such an individual to take the remnant of that momentary illumination and draw it into the continued performance of mitzvot, it also leaves open the possibility that being true to that remnant may necessitate going outside the system.

In concert with the halakhic discussion in the Talmudic passage, the Hanukkah lights do not supplant need for the Sabbath lights. Yet, the enlightened or illumined individual has the advantage over his or her unenlightened counterpart in the performance of the mitzvot by embellishing and elevating the nature of the mitzvot (permanence) via the extrahalakhic illumination of divine unity (illumination). What this amounts to is that the performance of the mitzvot are elevated and transformed when enacted by one who has overcome them. As discussed earlier, the incompatibility of the personality archetypes of Judah and Joseph in *Mei Ha-Shiloah* does not only arise when Judah acts outside the halakhic framework but is manifest even in the ways that both fulfill the law. The temporary illumination is a product of the protomessianic world, infusing messianic consciousness in a yet unredeemed world. Even though the temporality of the mitzvot may be overcome in the redemptive era, in the unredeemed world they are viewed in dialectical tension *with* but not in opposition *to* the mitzvot themselves. My contention is that R. Gershon Henokh's position is that personal illumination generally shares the same basic values with the halakhic system and, *in most cases,* enhances rather than opposes halakhic norms. However, the carrier of such an illumination draws his spiritual sustenance from a source other than a commitment to this system as the sole carrier of divine will. Therefore, acting outside (and against) the system "for the sake of heaven" (i.e., to oblige the divine will) is built into the system and is always possible. Therefore, it seems that mitzvot function best when performed by someone who no longer needs them.

This last point addresses critics who contend that R. Mordecai Joseph's position on personal illumination constitutes a case of Jewish antinomianism. Even if it would be correct to assert that, for this individual, the halakhic system cannot consume the spirit of divine will, extrahalakhic behavior can be absorbed by the system itself without rupturing its foundations. In R. Gershon Henokh's mind, there are two distinct yet interrelated purposes for halakhic practice, both of which reflect Maimonides' defense of the law in light of the threat of philosophical antinomianism discussed above. The first is that halakha is a catalyst for divine illumination. Adopting a position common in medieval Kabbala, the experience of illumination is largely dependent, although not contingent, upon the performance of mitzvot.[118] Although couched in Kabbalistic language, this resembles Maimonides' understanding of the law as facilitating "perfection of the body and soul."

For some Kabbalists the commandments are the vehicles for human perfection because they put one in contact with the divine realm. For both Maimonides and the Kabbalists, being fully human requires knowledge (or experience) of God. For this reason, perhaps, R. Moses Cordovero uses Maimonides as the basis of a chapter on the obligation to study Kabbala.[119] Maimonides distinguishes between the multitude and the elite on how each may attain this "knowledge." He states that "the perfection of the soul" constitutes "the *multitude* acquiring correct opinions corresponding to their respective capacity" (*Guide* 3:27). It is not at all clear that the *elite* (i.e., those with philosophical training) need the mitzvot to attain those "correct opinions." A reading of Maimonides influenced by Averroes's distinction between the philosopher and the masses would argue that the philosopher could attain true knowledge of God without the aid of the law, even as the law may help in that pursuit.[120] One could argue that the notion of spiritual lineage in Izbica/Radzin Hasidism corresponds in theory to reason in Maimonides' model. Both enable the individual to "know" God outside the performance of the mitzvot.[121] And both serve as the cornerstone of the antinomian threat. The difference, of course, is that, for Maimonides, the potential to achieve "knowledge of God" is theoretically accessible to all (although those with superior intelligence and training are at a clear advantage), while for R. Gershon Henokh the ability to achieve illumination is dependent on a spiritual inheritance that creates impermeable boundaries between the enlightened and the unenlightened.

Finally, Maimonides is well known for his seemingly antimystical assertion that the law will remain intact even after the onslaught of the messianic era.[122] This claim resonates in R. Gershon Henokh's statement above: "Nevertheless, these garments of Torah . . . like 'two who make claim on a prayer shawl' will never be nullified."[123] Maimonides' vision of the messianic era is one in which the world will be filled with a universally shared "knowledge of God." In the Izbica/Radzin tradition, messianism is a time when the "human will and divine will are permanently aligned," and that alignment will be recognized by the entire nation of Israel. In both cases, the law may remain but its purpose will radically change. In *Mei Ha-Shiloah* this era is marked by the archetype of Joseph understanding the archetype of Judah. Perhaps an Izbica/Radzin reading of Maimonides would have the messianic era marked by a pluralistic notion of how divine will can be fulfilled. Maimonides would argue, according to this Hasidic reading, that "knowledge of God" (which is really the telos of mitzvot and the covenantal experience) can be achieved in various ways, the practice of the law (the halakhists) being only one, *ta'amei ha-mitzvot* (the philosopher) being another, and pure contemplation of God's world (the mystic) a third. These different paths, while resulting in different visions of God and the world, and even different lifestyles, ultimately reach for the identical redemptive end and are all included under a much expanded category called "halakha."

Some Occupational Hazards of the Messianic Vocation

Another telos of halakha for R. Gershon Henokh is that it enables the integrated personality (i.e., those with the soul of Judah who see beyond the fragmented world of halakha) to avoid the danger of believing that his will and the divine will are permanently aligned, thus nullifying the need for divine grace. In other words, the recipient of personal illumination is always in danger of concluding that he has attained an independence *from* God by becoming one *with* Him. Such a deduction would necessitate erasing the final barrier of alienation initiated with Adam and Eve's sin, resulting in the end of exile and the onslaught of the messianic era. That is, such a figure could easily determine that he is the Messiah. This erasure and claims of messianic identity are common among Jewish antinomian ideologies and personalities, from Saint Paul to Sabbatai Sevi and beyond. Having inherited the aftershocks of the Sabbatean heresy, the Hasidic tradition is much more cautious in making (or at least externalizing) these assumptions. Therefore, it is predictable that the provocative leap outside halakha in *Mei Ha-Shiloah* is followed by a return to halakha in *Sod Yesharim*. Yet, R. Gershon Henokh's attempt to incorporate his grandfather's quasi-anarchic antinomianism into the framework of the law is not a conservative return to the law or an erasure of heightened messianic consciousness. It is, among other things, an attempt to justify halakha for one who has outgrown it and an attempt to expand the elasticity of the law to envelop acting outside its boundaries. The return to halakha in Izbica/Radzin Hasidism resembles the justification of the law for the philosopher, according to Joseph Stern's reading of Maimonides, even as the philosopher may no longer require it. R. Gershon Henokh claims that the halakha works as a sort of spiritual safety net even though it may no longer function as a catalyst for personal illumination.

For the illuminated personality the praxis of halakha remains, but its telos changes in two distinct ways. First, it keeps the messianic personality rooted in the protomessianic world, preventing him from moving beyond the boundaries of legitimate Judaism until the world catches up to him. Second, by living in tension *inside* the halakha, the messianic personality destabilizes the law, thereby extending the elasticity of the halakhic tradition. That is, the messianic personality brings collective redemption by abiding by a system that is, for him, obsolete, and he slowly, through observance, destabilizes the system until it is no longer necessary. This act of being simultaneously inside and outside forces its adherents to revisit the relationship between law and spirit in a way that moves them from the protomessianic (what is) to the messianic (what will be)—that is, from seeing spirit as ancillary to the law to seeing spirit as its center. This is arguably the underlying contribution of Hasidism in general as understood by many of the early and middle masters.

R. Gershon Henokh develops this idea in his reading of the rabbinic interpretation of Jacob's return over the Jabbok ford to gather his possessions (*pakhim katanim,* small vessels) (Genesis 32:25 and Rashi ad. loc.). Commenting on Jacob finding himself alone on the far side of the river, Rashi quotes a Talmudic source stating that he returned to gather "small vessels" (b.T. Hullin 91a).[124] Commenting on Rashi's rendering of Jacob's return over the river, R. Gershon Henokh states:

> After he passed back over the Jabbok ford, that is, after he reached the level where he could draw the light of God even into [the darkness] of nature,

> he needed to return to the *avodah* [i.e., the mitzvot] in order that he not [mistakenly] think that God is constantly shining through him without interruption. Therefore, he returned to the *avodah* which is called "small vessels" in order that he recognize that both the power of his influence as well as his vessels are small and that he understand that he should never say that his light [i.e., the light of God through him] is uninterrupted.[125]

R. Gershon Henokh offers two utilitarian approaches to answer the question as to why the integrated and enlightened personality must remain bound to the halakhic system: the first psychological, the second ontological. The psychological approach addresses the dangers faced by the integrated personality who carries with him the illumination and the apprehension of divine unity in the fragmented world. Jacob understands his unique capacity to draw down the light of God, that is, to reveal the will of God, even in the places where He is concealed (in nature). For Jacob, to imply that he has become divine would misconstrue his achievement as a vessel to contain divine effluence. This error would result in succumbing once again to the serpent's promise to Eve in Genesis 3:4–5.[126] The danger confronting the enlightened personality living in the protomessianic world is vulnerability to a belief that he has transcended his fallibility and humanness. For R. Gershon Henokh, the antidote to this danger is a return to the performance of mitzvot, to involve oneself in the "small vessels" of the fragmented world even as one apprehends their limited nature. It is not insignificant that the return to the minutia of halakha is depicted in the biblical Jacob who is viewed in the Zohar and subsequent Kabbalistic schools (including Hasidism) as the most perfected personality *(ta'am* or *shalem)* in the Torah (Genesis 25:27).[127] The return to mitzvot allows the fully integrated individual (Jacob) to continue his work of *tikun 'olam* without forfeiting his status as a vessel for God's will. It is precisely the archetype of the biblical Jacob, the perfected human being who no longer needs mitzvot, who shows the necessity of halakha for all others.

This psychological interpretation arguing for the continued need for mitzvot is coupled with an ontological interpretation of the "small vessels," suggesting that one must constantly return to the concealed world, the world where God is still absent and halakha is necessary, in order to fully integrate the messianic consciousness of divine presence into a yet unredeemed world. Jacob consciously converts his experience of divine unity back into the concealed world of mitzvot (the small vessels) to facilitate a full integration with the fragmented world in which he lives. That is, Jacob's action does not only insure his humility but also completes the process of gathering the lost sparks of divinity embedded in the material world. Breaking out of the exilic (halakhic) framework before the world is redeemed, the integrated personality would forfeit his ability to uplift the exilic world and to complete the final *tikun*. His salvation would be at the expense of all others. Yet, it is the very confrontation of these two realms of existence (the exilic and the messianic) that expedites the unfolding of redemption. Therefore, in the Izbica/Radzin tradition, Judah's confrontation with Joseph in Egypt (Genesis 44:18) is, in many ways, the apogee of the entire biblical narrative.

The confrontation between the archetype of the exilic character (Joseph) and the integrated messianic personality (Judah) in Egypt sets the stage for the history of Israel in exile. Both live in a covenant with God that requires mitzvot, albeit for very different reasons. The exilic personality needs halakha as the determinant of God's will. The integrated personality continues to need mitzvot either to avert the inherent danger of seeing oneself as a pure vessel of God's will, or to utilize his illumination to facilitate the perfection of the world—that is, to extend perfection from the self to the other. In either case, the carrier of the illumination should not forfeit the halakhic life as a consequence of his newly acquired apprehension of the unity between his will and God's. While mitzvot may no longer function as an essential part of the individual's personal religious life, they play an important role in his ability to contribute to the spiritual progress of the world at large.

The final alternative offered by R. Gershon Henokh to support the continued practice of halakha for the spiritually enlightened person is more common than the previous two, but it is important in that it serves as a pillar of the Radzin interpretation of Izbica Hasidism. He argues that the experience of illumination that lies at the core of *Mei Ha-Shiloah* is both achieved and maintained through the performance of mitzvot. In a somewhat ironic twist, he asserts that only by participating in what he calls the "small vessels" *(pakhim katanim)* of halakhic minutia can an individual transcend the fragmented nature of reality and apprehend the unity of creation and Creator. Furthermore, the experience that nullifies or overcomes the mitzvot is achieved *by* and sustained *through* the continued performance of the mitzvot. Below, I illustrate the ways in which R. Gershon Henokh attempts to integrate the mitzvot (nomos) as the catalyst for the illumined experience, which reaches beyond the need for mitzvot, yet does not result in an antinomian religious ideology.

> Behold, [regarding] the sanctity of home and wealth: one is called "home" and the other "wealth" when one is in a state of divine service

> [*avodot*] before clarification/perfection [*berur*]. However, when one becomes clear, when one perceives the light of God, the sanctity achieved is called "an enlightened woman" [*'isha maskolet*].[128] That is, man will apprehend that she is his source and she is the light that God gave to his source [soul]. There is no devotion that can reach this place, as it is said in Genesis [2:23], *Then the man said, This one at last is bone of my bones and flesh of my flesh. This one shall be called Woman, for from man was she taken.* The purpose of all devotion is that one should reach his source. When he reaches his source he will see that he is from God and that his source is connected to God through this light. Therefore, it will become clear that in this world he chose certain *avodot* [devotional practices] that would have a direct relation to the root of his [particular] soul and thus become obligatory from the root of his soul.[129]

In this intertextual reading of Genesis 2:23 through the lens of Proverbs 19:14, R. Gershon Henokh suggests that just as man can recognize the source of woman in himself, he can recognize his source in God through *avodah* (i.e., mitzvot).[130] The verse in Proverbs distinguishes between man's two most cherished possessions: that which is "bequeathed by inheritance" (property and wealth) and that which is a "a gift from God" (an enlightened or efficient woman). R. Gershon Henokh reads these as two perceptions of the same thing, two stages in self-awareness or enlightenment. This self-awareness comes about through devotion. Devotion for the unenlightened (i.e., before *berur*) is envisioned as something external to the worshipper, perhaps halakha as obligation. For the enlightened, however, devotion is an expression of intimacy with one's own spiritual makeup (the root of one's soul), both its strengths and weaknesses. When the mitzvot, which are the possessions of Israel, serve to facilitate the revelation of God, they are called "an enlightened woman," translated to mean "a mate who enlightens." As a result, the worshipper understands why he is more attracted to certain mitzvot, just as he is to certain women, each mitzvah representing a particular permutation of the divine will.[131] The common notion of a man finding his "soulmate" in a woman is used to understand why certain individuals are attracted to certain mitzvot and repelled by others.

The correlation of Eros and spirituality is intentional in this comparison. Just as Eve is described as Adam's "helpmate" (Genesis 2:18), mitzvot serve to help direct the desires of man toward spiritual ends.[132] The basic premise is that apprehending the source of one's soul is contingent on the performance of mitzvot. That is, only devotion *(avodah)* in an initial "unrefined" state, a state where halakha is still binding, can yield the clarification *(berur)* necessary for the illumination that overcomes the mitzvot as binding. The very notion of being bound by mitzvot seems to refer to the first stage, the stage of "home and wealth." When one lives in the mitzvot as an "enlightened woman," the mitzvot are no longer binding but are the product of the intimacy (devekut) between the worshipper and the commander. The mitzvot have become internalized.

In numerous ways, R. Gershon Henokh argues that his grandfather's position that individuals can indeed overcome the need for mitzvot does not negate the value of mitzvot and thus does not constitute a formal case of antinomianism. This is not to say that R. Gershon Henokh disagrees with his grandfather that the tension for the messianic personality is that he lives in a system (halakha) he no longer needs. Nor is he rejecting the possibility that this refined will can intuit divine will outside or even against halakha, thus sanctioning, at least in principle, the viability of extrahalakhic behavior. Even for those unique individuals, however, mitzvot continue to play an important role and should not be abandoned even as halakha may be bracketed in extenuating circumstances. It needs to be stressed that this temporary permissibility of transgressive behavior is not a reflection of the pragmatism underlying the rabbinic dictum of "desecrating one Sabbath in order to keep many Sabbaths." Rather, "holy transgression" in Izbica/Radzin Hasidism is the temporary eruption of the messianic temperament into the protomessianic world. It is, in a sense, a necessary heresy that is redemptive.

Perhaps R. Mordecai Joseph and R. Gershon Henokh feel that such behavior is necessary in order to ease the tension of the integrated personality whose living solely within the framework of halakha compromises his intimacy with God. Or, perhaps in line with the Lurianic notion of the infusion and retrieval of light from the vessels as a necessary part of the process of *tikun,* our thinkers maintain that this temporary eclipse of halakha strengthens the world's ability to eventually absorb the diffusion of halakha in the future.[133] Whatever the reason, it remains the case that R. Gershon Henokh's construction of halakha for the illumined messianic personality attempts to integrate extrahalakhic behavior into, and not distinguish it from, the halakhic system itself. Mitzvot remain the norm, even for one who has overcome them. However, through overcoming mitzvot, the system has overstepped its rabbinic boundaries. One can no longer conflate divine will and the law. Protomessianic halakha is a step away from premessianic halakha and a step toward Robert Cover's concept of the unknown nature of the messianic era. The rabbinic dictum limiting God's presence (and will) to the "four ells of halakha" has been irreparably shattered.

This last point is developed in a discussion on the nature of taking oaths that is the central theme in the final chapter of the Book of Numbers (chap. 30). Returning to the Kabbalistic concepts of "hovering light" *('or makif)* and "internal light" *('or penimi)* that serve as the foundation for his interpretation of Genesis 3 (the sin in the Garden of Eden), R. Gershon Henokh views both mitzvot and free will as necessary, yet containing the conditions for their own obsolescence.

> The idea of an oath is as follows: God gave this mitzvah to Israel in order to repair the root and source from which they were formed. Humanity is the telos of creation in that God concealed Himself after creating the world, as it says in *Sefer Raziel,* "After God created the world He turned His face from it. . . ." This means that the entire emanation which produced creation is surrounded by the will of God, which is the secret of the surrounding light [*'or makif*]. Hence, God's will surrounds the entire creation so that one can never turn from it. . . . Only human beings were given free will [*behira*] meaning they received the light of God as "inner light" [*'or penimi*]. This [inner light] is a garment [for the surrounding light] and allows this [surrounding] light to descend into the depths of human consciousness [*b'omek da'ato*]. This enables God to be drawn into this world via free will. The [uniqueness of the] human being [is that], apart from being surrounded by God's will [*mukaf b'razon*] he also surrounds His will [*makif l'razon*] [via the inner light within]. By being the garment for God's will one can turn God's face and stand "face to face" [*panim b'panim*] with God. This will result in the surrounding light also becoming face to face [with creation].[134]

Torah and free will exist so that one can draw God into the world even in His concealed state (i.e., after creation in *Sefer Raziel* cited above). Therefore, one can only live in concert with His will and can only live fully as a human being via Torah and mitzvot (i.e., revelation). However, in truth God's "face" surrounds creation *('or makif),* which makes us unable to "turn" away from Him. The uniqueness of humanity (really only Israel), an implicit reference to being created in the "image of God," is that as carriers of the inner light (the garment of God's infinitude) we can, via mitzvot, turn God's face and reveal the concealed state of God's presence. Until now, we have remained within the parameters of conventional interpretation. However, implicit in the entire Izbica/Radzin tradition is that certain individuals who have accomplished the necessary "refinements" *(berurim)* through spiritual inheritance and pious devotion can absorb and internalize the turning of God's face, thus overcoming the need for mitzvot.

Theosophical Kabbala based on the Zohar teaches that the natural state of creation is exilic, that is, God's face is turned away from us. The upward emanation *(mayim nukvin),* precipitated by human action in general and mitzvot in particular, turns God's face toward us via cosmic unification *(yihudim).* In this instance, however, the claim is that certain individuals have become so refined that God no longer needs to turn away from them because they are no longer living in exile. Being that the Kabbalistic telos of mitzvot is God turning toward us, for those individuals, the mitzvot cease to serve any constructive function vis-à-vis God's relation to them. The final turning of God's face (the messianic era) is therefore not a one-time event experienced by the entire nation (or world) simultaneously. Rather, certain individuals achieve this level of clarity and then must live in the tension of a world yet unredeemed. These individuals are no longer solely surrounded *by* God's will but, having internalized the surrounding light via the inner light, become carriers *of* His will. The barrier separating the inner light and the surrounding light is removed, liberating these refined beings from the confines of divine absence *(hester panim).*

Free will and mitzvot are the fundamental components in this redemptive process as they refine the messianic soul, thinning the veil between the external *(eyn sof)* and internal (human soul/*neshama*) light of God until the veil disappears. At that moment, God and the refined human soul stand "face to face" and all elements of doubt, which first arise from the absence of God's face, disappear.

Returning to the biblical context and rabbinic discussion of oaths, an oath is only necessary in a world of doubt and uncertainty. It is a divinely sanctioned and self-imposed suprahalakhic limitation of permissible behavior. The entire foundation of oaths becomes unnecessary for one who stands "face to face" with God as a result of identifying his will with the divine. For one who sees that "even the fear of heaven is in the hands of heaven," the oath becomes an outdated safeguard against human error. This last point is emphasized more poignantly in a text attributed to R. Jacob Lainer, R. Gershon Henokh's father.[135]

> God's dealing with an individual is only before his perfection [*kodem sh'nishlam*]. God has nothing more to do with him after his perfection. When he stands "face to face" with God [*nokakh Ha-Shem*] his actions are no longer attributed to him. Isaac is an example of this. We do not hear of him after he blesses Jacob, even though we know he remained alive. Before his perfection [i.e., before blessing Jacob] we are made aware of Isaac's seemingly trivial actions. This is because God was engaged with him, teaching him how to rectify [*yit'barer*] himself.[136]

R. Jacob Lainer's description of God "dealing" with an individual not yet purified refers to two things. First, it suggests that mitzvot are divine directives that lead one toward human perfection. God engages in the covenantal promise of reward and punishment in order to bring an individual to self-awareness and self-consciousness. Second, in this incomplete state, an individual is held responsible for his actions, therefore his actions "are attributed to him," for both good and evil. However, once one stands face to face with God, that is, once one's will becomes unified with divine will, he is no longer engaged in the same covenantal experience since he no longer acts from free will. His actions are no longer considered his own because he can no longer act otherwise. Therefore, R. Jacob Lainer states, "God has nothing more to do with him"—he has completed the process of perfection the mitzvot are intended to fulfill.

The covenant of mitzvot functions in an imperfect community for individuals who need external directives to achieve perfection. In many ways, this is aligned with Maimonides' idea that the purpose of mitzvot is to "perfect the body and the soul." However, when an individual achieves this perfection, either through spiritual inheritance and piety (Izbica/Radzin) or through philosophical reflection (Maimonides), many of the mitzvot become obsolete, and the binding nature of halakha, which is maintained, is reconfigured for those enlightened individuals. We have seen how our Hasidic thinkers grapple with the possibility of antinomianism before the advent of the messianic era while simultaneously supporting the continued necessity and relevance of the mitzvot. R. Jacob Lainer's comment above suggests that the conventional telos of mitzvot as the sole expression of divine will no longer applies for a messianic archetype. Throughout this chapter we have discussed numerous attempts by R. Gershon Henokh and his father R. Jacob Lainer to maintain the system, even as its boundaries become more and more permeable as the messianic era approaches.

In conclusion, even as I argue that Izbica/Radzin Hasidism does not constitute a case of Jewish antinomianism in the technical sense, I call it a soft antinomianism because it shatters the exclusivity of mitzvot as the sole arbiter of divine worship and raises the possibility that God can sometimes best be served outside the halakhic system. The halakhic system is maintained but its borders have become more transparent and permeable. The absolution of free will in the highest state of human perfection and the correlation between the divine will with the human will thereby makes any action of such an individual an act of God. This, I submit, sets Izbica/Radzin

Hasidism on the margins of any interpretation of Judaism. It is precisely this marginality that makes this Hasidic tradition such an important topic for scholarly inquiry. The creative impulse to move outside accepted religious doctrine, coupled with the acceptance of the yoke of the past, often yields fascinating and innovative ideologies in the history of religious traditions.

R. Gershon Henokh is noteworthy as a Hasidic thinker for various reasons. While primarily an exegete, he has a much broader agenda, one that seeks to integrate and synthesize the disparate parts of the Jewish literary canon and rethink the roots of the Hasidic-Mithnagdic debate that has dominated the most formative period of Hasidic creativity. More than many of his contemporaries, R. Gershon Henokh thinks in broad strokes and seems acutely aware of the wider implications of his teachings. I have argued that he is clearly not an apologist for his grandfather, even as he defends his grandfather's collected writings against its many critics.

While acknowledging the radical nature of *Mei Ha-Shiloah,* R. Gershon Henokh is also committed to offering a reading that maintains its radical foundation while remaining within the elastic boundaries of normative Judaism. His creative mind, combative disposition, and command of classical Jewish sources enable him to weave the mitzvot back into the cryptic and often startling assertions of his grandfather, setting R. Mordecai Joseph's ideology within the halakhic tradition without sacrificing his belief in the ability to "overcome" the mitzvot in the protomessianic world.

In this final chapter, I attempt to arrive at a working definition of classical antinomianism in order to demonstrate how the pietistic Hasidic ideology of Izbica/Radzin does not fulfill the necessary requirements of antinomianism as classically defined. Yet, R. Gershon Henokh is aware of the sensitive nature of some of his grandfather's assertions and thus strives to make certain the mitzvot continue to play a part in his soft antinomian framework. The question that looms large above all of the previous scholarly studies on Hasidism in general and Izbica/Radzin Hasidism in particular is how and why these clearly radical thinkers were able to remain within the halakhic tradition and not take the route of the Sabbateans, who either repudiated the radical antinomian doctrines of Sabbatai Sevi and Nathan of Gaza and became reabsorbed into traditional communities or, like the Frankists, abandoned Judaism altogether. Although the definitive answer to this question remains a desideratum, this study has shown that the Izbica/Radzin Hasidic tradition represents an imposing and unique example of "Judaism on the margin."

Conclusion

The scholarly study of Hasidism has, to a large degree, been oriented toward either history or theology. Primarily as a response to nineteenth-century historians such as Henrich Graetz and Simon Dubnow, twentieth-century scholars have painstakingly reconstructed the history of Hasidic life, printing, literature, and ideas. Theologians, following the lead of Samuel Abba Horodetzky and Martin Buber, have used Hasidic doctrine as a basis for contemporary theological reflections on the nature of Jewish spirituality. Some scholars have seriously engaged with Hasidic doctrine in its own right, doing so largely to present Hasidism as a viable and sophisticated response to its social and intellectual environment. Here I have attempted to take Hasidism in a different direction: to view Hasidic thinking as part of the long trajectory of Jewish philosophy and Kabbala, and to argue that this can only be accomplished by viewing Hasidic texts through a hermeneutical lens. That is, I have attempted to show Hasidic creativity in its utilization of hermeneutical principles founded on a philosophy of esotericism and secrecy. I argued that while the social and intellectual contexts of these thinkers remains relevant, to focus primarily on that dimension of Hasidic literature diminishes the philosophical breadth and depth of these texts.

In this book I set out to investigate the nature of mid- to late-nineteenth-century Polish Hasidism through the lens of the Izbica/Radzin dynasty. I focus on a few fundamental issues central to the study of religion in general and the study of Jewish philosophy and mysticism in particular. My claim throughout has been that Hasidism shares a great deal with other religious pietistic traditions, even as it speaks in an insular and private language, yet these parallels cannot be fully disclosed as long as Hasidism is viewed myopically through such a narrow lens. I argue from the particular case of the Izbica school, which is admittedly radical but not atypical, that the fundamental principle of Hasidism, and its contribution to Jewish pietism, is its notion of esotericism and secrecy. In this school it is manifest as a primordial Torah that is both concealed and disclosed throughout the long history of Jewish literature. The key to redemption is not solely in the adherence to the mitzvot but also (or even more importantly) in the disclosure and accessibility of this hidden Torah, a Torah that predates mitzvot. Hasidism is presented here as the final frontier of Jewish esotericism, the culmination of thousands of years of disclosure and concealment of this primordial Torah, finally revealed in its fullness, and simplicity, in the teachings of the Baal Shem Tov.

The notion of philosophical perennialism, common in esoteric traditions, also touches on issues central to the Jewish philosophical tradition. The theory of a hidden yet present Torah, an extension of a hidden yet manifest God (two ideas common in classical Judaism), also serves to represent faith as a primordial experience of secrecy through which the recipient attains a level of knowing that is beyond discursive knowledge but does not cancel it out. That is, faith, which produces this metacognition, does not stand in opposition to reason but is founded on a kind of knowledge beyond reason, an experience of the divine that is then incorporated into one's cognitive life and serves as the foundation of piety. Primordial faith (as distinct from simply "believing in" something) is the result of the disclosure of an "understanding" based on a superrational experience that makes cognition possible. While faith (as metacognition) must precede knowing, the full unfolding of this faith results in knowledge, wisdom, and finally action.

Thus, true knowledge can never be isolated from human action. It is embodied in human behavior, known *through* the body in the form of piety and devotion. Yet action does not exclusively mean mitzvot, devekut serving here as a wedge separating piety and halakha. By this I mean that in Hasidism, devekut is an experience of proximity to the divine that may be a consequence of mitzvot but is not dependent on mitzvot. Devekut is not the necessary outgrowth of living according to halakha, nor is halakha a necessary precondition for the experience. Hasidic "knowing," at least according to R. Gershon Henokh, is the enactment of faith through living *for* and *toward* that initial moment of primordial faith which, when that faith is made accessible to the collective, yields God's redemptive disclosure. This religious ideal is envisioned as the true Abrahamic religion, the (literal) embodiment of faith that precedes, in fact precludes, commandment. It is only when human beings can no longer access this primordial faith that commandment (and Sinai) become necessary.

The goal of disclosing this primordial Torah, of revealing the secret that underlies Judaism as we know it, is to recapture the Abrahamic religion that is its true expression. The secret upon which Judaism is built, and where it must return, is that which reformats mitzvah-centered Judaism embedded in halakha. As ultratraditionalists, however, these Hasidic thinkers could not easily forego the Judaism of mitzvot that has sustained them and their ancestors for so many generations and that serves as the foundation of their construction of the world. Therefore, what emerges from this tension—on the one hand, to transcend the need for Judaism by disclosing this primordial faith, and on the other hand, remaining true to the Judaism of Sinai that they believe is still valid and necessary—is the unfolding of a fascinating drama on the margins of Judaism.

This notion of esoteric disclosure thus has three pieces: (1) the discovery of a buried Abrahamic religion in need of renewal; (2) the discovery of primordial faith that creates a new foundation for embodied knowledge achieved through devotion; and (3) a source with which to synthesize the disparate traditions of philosophy and Kabbala in order to rectify the exilic construction of Torah and give birth to a new Torah for the future. These are the three pieces that make up R. Gershon Henokh's "Introduction to Hasidism," the preface to the reconstruction of the Jew in his and his grandfather's commentaries to the Torah, the Festivals, and the Zohar.

The second part of this book is an extended essay on Hasidic hermeneutics, focusing on the way certain philosophical ideas are played out in creative readings of the biblical narrative. In his conclusion to his *Through a Speculum that Shines* (394), Elliot Wolfson makes a general comment about classical Kabbala that is also applicable to Hasidic literature. "Whatever other religious influences have been operative in the various trends of Jewish mysticism, it is evident that the Jewish mystics are primarily interpreters of Scripture. . . . No experience is without context, and no context in Judaism is without Scripture." Although this seems obvious to any close reader of Hasidic texts, most scholarly literature on Hasidism does not focus on this "context," that is, it does not acknowledge that, in Hasidic literature, doctrine simply cannot be decontextualized from the Bible and its Hasidic reading. Discussing Hasidic doctrine outside its hermeneutical circle can yield interesting historical, sociological, and theological results but it cannot uncover the complex ways Hasidic literature serves as an extension of, and contribution to, the metahalakhic tradition of Jewish ideas. While scholarly literature surely uses Hasidic comments on Scripture as the basis of its analysis, it has not, in my view, adequately addressed the question of hermeneutical schemes and methods employed by Hasidic exegetes. In this book I explore some of these methods as they address two basic philosophical questions: first, determinism and the dissolution of free will as a goal of Hasidic devotion; and second, antinomianism and the dissolution of mitzvot as a goal of Hasidic messianism, existing in the present and not in some distant future.

This exercise highlights another innovative dimension of Hasidic thinking—its focus on the Bible as the blueprint for the person, as opposed to history, doctrine, or peoplehood. The biblical narrative, as read through the eyes of R. Mordecai Joseph of Izbica and R. Gershon Henokh of Radzin, is about the depiction and development of various personality archetypes, all of whom play a role in the emergence of the perfected or, as I prefer, reconciled person. This reconciled person is the archetype of the messianic personality, culminating in the biblical Jacob and then bifurcated in his sons, none of whom contain the requisite integration and fullness of their perfected father. Exile is framed as the dysfunctionality of the Israelite family, specifically the two dimensions of Jacob (Jacob and Israel/revealed and concealed perfection) who cannot understand each other because they cannot understand the concealed dimension of themselves. In particular, it is the Joseph archetype—the halakhist—who simply cannot comprehend and thus cannot tolerate the Judah archetype, who in turn refuses to allow divine will to be limited to the four ells of the law. This confrontation plays itself out in numerous scenarios in the Bible and rabbinic literature. I argue that the point of this exercise is to claim that redemption does not bring us the messianic person—the messianic person(ality) brings us redemption, brought about by expanding our notion of divine will and questioning our belief in free will as a model for human action and devotion. There is clearly a conventionality to all this, especially as read through the lens of classical Kabbala. Hasidism is innovative in its focus on the individual (the perfected person as the true servant of God) and the notion that a messianic personality lives (and sacrifices himself) on the margins of Judaism precisely to expand those margins and, in doing so, reveal a dimension of the halakhists heretofore concealed. Thus the reconciliation of the messianic person (the unity of divine and human will revealed) eventually becomes the reconciliation of Israel, accomplished by revealing the concealed dimension of the halakhist's limited personality.

The vision of Hasidism that emerges from this analysis is a traditional subversion of tradition. This is not a new observation but, in fact, is held by both critics and scholarly advocates of Hasidism in the last two centuries. What differs here is that I argue that Hasidism succeeds in the mid- to late nineteenth century not because it recedes back into traditionalism but because it successfully realigns the boundaries of what is legitimate in traditional Judaism. That is, it reconstructs Judaism in its own image. It is radical not because it is anarchic or antinomian but because it succeeds in translating religious anarchy into a pietistic framework that does not blow apart the halakhic tradition but radically reforms it under the very noses of halakha's great practitioners in Eastern Europe. Reform here is not instituted by the eradication of rituals or ceremonies but by reconstructing religious intentionality *(kavvanah),* thereby changing the very foundation of religious practice while maintaining its basic edifice. And, it bolsters the law by demanding that the law must always exist in a state of liminality and instability. The law survives because it is always on the verge of collapse.

This is all implemented by a hermeneutical method of reading classical texts against themselves to yield innovative results from texts that, on a more conventional reading, stand in stark opposition to the Hasidic reading. Ironically, largely through Hasidism's apologetic reception, these subversive readings have themselves become canonical. By never disclosing its reformist agenda, unlike Nathan of Gaza, the great Sabbatean hermeneut, this Hasidic tradition is able to reform Judaism from within and create the possibility of an alternative model of Jewish pietism that, in the future, can become the foundation for more explicit religious reform. It is therefore no surprise that contemporary Jewish Renewal, a movement that, in effect, combines liberal religious critique, neo-Sabbatean religious reform, and Hasidic pietism, views itself as the spiritual inheritor of these Hasidic texts. While one can surely argue whether and to what extent these reformers are accurately reading and interpreting these texts, it is certainly the case that these texts at least lend themselves to be read in such an expansive fashion.

In many respects this leads me to a final point that underlies this whole project: the definition of heresy and its place in the study of Hasidism. While I only touched on heresy in the body of the book, this important phenomenon in the study of Hasidic textuality is really the subtext of the entire book. By heresy I do not mean the overt and blatant abrogation of traditional norms, but the more subtle and nuanced way critics of a religious status quo affect change hermeneutically, that is, through subversively reading canonical texts. What I mean when I say that the masters of the Izbica and Radzin tradition, and other masters in mid- to late-nineteenth-century Polish Hasidism more generally, are heretics, is that they created the religious critique inside tradition sufficient for those who followed them to read (or misread) them and implement that critique in a more overt fashion. This does not mean that they would agree with this "heretical" extension, as I am quite certain they would not. However, I do think they would understand such deviance more than their more traditional inheritors maintain.

Many of these radical Hasidic schools were followed by generations of apologetic readers who, committed to the maintenance of ultra-Orthodox Judaism, simply could not accept, or perhaps could not afford, to let these opaque and provocative texts go uninterpreted. The result is that "legitimacy" is defined by those readings, and not the texts themselves, all of which fit these Hasidic texts solidly inside the doctrinal framework of ultra-Orthodoxy as presently construed. The apologetic reader saves the text by reading it totally within a doctrinal framework that the text may have been challenging. In short, apologetics here subverts the subversion. While many of these readings are surely well informed and sometimes even quite sophisticated, they fail, in my view, because they are unwilling to engage in two things: hermeneutical and comparative analysis. That is, they are not engaged in unraveling the underlying hermeneutical principles upon which these texts are constructed and, viewing this tradition as *sui generis,* at least in terms of extra-Judaic literature, they are unwilling to view the text's subtle conclusions in light of other religious traditions. This type of apologetic reading succeeds largely because the texts themselves are esoteric enough that they can be read in spite of their subversive critique, and the attempt to disclose the "subversive" agenda can never be definitively defended. This phenomenon speaks to the success of these texts as esoteric. The result of this apologetic reading is that it salvages the text from heretical reading, viewing it as both canonical, and thus sacred, and yet still critical of the status quo (i.e., Lithuanian Talmudism). In the late twentieth century, even this last point is muted, as Hasidic and non-Hasidic ultra-Orthodox Judaisms have collapsed into one largely homogenous haredi Judaism. What distinguishes Hasidic and non-Hasidic ultra-Orthodoxy is no longer the polemic against Hasidism. Hasidic texts, whether they are studied or not, are part of the sacred canon in contemporary haredi Judaism. My claim is that the canonization of Hasidic literature is, in one sense, its failure as it suppresses the very heretical elements that made Hasidism so compelling and attractive to those interested in religious reform.

What I have attempted to do in this book is argue that these Hasidic texts (at least) exhibit a "dialectic of heresy." That is, a heresy that is the very thing that enables a tradition to survive by expanding the boundaries of legitimacy in order to push the tradition towards its redemptive end. I argue that the Izbica and Radzin Hasidic legacy presents us with a reading of Scripture that undermines, and simultaneously supports, the biblical message as interpreted by the rabbinic sages arguing, by implication, that the biblical message (Abrahamic Torah) is supported, and even salvaged, by subversively reading through the rabbis in order to read against them. By this I do not mean that our Hasidic masters openly argued with authoritative rabbinic interpretation. Rather, they read the rabbis while proposing a different narrative about what Judaism is, and a different program about how Israel can hasten the end, a narrative that viewed halakha as a necessary but ultimately deficient vehicle for redemption. The complexity of this project, I maintain, eludes one who does not read for the hermeneutic strategies and is not willing to see the texts as a reflection of a larger esoteric exercise, sharing a great deal with other esotericisms both inside and outside Judaism. What results from such a reading is a pietistic Judaism on the margin, a Judaism that expands the margin as it works through the labyrinth of the middle, preparing Judaism for what it believes is the impending era of redemption and the text's final disclosure.

Notes

Bibliography

Index

Notes

Biographical Introduction

1. For a biographical sketch of R. Mordecai Joseph, see Morris Faierstein, *All Is in the Hands of Heaven* (1989), 11–19. On R. Gershon Henokh, see my "'A Thread of Blue': Rabbi Gershon Henokh Lainer of Radzyn and his Search for Continuity in Response to Modernity," *Polin* 11 (1998): 31–52.

2. See A. Penkalla, "The Socio-Cultural Integration of the Jewish Population in the Province of Radom 1815–1862," *Polin* 3 (1998); and Gershon Hundert, "An Advance to Peculiarity: The Case of the [Jews in the] Polish Commonwealth," *AJS Review* 6 (1981): 21–38.

3. See R. F. Leslie, *Polish Politics and the Revolution of November 1830* (1956).

4. On this see *The Jews in Warsaw,* W. T. Bartoszewski and A. Polonsky, eds. (1991), 14, 174; and Y. Ba'artish, "The Agricultural Settlement of the Jews in Congress Poland in the Period Preceding the Freedom of the Serfs" (in Hebrew), *Zion* 32:3, no. 4 (1967): 46–75. Cf. Arthur Eisenbach, *The Emancipation of the Jews in Poland 1780–1870,* Antony Polonsky, ed., and Janina Dorosz, trans. (1991), 207–33. Cf. Leslie, *Reform and Insurrection in Russian Poland 1856–1865* (1963).

5. On the general problem of Hasidic "history," see Ada Rapoport-Albert, "Hagiography with Footnotes: Edifying Tales and the Writing of History in Hasidism," in Ada Rapoport-Albert and Steven Zipperstein, eds., *Essays in Jewish Historiography* (1991), 119–59.

6. See R. Rurup, "The European Revolutions of 1848 and Jewish Emancipation," in *Revolution and Evolution: 1848 in German Jewish History,* Werner E. Mosse, ed. (1981); and H. S. Blejwas, "Polish Positivism and the Jews, " in *Journal of Jewish Studies* 46 (1984): 21–36.

7. On this see Raphael Mahler, *Hasidism and the Jewish Enlightenment* (1985), esp. 171–243. Although Mahler argues that the Haskalah (Jewish Enlightenment) failed to take root in Poland the way it did in Galicia, the threat of the Haskalah became an integral part of Hasidic writing, even in those areas not inundated with the progressive politics and culture of Haskalah society.

8. See the hagiographies by Zvi Meir Rabinovitz, *R. Simha Bunim of Pryzsucha* (1944); and Yohanan Levi Eyebshutz, *Simha Bunim of Pryzsucha* (1973). More

recently, see Alan Brill, "Grandeur and Humility in the Writings of R. Simha Bunim of Pryzsucha," in *Hazon Nahum,* Y. Elman and J. Gorock, eds. (1998), 419–48.

9. Rabbi Simha Bunim of Pryzsucha was the spiritual heir to R. Isaac Jacob Rabinovitz, known as the Holy Jew, who years earlier departed from the court of the R. Jacob Isaac Horowitz, Seer of Lublin.

10. The history of succession in Hasidism is quite complex and contains many different variations. During the first two generations of Hasidism, the master-disciple model of succession was often in considerable conflict with the father-son model, which became the dominant mode of transmission in the nineteenth century. See Ada Rapoport-Albert, "The Parable of Succession in the Hasidic Leadership with Special Emphasis to the Circle of R. Nahman of Bratzlav" (Ph.D. diss., University of London, 1970), esp. 87ff. Cf. idem, "Hasidism after 1772: Continuity and Change," in *Hasidism Reappraised,* Ada Rapoport-Albert, ed. (1996), 76–140. This article also appears in Hebrew in *Zion* 55 (1990): 187–215. This controversy became particularly acute in the second battle over the Habad dynasty between R. Dov Baer Schneersohn, the son of R. Shneur Zalman of Liady (the first master of Habad), and R. Shneur Zalman's pupil, R. Aaron Ha-Levi Horowitz of Staroselye. For the most recent study of this phenomenon see Moshe Rosman, *Founder of Hasidism: A Quest for the Historical Ba'al Shem Tov* (1996), 187–215.

11. The young Mordecai Joseph was introduced to R. Simha Bunim by his childhood friend Menahem Mendel Halperin (aka Morgenstern), later of Kotzk. See Yizhak Alfasi, *Ha-Hozeh Me-Lublin* (1969), 91; and Faierstein, *All Is in the Hands of Heaven,* 12.

12. Yizhak Alfasi, *Ha-Saba ha-Kadosh me-Radoshits* [The Holy Grandfather of Radoshits] (1967), 86–89. For an account of how non-Hasidim also viewed this date as auspicious, see Arie Morgenstern, *Bi-shelihut Yerushalayim: Toldot mishpahat H. Rozental, 1816–1839* [Emissary to Jerusalem: the history of the H. Rozenthal family] (1985), 52–78. Cf. idem, "Messianic Expectation in the Wake of the Year 1840" (in Hebrew), *Messianism and Eschatology* (1983), 343–64.

13. There are many "accounts" of R. Menahem Mendel's life, but almost all are written by students and descendants of students who are hardly objective in their research. The latest studies of this type are Yehudah Leyb Levin, *Beit Kotzk* (1990), which is a collection of literary fragments and oral traditions about Menahem Mendel and his students; and Pinhas Sade, *Eish be Heder Sagur* [Man in a Closed Room] (1993). In the scholarly world, Abraham Joshua Heschel's two-volume Yiddish study, *Kotzk* (1973), contains some historical data but is primarily devoted to a presentation of the Pryzsucha/Kotzk Hasidic ideology. Morris Faierstein, "The Friday Night Incident in Kotzk: History of a Legend," *Journal of Jewish Studies* 34 (1983): 179–89; and a slightly revised version in his *All Is in the Hands of Heaven,* 89–98, attempts to gain some historical clarity on the incident which preceded R. Menahem Mendel's seclusion.

14. Apart from the fact that thirteen years has significance in the Zohar, it is also the period of time R. Simha Bunim served as rebbe in Pryzsucha before his untimely death. This time period continues to have significance for R. Gershon Henokh. R. Hayyim Simcha Lainer, in *Dor Yesharim,* 83: "He [R. Gershon Henokh] told us that most leaders of Israel do not remain leaders more than thirteen years." He was thinking about R. Simha Bunim and the author of *Mei Ha-Shiloah* (his grandfather) as well as others. He was also referring to his father (R. Jacob Lainer) and said that he had remained the rebbe in Izbica until the twelfth year of his reign after which he moved to Radzin. "When he related this to us we didn't think he was referring also to himself . . . but afterward we realized that his intention was to change his residence and move away from Radzin."

15. The great rift in the community was healed decades later when R. Mordecai Joseph Eliezer Lainer, the great-grandson of R. Mordecai Joseph of Izbica, befriended R. Israel Pilov, the grandson of R. Menahem Mendel, in the resort of Marienbad in 1900. See Z. Glicksman, *Der Kotzker Rebbe* (1938), 48; and Faierstein, *All Is in the Hands of Heaven,* 19.

16. One version, R. Hayyim Simha Lainer, in *Dor Yesharim* (1925), 34, states that the split was friendly, even saying that R. Menahem Mendel escorted R. Mordecai Joseph to his carriage that Simhat Torah night. Note that this is the second edition of *Dor Yesharim,* and it may soften the break with Kotzk in an attempt to end the feud. I have not seen the first edition. Another account, Glicksman, *Der Kotzker Rebbe,* 53, depicts the split as much more dramatic and sensational, and there are similar versions in *Sefer Kotzk,* 111; and Yehudah Leyb Levin, *Ha-Admorim me-Izbica.* Levin was a Gerer Hasid whose allegiance was clearly with R. Menahem Mendel (R. Isaac Meir of Warsaw [later of Ger] succeeded R. Menahem Mendel as the Rebbe of the Kotzker community). For a later Izbica version of the split see S. Z. Shragai, *Be-Netive Hasidut Izbica-Radzin* (1972), vol. 1, 72. In conversations with the Lainer family, I have felt that neither the Lainers nor the Gerer Hasidim are interested in getting at the truth of this incident.

17. *Dor Yesharim,* 12; Faierstein, *All Is in the Hands of Heaven,* 79–84.

18. *Sefer Temunah* influenced the extent to which Hasidic versions of messianism and its theory of *torat ha-shemittot* is an interesting point worth pursuing. On *Sefer Ha-Temunah* see Gershom Scholem, *Origins of the Kabbala* (1962), 460–75; and idem, *The Kabbala of Sefer Temunah and Abraham Abulafia* (in Hebrew), Ben Shlomo, ed. (1969). It should be noted that the messianic implications of this incident in Kotzk are never made explicit during R. Mordecai Joseph's life but are the result of reflections of subsequent generations of the Izbicer dynasty. For a recent discussion of R. Mordecai Joseph's messianism see Morris Faierstein, "Personal Redemption in Hasidism," in *Hasidism Reappraised,* 215–24.

19. R. Hayyim Simha Lainer suggests that R. Mordecai Joseph chose Izbica to fulfill a prophecy made by R. Jacob Isaac (the Seer) of Lublin, who once passed through Izbica and said that it would one day be the home of a great scholar. *Dor*

Yesharim, 34. Another tradition has it that R. Aaron of Karlin, while passing through Izbica, once said, "I feel here the air [spirit] of Eretz Yisrael." R. Jacob of Izbica replied to R. Aaron of Karlin that the Seer of Lublin had once made a similar comment. See Yehudah Leyb Levin, *Ha-Admorim me-Izbica,* 62. Izbica was indeed set on the top of a mountain surrounded by hills similar to the Judean hills outside Jerusalem. Still others suggest that it was chosen for its close proximity to Kotzk. Faierstein suggests that he moved to Izbica because the opposition to him from Kotzker Hasidim in Tomaszow was too great. See Faierstein, *All Is in the Hands of Heaven,* 17.

20. Levin, *Ha-Admorim,* 56, 57.

21. R. Liebele Eiger was considered a prodigy of R. Mordecai Joseph from the beginning. See *Dor Yesharim,* 24. On R. Liebele Eiger in general, see Yehudah Leyb Levin, *Beit Kotzk* (1990); and Nahman Shemen, *Lublin* (in Yiddish) (1951).

22. On *Sidrei Taharot,* see Shlomo Zalman Shragai, *B'Netivei Hasidut Izbica-Radzin* (1972), vol. 2, 150ff; and R. Hayyim Simha Lainer, *Dor Yesharim* (1925), 175, 176. Cf. Yehuda Leib Ha-Cohen Maimon, *Midei Hodesh be Hodshov* (1959), vol. 5, 128–32.

23. For one of the earliest mentions of the *hilazon,* see Mishna Bekhorot 2:8. Cf. Herzog, *The Royal Purple and the Biblical Blue,* 57–61.

24. R. Gershon Henokh discusses the various opinions when the *hilazon* disappeared. See *Shipunei Temunei Hol,* 10; and *'Ayin Tekhelet,* 112b. Cf. Isaac Herzog, "When Did *Tekhelet* Disappear from Israel" (in Hebrew), in R. I. Wolfsberg, *Shai l' Yeshayahu: Sefer Yovel l'* (1987).

25. This discovery is meticulously documented in *Ma'amer Petil Tekhelet.*

26. A refutation of R. Gershon Henokh's claims regarding his *tekhelet* can be found in Isaac Herzog, *The Royal Purple and the Biblical Blue: Argamon and Tekhelet* (1987), esp. 114–19.

27. See Jacob Dienstag, "Ha-Moreh Nevuchim ve Sefer Ha Madda Be Sifrut Ha-Hasidut," in *Abraham Weiss Jubilee Volume* (1964), 307–38; and Samuel Abba Horodetzky, "The Rambam in Kabbala and Hasidism" (in Hebrew), *Moznaim* 3 (1943): 441–45.

28. Heinrich Graetz, *History of the Jews* (1956), vol. 4, 1–46, 477–528. Cf. Graetz, *The Structure of Jewish History and Other Essays,* Ismar Schorch, trans. and ed. (1975), 104.

29. Gershom Scholem, *Origins of the Kabbala* (1962), 3–12; and "The Science of Judaism—Then and Now," in Scholem, *The Messianic Idea in Judaism* (1971), 304–13. See also the discussion of these and other texts in David Biale, *Gershom Scholem: Kabbala and Counter History* (1979). Scholem's theory has been challenged from two different angles. For a critique that moves back in the direction of Graetz see Eliezer Schweid, *Judaism and Mysticism According to Gershom Scholem,* D. A. Weiner, trans. (1985), 21–38, 145–63, 168–71. Another critique which argues that mysticism was even more an integral part of Judaism than Scholem's initial claim can be found in Moshe Idel, *Kabbala: New Perspectives* (1988), 1–17; and

more directly in Moshe Idel, "On Kabbalism vs. Rabbinism: On Gershom Scholem's Phenomenology of Judaism," in *Modern Judaism* (1991): 281–96.

30. See Jay Harris, "The Image of Maimonides in Nineteenth-Century Jewish Historiography," *Proceedings of the American Academy of Jewish Research* 54 (1997): 117–39.

31. *Ha-Zefirah,* Adar 14 (1886).

1. Retrieving the Origins of Kabbala

1. *Ha-Hakdama ve Ha-Petikha* was first published with R. Jacob Lainer's *Beit Ya'akov 'al Sefer Bereshit* (1890). R. Yeruham Lainer subsequently published it separately in New York in 1940. A new edition was published under the new title *Sha'ar Ha-Emunah ve Yesod Ha-Hasidut* (1996).

2. The question as to whether the Besht was as anti-ascetic as is commonly thought is a point of scholarly debate. See for example Abraham J. Heschel, "Rabbi Pinhas of Korzec" and "Rabbi Nahman of Kosow: Companion of the Baal Shem," both in his *Circle of the Baal Shem Tov,* S. Dresner, ed. (1985), 1–43, 113–51. Heschel argues that the Besht indeed was anti-ascetic in opposition to R. Pinhas and R. Nahman of Kosow, who were both more aligned with pre-Hasidic pietism which included the intense study of Kabbala accompanied by ascetic practices. However, see Ada Rapoport-Albert, "God and the Zaddik as the Two Focal Points of Hasidic Worship," *History of Religions* 18 (1979): 296–324. Rapoport-Albert argues that the Besht and his circle were quite elitist and ascetic and were not very distinguishable from pre-Hasidic pietists of that geographical area. Cf. Moshe Rosman, *Founder of Hasidism* (1996), esp. 173–86.

3. The ascetic ideal dominates much of mystical Jewish pietism. On asceticism in sixteenth-century Safed, which had a deep impact on Hasidism, see Hayyim Hillel Ben Sasson, *Studies in Medieval Jewish History* (in Hebrew) (1958), 286–89; Joseph Dan, *Jewish Mysticism and Jewish Ethics* (1986), esp. 76–103; Lawrence Fine, *Safed Spirituality* (1984), 11–16; and Gershom Scholem, *On the Kabbala and Its Symbolism* (1969), 135–53. On the asceticism of Bahya ibn Pakuda, whose *Duties of the Heart* was widely read in Hasidic circles, see Menahem Mansoor, trans. and ed., *The Book of Direction to the Duties of the Heart* (1973), 3–11, 402, 425; and A. Lazeroff, "Bahya's Asceticism Against Its Rabbinic and Islamic Background," *Journal of Jewish Studies* (1970): 11–38. Cf. Elliot R. Wolfson, "Eunuchs who Keep the Sabbath: Becoming Male and the Ascetic Ideal in Thirteenth-Century Jewish Mysticism," in *Becoming Male in the Middle Ages,* J. J. Cohen and B. Wheeler, eds. (New York, 1997), 151–85. More generally see Bernard McGinn, "Asceticism and Mysticism in Late Antiquity and the Early Middle Ages," and E. A. Clark, "The Ascetic Impulse in Religious Life: A Response," both in *Asceticism,* V. L. Wimbush and R. Valantasis, eds. (1995), 58–74, 505–11. This dualistic ascetic idea also plays a prominent role in early Hasidism, especially by those Hasidic masters who were strongly influenced by Kabbala. See Mendel Piekarz, *Biyemei Zemihat Ha-Hasidut*

(1978), 37–50, 153–68; Arthur Green, *Tormented Master* (repr., 1992), 35–52; and Miles Krassen, *Uniter of Heaven and Earth* (1998), 43–79.

4. See for example Antoine Faivre, *Access to Western Esotericism* (1994), 49–57.

5. On this see Elliot R. Wolfson, *Abraham Abulafia—Kabbalist and Prophet: Hermeneutics, Theosophy, and Theurgy* (2000), 9–38.

6. Faivre, *Access to Western Esotericism.*

7. Zohar 2.147a. This seems to be a play on b.T. Kiddushin 66a, "The world was in a state of destruction until Shimon ben Setah came and restored Torah to her former condition." See Daniel Matt, "New Ancient Words: The Aura of Secrecy in the Zohar," in *Gershom Scholem's Major Trends in Jewish Mysticism Fifty Years After: Proceedings of the Sixth International Conference on the History of Jewish Mysticism,* Peter Schafer and Joseph Dan, eds. (1993), 185, 186.

8. See Scholem, *On Kabbala and Its Symbolism,* 19–21.

9. R. Hayyim Vital, "Introduction to *Sha'ar Ha-Hakdamot,*" printed as the "Introduction to *Etz Hayyim*" in standard editions. Rachel Elior has suggested that Vital's "Introduction" is a sweeping summary of postexpulsion attitudes to Kabbala. This sets the stage for the Lurianic corpus, which revolutionizes Kabbala by taking the antiphilosophic bent of his predecessors (excluding Cordovero) and configuring a spiritualization of religious praxis and rereading of the entire halakhic and metahalakhic tradition. See Rachel Elior, "Messianic Expectations and the Spiritualization of Religious Life in the Sixteenth Century," in David Ruderman, ed., *Essential Papers on Jewish Culture in Renaissance and Baroque Italy* (1992), esp. 287–89.

10. See Bracha Sack, "R. Moshe Cordovero's Relationship to the Zohar Literature, R. Shimon bar Yohai and His Circle," *Frank Talmage Memorial Volume, Jewish History* 6:1–2 (1983), 63–83; idem, *Sha'arei ha-Kabbala shel R. Moshe Cordovero* (1995), 11–33; and Pinhas Giller, *Reading the Zohar: The Sacred Text of the Kabbala* (2001), 16–18, 140–44.

11. See Scholem, *Kabbala* (1974), 420–29.

12. *Ha-Hakdama,* 40, 41.

13. I heard this locution from Elliot Wolfson in a public lecture.

14. See Moshe Idel, *Hasidism: Between Ecstasy and Magic* (1995), 31–102. Cf. idem, "One from a Town—Two from a Clan: A New Look at the Problem of the Diffusion of Lurianic Kabbala and Sabbateanism," *Jewish History* 7 (1993): 79–104.

15. See for example Rivka Shatz-Uffenheimer, "Anti-Spiritualism in Hasidism: Studies in the Thought of R. Shneur Zalman of Liady" (in Hebrew), *Molad* 71 (1962): 513–28.

16. In fact, one of the earliest (and most important) sources of the Hasidic-Mithnagdic controversy was R. Shneur Zalman of Liady's accusation that the Gaon of Vilna did not unequivocally accept the authority of Lurianic interpretation. See R. Shneur Zalman of Liady, *Iggrot Baal Ha-Tanya,* in Mordecai Wilensky, *Hasidim u'Mithnagdim: L'Toldot ha-Pulmus Beynehem,* 2 vols. (1970), 2:84–85. Cf. Aaron Ze'ev Aescoly, *Ha-Hasidut b'Polin,* David Assaf, ed. (repr., 1999), 27–29.

17. See Abraham Rubinstein, ed., *Shivhei Ha-Besht* (1991), 340, 341.

18. There are many traditions as to the book studied in this story. See for example in ibid., 128, 129; Joseph Dan, *The Hasidic Story: Its History and Development* (in Hebrew) (1975), 127, 128; Moshe Idel, *Hasidism: Between Ecstasy and Magic,* 172, 353nn. 3, 4.

19. On Hasidic interpretations of Lurianic *kavvanot,* see Menahem Kallus, "The Relation of the Baal Shem Tov to the Practice of Lurianic *Kavvanot* in Light of his Comments in *Siddur Rashov,*" *Kabbala* 2 (1997): 151–68. On the Baal Shem Tov's Kabbalistic commentary to Psalm 107, see Rivka Shatz-Uffenheimer, *Kabbala as Mysticism* (1993), 342–54. Cf. R. Yizhak Isik Yehudah Yehiel Safrin's commentary to the Siddur, *Hekhal Ha-Berakha* (repr., 1990), which contains Lurianic *kavvanot* through the lens of the Komarno Hasidic tradition.

20. See Isaac Barzilay, "The Ideology of the Berlin Haskalah," *Proceedings of the American Academy of Jewish Research* 25 (1956): 7ff; James H. Lehmann, "Maimonides, Mendelssohn and the *Me'asfim:* Philosophy and the Biographical Imagination in the Early Haskalah," *Leo Baeck Institute Year Book* (1975): 87–108; and Jay Harris, "The Image of Maimonides in Nineteenth-Century Jewish Historiography," in *Proceedings of the American Academy of Jewish Research* 54 (1987): 117–39. Cf. Shmuel Feiner, "Faith Alone!: R. Nathan of Nemirov's Battle Against Atheism and the Enlightenment" (in Hebrew), *Mekharei Yerushalayim b'Makhshevet Yisrael* 15 (1999): 110–24; and Mendel Piekarz, "*'Al Mah Avdah Galut Sefard:* A Response Against the Enlightenment in Eastern Europe: Hasidism in the Eyes of R. Zvi Elimelekh of Dinov" (in Hebrew), in Piekarz, *Ha-Hanhaga Ha-Hasidit* (1999), 336–62.

21. New responses came from both the Lithuanian and Hasidic camp. See for example Michael Silber, "The Emergence of Ultra-Orthodoxy—the Intention of a Tradition," in J. Wertheimer, ed., *The Uses of Tradition* (1992), 84–105; J. J. Schachter, "Haskala, Secular Studies and the Close of the Yeshiva in Volozhin in 1892," *The Torah U-Maddah Journal* 2 (1990): 76–134.

22. *Mei Ha-Shiloah*'s reading of biblical personalities is the topic of the second part of this study.

23. The important exception to this rule is the Kabbala of the Italian Renaissance, especially in the seventeenth century. Kabbalists such as R. Abraham Ha-Kohen Herrera, among many others, offered a philosophical interpretation of the Lurianic tradition. On this see Nisim Yosha, *Myth and Metaphor* (in Hebrew) (1994). The Kabbala of Cordovero, while not philosophical in the same way as Herrera, does engage with the medieval Jewish philosophical tradition. On this see Joseph Ben Shlomo, *Torah Ha-Elohut shel R. Moshe Cordovero* (1986), esp. 281–374.

24. On Ibn Latif, see Sara O. Heller-Wilensky, "Isaac Ibn Latif—Philosopher or Kabbalist," in *Jewish Medieval and Renaissance Studies,* Alexander Altmann, ed. (1967), 185–223; idem, "Between Mysticism and Philosophy—In Light of the Thought of R. Isaac Ibn Latif" (in Hebrew), *Jerusalem Studies in Jewish Thought* 4 (nos. 3–4) (1987): 362–82; and "The Dialectical Influence of the Rambam on Ibn

Latif and the Beginning of the Kabbala in Spain" (in Hebrew), in *Sefer Ha-Yovel le Shlomo Pines—Jerusalem Studies in Jewish Thought* (1988), 289–306. For Abulafia, see Idel, "Maimonides and Kabbala," in *Studies in Maimonides,* 54–79; and Elliot R. Wolfson, *Abraham Abulafia,* 52–93, 152–85.

25. Maimonides himself alludes to such a claim. See Alexander Altmann, "Maimonides' Attitude toward Jewish Mysticism," *Studies in Jewish Thought: An Anthology of German Jewish Scholarship,* A. Jospe, ed. (1981), 206–7. Cf. Moshe Idel, "Maimonides and Kabbala," in *Studies in Maimonides,* I. Twersky, ed. (1990), 34, 35, and n.10.

26. Abraham Abulafia is an important exception to the Kabbalistic attitude toward philosophy in general and toward Maimonides in particular. Unlike R. Gershon Henokh, Abulafia held that Maimonides (and perhaps Jewish philosophy in general) intentionally concealed its secrets from the masses in order to limit the community's exposure to its true doctrine. Abulafia's "Straussean" reading of Maimonides is striking. R. Gershon Henokh believed that Maimonides may not have known the extent to which his own writing contained these esoteric secrets, as he received them as fragments of some ancient tradition. On Abulafia and Maimonidean esotericism, see Elliot R. Wolfson, *Abraham Abulafia,* 38–52; and Moshe Idel, "Maimonides and Kabbala," 54–79.

27. An early-twentieth-century example of this can be found in R. Elijah Dessler's *Mikhtav m'Eliahu,* 5 vols. (1964), vol. 3, 115–47. See also R. Kalonymous Kalman Shapira of Piasczeno, *Hakhsharat Avreikhim* (1962).

28. On this see Moshe Halbertal, *People of the Book: Canon, Meaning and Authority* (1997), 109–28; and Boaz Huss, "*Sefer Ha-Zohar* as a Canonical, Sacred and Holy Text," in *Journal of Jewish Thought and Philosophy* 7 (1998): 257–307.

29. R. Gershon Henokh acknowledged that the Enlightenment was not the first distortion of Maimonides' *Guide* and its philosophical agenda. See *Ha-Hakdama,* 51.

30. The mutuality of Kabbala and philosophy is not new here but has a long history among both Kabbalists and philosophers. On the philosophical side, see Colette Sirat, *A History of Jewish Philosophy in the Middle Ages* (1990), esp. 205–72.

31. See for example Heinrich Graetz, *History of the Jews* (1891–1895), vol. 4, 1–45, 447, 528; and vol. 5, 374–94.

32. The messianism of the Besht and Hasidism in general is a debated issue among scholars. See Ben Zion Dinur, "The Messianic-Prophetic Role of the Baal Shem Tov," reprinted in *Essential Papers on Messianic Movements and Personalities in Jewish History,* Marc Saperstein, ed. (1992), 377–88; Mendel Piekarz, "The Messianic Idea in the Beginning of Hasidism in Light of *Drush* and *Mussar* Literature" (in Hebrew), in *The Messianic Idea in Israel: A Study Conference in Honor of the Eightieth Birthday of Gershom Scholem* (1990), 237–53; and most recently, Mor Altshuler, "Messianic Strains in Rabbi Israel Baal Shem Tov's 'Holy Epistle,'" *Jewish Studies Quarterly* 6 (1999): 55–70.

33. On orality as the foundation of esotericism in Kabbalism see Idel, *Kabbala: New Perspectives* (1988), 20–22; and Wolfson, *Abraham Abulafia,* 52–58.

34. See Alan Nadler, *The Faith of the Mithnagdim,* 29–49: "The established rabbinate's consternation at the specter of a new sect of mystical enthusiasts eerily reminiscent of the Sabbateans also began, in the earlier generations, to manifest itself as a deep and thorough respectful reticence toward Kabbala, rooted in the unhappy experience with its potent antinomian capabilities. Ultimately, however, this initial circumspection was to evolve into an almost complete indifference to an ignorance of Jewish mysticism among the later Mithnagdim" (35).

35. The Kabbala of the Vilna Gaon has recently received some attention in Jewish scholarship. See for example Joseph Avivi, *Kabbalat Ha-GRA* (1992); Alan Brill, "The Mystical Path of the Vilna Gaon," *Journal of Jewish Thought and Philosophy* 3 (1993): 131–51; E. R. Wolfson, "From Sealed Book to Open Text: Time, Memory and Narrativity on Kabbalistic Hermeneutics," in *Interpreting Judaism in a Postmodern Age,* Steve Kepnes, ed. (1996), 145–80; and my "Deconstructing the Mystical: The Anti-Mystical Kabbalism in Rabbi Hayyim of Volozhin's Nefesh Ha-Hayyim," *Journal of Jewish Thought and Philosophy* 9 (2000): 21–67.

36. See Immanuel Etkes, *Rabbi Yisrael Salanter and the Beginning of the Mussar Movement* (in Hebrew) (1984), 129–65. While Salanter emerges out of the world of Volozhin, and continues to see himself as a product of Lithuanian Jewry, his movement departs from the strict Talmudism indicative of that world.

37. See Rafael Mahler, *Hasidism and the Jewish Enlightenment* (1985). Many of the historians of that period, as members of the Jewish Enlightenment, offered negative responses to the rise of Kabbalism and Hasidism. For an analysis of some of these historians on their attitude toward mysticism and Hasidism, see Robert Seltzer, "The Secular Appropriation of Hasidism by an Eastern European Intellectual: Dubnow, Renan and the Besht," *Polin* 1 (1986): 151–62; M. Waxman, "Hoker Ha-Hasidut," in *Sefer Simon Dubnow,* Simon Rawidowicz, ed. (1934), 149–65; and David Weintraub, "Dubnow and Jewish Historiography" (in Hebrew), in *Sefer Simon Dubnow,* Simon Rawidowicz, ed. (1934), 67–75. Cf. Shmuel Feiner, *Haskala and History: The Emergence of Modern Jewish Awareness of the Past* (in Hebrew) (1995).

38. R. Simha Bunim of Pryzsucha is perhaps the most outspoken in his ambivalence toward Kabbala. For example, "As I [Simha Bunim] have said, I am not able to learn Kabbala since the study of Kabbala necessitates an apprehension [experience] of the Holy Lights [referring to mystical illuminations]. As it is said in the Zohar: 'Come and see. . . .' This is known from the Baal Shem Tov." See *Ramatayim Zofim* commentary to *Tanna D'Be Eliahu,* collected by R. Shmuel of Shinov (1942), 227. See also Binyamin Mintz, *Mivhar Ketavim* (1954), 101–3; Zvi Meir Rabinowitz, *R. Simha Bunim of Pryzsucha* (1944), 64ff; and Mahler, *Hasidism,* 267 ("Whereas the dignity of the Talmud was elevated, that of the Kabbala was lowered. The system of mystery in general no longer held a significant place in the

doctrine of the school of Pryzsucha"). It should be noted that the teachings we have from R. Simha Bunim are replete with Kabbalistic terminology, thereby questioning Mahler's assertion. I would suggest, however, that Mahler is essentially correct and the Kabbalistic terminology is more a reflection of the adaptation and canonization of the Lurianic lexicon than any sincere interest in Kabbalistic theosophy. I would like to thank my friend Yehudah Gellman for bringing this issue to my attention. Although this may have held true for Pryzsucha as it became Kotzk and then Ger (through R. Isaac Meir Alter) and Amshinov (through R. Isaac of Worka), the Izbica tradition, in R. Gershon Henokh, R. Zaddok Ha-Kohen, and R. Leibele Eiger, clearly adopted the Zohar and Lurianic Kabbala as a foundation for their thinking.

39. See Raphael Mahler, *Hasidism,* 267–303; and Alan Brill, "Grandeur and Humility in the Writings of R. Simha Bunim of Pryzsucha," in *Hazon Nahum,* Y. Elman and J. S. Gorock, eds. (1999), 419–48.

40. Even though most of our knowledge of Izbica's teachings is from R. Gershon Henokh, one can immediately see a distinction between the role of Kabbala in R. Mordecai Joseph's *Mei Ha-Shiloah* and R. Gershon Henokh's *Sod Yesharim.*

41. By "rational" I simply mean a presentation of Maimonides not synthesized in any way with either Kabbala or standard rabbinic tradition. One of the things the Maskilim forced traditionalists to do was to confront Maimonides anew by presenting him in a rationalist framework. On this see Lachover, "Maimonides in the Early Enlightenment Literature," *Gevul Ha-Yashan ve Ha-Hadash* (1951), 97–109. This was also the position taken by the anonymous Hasidic author of *Kina'at ha-Shem Ziva'ot* (1870). On this see Mendel Piekarz, *Hasidut Bratslav* (1972), 197–202.

42. Zohar 3.152a. For a full English translation of this text see Scholem, ed., *Zohar—The Book of Splendor: Basic Readings from the Kabbala* (1963), 121ff.

43. For a recent survey on the history of the interpretation of the Zohar in general and the circle of Luria in particular see Pinhas Giller, *Reading the Zohar: The Sacred Text of the Kabbala* (2001), esp. 3–33.

44. *Ha-Hakdama,* 42, 43.

45. Ibid., 43.

46. The importance of symbolic and mythic language of the Kabbala is a topic of great concern to scholars. See for example Scholem, "The Name of God and Linguistic Theory in Kabbala," *Diogenes* 79 (1972): 164–94; Yehuda Liebes, "Myth versus Symbol in the Zohar and in Lurianic Kabbala," in Lawrence Fine, ed., *Essential Papers on Kabbalah* (1995), 212–42; E. R. Wolfson, *Through a Speculum That Shines,* 55–392; Joseph Dan, "Beyond the Kabbalistic Symbol" (in Hebrew), *Jerusalem Studies in Jewish Thought* 5 (1986): 363–85; and idem, "Midrash and the Dawn of Kabbala," in *Midrash and Literature,* G. Hartmann and S. Budick, eds. (1986). Cf. David Stern, *Parables in Midrash* (1991), 216–24, 227–33.

47. On Abulafia and the linguistic distinction between philosophy and Kabbala, see Scholem, "The Name of God and Linguistic Theory in Kabbala," 183–86;

Idel, *Language, Torah and Hermeneutics* (1989), 16ff; and Wolfson, *Abraham Abulafia,* 58–70.

48. This is taken up in a much more conventional manner by R. Gershon Henokh's descendant R. Yeruham Lainer in his *Zohar Ha-Rakiya,* reprinted in the back of R. Yizhak Izik Haver's *Magen ve Zina* (1985), 118–60.

49. See the essays collected in *The Sword of Gnosis: Metaphysics, Cosmology, Tradition, Symbolism,* Jacob Needleman, ed. (1974); and Antoine Faivre, *Access to Western Esotericism,* 35–49.

50. Ibid., 37.

51. Thus we have the collected works of Rene Guenon and the comprehensive work by Hossein Seyyed Nasr, *Knowledge of the Sacred* (1981).

52. On this see Idel, *Hasidism: Between Ecstasy and Magic,* 227–39; and Scholem, "The Neutralization of the Messianic Element in Early Hasidism," in *The Messianic Idea in Judaism* (1971), 176–202.

53. See Rivka Shatz-Uffenheimer, "Self-Redemption in Hasidic Thought," in *Types of Redemption,* R. J. Z. Werblowsky and C. J. Bleeker, eds. (1970), 207–12; idem, "The Messianic Element in Hasidic Thought" (in Hebrew), *Molad* 1 (1967): 105–11; Mendel Piekarz, "The Messianic idea in the Early Days of Hasidism Through the Lens of Ethical and Homiletical Literature" (in Hebrew), in *The Messianic Idea in Israel* (1990), 237–53; Morris Faierstein, "Personal Redemption in Hasidism," in *Hasidism Reappraised,* A. Rapoport-Albert, ed. (1996), 215–24; and most recently, Idel, *Messianic Mystics* (1998), 212–47.

54. From a historical perspective, Gershom Scholem made a similar claim in addressing the similarities between the Gnosticism in *The Book Bahir* and ancient Gnostic texts. That is, instead of arguing that one influenced the other, he suggested that both drew from a third Jewish source, no longer available to the modern scholar. See Scholem, *Reshit Ha-Kabbala* (1948), 31–35.

55. Miles Krassen argues that this shift of emphasis in Hasidism may be the result of Cordovero's influence, which does not contain the strong Gnostic tones of Luria. See Krassen, *Uniter of Heaven and Earth* (1998), 81–93.

56. An exception may be Abraham Abulafia. See Moshe Idel, *Studies in Ecstatic Kabbala* (1988), 16. Idel suggests that Abulafia's commentaries to Maimonides' *Guide* may have been based on his belief that he lived in the final prelude to redemption that necessitated, or perhaps allowed, the "secrets" of the *Guide* to be revealed. Cf. Wolfson, *Abraham Abulafia,* 53, 54. In R. Gershon Henokh's case, it was clear that the philosophy/Kabbala synthesis was the necessary prelude to redemption.

57. An analysis of these works can be found in the next chapter.

58. The notion of Torah as revealing the concealment of God in the world is not new in R. Gershon Henokh but is a central theme in the teachings of the Maggid of Mezeritch. See for example in R. Meshullam Feibush of Zbarazh, *Yoshar Divrei Emet* (1974), 33. Compare this with ibid., 15, 22. This is also the way R. Abraham Isaac Ha-Kohen Kook describes an expression of holiness, understood

as revealing that which is concealed. See his "Orot Tehiyah," in *Orot* (1983), 67–69; and idem, *'Olat Ha-Reiyah,* vol. 2 (1983), 3–5.

59. See *Ha-Hakdama,* 12. This interpretation is developed further both in *Mei Ha-Shiloah* and *Sod Yesharim on the Torah,* 20–22. See also Bereshit Rabba 14. It seems this interpretation points to another component in the second part of this Treatise which speaks of "overcoming" the ascetic nature of Jewish worship so common in pre-Beshtian traditions. For a study devoted specifically to the biblical figure Melchizedek, see James R. Davila, "Melchizedek: King, Priest, and God," in *The Seductiveness of Jewish Myth: Challenge or Response,* S. Daniel Breslauer, ed. (1977), 217–34. On Melchizedek in Christian Scripture and late antiquity see F. L. Horton Jr., *The Melchizedek Tradition: A Critical Examination of the Sources to the Fifth Century* A.D. *and in the Epistle to the Hebrews* (1976).

60. Maimonides does say in "Laws on the Foundation of the Law" and his commentary to Mishna Sandhedrin that "nothing is outside of Him," but this is not the same as God filling the world, which is the basis of the Zohar's theology. For example, Maimonides, in his *Mishneh Torah,* "Laws of Idolatry," chap. 1:3, claims that Abraham, via reflection and rational analysis, comes to the conclusion that, "there is one God, who directs the planets, and creates everything." But Maimonides never claims that God can be found in the world. Maimonides' Abraham is thus quite different from the Abraham presented here.

61. On this rendering of Abraham, see Maimonides, *Mishneh Torah,* "Laws of Idolatry," 1:1–4. Cf. also the discussion in Lenn Goodman, *The God of Abraham* (1996), esp. 167–215.

62. See *Sod Yesharim Tinyana,* 112a.

63. The significance of circumcision as an act that elevates the consciousness of the circumcised is a central theme in the Zohar as well as Maimonides. See for example Zohar 1:70b–71a; and E. R. Wolfson, "Circumcision and the Divine Name: A Study in the Transformation of an Esoteric Doctrine," *Jewish Quarterly Review* 78 (1987): 77–112; idem, "Circumcision, Vision of God, and Textual Interpretation: From Midrashic Trope to Mystical Symbol," *Circle in the Square* (1995), 29–48; and Joseph Stern, "Maimonides on the Covenant of Circumcision and the Unity of God," *Midrashic Imagination: Jewish Exegesis, Thought and History,* M. Fishbane, ed. (1993), 131–54. Stern notes (144), "For Abraham is portrayed not only as the first person to practice circumcision but also, in Maimonides' writings, as 'the first to make known the belief in Unity' [*Guide* 3:24, 502]." Stern argues that although Maimonides does not adopt a mystical notion of the act as affecting Abraham's consciousness, circumcision does represent for the community a move toward recognizing the unity of God. The correlation between circumcision and the revelation of the unity between God and world is integral to R. Gershon Henokh's theory of recovering the esoteric Abrahamic tradition. It is interesting that R. Gershon Henokh failed to notice this reference in *Guide* 3:24.

64. This idea of circumcision is not limited to the Zohar but exists throughout medieval Kabbala. In particular, Abulafia stresses how the act ritualizes the essence

of the mystical path, which is the disclosure of secrets. See Elliot R. Wolfson, *Abraham Abulafia,* 87–93, 216–28.

65. Thus circumcision for the Kabbalists, the act which typifies Abraham's contribution to the covenant, is infused with messianic implications. This is a central theme in another student of Izbica, R. Aryeh Leib Eiger of Lublin. See his *'Imre Emet* (1973); and his *Torat Emet,* 3 vols. (1889). R. Zaddok Ha-Kohen of Lublin, also a student of R. Mordecai Joseph, develops the notion of *brit* in a similar way.

66. *Ha-Hakdama,* 12, 13. The use of circumcision imagery (foreskin—*'orlah*) to describe the acquisition of knowledge *(hasagot)* is intentional. The acquisition of the light of God as knowledge *(da'at elohim)* is a model of describing the messianic process, which has roots in rabbinic interpretations of prophetic texts and is canonized in Maimonides' description of the messianic age at the end of "Laws of Kings," in his *Mishneh Torah*. See how this also reflects Maimonides' position in *Guide* 3:39 and 1:63, where the distinction is made between the spiritual apprehension of Abraham and its legalistic formulation in Moses. The motif of circumcision is, of course, rooted in medieval Kabbala as well. Joseph Stern notes the relationship between the circumcision of Abraham and its renewal in the covenant at Sinai. See Stern, "On the Covenant of Circumcision," 137: "By ceasing circumcision, the Israelites annulled or abolished a *covenant:* they surrendered their identity as a distinct community. And having abrogated the previous [Abrahamic] covenant through assimilation, nothing less than a new covenant fathered by Moses was necessary. Hence, Maimonides emphasizes that it was Moses who circumcised the nation, just as the obligation of circumcision falls on the father of the uncircumcised infant according to Mosaic law." Stern claims that Maimonides viewed the covenant of Moses as necessary due to the failure of the people to adhere to the covenant of Abraham. R. Gershon Henokh would argue that the covenant of Moses was not new but rather a renewal of the Abrahamic covenant which was lost due to its refragmentation in the sons of Jacob.

67. See R. Gershon Henokh, *Tiferet Hanokhi,* 11b.

68. See Zohar 3.14a.

69. The correlation between circumcision as covenant and the covenant at Sinai is developed in both *Sefer Yezirah* 1:3 and Zohar 3:91b. See also Abraham Abulafia, *Ozar Eden Ganuz,* MS Oxford 1580, fol. 5a, "If not for the covenant of circumcision one could not fulfill the covenant of the tongue [i.e., the Torah]"; and Joseph Gikatillia, *Sha'are 'Orah,* Ben Shlomo, ed., 1:114–16. Whereas these medieval texts create a correlation between the ability to enter into the covenant of Torah and being circumcised, R. Gershon Henokh uses these two models as part of a process toward the fulfillment of Torah as "uncovering the sheath behind which hides the divine will." One is then not a prerequisite for the other, but rather circumcision is symbolic of the spiritual nature of Abraham, which is only completed in the revelation at Sinai, and the fully integrated personality of Moses. On the image of "seeing voices" and the instrument of the shofar understood as the vehicle which facilitates this experience, see Zohar 2.81b. R. Gershon Henokh

reads the voices and the shofar as parallel to the circumcision of Abraham. See *Sod Yesharim on the Torah,* 26, 27.

70. Zohar 3.13b. Cf. Zohar 1.95b, and Midrash Tanhuma, parshat Shemimi, 8.

71. Zohar 1.98a.

72. In this sense, Buber's statement that Hasidism "overcomes" Kabbala may very well be in place. The ambivalence that Idel speaks about regarding the Hasidic attitude toward Lurianic Kabbala may partially be the result of the unconscious Hasidic belief in Hasidism as completing rather than rejecting the Kabbalistic system. For Buber's statement see Buber, "The Faith of Judaism," in *Mamre: Essays in Religion,* Greta Hort, trans. (1970), 149–82. Also see Idel, *Hasidism: Between Ecstasy and Magic,* 35–45, 103–47. Arthur Green views this "overcoming" of Kabbala in Hasidism as internal to the tradition itself. Noting the lack of Kabbalistic terminology in the Hasidic writings of R. Judah Leib Alter's (1847–1905) *Sefat Emet,* he argues that *Sefat Emet* is the beginning of a "post-Kabbalistic" yet highly mystical trend in Hasidism. Green attributes numerous factors to this "turn," including the rejection of Kabbala in the Kotzk tradition, the spiritual cornerstone of the Ger dynasty. The connection, if any, between Buber's notion of Hasidism "overcoming" Kabbala and Green's depiction of "post-Kabbalistic" Hasidic mysticism remains to be seen. See Arthur Green, *The Language of Truth* (1997), 6–21.

73. See Zohar 3.53b; and R. Ya'akov Lainer, *Sefer Ha-Zemanim* on Shavuot (1984), 10b, 11a. Cf. R. Meshullam Feibush of Zbarazh, *Yoshar Devrei Emet,* 3. An explicit example of Torah as teaching in nineteenth-century Jewish thought can be found in R. Shimshon Raphael Hirsch's *Nineteen Letters to Ben Uziel,* Bernard Drachman, trans. (1942), 13.

74. This notion may be utilizing the double *brit* language in *Sefer Yezirah:* the *brit* (covenant) of the tongue (Sinai) adds the *brit me'or* (membrum) of Abraham. See *Sefer Yezirah* 1:3. On the relationship between language and circumcision, see the commentary of the Gaon of Vilna on *Sefer Yezirah,* standard editions (1989), 6d–7b; Elliot R. Wolfson, "Circumcision, Vision of God, and Textual Interpretation: From Midrashic Trope to Mystical Symbol," *Circle in the Square* (1995), 29–48; and Shaul Magid, "Conjugal Union, Mourning, and Talmud Torah" in R. Isaac Luria's *Tikkun Hazot, Da'at* (1996): xvii–xlv.

75. At the conclusion of *Ha-Hakdama,* R. Gershon Henokh seems to change his position and suggest that, after the Beshtian interpretation of faith which ushered in the messianic period in Jewish history, it is faith and not Kabbala which is seen as identical to Torah. See later in this chapter. As well, there are Christian counterparts to this theory. See Bernard McGinn, *The Foundations of Mysticism: From Its Origins to the Fifth Century* (1992), 282, "The mystical life in its foundation is nothing less than the Christian life; in its restricted sense (the sense in which we call only some Christians mystics) it is the higher development of that root and foundation." On the progression of Torah as textual study to Torah as mystical experience, see Louis Jacobs, *The Jewish Mystics* (1990), 4, "Once such a

step is taken (i.e., that of making experience part of Torah) mystical experience is equated with the 'study' of the Torah, i.e., in its esoteric aspect, and thus becomes in its turn part of the highest mitzvah."

76. See *Ha-Hakdama,* 20–22, where this position is developed further. This dichotomy was extremely popular in mid- to late-nineteenth-century Polish Hasidism. It was a major interest of R. Gershon Henokh's contemporary, R. Zaddok Ha-Kohen of Lublin.

77. The status of the oral law was also extremely important to a contemporary of R. Gershon Henokh's, R. Zaddok Ha-Kohen Rabinovitz of Lublin. R. Zaddok was a disciple of R. Mordecai Joseph of Izbica, settling in Lublin after his master's death in 1854. For an important study on R. Zaddok's position on Oral Law, see Ya'akov Elman, "R. Zaddok Ha-Kohen and the History of Halakha," *Tradition* (1985): 1–27.

78. This dichotomy is found in the later strata of the Zohar. See Pinhas Giller, *The Enlightened Will Shine* (1993), 59–81. Another noteworthy reading of the Zohar's relationship between the written and oral Torah can be found in *Sefer 'Or Yashar,* edited by R. Zvi Hirsch Hazan, printed in the 1842 Premeshlayan edition of R. Moshe Cordovero's *Tefilla le Moshe,* 1a: "The cloud which followed the Jews in the desert is the Written Law. The pillar of fire is the Oral Law. These are the pillars which come before a man's bed who busies himself with them [the Written and Oral Law]. As we have found numerous times, 'Happy is the one who merits this.' The Written Law is that [Torah] which is studied during the day, the Oral Law is that which is studied at night."

79. *Sod Yesharim on the Festivals,* Purim, 16a. A strikingly similar presentation of this issue can be found in R. Yizkah Hutner's *Pahad Yizhak* on Hanukkah, sermon 10 (1978), 84–96. Hutner studied at the Ger Yeshiva in Warsaw as a young adult and retained a strong connection to the world of Polish Hasidism.

80. See Tikkunei Zohar 21, 58a.

81. For the notion of disclosure and concealment as a trope in the Zohar see Liebes, *Studies in the Zohar,* 26–34. The conventional use of the term "Kabbala" usually refers to the Jewish mystical tradition as it became concretized in the early twelfth century. Scholem's *Origins of the Kabbala* thus begins in the twelfth century and excludes Hekhalot Literature and *Sefer Yezirah,* which appeared before that time. Mystical literature and traditions prior to that century are referred to as pre-Kabbalistic Jewish mysticism (or some such term). Not concerned with the periodization of Jewish mystical literature, R. Gershon Henokh used the term "Kabbala" in a much looser fashion to incorporate the entirety of the Jewish mystical tradition.

82. See this notion introduced in Pico della Mirandola's *Orations on the Dignity of Man.* Mirandola views Jewish esotericism as a calculated attempt to conceal the "true position" from the masses. The dichotomy between the spiritual authority of the prophets and the legal activity of the rabbis is a basic premise of Wellhausen and the nineteenth-century school of biblical criticism. See for example

Wellhausen, *Prolegomena to the History of Israel,* J. Sutherland Black and Allan Menaies, trans. (n.d.), 398. Wellhausen's Protestant agenda was meant to attack the rabbinic authority (which he viewed as the basis of contemporary Judaism) and thus described a spiritualistic prophetic religion which reflected the nature of Protestant Christianity. Another example of this can be found in Max Weber's distinction between charismatic and institutional authority. See *Economy and Society: An Outline of Interpretive Sociology,* Guenther Roth and Claus Wittich, eds., and Ephraim Fischolf, trans., 2 vols. (1978), vol. 1, 240ff. Although the critical school is quite different in both method and substance from the Hasidic position exhibited here in R. Gershon Henokh, it is interesting to see how both are spiritualistic (quasi-anarchic) critiques of a legalist tradition which limited the free expression of one's yearning for God.

83. See as reprinted in *Etz Hayyim,* 1d; cf. 2c. See also Zohar 3.244b. Another variant of this tradition can be found in R. Nathan of Gaza's interpretation of a Zoharic passage in his description of the inability of the sages to accept the messianic figure. See "The Letter of Nathan of Gaza on Sabbatai Zevi and his Leadership" (in Hebrew), printed in Scholem, *Studies and Texts Concerning the History of Sabbateanism and Its Metamorphoses* (in Hebrew) (1982), 242, 243.

84. *Etz Hayyim,* 1d.

85. *Ha-Hakdama,* 22.

86. The notion of the progressive overcoming of Torah to yield a "new" Torah is rooted in the cosmic eon theory *(torat ha-shmitot)* in *Sefer Temunah* (c. 1300). Although I have not found any explicit reference to *Sefer Temunah* in R. Gershon Henokh's writings, such influence is not unlikely considering that *Sefer Temunah* was published in Koretz in 1788 and is mentioned in earlier Hasidic literature that may have influenced Polish Hasidism.

87. See *Ha-Hakdama,* 21. For a precedent in the Zohar, see Tikkunei Zohar 46a. The notion of the Zohar being the concealed dimension of Torah, only to be fully revealed in the messianic era, is a popular idea in Jewish mysticism and served a foundation for the folk festival of *Lag B'Omer.* See for example in R. Zvi Elimelekh's *Bnei Yissakhar,* 2 vols. (1968), sermon for the month of Iyar, vol. 2, 88a: "Behold R. Shimon bar Yohai is called the Holy Spark [*Bozina Kadisha*] because through him the secrets of Torah were revealed. This is the secret of the Light of Goodness concealed in the Torah [*'or ha-tov*—which was created the first day of creation and hidden for the zaddikim in the future]. Therefore his book was called Zohar meaning the brilliant light that shines from one end of the world to the other." This source also appears in a different form in *Zohar Hadash,* 33b, 34a.

88. This is largely the way in which the Zohar viewed itself. See Y. Liebes, *Studies in the Zohar,* esp. 43–52. R. Gershon Henokh appears to adopt a dialectical position among the myth/transcendentalism/mysticism that is suggested by Scholem in numerous places. R. Gershon Henokh suggests that the Zohar is the renewal of a tradition that had its roots in Sinai but was intentionally concealed by

the legalistic garb of the rabbis. This dialectic of Kabbala suggested by Scholem was challenged by Moshe Idel in a paper entitled "Kabbala and the Phenomenology of Religions," given at the Harvard Center for World Religions during the winter of 1992. Some similar views were expressed by Idel in "Kabbalism and Rabbinism," 281–96. The dialectical position of Scholem is, of course, not his own. Scholem appears to be developing a trend in Kabbalistic literature that sees the halakhic tradition as a garment for esoteric doctrine. As Scholem himself notes, this doctrine periodically appears and disappears throughout Jewish intellectual history. See for example in del Medigo's *Mazref la Hokhma,* 41a, where del Medigo argues that although the Talmud is, by and large, a nonmystical or amystical body of literature, there existed a second esoteric literature which was available only to an elite group of mystics. "Rather, there were specific books [the rabbis had] in the Houses of Learning where these deep secrets was transmitted, like other forms of wisdom."

89. *Ha-Hakdama,* 22. On this see *Mei Ha-Shiloah,* vol. 1, 29c–30b; and *Tiferet Ha-Hanokhi,* 22b, 61b.

90. It is interesting to note that circumcision is done with a physical object (a knife) and the shofar at Sinai was a miracle of "seeing the voices" (Exodus 20:15), an experience of the senses. The uncovering done by R. Shimon and those after him is an intellectual act of interpretation by means of a divine directive. With the Besht, R. Gershon Henokh suggests it is an emotional experience of unity, reaching beyond or deeper than the intellect. There appears to be a progression from the mundane act of cutting to the lofty experience of unity, all as the unfolding of the will of God, which R. Gershon Henokh calls Kabbala.

91. This explanation of esotericism is not unique in western literature. See for example the essays contained in *Modern Esoteric Spirituality,* Antoine Faivre and Jacob Needleman, eds. (1992); and Antoine Faivre, *Access to Western Esotericism,* esp. 3–35. This dichotomy is viewed in a different light in Gershom Scholem's historiosophy of Kabbala, whereby rabbinism and kabbalism are viewed as competing intellectual pursuits.

92. See Moshe Idel, "On Kabbalism vs. Rabbinism: On Gershom Scholem's Phenomenology of Judaism," in *Modern Judaism* 11 (1991): 281–96.

93. For examples of the source material he uses for this interpretation, see Zohar 1.224b; Midrash Tanhuma, *parshat Ki Tisa,* 31; and b.T. Sanhedrin 24a.

94. See Amos Funkenstein, "Maimonides' Political Theory and Realistic Messianism," in *Miscellanea Mediaevalia* 11 (1977): 81–103. Funkenstein's assumption is that Maimonides' true messianic stance emerges from his "Epistle to the Jews of Yemen" *(Iggeret Taman)* and not from his Commentary to the Mishna and the last chapters of "Laws of Kings" in *Mishneh Torah.* David Hartman challenges Funkenstein's thesis and argues that Funkenstein's "Hegelian" reading of Maimonides does not do justice to the complexity of Maimonides' position. See David Hartman, *Crisis and Leadership: Epistles of Maimonides* (1985), 150–207. Hartman's critique of Funkenstein can be found on 171f.

95. This idea serves as an essential core of Lurianic cosmology. For the most comprehensive presentation, see R. Hayyim Vital, *Etz Hayyim,* vol. 1, Seventh Gate, *Mate ve lo Mate,* 30a–34a.

96. This simply means that the philosophers and their interpreters were not aware of the extent to which they were drawing from fragments of this Sod tradition. R. Gershon Henokh's synthesis of the *Guide* and the Zohar, the subject of the next chapters, addresses this phenomenon more closely.

97. See b.T. Ketubot 111a. The anti-Zionist ideology of R. Hayyim Elazar Shapira of Munkacz, and later his disciple R. Yoel Teitelbaum of Satmar, is founded on the notion of Zionism as guilty of the transgression of "forcing the end." See Aviezer Ravitsky, *Messianism, Zionism and Jewish Religious Radicalism* (1993), 40–78, esp. 63–66, 211–34; and Alan Nadler, "A War on Modernity of R. Hayyim Elazar Shapira of Munkacz," *Modern Judaism* 14 (1994): 233–64.

98. There are many references in the Zohar that imply this very notion. See for example Zohar 3.61a, Zohar 3.65a. The central belief in these sources is that R. Shimon bar Yohai experienced a revelation of Elijah the Prophet who taught him the method of revealing the lost mystical doctrine from the legalistic teachings of the rabbis. See also the introduction to Tikkunei Zohar.

99. R. Mordecai Joseph notes that limiting God's presence to the four ells of halakha is largely the result of exile. "When the Cloud of Glory departed [in lieu of Aaron's death] the Israelites began to act in the realm of the general principle of Torah [i.e., halakha]. This is likened to the present, after the destruction, when God's presence is only within the four cubits of halakha." *Mei Ha-Shiloah,* vol. 1, 52b. Cf. R Zaddok Ha-Kohen, *Dover Zedek,* 20c, "This is what is meant in b.T. Berakhot 8b that God only dwells in the four cubits of halakha. These [four cubits] are the dwelling place of God, it is the 'image of God' as it hovers over the individual and dwells within his consciousness as he contemplates halakha and God's Torah. Moreover, when the Temple was destroyed, the Temple being the dwelling place of God, God was still found in the [human] soul as all of its parts are likened to the Temple, as is developed in the Zohar. Hence God returned to dwell in the human soul that is confined in the body. The soul itself is spatially confined [i.e., it is material substance] and thus confined to 'the world.' Now we can better understand the 'four ells' [in the Talmud] as the place of humankind. Each individual contains four cubits of halakha at each moment he walks or behaves according to the halakha."

100. The idea of God or, more exactly, the will of God as existing outside the halakhic system is a central theme in Izbica/Radzin Hasidism. We see here how R. Gershon Henokh attempts to graft the antinomian tendency in his Hasidic tradition onto the authentic tradition of the Zohar. Moreover, the acceptance in principle of the possibility of God's will existing outside the halakhic system is viewed as the contribution of Abraham, R. Shimon bar Yohai, and the entire mystical tradition. Rabbinic legalism is, by implication, compared to the limited theological position of Melchizedek in the Book of Genesis, chap. 14. The comparison of rabbinic

legalism to the transcendent God of Melchizedek may be seen in the theological view of R. Hayyim of Volozhin in the third part (chaps. 2–6) of *Nefesh Ha-Hayyim.* R. Hayyim argues that the authority of halakha can only survive when the transcendent nature of God is the matrix as opposed to the immanent nature of God that was the matrix of early Hasidic worship. For a discussion on this in R. Hayyim of Volozhin see Mordecai Pachter, "Between Acosmism and Theism in R. Hayyim of Volozhin" (in Hebrew), *Mehkarim be Hagot Ha-Yehudit* (1989), 139–57; and my "Deconstructing the Mystical: The Anti-Mystical Kabbalism in R. Hayyim of Volozhin's *Nefesh Ha-Hayyim,*" in *Journal of Jewish Thought and Philosophy* 9 (2000): 21–67. R. Mordecai Joseph of Izbica argues against the anti–immanentist position of R. Hayyim of Volozhin, although never quoting him by name. See for example *Mei Ha-Shiloah,* vol. 1, 14. On how the Zohar renews this ancient tradition, see *Ha-Hakdama,* 25. Cf. Daniel Matt, "New Ancient Words: The Aura of Secrecy in the Zohar," in *Gershom Scholem's Major Trends in Jewish Mysticism Fifty Years After,* P. Schaefer and J. Dan, eds.(1993). The fact that R. Shimon was only revealing of that which other sages were also aware is not new in R. Gershon Henokh. See for example R. Isaac Eisek Haver, *Magen ve Zinah,* 46 a/b.

101. See Zohar 3.287a.

102. See b.T. Sanhedrin 97a; and b.T. Avodah Zara 9z. See *Ha-Hakdama,* 24, 25. This Torah of Spirit may also be drawing from the notion of the Primordial Torah *(Torah Kadumah)* in earlier Kabbala, specifically *Sefer Temunah* (around 1300). Cf. *Sefer Temunah* (1892), 26ff.

103. R. Gershon Henokh would appear to reject the opinion that the patriarchs lived within the framework of halakha. Although, to my knowledge, he never uses this source, his general position would imply that such a pre-Sinaitic Judaism could not have included the halakhic system as we know it.

104. This distinction is, of course, not new but utilizes the Zoharic distinction of the Torah of Emanation and the Torah of Creation common in *Ra'aya Mehemna* and Tikkunei Zohar.

105. This idea was developed in a different way by R. Menahem Azaria da Fano regarding halakha and Kabbala. See for example in Robert Bonfil, "Halakhah, Kabbala and Society: Some Insights into Rabbi Menahmen Azaria da Fano's Inner World," *Jewish Thought in the Seventeenth Century* (1987), 45, "Perhaps we might even see it [*Kabbalistica veritas*] implicitly contained in RMA's clearly expressed view that, although Talmudic literature has undergone redactional processes, following principles not held by the totality of the Rabbis in Mishnaic and Talmudic times, one must be allowed to search between the lines for hints of the lost *testimonia veritatis,* as recently revealed more explicitly in the zoharic literature." It is not at all unlikely that R. Gershon Henokh was influenced by such a position.

106. See for example in Zohar 2.34 and *Dor Yesharim,* 16, "And so [esoteric] knowledge was diminished until the culmination of the Talmud at which point the secrets of Torah only existed among the elite of the generation, sealed with an iron seal." Cf. *Ha-Hakdama,* 28.

107. R. Gershon Henokh is aware that certain rabbinic statements may have indeed preceded Sinai. He suggests that texts, which are not based upon Scripture, may be remnants of a pre-Sinaitic tradition. "Regarding those rabbinic statements [*braitot*] which do not mention a verse from the Torah, such statements are not rooted in a verse from the Torah because their source reaches back before the giving of the Torah [at Sinai]. From the days of old [from the time of R. Shimon bar Yohai], God revealed that everything is ultimately from the Torah" (*Ha-Hakdama,* 13, 14). R. Shimon's contribution is that he integrates all of what may have preceded Sinai into the narrative of Scripture. His work brings together the authentic Abrahamic tradition with the legalistic tradition of Sinai, creating a synthesis between a prescriptural and a postscriptural tradition. See for example in Zohar 2.70b, "Even that which was from 'the Book of Adam' was taught again to Moshe in the Torah." This statement suggests that R. Gershon Henokh held that, before Sinai, not only was there not halakha as we know it, but there was not Scripture either. It appears that the nature of pre-Sinaitic Judaism, according to R. Gershon Henokh, is one of a pure spiritual nature, void of halakha and literary interpretation. It appears to reflect a time when God was revealed and man had direct access to Him. In short, it was the life of the mystic. R. Isaac Eisek Haver supports this position in his *Magen ve Zina.* Haver argues that although *Sefer Yezirah* is traditionally attributed to Abraham, this does not mean that the book that has come down to us was from the pen of Abraham. Rather, the technique of using permutations of the letters of the divine Name to facilitate the mystical experience and the performance of miracles was known to and practiced by Abraham.

108. For the most recent study on *ta'amei ha-mitzvot* in medieval Jewish thought see Joseph Stern, *Problems and Parables of the Law: Maimonides and Nahmanides on Reasons for the Commandments* (1998), esp. 1–49. Cf. Isadore Twersky, "Concerning Maimonides' Rationalizations of the Commandments: An Explication of *Hilkhot Me'ilah*" (in Hebrew), in *Studies in the History of Jewish Society in the Middle Ages and Modern Period* (1980), viii, 8; and Isaac Heinemann, *Ta'amei Ha'Mitzvot b'Sifrut Yisrael,* 2 vols. (1954). Heinemann's history of *ta'amei ha-mitzvot* begins with Talmudic literature and moves through the philosophical literature of the Middle Ages, almost ignoring the Kabbalistic tradition. On *ta'amei ha-mitzvot* in Kabbala, see Daniel Matt, "The Mystic and the Mitzvot," in *Jewish Spirituality I,* Arthur Green, ed. (1986), 364–404; Elliot R. Wolfson, "Mystical Rationalization of the Commandments in *Sefer Ha-Rimon,*" *Hebrew Union College Annual* 59 (1988): 103–79; and idem, "Mystical Rationalization of the Commandments in the Prophetic Kabbala of Abraham Abulafia," in *Perspectives on Jewish Thought and Mysticism,* Alfred Ivry, E. R. Wolfson, and A. Arkush, eds. (1998), 331–80.

109. On this see Yehuda Liebes, "The Messiah of the Zohar" (in Hebrew), in *Ha-Ra'ayon Ha-Meshihi b'Yisrael* (1982), 87–236; and also (in English), Liebes, "The Messiah of the Zohar: On R. Shimon bar Yohai as a Messianic Figure," in *Studies in the Zohar* (1993), 1–84.

110. Although this notion was common in the Middle Ages, it is highly uncommon among Hasidic authors. For a statement against such a position, see R. Hayyim Elazar Shapira of Munkacz, *Divrei Torah* (1929–36), vol. 6, 25. Both R. Gershon Henokh and his contemporary R. Zaddok Ha-Kohen of Lublin (for very different reasons) seem to have reinvigorated the medieval notion that a symmetry exits between Greek and Jewish wisdom. However, the myth of confluence, based on Plato's interaction with the Hebrew prophets, is not prominent in these Hasidic texts.

111. See William Graham, *Beyond the Written Word: Oral Aspects of Scripture in the History of Religions* (1987), 9–48.

112. There are many references to R. Shimon's death in the Zohar and the implications of such a loss. See for example Zohar 1.217a, "When R. Shimon was laid to rest wisdom left the world." See also 2.149a: "Woe to the generation of R. Shimon's passing. The wise became few in number and wisdom was lost from the world." Cf. Zohar 2.201b. The Zohar's description of the death of R. Shimon is strikingly similar to its depiction of the death of Moses. See for example in Zohar 2.156a, "At the time when Moshe died the sun became darkened and the Written Law was closed like the teaching of the speculum that shines." Cf. Zohar 2.34b, 149, 201b.

113. *Ha-Hakdama,* 27, 28. The focus on the essential oral component of transmission of knowledge in Judaism is just now being excavated. See Martin Jaffe, "Writing and Rabbinic Oral Tradition: On Mishnaic Narrative, Lists, and Mnemonics," in *Journal of Jewish Thought and Philosophy* 4 (1994): 123–46; idem, "The Oral-Cultural Context of the Talmud Yerushalmi: Comparative Perspectives on Rhetorical Paideia, Discipleship, and the Concept of Oral Torah," in *Text and Context: The Greco-Roman Setting of the Talmud Yerushalmi,* Peter Schafer, ed. (forthcoming); and idem, "A Rabbinic Ontology of the Written and Spoken Word: On Discipleship, Transformative Knowledge, and the Living Texts of Oral Torah," *Journal of the American Academy of Religion* (forthcoming). For a more general discussion see Jack Goody, John Rankine, and Ian Watt, "The Consequences of Literacy," in Jack Goody, ed., *Literacy in Traditional Societies* (1978), 27–84; Walter Ong, *Orality and Literacy* (1982), esp. 78–117; and William A. Graham, *Beyond the Written Word: Oral Aspects of Scripture in the History of Religions* (1987), 9–48. The difficulty in transmitting the mystical experience in a literary form is present in Christianity as well. See Bernard McGinn, *The Foundations of Mysticism: From Its Origins to Fifth Century* (1992), xvii, "One thing that all Christian mystics have agreed on is that the experience itself defies conceptualization and verbalization, in part or in whole. Hence, it can only be presented indirectly, partially by a series of verbal strategies in which language is used not so much informationally as transformationally, that is, not to convey content but to assist the hearer or reader to hope for or to achieve the same consciousness."

114. The significance of the words of the sage as opposed to the written word is an important dimension in Geronese Kabbala and Hasidism as well. See for

example Daniel Abrams, "Orality in the Kabbalistic School of Nahmanides: Preserving and Interpreting Esoteric Traditions and Texts," *Jewish Studies Quarterly Review* 3, no. 1 (1996): 85–102. Cf. R. Nahman of Bratslav, *Likkutei MoHaRan,* 1: 20, 28a–29a; and 1:110.

115. The notion of the deficiency of R. Shimon's disciples to accurately transmit the teachings of R. Shimon and the implications of R. Shimon's death form the central core of the Idra Rabba, one of the most opaque and important books of the Zohar. On this see Liebes, *Studies in the Zohar,* 63–84. The acknowledgment of the limitations of the text to transmit the experience of its author is a common theme in Hasidism. See for example R. Meshullam Feibush of Zbarazh in the early Hasidic text *Yosher Divrei Emet,* 1.22. For an English translation of this text see Louis Jacobs, *Turn Aside from Evil and Do Good: An Introduction and a Way to the Tree of Life* (1995), xxxii–xxxiii.

116. See b.T. Sota 13b, 14a; b.T. Temurah 15b, 16a; and Zohar 1.37b, 38a. Cf. R. Yonatan Eyebshutz, *Ya'arot Devash,* 2 vols. (1983), vol. 1, sermon 8, 158–64.

117. *Ha-Hakdama,* 29.

118. For a discussion on the centrality of the revelation of Elijah as authoritative in the history of Kabbala, see Scholem, *On the Kabbala and Its Symbolism* (1965), 19–29.

119. This is true of the circle of R. Isaac Luria. After his death, R. Hayyim Vital and R. Moses Yonah attempted to prevent at all costs the publication of Lurianic doctrine for "at least 100 years." The appearance of Lurianic Kabbala in Italy, made available by R. Israel Sarug, caused much controversy among Kabbalists in Palestine. For a lengthy discussion on this, see Joseph Avivi, "The Lurianic Corpus in Italy Before 1620" (in Hebrew), *'Aley Sefer* 11 (1984): 134–91.

120. *Ha-Hakdama,* 29.

121. This echoes Abulafia's position as well. See his *Sitrei Torah,* MS Paris-BN heb. 774, fol. 143a; cited and discussed in Wolfson, *Abraham Abulafia,* 75, 76.

122. *Ha-Hakdama,* 29. See also Zohar 2.69b; and Zohar Hadash cited in R. Zvi Hirsch Eichenstein's *Sur m'Ra ve Aseh Tov,* 133. A more unequivocal rejection of philosophy is given by R. Shneur Zalman of Liady in *Likkutei Amarim Tanya,* chap. 8, 26, "Likewise, he who occupies himself with the science of the nations of the world is included among those who waste their time in profane matters, insofar as the sin of neglecting the Torah *(bittul Torah)* is concerned. . . . Moreover, the defilement of the sciences of the nations is greater than that of profane speech." This is similar to statements made by R. Abraham Isaac Ha-Kohen Kook a few decades later. See for example, *Orot Ha-Kodesh* (1981), vol. 1, nos. 7, 9, 10. For a Hasidic example where philosophy is criticized more vociferously, see the anonymous Bratslav monograph *Kinat Ha-Shem Ziva'ot* (1860–1865).

123. The distinction between Kabbala as tradition and Kabbala as *s'vara* (logic) is a long-standing debate. R. Isaiah Horowitz suggests such a distinction between R. Isaac Luria and R. Moses Cordovero. See Elliot R. Wolfson, "The Influence of the Ari on the Shelah" (in Hebrew), *Jerusalem Studies in Jewish Thought* 10 (1992):

443, n.114; and Isaiah Tishby, "The Conflict between Kabbalat Ha-Ari and Kabbalat Ha-Ramak in the Writings of Ra'abam" (in Hebrew), *Zion* 39 (1979): 28ff.

124. The issue of the symbolic language of Kabbala in general and the language of the philosophers is addressed in many studies on Jewish mysticism. See for example Gershom Scholem, "The Name of God and Linguistic Theory in Kabbala," 164–94; Idel, *Language, Torah and Hermeneutics in Abraham Abulafia* (1989), esp. 1–29; idem, "Reification of Language in Jewish Mysticism," in *Mysticism and Language,* Steven Katz, ed. (1992), 3–41.

125. *Ha-Hakdama,* 29. On this see R. Dov Baer Schneersohn, *Ner Mitzvah ve Torah 'Or* (repr., 1995), 160b–161a, where the question of the limitations of the use of *mashal* (a central tenet of medieval philosophical discourse) is discussed at length.

126. The notion of "prophecy" or "illumination" among medieval Jewish philosophers, specifically Maimonides, is a complex matter. See the discussion in A. J. Heschel, "Prophetic Inspiration in the Middle Ages" and "Did Maimonides Believe He Had Attained Prophecy?" both in A. J. Heschel, *Prophetic Inspiration after the Prophets,* Morris Faierstein, ed. (1996). For a counterargument see Ben Sommer, "Did Prophecy Cease?" *Journal of Biblical Literature* 115 (1996): 31–47.

127. A similar formulation of this idea can be found in the Lurianic text entitled *"Pesiutav shel Avraham Avinu,"* reprinted in *Ketavim Hadashim l'Rabbenu Hayyim Vital* (1989), 18. The Lurianic text makes a much more severe distinction between Kabbala and philosophy by claiming that the philosophical enterprise vis-à-vis the interpretation of Scripture is the mistaken belief that *peshat* (plain-sense meaning) can be fully understood without Sod. "The plain-sense meaning of Torah is necessarily similar to the soul of Torah and its inner-meaning as the form of the body [*zelem*] is to the soul [*nefesh*]. This being so, until one has a firm grasp of the inner-meaning of Torah, one is sure to be mistaken in its plain-sense meaning [*p'shat*]." Thus, argues this Lurianic text, when the plain-sense meaning eludes the interpreter, he moves to a philosophical interpretation rather than acknowledging that the plain-sense meaning cannot be understood without its esoteric counterpart. Even though R. Gershon Henokh speaks only of the inadequacy of philosophical language to fully convey the meaning of Scripture, his orientation is the result of the later Kabbalistic attitude toward philosophy in general reflected in this Lurianic text. Cf. *Pesiutav,* 3, 8, 17; and R. Hayyim Vital's Introduction to *Sha'ar Ha-Hakdamot,* printed as the Introduction to *Etz Hayyim,* 2d.

128. The advantage of poetic language to depict and describe the prophetic and mystical experience is common in the Jewish tradition. See for example R. Yizhak Abrabanel, *Perush 'al Ha-Torah* to Exodus 15:1; and his *Perush 'al Neviim Ahronim,* 40–42. Cf. Maimonides' *Guide of the Perplexed,* 1:36, 2:45; and Gersonides' commentary to Song of Songs, "Hakdama," and chapter one, in *Commentary to Song of Songs,* Menahem Kellner, trans. (in English) (1998), 3–30. Cf. Alan Cooper, "Imagining Prophecy," in *Poetry and Prophecy: The Beginnings of a Literary Tradition,* James Kugel, ed. (1990), 26–44.

129. According to R. Gershon Henokh in *Ha-Hakdama,* Kabbala as a concept (i.e., revealing the concealed God) begins with Abraham and is developed further in his commentary to Genesis in *Sod Yesharim*. Abraham represents for R. Gershon Henokh the first individual who recognized the immanent nature of God and the ability of humankind to approach Him. Therefore, the attempt to lift the veil which conceals the divine becomes the vocation of Abraham as patriarch and a motif for the vocation of the Jewish mystic.

130. The notion of Kabbala as precisely that which reveals the secret and, in doing so, conceals the secret, is the foundation of Elliot Wolfson's recent study on Abraham Abulafia. See Wolfson, *Abraham Abulafia*,, 9–38.

131. The absence of any direct illumination by Elijah the Prophet during the Middle Ages (until R. Isaac Luria) is not at all a popular notion among mystics. The author of *Brit Menuha* states explicitly that R. Abraham ben David (Rabad) had experienced such a direct illumination. See *Brit Menuha,* 2b, 3a. R. Hayyim Vital draws a distinction between the formal category of *Ruah Ha-Kodesh,* which he believed no longer existed, and the illumination of Elijah the Prophet, which he believed was the source for R. Isaac Luria's Kabbalistic doctrine. See his Introduction to *Sha'ar Hakdamot,* 4d, 5a. The illumination of Elijah was often used by Kabbalists to give Kabbalistic doctrine the authority it needed to be considered an authentic mode of Jewish spirituality. On this see Scholem, *On the Kabbala and Its Symbolism,* 19ff. It is worth noting that R. Gershon Henokh, in his treatment of the Middle Ages, never directly confronts the development of Kabbala during those philosophical times. Many medieval Kabbalists such as Abraham Abulafia, his student Joseph ibn Gikatillia and Abraham ben Isaac Gerondi claimed to have had a direct illumination of the divine. According to R. Gershon Henokh, the direct illumination seems to end with R. Shimon (perhaps remnants remained until Nahmanides [later part of the thirteenth century]) and only pick up again with R. Isaac Luria, culminating with the Besht. Placing this referent into the theory that Elijah was a tool to authenticate innovation, the whole Lurianic tradition appears to see itself as a renewal of an age-old direct (or full) tradition which was concealed (even to the Kabbalists) in the thirteenth century.

132. On this see *Ha-Hakdama,* 41. See also his *Ayin Ha-Tekhelet,* 67b, where he states regarding Rabad, "It is known that many pamphlets from the holy Zohar were in the hands of the Gaonim." However, R. Gershon Henokh may have also argued that Nahmanides, like all other medieval philosophers (also mystics) used a Kabbalistic hermeneutic, which contained within it a partial Sod tradition to interpret Scripture.

133. The Hasidic use of Abraham and his natural and liberated form of service to God is frequent in Hasidism. See Arthur Green, *Devotion and Commandment,* 9ff. Cf. Jerome Gellman, *The Fear, The Trembling and the Fire: Kierkegaard and the Hasidic Masters on the Binding of Isaac* (1994), 73–98.

2. Recircumcising the Torah

1. See Abraham Joshua Heschel, "Hasidism as a New Approach to Torah," reprinted in *Moral Grandeur and Spiritual Audacity,* S. Heschel, ed. (1996), 33–39. This is also the assumption of Buber in *The Origin and Meaning of Hasidism* (1988), 59–112. On Talmud Torah in Hasidism and its relationship to Mithnagdic ideals, see Joseph Weiss, "Talmud Torah lefi Ha-Besht," in *Sefer Ha-Yovel Tiferet Yisrael: Essays in Honor of Rabbi Israel Brodie* (1967), 151–69; and idem, "Talmud Torah in Early Hasidism," in *Studies in Eastern European Jewish Mysticism* (1985), 55–68. Cf. Rivka Shatz-Uffenheimer, *Hasidism as Mysticism,* Jonathan Chipman, trans. (1978), 343–56.

2. On this, see Nahmanides' commentary to Leviticus 19:2.

3. Abraham's place in the Hasidic imagination is the focus of Arthur Green's *Devotion and Commandment* (1989). For another view that stresses the more elitist origins of Hasidism see Ada Rapoport-Albert, "God and the Tzadik as the Two Focal Points of Hasidic Worship," *History of Religions* 18 (1979): 296–324.

4. See Elliot R. Wolfson, "Circumcision, Vision of God, and Textual Interpretation: From Midrashic Trope to Mystical Symbol," *Circle in the Square* (1995), 29–48; and idem, "Circumcision and the Divine Name: A Study in the Transformation of an Esoteric Doctrine," *Jewish Quarterly Review* 78 (1987): 77–112. For a Hasidic view on circumcision, see Wolfson, "The Cut That Binds: Time, Memory, and the Ascetic Impulse (Reflections on Bratslav Hasidism)," in *God's Voice from the Void: Old and New Studies in Bratslav Hasidism,* Shaul Magid, ed. (2001), 103–54.

5. See R. Hayyim Vital, "Introduction to *Sha'ar Ha-Hakdamot,*" printed as the "Introduction to *Etz Hayyim,*" in *Etz Hayyim,* Mekor Hayyim edition, 3b: "One who reads Mishna and Talmud is called 'a slave who serves his master to receive reward.' This is not the case with Kabbala *(Hokhmat Ha-Emet).* [The one who reads Kabbala] rectifies [the world], as it were, and gives strength to the supernal worlds above. This is without a doubt called '*torah lishma.*' Moreover, man was only created to study the wisdom of the Kabbala!"

6. On this see Jerome Gellman, *The Fear, the Trembling and the Fire* (1994), esp. 23–44, 73–98.

7. On this see Aviezer Ravitzky, "Samuel Ibn Tibbon and the Esoteric Character of the *Guide of the Perplexed,*" *AJS Review* 6 (1981): 87–123; Moshe Idel, "*Sitrei 'Arayot* in Maimonides' Thought," in *Maimonides and Philosophy,* S. Pines and Y. Yovel, eds. (1986), 79–91; Sarah Klein-Bratzlavy, *King Solomon and the Philosophical Esotericism in the Thought of Maimonides* (in Hebrew) (1996); and most recently Elliot Wolfson, *Abraham Abulafia* (2000), 38–52. Cf. R. Abraham Isaac Ha-Kohen Kook, *'Orot Ha-Kodesh* (1981), vol. 1, nos. 7, 9, 10 where a similar idea is expressed vis-à-vis the limited nature of philosophy, focusing on its objective and language.

8. See Moshe Idel, "Maimonides and Kabbala," esp. 54–80.

9. On this see Alfred Ivry, "Maimonides and Neoplatonism: Challenge and Response," in, *Neoplatonism and Jewish Thought,* Lenn Goodman, ed. (1992), 137–56; and idem, "Neoplatonic Currents in Maimonides' Thought," in *Studies in Maimonides' Thought and Environment,* J. Kraemer, ed. (1990), 149–74.

10. On Ha-Levi and the mystical tradition, see Elliot R. Wolfson, "Merkavah Traditions in Philosophical Garb: Judah Ha-Levi Reconsidered," *Proceedings of the American Academy of Jewish Research* 57 (1991): 179–242; and Aaron Hughes, "Two Approaches to the Love of God in Medieval Jewish Thought: The Concept of *Devekut* in the Works of Ibn Ezra and Ha-Levi," *Studies in Religion* 28–2 (1999): 139–51.

11. *Ha-Hakdama,* 20–22.

12. In his book *Hasidism: Between Ecstasy and Magic,* Moshe Idel argues that this is indicative of Hasidism in general. Although I still maintain that Lurianic Kabbala (and its reading of the Zohar) dominates the Hasidic imagination, Idel's observation that earlier Kabbalistic strands made their way into Hasidic literature is important. The Kabbala of the Italian Renaissance may be one catalyst for this influence. This is especially true in later Hasidism (after 1850), which had access to a wider assortment of medieval and Renaissance Kabbalistic texts.

13. However, the medieval philosophical tradition after Maimonides does suggest the existence of such an esoteric tradition in the *Guide.* See the discussion in Aviezer Ravitsky, "Mishnato shel R. Zerahyah ben Yizhak ben She'alti'ei Hen vehe-Hagut Ha-Maimonit-Tibonit b'Me'ah 13" [Ph.D. diss., Hebrew University, 1977]; and idem, "Samuel Ibn Tibbon and the Esoteric Character of the *Guide of the Perplexed,*" *AJS Review* 6 (1981): 87–123.

14. This is particularly true in Abulafia and those influenced by him. See Abraham Abulafia, *Sheva Netivot Ha-Torah,* in Adolph Jellinek, *Philosophie und Kabbala* (1854), reprinted in Abulafia, *Gan Na'ul* (1999), 86–136; Idel, "Maimonides and Kabbala," 55–70; and Wolfson, *Abraham Abulafia,* 38–52.

15. For short excerpts of Hasidic literature's use of the *Guide,* see Jacob Dienstag, "Ha-Moreh Nevuchim ve Sefer Ha Madda Be Sifrut Ha-Hasidut"(in Hebrew), in *Abraham Weiss Jubilee Volume* (1964), 307–38; idem, "Maimonides and the Kabbalists—Bibliography"(in Hebrew), *Da'at* 25 (1990): 53–84. Cf. Samuel Abba Horodetzky, "The Rambam in Kabbala and Hasidism"(in Hebrew), in *Moznaim* 3 (1943): 441–45.

16. On the Besht as the continuation of Luria in the Hasidic imagination, see Gershon Kitzis, "Hasidut Ha-Besht v' Kabbalat Ha-Ari," *Mahanayim* 6 (1994): 212–14. For another view see Moshe Idel, *Hasidism: Between Ecstasy and Magic* (1995), 33–102. Idel is dealing more with the question of the use of Lurianic models in Hasidism and less with the way Hasidism constructs the relationship between Luria and the Besht.

17. *Ha-Hakdama,* 43.

18. Ibid., 43.

19. Much of the second part of *Ha-Hakdama* (called *Ha-Petikha*) is devoted to addressing philosophical issues such as providence, epistemology, faith, and miracles, based on the Zohar. Using medieval philosophical and Kabbalistic sources to raise questions on these matters, the Zohar always serves as the proof-text for his answers. This will be examined in detail in the following chapter.

20. The most sophisticated presentations of this traditionalist position can be found in Marvin Fox, *Interpreting Maimonides* (1990), esp. 26–90; and David Hartman, *Torah and Philosophical Quest* (1974).

21. *Ha-Hakdama,* 40.

22. *Ha-Hakdama,* 49. Cf. Zohar 1.163b.

23. The notion of seeing philosophical and Kabbalistic esotericism as one is, as far as I know, unique to R. Gershon Henokh. Even among Kabbalists who used Maimonides in their esoteric projects, philosophical esotericism was seen as distinct, both in method and substance, from Kabbalistic esotericism. On this see Alexander Altmann, "Maimonides' Attitude toward Jewish Mysticism," *Studies in Jewish Thought: An Anthology of German Jewish Scholarship,* A. Jospe, ed. (1981), 200–219; and Wolfson, *Abraham Abulafia,* 39, n.94 for other scholarly sources.

24. On Isaac Arama's attitude toward Maimonides see Samuel Abba Horodetzky, "The Rambam in Kabbala and Hasidism" (in Hebrew), in *Moznaim* 3 (1943), 441–45. Cf. Seymour Feldman, "A Debate Concerning Determinism in Late Medieval Jewish Philosophy," *Proceedings of the American Academy for Jewish Research* 51 (1984): 15–54. Although Feldman focuses on the issue of determinism, he touches on the more general attitudes of late medieval Jewish writers, particularly after the expulsion, on the Maimonidean philosophical program.

25. For more on this see Antoine Faivre, *Access to Western Esotericism* (1994), 8ff.

26. *Guide* 1:73, 203. On the issue of free will in Maimonides and in medieval philosophy in general, see Alexander Altmann, "The Religion of the Thinkers: Free Will and Predestination in Saadia, Bahya and Maimonides," in *Religion in a Religious Age,* S. D. Goitein, ed. (1974), 25–52. On the popular belief of predestination among Jews in eleventh-century Egypt, see S. D. Goitein, "Religion in Everyday Life as Reflected in the Documents of the Cairo Geniza," *Religion in a Religious Age* (1974), 3–19.

27. I consulted the Soncino translation of the Zohar on this particular passage and changed it when I felt it did not adequately express the original. See *The Zohar* (1933), 1:331–32.

28. *Ha-Hakdama,* 31, 32. This text must be read in light of the general Izbica/Radzin position that free will is a negative consequence of the sin that is solely perspectival and has no ontological reality. The more one becomes spiritually refined, the more one realizes that free will is nonexistent. See for example *Sod Yesharim on the Torah,* 7b.

29. R. Hayyim of Volozhin, in his *Nefesh Ha-Hayyim,* 3:4–6, utilizes this method extensively. See also how these and other passages are discussed in

Mordecai Pachter, "Between Acosmism and Theism in R. Hayyim of Volozhin" (in Hebrew), *Mehkarim be Hagot Ha-Yehudit* (1989): 139–57; and my "Deconstructing the Mystical: The Anti-Mystical Kabbalism in Rabbi Hayyim of Volozhin's *Nefesh Ha-Hayyim,*" *Journal of Jewish Thought and Philosophy* 9 (2000): 21–67.

30. This distinction is central in Crescas's treatment of determinism. See his *'Or Adonay* (repr., 1992), part 3. Cf. Seymour Feldman, "Crescas' Theological Determinism," *Da'at* 9 (1982): 3–28; and Aviezer Ravitsky, "A Debate Concerning Determinism in Late Medieval Jewish Philosophy," *Proceedings of the American Academy for Jewish Research* 51 (1984): 15–54. This notion of perspectivity *(m'zido-m'zidanu)* is a common tool used in the Kabbalistic thinking of R. Moses Hayyim Luzzato and the Lithuanian Kabbalistic school of Sklov, particularly in R, Hayyim of Volozhin in his *Nefesh Ha-Hayyim,* and R. Yizhak Isaac Haver. See the sustained discussed in Haver's *Pithei Shearim* (repr., 1989), esp. 4b–10a. Cf. *Nefesh Ha-Hayyim,* 3:4.

31. This notion of knowledge is the foundation for the transition from metaphysics to mysticism in Plotinus and Christian and Jewish Neoplatonism. For a discussion on this see A. C. Lloyd, *The Anatomy ofNeoplatonism* (1990), chaps. 5, 6, and 7; Stephen Gersch, *From Iamblichus to Eriguena* (1972), esp. 261–82; and Rorem, *Pseudo-Dionysis* (1993), 214–39. Alfred Ivry has suggested in various studies that Maimonides adopts many of the Neoplatonic ideas of the Arab readers of Aristotle, thus becoming more of a Neoplatonist than he may have been aware. See for example Alfred Ivry, "Neoplatonic Currents in Maimonides Thought," in *Studies in Maimonides Thought and Environment,* J. Kraemer, ed. (1990), 149–74.

32. The attitude of the Zohar toward knowledge is quite complex. On the use of the word "zohar" as indicative of mystical knowledge, Yehuda Liebes notes, "*The enlightened ones will shine like the brilliance of the heavens* [Daniel 12:3]. This 'zohar' [illumination], which acts in the heavenly realm, also illumines the hearts of the true mystics. They are [called] the Enlightened Ones [Maskilim]. In another place [Zohar Hadash 105a] the Zohar distinguishes between the 'Knowers' [*Yodi'im*] who are the carriers of the secret doctrine which is established [perhaps as Tradition—my addition] and Enlightened Ones [Maskilim] who are able to illuminate the past via the illumination of the Torah which is illuminated through them. They are then able to dominate the secret teachings of their fathers in heaven [and are no longer merely the carriers—my addition]." See Yehuda Liebes, "Eros and the Zohar" (in Hebrew), *'Alpayim* 9 (1994): 73, 74, and n.52. The conflation of devekut and knowledge is also the subject of Moshe Cordovero's *'Ohr Ne'erav,* chap. 2, 17–19.

33. The idea that enlightenment is the correct understanding of providence is the central thesis in R. Samuel ibn Tibbon's reading of Job. See Robert Eisen, "Samuel Ibn Tibbon on the Book of Job," *AJS Review* 24, no. 2 (1999): 263–301.

34. R. Gershon Henokh uses a version of this perspectivity argument in his discussion of free will and the illusory distinction between miracle and nature. See *Ha-Hakdama,* 88, 89, 90. Cf. *Sod Yesharim on the Torah,* 39a.

35. Joseph Stern similarly reads Maimonides' ambiguity on the obligation of the law and philosophers' possible overcoming of that obligation in the *Guide*. See Joseph Stern, *Problems and Parables of Law* (1999), 1–48. Cf. my discussion of Stern in the final chapter of this study.

36. *Ha-Hakdama,* 32. It is interesting here to note that Goitein argues that the popular belief in Egypt among Jews was the deterministic one. Perhaps R. Gershon Henokh would agree with Maimonides in this sharp critique of this position in that it has no basis in the empirical world in which we live. However, it is important to note that R. Gershon Henokh's ideology is based on an intuitive experience, which is not based in the intellectual apprehension of the medievalists but in the emotional enthusiasm of the Besht's teachings.

37. Although R. Gershon Henokh and most of the Hasidic tradition held that Luria's teachings were a product of divine illumination through Elijah the Prophet (as stated by R. Hayyim Vital on the title page to all of his collected teachings), such a position is not without its dissenters. Another approach, expressed by R. Menahem Azaria da Fano in his commentary to R. Moshe Cordovero's *'Or Ne'erav* (1786), entitled "Pelekh Ha-Rimon," states, "Do not say [concerning the Ari] that his teaching was a product of prophecy. Rather, he found previously unknown ancient books which were hidden among our Fathers, the men of Ashkenaz" (4). See a similar statement in the responsa of R. Shlomo Luria, *Teshuvot Ha-Rashal,* no. 29.

38. See for example in *Guide* 3:2 where the four faces of the chariot are given philosophical readings.

39. See Abrabanel on the *Guide* 3:1 in the Ibn Tibbon edition (1970), 2a/b, 3a. Although Abrabanel does not comment on the Introduction itself, his lengthy comments on Maimonides' interpretation of the four faces of the chariot in *Guide* 3:1 are based on the more general question (stated at the end of those comments on 3a) regarding the prohibition in light of Maimonides' claim to give "the plain-sense meaning" *(peshuto shel mikra).*

40. The source of R. Gershon Henokh's assertion is not made explicit in his discussion. It is likely that he may have utilized the delineation of God's thirteen attributes of mercy and their relation to the ten *sephirot* as described in a responsa by R. Hai Gaon. R. Gershon Henokh likely knew of Hai Gaon's responsa from Cordovero's *Pardes Rimonim*. R. Hai Gaon's position is cited and interpreted by R. Moshe Cordovero in *Pardes Rimonim* (1787; repr., 1962), "Sha'ar 'Eser ve lo Tesha," chaps. 6, 5b, 6a.

41. See Gershom Scholem, *On the Kabbala and Its Symbolism* (1965), 110–11; Moshe Idel, "On The Concept of *Zimzum* in Kabbala and Its Research" (in Hebrew), *Jerusalem Studies in Jewish Thought* 10 (1992): 59–110; David Novak, "Self-Contradiction of the Godhead in Kabbalistic Theosophy," in *Neoplatonism and Jewish Thought,* Lenn Goodman, ed. (1992), 299–318; and Shaul Magid, "Origin and Overcoming the Beginning: *Zimzum* as a Trope of Reading in Post-Lurianic Kabbala," in *Beginning/Again: Toward a Hermeneutic of Jewish Texts,* Aryeh Cohen and Shaul Magid, eds. (2001), 163–213.

42. See *Etz Hayyim,* "Seventh Palace, Palace of ABYA," 1:94b. Other sources in Lurianic Kabbala and how R. Gershon Henokh uses these categories in his Torah commentary *Sod Yesharim* are discussed in the later chapters of this study.

43. See Pinhas Giller, *Reading the Zohar: The Sacred Text of the Kabbala* (2001), 35–62.

44. For a historical discussion on the development of these two elements in Lurianic Kabbala see Mordechai Pachter, "Igullim ve Yosher Toldoteha shel Idea," *Da'at* 18 (1987): 59–90. These categories are used by R. Gershon Henokh in his reading of the relationship between the human (divine) soul and the serpent.

45. The ambiguity of recension of Lurianic literature is one of the most complex episodes in the history of Jewish bibliography. Scholars have determined three or perhaps of late four basic periods of recension of Lurianic material: the early recension, the middle recension, and the later recension. More recent scholarship has suggested a fourth "hidden" recension *(Madurah Genuzah)* that may be a missing link in mapping out the development of Lurianic Kabbala among his many disciples. For some elaborate discussions on these see Joseph Avivi, *Binyan Ariel* (1987); and R. Ya'akov Moshe Hillel's preface to R. Ya'akov Zemah's *Kehillat Ya'akov* (1992), 11–56.

46. *Etz Hayyim,* Introduction to "Seventh Palace, Palace of ABYA," 1:95a.

47. Ibid., 1:95a.

48. *Ha-Hakdama,* 35. Cf. *Etz Hayyim,* "Sha'ar Ha-Kelippot," chap. 3, 110a–d.

49. Note that in Jewish tradition the angels who, in Lurianic Kabbala, reside in the world of creation *(beriah)* do not have free will because in their world no distinction has yet been made between good and evil. Moreover, the Lurianic tradition suggests that the two highest worlds *(azilut* and *beriah)* were not affected by the first sin. On this, see R. Hayyim Vital's *Sha'ar Ha-Pesukim ve Sha'ar Ha-Lekutim,* 2–4b.

50. *Ha-Hakdama,* 35, "Therefore in the world of *yezirah* the power of concealment increases. Hence it was God's will that the vision of Ezekiel was rooted in the concealed [state of the divine] as is stated in Zohar 2.2b and 3.118b."

51. Ibid, 35. "The reason there were those who criticized him [Maimonides] in attempting to understand the vision as being rooted in a lower sphere was because they understood the vision as rooted in the upper sphere [*gevoah m'al gevoah*]. Even though he attempted to interpret it in a lower sphere, nevertheless his interpretation contains [elements of] a true Kabbalistic tradition that he concealed and merely hinted with the sweetness of his words [*b'matok sefatav*]." Compare this with Ibn Gabbai's critique of Maimonides in *Avodat Ha-Kodesh,* 2:3, 3:63.

52. Although many answers were given to this obvious question, see in particular R. Shem Tov ibn Falaquera's comment to the introduction in Ibn Tibbon's standard edition.

53. See Afodi to *Guide* 3, "Introduction."

54. The use of philosophical garb to explain mystical principles is a central theme in R. Gershon Henokh's theory. In another case, where he attempts to

uncover the mystical interpretation embedded in the seemingly rational understanding of the reason for the incense in the Sanctuary in *Guide* 3:45, he states, "and he [Maimonides] held the position [of the Zohar] using the garment for *p'shat*."

55. On this see Moshe Idel, "Secrecy, Binah, and Derisha," in *Secrecy and Concealment,* H. G. Kipperberg and G. G. Stroumsa, eds. (1995), 310–43; idem, "*Sitrei 'Arayot* in Maimonides' Thought," in *Maimonides and Philosophy,* S. Pines and Y. Yovel, eds. (1986), 79–91; and Elliot R. Wolfson, *Abraham Abulafia,* 38–52. Cf. Sarah Klein-Bratzlavy, *King Solomon and the Philosophical Esotericism* (1996).

56. See in the Ibn Tibbon edition, 2b of part 3.

57. R. Gershon Henokh also quotes from Abraham Maimonides' "Pirke Ha-Hazlaha" *(Treatise on Beatitude),* which he claims to have seen printed in *Teshuvot Ha-Rambam (The Responsa of Maimonides)* and believed, as most did in the nineteenth century, that this treatise was authored by Maimonides himself. Scholarship has determined that this work was most probably authored by Maimonides' son, Abraham Maimonides, and reflects the Jewish/Sufi perspective common in Egypt in the twelfth century. See for example Paul Fenton, *Treatise of the Pool* (1987), introduction entitled, "Judaism and Sufism." On the authorship, translation, and analysis of "Pirke Ha-Hazlaha," see Samuel Rosenblatt, *The High Ways to Perfection of Abraham Maimonides* (1927), vol. 2, "Introduction."

58. For another clear example of this, see R. Hayyim Vital, *Sha'arei Kedusha* (1976), part 3, gate 22: "One light in the form of Adam emanates through the four worlds until the end of the four foundations [*yesodot*] in this lowly world. This [light in the lowest world] is connected to the lights in the upper worlds which are called *sephirot.*" Compare this with the *Sha'arei Kedusha,* second gate, 71a.

59. The human face, particularly its seven openings, the hair and the corners of the head, are the places where divine light begins its emanation into the empty space created by *zimzum*. See Vital, *Etz Hayyim,* 24b–30a; and an abbreviated version in idem, *'Ozrot Hayyim,* "Sha'ar Ha-Adukim," 2b–5a; and *Adam Yashar,* 85b–85d.

60. Cf. *Guide of the Perplexed,* 3:24, 497–99, containing Maimonides' most sustained discussion of the binding of Isaac in the *Guide*. Cf. *Mishneh Torah,* "Laws on the Foundations of the Torah," chap. 8 on the uniqueness of Moses' prophecy. For a discussion of the relationship between Maimonides' interpretation of Genesis 22 and the Izbica tradition, see Jerome Gellman, *The Fear, the Trembling and the Fire* (1994), 28–44.

61. For an example of the Aramaic term *'umei* as swearing, see Targum Onkelos to Genesis 50:25 and Exodus 13:19.

62. Zohar, *Ra'ayah Mehemna,* 3:130a.

63. *Ha-Hakdama,* 94.

64. Maimonides, *Mishneh Torah,* "Laws of the Foundation of the Torah," chaps. 8 and 9.

65. On this interpretation, see R. Jacob Lainer's *Beit Ya'akov* to Genesis, 65bff. R. Jacob Lainer's discussion of the uniqueness of Abraham's prophecy focuses on the continuous prophecy initiated via circumcision rather than the Akedah.

66. See Moshe Idel, "Maimonides and Kabbala," 31–54. For a comprehensive discussion on the notion of *ta'amei ha-mitzvot* in Maimonides see Isadore Twersky, *Introduction to Maimonides' Mishneh Torah* (1980), 374–407. On Kabbala, see Daniel Matt, "The Mystic and the Mitzvot," in *Jewish Spirituality II,* A. Green, ed. (1986), 367–404. The notion of *ta'amei ha-mitzvot* stands as one of the most pressing points of contention between traditionalists and philosophers. Ironically, philosophers and Kabbalists stand on the same side of this polemic in that both engaged in a form of *ta'amei ha-mitzvot.* David Novak states that, "Maimonides and Nahmanides, both *committed* [my emphasis] to the thesis that there are reasons for all the commandments, developed their own distinctive means of explaining the more difficult commandments of the Torah. It is at this level of exegetical challenge that their fundamental theological differences become most apparent. Indeed, it is against the background of Maimonides' treatment of these commandments that Nahmanides' position emerges most clearly by the contrast." See David Novak, *The Theology of Nahmanides Systematically Presented* (1992), 9. Compare Novak with the following statement by Nahmanides in his "Sermon on Ecclesiastics," in *Kitve Ramban,* 1:190: "With respect to these matters and others like them one cannot understand their truth from one's own mind but only through tradition [*be-kabbala*]. This matter is explained in the Torah to whosoever has heard the rationale for the commandments through tradition as is fitting. This refers to one who has received from a mouth which has received, going back to Moses, our teacher, [who received] from God." On this see also E. R. Wolfson, "Maiden without Eyes: *Peshat* and *Sod* in Zoharic Hermeneutics," 160, 161.

67. The most comprehensive study of this phenomenon in Jewish thought is in Isaac Heinemann, *Ta'amei Ha-Mitzvot,* 2 vols. (1949). However, that Heinemann ignores the whole Kabbalistic tradition of *ta'amei ha-mitzvot,* including obvious studies of this nature by Kabbalists such as R. Menahem Recanati's *Ta'amei Ha-Mitzvot, Likkutei Torah,* R. Meir Poppers, ed. (1880), including a running gloss entitled *ta'amei ha-mitzvot;* and R. Menahem Mendel Schneersohn's *Derekh Mitzvotekha (Ta'amei Mitzvot).* The inclusion of the Kabbalists in the genre of *ta'amei ha-mitzvot* and even the identification of the philosophical enterprise with Kabbalistic discourse is the subject of a recent study by Isadore Twersky, who views metahalakha as one of the brilliant gems of medieval Jewish intellectual activity. See Twersky, "Talmudists, Philosophers, Kabbalists: The Quest for Spirituality in the Sixteenth Century," B. Cooperman, ed., *Jewish Thought in the Sixteenth Century* (1983), 431–60. Cf. Jacob Katz, *Halakha and Kabbala: Studies in the History of Jewish Religion, Its Various Faces and Social Relevance* (in Hebrew) (1984), 9–33; E. R. Wolfson, "Mystical Rationalization of the Commandments in the Prophetic Kabbala of Abraham Abulafia," *Perspectives on Jewish Thought and Mysticism,* A. Ivry, E. R. Wolfson, and A. Arkush, eds. (1998), 331–80; and Morris Faierstein, "God's Need for the Commandments in Medieval Kabbala," *Conservative Judaism* 36, no. 1 (1982): 45–59. R. Joseph Baer Soloveitchik, a leading spokesperson for twentieth-century Orthodoxy in America and an ardent defender of the

Maimonidean program, is surprisingly critical of Maimonides' *ta'amei ha-mitzvot*. See Soloveitchik, *The Halakhic Mind,* Lawrence Kaplan, trans. (1986), 93, where he claims that Maimonides' rationalizing of the commandments turned Judaism into a "religious instrumentalism" and converted the Jewish religion into "technical wisdom."

68. The Lurianic treatise by R. Meir Poppers, *Pri Etz Hayyim,* is entirely devoted to *ta'amei ha-mitzvot,* as is *'Olat Tamid* (1854); and R. Hayyim Vital's *Sha'ar Ha-Mitzvot* (1852).

69. See Scholem, *On the Kabbala and Its Symbolism,* 118–57; Ya'akov Gartner, "The Influence of the Ari on the Custom of Wearing Two Pair of *Tefillin*" (in Hebrew), *Da'at* 28 (1992): 51–64; Magid, "Conjugal Union, Mourning, and Talmud Torah in Luria's *Tikun Hazot,*" *Da'at* 36 (1996): xvii–xlv; and Moshe Idel, *Messianic Mystics* (1998), 308–20.

70. See Ronit Meroz, "Redemption in the Lurianic Teaching," (Ph.D. diss., Hebrew University, 1988), part 2; and Scholem, *Major Trends in Jewish Mysticism* (1941), 244–86. This claim admittedly requires much more evidence. However, I would like to suggest here that the uniqueness of Lurianic Kabbala regarding *ta'amei ha-mitzvot* is that this dimension of mystical thought that almost always played a role in Kabbala now becomes the central focus of Kabbalistic doctrine. Many earlier Kabbalistic works are dedicated to *ta'amei ha-mitzvot* such as the late-thirteenth-century *Ra'aya Mehemna* and *Sefer Ha-Tikkunim,* R. Menahem Recanati's *Ta'amei Ha-Mitzvot,* and the anonymous fourteenth-century *Sefer Ha-Kaneh*. A detailed analysis as to the innovative element in Luria's *ta'amei ha-mitzvot* is beyond the scope of this work. However, it is noteworthy that Hasidic readings of Luria are by and large adaptations of his *ta'amei ha-mitzvot*. Yet, in the more antinomian mood of Izbica/Radzin, R. Gershon Henokh is quite adamant about the ultimate importance of the act itself as a necessary catalyst for cosmic change. See for example in his *'Ayin Tekhelet,* 134a, where he qualifies a statement in the Zohar 2.150b that suggests that, under certain extreme circumstances, intention can replace action. R. Gershon Henokh responds, "In truth, the deep value of the act [*ma'aseh ha-mitzvah*] is higher than all the *kavvanot*. Even to the elite who knows the *ta'amei ha-mitzvot,* nevertheless, the action is higher than the *kavvanah* that will not enable one to reach its ultimate purpose. Rather, the action encompasses all of the *kavvanot*." This is strikingly similar to Maimonides' seemingly unequivocal stance on action as independent of the "reason" in *Mishneh Torah,* "Laws on the Foundations of the Torah," 9:1, and Nahmanides' comment to Exodus 13:16. Whether Maimonides and Nahmanides as well as R. Gershon Henokh felt the same need to qualify their potentially problematic stances regarding *ta'amei ha-mitzvot* and antinomianism, respectively, is left open to discussion. I would suggest that in Hasidic thought, R. Gershon Henokh being merely an isolated example, the term *kavvanah* has taken on the meaning of the earlier *ta'amei ha-mitzvot*. Perhaps the unique element in Luria's *ta'amei ha-mitzvot* juxtaposed to its earlier Kabbalistic counterpart is that, for Luria, the *kavvanah* is the *ta'am*

(telos). In this sense, earlier Kabbalistic *ta'amei ha-mitzvot* are more a reflection of Maimonidean teleology than Lurianic *kavvanah*.

71. See Menahem Kallus, "The Relationship of the Baal Shem Tov to the Practice of Lurianic *Kavvanot* in Light of his Comments to the *Siddur Rashkov*," in *Kabbala: Journal for the Study of Jewish Mystical Texts* 2 (1997): 151–68.

72. The Kabbalistic critique of Maimonides' *ta'amei ha-mitzvot* largely focused on this relativism. See for example Shem Tov ibn Shem Tov, *Sefer Ha-Emunot* (1969), 1:1, 7a; and R. Isaac of Acre, *Meirat Einayim* (1975), 203. Cf. Louis Jacobs, "Attitudes of the Kabbalists and Hasidism toward Maimonides," *The Solomon Goldman Lectures* 5 (1990): 46, 47.

73. On this see Isadore Twersky, *Introduction to the Code of Maimonides*, 408–11; Joseph Stern, *Problems and Parables of Law*, 15–48; and the last chapter of this study.

74. The Sin of Adam and Eve is the focus and hub of the entire Lurianic system. See Isaiah Tishby, *Torat Ha-Ra ve' Ha-Kelippah* (1984), 91–105; and Magid, "From Theosophy to Midrash: Lurianic Exegesis and the Garden of Eden," *AJS Review* 22, no. 1 (1997): 37–75.

75. One striking case can be found in Zohar 3.113b, where charity is de-ethicized and interpreted solely as the unification of *Tiferet* and *Malkhut*. The Zohar states that the proper attitude for performing this mitzvah *(lishma)* is to have this cosmic unity in mind and not compassion for the poor, etc. For the general attitude of *ta'amei ha-mitzvot* in the Zohar see Isaiah Tishby, *Wisdom of the Zohar*, 3 vols., David Goldstein, trans. (1989), vol. 3, 1155–171.

76. On the antagonistic relationship between Hasidic authors and their philosophical Enlightenment counterparts, see Rafael Mahler, *Hasidism and the Enlightenment* (1985). On the lack of common ground between philosophy and Lurianic Kabbala in eighteenth-century Europe see Idel, "Perspectives of Kabbala in the Second Half of the Eighteenth Century," *Journal of Jewish Thought and Philosophy* 1 (1991): 55–114. See also I. Twersky, *Introduction to the Code of Maimonides*, 378–80. This is not to say that *ta'amei ha-mitzvot* had been abandoned. Rather, Hasidic literature readdressed *ta'amei ha-mitzvot* in the form of *kavvanot*. See for example R. Yizhak Isik Yehudah Safrin of Komarno, *Nativ Mitzvotekha* (1858; repr., Jerusalem, n.d.).

77. An interesting example of this is R. Nahman of Bratslav who was outspoken in his disdain for medieval Jewish philosophy and warned his Hasidim not to read the works of everyone from Sa'adia Gaon to Gersonides. In a somewhat provocative statement, recorded by R. Nahman of Tulchin, a student of R. Nathan Sternharz of Nemerov, R. Nahman implies that in the future Maimonides' problematic stance will become apparent. See R. Nahman of Tulchin, *Haye Moharan*, 48–55. Cf. *Sihot Ha-Ran* (1961), no. 40, 44–50. R. Nathan Sternharz apparently wrote two treatises entitled *Kina'at Ha-Shem Zeva'aot* and *Makhni'a Zadim*, devoted to a sustained attack against Maimonides' *Guide*. See Shmuel Feiner, "R. Nathan of

Nemirov's Polemic Against Atheism and the Enlightenment" (in Hebrew), in *Mekhkarei Yerushalayim b'Makhshevet Yisrael—Mekharei Hasidut* 15 (1999), 89–124. Non-Hasidic Kabbalists in Eastern Europe, the Gaon of Vilna for example, were also ambivalent about the philosophical works of Maimonides although no Hasidic writer with whom I am familiar ever vilified Maimonides like R. Nahman of Bratslav. On this see Dienstag, "Was the Gaon of Vilna Opposed to the Philosophy of Rambam?" (in Hebrew), in *Talpiot* 4 (1929): 253–69. Another example of a harsh critique of medieval Jewish philosophy in Hasidic literature can be found in R. Zvi Hirsch Eichenstein of Zhidachov's *Sur m'Ra ve Aseh Tov* (1942), especially in the section "*Ktav Yosher Divre Emet,*" 117–22. Other Hasidic masters, such as R. Moshe Teitelbaum of Ohel in his *Yismakh Moshe,* readily cite R. Joseph Albo, R. Hasdai Crescas, and R. Yizhak Arama, among others. Hillel Zeitlin transmits a tradition in the name of R. Pinhas of Koretz, a disciple and older contemporary of the Besht. When R. Pinhas's son wanted to remove a copy of Maimonides' *Guide* from his home, R. Pinhas refused, saying, "when the *Guide of the Perplexed* is in the house it brings in 'awe of heaven' [*yerat shamayim*]." See Hillel Zeitlin, "*Die svivah in velkher s'iz oisgevoksen der Rogatchover Iluy zt'l,*" in the Warsaw daily Yiddish newspaper, *Der Moment,* Friday, 13 March 1936. An English translation appeared in *The Chasidic Historical Review* 2, no. 1 (June/July 1977): 26–31.

78. An exception to this is R. Barukh of Kosov who, in his *Amud Ha-Avodah,* is quite supportive of the whole medieval philosophical worldview. See Esther Liebes, "Kabbalat Ha-Sekhel: Perakim b' Mishnato shel R. Barukh of Kosov—b'Ma'amado bein Hasid l'Mekubal" (M.A. thesis, Hebrew University). Both Dienstag and Horodetzky list the many references in early Hasidic material to the *Guide.* There are many such references in R. Schneur Zalman of Liady's *Likkutei Amarim Tanya* and R. Moshe Teitelbaum of Ohel's *Yismah Moshe.* Regarding the *Tanya* and Habad Hasidism, I would suggest that although many references are made to the *Guide,* there is no systematic attempt to argue for the Kabbalistic nature of the text. There may very well be systematic expositions of Lurianic symbolism in Habad Hasidism, but there is hardly a philosophical interpretation of Kabbala the likes of Abraham Ha-Kohen Herrera. See for example Rachel Elior, *The Paradoxical Ascent to God* (1992), particularly chaps. 4, 5, and 24. On R. Moshe Teitelbaum's *Yismah Moshe,* no systematic scholarly work has yet been done.

79. See *Ha-Hakdama,* 59, 60.

80. Maimonides' introduction to the first part, instruction 15. On this, see Leo Strauss, "How to Begin to Study the *Guide of the Perplexed,*" in *The Guide of the Perplexed,* Leo Strauss and Shlomo Pines, trans. (1963), xi–lvii. Cf. Leo Strauss, *Persecution and the Art of Writing* (1987), 22–37, 38–95; and Aviezer Ravitzky, "The Secrets of the *Guide of the Perplexed:* Between the Thirteenth and Twentieth Centuries," in *Studies in Maimonides,* I. Twersky, ed. (1990), 159–207, esp. 159–69.

81. Ibid, 3–21; Aviezer Ravitzky, "Samuel Ibn Tibbon and the Esoteric Character of the *Guide of the Perplexed,*" *AJS Review* 6 (1981): 87–123.

82. See Marvin Fox, *Interpreting Maimonides* (1990), 3–25, 47–90; and Lawrence Kaplan, "Maimonides and the Miraculous Element in Prophecy," *Harvard Theological Review* 70 (1977): 233–56.

83. The shared fate *(shituf-goral)* of Torah and Israel is not new in R. Gershon Henokh and is not unique to his ideology. R. Judah Loew ben Bezalel (MaHaRal of Prague) makes this correlation of the shared fate of Israel and Torah in his interpretation of the rabbinic tradition of R. Shimon bar Yohai in b.T. 138b and 139a. See his *Drush 'al Ha-Torah* (1964), 37; and *Tiferet Yisrael* in *Sifrei MaHaRal* (1972), chap. 64. MaHaRal's idea is expanded and interpreted by R. Isaac Hutner in his *Pahad Yizhak* (1995), "Hanukkah," no. 10, 84–89.

84. See R. Moshe Isserles, *Torat Ha-Olah* (1858), 75a. Cf. ibid., 75b, "The wisdom of Kabbala is like the wisdom of philosophy except they speak in two different languages." This position is close to the position of Moses Botreil in his introduction to his commentary to the *Sefer Yezirah* (24) in standard editions. The difference between Ramah and Botreil is discussed in Jonah Ben-Sasson's *The Philosophical System of Rabbi Moses Isserles* (in Hebrew) (1984), 34, n.71. Compare this with R. Azriel of Gerona's *Perush 'al Ha-Aggadot,* I. Tishby, ed. (1945), 83.

85. *Ha-Hakdama,* 43.

86. *Ha-Hakdama,* 41. Compare this with R. Hayyim Vital's Introduction to *Sha'ar ha-Hakdamot,* printed as the Introduction to *Etz Hayyim.*

87. See for example R. Meir Solomon ibn Sahula, *Biur Sodot Ha-Ramban,* and R. Isaac of Acre's *Me'irat Eynayim* (1993), both of which are devoted to extrapolating on Nahmanides' Kabbalistic allusions in his commentary to the Torah. Scholem claimed that *Biur Sodot Ha-Ramban* was really written by R. Meir's teacher, R. Joshua ibn Shu'ab of Tudela. See Scholem, *Kabbala,* 61.

88. The debate as to whether Kabbala was a received tradition and not a hermeneutic method in Nahmanides is discussed in studies on Nahmanides by Idel and Wolfson. See Idel, "We Have No Kabbalistic Tradition On This," in *Rabbi Moses ben Nahman,* I. Twersky, ed. (1983), 51–73; and Wolfson, "By Way of Truth: Aspects of Nahmanides' Kabbalistic Hermeneutics," *AJS Review* 14 (1989): 103–79. This issue was a concern for later Kabbalists, particularly those who waged a battle against philosophy that was viewed as solely the product of the intellect and not of direct revelation. See for example R. Meir ibn Gabbai's introduction to *Tola'at Ya'akov* (1799), and its treatment in R. Joseph Shlomo del Medigo's *Mazref la Hokhma,* 29b.

89. Vital's position could then support Elliot Wolfson's theory concerning Nahmanides' Kabbalistic hermeneutic as explicated in Wolfson, "By Way of Truth."

90. See *Ha-Hakdama,* 41. In R. Gershon Henokh's mind this accounts for the various redactions of Luria's disciples, even among his closest circle of students. Although R. Hayyim Vital became the definitive spokesmen in his *Etz Hayyim* and the compendium eight gates of his Lurianic corpus, many other students of that circle published works, which offered distinctly different interpretations of Luria's

lectures. See for example Moses Yonah's *Kanfe Yonah* (much of this was the product of R. Menahem Azaria da Fano); *Drush Adam Kadmon;* R. Ephrayim Penzieri's *Sefer Ha-Derushim;* R. Joseph ibn Tabul's *Drush Hefzi Bah;* R. Ya'akov Zemah's *Kehillat Ya'akov;* and Israel Sarug's *Limud Ha-Azilut*. This is merely a sampling of some of the more influential texts. The Sephardic tradition of Lurianic Kabbala focuses on the extensive contradictions within the Lurianic system as compiled by R. Hayyim Vital. See for example R. Shaul Dweck's extensive gloss and commentary to Vital's *'Ozrot Hayyim,* "Efha Shelema," printed in the Mekor Hayyim edition. This is indicative of the Beit El school of R. Shalom Sharabi.

91. The messianic element in Lurianic Kabbala is crucial for this reading. According to Scholem, Luria offered a more sober and organic messianic vision than some other postexpulsion eschatological mystics such as David Reuveni, Abraham Eliezer Ha-Levi, and Solomon Molkho. For Molkho, see *Sefer Ha-Mefuar* and *Hayyat Kaneh,* reprinted in the 2-volume *Kitvei R. Shlomo Molkho* (1989). For a comprehensive discussion on the messianic components in Lurianic Kabbala, see the sources in A. Z. Aescoly, *Jewish Messianic Movements* (in Hebrew) (1956), 253ff.; and Idel, *Messianic Mystics* (1998), 154–82.

3. What Is Hasidism?

1. For some new questions on the study of Hasidism, see Arthur Green, "Early Hasidism: Some Old/New Questions," in *Hasidism Reappraised,* Ada Rapoport-Albert, ed. (1997), 441–46.

2. There were, of course, many Hasidic masters who were Kabbalists by training. Moreover, the Baal Shem Tov's expertise in Kabbala has a long tradition in the hagiographical literature on Hasidism and in some scholarly literature as well. See for example Menahem Kallus, "The Relation of the Baal Shem Tov to the Practice of Lurianic *Kavvanot* in Light of his Comments on the Siddur Rashkov," *Kabbala* 2 (1997): 151–67; and Rachel Elior, "Kabbalat Ha-Ari, Sabbateanism and Hasidism: Historical Continuity, Spirituality and Differences" (in Hebrew), in *Mekhkarei Yerushalayim* 13 (1996): 339–97.

3. On this see Lawrence Fine, "The Contemplative Practice of *Yihudim* in Lurianic Kabbala," in *Jewish Spirituality II,* Arthur Green, ed. (1987), 64–98. I intentionally excluded the entire ecstatic tradition of Abulafia since, according to Moshe Idel, Abulafia's contemplative methods are more anomian than nomian. Even Elliot Wolfson's correction to Idel's general theory by exhibiting the use of *ta'amei ha-mitzvot* in Abulafia's system leaves Abulafia's mystical corpus less intertwined with the performance of mitzvot than the theosophic Kabbala. On the anomianism of Abulafia, see Moshe Idel, *Language, Torah and Hermeneutics in Abraham Abulafia* (1989), xii–xiii; and Elliot R. Wolfson, *Abraham Abulafia,* 178–86, esp. n.3.

4. The use and transformation of Kabbala in Hasidism has been the subject of some recent research. See Rachel Elior, "Hasidism: Historical Continuity and

Spiritual Change," in *Gershom Scholem's Major Trends in Jewish Mysticism Fifty Years After: Proceedings of the Sixth International Conference on the History of Jewish Mysticism,* Peter Schafer and Joseph Dan, eds. (1996), 303–36; and idem, "Ha-Zika she-beyn Kabbala la-Hasidut," *Proceedings of the Ninth World Congress of Jewish Studies* (1986), 107–14.

5. Moshe Idel's book on Hasidism makes a counter argument that Hasidism is more magical and ecstatic than psychological. My claim about Hasidism is only from this late-nineteenth-century perspective, one that clearly envisions Hasidism as an existential manifestation of Kabbalistic theosophy. Given the multivalent nature of Hasidic thinking, there is surely room for both visions of Hasidic spirituality.

6. Arthur Green notes, "I would say that [what is new in Hasidism] is a focusing of Judaism on worship—a sense that simple prayer life . . . is the very center of Judaism. For the Hasidic masters, Judaism is all about the act of devotion, and especially prayer . . . this seems to constitute a core that is unique and definable, a Gestalt of Hasidic piety as distinct from that of other Judaisms. The typology of this view *al derekh ha'avodah* is in need of further clarification and definition." See Arthur Green, "Early Hasidism: Some Old/New Questions," in *Hasidism Reappraised,* 445.

7. Most recently, see Moshe Idel, *Messianic Mystics* (1998), 212–41.

8. The type of Platonism I have in mind is only the notion that the ideal always eludes the seeker, and the striving for the ideal continues as the result of this unachieved and unachievable end. The notion of negative theology, so common in the Maimonidean tradition, is one example of this type of Platonism. It is true that Maimonides had absorbed quite a bit of the Middle Platonist and Neoplatonic revisions of Platonism, which served as a foundation for his understanding of prophecy, among other things. On the question of mystical experience, however, I would argue that Maimonides was closer to the Platonic stance mentioned above. See Michael Sells, "Apophasis in Plotinus: A Critical Approach," *Harvard Theological Review* 78 (1985): 47–65; Alfred Ivry, "Neoplatonic Currents in Maimonides' Thought," in *Studies in Maimonides' Thought and Environment,* J. Kraemer, ed. (1990), 149–74; and idem, "Maimonides and Neoplatonism: Challenge and Response," in *Neoplatonism and Jewish Thought,* Lenn Goodman, ed. (1992), 137–56. Cf. Elliot R. Wolfson, "Negative Theology and Positive Assertion in the Early Kabbala," *Da'at* 32–33 (1994): v–xxii.

9. Kenneth Seeskin, *Jewish Philosophy in a Secular Age* (1990), 5. Cf. Steven Schwarzschild, "The Lure of Immanence," in *The Pursuit of the Ideal: Jewish Writings of Steven Schwarzschild,* Menahem Kellner, ed. (1990), 61–81.

10. On this see R. Aaron of Optaw, *Keter Shem Tov* (1987), 43d–44b.

11. This of course is based on the Besht's Holy Epistle, where the Besht ascends to heaven and is told that the Messiah will come only when "his teachings are spread out to the world." This Epistle is first published as an appendix to R. Jacob Joseph of Polnoy's *Ben Porat Yosef* (1781). On this see Avraham Rubinstein,

"Iggeret ha-BESHT l'Rabbi Gershon m'Kutov" (in Hebrew), *Sinai* 67 (1970): 120–39; Moshe Rosman, *Founder of Hasidism* (1996), 97–113; and most recently Mor Altshuler, "Messianic Strains in Rabbi Israel Baal Shem Tov's 'Holy Epistle,'" *Jewish Studies Quarterly* 6 (1999): 55–70.

12. Asceticism often accompanied the mystical life. On this see Bernard McGinn, "Asceticism and Mysticism in Late Antiquity and the Middle Ages," in *Asceticism,* Vincent L. Wimbush and Richard Valantasis, eds. (1995), 58–75, 505–11. For a study of the asceticism of the Kabbalists (and Hasidism) see Joseph Dan, *Jewish Mysticism and Jewish Ethics* (1986), esp. 104–18; and E. R. Wolfson, "Eunuchs Who Keep the Sabbath: Becoming Male and the Ascetic Ideal in Thirteenth-Century Jewish Mysticism," in *Becoming Male in the Middle Ages,* J. J. Cohen and B. Wheeler, eds. (1997), 151–85.

13. See Gershom Scholem, "*Devekut,* or Communion with God, " in *The Messianic Idea in Judaism* (1971), 203–27; Mendel Piekarz, "Hasidism as a Social-Religious Movement and the Evidence of *Devekut,*" in *Hasidism Reappraised,* 225–48; Mordecai Pachter, "*Devekut* in the Sixteenth Century Homiletical and Ethical Literature" (in Hebrew), *Mekharei Yerushalayim* 1, no. 3 (1982): 51–121; Gedalyah Nigal, "The Sources of *Devekut* in Early Hasidic Literature" (in Hebrew), *Kiryat Sefer* 46 (1971): 343–48; and Miles Krassen, *Uniter of Heaven and Earth* (1998), 43–80. Cf. Idel, *Hasidism,* 237–38.

14. Although R. Gershon Henokh never explicitly mentions his choice of "Preparation" and "Opening" for his Introduction, it appears obvious that the "Preparation" presents the historical setting of integration and synthesis for the second (and final) "Opening," which is his presentation of the innovative and redemptive nature of Hasidism.

15. The centrality of faith is a well-known characteristic of Hasidic piety. For a useful, albeit brief, introduction to faith in Hasidism see Norman Lamm, *The Religious Thought of Hasidism: Text and Commentary* (1999), 67–71, and the selected texts, 71–98.

16. *Ha-Hakdama,* 62. See also Deuteronomy 10:12, *Now Israel, what does God require of you except to fear the Lord your God;* Proverbs 1:7, *The fear of God is the beginning of knowledge;* and Proverbs 31:30, *A woman who fears God is praised.*

17. Zohar 1.11b. See the use of this passage as the obligation to study Kabbala in R. Moshe Cordovero, *'Or Ne'erav* (repr., Jerusalem, 1992), 17.

18. Tikkunei Zohar, 5a/b.

19. *Ha-Hakdama,* 63.

20. On this see H. H. Price, "Belief 'In' and Belief 'That,'" *Religious Studies* 1, no. 1 (October 1965): 1–27. Cf. Martin Buber, *Two Types of Faith* (1951), 36–42.

21. Ibid., 36–42.

22. See Maimonides, *Sefer Ha-Mitzvot,* positive commandment no. 1; and idem, *Mishneh Torah,* "Laws on the Foundation of the Torah," 1:1–3. Cf. R. Moses Nahmanides' gloss to Maimonides' *Sefer Ha-Mitzvot,* negative commandment no. 1. The absence of creator language in these passages is even more curious since

Maimonides freely uses such language in other parts of his *Mishneh Torah.* See for example "Laws on the Foundations of the Torah," 2:8, 2:9, 2:10, 4:1, and 4:9. He intermittently uses the phrase "*Bore*" (Creator) when referring to God but he never specifies what he means by that.

23. See Nahmanides on Genesis 1:1 as a possible source for this synthesis of creation *ex nihilo* and Maimonides' notion of faith. On the most explicit statement of creation *ex nihilo* in the Zohar, see Zohar Hadash, "Genesis," 17b; and Tishby, *Wisdom of the Zohar 2,* David Goldstein, trans. (1989), 572, 573. Cf. Gershom Scholem, "Schöpfung aus Nichts und Selbstuerschrankung Gottes," in *Eranos Jahrbuch* 25 (1956): 87–119.

24. This is not the case for Maimonides, since God as Creator *ex nihilo* is not the subject of either the *Mishneh Torah* or *Sefer Ha-Mitzvot.*

25. *Ha-Hakdama,* 71.

26. On this, see *Tiferet Ha-Hanokhi,* 2b.

27. Ibid., 2b.

28. See *Tiferet Ha-Hanokhi,* Introduction, 10 (English pagination).

29. See David Novak, *Natural Law in Judaism* (1998), esp. 122–49. Cf. idem, *The Image of the Non-Jew in Judaism* (1983), 65 f.

30. Novak, *Natural Law in Judaism.*

31. Zohar 2.231b.

32. Isaiah 40:26 is a central verse in the Pryzsucha tradition that produced R. Mordecai Joseph of Izbica. See R. Israel Berger, *Simhat Yisrael* (1911), "Torat Simha," 310. Cf. Alan Brill, "Grandeur and Humility in the Writings of R. Simha Bunim of Pryzsucha," in *Hazon Nahum,* Y. Elman and J. Gorock, eds. (1998), 419–48, esp. 422, 423.

33. *Ha-Hakdama,* 89. Cf. *Sod Yesharim on the Torah,* 31a.

34. See *Sod Yesharim on the Torah,* 20a.

35. Zohar 2.184a. Cf. Elliot R. Wolfson, "Left Contained in the Right: A Study in Zoharic Hermeneutics," *AJS Review* 11 (1986): 27–52.

36. See *Mei Ha-Shiloah,* vol. 2, 6c.

37. One will see a very different depiction of Abraham in Maimonides' *Mishneh Torah,* "Laws of Idolatry," 1: 1–3. Maimonides portrays Abraham there as a kind of itinerant philosopher in the model of Socrates, who discovers God through logic and then travels around to teach monotheism using the Socratic method.

38. See Arthur Green, *Devotion and Commandment* (1989), 34–62.

39. Perhaps the earliest Jewish expositor of this idea is Philo of Alexandria who, while not overly messianic, described the law as a means to an end rather than an end in itself. See his *On the Migration of Abraham,* Loeb Classic Library, no. 4, 183–85. The coupling of this idea with messianism resulted in Paul's critique of the law (Gal. 3:24) and finally to his repudiation of the law (2 Corinthians 3:6). On this see Robert Goldenberg, "Law and Sprit in Talmudic Religion," in *Jewish Spirituality I,* A. Green, ed. (1986), 232–34. On how these ideas play out in medieval kabbalism

see Gershom Scholem, "The Messianic Idea in Kabbalism," in his *The Messianic Idea in Judaism,* 37–48; and Moshe Idel, *Messianic Mystics,* 273–79.

40. Zohar, Idra Rabba, 3.130a. Cf. Zohar Hadash, 51d, which stresses the messianic elements in this passage. What Abraham received in that verse was the revelation of the Primordial Day [*Yoma Kadma'ah*], "the day that is not day and not night." Cf. Tikkunei Zohar, 17b. See also *Mei Ha-Shiloah,* vol. 2, 6b.

41. *Ha-Hakdama,* 94; *Sod Yesharim on the Torah,* 31b/c.

42. R. Jacob Lainer, *Beit Ya'akov on Genesis,* 82d–83a, no. 57.

43. *Ha-Hakdama,* 94.

44. *Mei Ha-Shiloah,* vol. 2, 6c.

45. Zohar 1.11b, "In the beginning God created . . . the first commandment is the commandment of fear of God [*yeriat Ha-Shem*] which is called *reshit,* as it says (Psalm 111:10) *The beginning of wisdom is fear of God* and [Proverbs 1:7] *The fear of God is the beginning of knowledge* [*da'at*]. Because the word *reshit* is used [in both of these verses] it refers to a higher fear that is faith [*m'hemanuta*]. On this commandment, the world stands." The Zohar is ambiguous as to whether the commandment is fear of God, knowledge of God, or faith in God. Apparently, in this passage either: (1) there is no substantive distinction in these three phases; or (2) the author intends to conflate them. From the continuation of this passage in the Zohar, which speaks only about fear, it seems that fear and beginning are conjoined, the other two (knowledge and faith) being different manifestations of fear.

46. The Kabbalistic utilization of negative theology and its Maimonidean presentation is well known. See for example Elliot R. Wolfson, "Negative Theology and Positive Assertion in the Early Kabbala," *Da'at* 32–33 (1994): v–xxii.

47. *Ha-Hakdama,* 79.

48. *Ha-Hakdama,* 82, 83. This passage is based on a series of comments made in the introduction to *Sefer Yezirah* attributed to Rabad (R. Abraham ben David of Posquiéres). The attribution of this commentary to Rabad has been discredited, even by the Lurianic Kabbalist R. Hayyim Vital, who said quite definitively in his Introduction to *Sha'ar Ha-Hakdamot,* "The commentary of *Sefer Yezeria* attributed to Rabad is not from Rabad." It has been attributed to R. Joseph ben Shalom Askenazi. See Gershom Scholem, "*Ha-Mehaber ha-Amiti shel Perush Sefer Yezirah*" (1931), 2–17. Cf. Isadore Twersky, *Rabad of Posquiéres: A Twelfth-Century Talmudist* (repr., 1980), 286–300.

49. *Sod Yesharim on the Festivals,* Passover, 11b.

50. See *Ha-Hakdama,* 64, 65, where R. Gershon Henokh draws a sharp distinction between the fear of God of the Gentile nations and the fear of God of the Jews. The first is a fear that is a value in and of itself, while the second is a fear that facilitates action. It appears that R. Gershon Henokh is pointing to the notion of faith in nineteenth-century Protestantism that is valued as an end in itself and not a means toward the fulfillment of mitzvot as it is in Judaism.

51. I have intentionally excluded the pietistic tradition from the list. One of the difficulties of R. Gershon Henokh's reading of the innovative nature of Hasidism

is that he mostly ignores the medieval pietistic tradition, which seems to reflect many of the "innovative" elements in Hasidism. This is also true of the pre-Hasidic *Mussar* and *Drush* literature. On a later Hasidic discussion on the differences between Kabbala and Hasidism see R. Kolonymous Kalman Shapira of Piasceno, *Mevo Ha-She'arim* (1962), chaps. 3, 4, and 5; and 18–31.

52. On this point, R. Gershon Henokh suggests that even prophecy is a product of creation. See *Ha-Hakdama,* 6, "Even the apprehension of prophesy and the Prophets is only according to the power of understanding given to them by God." This idea was discussed by Joseph Weiss in *Studies in Eastern European Jewish Mysticism,* 47–55. It is somewhat surprising that Weiss, being quite familiar with the whole Izbica/Radzin tradition, failed to mention R. Gershon Henokh's elaborate discussion on this topic. Cf. idem, "Torat Ha-Determinism Ha-Dati le R. Mordecai Joseph Lainer M'Izbica," in *Sefer Yovel Shel Yitzchak Baer* (1964), 447–53.

53. See Zohar, Idra Rabba, 135a. See also Zohar 3.104b.

54. Therefore, many Kabbalists who wanted to include Maimonides in the orbit of Kabbala interpret his charge to know God through divine action as a charge to study the world of the *sephirot* through the Kabbala. For an example see R. Moses Cordovero, *'Or Ne'erav,* 17a–19a; and Joseph Ben-Shlomo, *Torat Ha-Elohut Shel Moshe Cordovero* (1965), 31–38.

55. On this see *Sod Yesharim on the Torah,* 11–13, on the verse, *All who call My Name, Whom I have created* (Isaiah 43:7). The importance of the study of Kabbala is a common theme among Kabbalists, many of whom regard Kabbala as the "true" Torah, the only dimension of Torah which can facilitate redemption. For a discussion on this and a list of relevant medieval sources, see R. Mordechai Attia's preface to his edition of M. Recanati's *Sefer Recanati* (1961). Cf. R. Naftali Bacharach's *Emek Ha-Melekh* (1648; repr., 1973), second introduction, 7a–10a. Cf. R. Zvi Hirsch Eichenstein of Zhidochov, *Sur m' Ra ve Aseh Tov,* 131, "Believe me, my brother, one who does not study this wisdom [Kabbala,] it is as if he lives in the Diaspora [*huz l'aretz*] and is like one who has no God!" Cf. R. Abraham Isaac Ha-Kohen Kook, *'Orot Ha-Kodesh,* vol. 1, 92; and idem, *'Orot Ha-Teshuvah,* chap. 10: "Complete repentance in truth requires a higher gazing in order to become uplifted to the preciousness of the world, which is full of truth and holiness. This is impossible without being involved with the deeper realms of Torah [*'amkei ha-torah*] and divine wisdom [*hokhma elohit*], the secret dimension of the world [*raze 'olam*]." This was not the case with all Hasidism. The Pryzsucha tradition, out of which Izbica/Radzin emerged, discouraged the study of Kabbala and, in some extreme cases, even forbade it. See R. Schmuel of Shimov, *Ramataym Tzofim,* commentary on *Tana Debe Rabbi Eliahu* (1942), 22; Raphael Mahler, *Hasidism and the Jewish Enlightenment,* 267; and Zvi Meir Rabinovitz, *Rabbi Simha Bunim of Pryzsucha,* 64.

56. See R. Hillel of Patrich, *Pelah Ha-Rimon* (1957), vol. 2, 78; cited and discussed in Idel, *Hasidism,* 235, 236.

57. See for example in Zohar 2.184a, "Divine service only exists because of [or within] darkness." For a discussion of this text see Elliot R. Wolfson, "Light Through Darkness: The Ideal of Human Perfection in the Zohar," *Harvard Theological Review* 81 (1988): 73–95. In Hasidism, this became a central theme as well. See for example R. Nahman of Bratslav's teaching that prayer only can emerge from an "empty space" created in the heart and that the light of redemption comes from the power of destruction in *Likkutei MoHaRan,* 1:49, 57a–58b.

58. This is a common trope in the rabbinic imagination, although it becomes more pronounced in Kabbalistic and philosophical literature of the Middle Ages. On this see Shalom Rosenberg, "Return to the Garden of Eden: Reflections on the History of the Idea of Restorative Redemption in Medieval Jewish Philosophy" (in Hebrew), in *Ha-Ra'ayon Ha-Meshihi b'Yisrael* (1990), 37–86.

59. See my "From Theosophy to Midrash: Lurianic Exegesis and the Garden of Eden," *AJS Review* (1997): 37–75; and Gershom Scholem, *Ha-Kabbala shel Sefer Ha-Temunah v'shel Avraham Abulafia,* Joseph Ben-Shlomo, ed. (1969), 41–84. Cf. Moshe Idel, *Messianic Mystics,* 169–78.

60. See *Etz Hayyim,* vol. 1, Gate 36, chap. 1, 45d; vol. 2, Gate 34, chap. 2, Principle 17, 47a; *Likkutei Torah,* 4d; other sources in my "From Theosophy to Midrash; Lurianic Exegesis and the Garden of Eden," 58–75; and Isaiah Tishby, *Torat Ha Ra v' Ha-Kelippah b'Kabbalat Ha-Ari* (1992), 91–105.

61. *Ha-Hakdama,* 76–77. Cf. another version of this in *Sod Yesharim on the Torah,* 295b. Cf. Tikkunei Zohar, tikun 69, 117b.

62. *Tiferet Ha-Hanokhi,* 9d. R. Gershon Henokh notes that Noah repeated Adam's sin. It was only Abraham, who willingly descended to Egypt, who finally overcame the sin of Adam and began the process of repair. The use of this Zoharic passage to reiterate the primacy of action can also be found in R. Azaria da Fano, *"Ma'amar Hikur Ha-Din,"* in *'Eser Ma'amarot* (1988), chap. 6, 256, 257, commenting on the rabbinic dictum, "action and not study is the most important thing." Cf. R. Aryeh Leib ben Shimon's gloss on da Fano's essay, "Yad Yehuda," 16.

63. *Ha-Hakdama,* 77. Cf. *Sod Yesharim on the Torah,* 13a.

64. b.T. Hagigah 14b.

65. *Ha-Hakdama,* 77.

66. On the heresy of Elisha ben Abuya, see Yehuda Liebes, *The Sin of Elisha: Four Who Entered Pardes and the Nature of Talmudic Mysticism* (in Hebrew) (1990); Jeffrey Rubinstein, "Elisha ben Abuya: Torah and Sinful Sage," *Journal of Jewish Thought and Philosophy* 7 (1998): 139–228; and Alon Goshen-Gottstein, *The Sinner and the Amnesiac: The Rabbinic Invention of Elisha ben Abuya and Elazar ben Arach* (2000), esp. 37–124.

67. This apparently refers to his observation of the space between the higher and lower waters in b.T. Hagigah 15a.

68. b.T. Hagigah, 15a.

69. b.T. Hagigah, 15a.

70. The term *"b'hutz"* is unclear. Hai Gaon understands this to mean "insane." This has become the conventional interpretation.

71. *Ha-Hakdama,* 78, 79. The Talmudic passage in question is quite complex and has been the subject of much scholarly inquiry. See Gershom Scholem, *Jewish Gnosticism, Merkabah Mysticism, and Talmudic Tradition* (1960), 9–19; and Alon Goshen-Gottstein, "Four Who Entered Paradise Revisited," *Harvard Theological Review* 88 (1995): 69–133, esp. 106–16.

72. In the following chapters the distinction between the serpent and Esau as embodying two heretical stances is analyzed. Esau, like Elisha ben Abuya in the Talmud, is read as a fatalist.

73. *Ha-Hakdama,* 95.

74. Ibid., 91. The diffusion of any theory of natural law as a result of miracle supports David Novak's claim that Kabbala has no natural law precisely because it does not see creation outside the context of revelation. More exactly, Novak claims that Kabbala "confines God's relationship to the world to God's relationship with Israel [i.e., revelation]." See David Novak, *Natural Law in Judaism* (1998), 145.

75. Ibid., 91, 92

76. Ibid., 92.

77. See Exodus 3:7, 3:9, 11:6, 12:30, 22:22. On this see R. Nahman of Bratslav, *Likkutei MoHaRan,* 1:8.

78. *Higayon Ha-Lev* is a common term in the Zohar. See for example Zohar 1.169a. I translated it above as "control." In the Zohar it refers to something closer to intuition—that which is understood but cannot be explained in words.

79. See most recently Pinhas Giller, *Reading the Zohar: The Sacred Text of the Zohar* (2001), 89–157.

80. See Yehuda Liebes, *Studies in the Zohar,* 19–22, 55–63; and Elliot R. Wolfson, *Abraham Abulafia,* 9–38. Cf. idem, *Through a Speculum That Shines,* 326–33, 355–68, 377–80.

81. On the history of the Idra Rabba and its importance to the entire Zoharic corpus, see Liebes, *Studies in the Zohar,* 12–82.

82. The relevance of this verse rests on a play of the word "treasure" *('ozar)* which can also mean "receptacle" *(kli kibul).* The verse is reread to mean "Fear of God—that is his receptacle."

83. *Sod Yesharim on the Festivals,* Passover, "Sermon for the Seventh Night of Pesach," 68c/d.

84. Yehuda Liebes, *Studies in the Zohar,* 74–82. See the more expanded version in idem, "Ha-Meshiah shel Ha-Zohar: l'Demuto Ha-Meshihit shel R. Shimon bar Yohai" (in Hebrew), in *Ha-Ra'ayon Ha-Meshihi b'Yisrael,* 208–15.

85. *Lag b'Omer* is the thirty-third day of the counting of the Omer that begins with Passover and ends seven weeks later with *Shavuot.* It has mystical significance because it is thought to be the day R. Shimon bar Yohai died a mystical death after revealing the secrets to his disciples. See the discussion in Liebes, "Ha-Meshiah shel Ha-Zohar," 110, n.99.

86. Zohar, Idra Rabba, 3.130a; and Zohar Hadash, 51d.

87. *Ha-Hakdama,* 97. It is interesting that the initial pragmatic affirmation of free will in Izbica/Radzin, which is erased later on, resembles Maimonides' pragmatic affirmation of creation *ex nihilo* in the Guide 2:25, 2:26, especially for those who argue that Maimonides rejects creation *ex nihilo* on philosophical grounds.

88. Zohar 1.169a. This appears to be a paraphrase of the Zohar cited. The closest thing I found in the Zohar is, "I know that all of your actions are conditional," referring to God's promise to bring goodness to Jacob and his descendants.

89. *Ha-Hakdama,* 97, 98.

90. The apparent meaning of "children of a whore" is a whore who bore children from her whoredom. See *Mesudat David,* ad loc.

91. I follow Rashi's reading of the verse as opposed to *JPS Tanakh,* which is more awkward in this context.

92. *Ha-Hakdama,* 102.

93. The relationship between prophecy and the law is complicated in the rabbinic and postrabbinic tradition. See Ephrayim Urbach, "Halakha u Nevuah" (in Hebrew), *Tarbiz* 18, no. 1 (1947): 1–27.

4. The Redemptive Foundation of Sin

1. On this see Yehuda Liebes, "Myth versus Symbol in the Zohar and in Lurianic Kabbala," in *Essential Papers on Kabbala,* Lawrence Fine, ed. (1995), 212–42; Michael Fishbane, "The Book of Zohar and Exegetical Spirituality," in his *The Exegetical Imagination* (1998), 105–22; Moshe Idel, "PaRDeS: Some Reflections on Kabbalistic Hermeneutics," *Death, Ecstasy and Other Worldly Journeys,* J. Collins and M. Fishbane, eds. (1995), 249–68; Elliot R. Wolfson, "Beautiful Maiden without Eyes: Peshat and Sod in Zoharic Hermeneutics," in *The Midrashic Imagination: Jewish Exegesis, Thought, and History,* M. Fishbane, ed. (1993), 155–203; Shaul Magid, "From Theosophy to Midrash: Lurianic Exegesis and the Garden of Eden," *AJS Review* 22, no. 1 (1997): 37–75. More generally see Frank Talmage, "Apples of Gold: The Inner Meaning of Sacred Texts in Medieval Judaism," in *Jewish Spirituality I,* A. Green, ed. (1987), 313–55.

2. In Hasidism, the exception that proves the rule is the very systematic approach of Habad Hasidism, especially during the early period. On this see Naftali Loewenthal, *Communicating the Infinite* (1990); Rachel Elior, *The Paradoxical Ascent to God,* J. M. Green, trans. (1993), esp. 5–36; and Roman A. Foxbrunner, *Habad: The Hasidism of R. Shneur Zalman of Lyady* (1992).

3. See Zeev Gries, *The Book in Early Hasidism* (in Hebrew) (1992), 47–67.

4. For a study devoted to just this issue see Arthur Green, *Devotion and Commandment: The Faith of Abraham in the Hasidic Imagination* (1989).

5. On the importance of the "return to Eden" as a messianic desideratum in Jewish philosophy, see Shalom Rosenberg, "The Return to the Garden of Eden:

Reflections on the History of the Idea of Restorative Redemption in Medieval Jewish Philosophy" (in Hebrew), in *Ha-Ra'ayon Ha-Meshihi b'Yisrael* (1990), 37–86.

6. See Shalom Carmy and David Shatz, "The Bible as a Source for Philosophical Reflection," in *History of Jewish Philosophy,* Daniel Frank and Oliver Leaman, eds. (1997), 13–37. For another view, see Umberto Cassuto, *A Commentary on the Book of Exodus* (in Hebrew) (1967), 55: "When we come to consider these two questions [i.e., relating to the hardening of Pharaoh's heart in Exodus] we must first of all realize that we are not dealing with philosophical issues. . . . The Torah does not seek to teach us philosophy; not even what is called religious philosophy. When the Torah was written, Greek philosophy had not yet been thought of; and Greek logic was likewise non-existent." Cassuto's mistake was to conflate "Philosophy" with philosophy. While the former (Greek philosophy, etc.) was surely nonexistent in the time of the Bible, it does not mean that the Bible was not addressing philosophical issues, as these issues were not created by philosophers in ancient Greece. Arguably, the Greeks merely took issues of human existence that were perennial and dealt with them in specific, systematic ways. Therefore, while the Bible may not teach us philosophy in any formal sense, it surely grappled with fundamental issues of human existence and offered its view on these issues.

7. One classic example of this is Maimonides' reading of the Garden of Eden story in *Guide of the Perplexed,* 1:2.

8. See David Stern, *Midrash and Theory: Ancient Jewish Exegesis and Contemporary Literary Studies* (1996), 39–54; and more generally in idem, *Parables in Midrash: Narrative and Exegesis in Rabbinic Literature* (1991). Cf. Michael Fishbane, "Midrash and the Nature of Scripture," in idem, *The Exegetical Imagination* (1998), 9–21.

9. For an example of how the question of free will and responsibility is addressed by the midrash in relation to the hardening of Pharaoh's heart using *mashal,* see Exodus Rabba 13:1, 13:2.

10. This is not to say that there is no rabbinic theology. But rabbinic theologians, just like biblical theologians, must construct their theologies, or the theologies of the texts they read, out of a series of texts that do not easily lend themselves to such analysis. This is quite different than an analysis of Maimonides' position on human freedom, for example.

11. For an interesting thesis on the "rationality" of the rabbis see Menahem Fisch, *Rational Rabbis: Science and Talmudic Culture* (1997).

12. Cf. b.T. Shavuot 39a.

13. The necessity of free will became commonplace, even among Jewish mystics. One clear example can be found in R. Moshe Hayyim Luzatto's *Derekh Ha-Shem,* a simplified presentation of Jewish ideas drawn from the Kabbala. See *Derekh Ha-Shem* (1981), part 1, chap. 3, 22: "[Devekut] must be achieved via free will. If one was compelled toward perfection, he would not be the master of that perfection and the highest will of God [i.e., that man himself to Him] would not be fulfilled."

14. See Maimonides, *Mishneh Torah,* "Hilkhot Teshuva," 5:9, 10. Cf. idem, *Perush 'al Ha-Mishna,* "Introduction to Avot," chap. 8, and *Guide* 3:20.

15. *Mishneh Torah,* "Hilkhot Teshuva," 5:11.

16. For Maimonides' approach, see most recently Moshe Sokol, "Maimonides on Freedom of the Will and Moral Responsibility," 25–39. Sokol argues that Maimonides, especially in *Guide* 2:48, argues against free will, in opposition to his more popular works ("Commentary to the Mishna," *Mishneh Torah*) where he advocates a position of free will. Yet, he continues, the rejection of free will is not, for Maimonides, an excuse for abandoning moral responsibility. In this sense, Maimonides is more aligned with the pietists who also equivocate free will in order to protect the doctrine of providence and omniscience.

17. See Gersonides, *Milkhamot Ha-Shem,* book 3, chaps. 2 and 3 (Seymour Feldman's translation, *Wars of the Lord,* vol. 2, 102–5). On Gersonides' unique position on free will *(behira)* see Norbert M. Samuelson, "The Problem of Free Will in Maimonides, Gersonides, and Aquinas," *CCAR Journal* 17 (1970): 2–20; Tamar Rudavsky, "Divine Omniscience, Contingency and Prophecy in Gersonides," in *Divine Omniscience and Omnipotence in Medieval Philosophy,* T. Rudavsky, ed. (1985), 143–59; and Sarah Klein-Bratzlavy, "Gersonides on Determinism, Possibility and Choice" (in Hebrew), *Da'at* 22 (1989): 5–54. Gersonides is not the only Jewish philosopher who rejected divine foreknowledge in order to salvage free will. His position is largely adopted by the sixteenth-century thinker R. Eliezer Ashkenazi in his *Ma'aseh Ha-Shem.* On this see the discussion in Leonard Levin, "Seeing with Both Eyes: The Intellectual Formation of Ephraim Luntshitz" (Ph.D. diss., Jewish Theological Seminary of America, 2002), 95–98.

18. Leo Strauss argued that the use of this type of esotericism is common among radical thinkers who wish to remain within the confines of a normative tradition. Izbica/Radzin Hasidism represents an example of such esotericism, even as the authors themselves did not write under a state of formal persecution and may not have been fully conscious of the logical conclusions of their discourse. See Leo Strauss, *Persecution and the Art of Writing* (1980), 22–37.

19. Both R. Joseph Albo and R. Isaac Arama accused R. Hasdai Crescas of such a semantic distinction. Joseph Weiss argued that, in Izbica, no distinction is made between divine will and human action. We find in Izbica, particularly later in R. Jacob Lainer's *Beit Ya'akov,* R. Mordecai Joseph Eliezar Lainer's *Tiferet Joseph,* and his son R. Yeruham Lainer's *Tiferet Yeruham,* a clear attempt to reformulate *Mei Ha-Shiloah*'s radical determinism. Therefore, Joseph Weiss correctly raises the issue of antinomianism as a product of any minimization of human will vis-à-vis divine will. See Weiss, "Torat Ha-Determinism Ha-Dati shel R. Mordecai Joseph Lainer m'Izbica," *Sefer Ha-Yovel shel Yizhak Baer* (1964), 448ff.

20. The corollary between Hasidic faith and pietistic trust or obedience is evident in early Hasidic thinking. On its place in the thinking of Rabbi Nahman of Bratslav, see Arthur Green, *Tormented Master* (1979), esp. 299, 300. I would argue that faith in R. Gershon Henokh moves in a different direction. R. Nahman's

ambivalence about mystical experience has been discussed by Green (see ibid., 285–336); also see Joseph Weiss, *Studies in Bratslav Hasidism* (in Hebrew) (1974), 87–95. The teacher of R. Mordecai Joseph, R. Menahem Mendel of Kotzk, adopts a similar idea. See for example Abraham J. Heschel, *A Passion for Truth* (1973), esp. 183–96. For R. Gershon Henokh, however, the experience of unity is the pillar of his ideology. Faith is not the acknowledgement of the unity of the world but rather the vehicle toward experiencing it. Whereas R. Nahman of Bratslav and the Kotzker Rebbe both retreat from the confrontation with doubt into the world of halakha, R. Gershon Henokh confronts doubt with faith as a way of reaching beyond doubt to an experience of divine unity. See for example his discussion of doubt in *Sod Yesharim on the Torah,* 7, 8.

21. The nature of such an illumination is, of course, central in understanding Izbica/Radzin Hasidism. As Joseph Weiss relates, "Is the reality of this illumination experienced in exceptional physical or spiritual circumstances; is it the fruit of long contemplative seclusion; or is it a sudden certainty, totally unprepared for, which fills the consciousness of the person illuminated as if in a flash." See Weiss, *Studies in Eastern European Jewish Mysticism* (1985), 211. The necessary preparation for such an illumination raises certain questions that attracted the attention of both Jewish and Christian mystics. Maimonides, when speaking about the prophecy of Abraham, takes the position (stated by Rabbi Yohanan and Rabbi Hanina in b.T. Nedarim 32b) that Abraham was forty years old when he came to know God, rather than adopting the position of Reish Lakish that he was three years old, apparently unconvinced that prophecy descends upon one who has not first gone through the necessary steps of preparation. In his gloss on Maimonides' *Mishneh Torah,* Rabad raises the issue of why Maimonides adopts the forty-year-old position without even mentioning the second opinion. See *Mishneh Torah,* "Hilkhot Avodah Zarah," 1:3. Rabad seems to imply that, if prophecy is solely in the hands of God, even one who has not gone through the necessary preparation could be the recipient of prophecy. Weiss suggests that R. Mordecai Joseph's position is that the potential for such an illumination is predetermined by the nature of one's soul, i.e., whether it is of the lineage of Judah or that of Joseph.

22. These categories are discussed at length in the previous chapter.

23. This issue of the messianic idea in Hasidism has received much attention among scholars. See Scholem, "The Neutralization of the Messianic Idea in Hasidism," in *The Messianic Idea in Judaism* (1971), 176–202; Isaiah Tishby, "The Messianic Idea and Messianic Trends in the Development of Hasidism" (in Hebrew), *Zion* 32 (1967): 1–15; Rivka Shatz-Uffenheimer, "Self-Redemption in Hasidic Thought," in *Types of Redemption,* R. J. Z. Werblowsky and C. J. Bleeker, eds. (1970), 207–12; Mendel Pierkaz, "The Messianic Idea in the Beginning of Hasidism Seen Through *Mussar* and *Drush* Literature" (in Hebrew), *The Messianic Idea in Israel: Studies in Honor of the Eightieth Birthday of Gershom Scholem* (1990), 237–52; and Morris Faierstein, "Personal Redemption in Hasidism," in

Hasidism Reappraised, Ada Rapoport-Albert, ed. (1995), 215–24. Most recently see Idel, *Messianic Mystics* (1999), 212–47.

24. This seems to mean that all do not have equal access to God's will. There are individuals who have not yet achieved this state of purification whose access to divine will is solely through the mitzvot.

25. *Mei Ha-Shiloah,* vol. 1, 9a/b. Cf. R. Gershon Henokh of Radzin's gloss to *Mei Ha-Shiloah* called *gillyon* in *Mei Ha-Shiloah,* vol. 2, 65b.

26. *Ha-Hakdama ve Ha-Petikha,* 78. For a similar reading of the term *middot* used in this context see R. Mordecai Joseph Eliezer Lainer's *Tiferet Yoseph,* 55c–56b. The use of the term *middot* needs to be understood on various levels. R. Gershon Henokh appears to be referring to *middot* in its Zoharic meaning of supernal worlds or the flow of divinity from the infinite *eyn sof* to our physical world. However, the fragmented emanation of divinity is also represented in the mitzvot. Each mitzvah corresponds to a particular dimension of that emanation and returns it to its proper place in the Godhead. An individual who successfully accomplishes this unity through the performance of mitzvot will come to understand the temporal nature of the mitzvot himself or herself. The temporal character of mitzvot is developed in *Ra'aya Mehemna* and Tikkunei Zohar, texts with which R. Gershon Henokh was intimately familiar.

27. The Zoharic idea of divine directives became common nomenclature for Kabbalists who based themselves on the Zoharic corpus. For two examples, see Menahem Recanati's *Ta'amei Ha-Mitzvot* (1581; repr., 1962), 2–11; and Moses Cordovero, *Shiur Koma* (1883), 87–89 (English pagination). Cf. Rabbenu Bahya ben Asher's similar formulation in his "Introduction to Genesis," *Rabbenu Bahya 'al Ha-Torah* (1994), 9, "The 613 mitzvot are really 613 principles, for the particular mitzvot have no end and no intrinsic purpose [independent of the whole]."

28. It must be stated at the outset that knowledge *(da'at)* in the Hasidic tradition is different than knowledge among medieval Jewish philosophers. Hasidic "knowledge" is perhaps closer to the category of "intuition" or "speculative knowledge" in the writings of F. W. J. Schelling and other German philosophers of the Romantic period. On this see Samuel Abba Horodetzky, *Studies by Samuel Abba Horodetzky* (in German), Steven Katz, ed. (1980), 5–12; and Paul Tillich, *Mysticism and Guilt Consciousness in Schelling's Philosophical Development* (1974), part 3, "The Mysticism of Intellectual Intuition," 69–85. It is significant that R. Gershon Henokh, who sets his sights on a mystical illumination that reveals the unity of the divine will and the human will, strongly adopts the reading of mitzvot in the Zohar as "directives" *('ittin)* (i.e., a means) rather than an end in and of themselves. This, of course, is not new in Jewish mysticism. However, it does lie at the core of R. Gershon Henokh's whole ideological stance as well as his exegetical agenda.

29. One of the more prominent proponents of the importance of doubt for divine worship is R. Nahman of Bratslav. On this see Joseph Weiss, *Studies in Bratslav*

Hasidism (1974), 109–50; A. Green, *Tormented Master,* 285–336; and my "Through the Void: The Absence of God in R. Nahman of Bratslav's *Likkutei MoHaRan,*" *Harvard Theological Review* 88:4 (1995): 495–519. This is a central motif in the Zohar. Cf. Zohar 2.184a, "There is no light other than the light that emerges out of darkness. There is no worship of God except from darkness and no goodness without evil." This world (the premessianic world) is thus the world of "the Tree of Doubt [*'Ilana d'Sefeka*]," which necessitates free will. Cf. *Sod Yesharim on Passover,* 11b, and the discussion below on the sin of Adam and Eve.

30. See for example in b.T. Berakhot 28b; b.T. Niddah 61b; and *Midrash Tehillim,* S. Buber, ed. (1891), on Psalm 146, 268. Cf. Georges Vajda, *Recherches sur la philosophie et la Kabbala dans la pensée juive du Moyen Age* (1962), 345, n.6.

31. On this see Yehuda Liebes, *Studies in the Zohar,* 9–20. On Paul as a Jewish antinomian, see Alan Segal, *Paul the Convert* (1990), 144–45; and idem, "Paul and the Beginning of Jewish Mysticism," in *Death, Ecstasy, and Other Worldly Journeys,* 93–122.

32. This becomes the cornerstone of Sabbatean mysticism, which draws from the Lurianic tradition as well as earlier Kabbalistic schools such as the author(s) of *Sefer Temunah.* The nullification of mitzvot in the future has a long tradition in rabbinic and exegetical literature as well. See R. Jacob ben Sheshet, *Masiv Devarim Nohakhim* (1969), 81–82; R. Menahem Recanati, *Sefer Recanati* (1961), parshat Shemini, 60 c/d; and *R. Bahya ben Asher 'al Ha-Torah,* C. Chavel, ed. (1994), vol. 2, 358 (on Leviticus 11:4–7). The rabbinic texts inferring the nullification of mitzvot in the messianic future are discussed and softened by R. Isaac Abrabanel in his *Yeshu'at Meshikho,* "Fourth Inquiry", chaps. 3 and 4, 70–72. Cf. Shalom Rosenberg, "Return to the Garden of Eden: Reflections on the History of the Idea of Restorative Redemption in Medieval Jewish Philosophy," esp. 63–73.

33. See *Ha-Hakdama,* 117, "The truth is that the reason that they [mitzvot] are called *'ezot* [directives] is that through them continuous faith in God becomes embedded in the heart of the Jew. This faith remains in place forever."

34. On the history of the Lurianic notion of *zimzum,* which is the central tenet of Luria's rendering of creation, see Moshe Idel, "On the History of the Term *Zimzum* in Kabbala and Scholarship" (in Hebrew), *Jerusalem Studies in Jewish Thought* 10 (1992): 319–52. On original sin as an extension of *zimzum,* see my "From Theosophy to Midrash: Lurianic Exegesis and the Garden of Eden," *AJS Review* 22, no. 1 (1997): 37–75; and idem, "Origin and the Overcoming of Beginning: *Zimzum* as a Trope of Reading in Post-Lurianic Kabbala," in *Beginning/Again: Toward a Hermeneutic of Jewish Texts,* Aryeh Cohen and Shaul Magid, eds. (2002), 163–214.

35. For a concise rendition of this doctrine, see R. Ephraim Penzeri, *Sefer Ha-Derushim* (1996), 23–29.

36. See for example in Scholem, *Major Trends in Jewish Mysticism,* 244–86; and Tishby, *Torat Ha-Ra ve Ha-Kelippah* (1984), 91–143.

37. R. Gershon Henokh's use of these terms *('olam ha-safek—'ilana d'sfaka)* is intriguing. The Zohar never uses these terms to describe either the Tree of Knowledge or the world after the sin. Referring to the Tree, the most common term in the Zohar is *'ilana d'muta* (the Tree of Death). Cf. Zohar 1.2a, 35a/b, 36a, 51b–52a, 151a, 209a, 246a, 3.119a, 176b. The Tree of Eve is also used (Zohar 1.36a) as is the Tree of Falseness *('ilana d'shikra).* See Tikkunei Zohar, *tikun* 20, 106a. In another place, R. Gershon Henokh likens the body to the world of doubt: "at the time when the soul begins to descend from its lofty place into the physical body, it lets out a great scream. It is not pleasant for it to enter into concealment in the body, which is the Tree of Doubt." *Sod Yesharim on the Festivals,* Hoshana Rabba, 3b; and *Sod Yesharim on the Festivals,* "Pesach," 78d.

38. Although he does not mention it, it appears that R. Gershon Henokh is using the aggadic statement in b.T. Sanhedrin 97b that suggests that the 6,000 years of creation are divided into three basic parts. The first is 2,000 years of confusion *(tohu);* the second is 2,000 years of Torah (beginning with Abraham); and the third is the 2,000 years of redemption *(moshiah).* As we will see, alienation represents the period of confusion, when evil prevents the reunification between the human soul and the divine soul, whereas integration (through the covenant with Abraham) represents the reunion of the soul with its root above and thus the nullification of evil. David Berger developed the themes in this midrash in an unpublished paper entitled, "Torah and the Messianic Age: On the Polemical History of a Rabbinic Text." I'd like to thank Professor Berger for providing me with a copy of this paper.

39. For a concise definition of these terms in Hasidism, see R. Menahem Mendel Schneersohn (the Zemah Zedek), *Derekh Mitzvoteka* (1993), 14b–15a. For a general study of these terms see Mordecai Pacter, "Circles and Lines: The History of an Idea" (in Hebrew), *Da'at* 18 (1987): 59–90.

40. These distinctions are complex in the Lurianic corpus. See for example in *Mevo Sha'arim,* gate 2, part 1, chap. 3: "Know that between the circles [*'igullim*] each one contains lights and vessels. The light is divided into two parts, internal and hovering." See also gate 2, part 1, chap. 4: "We have already explained in our discussion of [the world that is] 'streaked' [a reference to Genesis 31:10] that there are lights and vessels. Each one is divided into two. The light is divided into internal and hovering [light] and the vessels are divided into internal and external [vessels]." For various reasons for this distinction, see *Etz Hayyim, "Sha'ar Ha-'Akudim,"* vol. 1, chap. 2, 24b–25b. For a discussion of the cosmic import of Jacob's "streaked, speckled, and mottled" sheep in Genesis 31:10 in Lurianic Kabbala, see *Etz Hayyim,* vol. 1; *"Sha'ar Ha-Zivugim,"* gate 16, chap. 1; and *'Ozrot Hayyim, "Sha'ar Ha-Akudim,"* 2a–5a.

41. The centrality of evil in Lurianic Kabbala is the topic of Isaiah Tishby's *Torat Ha-Ra ve Ha-Kelippah* (1984). For a more direct and perhaps more provocative statement on the subject, see R. Hayyim Friedlander's preface to the 1992

edition of R. Moshe Hayyim Luzzato's *138 Paths to Wisdom* (1992), 23, "True Wisdom [Kabbala] is largely devoted to the description of the possibility of evil. The purpose of such a discussion is not only concerned with the emergence of evil out of the *worlds* of creation, which are all brilliant and pure. Rather, how is it possible to understand in the world which is God's, whose goodness and kindness is limitless, can there be evil, suffering, destruction and death. The central purpose [of Kabbala] is, for us, a practical matter, i.e., to recognize the existence of evil in order to know how to fight against it and nullify it." According to this definition of Kabbala (i.e., to know the existence of evil) Hasidism is perhaps just the opposite. Taking the ontology of evil as described in Kabbala, Hasidism often attempts to show the transparency in the Kabbalistic ontology, i.e., to show that evil is a state of mind rather than a state of being.

42. Targum Onkelos, the standard Aramaic translator of the Hebrew Bible, renders *'arum* as "wise" *(hakim),* or, in the negative sense, "cunning."

43. The Zohar commonly defines the serpent as "darkness" *(hasukha).* See Zohar 2.284a, "There is no light that does not filter through darkness. . . . Darkness is the garment for light. By means of darkness light is recognizable." R. Gershon Henokh incorporates the Zoharic image of the serpent as darkness into his notion of the serpent as garment. See *Sod Yesharim on the Festivals,* Hoshana Rabba, 3c/d, "The serpent is also a garment just like darkness [is a garment for light in the Zohar]. However, this garment does not warm Adam at all for it is far from him. He receives no pleasure from it. Nor does any good emerge from it. In that sense the serpent is not a garment."

44. See *Sod Yesharim on the Torah,* 5b. Cf. a text attributed to R. Jacob Lainer's *Beit Ya'akov,* cited in S. Z. Shragai, *B'Ma'aynei Hasidut Izbica-Radzin* (1980), 19. The source of this citation is unknown. "God bases this world on the Tree of Doubt [*'ilana d'sfaka*]. Doubt means nothing in this world is completely clear. Just as there is no pure good, evil is never in a pure form distinct from goodness. If evil was completely detached from goodness it would cease to exist. This is what is meant in *Mei Ha-Shiloah* when it says that the future will bring about a synthesis of the verses *Eat from every tree, but from the Tree of Knowledge do not eat. . . .* This means that [in the future] we will eat the goodness from the Tree of Knowledge and thus separate goodness from evil. At that moment evil will cease to exist." The negative appraisal of the Tree of Knowledge is common in Jewish mystical literature. Abraham Abulafia, for example, calls the Tree of Knowledge the "Tree of Death, Good and Evil." See his "Sheva Netivot Ha-Torah," in *Philosophie und Kabbala, Erstes Heft,* A. Jellinik, ed. (1854), 9.

45. On the formulation of evil in the Zohar which, in many ways, is the source for R. Gershon Henokh's position, see Elliot R. Wolfson, "Light Through Darkness: The Ideal of Human Perfection in the Zohar," *Harvard Theological Review* 81 (1988): 73–95. Wolfson traces the notion of evil from the *Sefer Ha-Bahir* through the Zohar. He notes, "The underlying assumption here is that even the demonic derives from a stage in the emanative process" (79). On this point see Wolfson,

"Left Contained in the Right: A Study in Zoharic Hermeneutics," *AJS Review* 11 (1986): 29ff; and Daniel Matt, "The Mystic and the Mitzvot," in *Jewish Spirituality I,* A. Green, ed. (1986), 387, 388. Wolfson notes (ibid., 91) that, in the Zohar, "the ideal state is one of containment rather than eradication of the demonic." See Zohar 2.108 a/b. It would appear that R. Gershon Henokh suggests another interpretation. For R. Gershon Henokh, evil is the state of alienation that prevents the unity of the human will with the divine will. Hence, mitzvot are necessary to allow for a covenant to exist in the state of alienation or a "world of doubt," and also to fix that which caused the alienation to allow for a reunification. Perhaps the basic difference between R. Gershon Henokh and the Zohar on this point is that R. Gershon Henokh, in line with Hasidic teaching in general, gives no ontic quality to evil. Therefore, the whole question of eradicating or embracing evil falls away.

46. On this see the Zohar's comment that "the serpent's dominion is on the [read: her] flesh." See Zohar 1.65a and 2.269a. Cf. R. Nahman of Bratslav, *Likkutei MoHaRan* (1976), 1:19, 26a.

47. It is not surprising that the interaction between the serpent and Eve and subsequently between Eve and Adam is described in sexual terms, "and he [the serpent] placed poison within her." Cf. b.T. Shabbat 146a. Rashi, ad loc., attempts to diffuse the erotic overtones of the phrase by defining it as "giving her counsel to eat from the tree." Cf. b.T. Yebamot 103b; b.T. Avodah Zara 22b. Cf. *Likkutei Torah,* 18a, where the sexual nature of the sin is even more explicit. "*The serpent duped me, and I ate* [Genesis 3:13]. The rabbis teach: after the serpent came upon Eve and placed poison within her, she gave birth to Cain and Abel." This is taken from Zohar 3.231a, where Cain is viewed as the product of the insemination of Eve from the serpent. Cain and Abel are the product of an admixture of the semen of Adam and the serpent, which is used later to justify their sin. In Lurianic Kabbala, see the comments of R. Moses Negara in *Likkutei Torah,* 18a, "The correlation between Eros and eating is common in the medieval world in general and the Jewish mystical tradition in particular." See Joel Hecker, "Each Man Ate and Angel's Bread: Eating and Embodiment in the Zohar" (Ph.D. diss., New York University, 1996), 167–70; Elliot R. Wolfson, "Crossing Gender Boundaries in Kabbalistic Ritual and Myth," *Circle in the Square* (1995), 95; and Daniel Boyarin, *Carnal Israel: Reading Sex in Talmudic Culture* (1993), 70–75, 116, 117.

48. Evil does not begin with/in the serpent before the sin because evil has no independent status but needs to be empowered by engaging with holiness *(kedusha).* This is the basis of the danger of the *kelippot* in Lurianic Kabbala. See "Sha'ar Leah ve Rahel," *Etz Hayyim,* vol. 2, gate 39, chap. 1, 65a–67b; and Vital, *Sefer Ha-Gilgulim* (1986), chap. 1, 1–2. Cf. Tishby, *Torat Ha-Ra ve Ha-Kelippah,* 79–90. Cf. Elliot Wolfson, "Left Contained in the Right: A Study in Zoharic Hermeneutics," *AJS Review* 11 (1986): 27–52.

49. Although R. Gershon Henokh distinguishes between good and evil as integration and alienation, the Zohar (*Ra'aya Mehemna* and Tikkunei Zohar in particular) distinguishes between the Torah of Spirit, which is the Tree of Life, and

the Torah of Law, which is the Tree of Knowledge. R. Gershon Henokh draws a similar distinction. However, for him the Torah of Spirit, though it may be rooted in the creation before the sin (i.e., with Adam Ha-Rishon), first becomes manifest in Abraham. Abraham does not play such a role in the Zoharic reading. For references to the Torah of Spirit in the Zohar, see Zohar 3.125a–129a, 153a; and Tikkunei Zohar 106b–107b.

50. See *Sod Yesharim on the Torah,* 6a–6b.

51. The relationship between the first sin and redemption is quite complex yet essential in understanding any mystical ideology. In the words of Bezalel Safran, "To identify for a given writer the state from which Adam fell is to reconstruct that writer's concept of the ideal human being and the ideal human condition. This ideal will be found to be all pervasive in that writer's thought system. Thus, the messianic period will be viewed as a restoration of Adam's condition before the Fall, and for the period between the beginning and the End—the here and now—a program will be conceived to retrieve the lost ideal." See Bezalel Safran, "Rabbi Azriel and Nahmanides: Two Views of the Fall of Man," in *Rabbi Moses Nahmanides: Explorations in His Religious Virtuosity,* I. Twersky, ed. (1983), 75. The "necessity" of the sin is rooted in Lurianic reading of Genesis 3. In Lurianic Kabbala the sin was not in the act itself but rather the premature stage into which the act was performed. Cf. *Likkutei Torah,* 9a, "We already explained earlier that when *zeir anpin* only has a portion of the consciousness [*mohin*] from [*parzuf*] *imma* its only portion of *keter* is from the bottom third of the *sephirah tiferet* of *imma.* Adam Ha-Rishon in his action, his thought and his intention, thought to expand *keter* of *zeir anpin* until it absorbed the upper two-thirds of *tiferet* of *imma* before the proper time. That is, before the integration of the *mohin* of *abba.* This caused a profound blemish [*pegam gadol*]." Cf. my "From Theosophy to Midrash: Lurianic Exegesis and the Garden of Eden," 58–65.

52. This act in some way mirrors God's act of volitional alienation in the creation myth of *zimzum.* See my "Origin and the Overcoming of Beginning: *Zimzum* as a Trope of Reading in Post-Lurianic Kabbala," in *Beginning/Again: Toward a Hermeneutic of Jewish Texts,* Aryeh Cohen and Shaul Magid, eds. (2002), 167–75.

53. Alienation or in Lurianic terms, rupture *(shevirah),* as simultaneously the beginning of evil and the beginning of restoration, is a common theme in Lurianic Kabbala. For an example see *Mevo Sha'arim,* 5b, "The emanation of those worlds created the need for *tikun* in order to separate the 'extraneous matter' from the [eatable] food. This refinement [*berur*] could not occur without appropriate distancing and emanations. Each world renews the [need for] an additional *berur* and also introduces new dimensions of matter and extraneous matter."

54. See Tikkunei Zohar 69, 117b; and *Sod Yesharim on the Torah,* 295b.

55. This means that *malkhut,* empty of emanation, is pure nature without divine effluence.

56. *Sod Yesharim on the Torah,* 13a. Cf. *Ha-Hakdama,* 97, 98; and *Tiferet Ha-Hanokhi,* 9.

57. This entire program of integrating the serpent back into the divine is the telos of mitzvot in the Izbica/Radzin tradition. The possibility of this integration is also that which distinguishes between Judaism and the Greeks at the time of the Hanukkah story. In *Sod Yesharim Tinyana,* 120a, we read, "Said Caesar to Rabbi Joshua ben Haninah: How often does a serpent [*nahash*] give birth? Rabbi Joshua ben Haninah says, every two years. Behold the *Saba d'be Atunah* say every three years. . . . [b.T. Bekhorot 8b]. It is known the *Saba d'be Atunah* are the ancient Greek sages, and their argument with R. Joshua ben Haninah was an attempt to disprove the need for divine worship. The evil embedded in the redeemable *kelippot* [*kelippah noga*] becomes the *kelippot* of the serpent when it is disentangled from [good]. They say [the Greeks] that the *kelippot* of the serpent are incorporated into the primordial and continuous will of God. This follows from their position that everything is necessary [and nothing is contingent]." R. Gershon Henokh then gives a complex Lurianic rendition of this Talmudic passage which proves that the position of *Saba d'be Atunah* is founded on the principle of the necessity of existence and the lack of free will and the human capacity to change existence as we know it.

58. This obviously simplistic summary of one of the most complex issues in Lurianic Kabbala is merely intended to create a framework for understanding R. Gershon Henokh's reading of Luria's interpretation. For a discussion on the sin in Luria, see *Sha'ar Ha-Pesukim,* parshat Bereshit, and more importantly *Sha'ar Ha-Likkutim,* parshat Bereshit, 6a–6b. Although almost all Hasidic literature adapts the Lurianic (i.e., Zoharic) version of the sin, there is, to my knowledge, no major study on the various uses of the Lurianic version of the sin in Hasidic texts.

59. The locution, "he [Adam] *came upon* her" and its sexual implications is reflected in b.T. Shabbat 146a, "when he [the serpent] *came upon* Eve he injected poison into her." Even as Rashi (ad loc.) renders "[he] came upon her" as "giving her counsel to eat from the tree" the locution of injection or implantation is more suggestive of a sexual encounter. Adam's action repeats that of the serpent which strengthens R. Gershon Henokh's reading of the transformation of Adam into the serpent as a result of the sin. The explicit sexual reading of "he came upon her" is found in Zohar 1.126a/b, 2.231a, 3.153a, and 3.161a. Cf. Luria's rendition in *Etz Hayyim,* vol. 2, gate 32, chap. 7, 39a; and the discussion in Tishby, *Torat Ha-Ra ve Ha-Kelippah,* 79.

60. This refers back to Genesis 2:25 where Adam and Eve are called *'arum,* suggesting their state of mind rather than merely their physical state. See *Tanakh,* J. P. S. translation, 6, note g. In my translation of the passage in R. Gershon Henokh, I translated *'arum* as "naked," referring to the serpent, because the thrust of the comment is that the serpent was alienated or exposed.

61. For a similar use of this Talmudic passage in describing the formation of the evil inclination in Genesis, see R. Shlomo Ephraim of Luntshitz's *Kli Yakar* to Genesis 32:24 in standard editions. *Kli Yakar* was first included into the *Mikraot Gedolot* in the 1902 Warsaw edition.

62. See *Sod Yesharim on the Torah,* 7b. For the source in the Lurianic tradition, see *Pri Etz Hayyim,* Sha'ar Rosh Ha-Shana, chap. 6, 137b, 138a.

63. The etymology of *'arum* in both verses is discussed by R. Abraham ibn Ezra, in his lengthy comment to Genesis 3:1. He adopts Onkelos's translation of *'arum* as *hak'im* (lit., wise), which R. Abraham ibn Ezra understands as "having the power of speech." R. Gershon Henokh offers a synthesis between Onkelos's rendering of *'arum* as "wise" and the more figurative rendering of "shrewd." The serpent's wisdom was not in the knowledge of God (Truth) but in his ability to manipulate. For another Hasidic rendition of Ibn Ezra's translation see R. Moshe Teitelbaum, *'Ohel Yismakh Moshe,* vol. 1, 4a. His reading plays off the comments of language as garment in Maimonides' *Guide* 1:56.

64. See for example *Likkutei Torah,* 9a–10b; and *Sefer Ha-Derushim,* 143a–151a. Cf. R Naftali Bacharakh, *'Emek Ha-Melekh* (repr., 1973), 2b/c. Bacharakh, adopting R. Israel Sarug's position, that the protocreative act took place through divine "inner-pleasure" *(sha'ashuah)* and "shaking" *(na'anuah),* suggests that God's joy *(simha)* which facilitated the externalization of divine will (resulting in the creation of the I—Creator) was the result of His thought of the righteous in the future who would raise up the fallen sparks via mitzvot. This "joyous thought" implies, I would argue, the inevitability of the sin. Cf. R. Israel Sarug, *Limudei Azilut* (1897), 3a–3d. Cf. Elliot R. Wolfson, "Erasing the Erasure: Gender and the Writing of God's Body in Kabbalistic Symbolism," in *Circle in the Square* (1995b), 69–70 and nn.170–73. Cf. Yehuda Liebes, "*Zaddik Yesod 'Olam:* A Sabbatean Myth" (in Hebrew), *Da'at* 1 (1978): 105, n.167; and idem, "New Directions in the Research of Kabbala" (in Hebrew), *Pe'amim* 50 (1992): 155–56. However, see *Sefer Koah Ha-Shem,* printed at the end of *Likkutei Ha-Shas m'Ha-Ari* (1972), 40a–42a, where the Sarugian notion of *sha'ashuah* and *na'anuah* are explained in the context of *zimzum. Likkutei Ha-Shas,* first published in Karetz in 1788, largely consists of pp. 24–42 of R. Meir Poppers's *Nof Etz Hayyim,* which remains in manuscript although sections have been published under different names. Regardless of who is correct in the inner-Lurianic debate about the Sarugian doctrine, to my mind the Hasidic authors made no distinction between Sarug and Vital on the question of *zimzum.*

65. R. Gershon Henokh in numerous places argues that the birth of evil occurs only after Adam submitted to the serpent, thus consuming the fruit. Evil only exists when it confronts the possibility of good. Hence the serpent, before the sin, was alienated *('arum)* from the Good (the divine in the human) and thus was only evil in potential. Only after Adam ingested the alienated light represented by the serpent does evil exist in actuality.

66. See for example in Zohar 1.17a/b, where the creation of *gehenom* is understood to be a remnant of the "left" which departs from the initial dialectic with the "right" to become independent and thus unredeemable. This realm of the unredeemable is read in the Zohar as a "disagreement NOT for the sake of heaven," which is attributed in the Mishna to Korah and his community in Numbers 16. Although the connection between Korah and the serpent is not made in the

Zohar, they both appear to share the similar trait of perceived independence, which is, in essence, alienation from the dialectical process of creation *(uvdah d'be-reshit).* For the use of this Zohar source in Hasidic literature, see R. Moshe Hayyim Ephraim of Sudulkov, *Degel Mahene Ephraim* (1994), 181a–182a.

67. According to the Lurianic version of the sin narrative, Eve's encounter with the serpent (Genesis 3:1–6) is understood as an act of copulation, resulting in the serpent inseminating her. She then turns to Adam and couples with him (*She also gave the fruit to Adam, and he ate* [Genesis 3:6]), also resulting in insemination. Cain and Abel are viewed as containing the semen of both the serpent and Adam. The downfall of humanity in Cain's murder of his brother (Genesis 4:5–9) is understood as a result of this precarious admixture. See R. Meir Poppers, *Likkutei Torah* (1880), 11b–13a; and idem, *Sefer Ha-Gilgulim* (1986), chaps. 22–30, 41–61. Both texts are attributed to R. Hayyim Vital but were redacted and edited by R. Poppers. See Joseph Avivi, *Binyan Ariel* (1987), 70, 71.

68. The will of man will first appear again in the personality of Abraham. However, the first stage of this process will be an unconscious will which will not become conscious (integrated) until Jacob.

69. According to Elliot Wolfson's reading of the Zohar, knowledge of the demonic and the divine is a prerequisite for knowing their unity. It appears that R. Gershon Henokh adopts part of that conclusion but moves in a slightly different direction. For R. Gershon Henokh, evil is the very barrier that prevents such a vision of unity. For the Zohar, again according to Wolfson, nullifying evil is achieved by embracing it and thus seeing its unity with God; whereas for R. Gershon Henokh, evil, manifested as doubt, choice, and thus rationality is the alienated state of man and creation from the time of the sin until the covenant with Abraham. Evil is neither nullified nor embraced. Rather, it is integrated and thus transformed. Perhaps part of the difference between the Zohar and R. Gershon Henokh is that the Zohar, and much of medieval Kabbala, is far more willing to grant evil an ontic status. See for example in *Sefer Ha-Bahir,* Reuven Margaliot, ed. (1978), 162, 163. The dualistic nature of the Zohar and its Gnostic roots has long been a source for scholarly debate. See for example Isaiah Tishby, *Wisdom of the Zohar* (in Hebrew) (1961), 1.294–295 and 1.288–289. Although Wolfson challenges the sweeping assumptions of the Gnostic influences of the Zohar discussed in both Tishby and Scholem, he admits, "The Gnostic element of competing cosmic forces is likewise one of the essential doctrines of the Zohar. Like his Castilian predecessors, the author of the Zohar posits a demonic realm, *Sitra Ahra,* the 'Other Side,' which parallels the divine." See also Wolfson, "Left Contained in the Right," 29–30; and Scholem, *The Mystical Shape of the Godhead* (1991), 15–54. In Hasidism in general and R. Gershon Henokh in particular, the ontic character of evil is far less evident. From our present discussion it can be argued that it is not present at all. Evil is seen as a fragmented state of the world and a psychic state in man. It will pass, as it must, to yield integration and unity. Man serves merely as the catalyst for the transformation of history.

70. This idea is given a different twist in Nahmanides' reading of the fall. See for example in his commentary to Genesis 2:9. For Nahmanides, free will is not necessarily a negative consequence of the sin but only "evil" in potential. Although he does state that redemption will bring the world back to the place it was before the sin (see his comment on Deuteronomy 30:6), the result of the sin, i.e., free choice, is not inherently the darkened state of exile from God. For R. Gershon Henokh, the fall is the necessary state of alienation that must precede integration. On one hand his position resembles that of Azriel of Gerona, who offers a Neoplatonic reading of the fall where the soul is enveloped in the physical body only to be freed at the time of redemption. See his *Perush Ha-Aggadot le Rabbi Azriel,* I. Tishby, ed. (1942), 34, 39, 40, and 54. See also Bezalel Safran, "R. Azreil and Nahmanides," 76–81. However, R. Gershon Henokh's position is far less rooted in cosmology. For R. Azriel, the whole incident takes place in the cosmos and redemption is understood as the soul's return to its source in the cosmos. For R. Gershon Henokh, redemption (in this case, integration) is a psychic state which reaches fulfillment in Jacob and then becomes part of the dialectical process of Jewish history beginning with Sinai, becoming alienated in rabbinic Judaism and then reintegrated in the Zohar, Luria, and finally the Besht. In this sense R. Gershon Henokh resembles Nahmanides in that he views Paradise as a physical place (the redeemed world), which will once again return.

71. *Sod Yesharim on the Torah,* 13a, "[The sin was due to] the fact that he [Adam] took before the proper time, entering and wanting to elevate the world before [the appropriate moment]. This resulted in the concealment of knowledge and forgetting and the world remained in a material state. This is [what the Zohar means when it says] *'one who took malkhut without the other nine sephirot.'*" The idea that the sin was primarily a product of an ill-timed action is central in *Mei Ha-Shiloah* as well. See for example in *Mei Ha-Shiloah,* vol. 2, 5b, "In truth, all of the sins of Israel are likened to eating sacrificial meat outside of the appropriate time frame. They want to receive the light before the proper time." This is also viewed as the root of the sin of the Golden Calf in Exodus. See *Mei Ha-Shiloah,* vol. 1, 30b/c.

72. This sounds very much like medieval Gnostic interpretations of the alienated relationship between the human soul and God. R. Gershon Henokh's whole interpretive scheme is built on the medieval Kabbala of the Zohar, whose Gnostic elements have already been documented by Scholem, Tishby, and, most recently, Wolfson. The Hasidic position here is reflecting both the Zohar and Lurianic Kabbala in that the general Gnostic distinction between the physical and the spiritual (here alienation) is equivocated by the addition of the notion of *tikun,* which makes the disparity between the two opposites temporal. For more on this see Hans Jonas, "The Hymn of the Pearl: Case Study of a Symbol, and the Claims for a Jewish Origin of Gnosticism," 291–304; and "The Gnostic Syndrome: Typology of Its Thought, Imagination and Mood," 263–76, both in Hans Jonas, *Philosophical Essays: From Ancient Creed to Technological Man* (1974).

73. R. Gershon Henokh notes that the result of such alienation implies that to serve God in such a world one would have to deny the world completely. See *Sod Yesharim on the Torah,* 23b, "In the Sifra on Leviticus [we learn about] the Creator of the world and about divine service before the Patriarchs. One who wanted to serve [God] completely would have to . . . negate the world and nullify existence." See also Zohar 1.87b. This appraisal of what modern scholarship has called "world-renouncing asceticism" seems to be the product of a world before the covenant with Noah, which asserted the existence of God in the world of nature. Ironically, much of early Hasidism seemed to imply this very renunciation. See for example in R. Dov Baer Schneersohn's *Ner Mitzvah ve Torah Or,* 10b, "This self-nullification is truly the stripping away of one's entire self and substance and essence of everything until one no longer feels oneself at all, as if one were not within reality at all." R. Gershon Henokh, as a product of the nineteenth-century Pryzsucha School, not only moves away from this early stage of renunciation but also deems it a less developed form of worship.

74. *Sod Yesharim on the Torah,* 20b. See also 15b. Cf. *Sod Yesharim on the Festivals,* "Pesach," 2a, and *Mei Ha-Shiloah,* vol. 1, 8b/c.

75. *Sod Yesharim on the Torah,* 14b. As mentioned earlier, the alienation between the lower and upper worlds was the result of Adam's consumption of the fruit on the advice of the serpent, which created a barrier between the human will and the divine will.

76. It appears that the context for the Purim story is, according to R. Gershon Henokh, a similar situation. He reads the rabbinic hint of Esther in the Torah (Deuteronomy 31:18), *I will surely hide My face* (from b.T. Hullin 139a) to mean that not only was God hidden from the Jews in Shushan but even His concealment was hidden. However, in the case of Noah, God initiates the relationship through the covenant, whereas in Shushan the Jews themselves came to realize the divine source of their victory. See *Sod Yesharim on the Festivals,* Purim, 17b–18a.

77. The rainbow serves as an erotic motif in the Zohar, where the "upper unity" is perceived in the "lower unity." It serves as the vision for the mystic to envision dimensions of God's glory otherwise concealed. See Zohar 1.18a/b, 3.215a. Cf. Gershom Scholem, "Colors and their Symbolism in Jewish Tradition and Mysticism," *Diogenes* 109 (1980): 69–71; Michael Fishbane, "Zohar and Exegetical Spirituality," in *Mysticism and Sacred Scripture,* Steven T. Katz, ed. (2000), 112–13 and nn.39–42. On the important discussion of the rainbow as a phallic image ("the unveiling of the androgynous phallus"), see Elliot R. Wolfson, *Through a Speculum That Shines,* 336–45.

78. Actually, there is an ambiguity as to the nature of Ham's actions. Cf. b.T. Sanhedrin 70a which states, "[on the sin of Ham] Rav and Schmuel disagreed. One said he castrated him. One said he committed an act of sodomy [on him]." Rashi on Genesis 9:22 cites both possibilities.

79. *Sod Yesharim on the Torah,* 19a/b. It appears that the general upshot of this comment is that the covenant with Noah could not succeed. As long as the object

of covenant was outside the individual, it could never have the permanence we see in the covenant of circumcision. Ham, through castration, destroys the central organ of the covenant. Perhaps R. Gershon Henokh is implying that had Ham not castrated his father, the covenant of *brit milah* may have been given to him after the flood.

80. The translation of the phrase *"avirei lev"* in the verse in Isaiah is problematic. The *New JPS Tanakh* chooses "stubborn of heart" but notes that the *Septuagint* reads "who have lost heart." Targum Onkelos reads "*takifei lev,*" which implies a hard heart as in Pharaoh's heart in Exodus 10:1. R. Gershon Henokh's reading of the Zohar appears to be closer to "independent hearted." See Zohar 1.76b. This fits very well with R. Gershon Henokh's general position that Noah's covenant left him with recognition of God but a feeling of independence not dissimilar from what we see in the commentaries on Pharaoh.

81. *Sod Yesharim on the Torah,* 20a.

82. The two positions referred to here are either those of Rav and Shmuel or Rabbi Yohanan and Rabbi Eliezer in b.T. Berakhot 17b.

83. Isaiah 46:12, *Listen to me, you stubborn of heart, who are far from righteousness.*

84. *Sod Yesharim on the Torah,* 20a. Although the Zohar appears to use the term *"shalom"* to mean peace, R. Gershon Henokh plays on the word *"shalom"* to mean "perfection." We saw above how he holds that the covenant with Noah was incomplete or imperfect. This Zohar passage, using the word *"shalom,"* which can mean either peace or perfection, makes a connection between *"shalom"* and Torah. Further, in Zohar 1.86a we read "God is called *shalom*." The identification of God with Torah is a common theme in the Zohar that underlies a basic Kabbalistic theme of Torah as the catalyst to reveal God. Torah, both in the Zohar as well as in R. Gershon Henokh, means uncovering or revealing the divine. The covenant with Noah had no Torah because Noah, as a representative of humanity at that stage in history, did not believe in the possibility of one to reveal God through his actions.

85. See Genesis Rabba 35:15, Theodore/Albeck edition, 330–31. Cf. b.T. Ketubot 77a, where R. Shimon bar Yohai is asked whether he has ever seen a rainbow.

86. See *Beit Ya'akov on Genesis,* 40c. Cf. *Mei Ha-Shiloah,* vol. 2, 5d. Another comparison of the rainbow as the initial stage of the covenant that is overcome by circumcision can be found in R. Gershon Henokh's *Sod Yesharim on the Festivals,* Passover, 11a, citing Zohar 3.63: "Torah is called *brit,* God is called *brit,* and the holy remnant [of both of them] are called *brit* [circumcision, my addition]. They are all connected one to the other [i.e., Torah, God, phallus], they are never separated." The connection to the rainbow is made in Tikkunei Zohar, *tikun* 18, 36. R. Gershon Henokh then relates the vision of the colors of the rainbow as the moment of illumination experienced by Israel at the Exodus from Egypt. He continues with a comment by Tikkunei Zohar, which likens the cloud that Moshe ascended at Sinai to the clouds God relates to Noah in Genesis from the verse, *I have sent my rainbow in the clouds* (Genesis 9:13).

87. See *Sod Yesharim on the Torah,* 19.

88. *Mei Ha-Shiloah,* vol. 1, 5c. I'd like to thank Dr. Isaac Ely Stillman for bringing this text to my attention in this particular context.

89. For an interesting example of the fatalistic attitude given to the non-Jewish characters in the Bible see *Sod Yesharim on the Torah,* 83b, 84a, "Behold God created an explicit place in which worship is unnecessary because holiness has a permanent status." In this passage, R. Gershon Henokh equates the passive quality attributed to women in traditional Jewish law to the theological conclusions of Esau. This same attitude is attributed to Amalek in *Sod Yesharim on the Festivals,* Purim, 24. There is also a comparison between death and fatalism. R. Gershon Henokh argues, developing his grandfather's interpretation of the prohibition against a Kohen coming in contact with the dead, that death is the illusion of impotence or the inability to change. Divine service, particular to the Kohen, must accompany a belief in the ability to change. As expressed in the challenge of Amalek, the challenge of the fatalist is that divine service is superfluous in a world where God is hidden. See *Sod Yesharim on the Torah,* 227a—228b.

90. This dichotomy between true divine worship and fatalism is played out in various other ways in the Izbica/Radzin tradition. In *Sod Yesharim Tinyana,* collected from the disciples of R. Gershon Henokh, a similar theological battle is the central theme of the Hanukkah story. Cf. *Sod Yesharim Tinyana,* 116. Among the heretical nations the Greeks are "closest to the Jews," the basic difference being that the Greeks could not justify any correlation between the higher realms of divine will and human action. Therefore, they sought to nullify overt acts of devotion *(avodat ha-shem).* This is based on the rabbinic claim that the Greeks prohibited the public study of Torah and circumcision, the prototypic mitzvah.

91. See *Sod Yesharim on the Festivals,* Purim, 24b.

5. Human Perfection and the Fulfillment of Abrahamic Religion

1. For a discussion on various Hasidic perspectives on Abraham and the covenant see Arthur Green, *Devotion and Commandment* (1989). In these lectures, Green gives a wide variety of early Hasidic perspectives on the tension between the devotional dimension of Abrahamic religion and the nature of commandment and law. For another example in the Izbica/Radzin tradition where Abraham is viewed as the one to whom all is revealed, see R. Aryeh Leib (Liebele) Eiger, *'Imrei Emet* (1973), 12d–13b. R. Gershon Henokh views these figures progressively rather than synthetically. Whereas his grandfather R. Mordecai Joseph and his disciples see the completed personality in all of the patriarchs, R. Gershon Henokh sees the patriarchs developmentally, each one's deficiency being overcome by the other until we reach Jacob, who exhibits the perfected personality that cannot be sustained by his children. The larger scheme of this developmental theory is drawn from the Zohar's correlation between the biblical characters and divine potencies (i.e., the *sephirot*).

2. In *Sod Yesharim* the comparison is primarily between Abraham and Noah. The comparison made between Melchizedek and Abraham is secondary. See for example *Sod Yesharim on the Torah,* 51. A more elaborate depiction of the character of Melchizedek can be found in *Mei Ha-Shiloah,* vol. 1, 7b/c: "When he [Melchizedek] saw Abraham his student going to save Lot in Sodom, according to his own understanding he did not know what Abraham was doing. Actually [according to Melchizedek] it was proper for Abraham not to attempt to help Lot because from Lot's descendants would come Ammon and Moab who would destroy Jerusalem (b.T. Sanhedrin 96b). Moreover, God hated them in that he forbade them from entering into the community. How then, could Abraham have risked his life to save him? However, since he [Melchizedek] knew his student Abraham well, and knew him to be a perfect Zaddik, he concluded that any barrier would not threaten him. Therefore, he prayed that God open his eyes to reveal to him [Melchizedek] the reason behind Abraham's actions. . . . Afterward God did reveal to him that Abraham's actions were not fortuitous. Even though Ammon and Moab would emerge from this community, this decree only includes the men. However, the women would be permitted to enter immediately. Moreover, from this very community would rise the Kingdom of David and Solomon which is the foundation of the Kingdom of David and Jerusalem."

3. See *Sod Yesharim on the Torah,* 20a/b. The pantheistic implications of this equation are obvious. Although pantheism is more prevalent in other genres of Hasidic literature (e.g., the Maggid of Mezeritch and the first two generations of Habad), it is not absent from any Hasidic thinker. For a more general discussion on pantheism and Jewish mysticism, including Hasidism, see Joseph Ben Shlomo, "The Research of Gershom Scholem on Pantheism and Kabbala," in *Gershom Scholem: The Man and His Work* (in Hebrew), Paul Mendes-Flohr, ed. (1983), 77–91; and Mark Verman, "Pantheism and Acosmism in the Kabbala," *Studia Mystica* 10, no. 2 (1987): 24–37.

4. The term "garment" *(levush)* in R. Gershon Henokh has various meanings. Sometimes it is used to refer to the veil that represents the concealment of God in the world. See for example in *Sod Yesharim on the Torah,* 40: "Therefore, when the light is hidden it appears as if there is disagreement. So it is with [different] traits, for each trait is only the garment for the simple [divine] will, which contains no differentiation. However, when the will is weakened and descends to be enveloped in the world of distinction, it appears as if these traits are opposed one to the other." However, sometimes the Torah is called "the garment of Israel" implying that, in their perfected state, the will of Israel and the divine will are reconciled. Hence, the Torah (here meaning mitzvot) envelops the pure Spirit that is embodied in Israel. Paradoxically, whereas in the imperfect world Israel serves God through the performance of mitzvot, in the perfect world, the mitzvot serve Israel, who now become the internal core of spirit, while the Torah becomes the outer garment which, although it may have brought Israel to this state of perfection, now becomes, as a garment for the Spirit, obsolete. Cf. *Sod Yesharim on the Torah,* 296b.

5. See *Sod Yesharim on the Torah,* 22b. Compare this with R. Menahem Mendel of Kotzk, *'Emet ve 'Emunah* (1972), 44. The claim here that the light of God was only accessible through the covenant (circumcision) is an old motif in Kabbalistic literature. See for example in Elliot R. Wolfson, "Circumcision and the Divine Name: A Study in the Transformation of an Esoteric Doctrine," *Jewish Quarterly Review* 78 (1987): 77–112.

6. Interestingly, R. Gershon Henokh, true to Hasidic insularity, does not speak at all about other religions, e.g., Christianity and Islam, both of which are also part of the Abrahamic tradition. Especially when referring to the Noahides as Gentiles, this lacuna is quite problematic. This is even more striking in light of R. Gershon Henokh's close reading of Maimonides. Maimonides, especially in his "Epistle to the Jews of Yemen," clearly views both Christianity and Islam as part of the Abrahamic tradition and, as such, different in kind and not only in degree from all other nonscriptural religions.

7. Joseph Weiss stressed this point when he argued that the innovative element in Izbica Hasidism was not the determinism but the notion of religious anarchy. Although the unity of God and world is present in the earlier Hasidism of the Maggid of Mezeritch and Habad, neither trend ever entertained the possibility of questioning halakhic authority. It is only in Izbica/Radzin, where there is a clear distinction between the Torah of Spirit and the Torah of Law coupled with substantial messianic tendencies, that halakha faces a serious challenge. See Weiss, "A Late Jewish Utopia of Religious Freedom," in *Studies in Eastern European Jewish Mysticism,* 209–48.

8. The verse in question, i.e., Isaiah 51:4, reads, *For teaching shall go forth from me. . . .* The inclusion of the word *"hadasha"* (new) is an addition which first appears in Leviticus Rabba 12:3, which reads, "Says R. Avin bar Kahana, God says, 'A *new* Torah will go forth from Me.'" This midrashic play, which actually refers to a specific innovation in halakhic practice, became a popular reading of the Isaiah passage in Hasidic literature. Note, however, that the verse in Isaiah as interpreted by Rashi and other classical commentaries implies that the words of the prophets (Torah) are rooted in God *(will go forth from ME).* In the midrash cited above, the addition of the word "new" *(hadasha)* implies that temporary halakhic innovation (in this case regarding the instruments permissible for ritual slaughter) is also rooted in God. See for example the comment of R. Hanokh Zundel in his "Etz Yoseph," *Midrash Rabba,* vol. 2 (1974), 20a. However, the Hasidic masters read the addition of the word "new" in the midrash through the prism of the Zoharic distinction between the primordial "Torah of Emanation" and the mundane "Torah of Creation." Therefore, the "new" Torah is not temporary halakhic innovation but the revelation of the "Torah of Emanation," which is not halakhic at all! For examples of this "new" Torah in the Zohar, see Zohar *(Ra'aya Mehemna),* 3.124b–125a; and Tikkunei Zohar 44a, 98b. On the concept of this "new" Torah in the *Ra'aya Mehemna* and Tikkunei Zohar, see Isaiah Tishby, *Wisdom of the Zohar,* David Goldstein, trans. (1989), vol. 2, 1082–123. Cf. the Vilna Gaon's commentary

to Tikkunei Zohar, 67d: "such is the case with Torah in our time which contains no *hidush* [unprecedented reading]. We can only [try to] understand the teachings of old, as it says in numerous places 'a few ancient words' [*milin hadatin atikin*]. But in the future *A new Torah will go out from Me.*" In this passage, "new" implies a paradigmatic *hidush.*

9. The permanence of Torah mentioned here is the abolition of commandment, as we know it. Commandments are necessary precisely because Torah is not permanently established in the hearts of Israel.

10. See *Sod Yesharim on the Torah,* 72b–73a. On Torah as *zimzum,* see *Tiferet Ha-Hanokhi,* 3a; and *Sefer Ha-Zemanim,* 60.

11. This unconventional reading of the passage *For Torah shall go forth from me* (Isaiah 51:4), is interpreted by many Hasidic thinkers. See for example the interpretation given by R. Dov Baer, the Maggid of Mezeritch, in his *Maggid Devarav Le-Ya'akov* (1781; repr., 1972), chaps. 5, 17, 18. The Maggid's reading is similar to R. Gershon Henokh's in one way and different in another. The time frame of his "new Torah" is the messianic era. However, it is that "new Torah" which is truly the essential Torah (in R. Gershon Henokh, the Torah of Spirit). The Maggid suggests a somewhat radical reading of the word *"m'iti"* (meaning in the verse that the words of the prophets are from "Me") to mean from "Me," i.e., from my essence. Now the verse reads *the new Torah, it will emerge from My essence.* However, as the Maggid clearly states, this will only occur in the messianic era. He protects himself from the implications of his rereading of the verse. For another example see R. Zvi Elimelekh of Dinov's *Bnei Yissakhar,* "Sermon for the Month of Sivan," vol. 1, 5:9. Perhaps this notion of a "new Torah" is best expressed by Simon Rawidowicz, "On Interpretation," in *Studies in Jewish Thought* (1974), 60, when he said, "Some of the cabalists were yearning for a new era [*shmitah*] in which the Torah would be rearranged, read anew and thus free Israel from this given system of Law."

12. *Sod Yesharim on the Torah,* 31a. On this point see also midrash Genesis Rabba 15, 137, 138; and Zohar 1.32b. R. Mordecai Joseph introduces the idea by stating that the birth of Isaac *(gevurah)* is the recognition of divinity in what appears as its opposite. See *Mei Ha-Shiloah,* vol. 1, 8, "Sarah lied, saying, *I did not laugh,* for she was frightened [Genesis 18:15]. The deep meaning of this [verse] is as follows. The Talmud states [b.T. Berakhot 33b] that everything is in the hands of heaven excluding the fear of heaven, which is only according to the limitations and potential of the human intellect. However, in truth everything is in the hands of heaven including the fear of heaven. It is just that in this world God conceals His ways. The attribute of Isaac [as *gevurah*] was in order for us to understand that even fear of heaven [judgment—*gevurah*] is in the hands of God. However the world was not fit to accept this. This explains Sarah saying, 'my husband is old,' which appears to be questioning that everything (even fear of God) is in the hands of heaven. Therefore, God showed her measure for measure that even fear of heaven is in His hands. This is the meaning of the birth of Isaac." For a similar

reading that develops R. Mordecai Joseph's stance in a slightly different direction, see R. Leibele Eiger, *Torat Emet* (1989), vol. 1, 11a/b.

13. This topic is treated by Elliot Wolfson, "Circumcision, Vision of God, and Textual Interpretation: From Midrashic Trope to Mystical Symbol," *Circle in the Square* (1995), 29–49; and idem, "Circumcision and the Divine Name: A Study in the Transmission of Esoteric Doctrine," *Jewish Quarterly Review* (1987): 77–112.

14. Genesis Rabba 48:1, 479, cited in Wolfson, "Circumcision, Vision of God," 31. Cf. Zohar 1.97b–1.98b; and other sources in Wolfson.

15. Moshe Idel compares more classical mystical models and what he understands as Hasidism's amalgam of these models with its own unique stance. See his *Hasidism: Between Ecstasy and Magic* (1995), esp. 45–103.

16. I have intentionally translated *'adam* here as "man" instead of the gender-neutral "human," because this discussion focuses on the exclusively male mitzvah of circumcision as the transitional phase toward human perfection.

17. See for example Rachel Elior, *The Paradoxical Ascent to God* (1992), esp. 59–62; and Naftali Loewenthal, *Communicating the Infinite* (1990).

18. The sign of the covenant being the organ of man that procreates represents the active quality of Abraham's covenant. See *Sod Yesharim on the Torah,* 28a/b. Maimonides' initial reason for circumcision also focuses on the fact that the male sex organ exhibits an entirely different orientation. In *Guide of the Perplexed* 3:49, 609, Maimonides states that circumcision should result in "a decrease in sexual intercourse and a weakening of the organ in question." There are many other less "vulgar" reasons Maimonides suggests throughout his corpus, but the above-cited suggestion focuses on the procreative nature of the organ being "marked." Cf. Maimonides' *Guide,* 609, 610; *Guide* 3:24, 502; 3:27, 510; and *Mishneh Torah,* "Laws of Circumcision," 3:9. For a study of these and other sources in Maimonides, see Joseph Stern, "Maimonides on the Covenant of Circumcision and the Unity of God," *The Midrashic Imagination,* Michael Fishbane, ed. (1993), 131–54.

19. Paradoxically, the *via passiva* implicit in the nullification of the will as the result of the acosmic trend in R. Dov Baer, the Maggid of Mezeritch, R. Hayyim Haika of Amdura, and R. Shneur Zalman of Liady has the opposite result of what R. Gershon Henokh is suggesting. Whereas in the acosmic trend one nullifies oneself to see that all is God, in Izbica/Radzin, one can attain the limitless autonomy of the human spirit by realizing that "all is God." For examples in the Maggid, see R. Menahem Mendel of Prymeshlan, ed., *Likkutei Amarim,* 21b and 72a; *Maggid Devarav Le-Ya'akov,* 14c, "so man must abandon himself and forget his needs in order to reach the '*Olam Ha-Mahshava;* there it is all the same." See also Joseph Weiss, "*Via Passiva* in Early Hasidism," in *Studies in Eastern European Jewish Mysticism,* 69–83; idem, "Contemplation as Self-Abandonment in the Writings of Hayyim Haika of Amdura," 142–54; and Rivka Shatz-Uffenheimer, *Hasidut k'Mystica* (in Hebrew) (1968), 21–31.

20. The covenant with Abraham is not viewed as opposed to the covenant of Noah. In fact, R. Gershon Henokh mentions in various places that it is the

completion of Noah's covenant. See for example in *Sod Yesharim on the Torah,* 28, where he interprets why Noah was not able to give birth to generations who would sustain the covenant. "At the time that a person emanates influence [*mashbiah*] he adopts a masculine trait. As it is said, *a man's way is to conquer.*" The portrayal of Noah in R. Gershon Henokh is one who could not conquer because he lacked an active will. Thus he could not become the "man" who would give birth to generations who would sustain and develop his covenant. The distinction here between the covenant of Noah as outside the individual (the rainbow) and that of Abraham as integrated into the individual (circumcision) departs from the Zoharic reading which states that the covenant of Noah was also the phallus *('ish zaddik)* although Abraham's was more complete and perfect.

21. This point is developed by Rivka Shatz-Uffenheimer, "Autonomia shel Ha-Ruah ve Dat Moshe," *Molad* 21 (1963): 554–56. She argues that this point marks the innovative as well as the problematic dimension of Izbica Hasidism. Note, however, that R. Gershon Henokh draws an important distinction between desire and consciousness. While Abraham was the carrier of the desire to reveal God in the world, it was not until Jacob that this desire became conscious and thus fully integrated.

22. *Mei Ha-Shiloah,* vol. 1, 44c.

23. Referring to Isaiah 40:26, *Lift up your eyes and see who created all of this,* I intentionally changed the *JPS Tanakh* translation of *"kol 'eleh"* from "all these" to "all of this." The verse in Isaiah is referring to the heavenly hosts making "all these" appropriate. R. Mordecai Joseph is reading *"kol 'eleh"* as referring to the world, more specifically Abraham's discovery of the divine nature of the world. Hence, "all of this [nature]."

24. *Mei Ha-Shiloah,* vol. 1, 6b/c.

25. Ibid., vol. 2, 49a.

26. Ibid., vol. 1, 44c. Cf. vol. 1, 6b, 17d.

27. Zohar 1.120a. The Zohar's use of the term "dim glass" is quite different than that of R. Mordecai Joseph. The Zohar states, "[*He saw the mountain*] *from a distance* [Genesis 22:4]. He saw this from a dim glass. . . . Therefore the verse says that 'he saw it' as opposed to it being revealed to him clearly. From this dim glass Abraham acted in the appropriate manner." The Zohar's observation is closer to the verse itself, commenting on the phrase "from a distance" as pointing to the nature of the entire vision itself as opposed to his proximity to the mountain.

28. This is an important term in *Mei Ha-Shiloah.* It is conventionally translated as "strength," which would make sense in terms of the use of the divine name *Elohim.* However R. Mordecai Joseph uses this term to imply ever-expanding boundaries of divine will, even as that will may take him outside the boundaries of the law. His usage is closer to what we may call "transitory will," the word itself meaning "time periods" from the Hebrew *tekufah* (TKF) as a block of time. This may explain why R. Mordecai Joseph chooses not to follow the Zohar's linguistic base for the "dim glass," i.e., "from a distance" (Genesis 22:4). In his translation of this

passage Jerome Gellman chooses "strength," which is etymologically correct but I feel misses a central part of R. Mordecai Joseph's message. See Jerome Gellman, *The Fear, the Trembling, and the Fire: Kierkegaard and Hasidic Masters on the Binding of Isaac* (1994), 24. I consulted with his otherwise lucid translation of this passage.

29. *Mei Ha-Shiloah,* vol. 1, 8d, 9a. Cf. vol. 2, 6c.

30. For an interesting reading of the Akedah in the Izbica tradition that differs from this one see Jerome Gellman, *The Fear, the Trembling, and the Fire,* 23–71.

31. Compare this with Maimonides' reading of Genesis 22 in *Guide* 3:24, 501–2: "The second notion consists in making known to us the fact that the prophets consider as true that which comes to them from God in a prophetic revelation. . . . A proof for this is the fact that [Abraham] hastened to slaughter, as he had been commanded, *his son, his only son, whom he loved* [Genesis 22:2], even though this command came to him *in a dream* or *in a vision.* For if a dream of prophecy had been obscure for the prophets, or if they had doubts or incertitude concerning what they apprehended in a vision of prophecy, they would not have hastened to do what is repugnant to nature, and [Abraham's] soul would not have consented to accomplish an act of so great an importance if there had been *a doubt* about it."

32. This reading is taken from the Zohar but, as was the case in his use of the "dim glass" image, it deviates from the Zohar's intention. In Zohar 1.120a we read, "What is meant by the verse *And Isaac said to Abraham his father. And Isaac said 'my father,' and Abraham answered 'I am here, my son'* . . . [Genesis 22:7]? Why did Isaac repeat 'my father,' had he not already addressed him? Moreover, why did Abraham not answer him the first time [when Isaac said 'Abraham']? This is because at that moment Abraham's mercy of a father to a son left him. Therefore Abraham responds, *Here I am, my son.* This means, 'here I am as one whose mercy has been transformed to stern judgment [*dina*].' *And Abraham said 'God will show him the ram'* [Genesis 22:8]. It does not say 'and his father said' because Abraham no longer related to Isaac as his father but as one who is in opposition to him [*ba'al makhloket*]." The removal of Abraham's love for his son in the Zohar is given a more subtle treatment in *Mei Ha-Shiloah.* R. Mordecai Joseph's reading implies a kind of "suspension of the emotive" rather than a loss of love. In *Mei Ha-Shiloah* this was a conscious choice by Abraham in order to act and not become overcome by his uncertainty. In the Zohar, the implication is that Abraham's choice to act resulted in his loss of love or, stronger, in his wrath for Isaac.

33. *Mei Ha-Shiloah,* vol. 1, 44a. Cf. vol. 1, 17d. "Therefore we are presented with four levels of advice from which a person can ascertain the truth of the matter. Afterwards, when he knows for sure that this is from God then he is able to 'expand himself' as he will know that this act is either a mitzvah or the joy of a mitzvah [*simha shel mitzvah*]."

34. Of all the patriarchs, R. Mordecai Joseph views Abraham as the most unconscious yet the one who initiates human desire for unity with God. Abraham is driven by his will even as he himself is unaware of his own intentions. See for example in *Mei Ha-Shiloah,* vol. 1, 8–9 and vol. 2, 5–6.

35. See b.T. Sanhedrin 97b.

36. In actuality, Jacob is the completion of this process from desire to self-consciousness and should have been the recipient of Torah. His fully integrated soul becomes fragmented once again due to the sins of his sons and thus requires the exile of Egypt as a further clarification *(berur)* before the Sinai event. The jealousy of Jacob's son's vis-à-vis Joseph revisits the jealousy of Cain toward Abel, which expanded the fragmented nature of the human soul. The relationship (and correlation) between Jacob and Moses is a common theme in the Zohar. Cf. Zohar 1.21b–22a; Tikkunei Zohar, *tikun* 69, 101b; and Liebes, "Myth versus Symbol in the Zohar and in Lurianic Kabbala," in *Essential Papers on Kabbalah,* Lawrence Fine, ed. (1995), 213–19, and n.9. "The Zohar compares two men, Moses and Jacob. Both are considered to stand on a par with the *sephira* of *tiferet* as 'husbands' of the *Shekhina;* yet, both hold different ranks. Jacob's union with the *Shekhina* is said to be a union 'in form' or 'in spirit'—that is, symbolic—while his actual coupling takes place with the wives. Moses, on the other hand, is said to have actually and corporeally—that is mythically, united with the *Shekhina.*" (Liebes, 214). This depiction of Moses thus justifies his having to leave Zipporah, his wife. This correlation continues in Lurianic Kabbala. See *Sha'ar Mamre Razal* (1862), 15c, "Jacob emerges from the mist [*he'arah*] of *yesod* of [*parzuf*] *abba* within *zeir anpin*. . . . From [the cosmic rendition of] Jacob, who is called Torah—Torah is given. This is the secret of the verse, *When Moses charged us with the Teaching, as the heritage of the congregation of Jacob* [Deuteronomy 33:4]. Moses is from *yesod* of *abba* within *zeir anpin,* as we have explained. For Moses, Torah 'goes out' for it [i.e., Torah] is called *Kehillat Ya'akov* [the Congregation of Jacob]. These are the lights of Moses which are gathered in Jacob out of which Torah is made." According to Vital, Moses is composed of the substance of *yesod* of *abba* as opposed to the *he'arot* or mist. This may refer back to Liebes's summation of the Zohar's distinction between Jacob and Moses above when he states that the coupling of Jacob and the *Shekhina* is "in form" or "in spirit" whereas for Moses the coupling is corporeal.

37. See *Sod Yesharim on the Festivals,* Purim, 21a; and *Sefer Ha-Zemanim,* 9b, 61a.

38. For a succinct explanation in the Lurianic tradition of this phenomenon, see R. Hayyim Vital's *'Ozrot Hayyim,* 43–45.

39. *Parzufim* (lit., faces) are *sephirotic* clusters that comprise different dimensions of the Godhead. Although they exist in a rudimentary form in the Zohar, they are developed in Lurianic Kabbala and become the centerpiece of Luria's cosmology. In the Lurianic system there are twelve *parzufim,* each named after a biblical figure (Jacob, Rachel, Leah) or object (the staff of Moses, etc.). Lurianic cosmology is the mapping of these *parzufim* and how they interact with each other. Each *parzuf* is comprised as ten *sephirot* and each *sephirah* is further delineated into ten sub-*sephirot.*

40. Even as Moses is symbolic of the *sephirah nezah,* he is also situated in the realm of *da'at,* being the leader of the generation of the desert, known as *Dor Dea'h* (the generation of consciousness, i.e., those who experience Sinai). The issue of *da'at* in the *sephirotic* world of Lurianic Kabbala is quite complex. The important point here is that *tiferet* (which actually includes both the masculine aspect in the sub-*sephirah Yisrael Saba* and the feminine aspect in *Tevunah*), is situated in what we may call the "synthetic line" which includes either *keter* and/or *da'at, yesod,* and *malkhut.* This dimension is then read into the personality and spiritual prowess of Jacob as achieving the final integration.

41. See R. Shlomo Ha-Kohen, *Yafe Sha'ah "Drush Zeir Anpin,"* printed in the Mekor Hayyim edition of *Etz Hayyim,* vol. 2, 42b–44b. For a presentation of the *parzufim* in the Idrot see Pinhas Giller, *Reading the Zohar* (2001), 105–24.

42. Scholem notes that although this is the literal translation, the translation that reflects the original formulation in the Zohar and is reflected in the configuration of Luria's *Shevirat Ha-Kelim* and *Tikun* is "the impatient one." This rendition implies judgment or the need for *tikun* that is the essential character of this *parzuf.* Therefore, for our purposes, it is in Jacob *(zeir anpin)* where the final integration takes place. See Scholem, *Major Trends,* 270. For the elaborate development of Jacob as the symbol of integration in the Lurianic school see *Etz Hayyim,* vol. 1, palace 5, gate 1, 165–70. See also in *'Ozrot Hayyim,* 45–51; and *Mevo Sha'arim,* gate 5, part 1, chaps. 1–9, 37–45. Cf. *Mevo Sha'arim,* gate 2, part 2, chap. 2, 6, where Vital explains the unique characteristic of *zeir anpin* as the six lower *sephirot* which emanated in fragments rather than unified as opposed to the three higher *sephirot* which descended in unity and are thus able to withstand the moment of divine rupture. According to this reading, *zeir anpin* is perhaps better translated as "the fragmented one."

43. In Lurianic Kabbala, the *shevirah,* the result of which is the creation, only occurs in the seven lower "points" of *zeir anpin* in the "world of emanation" *('Olam Azilut);* the three higher points in *zeir anpin* as well as the three higher *parzufim* in the "world of emanation" did not descend to form the fabric of the "world of creation *('Olam Yezeriah).* See *Etz Hayyim,* "Sha'ar Ha-Nikudim," chaps. 2 and 7; *Sha'ar Ha-Hakdamot,* 20b; the comments of R. Shalom Sharabi in his *Shemen Sasson,* ad loc.; and *Mevo Sha'arim,* gate 2, part 2, chap. 3, 6b, 7a. There is an important distinction to be made in Lurianic Kabbala between the terms *shevirah* (rupture) and *pegam* (blemish). Although a blemish did occur in the head and upper body of Adam Kadmon, the term *shevirah,* which implies a descent from one world to the next, only takes place in the seven lower points of *zeir anpin,* labeled as the "seven kings who died" taken from Genesis 36:31–40. The trope of the seven kings from Edom who died is a centerpiece in the Lurianic discussion of *shevirah.* See *Etz Hayyim,* fourth gate, chaps. 1–10, 50a–55d; and *Mevo Shearim,* gate 2, part 2, chap. 3, 6cff.; and gate 2, part 3, chap. 7, 16aff. Cf. Isaiah Tishby, *Torat Ha-Ra ve Ha-Kelippah* (1984), 28–33.

44. See Idra Zuta, Zohar 2.292–295. Through the Lurianic reading of the Zohar, in Hasidism the doctrine of the *parzufim* in the Idrot becomes almost interchangeable with the doctrine of the *sephirot* in the main body of the Zohar. On this, see Pinhas Giller, *Reading the Zohar* (2001), 125–38, 153–57.

45. On this see Scholem, *Major Trends,* 270, 271. For a more comprehensive analysis, see Yehuda Liebes, "Myth versus Symbol in the Zohar and Lurianic Kabbala," 228–33; and Rachel Elior, "The Metaphorical Relation between God and Man and Significance of Visionary Reality in Lurianic Kabbala" (in Hebrew), *Jerusalem Studies in Jewish Thought* 10 (1992): esp. 50–57.

46. For a study on the relationship between Hasidism and Kabbala see Rachel Elior, "Ha-Zika beyn Kabbala la-Hasidut," *Proceedings of the Ninth World Congress of Jewish Studies* (1986): 107–14. The issue whether Hasidism was influenced more by Lurianic Kabbala or Cordoverean Kabbala is discussed by Elior. See also Rivka Shatz-Uffenheimer, "R. Moshe Cordovero ve Ha-Ari-bein Nominalism le-Realism," *Jerusalem Studies in Jewish Thought* 1, no. 3 (1982): 122–36.

47. See Joseph Weiss, *Studies in Eastern European Jewish Mysticism,* 216. Weiss uses as his source a statement in *Mei Ha-Shiloah* that suggests that the essential difference between Abraham and Isaac on the one hand and Jacob on the other is that Abraham and Isaac were not given a continuous illumination while Jacob was. I will attempt to show that R. Gershon Henokh, using the framework of the creation and the two covenants, develops this idea in a different direction. For the source in *Mei Ha-Shiloah* see vol. 1, 14a/b. Note that Weiss used the 1922 Lublin edition of *Mei Ha-Shiloah.* I used a 1984 reprint of the 1860 Vienna edition. Therefore, my page references will slightly differ from his.

48. See for example in *Mei Ha-Shiloah,* vol. 1, 18a–18b. See also Weiss, 242–43.

49. One should note that this whole discussion excludes Isaac, who is an important part of the process. I chose to ignore him here because his role in the process at hand is largely one of a catalyst between Abraham and Jacob and less an independent part of the overall process toward human perfection.

50. See *Sod Yesharim on the Torah,* 75a. It is interesting to note that the Russian existentialist Lev Shestov presents Abraham in a similar fashion when he says, "it is beyond a doubt that he alone will be able to attain the Promised Land who, like Abraham, decides to go forward without knowing where he is going." See Lev Shestov, *Athens and Jerusalem* (1966), 397. I'd like to thank Martin Kavka for bringing this to my attention.

51. See for example in Zohar 1.161b and 3.198b (which does not refer to Jacob in particular). R. Mordecai Joseph defines the process of perfection as *berur.* This notion of clarification or refinement *(berur)* is a central theme in *Mei Ha-Shiloah.* It appears less often in R. Gershon Henokh's writings but is nonetheless an integral part of *Sod Yesharim* as well. For a discussion on the concept of spiritual clarification in Izbica, see Morris Faierstein, *All Is in the Hands of Heaven* (1987), 44–48. An interesting formulation of this perfection which resembles that of our thinkers can be found in the writings of the Cistercian mystic St. William of St. Thierry, "Man's

perfection is to be like God . . . in unity of spirit, whereby man not only becomes one with God in the sense that he wills the same thing as God, *but in the sense that he is unable to will what God does not will.*" (*Epistola ad Fratres de Monte Dei,* vol. 2, no. 16, cited in Thomas Merton, *The Waters of Siloe* [1949], xx.)

52. The notion of Abraham not knowing where he was going, both in Genesis 12:1 and 22:1, supports the midrashic view of Abraham as "walking in darkness." On this see Jon D. Levenson, *The Death and Resurrection of the Beloved Son* (1993), 128–29.

53. The notion of the patriarchs being likened to a chariot that God sits upon is an old motif, which appears in Genesis Rabba (47:6, 474, 475): "Says Reish Lakish, the patriarchs are the chariot [*merkavah*]." See also Genesis Rabba 69:3, 792, 793; and 82:4, 983.

54. *Sod Yesharim on the Torah,* 83a/b. Note, however, that R. Gershon Henokh bases this distinction between Abraham and Jacob on the fact that the verse speaking of Abraham does not contain the phrase *with him.* However, if you look at the verse in full you will see that it indeed does contain that very phrase. Perhaps for R. Gershon Henokh the different position of the terminology in both verses is significant. In the verse regarding Abraham the term precedes the expression of God's parting. In the verse regarding Jacob, the term appears after God's parting. Therefore, Abraham may have had the consciousness of God when He was speaking to Him, but did not maintain it when God parted. Jacob, on the contrary, maintained the consciousness of being with God even after God's departure. For the Lurianic source for the realm of God which remains above see *Etz Hayyim,* vol. 1, "Sha'ar Anakh," 91a–92a. On this notion of a trace of sanctity as the latent power to be reconstructed, see R. Isaac Hutner, *Pahad Yizhak,* "Essays on Rosh Ha-Shana" (1990), 142–48.

55. For another example in Izbica/Radzin Hasidism, see R. Leibele Eiger's *Torat Emet,* vol. 3, 18d. See also Rachel Elior, "Ha-Zika she-beyn Kabbala la-Hasidut," in *Proceedings of the Ninth World Congress of Jewish Studies* (1986), 107–14. This is, of course, not to suggest that Lurianic Kabbala disregards the religious personality as a category in its system. See for example in R. Aaron of Optaw's "*Keter Nehora,*" published in *Siddur Tefilah Yeshara Berditchev,* Introduction, 9; and R. Hayyim Vital's *Sha'are Kedusha,* part 3, gate 5, 71a–74b, where the notion of prophecy as a result of Lurianic *kavvanot* is developed as a personal religious experience. In fact, often the theosophic structures in Lurianic Kabbala are applied anthropomorphically. Although Scholem chose to minimize the implications of such a move and designated Hasidism as the "mystical psychology" of Jewish mysticism, scholars have recently revisited the issue of the psychological and experiential nature of Lurianic Kabbala. See Elliot R. Wolfson, "The Influence of the Ari on the Shelah" (in Hebrew), *Jerusalem Studies in Jewish Thought* 10 (1992): 445, n.127; and Mordecai Pachter, "Clarifying the Terms *Katnut* and *Gadlut* in the Kabbala of the Ari and a History of Its Understanding in Hasidism" (in Hebrew), *Jerusalem Studies in Jewish Thought* (1992): 171ff.

56. Even as Idel has contributed to our understanding of the subtleties of the Hasidic use of other Kabbalistic schools beside Luria, when it comes to exegetical tools and lexicography, Hasidic authors remain largely within the Lurianic framework. Cf. Idel, *Hasidism,* 33–45.

57. This idea deviates sharply from the Lurianic concept of the ontic character of sin. See for example *Sha'ar Ha-Likkutim,* 10a. The transformation of the concept of sin in Izbica is a central theme in Rivka Shatz-Uffenheimer's study on Izbica, "Autonomia shel Ha-Ruah ve Torat Moshe," *Molad* 21 (1963): 554–56. Shatz-Uffenheimer claims that sin is better translated as mistake rather than transgression. Sin, in her reading, can only be seen as a mistake in intent and not a mistake in action. This reflects a similar statement by Tishby, *Torat Ha-Ra,* 97, which states, "The act of [the first] sin was not initially intended as a destructive [act] but rather to re-construct." A similar idea is found in Shragai when he states that the determinist nature of Izbica is that sin is only viable from an "external" perspective, while internally the Jewish covenant with God remains not only unbroken but undamaged. See Shlomo Zalman Shragai, "Hasidut Ha-Baal Shem Tov b'Tifisat Izbica/Radzin" in *Sefer Ha-Besht* (1960): 153–201. On this idea in R. Gershon Henokh, see *Sod Yesharim on the Torah,* 106. This idea is common in R. Zaddok Ha-Kohen as well. See for example his *Resisei Layla,* 23, where R. Zaddok interprets the rabbinic injunction of reaching a state of "until one does not know" as an understanding of the divine will inherent in sin. A collection of R. Zaddok's references to *Mei Ha-Shiloah* can be found in R. Abraham Joshua Heschel Frankel's *Mei Zedek* (1984).

58. See *Tiferet Ha-Hanokhi,* 4a.

59. A reader attuned to comparative analysis will immediately, and justifiably, see a comparison of the biblical Jacob presented here and Paul's depiction of Jesus in his Epistles.

60. This is not unequivocal. The depiction of Jethro, Moses' father-in-law, as a righteous Gentile needs to accompany the Izbica/Radzin presentation of the ontological differences between the inheritors of Jacob (Israel) and those who inherit only the preliminary reconciliation in Abraham and Isaac (the Gentile nations). For the Izbica portrayal of Jethro, see *Mei Ha-Shiloah,* vol. 2, 14c–15b.

61. See for example the description of Esau in *Mei Ha-Shiloah,* vol. 1, 10b, and the more general assertion in *Mei Ha-Shiloah,* vol. 1, 54b. The consequence that sin is a transgression of divine will is no longer applicable to the descendants of Jacob. This idea reflects numerous statements by R. Zaddok. See for example in *Resisei Layla,* 17a, "A deficiency in the root of Israel appears as a real deficiency but in reality it is not a deficiency at all!" Compare with *Mei Ha-Shiloah,* vol. 1, 8c, "Sinners of Israel are under the Providence of God. By means of this they will make God's name great and sanctify it." It is unclear whether the term "this" *(zeh)* refers to the Providence of God or the sinful act.

62. The implied correlation between Esau and the serpent in R. Gershon Henokh is made explicitly in the Lurianic text *Ma'amar Pesiutav shel Avraham Avinu,*

43, reprinted in *Ketavim Hadashim shel R. Hayyim Vital* (1988), 11: "Behold, Esau is the serpent and Dina was fit for him. Since Jacob concealed her, she was saved from him. However, Dina was one who journeyed, which is the secret of the verse, *And Dina went out* [Genesis 34:1]. If she would have remained in the place of holiness, the serpent would never have bound himself to her."

63. In midrash Genesis Rabba 63:27 (Albeck edition, 693), the language is different but the thrust is the same. Theodore notes in his gloss on the passage in Genesis Rabba that an earlier printing contains a version closer to the one in b.T. Berakhot 45b. For his comment in full, see Genesis Rabba, Theodore/Albeck edition, 693, n.4.

64. See *Mei Ha-Shiloah,* vol. 1, 10a. This comment reflects a much earlier Hasidic statement found in R. Jacob Joseph ben Yehuda Leib's *Rav Ya'abi* (1808; repr., 1970–71), 29c. The initial positive appraisal of Esau can be found as well in R. Yoakhim Kim Y. Kadish's three-volume collection of Polish Hasidism, *Siach Sarfe Kodesh* (1989), vol. 1, 36, in the name of R. Mordecai Joseph's teacher, R. Simha Bunim of Pryzsucha. See also R. Isaac Meir Alter of Gur's *Hiddushe Ha-Rim* (repr., 1990), 36.

65. *Sod Yesharim,* 75a.

66. See *Sod Yesharim,* 55a. The notion of Isaac being ill-equipped to take an active role in the act of revealing God begun by Abraham is dealt with in the midrashic as well as the literary tradition on the sacrifice of Isaac. See for example in Genesis Rabba 65:9, 718–20, where the blindness of Isaac is viewed as the result of the Akedah.

67. *Sod Yesharim,* 50.

68. *Sod Yesharim,* 56b.

69. For an example of how R. Gershon Henokh suggests that Isaac's lack of faith in himself is seen in a positive light, see *Sod Yesharim,* 53, "The power of repentance is to return everything to God by means of the individual contracting himself [*m'zamzem 'et 'azmo*], thus elevating everything to God. Through this one can come to understand that there is no power to act without God's will. This is also the trait of Isaac. . . . One can only see the light of God by means of contracting oneself [minimizing one's independence from God]. Through this one can see that the light of God is never severed from an individual even at the time of a sin even though it does not appear as such." The source for this statement can be found in Zohar 3.169, "There is a spark of light which remains in the individual even after death which is never destroyed. This bone is called *hokhma* which is hidden in the power of *bina*." See also Tikkunei Zohar, *tikun* 18, 35. It appears from this text that R. Gershon Henokh depicts Isaac as a model for the common Hasidic notion of self-nullification. However, this takes place within the context of mitzvot and does not lead to the fatalistic conclusion of Esau, who nullifies not only the potential of the self to act but faith in the covenant as well. This distinction is developed further in my discussion on antinomianism in the final chapter of this study.

70. See Genesis Rabba 63:8; and Rashi on Genesis 25:26.

71. R. Gershon Henokh essentially uses the biblical account of the sale of the birthright as the final distinction between Jacob and Esau. It appears that until that moment the potential of Jacob as the integrated individual worthy of election is not clear. Moreover, Esau remains potentially in the fold, even in his attempt to trick Isaac, until this crucial moment. See *Sod Yesharim on the Torah,* 55–56.

72. *Sod Yesharim,* 57a.

73. The connection between Adam and Jacob, rabbinic in origin, is commonly used in Hasidic discourse. For example, R. Ze'ev Wolf of Zhitomir reads the dictum that repentance reaches to the Throne of Glory in light of the midrashic statement that the face of Jacob is engraved on the Throne of Glory (Genesis Rabba 69:12). Repentance, the theme of Rosh Ha-Shana, is that which fixes the sin of Adam (having been created and having sinned on Rosh Ha-Shana) realigning the "face of Jacob" on the supernal throne with the distorted image of his face depicted as the Nation of Israel. Thus the unblemished, integrated face of Jacob on the supernal throne can be likened to Adam before the sin, repentance realigning the post-sin Adam (Israel) with his pre-sin image. See R. Ze'ev Wolf of Zhitomir, *'Or Ha-Meir* (1991), 260–66. For a comprehensive study of early mystical readings of the midrashic theme of Jacob's face being engraved on the Throne of Glory, see Elliot R. Wolfson, "The Image of Jacob Engraved upon the Throne: Further Reflection on the Esoteric Doctrine of the German Pietists," in *Along the Path* (1995), 1–63.

74. See *Sod Yesharim,* 63. R. Gershon Henokh interprets the Lurianic interpretation of the biblical account of Jacob's separating the sheep into *'akudim, nekudim, berudim* (Genesis 31:10–12). Luria uses this verse to suggest the three stages of creation from the beginning of the descent of the eternal light into the vessels *('akudim)* of Adam Kadmon to the breakage of the vessels *(nekudim)* to the final rectification *(berudim).* When speaking about the final reconciliation of the fragments in the erotic imagery of sexual intercourse "face to face," R. Gershon Henokh states, "This is achieved in the vocation of Jacob our father who recognized the 'root' [of the world] and returned everything *face to face* with God." Ibid., 64. Another example of this motif can be found in Zohar 1.156a where the phrase in Psalms, *how great are Your acts,* is interpreted to mean not only the breadth and scope of creation (space) but that all of these actions occur simultaneously (time). There are essentially three levels mentioned in the Zohar. The first is the river of light that is a bridge between the infinite and the finite and rationally incomprehensible. The second is the river of the supernal worlds (the world of *sephirot*), which can be perceived. The third is the fragmented dimension of our world. R. Gershon Henokh suggests that the first river of light can be experienced through *hirhur,* that which we have termed intuition. This is the world of Jacob.

75. On *gilgul,* see Gershom Scholem, *The Mystical Shape of the Godhead,* Joachim Neugroschel, trans. (1976), 197–250. Cf. Ephraim Gottlieb, "The Debate on *Gilgul* in Candia," in his *Studies in Kabbalistic Literature* (in Hebrew), J. Hacker,

ed. (1976), 370–96; Mikhal Oron, "Line of Influence in the Doctrine of the Soul and Reincarnation in the Thirteenth Century and in the Writings of R. Todros Ha-Levi Abulafia" (in Hebrew), in *Studies in Jewish Thought,* Sara O. Heller-Wilensky and Moshe Idel, eds. (1989), 277–90; Rami Sheqalim, *Reshit Torat Ha-Nefesh v' Ha-Gilgul b'Kabbala b'Meah 12–15* (1994); and the brief discussion of *gilgul* in the Zohar in Pinhas Giller, *Reading the Zohar,* 37–42.

76. On this see Louis Jacobs, "The Uplifting of Sparks in Later Jewish Mysticism," in *Jewish Spirituality II,* A. Green, ed. (1987), 99–126.

77. *Mei Ha-Shiloah,* vol. 1, 10a/b.

78. This character trait of Jacob comes to the fore in R. Mordecai Joseph's distinction between Judah (the true inheritor of Jacob) and Joseph. See *Mei Ha-Shiloah,* vol. 1, 14a–c.

79. See b.T. Hullin 81a. This interpretation was adopted by Rashi as an answer to the question as to why the Torah states that Jacob first saved his family and only then returned for his possessions (Genesis 32:23–25). Cf. b.T. Baba Kama 16b. For an alternate reading of Rashi's use of this rabbinic passage, see MaHaRal's "*Gur Aryeh,*" printed in *'Ozar M'Forshei Rashi 'al Ha-Torah* (1958), ad loc.

80. The notion of "forgetting" as indicative of a state of separation from God (rupture) is an important theme in Lurianic Kabbala. See for example in *Shulhan Arukh Ha-Ari zal,* 96, n.68; *Sha'ar Ha-Mitzvot,* 32a; and *Mevo Sha'arim,* gate 2, part 2, chap. 7, 9c, "It is explained that [the *parzufim*] *abba* and *imma* are two permutations of the tetragramaton (YHVH) whose numerical value equals *zakhor* [memory]. This is only when they are in the [unified] state of 'face to face.' However, the [numerical value of the] names in reverse [lit., when they are not unified] equals *tishkah* [forgetting]. Memory is drawn from the facial side [of the *parzuf*] and forgetting from the back since the *kelippot* [extraneous demonic matter] is found in the back." Forgetting as a positive trait is common in the mystical teachings of both Christianity and Islam. For examples in the mystic teaching of Meister Eckhart, see Louis Dupre, *The Other Dimension* (1979), 357–418. See also R. K. C. Forman, "Introduction: Mysticism, Constructivism, and Forgetting," in *The Problem of Pure Consciousness,* R. K. C. Forman, ed. (1990), 3–52; and William Stoddart, *Sufism* (1985), 41–76.

81. The motif of Jacob as "small," which is read by R. Gershon Henokh here to imply humility and the recognition of divine omnipotence, is most likely taken from the identification of Jacob as *zeir anpin,* the small face(s). However, both Scripture and rabbinic literature connote smallness to Jacob. See Amos 7:2, *When it had finished devouring the herbage in the land, I said, "Oh, God, pray forgive. How will Jacob survive? He is so small."* Compare with b.T. Hullin 60b. It is noteworthy that R. Gershon Henokh's rendering of the small vessels in Rashi's comment on this verse may be likened to Maimonides' comment in *Mishneh Torah,* "Hilkhot Yesodei Ha-Torah," 14:13, about the discrepancies of Abbaye and Rava (i.e., the halakhic discourse of the Talmud), as a "small thing" *(davar katan).*

82. *Sod Yesharim on the Torah,* 80a.

83. For a discussion on this text as a source for integrating mitzvot into the antinomianism of *Mei Ha-Shiloah,* see the final chapter of this study.

84. *Sod Yesharim on the Torah,* 68. Cf. Zohar Idra Zuta, 289b.

85. There is another passage in R. Gershon Henokh which draws the Lurianic distinction between the continuous union of the two higher *parzufim* of *abba* and *imma* and the apparently inconsistent union of the two lower *parzufim, zeir anpin* (Jacob) and *nukva* (consisting both of Rachel and Leah). Jacob's vocation, after achieving the consciousness of the highest union, is to reveal to the world that the apparently inconsistent lower union is constant as well. See *Etz Hayyim,* vol. 1, 117–22; *'Ozrot Hayyim,* 45a–47b; and *Sod Yesharim on the Torah,* 79a–b.

86. The dual nature of Jacob is developed in *Sod Yesharim on the Torah,* 68–69. See also R. Hayyim Vital, *Sha'ar Ha-Pesukim,* 17a.

87. This is one of the more fundamental principles in the Lurianic system. The significance of the *sephirah hod* is that the *parzuf imma* only extends within *zeir anpin* until *hod.* Therefore, the *sephirah yesod* of *zeir anpin* is empty of *imma* (although it contains a dimension of *abba*) and therefore called "orphaned" *(yatum).* As well, it is the revealed state of the forces of *parzuf abba,* which was, until this point, enveloped in *imma.* For more on this, see R. Shlomo Ha-Kohen in his *Yafah Sha'ah* [*drush zeir anpin*], included in *Etz Hayyim,* vol. 2, 42b–44a. This point will become more relevant when we discuss the uniqueness of Joseph, who represents the *sephirah yesod,* later in this chapter. See also R. Hayyim Vital, *Sha'ar Ha-Pesukim,* 15b, 17b; and R. Meir Poppers, *Sha'ar Ha-Likkutim,* 23a.

88. More accurately from the bottom third of *tiferet* of *zeir anpin* until the culmination of *yesod* (that includes *malkhut* or *ateret ha-yesod*).

89. This interpretation is based on the Lurianic concept of "the source which remains above" regarding light which, in order not to be damaged by sin, moves upward to the place in the cosmos where it is not susceptible to sin. In other contexts it is called "the returning light" *('or hozer).* See *Etz Hayyim,* "Sha'ar Ahaf," 3, 18a–19b; and *Mevo Sha'arim,* gate 2, part 1, chap. 5, 3b, 4a. See also *Sod Yesharim on the Torah,* 61 a/b, "The trait of *zeir anpin* when it is in a complete state, its foundation, which is *hesed* and *gevurah* is called Israel. However, when its traits are concealed [it is not completely revealed] it is called Jacob. The Ari z'l teaches that the bottom portion of the *parzuf* [*zeir apin*] is called Jacob and the upper half is called Israel."

90. See for example in *Sefer Ha-Gilgulim,* intro. 25–27, 48–53; and *Pri Etz Hayyim, "Sha'ar Hanukkah,"* 109b–109d.

91. According to Kabbalistic custom, the *tefillah shel yad* (worn on the arm opposite the heart) should be covered. Some say that the *tefillah shel rosh* should also be covered with the *talit.* See *Pri Etz Hayyim,* "*Sha'ar Ha-Tefillin,*" chaps. 6 and 7, 21a–22b; R. Ya'akov Zemah, *'Olat Tamid* (1907), 33bff; and *Shulkhan Arukh Ha-ARI z-'l* (1984), 19, 20, n.5.

92. The use of the Kabbalistic concept of *zimzum* is widespread in both R. Mordecai Joseph and R. Gershon Henokh. *Zimzum* is generally seen as the first act of

creation and will be nullified in the final redemption. For an example of *zimzum* as the temporal state of free will and *brit,* see *Sod Yesharim on the Torah,* 74; and *Mevo Sha'arim,* 4b.

93. R. Gershon Henokh is quite adamant about the fact that it is the grace of God and not human action that brings about this final revelation. Even as he is willing to relegate divine sanction to the performance of mitzvot, it is the result of the willful act of God and not theurgy. See *Sod Yesharim on the Torah,* 63b, where R. Gershon Henokh stresses that one's merit is dependent upon the extent to which he recognizes the presence of God in the world.

94. There are forty-nine days between Passover and Shavuot (Pentecost). According to Jewish law, these days constitute the forty-nine days of the Omer when a barley offering would daily be brought to the Temple, culminating with the two loaves of wheat that would be brought for the festival of Shavuot. According to Kabbalistic custom, these forty-nine days constitute the calculation of 7 X 7 of the *sephirot,* ending with the festival of receiving the Torah (on Shavuot, according to rabbinic tradition). The rabbinic tradition grafts onto this period of time the deaths of the students of R. Akiba during the Hadrianic persecutions of the first century. According to legend R. Shimon bar Yohai died on the thirty-third day of this period. His death was viewed as a retribution for Israel and, as a result, no further disciples of R. Akiba died. The thirty-third day of the Omer, according to the *sephirotic* system, is *hod sh'b'hod (hod of hod).*

95. In the Idrot, Rabbi Shimon dies in ecstasy after revealing the secrets of the esoteric tradition. See Idra Rabba, Zohar 3.142b–143a; Idra Zuta, Zohar 3.286a/b; and Yehuda Liebes, "The Messiah of the Zohar: The Messianic Portrait of R. Shimon bar Yohai" (in Hebrew), in *Ha-Ra'ayon Ha-Meshihi b'Yisrael* (1990), 191–94.

96. *Sod Yesharim on the Torah,* 63a. Cf. Zohar 1.162b and 3.262b.

97. See my discussion of this in "From Theosophy to Midrash: Lurianic Exegesis and the Garden of Eden."

98. The notion of Adam as the archetype of a future Israel resembles a more classical form of typology in biblical exegesis, where biblical figures of an earlier period return in a different person with a similar personality type later on. Such an interpretive scheme is also used to describe the biblical characters of Abraham and King David. See R. Clements, *Abraham and David: Genesis XV and Its Meaning for Israelite Religion* (1967), 55–60. On such a relationship between Moses and Ezekiel see Michael Fishbane, *Biblical Interpretation in Ancient Israel* (1985), 370, n.133. See also his more general discussion on biblical typology, 372–79. The interpretation of Adam as the future Israel in later Kabbala is built upon a Lurianic interpretation of the Zohar, which sees Adam as the cosmic primordial man who embodies both the alienation, as well as the subsequent integration, of creation to God. Cf. Tikkunei Zohar, *tikun* 69, 112b.

99. The reversion of Esau back to the Noahide covenant is my own reading of R. Gershon Henokh and is, to my knowledge, never explicitly stated in his

writings. In general, after Jacob, I did not find any substantive distinction between the descendants of Noah and the descendants of Esau except that, in line with the rabbinic and midrashic tradition, the enemy of Israel is always genealogically drawn back to Esau. This can be explained as follows: Esau's hatred is drawn from the biblical model of exclusion from the covenant. The direct descendants of Noah, on the other hand, do not have such a basis for animosity toward Israel. As I have suggested, this does not appear to be the way Esau is treated in R. Mordecai Joseph and R. Gershon Henokh. Esau's exclusion is the result of his own decision, which yields a fatalistic stance making the life of mitzvot untenable. Although I will not discuss the differences between Esau and the Noahide nations in this study, it is a desideratum. For one example of how a nineteenth-century Eastern European exegete treated the relationship between Israel and Esau in a cosmic framework, see R. Naftali Zvi Berlin, *She'er Yisrael,* printed in his commentary to Song of Songs, *Shir Ha-Shirim 'Im Pirush Ha-Natziv* (1967), 115–34. More generally, see Gerson Cohen, "Esau as a Symbol in Early Medieval Thought," in *Jewish Medieval and Renaissance Studies,* A. Altmann, ed. (1967), 19–48.

6. Reconciliation and Fragmentation

1. See *Mei Ha-Shiloah,* vol. 2, 9a.

2. *Sod Yesharim on the Torah,* 86b.

3. The legal exegetical category of "*klal u perat*" (general principle and specific cases) has often been used as a homiletic principle as well. The classic rabbinic delineation of this principle can be found in "Braita d'Rebbe Yishmael," printed in the beginning of Sifra to Leviticus, standard editions. In Kabbalistic exegesis, see the Vilna Gaon's essay at the end of his commentary to *Sefer Dezniuta* (1882), 38b; R. Moshe Hayyim Luzzato, *138 Paths to Wisdom* (in Hebrew) (1992), 39–42; R. Moshe Igras, *Pithei Sha'arim* (1974), 10 a/b; and R. Shlomo Elyashuv, *Leshem She Vo Ve-Ahlama* (1975), 36b. Even in modern scholarship, this principle has been used to understand different historical epochs in Jewish history. See for example in Simon Rawidowicz, "On Interpretation," in *Studies in Jewish Thought* (1974), 51, where he distinguishes between the First Temple (general law/prophecy) and Second Temple (particular law/rabbis). This reference is particularly appropriate here in that R. Gershon Henokh distinguishes between the two Temples as the prophetic Torah of Spirit and the rabbinic Torah of Law. Moreover, the general principle in R. Gershon Henokh represents the revealed spirit that is beyond the Law, while the particular represents halakha or the way toward the general principle when God is concealed.

4. The Lainer dynasty viewed itself as part of the Davidic family. The Kotzk tradition, which was the initial ideological framework of Izbica/Radzin Hasidism, also viewed itself in a messianic light. Much of this had to do with the fact that R. Menahem Mendel of Kotzk went into seclusion in the year 1840, the very year of the messianic prediction as extrapolated from the Zohar. It was the year R. Mordecai

Joseph split from his Rebbe, Menahem Mendel of Kotzk. For more on this, see Morris Faierstein, *All Is in the Hands of Heaven* (1987), 77–84; and Arie Morgenstern, "Messianic Expectation in the Wake of the Year 1840" (in Hebrew), in *Messianism and Eschatology* (1983), 343–64. Cf. Isaiah Tishby, "Messianic Ideas and Messianic Trends in the Development of Hasidism," (in Hebrew), *Knesset* 32 (1967): 1–15. Tishby's article is a good example of how later Hasidism (mid-nineteenth century onward) was almost ignored in the initial stages of Hasidic scholarship. In his very comprehensive and often illuminating article, Tishby basically ignores the messianic predictions of 1840 in the schools of Kotzk, Alexander, Warka, Sokochov, and Izbica.

5. This is perhaps best expressed in *Mei Ha-Shiloah,* vol. 1, 14b. The use of the spiritualist vs. legalist typology in Hasidic polemics is common, particularly in early Hasidism. See for example Gedalia Nigal's introduction to his edition of R. Jacob Joseph of Polnoy's *Zofnat Pa'aneah* (1989); and Samuel Dresner, *The Zaddik* (1974).

6. See b.T. Sukkah 52a, the oft-quoted Talmudic reference; and the "Tosefta" Targum on Zechariah 12:10, cited in Sperber, *The Bible in Aramaic* (1962), 3:495. Cf. Pseudo-Yonatan to Exodus 40:11; and Targum to Song of Songs 4:5, 7:4, which also mentions two messiahs (David and Ephraim). Cf. Joseph Klausner, *The Messianic Idea in Israel* (1955), 83–501; and Joseph Heinemann, "The Messiah of Ephraim and the Premature Exodus of the Tribe of Ephraim," in *Harvard Theological Review* 8, no. 1 (1975): 1–15.

7. It is interesting to note that R. Mordecai Joseph uses this verse containing the word *"m'lamdah"* as a reproach against the very nature he attributes to Ephraim. The word *"m'lamdah,"* meaning "learned by rote," is explicitly stated in regard to Ephraim in Hosea 10:11, *Ephraim became a trained [m'lamdah] heifer, but preferred to thresh.*

8. *Mei Ha-Shiloah,* vol. 1, 14d/15a. The antagonism between Ephraim (i.e., Joseph) and Judah (the true inheritor of Abraham through Jacob) is not new in Izbica/Radzin although it is developed in ways that are, in my view, innovative. For a precedent in Hasidism which draws a connection between Ephraim and Isaac (the patriarch who represents the outlook of Joseph) see R. Zvi Elimelekh of Dinov's *Bnei Yissachar,* vol. 2, "Sermon on Tishrei," 1a. On the use of the verse *[N]ow is the time to act for God* (Psalms 119:126) in the Zohar, see Zohar 3.148a where the term "*la'asot*" is read to mean "create" or "repair" the *parzuf* of *zeir anpin* via mitzvot rather than to "act" outside of the framework of mitzvot. Cf. Yehuda Liebes, "The Messiah in Sefer Ha-Zohar," in *The Messianic Idea in Israel* (in Hebrew) (1982), 166–70; and idem, "Eros in the Zohar" (in Hebrew), *'Alpayim* 9 (1994): 72 , n.34. This idea is reflected in R. Abraham Isaac Ha-Kohen Kook's thought as well. Cf. his *Mussar Ha-Kodesh,* 156, and *'Orot Ha-Teshuvah,* 12, n.6.

9. See Weiss, *Studies in Eastern European Jewish Mysticism,* 219, 220. This is also the case when Weiss notes that, "The radical determinism now hidden from man's eyes [perception] in the future will be revealed to the eyes of all." On this,

see Weiss, "Ha-Determinism Ha-Dati le R. Mordecai Joseph of Izbica," *Sefer Yovel shel Yizhak Baer* (1964), 499ff. I would add that the phrase "man's eyes" in Weiss's statement refers to those who carry the spiritual inheritance of Ephraim (Joseph).

10. See Morris Faierstein, *All Is in the Hands of Heaven,* 53, n.52.

11. See Zohar 1.136b and 3.62b where Simeon is seen either as deficient or as the embodiment of harsh judgment *(dine' kashia),* partially as the result of his active participation in revenge in the aftermath of the rape of his sister Dina in Genesis. This is viewed as a reason that Simeon does not receive an explicit blessing in the Torah, as did all of his brothers. Cf. *Tiferet Hanokhi,* 2b.

12. *Mei Ha-Shiloah,* vol. 1, 66d. Compare with R. Gershon Henokh's rendering in *Tiferet Hanokhi.* The reference to Genesis (25:28) can be found in *Mei Ha-Shiloah,* vol. 1, 10b. It is interesting to note that R. Mordecai Joseph is far more willing to acknowledge the viability and authenticity of Isaac's love for Jacob than most commentators and translators. For example, R. Hezekiah ben Manoah (Hizkuni) and R. David Kimha (Radak) on Genesis 25:28 both attempt to soften Isaac's love for Esau, making it conditional and diminishing. Onkelos translates the Hebrew *"veye'ehav"* as *"u'rahaim,"* which implies tolerance or mercy rather than love. This seems to be the base text for the *JPS Tanakh*'s translation of love as "favored," a status that also implies conditionality. In *Mei Ha-Shiloah,* Isaac's love for Esau was authentic and would have remained intact if Esau's actions were an accurate exemplification of his internal nature. It was Esau's deceptive personality, an insight R. Mordecai Joseph draws from rabbinic literature, that falsifies Isaac's initial love for his son.

13. See Faierstein, *All Is in the Hands of Heaven,* 44–51.

14. For a depiction of free will as the embodiment of the bones of Joseph, see *Sod Yesharim on the Festivals,* "Pesach," 78c/d. "The *behira* [choice] of Israel is called the 'bones of Joseph.'" This idea is developed around the notion of doubt. That is, doubt is a necessary prerequisite of free will. It is the tension of living in doubt (free will), yet knowing that one's holiness is not contingent upon choice, that distinguished Israel as a unique nation. Moses taking the bones of Joseph with him out of Egypt teaches this lesson.

15. *Mei Ha-Shiloah,* vol. 1, 10 b/c. Cf. *Beit Ya'akov to Genesis,* "parshat Toldot," 36.

16. The Lurianic tradition views the incident with Dina and Schem as fulfilling what could have happened if Leah had married Esau. Leah is likened to the first Eve, who was rejected by Adam because she contained elements of evil in need of repair. Her daughter Dina inherits Leah's spiritual makeup. Jacob, who physically and spiritually resembled Adam, was never attracted to Leah (Genesis 29:17, 31) but only Rachel (who is likened to Eve in Genesis). Leah purifies herself through her tears and repentance and is thus fit to marry Jacob. But, the Lurianic tradition relates, "Dina took Leah's place to marry Esau. However Jacob concealed her in a box, an action for which he was punished [Genesis Rabba 76:9]. She was fit to marry him and through her, he [Esau] would have been fixed for he still had

sparks of holiness [which could have been redeemed—my addition]." *"Ma'amar Pesiuto shel Avraham Avinu,"* in *Ketavim Hadashim shel R. Hayyim Vital* (1989), 11. Both Esau and Schem ben Hamor are likened to the serpent in Genesis 3. Hence Jacob, having ruined the chance to redeem the holy sparks of his brother, was uncharacteristically ambivalent about Dina's encounter with Schem ben Hamor and chastised his sons for their violent reaction. Apparently this reading is based on the fact that Jacob's final encounter with Esau in Genesis 33 and his realization that Esau cannot be purified is immediately followed by the Dina incident (Genesis 34: 1–30). On Leah as the first Eve, see R. Meir Poppers, *Likkutei Torah,* 7b, 8a.

17. The unique quality of the tribe of Judah is developed by R. Jacob Lainer in *Beit Ya'akov Ha-Kolel,* 40d, in his comment on Numbers 7:13: "In every tribe, the tribe elects the chief. . . . In the tribe of Judah Nahshon son of Aminadav [its chief] was the foundation [of the tribe and not its appointed leader], from whom arose the Davidic/messianic dynasty [Samuel 27:11]. Hence, in Judah, there was no appointment of a chief by the tribe. Rather, the tribe was elevated by means of the chief [Nahshon son of Aminadav]."

18. This Talmudic passage is developed in quite a different way by R. Hayyim of Volozhin to support his position on the superior status of Torah study. See for example *Nefesh Ha-Hayyim,* 4:20.

19. *Sod Yesharim on the Torah,* 87a/b. This statement is based on *Mei Ha-Shiloah,* vol. 1, 22b where R. Mordecai Joseph uses the decision of Moses to carry out the bones of Joseph as an expression of his doubt concerning the merit of the Jews to rid themselves of the Egyptians. Joseph here represents the trait of "fear of God" which Moses utilized to counter the doubt he felt about the Exodus.

20. Tikkunei Zohar, Introduction, 7b. This is developed in Lurianic Kabbala to mean that the female emanation (from *parzuf imma*) only reaches the *sephirah* of *hod.* Therefore, *yesod* has the positive characteristic of being the first moment where the male dimension (of *parzuf abba*) is revealed. Yet, it is also the first *sephirah,* which lacks the female emanation and is thus referred to as "orphaned."

21. On this, see Genesis Rabba 100:8, the Theodore/Albeck edition, 1292, 1293; and Midrash Tanhuma to Genesis 24. These midrashim suggest that as long as Jacob was alive, there was a sense of unity among the brothers. Once he died, the recognition of a common source and thus a common goal was lost.

22. As discussed in the last chapter, according to Luria, the influx of *imma* into *zeir anpin* only extends to *hod* of *zeir anpin.* Therefore, *yesod* is void or empty of the influence of *imma* and thus orphaned.

23. *Sod Yesharim on the Torah,* 87b. Cf. Zohar 1.150b.

24. The notion that the unique character of the exile of Egypt was in the unconsciousness of the Jews' awareness of being in exile is common in the midrashic tradition and in Lurianic Kabbala. See *Sha'ar Ha-Kavannot,* "Pesah," 1.79bff; and *Sha'ar Ha-Pesukim,* 20bff. For an example in Hasidism, see *Maggid Devarav Le-Ya'akov,* no. 7.7a. R. Mordecai Joseph expresses this same idea in his reading of the plague of darkness. He suggests that those Jews killed in the plague, according to

the midrash, were destroyed because they did not want to leave. Their doubts were rooted in the initial doubt of Abraham regarding his attempt to save Sodom. This doubt, which Abraham overcame with his intuition and faith, remained in the Jewish psyche until the Exodus. These individuals were an extreme type of the Joseph/Ephraim soul, limited to their empirical, naturalistic viewpoint and thus unable to integrate the miracles of the Red Sea and Sinai. See *Mei Ha-Shiloah,* vol. 1, 21b. Cf. R. Jacob Lainer, *Sefer Ha-Zemanim,* 62.

25. *Sod Yesharim Tinyana,* 116a.

26. Ibid., 116b.

27. See *Sod Yesharim on the Torah,* 108–9.

28. The parallels between Judah and Moses are common in both *Mei Ha-Shiloah* and *Sod Yesharim.* As we will see later in this chapter, the response of Moses when confronted about Zimri's sin is reflective of Judah's conflict with Ephraim and his confrontation with Joseph.

29. There are two tangential points worth noting here. First, the depiction of Joseph as *yesod* (the symbolic representation of the phallus) is significant in that the theosophic Kabbalistic tradition views the physical act of circumcision, particularly the act of *priah* or uncovering the corona of the phallus, as the quintessential redemptive act. In fact, the mitzvah of circumcision is seen to embody the entire larger framework of the 613 mitzvot. Judah's confrontation with Joseph is likened to the act of circumcision where the concealed identity of Joseph is revealed, enabling Jacob to descend into Egypt with the remnant of Israel and then be redeemed via Moses. See David J. Halperin, "A Sexual Image in Hekhalot Rabbati and Its Implication," *Jerusalem Studies in Jewish Thought* 6, nos. 1–2 (1987), esp. 120.

30. On Abrabanel and messianism, see Eric Lawee, "'Israel Has No Messiah,' in Late Medieval Spain," in *The Journal of Jewish Thought and Philosophy* 5 (1996): 245–79.

31. At first blush this reading resonates with Sabbatean doctrine, particularly regarding the notion of "redemption through sin" as Scholem presents it in his classic article on the subject. However, Izbica/Radzin Hasidism avoids the Sabbatean move in various ways. First, such a theoretical construct is never implemented, at least to our knowledge. Second, such activity was only legitimate for those who had the messianic soul, as it were, and not for those with the soul of Joseph or Ephraim. Finally, the transgressive act was not theoretically permitted as "sin" but rather as an attempt to challenge the conventional notion of halakha as containing the sum-total of divine will.

32. See *Mei Ha-Shiloah,* vol. 1, 16b, 17a. Although R. Mordecai Joseph suggests that, in the redemptive world, we will see how everything was the will of God, he stresses that Judah takes this position, i.e., "all is in the hands of heaven even the fear of heaven," even before redemption (in the biblical context, the Exodus). Judah is the redemptive personality living in the preredemptive world and is thus subject to suspicion and scorn by the preredemptive lineage of Isaac, Joseph, Ephraim, and

Rabbi Akiba. See also *Sod Yesharim on the Festivals,* "Pesach," 2b. Weiss uses this general idea to draw an important distinction in his reading of Izbica between messianism and anarchism: "In other words, religious anarchism in pre-eschatological history can be defined, as to its psychological character, as the occasional inroad of the absolute determinist character of the messianic age into the present premessianic world." See Joseph Weiss, *Studies in Eastern European Jewish Mysticism,* 242.

33. Both Rashi and R. David Kimhi (Radak), ad loc., advocate this position. Nahmanides rejects it as pure conjecture by stating, "The sin is never mentioned with Er just as it is not mentioned with his brother [Onan]."

34. The claim here of the adverbial form of devekut is debatable. It could be argued that devekut is not the description of the experience at all but rather the experience itself. That is, is devekut a term that collapses the object and subject by making one identical to the other? A scholarly study on the grammatical permutations of devekut in Hasidism has yet to be done. For some preliminary remarks see Gershom Scholem, "Devekut or Communion with God," in his *The Messianic Idea in Judaism* (1971), 203–27; and Miles Krassen, *Uniter of Heaven and Earth* (1998), 43–79.

35. The notion of semen as originating in the brain was common in the Middle Ages and adopted by the Zohar as well as other medieval Kabbalistic texts. Thus the Zohar 1.15a, 2.2a, calls the *sephirah da'at* the "higher phallus." On this, see *Gershom Scholem's Annotated Zohar* (1992), 1512; and Elliot R. Wolfson, *Through a Speculum That Shines,* 389, n.236. This is also what underlies R. Hayyim Vital's interpretation of the Kabbalistic notion of masculine and feminine waters *(mayyim dekhurin* and *mayyim nukvin)* in Vital's *Shar'ar Ma'amrei Rashbi,* 33c, and more explicitly 35d–36b. Cf. the early Lurianic text *Ma'amar Pesiutav shel Avraham Avinu,* 25, reprinted in *Ketavim Hadashim shel R. Hayyim Vital.* "The acronym of the word *kav* signifies *kedusha* [holiness] and *berakha* [blessing]. This means that the [seminal] drop which is drawn from the brain [*moah*] which is *hokhma,* is called *kodesh,* as is known. When it descends to *yesod* [the phallus] it is called *barukh.*" On this phenomenon as it relates to gender transformation in Lurianic Kabbala, see Elliot R. Wolfson, "Coronation of the Sabbath Bride: Kabbalistic Myth and the Ritual of Androgynisation," *Journal of Jewish Thought and Philosophy* 6 (1997): 320, n.60. For the general theory of spermogenesis in the Middle Ages see D. Jacqart and C. Thomasset, *Sexuality and Medicine in the Middle Ages,* M. Adamson, trans. (1988), 53f. For the use of this motif in later Hasidic writing, see my "Modernity as Heresy: The Introvertive Piety of Faith in R. Arele Roth's *Shomer Emunim,*" *Jewish Studies Quarterly* 4 (1996): 88, n.58.

36. *Mei Ha-Shiloah,* vol. 1, 15d, 16a.

37. Ibid., "The notion of the sin of Er can be explained in light of Jacob's request to live in tranquility, i.e., to be guarded against doubt. This, however, was not the will of God in this world" (b.T. Moed Katan 29a). Jacob also embodied this deficiency but in Jacob it was only in his divine service *(avodah).* However,

when this trait filters down into physical actions, it becomes explicit sin. This is true of all the problematic thoughts of the patriarchs. When they are in the minds of the patriarchs (combined with many other traits) these thoughts are quite small. However, when God chooses to create an individual out of that (problematic) thought, the inevitable will happen. See also *Mei Ha-Shiloah,* vol. 1, 3b, 4a; and 31a, 31b.

38. The later Hasidic correlation between Nadav and Avihu and Er and Onan is rooted in the Lurianic correlation of both sets of characters to Cain and Abel, the sons of Adam. In the Lurianic material this is complimented by the addition of Perez and Zerah, the sons of Judah and Tamar (one of whom becomes the beginning of the messianic lineage) coupled with Ruth and Boaz (the origin of the Davidic kingdom). This is finally filtered down into Shilo and Moses, "both of who together equal the numerical value of *Moshiah ben Dovid* [the Davidic Messiah] who is called Shilo. We also find that Moses is the secret of Messiah." See R. Meir Poppers, *Likkutei Torah* (1880), 50b, 51a. On Nadav and Avihu, see ibid., 71b–74a.

39. See Maimonides, *Mishneh Torah,* "Hilkhot Yesodei Ha-Torah," 7:6; and idem, *Guide* 3:33.

40. See Zohar 1.21b, 22a, 111, 187a; and the discussion in Liebes, "Myth versus Symbol in the Zohar and in Lurianic Kabbala," in *Essential Papers on Kabbala,* Lawrence Fine, ed. (1995), 213–16. Both Moses and Jacob are considered representations of *tiferet* (at least in the Zohar) and thus mates of the *Shekhina (malkhut).* Yet Jacob has two earthly wives while Moses has none (after separating from Zipporah). Moses is thus seen on a higher level since he had no corporeal mate at all, only cohabiting with the supernal realm of *Shekhina.* Hence, Moses is understood as the "inner aspect" of Jacob. In R. Gershon Henokh's mind this may be understood as Moses completing the reconciliation that Jacob began.

41. See R. Hayyim Vital, *Sha'ar Ha-Gilgulim,* Introduction 36, 181aff; and *Likkutei Torah,* "parshat vayashev," 44a–48a. This also may reflect a common Zoharic theme that the death of certain evolved individuals is the *tikun* that facilitates redemption. For a discussion of this in the Zohar, see Liebes, *Studies in the Zohar* (1993), esp. 63–65. The connection between *gilgul* and *yibum* (levirate marriage) is a central doctrine in the Zohar, specifically in *Sabba d'Mishpatim* (Zohar 2.94b–114a). The idea that the souls of Er and Onan would be reincarnated through the illicit relationship of Judah and Tamar is very much in line with Zoharic and later Lurianic thinking. See for example R. Jacob Zemah, *Zohar Ha-Rakiya* (1875), 97a. See the discussion in Pinhas Giller, *Reading the Zohar,* esp. 54–57. Cf. Mikhal Oron, "Lines of Influence in the Doctrine of Soul and Reincarnation in Thirteenth-Century Kabbala and the Worlds of R. Todros Abulafia" (in Hebrew), in *Studies in Jewish Thought,* Sara O. Heller-Wilensky and Moshe Idel, eds. (1989), 277–90.

42. See b.T. Sotah 10b. This Talmudic passage raises some serious questions on its own. First of all, in the Bible this assertion is made by Judah and not by God.

According to the Talmud's "intentional misreading," God asserts that the birth of Perez and Zerah are from Him and not Judah. This reading of the verse in b.T. Sotah is almost identical to the Targum Yerushalmi. R. Mordecai Joseph merely connects this obscure Talmudic discussion to the assertion in Lurianic Kabbala that Er and Onan were reincarnated in Perez and Zerah and adds on his own that this was due to the fact that Er's sin was actually a yearning for purity and devekut and not inappropriate behavior.

43. We have discussed in a previous chapter how Maimonides uses this verse. Another interpretation is suggested in *Zava'at Ha-Ribash* (repr., 1975) (collected sayings of the Baal Shem Tov and the Maggid of Mezeritch), 12. This suggestion implies that sometimes a mitzvah contains within it an element of sin. One should be careful not to refrain from performing such a mitzvah in an attempt to avoid the sin within it.

44. *Mei Ha-Shiloah,* vol. 1, 16a.

45. Thus Rashi, citing b.T. Yebamot 34b, is given little choice but to integrate the rabbinic reading connecting Onan's sin with Er's as the simple meaning of the text. Moreover, Rashi is able to integrate the added dimension of giving a reason why Er would not have sex with Tamar, a reason that has absolutely no basis in the text. The Zohar at least draws a linguistic connection between the word "evil" in reference to Er's actions and the same word in reference to the inappropriate sexual behavior of the generation of the flood.

46. B.T. Menahot 29b; midrash Bamidbar Rabba 19:6. Although I have not found any significant remark of Rabbi Akiba being referred to here as Akiba son of Joseph in either *Mei Ha-Shiloah* or *Sod Yesharim,* both read the midrash as reflecting the antagonistic confrontation between Judah and Joseph, Moses taking the part of Judah and Akiba of Joseph. For a possible precedent to the position taken here by Mordecai Joseph, see R. Menahem Mendel of Kotzk, *Emet ve Emunah* (1972), 28.

47. See also b.T. Shabbat 88b and 89a. For the mystical source of R. Akiba being substituted for Moses, see *Hekhalot Zutarti,* Rachel Elior's critical edition from MS New York 8128 in *Mekharei Yerushalayim, first supplement* (1982): lines 9, 21, 55. Cf. R. Yizhak Isik Yehuda Safrin, *Siddur Komarno,* 300, "One who is from the root of Cain . . . can elevate [divine light] from the *gevurah* of *atik* which is the secret of the 'concealed wisdom' [*hokhma setimah*] of *arikh* [*anpin*] and draw light from that source [above]. One who is [from the root] of Abel is from the *hasadim*. From this we learn that which was revealed to R. Akiba that was not revealed to Moses. This is what Moses meant when he said to God, 'You have a man like this and you are revealing the Torah through me?!' [b.T. Menahot 29b]. Behold, R. Akiba was able to apprehend that which Moses could not." Cf. Vital, *Sha'ar Mamrei Razal,* 15a.

48. See Liebes, "Myth versus Symbol," 23, 233; and Vital, *Sha'ar Ha-Kavannot,* 48 a/c. Luria places R. Akiba on a higher plane than Moses, using these figures as embodiments of the oral (Akiba) and written (Mosaic) law. On this see

Sefer Ha-Gilgulim, intro. 28, 76–77. According to Liebes, "This idea of the supremacy of the oral over written law is, I believe, an innovation of the Ari's, for, in ordinary Kabbalistic symbolism, the Oral Law represents the *Shekhina,* while the source of the Written Law is *Tiferet*" ("Myth versus Symbol," 232). Cf. R. Menahem Azaria da Fano, *"Ma'mar Yonat 'Elam,"* reprinted in *Ma'amarei Ha-RaMa,* 2 vols. (1997), vol. 1, 2a. In our Hasidic doctrine, it is Moses who reigns supreme, the messianic figure who overcomes the Oral Law (R. Akiba) and reinstates the written law, albeit in a new way. The oral law is viewed as the "law of exile" which, when completed, results in its own demise.

49. The portrayal of Moses as one unable to adequately understand (1) the people's difficulty in accepting revelation, and (2) the need for legal safeguards, is not new here. In his commentary to the Torah, Nahmanides offers such a portrait of Moses in his comments on Joshua's protest against Eldad and Medad in Numbers 11:28 when he says, "*Would that all the people of the Eternal were prophets, that the eternal would give His spirit upon them* [11:29] for God put His spirit directly upon them without taking of the spirit which was upon me, and this would happen to all the people." Nahmanides concludes his comment by saying, "But Moses answered [Joshua by saying] that he should not be zealous for his sake, for he wishes that they prophesy whether in his presence or outside it, since God had put His spirit upon them, either by transmission from Moses or [directly from God] without such a transition." See *Perush Ha-Ramban 'al Ha-Torah,* Charles B. Chavel, ed. (1960), vol. 2, 237–38. This comment suggests Moses' intolerance of Joshua's attempt to limit prophecy to any particular place or person. Moses, as a prophet, welcomed the notion of a nation of prophets. Relevant to our discussion, the apparent confrontation between Joshua and Moses in Numbers reflects the general conflict between Judah and Joseph beginning in Genesis. In Izbica/Radzin Hasidism, Joshua is placed among the spiritual descendants of Joseph, unable to comprehend the desire for an apprehension of the divine will (here depicted as prophecy).

50. See Northrop Frye, *The Great Code* (1982), 180–81

51. *Mei Ha-Shiloah,* vol. 1, 11a. This idea is elaborated in the third section of *Mei Ha-Shiloah* known as the *gilyon* (additional gloss). See *Mei Ha-Shiloah,* vol. 2, 68b. It is unclear who is the author of these additions. The present Radziner Rebbe in Brooklyn, R. Jacob Lainer, suggested that these additions were actually written by R. Gershon Henokh and constitute the beginning of his commentary to *Mei Ha-Shiloah* that he mentions writing but apparently never finished.

52. This common depiction of Moses reflects that of Maimonides who, in his discussion on prophecy, suggests that only Moses was able to unify, as it were, his imaginative faculty with his intellect. See *Mishneh Torah,* "Hilkhot Yesode Ha-Torah," 7; *Guide* 2:32; and *Commentary to the Mishna,* "Introduction to Sanhedrin Chapter 10," seventh article of faith.

53. Cf. Vital, *Sha'ar Mamrei Razal* (1862), 15b, "He [Moses] knew the entire Torah but his knowledge of it was *from his mouth* [*b'al peh,*] he didn't know how to

draw out such knowledge via Scripture." Cf. R. Jacob Joseph of Polnoy, *Ketonet Passim* [on Leviticus 1:1] (1884), 1b. Cf. Gedalyahu Nigal's critical edition with introduction and notes (1985), 2–3.

54. See *Mei Ha-Shiloah,* vol. 1, 51d, 52a.

55. The reference to Tikkunei Zohar, *tikun* 13, is only a small fragment of a larger discussion on the difference between Moses and Jacob. See *Sod Yesharim on the Torah,* 80b, 81a, "In the case of Moses, there was no distinction between the outside [lit., garment] and the inside. With Jacob, even though he internally had the same light as Moses, the light did not appear externally. This is why he wanted to return to gather the *small vessels* before crossing the Jabbok ford. The word *Ya'bok* [Jabbok] hints to a completion [a full spelling] of all the divine permutations of the YHVH, equaling 72 (AV), 63 (SaG), 45 (MaH), and 52 (BeN). He wanted the internal light to break through [its barriers] and enlighten even the exterior in order for him to reach in and reveal even the innermost light." Cf. Vital, *Sha'ar Mamrei Hazal,* 15c. For a description of the four permutations of the divine name see Vital, *'Ozrot Hayyim,* 1b and 1c.

56. Midrash Tanhuma, parshat *Zav,* 8: *"God spoke to Moses saying, 'take Aaron and his sons and the garments. . . .'* This is what is written, *[h]appy is the one who You choose and bring near to dwell in Your courts* [Psalms 65:5]. Happy is the one who is chosen even though he does not come near. Happy is the one who comes near even though he is not chosen. Who is the one who is chosen—this is Abraham. He was not brought near but he brought himself near, as it is written, *You are the Lord God, who chose Abram, who brought him out of the Ur of the Chaldeans and changed his name to Abraham* [Nehemiah 9:7]. Jacob was chosen by God, as it is written, *Jacob, whom I have chosen* [Isaiah 41:8]. But Jacob was not drawn near, he drew himself near as it is written, *Jacob was a mild man, who sat in the tent [of study]* [Genesis 25:27] (. . . . Moses was chosen but was not drawn close, as it says . . . *had not Moses His chosen one confronted him in the breach* [Psalm 106:23]). . . . Happy is Aaron 'the doubler' who was chosen and also was drawn close. How do we know that he was chosen? As it is written, *A man of God came to Eli and said to him 'Thus says the Lord: Lo, I revealed myself to your father's house in Egypt when they were tribes of Israel to be my priests . . .'* [Samuel 12:27]. How do we know that he was drawn close? As it is written, *bring near to you, Aaron your brother.*"

57. R. Mordecai Joseph seems to be intentionally misreading the midrash as cited above. The embodiment of "being drawn close and yet not being chosen" is Jethro and Rahav. "Happy are those who draw near and are not chosen. Come and see: Jethro was drawn close yet not chosen and Rahav the Zoneh whom God drew close but did not choose" (*Mei Ha-Shiloah,* vol. 2, 276b). In fact Aaron is the one figure who embodies both, as cited in the previous note. The dichotomy above should have been between Moses and Jethro, not Moses and Aaron. However, in the context of trying to justify the need for independent heads of tribes, R. Mordecai Joseph needed to juxtapose Moses and Aaron as one who was drawn close by choosing God. The way in which he reads this into the midrash remains unclear.

58. *Mei Ha-Shiloah,* vol. 2, 27c.

59. On this see R. Samuel Eliezer Ha-Levi Idlish (MaHaRSha), "Commentary to the Aggadot" to b.T. Makkot, fol. 23b, 4d, in standard editions.

60. *Mei Ha-Shiloah,* vol. 1, 22b. The notion stated here that the negative commandments merely constitute a framework for assuring that one's energy is not exhausted on the search for holiness is adopted by R. Gershon Henokh in his *Sod Yesharim on the Torah,* 43b, "The fundamental principle of negative commandments is only to focus one's spiritual strength so as to not exhaust and nullify one's energy for the glory of God and the greatness of awe."

61. See p. T. Peah, 9b.

62. R. Hayyim Vital, *Sha'ar Mamrei Razal,* 15b.

63. See for example in b.T. Baba Batra 12a; and Ephrayim Urbach, "Halakha u Nevuah," *Tarbiz 18* (1974): 9.

64. Scholem, *On the Kabbala and Its Symbolism* (1965), 21. Cf. ibid., 22, "It is the mystical experience which conceives and gives birth to authority."

65. *Halakha l'Moshe m'Sinai* is a complex idea in rabbinic tradition. One oft-cited source is Sifra on Numbers, end of chapter 8. Cf. Shmuel Safrai, "*Halakha l'Moshe m'Sinai:* History or Theology" (in Hebrew), *Mekharei Talmud,* J. Sussman and D. Rosenthal, eds. (1990), 11–38. Cf. David Weiss Ha-Livni, *Revelation Restored* (1997), 54–75 and 96, n.5. My assessment here is merely to highlight the way *Mei Ha-Shiloah* uses it as a nonexegetical (and thus nonrabbinic) source for law.

66. The polemical agenda of Vital is illustrated most prominently in his introduction to *Sha'ar Ha-Hakdamot,* printed as the introduction of *Etz Hayyim.* In that lengthy introduction Vital reiterates, and even deepens, the polemical stance of Tikkunei Zohar in its juxtaposition of the "masters of the Mishna" and the "masters of the Kabbala." Cf. Pinhas Giller, *The Enlightened Will Shine,* 59–90.

67. Shlomo Zalman Shragai devotes a whole section to his work on Izbica/Radzin Hasidism to exhibit the precedent for Mordecai Joseph's radical interpretation. See his *B'Netive Hasidut Izbica/Radzin* (1972), vol. 2, 81–99. As well, R. Yeruham Lainer, in his gloss on *Mei Ha-Shiloah,* also devotes a large comment attempting to find earlier precedents for seeing Zimri as R. Mordecai Joseph sees him. See *Mei Ha-Shiloah,* vol. 1, 54. The two most well-known and perhaps most influential sources for R. Mordecai Joseph appear in R. Hayyim Vital's claim that Zimri and Kozbi the daughter of Zur were destined for marriage from the sixth day of creation. In the introduction to R. Abraham Azulai's *Hesed Le-Avraham* (following a tradition attributed to R. Hayyim Vital), it is stated that Zimri was reincarnated as Rabbi Akiba. The second source is found in R. Yonatan Eyebshutz, *Tiferet Yonatan* (repr., 1974), 117b, 118a, "Regarding Zimri, it was revealed through prophecy that one of the heads of the tribes of Israel would take a woman from the seed of the Nations and give birth to a child which would lift [cleanse] the guilt from the Moabite people. Therefore, [Zimri] took Kozbi from who would go out a 'striking stone' to Moab. In truth [Zimri] made a mistake as it says in the Rambam that a judge is like a prince [the head of a tribe] in all matters but

only the prince of a tribe and not the prince [head] of a family. . . . Thus it was from heaven that a prince [of a tribe] would marry the daughter of a king of the Nations. However, Zimri was only the head of a family and thus not fit for this purpose." I would like to thank Alan Brill for pointing out this reference. Although this does suggest that the activity of Zimri was intended to fulfill a divine decree, it disregards the part Moses plays in the drama that is significant in R. Mordecai Joseph's depiction. This biblical story is also used to promulgate ultra-Orthodox ideology in nineteenth-century Hungarian Jewry. See for example in R. Israel David Margoliot-Jaffe's responsa, *Meholat Ha-Mahanaim* (1859), 3b. There Zimri is depicted as the "reformer" or one who "question(s) and ask(s) for clear-cut answers why it is forbidden to transplant customs of another religion into the vineyard of Israel." This refers to the fact that no explicit prohibition against having conjugal relations with a Midianite woman appears in the Torah until this event. Cf. the discussion in Michael K. Silber, "The Emergence of Ultra-Orthodoxy: The Invention of a Tradition," in *The Uses of Tradition: Jewish Continuity in the Modern Era,* J. Wertheimer, ed. (1992), 54 f. I used Silber's translation of the responsa in the above citation.

68. See b.T. Sanhedrin 82a. See also Rashi on Numbers 25:7.

69. The connection between Pinhas and Joseph is based on the Lurianic position of Pinhas having the reincarnated soul of Joseph, among others. See Vital, *Sefer Ha-Gilgulim,* intro. 35, 71, and 72.

70. The source in Lurianic Kabbala is *"Ma'amar Pesiuto shel Avraham Avinu,"* reprinted in *Ketavim Hadashim l'Rabbenu Hayyim Vital* (1988), no. 45, 12. This essay has a dubious history. It first appeared in print in Vital's *Sha'ar Mamrei Hazal* (1959), beginning from 9a, and many thought it was written by Vital himself. Scholars have determined that it originated in R. Meir Poppers's *Nof Etz Hayyim,* printed in Krakow in 1650. Poppers claims that Luria wrote it himself. The attribution to Vital, however, is found in various places in the generations following Poppers. Cf. R. Moses Hayyim Luzatto, *Ma'amar Ha-Vikuah,* 36. This fragment traces the genealogy of Zimri, who is identified as an incarnation of Shaul, son of the Canaanite, and Shlumiel, son of Zurishadai. Zimri was thus the son of Shimon and Dina. Shimon is called *Shem Avon* (the name of the sin). Both he and Dina were from the side of severe *gevurah.* Thus Zimri was infected with the poison of sin and was thus attracted to Kozbi, who was also infected. The text continues, "She [Kozbi] was his [Zimri's] soul mate except that she [or they] had eaten inappropriate food and thus was [were] not fit [for the encounter]." The next paragraph warns the reader that such an interpretation will be "strange to those who hear it." However, the text argues, with the proper preliminary foundations, it can be understood.

71. For an alternative interpretation as to why Moses could not judge Zimri, see Sifri Bamidbar, the end of parshat Balak. Cf. R. Bahya ben Asher, *Rabbenu Bahya 'al Ha-Torah,* C. Chavel, ed. (1994), vol. 2, 183–84; and R. Hayyim Vital's gloss to Zohar 3.205b in *Nizuzei Zohar* 2. This midrashic reading above that

Zimri's encounter with Kozbi was a direct challenge to Moses' marriage to Zipporah, a Midianite woman, is also mentioned in R. Yonatan Eyebshutz's *Tiferet Yonatan,* 119a, even as he seems to adopt the Lurianic position in his discussion of the Zimri/Kozbi episode.

72. R. Mordecai Joseph is utilizing the trope of *"na'ar"* or innocent one, which refers in the biblical narrative to Joseph (Genesis 37:2) to correlate the spiritual lineage of Joseph to the biblical figure Pinhas. This notion of innocence is also the justification for God's love for Pinhas as expressed in Numbers 25:11–12. Immediately following the verse describing Joseph as *"na'ar"* we read "[*a*]*nd Israel loved Joseph best from all of his sons*" (Genesis 37:3). The conclusion of this verse where Israel's love for Joseph is likened to Abraham's love for Isaac *(for he was the child of his old age)* is also important. God rewards Pinhas for his actions because, according to R. Mordecai Joseph, he was a *"na'ar"* and "could not see the depth of the matter." This is also the case with the Joseph/Ephraim lineage being unable to justify the actions of Judah discussed earlier and finally the inability of Isaac to see clearly the superiority of his son Jacob over Esau. R. Mordecai Joseph uses a biblical reference from Hosea 11:1, *I fell in love with Israel, when he was still a child "na'ar"* to liken the love of God for Pinhas to that of Joseph and Isaac. The reward each received was not for their actions per se but rather for maximizing their potential as premessianic figures unable to see divine will beyond the confines of halakha.

73. *Mei Ha-Shiloah,* vol. 1, 54 a/b. The translation begins four lines from the bottom of 45a. Cf. R. Jacob Lainer, *Beit Ya'akov Ha-Kollel,* 47b; and R. Zaddok Ha-Kohen, *Takanat Ha-Shavim,* 20a, 25b. R. Zaddok cites *Tiferet Yonatan,* cited above. He then continues, "In truth they depended on the fact that they had spent 40 years in the desert engaged in Torah, *avodah,* and the eating of the manna and that their bodies were completely purified. They consumed [lit., swallowed] the words of Torah in their bodies as the rabbis say, 'They recognized in themselves that they were pure from any desire and that the occurrence of a sin of a sexual nature would be impossible without it being the will of God.'"

74. See *Ma'amar Pesiuto shel Avraham Avinu,* 45.

75. The motif of the Gentile who sincerely desires the Israelite appears in numerous places in R. Zaddok Ha-Kohen's writings. Cf. *Takanat Ha-Shavim,* 20a/b. Speaking about the Kabbalistic term *kelipat nogah* (redeemable evil), R. Zaddok says, "Their dominion [the *kelipat nogah*] is with the souls of Israel. They do not convert . . . nevertheless they have a desire to bond with Israel. This is exemplified in the sexual impropriety of the Moabite daughters, as R. Yonatan Eyebshutz explains in *Tiferet Yonatan.*"

76. The notion that a child can be the outgrowth not only of the two sexual partners but of previous sexual partners of the woman bearing the child is common in Lurianic Kabbala. We see that Lurianic Kabbalists, interpreting Zohar 3.231a, view Cain [and to a lesser extent Abel] as the child of both Adam and the serpent, who inseminated Eve earlier. Thus Cain and Abel, containing the

admixture of good and evil, are reflections of the Tree of Knowledge, their birth being the product of the consumption of the tree. It is only Seth, conceived and born outside the Garden, who is solely the product of Adam and Eve. See Vital, *Likkutei Torah,* 18a.

77. *Mei Ha-Shiloah,* vol. 1, 13–14.

78. *Shimon and Levi are a pair; their weapons are a tool of lawlessness. Let not my person be included in their council, let not my being be counted in their assembly. For when* [*men are*] *angry, they slay men, and when pleased, they maim oxen. Cursed be anger so fierce. And their wrath so relentless. I will divide Jacob. Scatter them in Israel* [Genesis 49:5–7].

79. Zohar 1.141a.

80. This means that Judah has overcome the bifurcation of the human heart resulting from the sin of Adam and Eve, between the good and evil inclination. He sees indeed that no distinction exists between the human will and divine will. Cf. *Sod Yesharim on the Torah,* 7b.

81. *Mei Ha-Shiloah,* vol. 1, 66d.

82. I think this text renders "the seed of Jacob" from three different perspectives. The initial use of the term is to exclude Esau. The second, I believe, is to exclude those who are not from the lineage of Judah, that is, those who have not inherited the integrated (messianic) personality of Jacob. Those like Judah and Moses, who have inherited this lineage, can enter into the realm of doubt precisely because they understand via experience that everything is ultimately from God, even, as we saw earlier via Moses, the motivation for divine worship. The third usage is the conventional meaning of the Israelite nation in general. This usage usually appears when Israel is juxtaposed to the Gentile nations.

83. Cf. *Mei Ha-Shiloah,* vol. 2, 14c/d, on the distinction between converts whose intentions are pure and those who are still in need of clarification. Cf. R. Zaddok's discussion of R. Akiba as descended from converts in comparison with Shechem and then Zimri in his *Takanat Ha-Shavim,* 20a.

84. *Mei Ha-Shiloah,* vol. 1, 10c/d. Cf. *Tiferet Ha-Hanokhi,* 2b, on Zohar 1.236a.

85. The term "*na'ar*" more accurately refers to a prepubescent adolescent who is both self-centered and not really in control of his/her actions. A *na'ar* is not innocent in the sense of a baby but not responsible as an adult. See for example Exodus 2:6; and Nahmanides, ad loc.

86. This is Rashi's reading taken from b.T. Sanhedrin, fol. 82a. It is noteworthy that the provocative Izbica/Radzin reading of this biblical episode is maintained solely through reading the biblical text through the lenses of the rabbinic and later exegetical traditions. The attribution of "*na'ar*" to Pinhas and the use of the term "halakha" in this context is possible only through the Sanhedrin text.

87. *Ma'mar Pesiuto shel Avraham* appeared in the first printed edition of *Hesed l'Avraham* in 1685 and subsequent editions. The new Jerusalem edition of *Hesed l'Avraham* does not contain this essay. A new printing of this text appears in *Ketavim Hadashim shel R. Hayyim Vital* (1998).

7. In and Around the Law

1. On this see *Mei Ha-Shiloah,* vol. 1, 14d–15b; and *Beit Ya'akov Ha-Kolel,* 14c–15b.

2. This idea is expressed most explicitly by R. Gershon Henokh in *Sod Yesharim on the Festivals,* "Rosh Ha-Shana," 3b/c.

3. On the use of this term in Sabbatean ideology, see Gershom Scholem, "Redemption Through Sin," in *The Messianic Idea in Judaism* (1971), 86ff; Yehuda Liebes, "Sabbatei Zevi's Religious Faith," in his *Studies in Jewish Myth and Messianism* (1993), 107–13; and idem, *Sod Ha-Emunha Ha-Shabta'it* (1995), 9–19.

4. On the social and political agenda of Hasidism, see Ben Zion Dinur, "The Origins of Hasidism and Its Social and Messianic Foundations," reprinted in *Essential Papers on Hasidism,* Gershon Hundert, ed. (1991), 86–208; and Moshe Rosman, *Founder of Hasidism: A Quest for the Historical Baal Shem Tov* (1996), 11–94.

5. See Gershom Scholem, "Redemption Through Sin," in his *The Messianic Idea in Judaism,* 78–142. For a recent discussion of this essay and its impact on contemporary notions of antinomianism in the study of religion, see Steven M. Wassertrom, *Religion after Religion: Gershom Scholem, Mircea Eliade, and Henry Corbin at Eranos* (1999), 215–24.

6. In this light Hasidism may be fertile ground for Leo Strauss's theory of esoteric writing. As far as I know, no one has yet looked at Hasidism through the Straussean lens. See Leo Strauss, *Persecution and the Art of Writing* (1980), 22–37.

7. For some examples of Philo's position see David Winston, *Philo of Alexandria* (1981), 21–35, 164–74, 267–86. Scholem notes that Philo introduces the notion of law (halakha) as nomos into Judaism. Hellenistic Judaism conceived the law as the supreme expression of Jewish religious distinction. Hence, anything that would threaten the expression of the divine will through the fulfillment of the law would be a challenge to the unequivocal authority of the law. Thus, any religious reform, be it mystical or rational, would by definition contain latent antinomian tendencies. See Scholem's article on antinomianism in *Encyclopedia Judaica,* vol. 1, 67–71.

8. It is important to note here that Philo, who lived in Alexandria before the destruction of the Second Temple, wrote before the development of the rabbinic tradition in Palestine and Babylonia. See Alan Mendelson, "Orthopraxy," in *Philo's Jewish Identity* (1988), 51–76.

9. See Alan F. Segal, *Paul the Convert* (1980), 117, "In Paul's case, the change was from Pharisaism, in which Paul received his education, to a particular kind of gentile community of God-fearers, living without the law, and the change was powered by Paul's absorption into the Spirit." Paul's protestations in Romans 6:1 and 6:15 against defining sin solely as the abrogation of the law appears to be his attempt to distinguish between the law and the will of God. The question of heresy necessitates some kind of orthodoxy.

10. For a discussion of the law in this epistle, see Karl Barth, *The Epistle to the Romans* (1968), 77–90, 107–14; ibid., 143–49. Cf. in Romans 3:21–26, 3:31, 10:4; and Galatians 3:10, 5:4. The connection, if any, between Paul's antinomian streak and the generic antinomianism of early Kabbala has not been adequately researched. In general, Paul's relationship to early rabbinic forms of mysticism is a complex issue. Cf. Alan Segal, "Paul and the Beginning of Jewish Mysticism," in *Death, Ecstasy, and Other Worldly Desires,* J. H. Collins and M. Fishbane, eds. (1995), 95–122. However, both Scholem and Idel argue that antinomianism is a generic part of any mystical tradition that is founded and dependent on principles of law. See Scholem, "Redemption Through Sin," 89, regarding the mysticism of Sabbatai Sevi: "One so favored [with the mystical experience] was in certain respects no longer considered to be subject to the laws of everyday reality, having realized within himself the hidden world of divine light." Although Scholem's position in his "Religious Authority and Mysticism" tends to stress the more conservative character of Jewish mysticism, his conclusion is that by reinterpreting tradition, the mystic is actually transforming tradition to suit the conclusions of his mystical experience.

11. It has been suggested that Paul's antinomianism is the result of his rebellion against the strict nomian doctrine of Pharisaic Judaism. Paul's attempt to "destroy the law by the law" or to establish the law by its abrogation by suggesting the law as the "Torah of Angels" and not the "Torah of God," strikingly resembles the Tikkunei Zohar's distinction between the "Torah of Creation" (halakha) and the "Torah of Emanation" (the pure Torah of spirit).

12. See W. B. Stover, *"A Faire and Easie Way to Heaven": Covenant Theology and Antinomianism in Early Massachusetts* (1978), 161. Cf. John von Rohr, *The Covenant of Grace in Puritan Thought* (1986), 136, "In general, then, the Antinomian position was that the good works of the Christian life were the activity of the Holy Spirit in which the believer took little or no part." Robert Towne (in his *The Assertion of Grace*) spoke of the obedience of Christians as "the work of the Spirit in them; so it is passive to them." Cf. E. F. Kevan, *The Grace of Law: A Study in Puritan Theology* (1964), 220.

13. For an example of this, see the comments of Anne Hutchinson at her trial before the Church of Boston in 1638, in C. H. Adams, *Antinomianism in the Colony of Massachusetts Bay 1637–1638* (1894), 285–336.

14. See John von Rohr, *The Covenant of Grace in Puritan Thought,* 8. The notion that "even faith itself is solely a divine creation" is strikingly similar to R. Mordecai Joseph's reading of the Talmudic dictum, "All is in the hands of heaven except fear of heaven" (b.T. Berakhot 33b): "(All is in the hands of heaven except fear of heaven) is only according to the intellectual limitations of mankind. However, in truth, all is in the hands of heaven even the fear of heaven. It is just that in this world God conceals his ways." See *Mei Ha-Shiloah,* vol. 1, 8b.

15. This last statement became popular among Christian libertine antinomians in the Netherlands in 1525 as well as the more radical versions of Sabbateanism in

Jacob Frank in late-seventeenth- and early-eighteenth-century Germany. Although we will discuss libertinism later in this chapter, it is important to note here that most antinomian ideologues were not concerned with absolving themselves from ethical responsibilities or the adherence to Jewish law. Rather, coupled with a sincere belief in the advent of the messianic era, they could not submit to any authority which conflicted with their experience of sanctification or enlightenment.

16. For a Jewish parallel, see *Mei Ha-Shiloah,* vol. 1, 15b.

17. See Barth, *The Epistle of the Romans,* 107–14.

18. A common justification, known as the "practical syllogism," can be found in the work of J. Wollebius, quoted in Heinrich Heppe's *Dogmatik der evangelisch-reformierten Kirche, dargestellt und aus der Quellen belegt,* Ernst Bizer, ed., 122–23. This work is available in English as *Reform Dogmatics,* G. T. Thomson, trans. (1950). "In ascertaining our election analytically it is necessary to proceed from the means of execution to the degree, beginning from our sanctification, according to the following syllogism: Whoever perceives in himself the gift of sanctification, by which we die to sin and live to righteousness, is justified, calling or endowed with true faith, and elect. But by the grace of God I perceive this. Therefore, I am justified, called and elect" (I used the translation in Stover, 126). The antihalakhic act as fulfilling the will of God in *Mei Ha-Shiloah* raises a similar issue. He states that the personality of Joseph (the purely halakhic personality) can never understand the actions of Judah (the messianic personality) as long as the messianic era of integration has not yet arrived. See *Mei Ha-Shiloah,* vol. 1, 4a, 14d–15a, 57d. See also Morris Faierstein, *All Is in the Hands of Heaven* (1989), 44–48.

19. Nietzsche's thinking comes to mind here. Although Nietzsche often called himself an "amoralist" and is read by some as a nihilist, his disbelief in God and challenge of the religious foundations of ethics is not used as a justification for immorality but a call for a new morality built on human power. See Karen L. Carr, *The Banalization of Nihilism: Twentieth-Century Responses to Meaninglessness* (1992), 25–50; and "Nietzsche and Morality," in *Morality, Culture, and History,* Raymond Guess (1999), 167–98. Cf. Karl Lowith, *Martin Heidegger and European Nihilism,* Richard Wolin, ed. (1995), 192–208.

20. On hypernomianism and Kabbala, see Talya Fishman, "A Kabbalistic Perspective on Gender-Specific Commandments: On the Interplay of Symbols and Society," *AJS Review* 17, no. 2 (1992): 199–245, esp. 241–45; and Elliot R. Wolfson, "Mystical Rationalization of the Commandments in the Prophetic Kabbala of Abraham Abulafia," in *Perspectives on Jewish Thought and Mysticism,* A. Ivry, E. R. Wolfson, and A. Arkush, eds. (1998), 331–81, esp. 345–60. Wolfson argues that most "Jewish antinomianism" is actually hypernomian. A classic example of this (not raised by Wolfson) is the case of wearing two pair of *tefillin* (Rashi and Rabbenu Tam) in Lurianic texts. Although this custom arises from the Zohar (Zohar Hadash, 101d; Zohar 2.43a, 3.258a), in Lurianic texts it became part of the mitzvah of *tefillin* and no longer a voluntary stringency. See for example in R. Hayyim Joseph David Azulai, *Hayyim Sheal* (1792), 3a; and R. Natan Neta Shapira, *Mazat*

Shemurim [Laws of *Tefillin*] (1888), who states, "One who only wears the *tefillin* of Rashi . . . causes a great blemish [in the cosmos]." Cf. Ya'akov Gartner, "The Influence of the Ari on the Custom of Wearing Two Pair of *Tefillin*" (in Hebrew), *Da'at* 28 (1992): 51–64.

21. For an analysis of the debate among the Calvinists and the Armenians on the place of works in the salvation of the believing Christian, see "Covenant and Predestination," in John von Rohr, *The Covenant of Grace in Puritan Thought,* 113–33.

22. See Calvin, *Institutes,* in *Institutes of the Christian Religion,* Henry Beveridge, trans. (1989), vol. 3, 16:1, 98ff.

23. See Calvin, *Institutes,* vol. 3, 16, 98ff: "We are not justified at all without works, for as much as, in the participation in Christ in which our justification resides, sanctification is no less included." On this see François Wendel, *Calvin: The Origins and Development of His Religious Thought* (1950), 263–64.

24. Jonathan Edwards treated this theory in his partial support of the Great Awakening religious revival in New England. For Edwards's treatment of this issue, see *The Works of Jonathan Edwards,* Perry Miller, ed. (1957), vol. 1, 468ff.

25. This stance has precedent in rabbinic literature. See b.T. Rosh Ha-Shana 18b, reading Zechariah 8:19. The Talmud acknowledges that the days of mourning (fast days) will be days of joy and celebration in the future.

26. The notion that, in Judaism, the antinomian portends to fulfill and not abrogate the law was noted by Gershom Scholem in *Major Trends,* 293–94; and most recently by Elliot Wolfson in "Coronation of the Sabbath Bride: Kabbalistic Myth and the Ritual of Androgynisation," *Journal of Jewish Thought and Philosophy* 6 (1997), 301.

27. See, b.T. Niddah 61b, "Mitzvah will be nullified in the future [*l'atid l'vo*]."

28. See Conrad Cherry, *The Theology of Jonathan Edwards* (1966), 187. On Jonathan Edwards's debate with the Armenians and his rejection of neonomianism, see Claude Welch, *Protestant Thought in the Nineteenth Century,* 2 vols. (1972). Cf. Cherry, 186–216; and Welch, vol. 1, 26ff.

29. Although libertine activity is not always the product of an antinomian ideology, antinomianism will often lend itself to libertine actions. See John Dillenberger and Claude Welch, *Protestant Theology: Interpreted Through Its Development* (1954), 83, "The anti-nomians generally were men whose lives, lifted to new heights of achievement by the Gospels, were examples of Christian grace. On the other hand, the lack of concern for standards occasionally led instead to acts of license."

30. It is interesting that Paul, who is sometimes called the "first Jewish antinomian," spoke out very strongly against the libertine threat. Cf. I Corinthians, chaps. 5, 6.

31. See Hans Jonas, *The Gnostic Religion* (1934), vol. 1, 234; and Scholem, "Redemption Through Sin," 133. Jonas develops this further in his essay, "Gnosticism, Existentialism, and Nihilism," in Jonas, *The Phenomenon of Life* (1966), 224–32: "The subversion of the idea of law, or nomos, leads to ethical consequences in which the nihilistic implication of the Gnostic acosmism, and at the same time

the analogy to certain modern reasonings, become even more obvious than in the cosmological aspect. I am thinking of Gnostic antinomianism."

32. See for example in Stover, *"A Faire and Easie Way to Heaven": Covenant Theology and Antinomianism in Early Massachusetts,* 12: "Antinomianism, in short, took all the struggle out of religion by absolving individuals from personal responsibility for the observance that God demands of Christians. By implication, it appealed to people who were impatient of discipline, religiously lukewarm, or in search of an easy assurance of heaven." This is surely not the case for any Hasidic antinomianism, whose adherents were pious individuals hardly looking for an easy way out of divine service. Such a position is perhaps more indicative of the Frankists, whose sexual immorality was viewed as a necessary part of the redemptive process. See for example Gershom Scholem, *Du Frankisme au Jacobinisme,* Marc Bloch Lectures (Paris, 1981).

33. See Robert Cover, "Nomos and Narrative," in *Narrative, Violence and the Law: The Essays of Robert Cover,* M. Minow, M. Ryan, and A. Sarat, eds. (1995), 123, n.76.

34. Therefore, the distinction between Sabbatei Sevi and many of his early disciples and Jacob Frank is important. From written testimony, including letters from his disciple Nathan of Gaza, Sabbatei Sevi was a model of pietism and asceticism. Frank's descent into libertine acts should not be conflated with the pietism and hypernomianism of the Sabbatean movement. On the piety of Nathan of Gaza and early Sabbateanism see Scholem, *Sabbatai Sevi,* 818–20; and E. R. Wolfson, "Coronation of the Sabbath Bride: Kabbalistic Myth and the Ritual of Androgynisation," *Journal of Jewish Thought and Philosophy* 6 (1997): 301–43.

35. This is not true only of those antinomians who rejected the path of libertine behavior. As Tobias Crisp states regarding libertinism (in Works 1:114), "to be called a Libertine, is the gloriousest [*sic*] Title under Heaven, [for a Libertine is] one that is truly free by Christ." This passage was quoted in Kevan, *The Grace of Law: A Study in Puritan Theology,* 244. Although this definition was rejected by most antinomians, particularly the Puritans in America, it is significant to note that being "free" from the law did not necessarily mean that one is free from the adherence to ethical norms.

36. There is a Hasidic tale that a similar thing happened to R. Jacob Isaac Horowitz (the Seer of Lublin). "When the Seer was a young man, he underwent a spiritual trial decreed by heaven. The trial was that he forgot what was forbidden. The principle is that during a spiritual trial, all things that are not achieved through struggle are taken away. Only one thing remained clear to him at that time, the sole thing he achieved via struggle: do not act unless you know that the act will find favor in God's eyes. During this trial, even though he had no idea what was forbidden [by halakha], he was able to overcome his inclination to sin by the sole principle of not acting in a way that would not be pleasing to God." Cited in R. Shalom Noah Barzofsky of Slonim, *Netivot Shalom,* vol. 1 (1982), 140c.

37. The literal translation of the Hebrew reads, "advice external to Torah [*zulat divrei torah*]." I rendered this as "moral code" because I believe it best fits the context of the discussion. Judah had to resort to external criteria in order to decide that this act that appeared permissible (because God had concealed its transgressive nature) was actually immoral.

38. *Mei Ha-Shiloah,* vol. 1, 15b.

39. See Stover, *"A Faire and Easie Way to Heaven": Covenant Theology and Antinomianism in Early Massachusetts,* 162. In fact, perhaps the most popular antinomian crisis in Protestant Christianity, the trial of Anne Hutchinson in the Massachusetts Bay Colony, 1636–1638, was focused on an individual whose character was never brought into question. Even after her guilty verdict of holding antinomian doctrines, no one accused her of libertine or immoral behavior. See for example C. H. Adams, *Antinomianism in the Colony of Massachusetts Bay 1637–1638,* 157, 158.

40. For an exhaustive account of the Frankist heresy, see Heinrich Graetz, *Frank und die Frankisten* (1868). Scholem argues against both Graetz and David Kahana that Sabbateanism had a moderate as well as a "heretical" trend. Scholem's formulation of the moderate versus the radical Sabbateans is partially drawn from the position on Frankism held by Zalman Shazar, Scholem's friend and mentor during his youth in Berlin. Shazar wrote numerous essays on Frankism. See for example Shazar, *Light of Bygone Generations: Studies and Comments on Jewish History in Recent Centuries* (in Hebrew) (1971), 154–67.

41. See Arthur Green, *Devotion and Commandment* (1989), 2–8. Cf. Scholem, *On the Kabbala and Its Symbolism,* 5–32. Joseph Weiss suggested that Hasidism is far more radical and even antinomian than either Scholem or Green are willing to admit. Much of his research in Hasidism is devoted to the exposition of radical Hasidic thinkers who, even as they may have remained within the halakhic community, clearly put their mystical visions above it. His work is collected in English in J. Weiss, *Studies in Eastern European Jewish Mysticism* (1985). See also his important study on the origins of Hasidism, in Joseph Weiss, *"Reshit Zemihat Ha-Hasidut," Zion* 16 (1951): 46–105; and his Hebrew study of Izbica Hasidism, *"Torat Ha-Determinism Ha-Dati le R. Mordechai Joseph Lainer M'Izbica,"* in *Sefer Yovel Shel Yitzchak Baer* (1964), 447–53.

42. For example, R. Joseph Baer Soloveitchik is quite skeptical of the mystical path in general and its ability to remain within the halakhic system. Although he admits to being drawn to the mystical Jewish tradition and the desire to transcend the world of fragmentation, Soloveitchik ultimately rejects such a path as dangerous and fruitless. In his *Halakhic Mind,* 53, Soloveitchik states, "When reason surrenders its supremacy to dark, equivocal emotions, no dam is able to stem the rising tide of the affective stream. . . . It need hardly be stressed that this reduction of religion into some dark recondite, subjective current is absolutely perilous. It frees every dark passion and every animal impulse in man." It would appear that

Soloveitchik was quite pessimistic that any antinomian doctrine could avert libertine behavior. In this quasi-Hobbesian definition of halakha as a system which limits the animal impulses which otherwise would lead to immoral actions, Soloveitchik typifies the fears of normative Judaism rejecting the legitimacy of the mystical experience as an authority independent of halakha even if it does not contradict halakha.

43. R. J. Zwi Werblowsky, *"Messianismus und Mystik,"* in *Gershom Scholem's Major Trends in Jewish Mysticism Fifty Years After: Proceedings of the Sixth International Conference on the History of Jewish Mysticism,* Peter Schafer and Joseph Dan, eds. (1993), 15–24.

44. See Werblowsky, *Gershom Scholem's Major Trends,* 293, 294; and the critique by Barukh Kurzweil, "Notes on Gershom Scholem's *Sabbatai Zevi,*" in idem, *The Struggle Over Values in Judaism* (in Hebrew) (1970), 99ff.

45. Scholem's distinction between "radical" and "moderate" Sabbateans in "Redemption Through Sin" may fit into this category of hard versus soft antinomians. Yehuda Liebes is skeptical of Scholem's typology regarding Sabbateans and argues for a more fluid distinction. See his *"Ha-Emunah Ha-Shabta'it,"* in Liebes, *On Sabbateanism and Its Kabbala* (in Hebrew) (1995), 9–19; and Isaiah Tishby, *Hikrei Kabbala u Shelukhoteha,* vol. 3 (1993), 756–808.

46. Robert Cover, "Nomos and Narrative," 138.

47. See for example Rivka Shatz-Uffenheimer, "Self-Redemption in Hasidic Thought," in *Types of Redemption,* R. J. Z. Werblowsky and C. J. Bleeker, eds. (1970), 207–12.

48. Morris Faierstein, "Personal Redemption in Hasidism," in *Hasidism Reappraised,* Ada Rapoport-Albert, ed. (1997), 214–24.

49. See Joseph Weiss, *"Torat Ha-Determinism Ha-Dati le R. Mordechai Joseph Lainer M'Izbica,"* in *Sefer Yovel Shel Yitzchak Baer* (1964), 447–53; and idem, "A Late Jewish Utopia in Religious Freedom," in *Studies in Eastern European Jewish Mysticism,* 209–48. Cf. Rivka Shatz-Uffenheimer, *"Autonomia Shel Ha-Ruah ve Torat Moshe"* (in Hebrew), *Molad* 21 (1963): 554–66.

50. See Weiss, *Studies,* 77–85. Cf. Faierstein, *All Is in the Hands of Heaven,* 75–85. Faierstein argues that the existence of historical messianism in Izbica/Radzin is more the contribution of R. Gershon Henokh than R. Mordecai Joseph. Faierstein states, "messianism in the *Mei Ha-Shiloah* is closely associated with the concept of *berur* and is entirely individualistic. It is a term which applies to an internal spiritual state and not to external realities." Regardless of the messianic fervor in 1840, which coincided with the split between R. Menahem Mendel of Kotzk and R. Mordecai Joseph, R. Gershon Henokh is the one who pushed the idea of historical messianism with the publication of his *Sidre Tohorot* and the reinstitution of *tekhelet.*

51. Perhaps part of the difficulty in accepting Weiss's contention is that he never explicitly defines what he meant by antinomianism. This deficiency is what initially motivated the inclusion in this chapter of a general overview of antinomian

controversies. As I will argue, according to the common usage of the term in both Jewish and Christian circles, Izbica/Radzin constitutes at best a "soft" antinomianism, one that does not seek to usurp the halakhic system even by one who is a recipient of the illumination.

52. The only instance where this is explicit is in *Mei Ha-Shiloah,* vol. 1, 15a: "Even though he [i.e., the one whose soul is rooted in the biblical Judah] did something yesterday he cannot depend on himself but must always seek God's will anew. This notion will sometimes force him to perform an act against the halakha."

53. For an extensive discussion on how both R. Mordecai Joseph and R. Gershon Henokh portray Abraham, see the earlier chapters of this study. Note that the initial biblical character who makes this claim is Noah, after the deluge. See *Mei Ha-Shiloah,* vol. 1, 5c: "When a person is illumined [*nishlam,* lit., perfected] he is permitted to expand his activity in the world [beyond halakha] because at that time everything is the will of God."

54. Although the reason for the connection between listening to one's wife and moving outside the law to fulfill the will of God is never spelled out in the text, it appears that R. Mordecai Joseph is suggesting that a woman's word should have no authority over a man's action. However, it was God's will that she was given to him as a "helper" and companion and thus man should sometimes heed her advice. Yet, actions taken by man as a result of her advice are outside the framework of the formal relationship between man and God and thus fulfill the verse, *It is time to act for God. . . .*

55. *Mei Ha-Shiloah,* vol. 1, 7c.

56. R. Mordecai Joseph extends this avoidance of doubt in Abraham to Jacob as well. See *Mei Ha-Shiloah,* vol. 1, 10b/c, where he justifies Jacob's stealing of Esau's blessing from Isaac in a manner similar to the above passage about Abraham.

57. R. Mordecai Joseph introduces the nature of the nonintegrated personality and its relation to the integrated personality in his reading of Genesis 2:9, where the Tree of Knowledge is first introduced. The verse reads, *And from the ground the Lord God caused to grow every tree that was pleasing to the sight and good for food, with the tree of life in the middle of the garden, and the tree of knowledge, good and bad.* R. Mordecai Joseph comments, "This verse alludes to four types of trees [corresponding to four types of religious personalities—my addition]. . . . The tree of knowledge corresponds to one who is always in doubt as to the true will of God. . . . The tree of life is true repentance [read: transformation] which heals all of the deficiencies above." See *Mei Ha-Shiloah,* vol. 1, 3d. Thus the nonintegrated antinomianism of Abraham (the Tree of Knowledge) will be completed by the integrated antinomianism of Judah (the Tree of Life). For a more developed interpretation of the Tree of Knowledge as doubt, see *Sod Yesharim on the Torah,* 6a–9a.

58. See *Mei Ha-Shiloah,* vol. 1, 10b, where Jacob seeks to emulate Abraham by not entering into doubtful situations. Cf. ibid., 13a, where R. Mordecai Joseph states explicitly that Jacob was still in need of *berurim.* This experience of doubt precedes his wrestling with the angel, which signifies Jacob's completion.

59. The word *l'hitpashet* is a technical term in *Mei Ha-Shiloah* that refers to actions that are not in line with normative law. Weiss suggests the term implies the opposite of "according to the Torah." For some examples in *Mei Ha-Shiloah* see Weiss, *"Torat Ha-Determinism Ha-Dati,"* 450, n.10.

60. The halakha, drawing from the Talmudic discussion of burial and mourning, determines that a mourner should refrain from bathing from the time of death until the conclusion of *shiva,* the seven days of mourning.

61. *Mei Ha-Shiloah,* vol. 2, 6c/d. Cf. Mishna Rosh Ha-Shana 2:8 and 2:9, where the same Rabban Gamliel seems to act against conventional custom or law regarding the sanctification of the moon.

62. Ibid., vol. 1, 15a. A complete translation and discussion of this passage can be found in the previous chapter.

63. See Weiss, *Studies in Eastern European Jewish Mysticism,* 233ff. A further proof of Weiss's contention can be found in *Mei Ha-Shiloah,* vol. 1, 15d: "In truth, regarding Judah's actions with Tamar as with all actions of [the inheritors] of the tribe of Judah, God instilled [in them] such a strong desire, one which they had no ability to overcome . . . therefore, they were not guilty for actions which they had no ability to control." More than not being guilty, R. Mordecai Joseph would have to admit that these actions were not transgressions but actually fulfilled the will of God. They are only considered sins to those who do not or cannot see God's will beyond the perimeters of the halakha.

64. See for example his comments on Leviticus 19:1 in *Mei Ha-Shiloah,* vol. 1, 37a/b: "*You shall be holy, for I, the Lord your God, am holy.* This [holiness] is the language of preparedness. That is, God warns Israel that they should always be ready and prepared and should constantly be expecting God's redemption, which will redeem them and enlighten their eyes to the words of Torah." Cf. ibid., 38a/b.

65. *Mei Ha-Shiloah,* vol. 1, 51d, 52a.

66. See b.T. Yoma 67b; and R. Judah Loew (MaHaRal) of Prague's *"Gur Aryeh,"* on Rashi to Numbers 19:2.

67. See b.T. Shabbat 151b, where legal proscription is granted regarding the saving of a life: "It is permissible to desecrate one Sabbath in order to keep many." In the Talmudic text, this case is used to justify forbidding desecrating the Sabbath for a corpse, even if that corpse happens to be King David. However, in order to save the life of a day-old newborn, the Sabbath is desecrated.

68. See I Kings 18.

69. *Mei Ha-Shiloah,* vol. 1, 52b. Cf. *Beit Ya'akov Ha-Kolel,* 9d/10a.

70. See Alan Segal, *Paul the Convert,* 144–45.

71. Scholem, in his discussion of religious authority and mysticism, makes a similar distinction in his formulation of the "conservative" and "radical" character of the mystic's relationship with tradition. See for example in Scholem, *On the Kabbala and Its Symbolism,* 14: "It is very different with Paul, the most outstanding example known to us of a revolutionary Jewish mystic. Paul had a mystical experience that he interpreted in such a way that it shattered the traditional authority.

He could not keep it intact; but since he did not wish to forego the authority of the Holy Scriptures as such, he was forced to declare that it was limited in time and hence abrogated."

72. Paul's critique of the law is quite complex. Scholars have argued that Paul was more interested in shifting the emphasis from obedience to faith and not abolishing the law as such. See for example in *The Evangelical Dictionary of Theology,* W. Elweil, ed. (1984), 58: "He [Paul] concluded that the proper relationship was that of the stipulated works of the law flowing from the experience of saving grace, rather than vice versa." See *Romans,* chaps. 8 and 9.

73. See Mikhal Oron, "Exile and Redemption in *Sefer Ha-Peliah* and *Sefer Ha-Kanneh,*" 94–7; and Idel, *Messianic Mystics,* 192–94.

74. The correlation of the mitzvot to the divine elements in various parts of the body is an old Kabbalistic idea. However, Lurianic Kabbala, which appears to be the basis of R. Mordecai Joseph's mystical spirituality, interprets this correlation to affirm the need to fulfill all of the mitzvot. See for example in R. Hayyim Vital's *Sha'ar Ha-Mitzvot,* 1, "Know that all the sparks of the soul from every soul is obligated to fulfill all of the 613 commandments excluding those which are impossible to fulfill such as sacrifices. . . . As long as an individual has not fulfilled all of the 613 commandments which correspond to the 248 sinews and veins of the human body [soul], the soul is missing one of these parts and is thus called blemished, as it is said, *A blemished one cannot enter* [*the Sanctuary*]. . . . This is explained in *Sefer Ha-Tikkunim* [Tikkunei Zohar], 24, and *tikun* 70, 131b, where it states that no repair [of the soul] can occur until a person returns [transmigrates] and completes all of the 613 mitzvot." Interestingly enough, this affirmation of the need to complete all of the 613 commandments, in order to completely repair the blemished soul, is a preface to Vital's argument for the legitimacy of Kabbala as Talmud Torah. According to Vital, a complete *tikun* can only be achieved by involving oneself in all aspects of Torah study with Kabbala being central. Cf. Vital, *Likkutei MaHaRHu,* printed at the end of idem, *Sha'ar Mamrei Razal* (1998), 17a. For more on this last point, see R. Mordecai Attia's preface to his edition of *Ha-Recanati on the Torah* (1961).

75. For a list of Kabbalistic sources that treat this issue, see Scholem, *On the Kabbala and Its Symbolism,* 65. Cf. R Hayyim Vital, *'Etz Ha Da'at Tov* (1985), 76c–77b.

76. Joseph Weiss, *Studies in Eastern European Jewish Mysticism,* 212. Weiss's statement, although correct, ignores the entire Kabbalistic foundation that supports R. Mordecai Joseph's contention. The lack of proof-text material in *Mei Ha-Shiloah* is a serious deficiency that can easily allow one to think that this idea is original in Izbica. Thus, Weiss's conclusion that such a position is anarchic is correct but can easily be applied to any number of classical sources that make a similar claim.

77. Hasidic thinkers were aware of the dangers of their mystical assertions and often expressed reservations about a religious ideology that placed such a heavy

emphasis on personal experience. Concerning R. Nahman of Bratslav, Arthur Green notes, "In facing the assertion that God can be found [via the mystical experience—my addition] within the void, Nahman stands at the brink of religion's mystical self-transcendence, which viewed differently, is also its self-destruction." See Arthur Green, *Tormented Master* (1979), 326. For R. Nahman, whose dialectical thinking must have made it difficult for him to see the possibility of two modes of divine worship (faith and experience) sharing the same source of truth, the mystical life threatened the essential nature of the halakha. For R. Mordecai Joseph and R. Gershon Henokh, it appears that a unity between the divine will and the human will was such a fundamental principle, the inherent dangers of one obliterating the other seemed remote.

78. For example, see Scholem, "Mysticism and Society," *Diogenes* 58 (1967): 1–24; idem, *The Messianic Idea in Judaism,* 49–77; and idem, *On the Kabbala and Its Symbolism,* 5–31.

79. Compare with Morris Faierstein, *All Is in the Hands of Heaven,* 82–83.

80. Ibid., 79–84.

81. On this see Scholem, "The Messianic Idea in Kabbalism," in *The Messianic Idea in Judaism,* 37–48; and Moshe Idel, *Messianic Mystics,* 262–65,273–78. I have presented my position on this issue of originality, heresy, and canonicity in Hasidism in another study on the thought of R. Nahman of Bratslav. See my "Associative Midrash: Reflections on a Hermeneutic Theory of R. Nahman of Bratzlav's *Likkutei MoHaRan,*" in *God's Voice from the Void: Old and New Studies in Bratzlav Hasidism,* S. Magid, ed. (2001), 15–66.

82. For a discussion on this phenomenon in Kabbala, see Daniel Matt, "The Mystic and the Mitzvot," 367–405; Morris Faierstein, "God's Need for the Commandments in Medieval Kabbala," *Conservative Judaism* 36 (1983): 45–59; and Rivka Shatz-Uffenheimer, *Hasidism as Mysticism* (in Hebrew), 111–43. One glaring case that challenges this basic assumption is Abraham Abulafia. Moshe Idel has argued in numerous studies that Abulafia was an "anomian," i.e., that his own Kabbalistic system and relationship to God were not mediated by the mitzvot. See Idel, *The Mystical Experience of Abraham Abulafia* (1988), 8–10; and idem, *Language, Torah and Hermeneutics in Abraham Abulafia* (1989), xii–xiii. Compare with E. R. Wolfson, "Mystical Rationalization of the Commandments in the Prophetic Kabbala of Abraham Abulafia," esp. 331–41.

83. Joseph Stern, *Problems and Parables of Law,* 1. On this see also Frank Talmage, "Apples of Gold: The Inner Meaning of Sacred Texts in Medieval Judaism," in *Jewish Spirituality I,* A. Green, ed. (1986), 337–38.

84. Kabbalistic *ta'amei ha-mitzvot* is only now being studied. See for example Charles Mopsik, *Les Grandes texts de la Cabbala Les Rites qui font Dieu* (1993); E. R. Wolfson, "Mystical Rationalization of the Commandments in *Sefer Ha-Rimon,*" *HUCA* 59 (1988): 156–99; Idel, *Kabbala: New Perspectives,* 156–99; and Jacob Katz, *Halakha and Kabbala* (in Hebrew) (1984), 9–33. The classic study on *ta'amei ha-mitzvot* by I. Heinemann, *Ta'amei Ha-Mitzvot,* 2 vols. (1949), almost

entirely ignores the Kabbalistic tradition. For an interpretation of *ta'amei ha-mitzvot* as a potential contribution to the philosophy of religion in general, see R. Joseph B. Soloveitchik, *The Halakhic Mind* (1986), 91–99.

85. Although this has often been understood as only the case from theosophic Kabbala, Elliot Wolfson has recently argued that this also applies for the ecstatic Kabbala of Abulafia and his school. See E. R. Wolfson, *Abraham Abulafia: Kabbalist and Prophet,* 186–228. An interesting case here is Nahmanides. While engaging philosophically with Maimonides on *ta'amei ha-mitzvot* (e.g., his comment to Deuteronomy 22:6), he also takes a Kabbalistic stance. See his "Sermon of *Kohelet,*" in *Kitve Ramban,* vol. 1, 190.

86. Stern, *Problems and Parables of Law,* 14–48. Stern uses Twersky's framing of the problem in antinomian terms in *Introduction to the Code of Maimonides,* 407–11, but offers a very different reading.

87. Isadore Twersky was the first to view Maimonides' *ta'amei ha-mitzvot* as an answer to the threat of antinomianism. See his *Introduction to the Code of Maimonides,* 408–11. This has been developed by Joseph Stern, *Problems and Parables of Law,* esp. 36–48. I have largely followed Stern's analysis of Maimonides on this issue. For another important reading of Maimonides on *ta'amei ha-mitzvot,* see Amos Funkenstein, *Perceptions of Jewish History* (1993), 141–53.

88. Twersky, *Introduction,* 408. See also idem, "Clarifying the Words of Rambam in Hilkhot Me'eila 8:8 Regarding Ta'amei Ha-Mitzvot" (in Hebrew), in *Perakim b'Toldot Ha-Yehudim b'Yemei Ha-Benayim v'Et Ha-Hadasha 'l'Professor Yaakov Katz,* E. Etrkes and J. Salmon, eds. (1980), 24–33.

89. David Novak makes an important distinction between scriptural and rabbinic commandments on this point: "In the case of scriptural/divine law, the rule is always prior to the principle. . . . The principle functions more as an explanation [*ratio cognoscendi*] than a sufficient reason or ground. . . . However in the case of rabbinic/human law, the principle is prior to the rule in the sense that we do not know in advance the reasons for which the rule was originally devised. . . . The rule is thus derived from the principle as a means is derived from the ends it intends." See Novak, *Natural Law in Judaism* (1998), 74–75.

90. See *Guide* 2:16; and Twersky, *Introduction,* 410.

91. See *Guide* 3:36, "For if knowledge [of the mitzvot] is not achieved, no right action and no correct opinion can be achieved."

92. See *Guide* 3:31.

93. Besides Maimonides' pure philosophical belief that all consequences of God's will (mitzvot) have a reason, he argued that the arbitrariness of God's will and/or the inability of humans to understand it is far more dangerous. He criticizes the Kalamists and the Ash'arites as a basis for his argument. See *Guide* 3:25, 26, 31. See Twersky, *Introduction,* 407, "He should investigate them [i.e., mitzvot] the danger of antinomianism notwithstanding." Even Nahmanides, who disagrees with Maimonides on many issues surrounding *ta'amei ha-mitzvot,* states that one should strive to ascertain the reasons for the commandments as much as possible.

See Nahmanides' gloss to Maimonides' *Sefer Ha-Mitzvot,* section 5. Cf. Novak, *Natural Law in Judaism,* 68.

94. The dangers of *ta'amei ha-mitzvot* were already made explicit in the Talmud. See for example b.T. Sanhedrin 21b. Maimonides' most explicit warning can be found at the end of his *Sefer Ha-Miztvot* on negative commandment no. 365, in *Sefer Ha-Mitzvot l'Ha-Rambam,* C. Chavel, ed. (1981), 394.

95. Twersky, *Introduction,* 412.

96. David Novak noted that Maimonides' configuration of *ta'amei ha-mitzvot* from its conventional rabbinic understanding, as justification from a scriptural source to teleology, was one of his greatest accomplishments. See Maimonides, *Mishneh Torah,* "Laws of Mamrim," 1:4; and Novak, *Natural Law in Judaism,* 95, 99–105. Novak argues that while Maimonides' teleological system of mitzvot exhibits a philosophical orientation, such a teleology is deeply rooted in rabbinic tradition, specifically the teachings of the Amoraic sage Rava.

97. See Stern, *Problems,* 19. He agrees with Twersky under the assumption that *Guide* 3:50–54 are not part of *ta'amei ha-mitzvot.* But see ibid., 68, 69, where Stern reads "body" as the welfare of the general community and "soul" as the acquisition of "correct opinions." Maimonides argues in *Mishneh Torah, "Hilkhot De'ot,"* chaps. 1–3, that the utility of the law is largely engaged with the former and not the latter.

98. Stern, *Problems,* 47.

99. Maimonides does make an argument that philosophers must continue the performance of mitzvot in order to remain part of the community. See *Guide* 2:40, 3:27. However, this pragmatic response begs for a more philosophical justification.

100. Stern, *Problems,* 42. Stern's attempt to see *Guide* 3:49–53 as a protraction of *ta'amei ha-mitzvot* for the philosopher speaks to the difficulty many have had with understanding the place of these chapters in Maimonides' thinking. Novak notes parenthetically that these last chapters of the *Guide* have always confused Maimonides' readers. See Novak, *Natural Law in Judaism,* 115.

101. On the rationality for prayer in Maimonides, see Ehud Benor, *Worship of the Heart* (1995).

102. Cf. *Guide* 3:29, 3:32. In *Guide* 3:29 Maimonides makes his oft-cited claim that the entire purpose of mitzvot is to abolish idolatry and affirm the "correct belief" that there is only one Deity and humanity's purpose is to love and fear Him through worship.

103. Stern, *Problems,* 47.

104. What I mean here is that the conventional notion of "apologetics" is a weak and overly defensive stance toward tradition. In a positive sense, apologetics is a *pro vitam suam,* a "defense of one's own life," whereby provocative and innovative positions are viewed as compatible and not deviant from acceptable norms. In this latter sense, both Maimonides and R. Gershon Henokh are apologists on the question of antinomianism. Cf. Franz Rosenzweig, "Apologetic Thinking," in

Rosenzweig, *Philosophical and Theological Writings,* W. Franks and M. L. Morgan, trans. and eds. (2000), 95–108.

105. See David Shatz, "Worship, Corporeality, and Human Perfection: A Reading of the *Guide of the Perplexed* 3:51–54," in *The Thought of Moses Maimonides,* Ira Robinson, ed. (1991), 77–129.

106. This Talmudic discussion opens with Tractate Baba Meziah and is often cited as the paradigmatic discussion on civil law in the Talmudic corpus. R. Gershon Henokh uses it here to represent the halakhic system as a whole.

107. *Sod Yesharim on the Festivals,* "Simhat Torah" 31b. At first blush this resembles Maimonides' discussion of the messianic era in *Mishneh Torah,* "Laws of Kings," chap. 11. Maimonides appears to be implicitly addressing the rabbinic dictum suggesting the nullification of mitzvot in the messianic era and its popularization among many messianic movements throughout Jewish history.

108. This point is not uniquely Maimonidean but was argued earlier by Saadia Gaon in his *Emunot ve De'to* 3:7, R. Joseph Kafah, trans. and ed. (1972), 131a–135a.

109. In the Zohar the mitzvot are called "the body *(gufe)* of Torah." See, for example, Michael Fishbane, "The Garments of Torah—Or, To What May Scripture be Compared," in idem, *The Garments of Torah* (1989), 33–48. Cf. the oft-cited passage on garments in the Zohar 3:159b. For some examples, see Daniel Matt, "The Mystic and the Mitzvot," 367–404; and Elliot Wolfson, *Through a Speculum,* 355–67.

110. See for example in *Sod Yesharim on the Torah* 60a/b and its source in *Mei Ha-Shiloah,* vol. 1, 36, 37. R. Mordecai Joseph's personal stance on this important issue remains obscure because *Mei Ha-Shiloah,* as opposed to *Sod Yesharim,* is a very unreflective work that is intentionally structured in a cryptic manner.

111. See *Etz Hayyim,* vol. 2, gate 12, chap. 5, 51dff; *Sha'ar Ha-Kavannot,* 23d; *'Ozrot Hayyim, "Sha'ar Atik,"* 18c–22b; *"Sha'ar ha-Kelalim,"* chap. 12, printed at the beginning of standard editions of *Etz Hayyim;* and *Sha'ar Ma'amrei Rashbi,* 9d, 31a/b, 63b. Cf. my "From Theosophy to Midrash: Lurianic Exegesis and the Garden of Eden," 51–54. The Lurianic notion of the continuous union of *abba* and *imma (hokhma* and *bina),* and the temporal union of *zeir anpin* and *nukva,* is rooted in the Zohar. See Zohar 3.4a, 3.180b (Idra Zuta). Cf. R. Moses Cordovero, *Pardes Rimonim,* gate 8, chaps. 13 and 14. For a discussion on the difference between perpetual and temporal union in Lurianic Kabbala see Joseph Avivi, *Kabbalat Ha-GRA* (in Hebrew) (1991), 36–42.

112. On this see Idel, *Hasidism,* 33–44.

113. The tripartite appraisal of existence, space, and time, with soul, originates in *Sefer Yezirah* and becomes a popular theme in Hasidic thought. See *Sefer Yezirah,* 1:1, 4:5, 6.

114. See *Sod Yesharim on the Torah,* 79b. The eternally present state of God is reflected in the perpetual union of *abba* and *imma,* a union that is not affected by human transgression (i.e., *kelippot* and evil).

115. R. Gershon Henokh does mention that the result of illumination is the apprehension that the temporal union of the lower *parzufim* is also identical to the eternal higher union. See for example in *Sod Yesharim on the Torah,* 79b, "Sometimes, God will be revealed through the *avodah* [the performance of mitzvot] and man will come to understand that this [the lower temporal union] is also a constant union." From yet another perspective, R. Gershon Henokh uses the temporal state of the Sukkah juxtaposed to the permanent state of the Sabbath to suggest an interpretation as to why Jacob named the place he journeyed through Sukkot in Genesis 33:17. See *Sod Yesharim on the Festivals,* Rosh Ha-Shana, 49b/c. The notion of illumination as a flash that cannot be sustained resembles Maimonides' description of prophecy (and philosophical truth) as a "lightning flash," in *Guide,* "Introduction to the First Part," 7.

116. See *Sod Yesharim on the Torah,* 106b, 107a. Cf. *Sod Yesharim on the Festivals,* Sukkot 31a.

117. The normative halakhic precept is *tadir v eyno tadir, tadir kodem:* When a more frequent mitzvah is juxtaposed to a less frequent mitzvah, the more frequent mitzvah takes precedence.

118. This is not only true in the theosophical Kabbala but in the Kabbala of Abulafia as well. See for example in Abulafia's *Gan Na'ul,* MS Munich-BS 58 fol. 323a, cited and discussed in E. R. Wolfson, "Mystical Rationalization of the Commandments," 350. Cf. The Gaon of Vilna's illuminating comment in his commentary to the Zohar, *Biur l'Zohar* (1882), on Zohar 3.37c, "We have already explained above there are 613 parts to the human body and 613 dimensions of the human soul that are implanted in the body. . . . There are also 613 parts of the soul that are not implanted in the body but are emanated from the realm of spirit [*ruah*]. These 613 elements of spirit are drawn into the human being through the 613 mitzvot. This is the telos and perfection of the human being."

119. R. Moses Cordovero uses Maimonides' "Laws of the Foundations of the Torah" in the *Mishneh Torah* as the basis for his chapter on the obligation to study Kabbala (divine science). See his *'Or Ne'erav,* part 3. This is also apparent in the first section of R. Azriel of Gerona's *Perush 'al Ha-Eser Sephirot.* To "know God," for Cordovero, is to know "divine science," i.e., the *sephirot.* Apparently, Maimonides views "knowledge of God" as a universal principle of being human as opposed to believing in God, which he cites as particular to Israel (a mitzvah). When speaking of mitzvot in the beginning of *Sefer Ha-Mitzvot,* Maimonides uses "belief" and not "knowledge." If we follow his argument in "Laws on the Foundation of the Torah," we see there is nothing there unique to Israel, i.e., nothing a product of revelation alone. In *Sefer Ha-Mitzvot,* however, belief in God is based on the first words of the revelation *"Anokhi Ha-Shem Elokekha" (I am the Lord your God).*

120. There has been a great deal of scholarship on the Averroist nature of Maimonides' *Guide.* Much of the controversy surrounding the heretical nature of the *Guide* is based on its espousing Averroist doctrine. Averroes (Ibn Ahmad Ibn Rusd, 1126–1198) was an Islamic theologian born in Cordova, who became a chief

justice there around 1171. His theory about religion as a doctrine only for the masses was very influential in Islamic, Jewish, and Christian philosophical circles in the twelfth and thirteenth centuries. See Averroes, "The Decisive Treatise Determining What the Connection Is between Religion and Philosophy," in *Medieval Political Philosophy,* R. Lerner and M. Mahdi, eds., George F. Hourani, trans. (1963), 163–90.

121. One important distinction between Maimonides and our Hasidic thinkers is that Maimonides adamantly asserts that human will (i.e., the will to sin) never changes. "Though all miracles change the nature of some individual being, God does not change at all the nature of human individuals by means of miracles. . . . For if it were His will that the nature of any individual should be changed because of what He, may His name be exalted, wills from that individual, sending of prophets and all giving of a Law would have been useless" (*Guide* 3:32). The notion that there could be a unity of human and divine will is anathema for Maimonides and would destroy the entire purpose for the mitzvot that predicts the marginal nature of Izbica/Radzin Hasidism. However, they are similar in that Maimonides does entertain the possibility that the philosopher could attain "correct opinions" without the aid of Torah.

122. This is stated explicitly in his *Commentary on the Mishna,* b.T. Sanhedrin, chap. 10. It is also implied in *Mishneh Torah,* Laws of Kings, 10:1–3.

123. *Sod Yesharim on the Festivals,* "Simhat Torah" 31b.

124. The implications of the Hebrew term *pakhim katanim* in the Talmudic reading of this verse is a debated issue in traditional biblical exegesis. See for example MaHaRal of Prague's comment on Rashi in his *"Gur Aryeh,"* printed in *'Ozar M'Forshei Rashi 'al Ha-Torah,* vol. 1, 90b. See also Nahmanides' remarks in *Perush Ha-Ramban 'al Ha-Torah,* vol. 1, 185.

125. See *Sod Yesharim on the Torah,* 80a. Compare this with *Sod Yesharim,* 77a, where R. Gershon Henokh argues that, even for the illumined, a fence must be made to avert the hint of evil, which necessarily remains as part of the illumination. The interpretation on 80a is preceded by the use of a source in midrash Genesis Rabba 91, 1108, which states, "*Who commands the sun not to shine; Who seals up the stars* [Job 9:7]; *Who commands the sun not to shine;* this is Jacob. *Who seals up the stars;* these are the ten tribes [the sons of Jacob] who entered and exited Egypt and did not know that Joseph was alive. To Jacob it was revealed that Joseph was alive as it is said, *When Jacob saw that there were food rations to be had in Egypt* [Genesis 42:1]." Thus, Jacob is compared here to a sun, whose source of light is independent and not a reflection like the light of the moon. He also is said to have understood that Joseph was alive and thus sent his sons to Egypt in the hope that they would discover him. R. Gershon Henokh speaks of the vulnerability of such independence and how mitzvot serve as an antidote for that danger.

126. *And the serpent said to Eve, "You are not going to die but God knows that as soon as you eat of it* [*the fruit of the tree*] *your eyes will be opened and you will be like divine beings who know good and bad."*

127. See Zohar 1.172b, 1.203b; Tikkunei Zohar 29a, 55a (in standard editions).

128. This comment is built on Proverbs 19:14, *Property and riches are bequeathed to the fathers, but a brilliant* [alt., *efficient*] *wife comes from God.*

129. See *Sod Yesharim on the Torah,* 44b. On the connection of each soul to a particular mitzvah see *Mei Ha-Shiloah,* "Collected Writings on Proverbs," vol. 1, 5d: "The Torah purifies each individual, specifically in places where she knows there is a deficiency [in her soul]. For this, there is a specific mitzvah as it says in Shabbat [118b], 'Why was your father so careful in the mitzvah of *zizit*?' It is because he needed that particular mitzvah according to his own self-understanding. By means of this mitzvah, his deficiency was rectified."

130. On this, see Genesis Rabba 18:4 and R. Nahman of Bratslav, *Likkutei MoHaRan* 1:19, para. 3.

131. The notion that individuals have more pronounced relationships with certain mitzvot is not new here but is based on a Talmudic statement in b.T. Shabbat 118b. For a probable source of this idea in Izbica/Radzin Hasidism, see R. Moshe Cordovero's *Derasha be'Inyanei Malakhim,* Reuven Margolit, ed. (1945), 70; R. Hayyim Vital's *Sha'ar Ha-Kavannot,* 53b; and *Sha'ar Ha-Gilgulim* (1990), 26–27.

132. This is one of the overarching "reasons for the commandments" offered by Maimonides in the *Guide.*

133. See *Etz Hayyim,* "*Sha'ar Mate ve 'lo Mate,*" 30b–34b.

134. *Sod Yesharim on the Torah,* 270d, 271a.

135. The introduction to *Beit Ya'akov Ha-Kollel,* by R. Yeruham Lainer (R. Gershon Henokh's nephew), states that this text was written by R. Gershon Henokh and mostly contains the teachings he and others heard from his father R. Jacob during the years 1851–1852. Since R. Gershon Henokh is the author of this work, it reflects the style and substance of *Sod Yesharim* more than R. Jacob's other collections (*Beit Ya'akov* on Genesis, Exodus, and Leviticus).

136. *Beit Ya'akov Ha-Kollel,* 13a.

Bibliography

Works by R. Gershon Henokh Lainer of Radzin

'Ayin Tekhelet. New York, 1954.
'Esser Milin De-Hasiduta. New York, 1946.
Ha-Hakdama ve Ha-Petikha. New York, 1949.
Ma'amer Petil Tekhelet. N.p., 1952.
Mi-Pi Ha-Shemuah. Warsaw, 1887.
'Orhot Hayyim. New York, 1946.
Sha'ar Ha-Emunah ve Yesod Ha-Hasidut. Reprint of *Ha-Hakdama ve Ha-Petikha.* New York, 1996.
Shipunei Temunei Hol. N.p., 1952.
Sidrei Taharot. Petrikov, 1902.
Sod Yesharim on the Festivals. 2 vols. Brooklyn, N.Y., 1991.
Sod Yesharim on the Torah. Brooklyn, N.Y., 1971.
Sod Yesharim Tinyana. On the Torah. Brooklyn, N.Y., 1982.
Tekhelet Zizit Be-Yamenu. Vad Hasidut Radzin Bishrai, 1953.
Tiferet Ha-Hanokhi. Warsaw, 1900.

Works by R. Jacob Lainer of Izbica

Beit Ya'akov. 3 vols. *Genesis, Exodus, Leviticus.* New York, 1948.
Beit Ya'akov Ha-Kollel. New York, 1996.
Seder Hagaddah shel Pesach 'Im Sefer Ha-Zemanim. Lublin, 1903. Reprint. New York, 1990.
Sefer Ha-Zemanim. New York, 1973.

Works by R. Mordecai Joseph Lainer of Izbica

Mei Ha-Shiloah. Brooklyn, N.Y., 1976.

Works by R. Yeruham Lainer

Gilgulei Neshamot. Jerusalem, 1977.
Seder 'Olam. Warsaw, 1904.
Shemot She be-Mishnayot. Radzin, 1911. Reprint. New York, 1988.
Tiferet Yeruham. Brooklyn, N.Y., 1967.
Zikaron Rishonim. New York, 1950.
Zohar Ha-Rakiya. New York, 1951.

Works by Hayyim Simcha Lainer

Dor Yesharim. Lublin, 1925. Reprint. New York, 1988.

Works by Other Hasidic Masters

Akedat Yeshuah. R. Abraham Joshua Heschel Frankel. Brooklyn, N.Y., 1984.
Amud Ha-Avodah. R. Barukh of Kosov. Czernowitz, 1863.
Aspaklaria Ha-Me'ira [anthology of the teachings of R. Isaac Jacob Horowitz, the Seer of Lublin]. Jerusalem, n.d.
Ateret Zvi. 2 vols. R. Zvi Hirsch Eichenstein of Zhidochov. Brooklyn, N.Y., 1996.
Derekh Pikudekha, R. Zvi Elimelekh of Dinov Lvov. N.p., 1851.
Divrei Emet. R. Aryeh Leib Eiger of Lublin. Jerusalem, 1973.
Divrei Sofrim. R. Zaddok Ha-Kohen. Bnei Brak, 1973.
Emet ve Emunah. R. Menahem Mendel Morgenstern of Kotzk. Jerusalem, 1972.
'Imre Emet. R. Aryeh Leib Eiger of Lublin. Jerusalem, 1973.
Keter Shem Tov. R. Aaron of Zalakhov. Zolkiew, 1794/95.
Kol Mevaser—Likkutim Hadashim. R. Simha Bunim of Pryzsucha. Bnei Brak, 1991.
Kol Simha. R. Simha Bunim of Pryzsucha. Jerusalem, 1984.
Likuttei MoHaRan. R. Nahman of Bratslav. Brooklyn, N.Y., 1976.
Maggid Devarav Le-Ya'akov. R. Dov Baer of Mezeritch. Edited by Rivka Shatz-Uffenheimer. Jerusalem, 1976.
Mei Zedek. R. Abraham Joshua Heschel Frankel [collection of R. Zaddok Ha-Kohen's references to *Mei Ha-Shiloah*]. Brooklyn, N.Y., 1984.
Midrash Simha. R. Simha Bunim of Pryzsucha. Jerusalem, 1984.
'Ohel Torah. R. Menahem Mendel Morgenstern of Kotzk. Brooklyn, N.Y., 1952.
'Ohel Yitzhak. R. Aaron Waldman [the collected teachings of R. Isaac of Warka]. Israel, 1968.
'Or Ha-Meir. R. Ze'ev Wolf of Zhitomir. 2 vols. Jerusalem, 1996.
'Or Zarua La-Zaddik. R. Zaddok Ha-Kohen. Bnei Brak, 1973.
Pri Ha'artez [including *Pri Ha'etz*]. R. Menahem Mendel of Vitsbsk. Jerusalem, 1987.

Resise Layla. R. Zaddok Ha-Kohen of Lublin. Bnei Brak, 1967.
Siach Sarfe Kodesh [3 volume anthology of collected teachings of Hasidic masters of Poland]. R. Yoatz Ke'em Kadish of Parshitik. N.p., 1987.
Sur m'Ra ve Aseh Tov. R. Zvi Hirsch Eichenstein of Zhidochov. Jerusalem, 1996.
Tanna DeBeEliayhu with Ramatayim Zofim. R. Shmuel of Shinov. Jerusalem, 1975.
Torat Emet. R. Aryeh Leib Eiger of Lublin. 3 vols. Bnei Brak, 1970.
Yesod Ha-Emunah. R. Barukh of Kosov. Reprinted in *Seforim Kedoshim,* vol. 40. Brooklyn, N.Y., 1986.
Zidkat Ha-Zaddik. R. Zaddok Ha-Kohen. Bnei Brak, 1973.
Zikaron Zot. R. Isaac Jacob Horowitz, the Seer of Lublin. Jerusalem, 1973.
Zot Zikaron. R. Isaac Jacob Horowitz, the Seer of Lublin. Jerusalem, 1973.

General Bibliography

Abrabanel, R. Isaac. *Nahalat Avot.* New York, 1953.
Adams, C. H. *Antinomianism in the Colony of Massachusetts Bay 1637–1638.* New York, 1894.
Aescoly, A. Z. *Ha-Temunah Ha-Meshihit B'Yisrael.* Jerusalem, 1950.
Alfasi, Yizhak. *Ha-Hozeh Me-Lublin.* Jerusalem, 1969.
———. *Ha-Rebbe Me-Kotzk.* Tel Aviv, 1962.
———. *Ha-Saba ha-Kadosh me-Radoshits.* Tel Aviv, 1967.
Alter, Abraham Issacher. *Meir Einei Ha-Golah.* Tel Aviv, 1954.
Altmann, Alexander. "Jewish Mysticism." In *The Meaning of Jewish Existence: Theological Essays 1930–1939.* Hanover and London, 1990.
———. "Judaism and World Philosophy." *The Jews: Their History, Culture, and Religion,* vol. 1, edited by Louis Finkelstein. New York, 1949.
———. "Lurianic Kabbala in a Platonic Key: Abraham Cohen Herrera's Puerto Del Cielo." In *Jewish Thought in the Seventeenth Century,* edited by Isadore Twersky. Cambridge, Mass., 1987.
———. "Maimonides' Attitude toward Jewish Mysticism." In *Studies in Jewish Thought: An Anthology of German Jewish Scholarship,* edited by Alfred Jospe. Detroit, 1981.
———. "Metaphysics and Religion." In *The Meaning of Jewish Existence: Theological Essays 1930–1939.* Hanover and London, 1990a.
Anglin, W. S. *Free Will and the Christian Faith.* Oxford, 1991.
Assaf, David. "Hasidism in Poland in the Nineteenth Century—The State of Research and a Bibliographical Survey." In *Zaddikim ve Anshei Ma'asheh* (in Hebrew), edited by R. Elior, I. Bartal, and H. Shmeruk. Jerusalem, 1994.
———. "R. Israel of Ruzhin and His Role in the History of the Hasidic Movement in the First Half of the Nineteenth Century" (in Hebrew). Ph.D. dissertation, Hebrew University, 1993.
Augustine of Hippo, Saint. *On Free Choice of the Will.* New York, 1964.

Avivi, Joseph. *Introduction to the Homilies of R. Isaac Luria* (in Hebrew). Jerusalem, 1987.

———. *Kabbalat Ha-GRA.* Jerusalem, 1987.

———. "Kitvei Ha-Ari Be-Italia Lifne 1620." *'Aley Sefer* 11 (1984): 134–91.

Azriel of Gerona, R. *Perush Ha-Aggadot le Rabbi Azriel.* Edited by I. Tishby. Jerusalem, 1945.

Azulai, R. Hayyim Joseph David. "The Motif of the 'Shells' in Azriel of Gerona." In *Studies in Religious Philosophy and Mysticism,* edited by Alexander Altmann. Ithaca, N.Y., 1969.

———. "Notes on the Development of the Kabbalistic Doctrine of R. Menahem Azaria da Fano" (in Hebrew). *Jerusalem Studies in Jewish Thought* 3 (1983–84): 1–2.

———. "The Religion of the Thinkers: Free Will and Predestination in Saadia, Bahya, and Maimonides." In *Religion in a Religious Age,* edited by S. D. Goitein. Cambridge, Mass., 1974.

———. *Shem Ha Gedolim.* Reprint. Jerusalem, 1992.

———. *Shulkhan Ha-Arukh Ha-Ari z'l.* Jerusalem, 1962.

Ba'artish, Y. "The Agricultural Settlement of the Jews in Congress Poland in the Period Preceding the Freedom of the Serfs" (in Hebrew). *Zion* (1967): 46–75.

Bacher, W. "The Treatise on Eternal Bliss Attributed to Maimonides." *Jewish Quarterly Review,* o.s. 8 (1897): 270–89.

Bacon, Gershon. "Torah and Messianic Yearnings: On the Question of the Ideology of Aggudat Israel in Poland" (in Hebrew). *Tarbiz* 52, no. 3 (1983): 497–508.

Baer, Yizhak. "Ha Reka Ha-Histori Shel Ha-Ra'aya Mehemna." *Zion* 5 (1984): 1–44.

———. *A History of the Jews in Christian Spain.* Philadelphia, 1961.

Baker, M. "The Reassessment of Haskala Ideology in the Aftermath of the 1863 Polish Revolt." *Polin* 5 (1990): 221–50.

Bartoszewski, W. T., and Antony Polonsky, eds. *The Jews in Warsaw.* Cambridge, Mass., 1991.

Barzilay, Isaac. *Yoseph Shlomo Delmedigo Yashar of Candia: His Life, Works, and Times.* Leiden, 1972.

Benayahu, Meir. *Sefer Toldot Ha-Ari.* Jerusalem, 1967.

Ben Nahman, Moses. *Kitvei Ha-Ramban.* 2 vols. Edited by Hayyim Chavel. Jerusalem, 1976.

Ben Sasson, Jonah. *The Philosophical System of Rabbi Moses Isserles* (in Hebrew). Jerusalem, 1982.

Ben Sheshet, R. Isaac. *Teshuvot Ha-Ribash.* New York, 1964.

Ben Shlomo, Joseph. "The Research of Gershom Scholem on Pantheism and Kabbala" (in Hebrew). In *Gershom Scholem: The Man and His Work.* Jerusalem, 1983.

———. "R. Moses Cordovero's Relationship to Philosophy and Science" (in Hebrew). In *Sefer Safed,* edited by Y. Ben Zvi and M. Benayahu. Jerusalem, 1962.

———. *Torat Ha-Elohut Shel Moshe Cordovero*. Jerusalem, 1965.

Berofsky, Bernard. *Determinism*. Princeton, N.J., 1966.

———. *Free Will and Determinism*. New York, 1966.

Biale, David. *Gershom Scholem: Kabbala and Counter History*. Cambridge, Mass., 1978.

Blejwas, H. S. "Polish Positivism and the Jews." *Journal of Jewish Studies* 46, no. 1 (1984): 21–35.

Blickstein, Shlomo. "Between Philosophy and Mysticism: A Study of the Philosophical Writings of Joseph Gikatillia 1248–1322." Ph.D. dissertation, Jewish Theological Seminary, 1983.

Blumenthal, David. "Maimonides: Prayer, Worship and Mysticism." In *Prière, mystique et judaisme*. Strasbourg, 1987.

Bonfil, Robert. "Halakhah, Kabbala and Society: Some Insights into Rabbi Menahmen Azaria da Fano's Inner World." *Jewish Thought in the Seventeenth Century*. Cambridge, Mass., 1987.

———. *Jewish Life in Renaissance Italy*. Translated by Anthony Oldcorn. Berkeley, Calif., 1991.

Boyarin, Daniel. *Carnal Israel: Reading Sex in Talmudic Culture*. Berkeley, Calif., 1993.

Brill, Alan. "Grandeur and Humility in the Writings of R. Simha Bunim of Pryzsucha." In *Hazon Nahum*, edited by Yaakov Elman and Jeffrey Gorock. New York, 1998.

———. "The Mystical Path of the Vilna Gaon." *Journal of Jewish Thought and Philosophy* 3 (1993): 131–51.

Bruns, Gerald. *Hermeneutics Ancient and Modern*. New Haven, Conn., 1992.

Buber, Martin. *Mamre: Essays in Religion*. Translated by Greta Horn. Westport, Conn., 1970.

———. *The Origin and Meaning of Hasidism*. Atlantic Highlands, N.J., 1960.

Bulka, R. P. "The Rationale of Sacrifice: A Postscript on Abravanel's Defense of Maimonides." *Niv Hamidrashia* 18/19 (1984): 40–46.

Burrel, David. *Knowing the Unknowable God*. Bloomington, Ind., 1986.

Cala, A. "The Question of Assimilation of the Jews in the Polish Kingdom 1864–1892." *Polin* 1 (1982): 130–50.

Calvin, John. *Institutes of the Christian Religion*. Translated by H. Beveridge. Grand Rapids, Mich., 1989.

Carlebach, Elisheva. *The Pursuit of Heresy*. New York, 1990.

Chavel, Hayyim. *Ramban: His Life and Teachings*. New York, 1960.

Chenu, M. D. "Le Dernier Avatar de la théologie orientale en occident au XIIIe siècle." In *Melanges Auguste Pelzer*. Louvaine, 1947.

Cherry, Conrad. *The Theology of Jonathan Edwards*. Bloomington, Ind., 1966.

Clark, E. A. "The Ascetic Impulse in Religious Life: A General Response. In *Asceticism*, edited by V. L. Wimbush and R. Valantasis. New York and Oxford, 1995.

Cordovero, R. Moshe. *'Or Ne'erav.* Jerusalem, 1965.

Corrison, S. "Aspects of Population Change and the Acculturation of Jewish Warsaw at the End of the Nineteenth Century." *Polin* 3 (1988): 122–45.

Cover, Robert. *Narrative, Violence, and the Law: The Essays of Robert Cover.* Edited by Martha Minow, Michael Ryan, and Austin Sarat. Ann Arbor, Mich., 1995.

Da Fano, R. Menahem Azaria. *'Asara Ma'amarot.* Lemberg, 1858.

Dan, Joseph. "Ashkanazi Hasidism and the Maimonidean Controversy." Reprinted in *Jewish Mysticism: The Middle Ages.* Vol. 2. Northvale, N.J., 1988.

———. "The Beginning of the Messianic Myth in Thirteenth-Century Kabbala" (in Hebrew). In *Messianism and Eschatology: A Collection of Essays,* edited by Zvi Baras. Jerusalem, 1989.

Davila, James R. "Melchizedek: King, Priest, and God." In *The Seductiveness of Jewish Myth: Challenge or Response,* edited by S. Daniel Breslauer. Albany, N.Y., 1997.

Davis, S. T. "Divine Omniscience and Human Freedom." *Religious Studies* 15 (1979): 306–15.

———. *Faith, Skepticism and Evidence: An Essay in Religious Epistemology.* New York, 1978.

De Certeau, Michael. "Mystic Speech." In *Heterologies: Discourse on the Other,* translated by Brian Massumi. Minneapolis, 1982.

———. "Mystique au XVII siècle: Le problème du langage mystique." In *L'Homme devant Dieu: Mélanges offerts au Père Henri de Lubac.* 3 vols. Paris, 1964.

Del Medigo, R. Joseph Solomon. *Mazref la Hokhma.* Warsaw, 1890.

Dienstag, Jacob. "Ha-Moreh Nevuchim ve Sefer Ha-Madda Be Sifrut Ha-Hasidut." In *Abraham Weiss Jubilee Volume,* edited by Samuel Belkin. New York, n.d.

———. "Maimonides and the Kabbalists—Bibliography" (in Hebrew). *Da'at* 25 (1990): 53–84.

———. "Was the Gaon of Vilna Opposed to the Philosophy of Rambam?" (in Hebrew). *Talpiot* 4 (1929): 253–69.

Dienstag, Jacob, ed. *Eschatology in Maimonidean Thought: Messianism, Resurrection and the World to Come.* New York, 1983.

Dillenberger, John, and Claude Welch. *Protestant Theology: Interpreted through Its Development.* New York, 1954.

Dinur, Ben Zion. *Be Mifneh Ha-Dorot.* Jerusalem, 1972.

———. *Dorot u Rishumot.* Jerusalem, 1978.

———. "The Messianic-Prophetic Role of the Baal Shem Tov." In *Essential Papers on Messianic Movements and Personalities in Jewish History,* edited by Marc Saperstein. New York, 1981.

———. "The Origins of Hasidism and Its Social and Messianic Foundations." In *Essential Papers on Hasidism: Origins to the Present,* edited by Gershon Hundert. New York and London, 1991.

Dresner, Samuel. *The Zaddik: The Doctrine of the Zaddik According to the Writings of R. Yaakov Yosef of Polnoy.* New York, 1974.

Druker, A. G. "The Polish Insurrection's Missed Opportunity: Mochnacki's Views on the Failure to Involve the Jews in the Uprising of 1830–1831." *Journal of Jewish Studies* 28 (1966): 63–81.

Dubnow, Simon. "The Beginnings: The Baal Shem Tov and the Center in Podolia." In *Essential Papers on Hasidism: Origins to the Present,* edited by Gershon Hundert. New York and London, 1991.

———. *History of the Jews in Russia and Poland.* 3 vols. New York, 1975.

———. *Nationalism and History.* New York, 1970.

———. *Toldot Ha-Hasidut.* Tel Aviv, 1967.

Eisenbach, A. "About Emancipation of Jews in the Kingdom of Poland" (in Polish with English summary). *Bioletyn Zydowskiego Instytutu Historycznego* 92 (1974): 71–89.

———. "Die Judenemanzipation in den Polischen Gebeiten in 19 Jahrhundert von dem Europaische Hintergrund." *Bulletin des Leo Baeck Instituts* 68 (1984): 3–21.

———. *The Emancipation of the Jews in Poland, 1780–1870.* Translated by J. Dorosz. Edited by A. Polonsky. Oxford, 1991.

Elbaum, Yaakov. *Petihut ve Histagrut.* Jerusalem, 1990.

Elior, Rachel. "Between *Yesh* and *Ayin:* The Doctrine of the Zaddik in the Works of Jacob Isaac, the Seer of Lublin." In *Jewish History: Essays in Honor of Chimen Abramsky,* edited by Ada Rapoport-Albert and Steven Zipperstein. London, 1988.

———. "Ha-Zika she-beyn Kabbala la-Hasidut." In *Proceedings of the Ninth World Congress of Jewish Studies.* Jerusalem, 1986.

———. "Kabbalat Ha-Ari, Sabbateanism and Hasidism: Historical Continuity, Spirituality and Differences." *Mekharei Yerushalayim* 13 (1996): 339–97.

———. "Messianic Expectations and Spiritualization of Religious Life in the Sixteenth Century." In *Essential Papers on Jewish Culture in Renaissance and Baroque Italy,* edited by David B. Ruderman. New York, 1992.

———. "The Metaphorical Relation between God and Man and the Significance of Visionary Reality in Lurianic Kabbalah" (in Hebrew). *Jerusalem Studies in Jewish Thought* 10 (1992): 47–58.

———. "Spiritual Renaissance and Social Change in the Beginning of Hasidism" (in Hebrew). *'Aley Sefer.* Ramat Gan, Israel, 1990.

Elman, Yaakov. "R. Zaddok Ha-Kohen and the History of Halakha." *Tradition* 21, no. 4 (fall 1985): 1–27.

Ephrayim of Luntzshutz, R. Shlomo. *'Ollelot Ephrayim.* Zalkawa, 1865.

Erasmus, Desiderius, and Martin Luther. *Discourse on Free Will.* Translated by E. F. Winter. New York, 1961.

Etkes, Emanuel. "Hasidism as a Movement—The First Stage." In *Hasidism: Continuity or Innovation?* edited by Bezalel Safran. Cambridge, Mass., 1988.

———. "On the Question of the Enlightenment in Eastern Europe" (in Hebrew). *Tarbiz* 57, no. 1 (1989): 95–114.

———. *R. Yisrael Salanter and the Beginning of the Mussar Movement* (in Hebrew). Jerusalem, 1984.

Even Chen, Jacob. *Ramban* (in Hebrew). Jerusalem, 1977.

Eyebshutz, R. Yonatan. *Tiferet Yonatan.* Brooklyn, N.Y., 1974.

Eyebshutz, Yohanan Levi. *Simha Bunim of Pryzsucha.* Tel Aviv, 1973.

Faierstein, Morris. *All Is in the Hands of Heaven: The Teachings of Rabbi Mordecai Joseph Leiner of Izbica.* New Jersey, 1987.

———. "The Friday Night Incident in Kotzk: History of a Legend." *Journal of Jewish Studies* 34 (1983): 179–89.

———. "God's Need for the Commandments in Medieval Kabbala." *Conservative Judaism* 36, no. 1 (1982): 45–59.

———. "Personal Redemption in Hasidism." In *Hasidism Reappraised,* edited by A. Rapoport-Albert. London, 1996.

Faivre, Antoine. *Access to Western Esotericism.* Albany, N.Y., 1994.

Faivre, Antoine, and J. Needleman, eds. *Modern Esoteric Spirituality.* Albany, N.Y., 1992.

Feiner, Samuel. "The Enlightenment in Relation to History: The Recognition of the Past and Its Purpose in the Jewish Enlightenment 1782–1881" (in Hebrew). Ph.D. dissertation, Hebrew University, 1990.

———. "Faith Alone!: R. Nathan of Nemirov's Battle Against Atheism and the Enlightenment" (in Hebrew). *Jerusalem Studies in Jewish Thought* 15 (1999): 110–24.

Feldman, Seymour. "A Debate Concerning Determinism in Late Medieval Jewish Philosophy." *Proceedings of the American Academy for Jewish Research* 5 (1984): 15–54.

Fine, Lawrence. *Safed Spirituality: Rules of Mystical Piety, the Beginning of Wisdom.* New York, 1984.

Fishbane, Michael. *Biblical Interpretation in Ancient Israel.* Oxford, 1985.

———. *The Exegetical Imagination: On Jewish Thought and Theology.* Cambridge, Mass.: 1998.

———. *The Garments of Torah: Essays in Biblical Hermeneutics.* Bloomington, Ind., 1989.

Forman, R. K. C., ed. "Introduction: Mysticism, Constructivism, and Forgetting." In *The Problem of Pure Consciousness: Mysticism and Philosophy,* edited by R. K. C. Forman. New York and Oxford, 1990.

Fox, Marvin. *Interpreting Maimonides: Studies in Methodology, Metaphysics and Moral Philosophy.* Chicago, 1990.

Frankel, R. Abraham Joshua Heschel. *Mei Zedek.* Brooklyn, N.Y., 1984.

Funkenstein, Amos. "Maimonides' Political Theory and Realistic Messianism." *Miscellanea Mediaevalia* 11 (1977): 81–103.

———. *Perceptions of Jewish History.* Berkeley, Calif., 1993.

______. "The Typological Exegesis of Ramban" (in Hebrew). *Zion* 45 (1980): 35–59.

Gabbai, R. Meir Ibn. *Avodat Ha-Kodesh.* Jerusalem, 1973.

Gataker, T. *Antinomianism Discovered and Confuted.* London, 1655.

Gellman, Jerome. *The Fear, the Trembling and the Fire: Kierkegaard and Hasidic Masters on the Binding of Isaac.* New York and London, 1994.

Gerondi, R. Jacob ben Sheshet. *Ha-Emunah ve Ha-Bitahon.* In *Kitvei Ha-Ramban,* 2 vols., edited by Hayyim Chavel. Jerusalem, 1976.

Gerondi, R. Perez ben Isaac. *Ma'arekhet Ha-Elohut.* Mantua, 1558. Reprint. Jerusalem, 1963.

Gikatillia, R. Joseph. *Sha'are 'Orah.* Preface by Joseph Ben Shlomo. Jerusalem, 1970.

Giller, Pinhas. *The Enlightened Will Shine: Symbolization and Theurgy in the Later Strata of the Zohar.* Albany, N.Y., 1993.

______. *Reading the Zohar: The Sacred Text of the Kabbalah.* Oxford, 2000.

Glicksman, P. Z. *Tiferet Adam.* Lodz, 1933.

Ginsburg, Elliot. *The Sabbath in the Classical Kabbala.* Albany, N.Y., 1989.

Goitein, S. D. "Abraham Maimonides and His Pietist Circle." In *Jewish Medieval and Renaissance Studies,* edited by A. Altmann. Cambridge, Mass., 1967.

Gottlieb, Efrayim. *Mekharim be Sifrut Ha-Kabbala.* Edited by Joseph Hacker. Tel Aviv, 1976.

Graetz, Heinrich. *Frank und die Frankisten: Eine Sekten-Geschichte aus der letzten Hälfte des vorigen Jahrhundertes.* Breslau, 1868.

______. *History of the Jews.* Vol. 4. Philadelphia, 1956.

Graham, William. *Beyond the Written Word: Oral Aspects of Scripture in the History of Religion.* Cambridge, 1987.

Green, Arthur. *Devotion and Commandment: The Faith of Abraham in the Hasidic Tradition.* Cincinnati, 1989.

______. "Three Warsaw Mystics." *Jerusalem Studies in Jewish Thought* 13 (1996): 1–58.

______. *Tormented Master: A Life of Rabbi Nahman of Bratslav.* Birmingham, Ala., 1979.

______. "Typologies of Leadership and the Hasidic Zaddik." In *Jewish Spirituality II,* edited by Arthur Green. New York, 1989.

Gries, Zeev. *The Book in Early Hasidism* (in Hebrew). Tel Aviv, 1992.

______. *Conduct Literature: Its History and Place in the Life of Beshtian Hasidism* (in Hebrew). Jerusalem, 1989.

______. "Hasidism: The Present State of Research and Some Desirable Priorities." *Numen* 34, no. 2 (1987): 97–108, 179–213.

______. "Mi-Mytos le-Etos-Kavim li Demuto shel Avraham mi-Kalish." *Umah ve Toldoteha* 2 (1984): 117–47.

______. "Sifrut Ha-Hanhagot Ha-Hasidit." *Zion* 46, nos. 3–4 (1981): 198–236, 278–305.

Grozinger, K. E. "Neoplatonische Denken in Hasidismus und Kabbala." *Frankfurter Judaistiche Beiträge* (1983).

———. "Principles and Aims in Lurianic Cosmology." *Jerusalem Studies in Jewish Thought* 10 (1992): 37–46.

Gutmann, Julius. *Philosophies of Judaism: The History of Jewish Philosophy from Biblical Times to Franz Rosenzweig*. New York, 1964.

Haack, S. "On a Theological Defense for Fatalism." *Philosophical Quarterly* 24 (1974): 156–59.

Hallamish, Moshe. "Kabbala in the Legal Decisions of R. Joseph Karo" (in Hebrew). *Da'at* 21 (1988): 85–102.

———. "Luria's Status as a Halakhic Authority" (in Hebrew). *Jerusalem Studies in Jewish Thought* 10 (1992): 259–85.

———. "Mishnato Ha-Iyunit shel R. Schneur Zalman mi-Liadi ve-Yahasa Le-Torat Ha-Kabbala u-Le-Reshit Ha-Hasidut." Ph.D. dissertation, Hebrew University, 1976.

Handelman, Susan. *Fragments of Redemption: Jewish Thought and Literary Theory in Benjamin, Scholem, and Levinas*. Bloomington, Ind., 1991.

Harris, Jay M. "The Image of Maimonides in Nineteenth-Century Jewish Historiography." In *Proceedings of the American Academy of Jewish Research* 54 (1987): 117–39.

Hartman, David. *Crisis and Leadership: Epistles of Maimonides.* Translated by Abraham Halkin. David Hartman Commentaries. Philadelphia, 1985.

———. *Maimonides: Torah and Philosophical Quest.* Philadelphia, 1974.

Haver, R. Yizhak Eisek. *Magen ve Zina.* Bnei Brak, 1985.

Hecker, Joel. "Each Man Ate an Angel's Bread: Eating and Embodiment in the Zohar." Ph.D. dissertation, New York University, 1996.

Heinemann, Isaac. *Ta'amei Ha-Mitzvot.* 2 vols. Jerusalem, 1949.

Heller-Wilensky, Sara O. "Between Mysticism and Philosophy: In Light of the Thought of R. Issac Ibn Latif" (in Hebrew). *Jerusalem Studies in Jewish Thought* 4, nos. 3–4 (1987): 362–82.

———. "The Dialectical Influence of the Rambam on Ibn Latif and the Beginning of the Kabbala in Spain" (in Hebrew). Vol. 7. *Shlomo Pines Jubilee Volume, Part 1, Jerusalem Studies in Jewish Thought.* Jerusalem, 1988.

———. *R. Yizhak Arama u Mishnato.* Jerusalem, 1957.

Hendel, Ronald S. "The Poetics of Myth in Genesis." In *The Seductiveness of Jewish Myth: Challenge or Response,* edited by Daniel Breslauer. Albany, N.Y., 1997.

Herschler, M., ed. *Hidushei Ha-Ramban Ha-Shalem.* 4 vols. Jerusalem, 1970–87.

Hertz, A. *The Jews in Polish Culture.* Evanston, Ill., 1988.

Herzog, Isaac. *The Royal Purple and the Biblical Blue: Argamon and Tekhelet.* Jerusalem, 1987.

Heschel, A. J. *Kotzk* (in Yiddish). 2 vols. Tel Aviv, 1973.

Heschel, Abraham Joshua. *The Circle of the Baal Shem Tov: Studies in Hasidism.* Chicago, 1985.

———. "The Eastern European Era in Jewish History." In *Studies in Modern Jewish Social History,* edited by J. Fishman. New York, 1972.
———. *Maimonides: A Biography*. New York, 1982.
———. *A Passion for Truth.* New York, 1973.
———. *Prophetic Inspiration after the Prophets: Maimonides and Other Medieval Authorities*. Edited by Morris M. Faierstein. New Jersey, 1996.
Horodetzky, Samuel Abba. *Ha-Hadisut ve Ha-Hasidim.* 4 vols. Tel Aviv, 1953.
———. "The Rambam in Kabbala and Hasidism" (in Hebrew). In *Moznaim* 3 (1943): 441–45.
———. *Studies by Samuel Horodetzky* (in German). Edited by Steven Katz. New York, 1980.
———. *Torat Ha-Kabbala Shel Moshe Cordovero.* Jerusalem, 1951.
———. *Torat Ha-Kabbala shel R. Yizhak Ashkenazi ve R. Hayyim Vital.* Palestine, 1947.
Horowitz, Elliot. "Coffee, Coffee Houses, and the Nocturnal Rituals of Early Modern Jewry." *AJS Review* 14, no. 1 (1989): 17–46.
Hundert, Gershon. "An Advantage to Peculiarity? The Case of the [Jews in the] Polish Commonwealth." *AJS Review* 6 (1981): 21–38.
———. "Jewish Urban Residence in the Polish Commonwealth in the Early Modern Period." *Journal of Jewish Studies* 26, no. 1 (1984): 25–34.
———. "Some Basic Characteristics of the Jewish Experience in Poland." *Polin* 1 (1986): 28–34.
Husik, Isaac. *A History of Medieval Jewish Philosophy*. Philadelphia, 1948.
Huss, Boaz. "*Sefer Ha-Zohar* as a Canonical, Sacred and Holy Text." *Journal of Jewish Thought and Philosophy* 7 (1998): 257–307.
Ibn Gaon, R. Shem Tov. *Migdal 'Oz.* Commentary to Maimonides' *Mishneh Torah.* In standard editions.
Ibn Pakuda, R. Bahya. *Hovot Ha-Levavot.* Jerusalem, 1969.
Idel, Moshe. "Between the Kabbala of Jerusalem and the Kabbala of Israel Sarug" (in Hebrew). *Shalem* 6 (1992): 165–73.
———. "Differing Conceptions of Kabbala in the Early Seventeenth Century." In *Jewish Thought in the Seventeenth Century,* edited by I. Twersky and B. Septimus. Cambridge, Mass., 1987.
———. "Divine Attributes and Sefirot in Jewish Theology." In *Studies in Judaism,* edited by S. O. Heller-Wilensky. Jerusalem, 1989.
———. "Ha-Sefirot me 'al Ha-Sefirot." *Tarbiz* 51 (1982): 239–80.
———. *Hasidism: Between Ecstasy and Magic.* Albany, N.Y., 1995.
———. *Infinities of Torah in Kabbala, Midrash and Literature.* Edited by Geoffrey H. Hartman and Sanford Budick. New Haven, Conn., 1986.
———. "Jewish Kabbala and Platonism in the Middle Ages and the Renaissance." *Neoplatonism and Jewish Thought,* edited by Lenn Goodman. Albany, N.Y., 1992.

______ "Kabbala and Philosophy in R. Isaac and Yehuda Abrabanel" (in Hebrew). In *The Philosophy of Leone Ebreo,* edited by M. Dorman and Z. Levy. Tel Aviv, 1985.

______. *Kabbala: New Perspectives.* New Haven, Conn., 1988.

______. *Language, Torah and Hermeneutics in Abraham Abulafia.* Albany, N.Y., 1989.

______. "Magical and Neoplatonic Interpretations of Kabbala in the Renaissance" (in Hebrew). *Jerusalem Studies in Jewish Thought* 4 (1982): 60–112.

______. "Maimonide et la Cabala." In *Maimonide et la Mystique Juive.* Paris, 1991.

______. "Maimonides and Kabbala." In *Studies in Maimonides,* edited by Isadore Twersky. Cambridge, Mass., 1991.

______. "Midrashic versus Other Forms of Jewish Hermeneutics: Some Comparative Reflections." In *The Midrashic Imagination: Jewish Exegesis, Thought and History,* edited by M. Fishbane. Albany, N.Y., 1993.

______ "Nahmanides: *Kabbalah, Halakha,* and Spiritual Leadership." In *Jewish Mystical Leaders and Leadership in the Thirteenth Century,* edited by Moshe Idel. Northvale, N.J., 1998.

______. "One from a Town, Two from a Clan: A New Look at the Problem of the Diffusion of Lurianic Kabbala and Sabbateanism." *Jewish History* 7 (1993): 79–104.

______. "On Kabbalism vs. Rabbinism: On Gershom Scholem's Phenomenology of Judaism." In *Modern Judaism* 11, no. 3 (1991): 281–96.

______ "On the History of the Term *Zimzum* in Kabbala and Scholarship" (in Hebrew). *Jerusalem Studies in Jewish Thought* 10 (1992): 59–112.

______. "Perspectives of Kabbala in the Second Half of the Eighteenth Century." *Journal of Jewish Thought and Philosophy* 1, no. 1 (1991): 55–114.

______. "R. Abraham Abulafia: Works and Doctrine" (in Hebrew). Unpublished Ph.D. dissertation, Hebrew University, Jerusalem, 1976.

______. "Reification of Language in Jewish Mysticism" In *Mysticism and Language,* edited by Steven Katz. Oxford, 1992.

______. *R. Menahem Recanati: The Kabbalist* (in Hebrew). Tel Aviv, 1998.

______. "Universalization and Integration: Two Conceptions of Mystical Union in Jewish Mysticism." In *Mystical Union and Monotheistic Faith: An Ecumenical Dialogue,* edited by Louis Dupre. New York, 1989.

Isaac of Granada, R. Abraham. *Brit Menuha.* Jerusalem, 1958–59.

Isserles, R. Moshe. *Teshuvot Ha-Rama.* New York, 1954.

______. *Torat Ha-'Olah.* Lemberg, 1858.

Ivry, Alfred. "Islamic and Greek Influences on Maimonides' Philosophy." In *Maimonides and Philosophy,* edited by Shlomo Pines and Yermiyahu Yovel. Nijhoff, Netherlands, 1986.

______. "Maimonides and Neoplatonism: Challenge and Response." In *Neoplatonism and Jewish Thought,* edited by Lenn Goodman. Albany, N.Y., 1992.

———. "Neoplatonic Currents in Maimonides' Thought." In *Studies in Maimonides' Thought and Environment,* edited by Joel Kraemer. Oxford, 1990.

———. "Providence, Divine Omniscience and Possibility: The Case of Maimonides." Reprinted in *Maimonides: A Collection of Critical Essays,* edited by J. A. Buijs. Notre Dame, Ind., 1988.

Jacobs, Louis. "Aspects of Scholem's Study of Hasidism." In *Gershom Scholem,* edited by Harold Bloom. New York, 1987.

———. "Attitudes of the Kabbalists and Hasidism towards Maimonides." Samuel Goldman Lecture Series, no. 5. 1990.

———. "Divine Foreknowledge and Human Free Will." *Conservative Judaism* 34 (1980): 4–16.

———. *The Jewish Mystics.* London, 1990.

———. *Seeker of Unity: The Life and Works of R. Aaron of Staroselye.* New York and London, 1966.

———. *Turn Aside from Evil and Do Good: An Introduction and a Way to the Tree of Life.* London, 1995.

Jacobson, Yoram. *From Lurianic Kabbalism to the Psychological Theosophy of Hasidism* (in Hebrew). Israel, 1984.

James, William. *Essays on Faith and Morals.* Cleveland, 1962.

———. *Pragmatism.* Indianapolis, 1981.

Jellinek, Adolph. *Philosophie und Kabbala.* Leipzig, 1854.

Jonas, Hans. *The Gnostic Religion.* Boston, 1963.

———. "Myth and Mysticism: A Study of Objectification and Interiorization in Religious Thought." *Journal of Religion* 49 (1969): 315–29.

———. "The Soul in Gnosticism and Plotinus." In *Le Néoplatonisme,* Colloques internationaux du Centre national de la recherche scientifique: Sciences humaines. Paris, 1971.

Jospe, Raphael. "Ramban and Arabic" (in Hebrew). *Tarbiz* 57, no. 1 (1988): 67–93.

Kadish, Y. K. *Tiferet Ha-Yehudi.* Jerusalem, 1975.

Kallus, Menahem. "The Relationship of the Baal Shem Tov to the Practice of Lurianic Kavvanot in Light of His Comments on the Siddur Rashkov." *Kabbala: Journal for the Study of Jewish Mystical Texts* 2 (1997): 151–68.

Kaplan, Abraham Elijah. *Be-Ikvot Ha-Yerah.* Jerusalem, 1960.

Kaplan, Aryeh. *The Bahir: Illumination.* New York, 1979.

———. *Inner Space: Introduction to Kabbalah, Meditation, and Prophecy.* Jerusalem, 1990.

Kaplan, Lawrence. "Maimonides and the Miraculous Element in Prophecy." *Harvard Theological Review* 70 (1997): 233–56.

Katz, Jacob. "Halakha and Kabbala as Competing Disciplines of Study." In *Jewish Spirituality II,* edited by Arthur Green. New York, 1989.

———. *Halakha and Kabbala: Studies in the History of Jewish Religion, Its Various Faces and Social Relevance* (in Hebrew). Jerusalem, 1984.

_______. "Post-Zoharic Relations between Halakhah and Kabbalah." In *Jewish Thought in the Sixteenth Century,* edited by Bernard Dov Cooperman. Cambridge, Mass., 1983.

Katz, Steven. "The Conservative Character of Mysticism." In *Mysticism and Religious Tradition,* edited by Steven Katz. Oxford, 1983.

_______. *Jewish Neo-Platonism.* New York, 1980.

_______. "Language, Epistemology, and Mysticism." In *Mysticism: Philosophical Analysis,* edited by Steven Katz. New York, 1978.

Kellner, Menahem. "Jewish Dogmas after the Spanish Expulsion: Rabbi Isaac Abravanel and Joseph Ya'bes on Belief in Creation as an Article of Faith." *Jewish Quarterly Review* 72 (1982): 178–87.

_______. *Principles of Faith: Rosh Amanah of R. Isaac Abravanel.* Translated with commentary by Menahem Kellner. London and Toronto, 1982.

Kevan, E. F. *The Grace of Law: A Study in Puritan Theology.* London, 1964.

Kieniewicz, S. "The Jews of Warsaw, Polish Society and the Partitioning Powers 1765–1861." *Polin* 3 (1988): 102–21.

_______. *History of Poland.* Warsaw, 1968.

Kimelman, Reuven. "The Seduction of Eve and the Exegetical Politics of Gender." In *Biblical Interpretation.* Leiden, 1996.

King, Sallie B. "Two Epistemological Models for the Interpretation of Mysticism." *Journal for the American Academy of Religion* 56 (1988): 257–79.

Kreisel, Howard T. "Theories of Prophecy in Medieval Jewish Philosophy." Ph.D. dissertation, Brandeis University, 1981.

Lehmann, J. H. "Maimonides, Mendelssohn and the *Me'asfim:* Philosophy and the Biographical Imagination in the Early Haskalah." *Leo Baeck Institute Year Book* (1975): 87–108.

Leslie, R. F. *Polish Politics and the Revolution of November 1830.* London, 1956.

_______. *Reform and Insurrection in Russian Poland, 1856–1865.* London, 1963.

Levin, Yehudah Leyb. *Beit Kotzk.* Jerusalem, 1990.

_______. *Ha-Admorim me-Izbica.* Jerusalem, n.d.

Liebes, Yehuda. "Eros and the Zohar" (in Hebrew). *'Alpayim* 9 (1994): 67–119.

_______. "How Was the Zohar Written?" (in Hebrew). *Jerusalem Studies in Jewish Thought* 9 (1989): 1–71.

_______ "The Messiah in *Sefer Ha-Zohar*" (in Hebrew). In *Ha-Ra'ayon Ha-Meshihi be Yisrael.* Jerusalem, 1982.

_______. "Myth Versus Symbol in the Zohar and in Lurianic Kabbala." In *Essential Papers on Kabbalah,* edited by Lawrence Fine. New York, 1995.

_______. "New Directions in the Research of Kabbala" (in Hebrew). *Pe'amim* 50 (1992): 150–70.

_______. *On Sabbateanism and Its Kabbala: Collected Essays.* Jerusalem, 1995.

_______. *Studies in the Zohar.* Albany, N.Y., 1993.

_______. "*Zaddik Yesod 'Olam:* A Sabbatean Myth" (in Hebrew). *Da'at* 1 (1978): 159–73.

Lord, Albert B. "Patterns of Lives of the Patriarchs from Abraham to Samson and Samuel." In *Text and Tradition: The Hebrew Bible and Folklore,* edited by Susan Niditch. Atlanta, Ga., 1990.

Lowenthal, Naftali. *Communicating the Infinite: The Emergence of the Habad School.* Chicago, 1990.

______ "The Concept of 'Mesirat Nefesh' in the Teachings of R. Dov Baer of Lubavitch." Ph.D. dissertation, University of London, 1981.

Luria, R. David. *Kadmut Sefer Ha-Zohar.* Bnei Brak, 1985.

Luzatto, R. Moshe Hayyim. *Da'at Tevunot.* Bnei Brak, 1975.

______. *Kelakh (148) Pithai Hokhma.* Bnei Brak, 1992.

______. *Sefer Ha-Klalim.* Bnei Brak, 1975.

Magid, Shaul. "Associative Midrash: Reflections on a Hermeneutical Theory in Rabbi Nahman of Bratslav's *Likkutei MoHaRan.*" In *God's Voice from the Void: Old and New Studies in Bratslav Hasidism,* edited by S. Magid. Albany, N.Y., 2001.

______. "Conjugal Union, Mourning, and Talmud Torah in R. Isaac Luria's *Tikkun Hazot.*" *Da'at* 36 (1996): xvii–xlv.

______. "From Theosophy to Midrash: Lurianic Exegesis and the Garden of Eden." *AJS Review* 22, no. 1 (spring/summer 1997): 37–75.

______. "Modernity as Heresy: The Introvertive Piety of Faith in R. Areleh Roth's *Shomer Emunim.*" *Jewish Studies Quarterly* 4 (1996): 74–104.

______. "Origin and the Overcoming of Beginning: *Zimzum* as a Trope of Reading in Post-Lurianic Kabbala." In *Beginning/Again: Toward a Hermeneutic of Jewish Texts,* edited by Aryeh Cohen and Shaul Magid. New York, 2002.

______. "Through the Void: The Absence of God in R. Nahman of Bratzlav's *Likkutei MoHaRan.*" *Harvard Theological Review* 88, no. 4 (1995): 495–519.

Mahler, Raphael. *Hasidism and the Jewish Enlightenment.* Philadelphia, 1985.

Maimon, Yehuda Leib Ha-Cohen. *Midei Hodesh be Hodshov.* Vol. 5. Jerusalem, 1959.

Maimonides, Obadya. *Treatise of the Pool.* Translated by Paul Fenton. London, 1987.

Maimonides, R. Moses. *Guide for the Perplexed.* Translated by Samuel Ibn Tibbon. Jerusalem, 1970.

______. *Guide of the Perplexed.* Translated by Shlomo Pines. Chicago, 1963.

______. *Sefer Ha-Mitzvot l'Ha-Rambam.* Gloss by Maimonides. R. Hayyim Chavel, ed. Jerusalem: Mossad Ha-Rav Kook, 1981.

Mansoor, Menahem. *The Book of Direction of the Duties of the Heart.* London, 1973.

Marcus, Aaron. *Der Chasidismus.* Pleschen, 1901.

Marcus, Ivan. "Beyond the Sephardic Mystique." *Orim* (1985): 35–58.

Margoliot, Reuven, ed. *Sefer Ha-Zohar.* 3 vols. Jerusalem, 1984.

Marty, Martin. *Varieties of Unbelief.* New York, 1966.

Marx, Alexander. "Texts By and About Maimonides." *Jewish Quarterly Review* 25 (1934–35): 374–81.

Matt, Daniel. *Zohar: The Book of Enlightenment.* New Jersey, 1983.
______ "The Mystic and the Mitzvot." In *Jewish Spirituality I,* edited by Arthur Green. New York, 1986.
______. "New Ancient Words: The Aura of Secrecy in the Zohar." In *Gershom Scholem's Major Trends in Jewish Mysticism Fifty Years After: Proceedings of the Sixth International Conference on the History of Jewish Mysticism,* edited by Peter Schafer and Joseph Dan. Tubingen, 1993.
McGinn, Bernard. "Asceticism and Mysticism in Late Antiquity and the Early Middle Ages." In *Asceticism,* edited by V. L. Wimbush and R. Valantasis. New York and Oxford, 1995.
______. *Foundations of Mysticism: From Its Origins to the Fifth Century.* New York, 1992.
Melan, Paul. *Monopsychism, Mysticism and Metaconsciousness.* The Hague, 1963.
Meroz, Ronit. "Redemption in the Lurianic Teaching" (in Hebrew). Ph.D. dissertation, Hebrew University, 1988.
______. "R. Israel Sarug, Student of the Ari: A Re-Appraisal" (in Hebrew). *Da'at* 28 (1992).
______. "Selections from Ephraim Penzieri: Luria's Sermon in Jerusalem and the *Kavvanah* in Taking Food" (in Hebrew). *Jerusalem Studies in Jewish Thought* 10 (1992): 211–58.
Morgenstern, Arie. *Bi-shelihut Yerushalayim: Toldot mishpahat H. Rozental, 1816–1839* [Emissary to Jerusalem: The history of the H. Rozenthal family]. Jerusalem, 1985.
______. "Messianic Concepts and Settlement in the Land of Israel." In *Essential Papers on Messianic Movements and Personalities in Jewish History,* edited by Marc Saperstein. New York and London, 1992.
______. "Messianic Expectation in the Wake of the Year 1840" (in Hebrew). *Messianism and Eschatology* (1983): 343–64.
______. *Messianism and the Settlement of Eretz Yisrael.* Jerusalem, 1985.
Nadler, Allan. *The Faith of the Mithnagdim.* Baltimore, 1997.
______. "Religion of Limits." Ph.D. dissertation, Harvard University, 1988.
______. "The War on Modernity of R. Hayyim Elazar Shapira of Munkacz." *Modern Judaism* 14 (1994): 233–64.
Neher, Andre. *Jewish Thought and the Scientific Revolution of the Sixteenth Century: David Gans, 1541–1613, and His Times.* Translated by David Maisel. Oxford, 1986.
Neumann, Erich. "Mystical Man." In *The Mystic Vision,* edited by Joseph Campbell. Bollingen Series. Vol. 30, no. 6. Princeton, 1968.
Neumark, David. *Toldot Ha-Philosophia be Yisrael.* Jerusalem, 1971.
Novak, David. "The Doctrine of the Self-Contraction of God in Kabbalistic Theology." In *Neoplatonism and Jewish Thought,* edited by Lenn Goodman. Albany, N.Y., 1992.
______. *Natural Law in Judaism.* Cambridge, 1998.

———. *The Theology of Nahmanides Systematically Presented.* Atlanta, Ga., 1992.

Ong, Walter. *Orality and Literacy: The Technologizing of the Word.* London and New York, 1982.

Oppenheimer, I. "The History of Nineteenth-Century Polish Jewry from the Perspective of Twentieth-Century Polish Historiography" (in Hebrew). *Uma'ah ve Toldoteha* 2 (1984): 65–86.

———. "On the Question of the Jews in the Polish Newspaper *GLOS* [the Voice], 1880–1894" (in Hebrew). In *Bein Yisrael le 'Umot.* Jerusalem, 1987.

Otto, Rudolph. *The Idea of the Holy: An Inquiry into the Non-Rational Factor in the Idea of the Divine and Its Relation to the Rational.* London, 1925.

———. *Mysticism East and West: A Comparative Analysis of the Nature of Mysticism.* London, 1932.

Pachter, Mordecai. "Between Acosmism and Theism in R. Hayyim of Volozhin" (in Hebrew). *Mehkarim be Hagot Ha-Yehudit* (1989): 139–57.

——— "Circles and Lines: The History of an Idea" (in Hebrew). *Da'at* 18, 59–90.

——— "Clarifying the Terms *Katnut* and *Gadlut* in the Kabbala of the Ari and a History of Its Understanding in Hasidism" (in Hebrew). *Jerusalem Studies in Jewish Thought* 10 (1992): 171–210.

———. "The Concept of *Devekut* in the Homiletical Writings of Sixteenth-Century Safed." *Studies in Medieval Jewish History and Literature* 2 (1984): 171–230.

Penkalla, A. "The Socio-Cultural Integration of the Jewish Population in the Province of Radom 1815–1862." *Polin* 3 (1988): 214–38.

Penzeri, R. Eliahu. *Sefer Ha-Derushim.* Jerusalem, 1996.

Piekarz, Mendel. *Ha-Hanhaga Ha-Hasidit.* Jerusalem, 1999.

———. *Hasidut Bratslav.* Jerusalem, 1972.

———. "The Messianic Idea in the Beginning of Hasidism in Light of *Drush* and *Mussar* Literature" (in Hebrew). In *The Messianic Idea in Israel: A Study Conference in Honor of the Eightieth Birthday of Gershom Scholem.* Jerusalem, 1990.

———. *Polish Hasidism between the Wars* (in Hebrew). Jerusalem, 1990.

——— *When Hasidism Was Flourishing* (in Hebrew). Jerusalem, 1978.

Pike, Nelson. "Divine Foreknowledge, Human Freedom and Possible Worlds." *Philosophical Review* 86 (1977): 209–16.

———. "Divine Omniscience and Voluntary Action." *Philosophical Review* 74 (1965): 27–46.

———. *God and Timelessness.* New York, 1970.

———. *Mystic Union: An Essay in the Phenomenology of Mysticism.* Ithaca, N.Y., and London, 1992.

Pines, Shlomo. "Abu'l-Barakat's Poetics and Metaphysics." *Scripta Hierosolymitana.* Vol. 6, *Studies in Philosophy.* Jerusalem, 1960.

Popkin, Richard. "Spinoza, Neoplatonic Kabbalist." In *Neoplatonism and Jewish Thought,* edited by Lenn Goodman. Albany, N.Y., 1992.

Poppers, R. Meir. *Derekh Etz Hayyim.* Karetz, 1784.

———. *Sefer Ha-Likuttim.* Jerusalem, 1913.

——— *Ta'amei Ha-Mitzvot.* Vilna, 1880.

Pressburg, R. Isaac Arama. *Akedat Yitzhak.* N.p., 1849.

Purtill, R. "Fatalism and the Omnitemporality of Truth." In *Faith and Philosophy.* N.p., 1988.

Rabinowitz, Zvi Meir. *R. Simha Bunim of Pryzsucha.* Tel Aviv, 1944.

———. *R. Ya'akov Yizhak of Pryzsucha.* Petrikov, 1916.

Rahner, Karl. *On Heresy.* Freiburg, 1964.

Rapoport-Albert, Ada. "God and the Tzadik as the Two Focal Points of Hasidic Worship." *History of Religions* 18 (1979): 296–324.

———. "Hagiography with Footnotes: Edifying Tales and the Writing of History in Hasidism." In *Essays in Jewish Historiography,* edited by A. Rapoport-Albert. Atlanta, Ga., 1991.

Ravitzky, Aviezer. *Al Da'at Ha-Makom: Studies in the History of Jewish Philosophy* (in Hebrew). Jerusalem, 1991.

———. "The Development of the Thought of Hasdai Crescas on the Issue of Free Will" (in Hebrew). *Tarbiz* 51 (1982): 445–69.

———. "The God of the Philosophers and the God of the Kabbalists: A Controversy in Fifteenth-Century Crete." In *History and Faith: Studies in Jewish Philosophy.* Amsterdam, 1996.

———. *Ha-Ketz Ha Meguleh u-Medinat Ha-Yehudim.* Tel Aviv, 1993.

———. "R. Shmuel Ibn Tibbon ve Sodo shel Moreh Nevuhim." *Da'at* (1984): 109–45.

Rawidowicz, Simon. "On Interpretation." In *Studies in Jewish Thought.* Philadelphia, 1974.

Recanati, R. Menahem. *Recanati 'al Ha-Torah.* Jerusalem, 1971.

———. *Ta'amei Ha-Mitzvot.* Basel, 1581.

Rosenberg, Shalom. *Good and Evil in Jewish Thought* (in Hebrew). Tel Aviv, 1985.

———. "On the Interpretation of Scripture in the *Guide*" (in Hebrew). *Jerusalem Studies in Jewish Thought* 1 (1982): 85–157.

———. "Return to the Garden of Eden: Reflections on the History of the Idea of Restorative Redemption in Medieval Jewish Philosophy" (in Hebrew). In *The Messianic Idea in Israel: A Study Conference in Honor of the Eightieth Birthday of Gershom Scholem.* Jerusalem, 1990.

Rosenblatt, Samuel. *The High Ways to Perfection of Abraham Maimonides.* Vol. 2. New York, 1927. Reprint. Baltimore, 1938.

Rosman, Moshe. *Founder of Hasidism: The Quest for the Historical Ba'al Shem Tov.* Berkeley, Calif., 1996.

Rosner, Fred. *Six Treatises Attributed to Maimonides.* Translated and annotated from the Hebrew editions. Northvale, N.J., and London, 1988.

Ross, Tamar. "Shnei Perushim le-Torat Ha-Zimzum: R. Hayyim of Volozhin ve-R. Shneur Zalman mi-Liady." *Jerusalem Studies in Jewish Thought* 2 (1982): 153–69.

Rubin, Zvia. "The Way of Joseph Ibn Tabul as a Commentator to the Zohar" (in Hebrew). *Jerusalem Studies in Jewish Thought* 10 (1992): 363–88.

Rubinstein, Abraham, ed. *Shivhei Ha-Besht*. Jerusalem, 1991.

Ruderman, David. "The Italian Renaissance and Jewish Thought." In *Renaissance Humanism: Foundations and Forms,* edited by A. Rabil Jr. Philadelphia, 1988.

———. *Jewish Thought and Scientific Discovery in Early Modern Europe*. New Haven, Conn., 1995.

Rurup, R. "The European Revolutions of 1848 and Jewish Emancipation." In *Revolution and Evolution 1848 in German-Jewish History,* edited by Werner Eugen Mosse. Tubingen, 1981.

Sack, Bracha. "Ha Ramak ve Ha-Ari." *Jerusalem Studies in Jewish Thought* 10 (1992): 311–40.

——— "The Influence of Cordovero on Seventh-Century Jewish Thought." In *Jewish Thought in the Seventeenth Century,* edited by I. Twersky. Cambridge, Mass., 1987.

——— "On the Relation of R. Moshe Cordovero to *Sefer Temunah*." In *Masu'ot: Studies in Kabbalistic Literature and Jewish Thought,* edited by Michael Oron and Amos Goldreich. Jerusalem, 1994.

———. "The Relationship of R. Shlomo Alkabetz to Philosophical Inquiry" (in Hebrew). *'Eshel Beer Sheva* (1976): 288–306.

——— *Sha'arei Ha-Kabbala Shel R. Moshe Cordovero*. Jerusalem, 1995.

Sade, Pinhas. *'Eish Be-Heder Sagur*. Jerusalem and Tel Aviv, 1993.

Safran, Bezalel. "Rabbi Azriel and Nahmanides: Two Views of the Fall of Man." In *Rabbi Moses Nahmanides: Explorations in His Religious and Literary Virtuosity*. Cambridge, Mass., 1983.

Samuelson, Norbert. "The Problem of Free Will in Maimonides, Gersonides and Aquinas." *CCAR Journal* 17 (1970): 2–20.

Sarachek, Joseph. *Faith and Reason: The Conflict Over Rationalism in Maimonides*. Williamsport, Pa., 1935.

Sarug, R. Israel. *Limmudei Azilut*. Munkacs, 1897.

Schafer, Peter. *The Hidden and Manifest God*. Translated by A. Pomerance. Albany, N.Y., 1992.

Schochat, Azriel. "Al Ha-Simha Be-Hasidut." *Zion* 16 (1951): 30–43.

Scholem, Gershom. "Alchemie und Kabbala." *Monatsschrift für Geschichte und Wissenschaft des Judentums* 69 (1925): 13–30.

———. "The Authentic Writings of the Ari in Kabbala" (in Hebrew). *Kiryat Sefer* (1952/53): 184–99.

———. *Avraham Cohen Herrera: Ba'al Sha'ar Ha-Shamayim* (in Hebrew). Jerusalem, 1978.

———. "The Beginning of Kabbala" (in Hebrew). *Knesset* 10 (1947): 179–228.

———. "The Biography of Ya'akov Zemah and his Literary Activity" (in Hebrew). *Kiryat Sefer* 26 (1950): 185–94.

_______. *Das Buch Bahir*. Leipzig, 1923.
_______. "*Devekut* or Communion with God." In *The Messianic Idea in Jewish Mysticism*. New York, 1971.
_______. "Documents on the Life of Nehemiah Hayyun and Sabbatianism" (in Hebrew). *Zion* 3 (1932): 172–79.
_______. *Ha-Kabbala be Gerona*. Jerusalem, 1964.
_______. *Ha-Kabbala Be-Provence*. Edited by Rivka Shatz. Jerusalem, 1976.
_______. *Ha-Kabbala be Provence Hug Ha-Rabad u beno R. Yizhak Sagi Nahor*. Jerusalem, 1962.
_______. "The Historical Image of R. Israel Baal Shem Tov." *Devarim beGo* (1976): 287–324.
_______. *Jewish Gnosticism, Merkaba Mysticism and Talmudic Tradition*. New York, 1960.
_______. *Judaism and Gnostic Man*. Eranos Lectures, Series 3. Dallas, 1972–73.
_______. *Kabbala*. New York, 1974.
_______. *The Kabbala of Gerona*. Edited by Ben-Shlomo. Jerusalem, 1973.
_______. *The Kabbala of Sefer Temunah and Abraham Abulafia* (in Hebrew). Edited by Ben-Shlomo. Jerusalem, 1969.
_______. "Kabbalat Yizhak ben Shlomo ben Avi Sahula ve Sefer Ha-Zohar." *Kiryat Sefer* 6 (1929): 109–18.
_______. *Major Trends in Jewish Mysticism*. New York, 1941.
_______. "Martin Buber's Hasidism: A Critique." *Commentary* 32 (1961): 305–16.
_______. "Me-Hoker Le-Mekubal." *Tarbiz* 6 (1935): 334–42.
_______. "Mysticism and Society." *Diogenes* 58 (1967): 1–24.
_______. *The Mystical Shape of the Godhead*. Translated by Joachim Neugroschel. Edited by Jonathan Chipman. New York, 1991.
_______. "The Name of God and Linguistic Theory in Kabbala." *Diogenes* 79 (1972): 164–94.
_______. "The Neutralization of the Messianic Element in Early Hasidism." In *The Messianic Idea in Jewish Mysticism*. New York, 1971.
_______. *On the Kabbala and Its Symbolism*. New York, 1965.
_______. *Origins of the Kabbala*. Princeton, N.J., 1962.
_______ "Philosophy and Jewish Mysticism." *Review of Religion* 2 (1937–38): 53–64.
_______ *Pirkei Yesod b'Havanat Ha-Kabbala u' Semalehah*. Jerusalem, 1976.
_______. "Redemption through Sin." In *The Messianic Idea in Judaism*. New York, 1971.
_______. *Sabbatai Sevi: The Mystical Messiah*. Princeton, 1973.
_______ "The Science of Judaism Then and Now." In *The Messianic Idea in Judaism*. New York, 1971.
_______. "Schöpfung aus Nichts und Selbstuerschrankung Gottes." *Eranos Jahrbuch* 25 (1956): 87–119.

———. *Studies and Texts Concerning the History of Sabbetianism and Its Metamorphoses* (in Hebrew). Jerusalem, 1982.

———. "The Unknown and the Expression *Kadmut Ha-Sekhel* in Hasidic Literature." *Devarim beGo* (1976): 351–60.

———. "Yisra'el Sarug—Talmid Ha-Ari ?" (in Hebrew). *Zion* 8 (1940): 214–43.

———. *Zohar: The Book of Splendor*. New York, 1949.

Schorsch, Ismar. *Henrich Graetz's The Structure of Jewish History and Other Essays.* Translated and edited by Ismar Schorsch. New York, 1975.

Schwartz, Dov. "Between Conservatism and Rationalism: The Speculative Thought of the Circle of the Rashba" (in Hebrew). *Da'at* 32–33 (1985): 143–80.

———. "Contacts between Jewish Philosophy and Mysticism at the Beginning of the Fifteenth Century" (in Hebrew). *Da'at* 29 (summer 1992): 41–68.

Schweid, Eliezer. *Judaism and Mysticism According to Gershom Scholem.* Translated by D. A. Weiner. Atlanta, Ga., 1985.

Sefer Hayye Ha-Ari Z'L: Mikhavei M'R. Hayyim Vital. Jerusalem, 1990.

Sefer Kotzk. Jerusalem, 1961.

Sefer Yezirah. Commentary by Moshe Botreil. In standard editions. Brooklyn, N.Y., 1988.

Segal, Alan F. *Paul the Convert.* New Haven, Conn., 1990.

Seltzer, Robert. "The Secular Appropriation of Hasidism by an Eastern European Intellectual: Dubnow, Renan and the Besht." *Polin* 1 (1986): 151–62.

Septimus, Bernard. *Hispano-Jewish Culture in Transition.* Cambridge, Mass., 1982.

———. "'Open Rebuke and Concealed Love': Nahmanides and the Andalusian Tradition." In *Rabbi Moses Nahmanides: Explorations in His Religious and Literary Virtuosity.* Edited by Isadore Twersky. Cambridge, Mass., 1983.

Shacher, Y. *Criticism of Society and Leadership in the Mussar Movement and Drush Literature in Eighteenth-Century Poland* (in Hebrew). Jerusalem, 1993.

Shatz-Uffenheimer, Rivka. "Autonomia Shel Ha-Ruah ve Torat Moshe." *Molad* 21 (1963): 554–56.

———."The Interpretation of Hasidism in the Idealistic Ideology of Gershom Scholem" (in Hebrew). In *Gershom Scholem: The Man and His Work.* Jerusalem, 1984.

———. *Quietistic Elements in Eighteenth-Century Hasidic Thought* (in Hebrew). Jerusalem, 1968.

———. "R. Moshe Cordovero and Ha-Ari: Between Nominalism and Realism" (in Hebrew). *Jerusalem Studies in Jewish Thought* 1, no. 3 (1982): 122–36.

———. "Self-Redemption in Hasidic Thought." In *Types of Redemption,* edited by R. J. Zwi Werblowsky and C. J. Bleeker. Leiden, 1970.

Shazar, Zalman. *Light of Bygone Generations: Studies and Comments on Jewish History in Recent Centuries.* Jerusalem, 1971.

Shemen, Nahman. *Lublin* (in Yiddish). Toronto, 1951.

Shivhei Ha-Ari. Warsaw, 1875.
Shmidman, Michael. "On Maimonides' 'Conversion' to Kabbala." *Studies in Medieval Jewish History and Literature 2*. Cambridge, Mass., 1984.
Shohet, Azreil. "Berurim be-Farashat Ha-Pulmus Ha-Rishon 'al Sifrei Ha-Rambam." *Zion* 36 (1971): 27–60.
Shragai, Shlomo Zalman. *Be-Ma'ayane Hasidut Izbica-Radzin*. Jerusalem, 1980.
———. *Be-Netive Hasidut Izbica-Radzin*. 2 vols. Jerusalem, 1972.
———. "Ha-Lehut Ha-Geula B'Mishnat Hasidut Izbica-Radzin." *Sinai* 79, no. 1 (1976): 44–54.
———. "Hasidut Ha-Baal Shem Tov B'T'fisat Izbica/Radzin." In *Sefer Ha-Besht*. Jerusalem, 1960.
———. "Redemption in Izbica-Radzin Hasidism" (in Hebrew). In *Chassidismus und Zion,* edited by Simon Federbusch. Jerusalem, 1963.
Shragai, Shlomo Zalman, and Abraham Bik. *B'Hechal Izbica-Lublin*. Jerusalem, 1977.
Silber, Daniel. *Maimonidean Conflict and Maimonidean Controversy*. Leiden, 1965.
Silber, Michael. "The Emergence of Ultra-Orthodoxy: The Invention of a Tradition." In *The Uses of Tradition,* edited by Jack Wertheimer. Cambridge, Mass., 1992.
Skarbek, J. "Lublin Province Jews in the November Insurrection." *Bioletyn Zydowskiego Instytutu Historycznego* 23 (1975): 63–81.
Smith, John E. "Freedom as Self-Determination." In *On Freedom,* edited by Leroy S. Rouner. Notre Dame, Ind., 1989.
Sommer, Benjamin. "Did Prophecy Cease?" *Journal of Biblical Literature* 115 (1996): 31–47.
Stace, Walter. *Mysticism and Philosophy*. Philadelphia, 1960.
———. *The Teachings of the Mystics*. New York, 1960.
Stern, David. *Parables in Midrash: Narrative and Exegesis in Rabbinic Literature*. Cambridge, Mass., 1991.
Stern, Greg. "Menahem Ha-Meiri and the Second Controversy Over Philosophy." Ph.D. dissertation, Harvard University, 1995.
Stern, Joseph. "Maimonides on the Covenant of Circumcision and the Unity of God." In *Midrashic Imagination: Jewish Exegesis, Thought and History,* edited by Michael Fishbane. Albany, N.Y., 1993.
———. *Problems and Parables of Law: Maimonides and Nahmanides on Reasons for the Commandments Ta'amei Ha-Mitzvot*. Albany, N.Y., 1998.
Stover, W. B. *"A Faire and Easie Way to Heaven": Covenant Theology and Antinomianism in Early Massachusetts*. Middletown, Conn., 1978.
Strauss, Leo. "Notes on Maimonides' Book of Knowledge." *Studies in Mysticism and Religion Presented to Gershom Scholem*. Jerusalem, 1967.
———. *Persecution and the Art of Writing*. Chicago, 1980.
———. *Philosophy and Law: Essays toward an Understanding of Maimonides and His Predecessors*. Philadelphia, 1975.

Talmage, Frank. "Apples of Gold: The Inner Meaning of Sacred Texts in Medieval Judaism." In *Jewish Spirituality I,* edited by Arthur Green. New York, 1986.

Thackeray, F. W. *Antecedents of Revolution: Alexander I and the Polish Kingdom.* New York, 1980.

Tikkunei Ha-Zohar. Vilna, 1867.

Tirosh-Rothschild, Hava. "Continuity and Revision in the Study of Kabbala." *AJS Review* 16, nos. 1–2 (1991): 161–92.

Tishby, Isaiah. "The Attitude of R. Joseph Hayyim David Azulai toward Cordoverean and Lurianic Kabbala" (in Hebrew). *Sefunot* 16 (1980): 191–203.

———. "Between Sabbatianism and Hasidism" (in Hebrew). In *Knesset* 9 (1945): 238–68.

———. "The Conflict between Kabbalat Ha-Ari and Kabbalat Ha-Ramak in the Writings of Ra'abam" (in Hebrew). *Zion* 39 (1979): 8–85.

———. "The Confrontation between Lurianic Kabbala and Cordoverean Kabbala in the Writings and Life of R. Aaron Berehiah of Modena" (in Hebrew). *Zion* 39 (1974): 8–85.

———. *The Doctrine of Evil and the "Kelippah" in Lurianic Kabbala* (in Hebrew). Jerusalem, 1984.

———. *Hikre Kabbala u Shelukhoteha.* 3 vols. Jerusalem, 1982.

———. "The Messianic Idea and Messianic Trends in the Development of Hasidism" (in Hebrew). *Zion* 32 (1967): 1–15.

———. *Mishnat Ha-Zohar.* 2 vols. Jerusalem, 1961.

———. *Netive Emunah u Minut.* Jerusalem, 1982.

———. *The Wisdom of the Zohar.* 3 vols. Translated by Jonathan Goldstein [English translation of *Mishnat Ha-Zohar*]. Oxford, 1989.

Torat Ha-Gilgul. 2 vols. R. Hayyim Vital, *Sha'ar Ha-Gilgulim* and *Sefer Ha-Gilgulim.* R. S. Agasi's commentary to *Sha'ar Ha-Gilgulim, Bnei Aaron, Hezyonot v'Gilluye Eliahu,* and *Sefer Megillat Setarim.* R. Elijah Mani, *Mazkir Shalom* on *Sha'ar Ha-Gilgulim.* R. Meir Poppers, *'Ohr Ner.* Jerusalem, 1982.

Twersky, Isadore. "The Beginnings of the Mishneh Torah Criticism." In *Biblical and Other Studies,* edited by A. Altmann. Cambridge, Mass., 1963.

———. *Introduction to the Mishneh Torah.* New Haven, Conn., 1980.

———. *Rabad of Posquiéres.* Cambridge, Mass., 1962.

———. "Some Non-Halakhic Aspects of the Mishneh Torah." In *Jewish Medieval and Renaissance Studies,* edited by Alexander Altmann. Cambridge, Mass., 1967.

———. "Talmudists, Philosophers, Kabbalists: The Quest for Spirituality in the Sixteenth Century." In *Jewish Thought in the Sixteenth Century,* edited by Bernard Cooperman. N.p., n.d.

Underhill, Evelyn. *Mysticism.* Reprint. New York, 1990.

———. *Worship.* New York, 1936.

Unger, M. *Pryzsucha und Kotzk* (in Yiddish). Buenos Aires, 1948.

Urbach, Efrayim. "Halacha and Prophecy" (in Hebrew). *Tarbiz* 18 (1947): 1–27.
———. "The Role of the Scholars of France and Germany in the Maimonidean Controversy" (in Hebrew). *Zion* 12 (1947): 149–59.
———. *The Sages: Their Concepts and Beliefs* (in Hebrew). Jerusalem, 1978.
Vajda, Georges. *La Théologie ascétique de Bahya ibn Pakuda.* Paris, 1947.
———. "The Mystical Doctrine of R. Obadya, Grandson of Maimonides." In *Journal of Jewish Studies* 6 (1955): 213–25.
———. *Recherches sur la philosophie et la Kabbala dans la pensée juive du Moyen Age.* Paris, 1962.
Verman, Mark. *The Books of Contemplation: Medieval Jewish Mystical Sources.* Albany, N.Y., 1992.
———. "Pantheism and Acosmism in the Kabbala." *Studia Mystica* 10, no. 2 (1987): 25–37.
Vital, R. Hayyim. *'Adam Yashar.* Cracow, 1885. Reprint. Jerusalem, 1994.
———. *Etz Hayyim.* Gloss by R. Shlomo Elyahshuv. Mekor Hayyim edition. Jerusalem, n.d.
———. "Hakdama of R. Hayyim Vital to *Sha'ar Ha-Hakdamot.*" Reprinted in the Mekor Hayyim edition of *Etz Hayyim.* N.p., n.d.
———. *Ketavim Hadashim l'Rabbenu Hayyim Vital.* Jerusalem, 1989.
———. *Mevo Sha'arim.* Tel Aviv, 1960.
———. *'Olat Tamid.* Jerusalem, 1907.
———. *'Ozrot Hayyim.* Commentary by R Shaul Dweck. Mekor Hayyim edition. Jerusalem, n.d.
———. *Sha'ar Ha-Gilgulim.* Commentary by R. Shimon Agasi. Jerusalem, 1990.
———. *Sha'ar Ha-Kavvanot.* Solonika, 1852. Reprint. Jerusalem, n.d.
———. *Sha'ar Ha-Mitzvot.* Solonika, 1852. Reprint. Jerusalem, n.d.
———. *Sha'ar Ha-Pesukim.* Jerusalem, 1912.
———. *Sha'ar Ha-Yihudim.* Mekor Hayyim edition. Jerusalem, n.d.
———. *Sha'arei Kedusha.* Jerusalem, 1976.
———. *Sha'ar Mamarei Rashbi, Sha'ar Mamarei Razal.* Jerusalem, 1898. Reprint. Jerusalem, n.d.
———. *Sha'ar Mamrei Razal.* Jerusalem, 1998.
———. *Sha'ar Ruah Ha-Kodesh.* Jerusalem, 1874.
Vital, R. Hayyim (attributed). *Pri Etz Hayyim.* Gloss by R. Shlomo Elyashuv. Mekor Hayyim edition. Jerusalem, n.d.
———. *Sefer Ha-Gilgulim.* Bnei Brak, 1986.
Von Rohr, John. *The Covenant of Grace in Puritan Thought.* Atlanta, Ga., 1986.
Wach, Joachim. *Types of Religious Experience.* Chicago, 1954.
Wald, Stephen. *The Doctrine of the Divine Name: An Introduction to Classical Kabbalistic Theology.* Atlanta, Ga., 1988.
Walis, R. T. *Neoplatonism.* London, 1972.
Wasserstrom, Steven M. "Defeating Evil from Within: Comparative Perspectives

on 'Redemption Through Sin.'" *Journal of Jewish Thought and Philosophy* 6 (1997): 37–57.

———. *Religion after Religion*. Princeton, N.J., 1998.

Watt, W. M. *Free Will and Determinism in Early Islam*. London, 1948.

Waxman, Meir. "Hoker Ha-Hasidut." In *Sefer Simon Dubnow*, edited by Simon Rawidowicz. Jerusalem and London, 1934.

Weinryb, Bernard D. *The Jews of Poland*. Philadelphia, 1973.

Weiss, Joseph. "Reshit Z'michat Ha-Derekh Ha-Hasidit." *Zion* 16 (1951): 46–105.

———. *Studies in Bratzlav Hasidism* (in Hebrew). Jerusalem, 1974.

———. *Studies in Eastern European Jewish Mysticism*. Oxford, 1985.

———. "Torat Ha-Determinism Ha-Dati le R. Mordechai Joseph Lainer M'Izbica." In *Sefer Yovel Shel Yitzchak Baer*, edited by Haim Beinart. Jerusalem, 1964.

Welch, Claude. *Protestant Thought in the Nineteenth Century*. 2 vols. New Haven, Conn. 1972.

Wendel, François. *Calvin: The Origins and Development of His Religious Thought*. New York, 1950.

Werblowsky, R. J. Zwi. "Messianismus und Mystik." In *Gershom Scholem's Major Trends in Jewish Mysticism Fifty Years After: Proceedings of the Sixth International Conference on the History of Jewish Mysticism*, edited by Peter Schafer and Joseph Dan. Tubingen, 1993.

Wilensky, Mordecai. "Hasidic-Mithnagdic Polemics in the Jewish Community of Eastern Europe: The Hostile Phase." Reprinted in *Essential Papers on Hasidism: Origins to the Present*, edited by Gershon Hundert. New York and London, 1991.

———. *Hasidim u-Mitnaggdim*. 2 vols. Jerusalem, 1970.

Winston, David. "Freedom and Determinism in Greek Philosophy and Jewish Hellenistic Wisdom." *Scripta Philonica* 2 (1973): 40–50.

———. "Freedom and Determinism in Philo of Alexandria." *Studio Philonica* 3 (1974/75): 47–70.

Wirszubski, Hayyim. *Between the Lines: Kabbalah, Christian Kabbalah and Sabbatianism* (in Hebrew). Jerusalem, 1990.

———. *Pico della Mirandola's Encounter with Jewish Mysticism*. Cambridge, Mass., 1989.

Wolfson, Elliot R. *Abraham Abulafia—Kabbalist and Prophet: Hermeneutics, Theosophy, and Theurgy*. Los Angeles, 2000.

———. *The Book of the Pomegranate: Moshe de Leon's Sefer Ha-Rimon*. Atlanta, Ga., 1987.

———. "By Way of Truth: Aspects of Nahmanides' Kabbalistic Hermeneutic." *AJS Review* (1989): 103–79.

———. "Circumcision and the Divine Name: A Study in the Transformation of an Esoteric Doctrine." *Jewish Quarterly Review* 78 (1987): 77–112.

———. "Circumcision, Vision of God, and Textual Interpretation: From

Midrashic Trope to Mystical Symbol." In *Circle in the Square: Studies in the Use of Gender in Kabbalistic Symbolism.* Albany, N.Y., 1995.

______. "Coronation of the Sabbath Bride: Kabbalistic Myth and the Ritual of Androgynisation." *Journal of Jewish Thought and Philosophy* 6 (1997): 301–43.

______. "Crossing Gender Boundaries in Kabbalistic Ritual and Myth." In *Circle in the Square: Studies in the Use of Gender in Kabbalistic Symbolism.* Albany, N.Y., 1995.

______. "The Doctrine of Sephirot in the Prophetic Kabbala of Abraham Abulafia 1." *Jewish Studies Quarterly* 2, no. 4 (1995): 336–71.

______. "The Doctrine of Sephirot in the Prophetic Kabbala of Abraham Abulafia 2." *Jewish Studies Quarterly* 3, no. 1 (1996): 47–84.

______. "The Engenderment of Messianic Politics: Symbolic Significance of Sabbatai Sevi's Coronation." In *Toward the Millennium: Messianic Expectations from the Bible to Waco,* edited by Peter Schafer and Martin Cohen. Leiden, 1998.

______. "Erasing the Erasure: Gender and the Writing of God's Body in Kabbalistic Symbolism." In *Circle in the Square: Studies in the Use of Gender in Kabbalistic Symbolism.* Albany, N.Y., 1995.

______. "Eunuchs Who Keep the Sabbath: Becoming Male and the Ascetic Ideal in Thirteenth-Century Jewish Mysticism." In *Becoming Male in the Middle Ages,* edited by Jeffrey J. Cohen and Bonnie Wheeler. New York, 1997.

______. "From Sealed Book to Open Text: Time, Memory and Narrativity in Kabbalistic Hermeneutics." In *Judaism in a Postmodern Age,* edited by Steven Kepnes. New York, 1994.

______. "The Influence of the Ari on the Shelah" (in Hebrew). *Jerusalem Studies in Jewish Thought* 10 (1992): 423–48.

______. "Left Contained in the Right: A Study in Zoharic Hermeneutics." *AJS Review* 11 (1986): 27–52.

______. "Letter Symbolism and Merkava Imagery in the Zohar." In *'Aley Sefer: Studies in the Literature of Jewish Thought,* edited by M. Hallamish. Ramat Gan, Israel, 1990.

______. "Light Through Darkness: The Ideal of Human Perfection in the Zohar." *Harvard Theological Review* 81 (1988): 73–95.

______. "Maiden without Eyes: *Peshat* and *Sod* in Zoharic Hermeneutics." In *The Midrashic Imagination: Jewish Exegesis, Thought and History,* edited by Michael Fishbane. Albany, N.Y., 1993.

______. "Mystical Rationalization of the Commandments in the Prophetic Kabbala of Abraham Abulafia." In *Perspectives on Jewish Thought and Mysticism,* edited by A. Ivry, E. R. Wolfson, and A. Arkush. Amsterdam, 1998.

______. "Mystical Rationalization of the Commandments in *Sefer Ha-Rimon.*" *HUCA* 59 (1988): 217–52.

______. "Sefer Ha-Rimon." Ph.D. dissertation, Brandeis University, 1986.

———. *Through a Speculum That Shines: Vision and Imagination in Medieval Jewish Mysticism.* Princeton, N.J., 1995.

Wolfson, Harry Austryn. "The Double-Faith Theory in Clement, Sa'adia, Averroes and St. Thomas." *Jewish Quarterly Review* 33 (1942–43): 213–64.

———. "Maimonides on Negative Attributes." *Louis Ginzberg Jubilee Volume.* American Academy of Jewish Research. New York, 1945.

———. *Philo.* 2 vols. Cambridge, Mass., 1948.

Yerushalmi, Joseph Hayyim. *Zakhor.* New York, 1982.

Yosha, Nissim. "Abraham Ha-Cohen Herrera's Philosophical Interpretation of Lurianic Kabbala" (in Hebrew). Ph.D. dissertation, Hebrew University, 1991.

———. "The Lurianic Concept of Prophecy in the Writings of Abraham Cohen Herrera" (in Hebrew). *Jerusalem Studies in Jewish Thought* 10 (1992): 389–422.

———. *Myth and Metaphor* (in Hebrew). Jerusalem, 1991.

Zagzebski, L.T. *The Dilemma of Freedom and Foreknowledge.* Oxford and New York, 1991.

Zemah, R. Jacob Hayyim. *Nagid u Mitzvah.* Jerusalem, 1965.

———. Jacob Hayyim. *Tiferet Adam.* Bnei Brak, 1982.

Zohar Hadash. Bnei Brak, n.d.

Index

MODERN JEWISH PHILOSOPHY AND RELIGION

Translations and Critical Studies

Barbara E. Galli and Elliot R. Wolfson, series editors

Hermann Cohen
Ethics of Maimonides
Translated with commentary by Almut Sh. Bruckstein, wih a foreword by Robert Gibbs

Emil Fackenheim
An Epitaph for German Judaism: From Halle to Jerusalem

Shaul Magid
Hasidism on the Margin: Reconciliation, Antinomianism, and Messianism in Izbica/Radzin Hasidism

Franz Rosenzweig
On Jewish Learning